UGC NET

Economics (Paper II)

Latest Edition
Practice Kit

12 Tests

12 Mock Test

Based On Real Exam Pattern

✓ Thoroughly Revised and Updated

✓ Detailed Analysis of all MCQs

Title	: UGC NET Economics (Paper II)
Author Name	: Mr. Rohit Manglik
Published By	: EduGorilla Community Pvt. Ltd.
Publishers Address	: 12/651, First Floor Opp. Arvindo Park, Near Jama Masjid, Indira Nagar, Lucknow, Uttar Pradesh-226016, India

Copyright EduGorilla

ISBN : 978-93-90297-29-0

Second Edition

Disclaimer EduGorilla

Compiled and created by EduGorilla Community Pvt. Ltd

Printed By EduGorilla Community Pvt. Ltd.

ROHIT MANGLIK
CEO, EduGorilla

Dear Applicants,

People say *"Success comes to those who work hard."* But I've seen people working hard for their exams day in and day out for marginal success. While others succeed in their examinations by putting in just half the work. So are they God Gifted? No! I believe that it's because they work *smart* and not just *hard*. Similarly, for your exams, you should strategize your preparation so as to increase the likelihood of success. Well with EduGorilla get ready to increase your *chances of selection* in your exam by *16x*.

EduGorilla helps you in not only working *hard* but also working in a *smart and strategic* manner. With EduGorilla's preparation package, you get a chance to make your exam preparation easy, and a fun learning path towards selection. Finding the right path to your preparations can be difficult if you don't know in which direction to head. Don't worry, we have you covered! EduGorilla will be your guide to success in your journey. With our Preparation Package, you can prepare strategically and beat the exam in just one attempt.

EduGorilla's Preparation Package includes-

• **Test Series**   • **Books**

Our preparation package is handcrafted as per the latest changes, expert opinions, and students' discretion. Thus, enabling you to get through each stage of the selection process for your exam.

Our Books are designed by the teachers and experts of the respective exam with a combined 150+ years of experience; to provide you with easy, efficient, and effective learning. Our books are smart, in the sense that not only do they give you the answers to the questions but also provide similar questions for practice.

EduGorilla's competent Test Series gives you real-time experience and confidence through which you can clear your offline or online exam in just one attempt. We currently host 82,000+ mock tests for 1,440+ competitive and academic exams.

Thus, EduGorilla misses no chance to assist you in your preparation and covers all stages of the exam, so that you don't have to look anywhere else.

We provide complete preparation packages for defense, banking, teaching, and other National & State-Level exams. Hence, it doesn't matter which exam you aspire to because you will reach your success.

ALL THE BEST !

Let EduGorilla be your Guide to Success.

Rohit Manglik,
Founder and CEO, EduGorilla

INTRODUCTION

EduGorilla focuses on guiding students to succeed in their examinations. With that in mind, our book, titled "UGC NET : Economics (Paper II)", has been drafted through the collective efforts of our distinguished experts with 150+ years of combined experience. This book consists of questions that are created following the latest changes in the syllabus and exam pattern. We compiled the book on the basis of questions that are most likely to appear in the NTA UGC NET Economics. Through EduGorilla's "UGC NET : Economics (Paper II)" your chances of success will increase 16x.

EduGorilla does this through our Complete Preparation Package. This package consists of well-conceptualized and structured content in the form of questions that are tailor-made according to your needs and will help you practice for exams in a smart way by pinpointing all the necessary information. It also provides hints and solutions, along with a smart answer sheet for your self-evaluation. You can assess your shortcomings and work accordingly on areas that may require more of your attention.

EduGorilla promises to help you succeed in your examination and accomplish your dream goals. We believe in our aspirants and see them at the top of the merit list. And the first step towards the top is to start preparing with us. EduGorilla's "UGC NET : Economics (Paper II)" includes the following attributes.

➤ Well-Researched Content

➤ Top-Notch Quality

➤ Detailed Answers and Analysis

➤ Smart Answer Sheet

➤ Exam Relevant Questions

Therefore, EduGorilla fortifies your preparation and makes it durable enough to help you stand tall and beat the examination.

NTA UGC NET Economics
Scan QR code for Eligibility, Exam Pattern, Syllabus and more.

Book ID: 0027

TABLE OF CONTENTS

Q.1 Which state has achieved 100 percent success in implementing ambitious Pradhan Mantri Jan Dhan Yojna?

A. Gujarat
B. Assam
C. Kerala
D. All of above

Q.2 The Reserve Bank of India (RBI) has revised regulations for ____ lenders by directing them to get themselves rated by March 2016.

A. Non-Banking finance
B. Core-banking
C. Stock
D. Home based

Q.3 Name the country invited by India to participate in creating mega industrial manufacturing corridors including Delhi-Mumbai industrial corridor?

A. China
B. Japan
C. Canada
D. Qatar

Q.4 What amount of money was fetched by the government in the Spectrum auction that concluded on 25th Mar 15?

A. 1 Thousand Crore
B. 1.10 Lakh Crore
C. 110 Lakh Crore
D. 1100 Crore

Q.5 In which state the two open-cast coal mines – Makardhokra and Bhanegaon were dedicated to the nation on 21st Mar 15?

A. Chhattisgarh
B. Jharkhand
C. Maharashtra
D. Andhra Pradesh

Q.6 How many Central Public Sector Enterprises (CPSEs) have been decided to be closed down by the Union Cabinet?

A. 10
B. 9
C. 8
D. 7

Q.7 Consider the following statements:

1. The Basel Accord is the banking supervision recommendation issued by RBI.

2. Basel norms focus on minimum capital requirements, internal assessment processes, and encourage sound banking practices including supervisory review.

3. The Basel committee has the authority to enforce its recommendations.

Which of the above options are correct:

A. Only 1
B. Only 2
C. Only 1 and 3
D. All of the above

Q.8 By what percent India's exports declined during February-2015?

A. Over 15%
B. Below 10%
C. Over 10%
D. 12%

Q.9 What was the retail inflation observed in Feb 15 in comparison to 5.11% in Jan 15?

A. 5.79%
B. 6.01%
C. 6.70%
D. 5.9%

Q.10 Which state government has launched a special project for installing solar photo voltaic panels in 80 schools and 20 primary health centers in 10 districts of the state on 12th Mar 15?

A. Odisha
B. Haryana
C. Kerala
D. West Bengal

Q.11 The International Monetary Fund (IMF) has raised India's growth forecast for the current fiscal to ____.

A. 6%
B. 6.7%
C. 7.5%
D. 7.9%

Q.12 Upto what limit Reserve Bank of India eased the norms for home loans by allowing banks to include stamp duty and registration charges to the cost of a unit?

A. 20 Lakh
B. 10 Lakh
C. 15 Lakh
D. 30 Lakh

Q.13 Which bank became the first major bank to announce rate cut after RBI's second Repo rate cut of the year was announced on March 2015?

A. State Bank of Travancore
B. State Bank of India
C. Punjab National Bank
D. ICICI Bank

Q.14 By what percent, the Foreign Direct Investment into the services sector increased during April - Dec 2014?

A. 15%
B. 50%
C. 33%
D. 44%

Q.15 How many points were cut in Repo Rate by the Reserve Bank of India on 4th Mar 15?

A. 50 Basis Point
B. 80 Basis Point
C. 35 Basis Point
D. 25 Basis Point

Q.16 In which state, did the Prime Minister Narendra Modi inaugurate the first phase of Shri Singaji Thermal Power Project on 5th Mar 15?

A. Uttar Pradesh
B. Madhya Pradesh
C. Arunachal Pradesh
D. Himachal Pradesh

Q.17 On which framework the government and the Reserve Bank of India signed an agreement whereby the government has set a target for RBI to bring down inflation below 6% by January 2016?

A. Monetary Policy Framework
B. Fiscal Deficit Framework
C. Inflation Policy Framework
D. Commercial Framework

Q.18 What is the growth forecast for the 2015-16 year as announced by Union Home Minister while presenting the Economic Survey for 2015-16 on 27th Feb 15?

A. Below 8%
B. Below 7%
C. Above 8%
D. Above 9%

Q.19 DMIC will include the development of the 1540 km long Western Dedicated Freight Corridor(WDFC) with how many nodes?

A. 24 **B.** 21 **C.** 20 **D.** 26

Q.20 How many new trains were announced in the Railway Budget 2015-16?

A. Eleven **B.** One **C.** Twelve **D.** Zero

Q.21 Which edition of Finance Commission recommended that a dedicated panel should be constituted for domestic financial institutions (DFIs)?

A. 12th **B.** 13th **C.** 14th **D.** 15th

Q.22 Name the commission that has recommended increasing state's share in the centre's tax revenue to 42% from current 32%?

A. Y. V. Reddy Commission
B. Justice C Rangarajan Commssion
C. Bajpai Panel
D. Bimal Jalan Committee

Q.23 What is the full form of MGNREGA?

A. Maharani Gangubai National Reconstruction Employment Guarantee Act
B. Mahadevi Gunabati National Rural Employment Guarantee Act
C. Mahatma Gandhi National Rural Employment Generation Act
D. None of the above

Q.24 Name the organisation that launched the virtual form of RuPay debit card?

A. SBI **B.** NPCI **C.** EPFO **D.** RBI

Q.25 In which month of 2015, inflation declined to a five-and-a-half year low of minus 0.39 per cent?

A. January **B.** February **C.** March **D.** April

Q.26 Which Indian Currency Note will be brought back by the Reserve Bank of India after a gap of almost two decades?

A. One Rupee **B.** Two Rupee
C. Three Rupee **D.** Five Rupee

Q.27 As per the new forecast of annual economic growth on 9th Feb 15, what was the new growth forecast for the year ending 2014-15?

A. 7.5% **B.** 6.9% **C.** 5.7% **D.** 8%

Q.28 How many public sector banks will get capital infusion as per the announcement made by the Finance Ministry on 7th Feb 15?

A. Nine **B.** Eight **C.** Ten **D.** Twelve

Q.29 Name the head of the committee constituted by the Reserve Bank of India on 3 February 2015 to evaluate applications received for the proposed small finance banks?

A. R Gandhi **B.** Usha Thorat
C. Dr. Nachiket Mor **D.** None of these

Q.30 The first bi-monthly monetary policy statement for fiscal year 2015-16 was released in which month?

A. March **B.** May **C.** April **D.** August

Q.31 A change in base year for computing national accounts pushed up the economic growth rate for 2013-14 to ___ percent, while earlier estimate on the basis of old series was 4.7 percent.

A. 5.5% **B.** 5.1% **C.** 6.5% **D.** 6.9%

Q.32 What is the new base year being used for computing the economic growth rate in India?

A. 2014-15 **B.** 2011-12 **C.** 2013-14 **D.** 2010-11

Q.33 The Cabinet Committee on Economic Affairs (CCEA) on 28th Jan 15 approved a proposal of which bank to raise the foreign holding limit to 74 per cent?

A. Reserve Bank of India
B. Punjab National Bank
C. State bank of India
D. HDFC Bank

Q.34 Which bank has released a report on 28th Jan 15 titled 'Scaling the Heights: Social Inclusion and Sustainable Development in Himachal Pradesh', first report of its kind for Himachal Pradesh?

A. World Bank
B. Reserve bank of India
C. Federal bank of India
D. Swiss Bank.

Q.35 As per the sixth bi-monthly monetary policy statement made by RBI in Mumbai on 3rd Feb 15, by how many basis points has the Statutory Liquidity Ratio been slashed?

A. 25 basis points **B.** 35 basis points
C. 50 basis points **D.** Unchanged

Q.36 By what percent India's Core sector growth dropped to a 3-month low in Dec 14 compared to 6.7% growth witnessed in the previous month of Nov 14?

A. 4.7% **B.** 5.7% **C.** 3.3% **D.** 2.4%

Q.37 To meet the fiscal deficit, the government decided sell up to ___ per cent stake in state owned Coal India Ltd.

A. 5% **B.** 10% **C.** 25% **D.** 25%

Q.38 Reserve Bank of India (RBI) has lifted a ban on carrying Indian bank notes of Rs 1,000 and 500 denominations to and from _____.

A. Pakistan **B.** Nepal
C. Bangladesh **D.** Myanmar

Q.39 How many MoUs have been signed between India and United States on 25th Jan 15 as part of Indian Government ambitious "Smart Cities" Scheme?

A. 4 **B.** 3 **C.** 5 **D.** 11

Q.40 After Sep 2011, in which year India's foreign exchange reserves touched an all-time high of $322.135 billion on account of a surge in foreign currency assets?

A. 2012 **B.** 2013 **C.** 2014 **D.** 2015

Q.41 Which edition of the Status paper on Government Debt has been released by the Central Government on 21st Jan 15?

A. First   **B.** Second   **C.** Third   **D.** Fourth

Q.42 Central government wants to construct Ram Janki Marg at a cost of Rs. 2000 Crore. Ram Janki Marg connects which two cities?

A. Rampur-Jankinagar
B. Ayodhya-Janakpur
C. Ayodhya-Haridwar
D. Rampur- Janaknagar

Q.43 The capital that is consumed by an economy or a firm in the production process is known as

A. Capital loss   **B.** Production cost
C. Dead-weight loss   **D.** Depreciation

Q.44 With which country, India's trade deficit increased to 37.8 billion US dollars in 2014 despite the increase in bilateral trade by 7.9 percent?

A. China
B. United States of America
C. Pakistan
D. Bangladesh

Q.45 How many funds are allocated for the health & wellbeing sector in the Union Budget 2021-22?

A. Rs 2,23,846 crore   **B.** Rs 2,87,000 crore
C. Rs. 1,97,000 crore   **D.** Rs. 1,10,550 crore

Q.46 By what basis points, Reverse Repo Rate was cut by Reserve bank of India on 15th January 2015?

A. 50 basis points   **B.** 70 Basis points
C. 80 basis points   **D.** 25 basis points

Q.47 IRDA was concerned over the skewed penetration of health insurance in India with four states accounting for 62% of premium. Name the four states.

A. Delhi, Maharashtra, Chennai & West Bengal
B. J&K, Assam, Punjab & Rajasthan
C. Maharashtra, Tamil Nadu, Karnataka and Union Territory of Delhi
D. Gujarat, Punjab, Maharashtra & Tamil Nadu

Q.48 Risks in the business arise because of

A. Introduction of the new products
B. Uncertain policy of rival firms
C. Changes in tastes
D. All of the above

Q.49 Indifference curves are convex to the origin because

A. Two goods are perfect substitutes
B. Two goods are imperfect substitutes
C. Two goods are perfect complementary goods
D. None of the above

Q.50 Standard of living of a country can be raised if it increases

A. Labour force   **B.** Production
C. Money supply   **D.** Exports

Q.51 According to Malthus, population increases by progression of which kind?

A. Systematic   **B.** Arithmetic
C. Geometric   **D.** Automatic

Q.52 Profit is maximum when

A. Distance between TR and TC is maximum
B. Distance between AR and AC is maximum
C. Distance between MR and MC is maximum
D. None of the above

Q.53 In Monopoly at various output levels

A. AR=MR   **B.** AR
C. AR>MR   **D.** None of the above

Q.54 All labour is

A. Homogeneous   **B.** Heterogeneous
C. Lazy   **D.** Intelligent

Q.55 Mobility of labour

A. Increases efficiency of labour
B. Spoils labour
C. Increases division of labour
D. '1' and '3' both

Q.56 Profit is maximum when

A. Slope of MC and Mr is the same
B. Slope of TC and TR is the same
C. Slope of AC and AR is the same
D. None of the above

Q.57 Excise tax is a part of

A. Fixed cost   **B.** Variable cost
C. Implicit cost   **D.** Is not a part of cost

Q.58 Unemployment due to mechanization of agriculture is

A. Seasonal   **B.** Structural
C. Industrial   **D.** Personal

Q.59 The labour force participation rate is the

A. Proportion of population that is working
B. Proportion of population working or looking for work
C. Proportion of skilled workers population
D. Proportion of female workers to male workers

Q.60 At the point of equilibrium of firm (under perfect competition)

A. MC curve must be rising
B. MC curve must be falling
C. MR cure must be rising
D. None of the above

Q.61 The shape of rectangular hyperbola is made by

A. MC   **B.** AFC
C. AVC   **D.** None of the above

Q.62 Unemployment of labour means that

A. A worker does not get full time job
B. A worker is not happy with his present job
C. A person does not get job according to his qualification
D. '1' and '3' both

Q.63 The human effort applied to the production of goods is called in economics

A. Labour   B. Skill
C. Experience   D. Service

Q.64 Normal profit is

A. Part of total cost
B. Part of economic profit
C. Total revenue minus total cost
D. Total revenue minus implicit cost

Q.65 As output increases

A. MC curve initially falls and then rises
B. MC initially rises and then falls
C. MC continuously rises
D. None of the above

Q.66 Which of the following is a producer good?

A. Pen   B. Cycle
C. Mobile phone   D. Hammer

Q.67 He described economics as a science of material welfare

A. Robbins   B. Marshall   C. Ricardo   D. Keynes

Q.68 Economic profit is

A. Part of total cost
B. Total revenue minus total cost
C. Total revenue minus explicit cost
D. Total variable cost minus total fixed cost

Q.69 Unit cost is another name for

A. MC   B. AVC   C. ATC   D. AFC

Q.70 Which statement relates to macroeconomics?

A. Oil prices are rising in Pakistan
B. Profit rate is high on textile industry
C. The firms try to make huge profits
D. The government has failed to control inflation

Q.71 Ceteris Paribus means

A. Other things remaining same
B. All variables are independent
C. Enable economists to simplify reality
D. That no other assumptions are made

Q.72 A firm earns economic profit when total profit exceeds

A. Normal profit   B. Implicit costs
C. Explicit costs   D. Variable costs

Q.73 All inputs can be varied in

A. Short run   B. Long run
C. Both periods   D. None of the period

Q.74 Scarcity means

A. Non-availibility of goods
B. High price of goods
C. Less supply than demand
D. High profit of the firms

Q.75 Who is the 'father of economics'?

A. Max Muller   B. Adam Smith
C. Karl Marx   D. None of the above

Q.76 Passive factor of production is

A. Only Land
B. Only Capital
C. Both Land & Capital
D. Neither Land nor Capital

Q.77 Under law of demand

A. Price of commodity is an independent variable
B. Quantity demanded is a dependent variable
C. Reciprocal relationship is found between price and quantity demanded
D. All of the above

Q.78 For inferior commodities, income effect is

A. Zero   B. Negative   C. Infinite   D. Positive

Q.79 Mixed economy means an economy where

A. Both agriculture and industry are equally promoted by the state
B. There is co-existence of public sector along with private sector
C. There is importance of small scale industries along with heavy industries
D. Economy is controlled by military as well as civilian rulers

Q.80 When total utility becomes maximum, then marginal utility will be

A. Minimum   B. Average
C. Zero   D. Negative

Q.81 Utility means

A. Power to satisfy a want
B. Usefulness
C. Willingness of a person
D. Harmfulness

Q.82 Marginal utility is equal to average utility at that time when average utility is

A. Increasing   B. Maximum
C. Falling   D. Minimum

Q.83 Which one of the following is the task of the Planning Commission?

A. Preparation of the plan
B. Implementation of the plan
C. Financing of the plan
D. None of the above

Q.84 At the point of satiety, marginal utility is

A. Zero   B. Positive
C. Maximum   D. Negative

Q.85 Total utility of a commodity is measured by which price of that commodity?

A. Value in use   B. Value in exchange
C. Both of above   D. None of above

Q.86 According to Marshall, the basis of consumer surplus is

A. Law of diminishing MU
B. Law of Equi-MU
C. Law of proportions
D. All of the above

Q.87 Which of the following bodies finalizes the Five Year Plan Proposals?
A. Planning Commission
B. Union Cabinet
C. National Development Council
D. Ministry of Planning

Q.88 What implication does resource scarcity have for the satisfaction of wants?
A. Not all wants can be satisfied
B. We will never be faced with the need to make choices
C. We must develop ways to decrease our individual wants
D. The discovery of new natural resources is necessary to increase our ability to satisfy wants

Q.89 Who expressed the view that 'Economics should be neutral between ends'?
A. Robbins
B. Marshall
C. Pigou
D. Adam Smith

Q.90 Price-taking firms i.e., firms that operate in a perfectly competitive market, are said to be 'small' relative to the market. Which of the following best describes this smallness?
A. The individual firm must have fewer than 10 employees
B. The individual firm faces a downward-sloping demand curve
C. The individual firm has assets less than Rs. 20 lakhs
D. The individual firm is unable to affect market price through its output decisions

Q.91 Which one of the following is true about Planning Commission?
A. It is a Ministry
B. It is a Government Department
C. It is an Advisory Body
D. It is an Autonomous Corporation

Q.92 A firm encounters its 'shutdown point' when
A. Average total cost equals price at the profit-maximizing level of output
B. Average variable cost equals price at the profit-maximizing level of output
C. Average fixed cost equals price at the profit-maximizing level of output
D. Marginal cost equals price at the profit-maximizing level of output

Q.93 Under _____ market condition, firms make normal profits in the long run.
A. Perfect competition
B. Monopoly
C. Oligopoly
D. None of the above

Q.94 Larger production of __ goods would lead to higher production in future
A. Consumer goods
B. Capital goods
C. Agricultural goods
D. Public goods

Q.95 Economic survey is published by
A. Ministry of Finance
B. Planning Commission
C. Government of India
D. Indian Statistical Institute

Q.96 A horizontal supply curve parallel to the quantity axis implies that the elasticity of supply is
A. Zero
B. Infinite
C. Equal to 1
D. Greater than 0 but less than 1

Q.97 When _____, we know that the firms are earning just normal profits.
A. AC = AR
B. MC = MR
C. MC = AC
D. AR = MR

Q.98 The economic analysis expects the consumer to behave in a manner which is
A. Rational
B. Irrational
C. Emotional
D. Indifferent

Q.99 Consumer surplus is highest in case of
A. Necessities
B. Luxuries
C. Comforts
D. Conventional necessities

Q.100 The vertical difference between TVC and TC is equal to
A. MC
B. AVC
C. TFC
D. None of the above

// Smart Answer Sheet //

Correct   Indicates percentage of students who answered questions correctly.

Skipped   Indicates percentage of students who skipped questions.

Q.	Ans.	Correct / Skipped	Q.	Ans.	Correct / Skipped	Q.	Ans.	Correct / Skipped	Q.	Ans.	Correct / Skipped	Q.	Ans.	Correct / Skipped
1	D	22.01 % / 14.2 %	17	A	30.87 % / 28.65 %	33	D	14.94 % / 17.3 %	49	B	19.16 % / 29.01 %	65	A	31.12 % / 28.52 %
2	A	41.72 % / 22.94 %	18	C	20.09 % / 31.74 %	34	A	24.61 % / 23.25 %	50	B	31.25 % / 26.65 %	66	D	47.61 % / 26.04 %
3	D	12.71 % / 21.2 %	19	A	21.76 % / 16.18 %	35	C	13.39 % / 26.29 %	51	C	49.1 % / 19.84 %	67	B	30.07 % / 27.65 %
4	B	27.09 % / 29.88 %	20	D	9.42 % / 14.08 %	36	D	7.38 % / 25.04 %	52	A	43.03 % / 17.35 %	68	B	37.88 % / 28.33 %
5	C	16.55 % / 30.63 %	21	C	28.33 % / 16.62 %	37	B	21.82 % / 29.95 %	53	C	40.92 % / 25.42 %	69	C	20.27 % / 27.78 %
6	D	10.73 % / 28.7 %	22	A	31.25 % / 24.11 %	38	B	24.3 % / 29.51 %	54	B	37.76 % / 26.03 %	70	D	50.77 % / 28.9 %
7	B	12.03 % / 29.69 %	23	D	12.15 % / 18.04 %	39	B	14.88 % / 31.87 %	55	D	56.23 % / 23.06 %	71	A	63.73 % / 16.8 %
8	A	8.99 % / 31.43 %	24	B	21.51 % / 21.64 %	40	D	13.76 % / 32.06 %	56	B	18.97 % / 27.53 %	72	A	34.84 % / 14.08 %
9	A	12.09 % / 31.8 %	25	A	8.37 % / 31.87 %	41	D	8.49 % / 21.52 %	57	B	21.08 % / 28.7 %	73	B	47.06 % / 26.16 %
10	D	8.0 % / 30.25 %	26	A	29.26 % / 30.07 %	42	B	34.16 % / 24.92 %	58	B	35.65 % / 26.35 %	74	C	38.75 % / 27.09 %
11	C	23.5 % / 24.11 %	27	A	17.79 % / 20.46 %	43	D	22.26 % / 24.55 %	59	C	13.21 % / 23.12 %	75	B	68.51 % / 26.84 %
12	B	22.38 % / 29.39 %	28	A	13.02 % / 25.11 %	44	A	24.8 % / 28.45 %	60	A	42.72 % / 19.83 %	76	C	31.37 % / 25.54 %
13	A	9.92 % / 20.46 %	29	B	22.32 % / 21.95 %	45	A	19.47 % / 22.75 %	61	B	42.22 % / 25.11 %	77	D	40.67 % / 27.4 %
14	D	8.25 % / 27.34 %	30	C	27.77 % / 23.44 %	46	D	23.0 % / 27.28 %	62	D	45.88 % / 26.72 %	78	B	48.98 % / 27.65 %
15	D	18.97 % / 24.92 %	31	D	7.32 % / 25.35 %	47	C	26.47 % / 26.97 %	63	A	49.16 % / 23.07 %	79	B	68.51 % / 15.93 %
16	B	28.39 % / 22.63 %	32	A	22.88 % / 21.01 %	48	D	57.04 % / 27.71 %	64	A	7.94 % / 27.4 %	80	C	60.82 % / 16.49 %

Q.	Ans.	Correct		Q.	Ans.	Correct		Q.	Ans.	Correct		Q.	Ans.	Correct		Q.	Ans.	Correct
		Skipped				Skipped				Skipped				Skipped				Skipped
81	A	69.81 %		85	A	16.43 %		89	A	23.56 %		93	A	61.56 %		97	A	19.71 %
		14.94 %				28.08 %				28.21 %				18.91 %				27.78 %
82	B	31.62 %		86	A	29.94 %		90	D	34.1 %		94	B	44.82 %		98	A	58.59 %
		22.44 %				27.22 %				30.44 %				25.73 %				27.65 %
83	A	39.93 %		87	C	15.56 %		91	C	41.66 %		95	A	33.79 %		99	A	30.87 %
		27.27 %				28.02 %				29.02 %				24.36 %				23.0 %
84	B	11.16 %		88	A	26.47 %		92	B	34.04 %		96	B	44.82 %		100	C	54.37 %
		26.29 %				30.38 %				29.44 %				24.8 %				21.58 %

Performance Analysis

Avg. Score (%)	29.0%
Toppers Score (%)	100.0%
Your Score	

//Hints and Solutions//

1. As per the statement made by Officials of the State Bank of India, all the districts have able to open at least one bank account of every household under the scheme.

2. In the revised regulatory framework on NBFCs notified late last evening, RBI further said, those asset finance companies (AFCs) failing to achieve investment grade ratings by the end of March 2016, should not accept fresh public deposits and renewing existing ones. In such an event, all existing deposits should runoff to maturity and NBFCs should report to the concerned RBI's Regional Offices within 15 days.

3. On 26th Mar'15 a joint statement issued in New Delhi at the end of two day visit of the Emir of Qatar Sheikh Tamim bin Hamad Al Thani said, the Indian side highlighted the considerable experience and expertise its companies had acquired in infrastructure development including power generation and transmission.

4. The auction concluded today after 19 days and 115 rounds of bidding. However, 11 percent airwaves stayed unsold. The process of auction was conducted for 800 MHz, 900 Mhz, 1800 MHz and 2100 MHz covering both mobile telephony and broadband, including 4G.

5. The two open-cast coal mines at Makardhokra and Bhanegaon, having a capacity of 2-million tonne and one million tonne respectively, were formally dedicated to the nation on 21 March by Union Power Minister Piyush Goyal.

6. The Seven CPSEs are HMT Bearings, HMT Watches, HMT Chinnar Watches, Tungabhadra Steel Products, Hindustan Photo Films Manufacturing Co., Hindustan Cables and Spices Trading Corporation Ltd.

7. The Basel Accord is the banking supervision recommendation issued by the Basel Committee on Banking Supervision (BCBS). All the G-20 major economies are represented in Basel Committee. Basel accord is a set of international banking regulations put forth by the Basel Committee on Bank Supervision (BCBS) that sets out the minimum capital requirements of financial institutions with the goal of minimizing credit risk. Banks that operate internationally are required to maintain a minimum amount (8%) of capital based on a percent of risk-weighted assets.

Hence, the correct option is (B).

8. India's export was declined by more than 15 percent to 21.5 billion dollars in February 2015.

9. It increased due to higher prices of food items, including vegetables. According to official data, food inflation rose to 6.79 percent in February this year, from 6.06 percent in January. Inflation in vegetables rose to 13%, and in pulses and products to 10.61% during the month under review. Inflation in rural areas stood at 5.79 percent, and in urban areas at 4.95 percent in February.

10. The State Government has also decided to introduce roof top solar power system particularly for high rise buildings. The government is also considering providing subsidy to the solar power user to encourage the use of Green Energy.

11. Last year, IMF had forecast a growth rate of 5.6 percent for the current fiscal, and 6.4 per cent for the next fiscal. In its annual assessment report for the country, IMF said that India has emerged as one of the fastest-growing big emerging market economies and the growth rate would grow by 7.5 per cent.

12. Upto the limit of 10 lakhs the Reserve Bank of India eased the norms for home loans by allowing banks to include stamp duty and registration charges to the cost of a unit. but at present, Banks do not include stamp duty, registration and other documentation charges in the cost of housing property.

13. It is a associate bank of the State Bank Group announced a 10 basis-point cut in the base rate to 10.15% on 8th Mar 15.

14. The Foreign Direct Investment into the services sector jumped 44 per cent to 2.29 billion dollars in the April to December period of the current fiscal. The services sector contributes over 60 percent to India's GDP.

15. The Reserve Bank of India on 4th Mar 15 cut repo rate by 25 basis points to 7.5 percent, signaling that it was convinced by the fiscal consolidation measures announced in the Budget. This is the second out of turn 25 basis point-cut after the one in January.

16. The first phase of project will be inaugurated at Dongliya village in Khandwa district of Madhya Pradesh. The Shri Singaji Thermal Power Project will give impetus to the state government's Atal Jyoti Abhiyan which aimed at providing 24 X 7 power supply across the state. The first phase of the Shri Singaji Thermal Power Project is of 12 hundred mega watt capacity. The Madhya Pradesh Power Generation Company has incurred 7820 crore rupees on this phase. With commissioning of two plants of this phase, the total thermal power generation capacity of the state will be 4500 mega watt.

17. The Agreement, which was signed on February 20 but made public on 2nd Mar 15, veers round to RBI Governor Raghuram Rajan's view that India too should move towards inflation targeting, which is common in developed economies. Currently, the Centre and the RBI give inflation estimates, but don't set targets.

18. The growth forecast is for fiscal year 2015-16 as disclosed in the Survey was 8.1 to 8.5%.

19. DMIC will include the development of the 1540 km long Western Dedicated Freight Corridor (WDFC) with 24 nodes (investment regions and industrial areas) including six large investment regions of 200 square kilometers and will run through 6 states- Delhi, western Uttar Pradesh, southern Haryana, eastern Rajasthan, eastern Gujarat and western Maharashtra.

Hence, the correct option is (A).

20. With this No increase in Passenger fares was also announced.

21. As per the 14th Finance Commission stated that domestic financial institutions (DFIs), such as public sector banks have a dominant role in the financial framework of the economy hence it is recommended that a Financial Sector Public Enterprises Committee (FSPEC) be appointed to examine and recommend parameters for appropriate future fiscal support to financial sector public enterprises.

22. According to an Action Taken Report on the recommendations given by the Commission, the Centre has decided to devolve a much higher share of 42% of the Union's tax receipts to the States.

23. The full form of MGNREGA is the "Mahatma Gandhi National Rural Employment Guarantee Act".

- MGNREGA is a flagship Programme of the Government of India.

- The scheme was introduced as a social measure that guarantees "the right to work".

- The key tenet of this social measure and labor law is that the local government will have to legally provide at least 100 days of wage employment in rural India to enhance their quality of life.

- The Mahatma Gandhi National Rural Employment Guarantee Act (MGNREGA) was passed in 2005.

- The Acts guarantees the " Right To Work" and aims at enhancing the livelihood security of rural peoples.

Hence, the correct option is (D).

24. National Payments Corporation of India (NPCI) is the nodal agency for all retail payment systems under the Pradhan Mantri Jan Dhan Yojana. The physical plastic RuPay card carries a 16-digit number. Under its virtual form, there will be no need of a physical card and a transaction can be done with the help of this 16-digit number alone. Currently, only around 20 per cent of the total transactions of around 8,000 crore rupees are taking place through IMPS or immediate payment service per month.

25. It happened due to falling prices of food items. But inflation in food articles remained high. Food inflation rose to scale a six month high of 8 percent in January, according to government data released on 16th Feb 15.

26. An RBI press release issued from Mumbai has informed that the notes, to be printed by the Government of India will soon be back into circulation. The government had discontinued printing of one rupee notes in November 1994 due to higher printing costs.

27. With this new forecast of annual economic growth it makes India the fastest growing major economy in the world. Under the new method, the economy grew 7.5% in the quarter ending in December 2014, outpacing China's 7.3% growth in the latest quarter and making India the fastest growing major economy in the world.

28. These banks are SBI, Bank of Baroda, Punjab National Bank, Canara Bank, Syndicate Bank, Allahabad Bank, Indian Bank, Dena Bank and Andhra Bank. Among all SBI would get maximum capital infusion.

29. She is a former Deputy Governor of RBI.

30. The first bi-monthly monetary policy statement for fiscal year 2015-16 was released on 7th April, 2015.

31. A change in base year for computing national accounts pushed up the economic growth rate for 2013-14 to 6.9 percent, while earlier estimate on the basis of old series was 4.7 percent. These changes follow a revision in the base for calculating national accounts to 2011-12 from 2004-05.

32. The base year was last revised in January 2010. Earlier, year 2004-05 was the base year for computing the economic growth rate. India Ratings (Ind-Ra), a leading rating agency of the county, on 28th Jan 15 said that the revision in base year of India's national accounts will increase the size of the economy to Rs. 111.7 trillion in the financial year 2014-15.

33. HDFC Bank would raise the fund through issuing of equity shares to non-resident Indians (NRIs) or foreign institutional investors (FIIs) or foreign portfolio investors (FPIs) subject to aggregate foreign shareholding not exceeding 74 percent of the post issue paid-up capital.

Hence, the correct option is (D).

34. As per the report, Per capita income in Himachal Pradesh is the second highest in the country – an impressive achievement given that more than 90 percent of its residents live in rural areas.

35. The RBI has decreased SLR of scheduled commercial banks by 50 bps to 21.5% to improve the liquidity in the market.

36. Slump in the production of crude oil and natural gas, pushed the growth rate of eight core sector industries to three-month low of 2.4 percent in December last year.

37. The decision will help the government to raise revenue of 24,000 crore rupees at the current market price. Currently, the government holds 89.65 per cent stake in CIL. As per the minimum shareholding norms for listed companies, the government needs to lower its stake in the state-run behemoth to 75 percent.

38. RBI issued a circular eased the restriction on export and import of bank notes of 1,000 and 500 denominations for Nepal and Bhutan that it had imposed since May, 2000. The Indian central bank, however, has put a limit of carrying such notes at Rs 25,000 per person.

39. Under these MOUs, the U.S. would assist India in developing three smart cities Allahabad, Ajmer and Visakhapatnam.

40. India's foreign exchange reserves touched an all time high of 322.135 billion US Dollars for the week ended 16th January 15. Strong FII inflows and reduction in import burden due to a record fall in oil prices have led to accumulation of the record forex reserves.

41. Since 2010-11, the Central Government has been bringing out an annual Status Paper on Government Debt giving detailed analysis of the government's debt position.The Fourth edition of the Status paper on Government Debt has been released by the Central Government on 21st Jan 15.

42. The road will connect Ayodhya with Janakpur in Nepal, to which Sita, the wife of Lord Rama in the epic 'Ramayana', belonged.

43. The capital that is consumed by an economy or a firm in the production process is known as Depreciation. In economics, depreciation is the gradual decrease in the economic value of the capital stock of a firm, nation or other entity, either through physical depreciation, obsolescence or changes in the demand for the services of the capital in question.

Hence, the correct option is (D).

44. India-China trade increased all time high of 73.9 billion US dollars in 2011 but declined to 66.57 billion US dollars in 2012 and 65.49 billion US dollars in 2013.

45. Union Budget 2021-22 allocates Rs 2,23,846 crore for the Health and Wellbeing sector for the fiscal year 2021-22 to strengthen three key areas: Preventive, Curative, and Wellbeing. Apart from this, the Budget allocation includes Rs 35,000 crore for COVID-19 vaccines.

Hence, the correct option is (A).

46. Reserve Bank of India (RBI) cut the reverse repo rate by 25 basis points to 7.75%. The move comes at a time when inflation is steadily coming down and cries for a rate cut were growing loud.

47. These four states contributed 62% of total health insurance premium; the rest 32 States/UTs contributed only 38% of total premium.

48. Risks in the business arise because of Introduction of the new products, Uncertain policy of rival firms and Changes in tastes.

49. Indifference curves are convex to the origin because two goods are imperfect substitutes.

50. Standard of living of a country can be raised if it increases Production. Labor productivity is a measure of the amount of goods and services that the average worker produces in an hour of work. The level of productivity is the single most important determinant of a country's standard of living, with faster productivity growth leading to an increasingly better standard of living.

51. According to Malthus, population increases by progression of Geometric.

52. Profit is maximum when Distance between TR and TC is maximum. At the equilibrium point, the firm earns maximum profits.

53. In Monopoly at various output levels AR>MR.

54. All labour is Heterogeneous.

55. Mobility of labour Increases efficiency of labour and also increases division of labour.

56. Profit is maximum when Slope of TC and TR is the same. To obtain the profit maximizing output quantity, we start by recognizing that profit is equal to total revenue (TR) minus total cost (TC).

57. Excise tax is a part of Variable cost. Excise duty is an indirect tax. That means the tax amount is included as part of the selling price. Excise duty, also known as excise tax, is ultimately passed on and paid by the consumer when he makes a purchase.

58. Unemployment due to mechanization of agriculture is Structural. Due to structural changes in the economy, structural unemployment may take place. Structural unemployment is caused by a decline in demand for production in a particular industry, and consequent disinvestment and reduction in its manpower requirements.

59. The labour force participation rate is the proportion of skilled workers population. It refers to the number of people who are either employed or are actively looking for work.

60. At the point of equilibrium of firm (under perfect competition) MC curve must be rising. If the firm is producing at an output level where the MC is falling, then this implies that it can further increase the profit by slightly raising the level of output. Equilibrium is established at the point where the MR is equal to MC and MC is rising.

61. The shape of rectangular hyperbola is made by AFC. The AFC curve is a rectangular hyperbola in the sense that all rectangles formed by AFC are of equal sizes.

62. Unemployment of labour means that a worker does not get full time job and a person does not get job according to his qualification.

63. The human effort applied to the production of goods is called Labour in economics. Labor is the human effort that can be applied to the production of goods and services.

64. Normal profit is Part of total cost. Normal profit is an economic term that describes when a company's total revenues are equal to its total costs in a perfectly competitive market.

65. As output increases when MC curve initially falls and then rises. The Marginal Cost curve is U shaped because initially when a firm increases its output, total costs, as well as variable costs, start to increase at a diminishing rate. Then as output rises, the marginal cost increases.

66. Hammer is a producer good. A hammer is a durable rival good.

67. Marshall described economics as a science of material welfare. Marshall's view is that economics studies all the actions that people take in order to achieve economic welfare. In the words of Marshall, "man earns money to get material welfare."

68. Economic profit is Total revenue minus total cost. Economic profit is the monetary costs and opportunity costs a firm pays and the revenue a firm receives. Economic profit = total revenue – (explicit costs + implicit costs).

69. Unit cost is another name for ATC. Average total cost (ATC): the per-unit cost of output.

70. The government has failed to control inflation relates to macroeconomics. Governments can use wage and price controls to fight inflation, but that can cause recession and job losses. Governments can also employ a contradictory monetary policy to fight inflation by reducing the money supply within an economy via decreased bond prices and increased interest rates.

71. Ceteris Paribus means other things remaining same. The Latin phrase ceteris paribus – literally, "holding other things constant" – is commonly translated as "all else being equal." A dominant assumption in mainstream economic thinking, it acts as a shorthand indication of the effect of one economic variable on another, provided all other variables remain the same.

72. A firm earns economic profit when total profit exceeds Normal profit. Economic profit is the profitability measurement that calculates the amount that revenues received from selling a product exceeds opportunity costs incurred from using resources to make and sell these products.

73. All inputs can be varied in Long run. The long run is defined as a period in which all INPUTS are variable. Because of that all costs are variable too. You're right that in the short run your rent and the cost of the machines you've already bought are fixed costs. But in the long term they aren't.

74. Scarcity means Less supply than demand. Scarcity refers to the basic economic problem, the gap between limited – that is, scarce – resources and theoretically limitless wants. This situation requires people to make decisions about how to allocate resources efficiently, in order to satisfy basic needs and as many additional wants as possible.

75. Adam Smith is the 'father of economics'. Adam Smith is called the father of economics for his work on The Wealth of Nations which he published in 1776.

76. Passive factor of production is both Land & Capital.

77. Under law of demand Price of commodity is an independent variable, Quantity demanded is a dependent variable and Reciprocal relationship is found between price and quantity demanded.

78. For inferior commodities, income effect is Negative. When price of an inferior good falls, its negative income effect will tend to reduce the quantity purchased, while the substitution effect will tend to increase the quantity purchased.

79. Mixed economy means an economy where there is co-existence of public sector along with private sector. All modern economies are mixed where the means of production are shared between the private and public sectors. Also called dual economy.

80. When total utility becomes maximum, then marginal utility will be Zero. It is based in the law of diminishing marginal utility which says 'as more and more units of a good are consumed, MU i.e level of satisfaction derived from each successive unit goes on falling because desire for that commodity tend to fall.

81. Utility means power to satisfy a want. It is a quality possessed by a commodity or service to satisfy human wants. Utility can also be defined as value-in-use of a commodity because the satisfaction which we get from the consumption of a commodity is its value-in-use.

82. Marginal utility is equal to average utility at that time when average utility is maximum.

83. Preparation of the plan is the task of the Planning Commission. The Planning Commission is charged with the responsibility of making assessment of all resources in the country, augmenting deficient resources, formulating plans for the most effective and balanced utilisation of resources and determining priorities.

84. At the point of satiety, marginal utility is positive. Goods where there is a point of satiety. This situation is common in

food. To the point of satiety, the marginal utility is positive; after that point, the marginal utility is negative.

85. Total utility of a commodity is measured by value in use price of that commodity. The utility theory of value was the belief that price and value were solely based on how much "use" an individual received from a commodity.

86. According to Marshall, the basis of consumer surplus is Law of diminishing MU. As per the law, as we purchase more of a commodity, its marginal utility reduces. Since the price is fixed, for all units of the goods we purchase, we get extra utility. This extra utility is consumer surplus.

87. National Development Council finalizes the Five Year Plan Proposals.

88. Resource scarcity for the satisfaction of wants implicates that not all wants can be satisfied. The classification of human wants is not a rigid concept.

89. Robbins expressed the view that 'Economics should be neutral between ends'. He believes that Economics is concerned merely with the utilization of scarce means far the satisfaction of multiple ends.

90. The individual firm is unable to affect market price through its output decisions best describes this smallness.

91. Planning Commission is an Advisory Body. The Planning Commission is a non-constitutional and non-statutory body and is responsible to formulate five years plan for social and economic development in India.

92. A firm encounters its 'shutdown point' when average variable cost equals price at the profit-maximizing level of output.

93. Under Perfect competition market condition, firms make normal profits in the long run. In sum, in the long-run, companies that are engaged in a perfectly competitive market earn zero economic profits.

94. Larger production of Capital goods goods would lead to higher production in future. If investment in capital good increases ,in turn it further increases the production of consumer goods in the long run. So, if an economy is investing more in capital goods, it shows signs of growth in near future, an increase in GDP.

95. The Department of Economic Affairs, Finance Ministry of India presents the Economic Survey in the parliament every year, just before the Union Budget.It is prepared under the guidance of the Chief Economic Adviser, Finance Ministry. It is the ministry's view on the annual economic development of the country.

96. A horizontal supply curve parallel to the quantity axis implies that the elasticity of supply is Infinite. The horizontal supply curve shows another extreme case, i.e., that of perfectly inelastic supply. The implication of such a supply curve is that a little price cut will cause the quantity supplied to fall to zero while a slightest increase in price will induce purchasers to offer an infinitely large quantity.

97. When AC = AR, we know that the firms are earning just normal profits.

98. The economic analysis expects the consumer to behave in a manner which is Rational. The assumption of rational behavior implies that people would rather be better off than worse off. Most conventional economic theories are based on the assumption that all individuals taking part in an action or activity are behaving rationally.

99. Consumer surplus is highest in case of necessities. Consumer surplus happens when the price that consumers pay for a product or service is less than the price they're willing to pay.

100. The vertical difference between TVC and TC is equal to TFC.

Q.1 Which of the following is/are assumption(s) of laws of returns to scale ?
A. All the factors of production keep changing
B. Organization is fixed
C. No change in technology
D. All of these

Q.2 Payment of interest as a factor reward is explained by:
A. Productivity Theory
B. Abstinence Theory
C. Time Preference Theory
D. All of the these

Q.3 In the light of the Revealed Preference Theory, consider the following axioms, and select the right answer from the code given below:
(a) Rationality
(b) Consistency
(c) Transitivity
(d) Non-satiation
A. (a) and (b) are correct.
B. All the four axioms are correct.
C. (a) and (c) are correct.
D. (a), (b) and (c) are correct.

Q.4 Starting from the earliest, arrange the following concepts in terms of their development in Demand Theory:
(i) Revealed Preference
(ii) Neumann and Morgenstern Utility Theory
(iii) Ordinal Utility
(iv) Cardinal utility
A. (iii), (i), (iv), (ii)   **D.** (iv), (iii), (ii), (i)
C. (i), (ii), (iii), (iv)   **D.** (iv), (iii), (i), (ii)

Q.5 Match the items in Group - I with those of Group - II and select the correct answer from the code given below:

Group - I	Group - II
(a) Kinked Demand Curve	(i) Baumol
(b) Full cost pricing	(ii) Bains
(c) Sales maximization	(iii) Sweezy
(d) Limit pricing model	(iv) Hall and Hitch
	(v) Modigilani

A. (iii), (i), (iv), (ii)   **B.** (ii), (i), (v), (iii)
C. (iii), (iv), (i), (ii)   **D.** (iv), (v), (ii), (iii)

Q.6 The notion of production function implies:
A. Economic Efficiency
B. Technical Efficiency
C. Allocative Efficiency
D. All of the above

Q.7 The 'core' of an economy contains
A. all Pareto optimal allocations
B. all competitive allocations
C. all Pareto improving allocations of the initial endowments
D. all the feasible allocations

Q.8 Demand for consumer durables and human capital forms part of the consumption demand model developed by which economist?
A. Friedman   **B.** Tobin
C. Rosenstein Rodan   **D.** Baumol

Q.9 Money multiplier determines:
A. Total supply of money in the economy
B. High powered money
C. Components of money supply
D. Employment and output in the economy

Q.10 Match the items in Group - I with those of Group - II and select the correct answer from the codes given below:

Group - I	Group - II
(a) $MV = PT$	(i) Marshall
(b) $MV = k\,PY$	(ii) Friedman
(c) $MV = f(r,\ y,\ w)$	(iii) Fisher
(d) $\hat{A}\ \dfrac{Md}{P} = \sqrt[4]{\dfrac{2bT}{r}}$	(iv) Baumol
$\hat{A}$	(v) Ando

A. (iv), (iii), (ii), (i)   **B.** (i), (ii), (iii), (iv)
C. (ii), (iv), (i), (iii)   **D.** (iii), (i), (ii), (iv)

Q.11 Estate duty was levied on the
A. incomes of the individuals
B. production of goods
C. export and import of goods
D. total property passing to the heirs on the death of a person

Q.12 Which of the following options arranges the given schemes in the correct chronological order?
(i) EAS
(ii) TRYSEM
(iii) JRY
(iv) RLEGP
A. (i), (ii), (iii), (iv)   **B.** (iv), (ii), (i), (iii)
C. (iv), (iii), (ii), (i)   **D.** (ii), (iv), (iii), (i)

Q.13 Which of the following options arranges the given points in the correct chronological order?
(i) General theory of employment, interest and money
(ii) Affluent society
(iii) Wealth of nation
(iv) Principles of economics

A. (iii), (iv), (i), (ii)   **B.** (iv), (ii), (i), (iii)
C. (i), (ii), (iii), (iv)   **D.** (iv), (iii), (ii), (i)

Q.14 Which of the following options arranges the given points in the correct chronological order?
(i) Commission for Agricultural Costs and Prices
(ii) Foodgrains Enquiry Committee
(iii) State Trading in Foodgrains
(iv) Foodgrain Policy Committee

A. (i), (ii), (iii), (iv)   **B.** (iv), (iii), (ii), (i)
C. (ii), (iii), (i), (iv)   **D.** (iv), (ii), (i), (iii)

Q.15 The Laffer Curve demonstrates the relationship between
A. inflation and the nominal interest rate
B. tax rate and total tax revenue
C. the real interest rate and investment demand
D. None of the above

Q.16 When government expenditure exceeds total government receipts, the budget deficit is
A. positive   **B.** negative
C. zero   **D.** intermediate

Q.17 Tax on inherited property is an example of
A. sales tax   **B.** income tax
C. wealth tax   **D.** VAT

Q.18 A temporary increase in marginal tax rate will
A. increase employment
B. increase output
C. raise the deficit
D. lower output

Q.19 VAT on any product is imposed
A. on the final stage of production
B. on the first stage of production
C. directly when a consumer buys it
D. at every stage between its production till it reaches a consumer

Q.20 'Pump Priming' should be resorted to at a time of
A. inflation   **B.** deflation
C. reflation   **D.** None of the above

Q.21 Union excise duties are a part of the Central government's
A. non-tax revenue   **B.** tax revenue
C. capital receipts   **D.** None of the above

Q.22 The tenth five year plan aims at reducing poverty by
A. 2%   **B.** 5%   **C.** 8%   **D.** 9%

Q.23 In the neo classical growth model, an increase in the marginal propensity to save
A. increases steady state output per person
B. increases the steady state growth rate of output
C. increases steady state capital per person
D. Both (1) and (3)

Q.24 Capital per person decreases if net investment per person
A. is less than the population growth rate
B. exceeds the population growth rate
C. exceeds savings per person
D. is less than savings per person

Q.25 In the Harrod–Domar model, if the growth rate of income is 5% and the capital-output ratio is 3, then what is the saving?
A. 5%   **B.** 3%   **C.** 8%   **D.** 15%

Q.26 The theory of unlimited supply of labour was proposed by
A. J.M. Keynes   **B.** Robert Solo
C. A. Lewis   **D.** Roy Harod

Q.27 The second five year plan was based on a model developed by
A. C.H. Hanumantha Rao
B. P.C. Mahalanobis
C. A.K. Sen
D. K.N. Raj

Q.28 Vicious cycle of poverty was proposed by
A. A. Marshall   **B.** J. M. Keynes
C. Ragner Nurkse   **D.** M. Friedman

Q.29 The trade off between inflation and unemployment remains stable only
A. during periods of stagflation
B. when the inertial rate of inflation remains unchanged
C. during the periods of slack demand
D. in the long run

Q.30 The money multiplier is the multiplicative inverse of the required reserve ratio as long as
A. currency leakages into circulation and/or foreign market do not occur
B. banks do not maintain excess reserves
C. the required reserve ratio is far in excess of the reserves that banks think are prudent given that they hold
D. All of the above

Q.31 With which of the following would Milton Friedman disagree?
A. Monetary policy has few short run effect on the real economy.
B. In the long run, changes in the money supply primarily effect the price level.
C. There is a little scope for using monetary policy actively to smooth out business cycles.
D. The reserve bank cannot be relied on to effectively smooth out business cycle.

Q.32 A person who left the job to find another job would be classified as
A. fractionally unemployed
B. structurally unemployed
C. cyclically unemployed
D. no longer in the labour force

Q.33 By which of the following is high powered money produced?
A. Commercial banks
B. Cooperative banks

C. Ministry of Finance
D. Reserve Bank of India

Q.34 The transaction version of the quantity theory of money was put forward by

A. Pigou   **B.** Marshall   **C.** Keynes   **D.** Fisher

Q.35 Crowding out will emerge in the economy if
A. government spending is on the rise
B. deficit financing is in control
C. government spending decreases
D. None of the above

Q.36 Which of the following is/are incorrect for a simple Y = AK model?
(a) Constant exogenous savings rate
(b) Non operation of diminishing returns to scale
(c) Constant endogenous savings rate
Choose the answer from the code given below.
A. (a) and (b)   **B.** (b) and (c)
C. Only (c)   **D.** Only (b)

Q.37 Value of Marginal Product (VMP) is
A. MPP X MR   **B.** MPP X AR
C. APP X MR   **D.** APP X AR

Q.38 The relevant age group for computation of a child sex ratio is
A. 0 - 1 years   **B.** 0 - 4 years
C. 0 - 6 years   **D.** 0 - 7 years

Q.39 Which of the following committees recommended abolition of tax rebates under Section 88 of the Income Tax Act?
A. Chellaiah Committee
B. Kelkar Committee
C. Shome Committee
D. None of the above

Q.40 The phenomenon of 'demographic dividend' of a country is related to
A. a sharp decline in the total population
B. a decline in the Infant Mortality Rate
C. an increase in the sex ratio
D. an increase in the population in the working age group

Q.41 Interim audit refers to an audit which
A. is conducted in two different accounting years
B. involves preliminary audit work
C. is conducted in between one statutory audit and an internal audit
D. None of the above

Q.42 A tax is said to be buoyant if tax revenue is proportionally
A. more responsive to changes in output
B. less responsive to changes in output
C. equally responsive to changes in tax base
D. less responsive to changes in tax base

Q.43 Segmented labour markets do not imply which of the following?

A. Labour discrimination
B. Labour paid wage less than MRP
C. MP theory of wage fails to determine market outcomes
D. Equality of wages of different types of labour

Q.44 In India, 'marginal farmers' hold land up to
A. 1 hectare   **B.** 2 hectares
C. 3 hectares   **D.** 4 hectares

Q.45 If there is balance of payments deficit, then in a floating exchange rate system,
A. the external value of the currency would tend to fall
B. the external value of the currency would tend to rise
C. the injections from trade are greater than the withdrawals
D. aggregate demand is increasing

Q.46 Devaluation will improve the balance of payment deficit, if sum of elasticity of exports and imports of the devaluing country is
A. greater than unity   **B.** less than one
C. equal to zero   **D.** negative

Q.47 Which of the following are examples of economic integration?
(1) Free Trade Area
(2) Customs Union
(3) Common Market
(4) Cartel
Select the correct answer from the given codes.
A. 1 and 2   **B.** 2 and 3
C. 1, 2 and 4   **D.** 1, 2 and 3

Q.48 Which of the following agencies estimates national income in India?
A. Central Statistical Organisation (CSO)
B. Reserve Bank of India (RBI)
C. National Sample Survey Organisation (NSSO)
D. Ministry of Finance, Government of India

Q.49 As used by economists, the word 'savings' means
A. the part of income not spent on consumption during some given time period
B. the total amount of money which people have accumulated in the past
C. the same thing as investment, since savings equals investment when the economy is in equilibrium
D. All of the above

Q.50 Match the following and choose the correct option.

List - I	List - II
(a) Trend	(i) (S.D./Mean) x 100
(b) Coefficient of variation	(ii) Normal
(c) Mean = np	(iii) Time series
(d) Symmetric distribution	(iv) Binomial

A. (ii), (i), (iii), (iv)   **B.** (i), (iii), (iv), (ii)
C. (iv), (i), (iii), (ii)   **D.** (iii), (i), (iv), (ii)

Q.51 If the Price Consumption Curve (PCC) of a commodity is bending backwards, then the commodity must be
A. an inferior commodity

B. a perfectly elastic commodity

C. normal commodity

D. giffen goods

Q.52 If the economy is in the liquidity trap, then

A. fiscal policy will be more effective

B. monetary policy will be more effective

C. crowding out effect will make fiscal and monetary policies effective

D. None of the above

Q.53 The rate at which the Central Bank discounts the bills of commercial banks is called

A. discount rate

B. bill rate

C. interest rate

D. lending rate

Q.54 Which of the following gives measure of price elasticity of demand?

A. $\frac{\Delta Q_x}{\Delta P_x} \times \frac{P_x}{Q_x}$

B. $\frac{\Delta P_x}{\Delta Q_x} \times \frac{P_x}{Q_x}$

C. $\frac{\Delta Q_x}{\Delta P_x} \times \frac{Q_x}{P_x}$

D. $\frac{\Delta P_x}{\Delta Q_x}$

Q.55 Green Box subsidies under WTO are allowed because they are considered to be

A. minimally trade distorting

B. higher among developed countries and relatively lower for developing countries

C. confined to agriculture sector

D. related to GATs provision

Q.56 Consider a Cobb-Douglas production function $q = AK^\alpha L^\beta$ which is a homogeneous function of degree 4. of what degree of homogeneity are its marginal products' functions (mpl and mpk), i.e. $\frac{\delta_q}{\delta L}, \frac{\delta_q}{\delta K}$?

A. 4

B. 3

C. 2

D. 1

Q.57 The balance of payments of a country on current account is equal to

A. balance of trade

B. balance of trade plus net invisible exports

C. balance of payment minus capital flows

D. balance of invisible trade plus imports

Q.58 Industrial Licensing Policy Inquiry Committee was set up in 1967 under the chairmanship of

A. R. K. Hazari

B. P. C. Mahalanobis

C. Subimal Dutt

D. V.K.R.V. Rao

Q.59 The term 'Hindu Rate of Growth' was coined by

A. Gagil

B. Chakravarthy

C. Bhagwati

D. Raj Krishna

Q.60 If $(32 > 3)$ then the curve is called

A. platykurtic

B. leptokurtic

C. mesokurtic

D. None of the above

Q.61 New Trade Policy 2015 - 20 has introduced a new scheme called

A. Merchandise Exports from India Scheme

B. Exports from India Scheme

C. Merchandise Trade from India Scheme

D. Trade from India Scheme

Q.62 Match the following and choose the correct option.

List - I	List - II
(a) Fiscal Deficit	(i) Revenue and interest receipts minus revenue expenditure
(b) Revenue Deficit	(ii) Revenue receipts and recovery of loans and other receipts minus total expenditure
(c) Budgetary Deficit	(iii) Receipts minus disbursements in capital account
(d) Capital Deficit	(iv) Total receipts minus total disbursements

A. (i), (ii), (iii), (iv)

B. (ii), (i), (iv), (iii)

C. (iii), (ii), (iv), (i)

D. (iv), (iii), (i), (ii)

Q.63 Match the following and choose the correct option.

List - I	List - II
(a) Keynesian theory of distribution	(i) W.S. Javons
(b) Time preference theory of interest	(ii) J.M. Keynes
(c) Sun-Spot theory of trade cycle	(iii) N. Kaldor
(d) Modern theory of income determination	(iv) Bohm Bawerk

A. (ii), (i), (iv), (iii)

B. (ii), (iv), (i), (iii)

C. (iii), (iv), (i), (ii)

D. (iii), (i), (iv), (ii)

Q.64 Which of the following theories is generally studied in microeconomics?

A. Price theory

B. Income theory

C. Employment theory

D. None of the above

Q.65 Net national product at market price minus net indirect taxes is equal to

A. net foreign investment

B. net foreign investment plus net domestic investment

C. net national product at factor cost

D. replacement expenditure

Q.66 Match the following and choose the correct option.

List - I	List - II
(a) Reaction of Ho when it is true	(i) Satisfied random sampling
(b) Mean is equal to degrees of freedom	(ii) Type I error
(c) Popular population heterogeneous	(iii) Positively skewed distribution
(d) Mean > mode	(iv) X^2 distribution

A. (ii), (iv), (iii), (i)

B. (i), (ii), (iii), (iv)

C. (ii), (iv), (i), (iii)

D. (iv), (i), (ii), (iii)

Q.67 Invisible items are included in

A. national income accounts

B. balance of payments accounts

C. international accounts

D. world bank accounts

Q.68 Personal disposable income is equal to personal income

A. minus personal direct taxes

B. plus indirect taxes

C. minus total taxes

D. minus subsidies

Q.69 Which of the following does satisfy factor reversal test?

A. Laspeyne & aposs index number

B. Marshell-Edgeworth index number

C. Fisher & aposs index number

D. Paache & aposs index number

Q.70 According to Keynes, the cause for the unprecedented global depression of the 1930's was

A. high interest rate in the USA

B. low interest rate in the UK

C. breakdown of the gold standard

D. lack of sufficient aggregate demand

Q.71 The table below consists of two lists of events/theories/models/statements and the other of authors. Match an item in one list with an item in the other and mark the correct option using the codes given below.

List - I	List - II
(a) Big push	(i) Joan Robinson
(b) Knife-edge	(ii) R. Rodan
(c) Golden age	(iii) Michael E. Phelps
(d) Golden rule of accumulation	(iv) Sir Henry Roy Forbes Harrod

A. (i), (ii), (iii), (iv)   **B.** (ii), (iv), (i), (iii)

C. (iv), (iii), (ii), (i)   **D.** (iii), (iv), (i), (ii)

Q.72 The table below consists of two lists of events/theories/models/statements and the other of authors. Match an item in one list with an item in the other and mark the correct option using the codes given below.

List - I	List - II
(a) Learning by doing	(i) R.R. Nelson
(b) Division of labour	(ii) John Stuart Mill
(c) Stationary state of bliss	(iii) Adam Smith
(d) Low level equilibrium trap	(iv) K. J. Arrow

A. (iv), (ii), (iii), (i)   **B.** (i), (ii), (iii), (iv)

C. (iv), (iii), (ii), (i)   **D.** (ii), (iv), (iii), (i)

Q.73 Which of the following options arranges the given points in the correct chronological order?
(i) WTO Ministerial Meeting at Cancun
(ii) WTO Ministerial Meeting at Hong Kong
(iii) WTO Ministerial Meeting at Singapore
(iv) WTO Ministerial Meeting at Doha

A. (ii), (i), (iii), (iv)   **B.** (iv), (iii), (ii), (i)

C. (iii), (iv), (i), (ii)   **D.** (ii), (iii), (i), (iv)

Q.74 Hedging in the foreign exchange market refers to

A. an act of devaluation

B. not covering a risk of foreign exchange in future

C. covering a risk of foreign exchange in future

D. None of the above

Q.75 Consider the following statements regarding Real Effective Exchange Rate and select the correct answer from the codes.
(A) It refers to average of value country's currency in relation to an index of basket of values major countries currencies.
(B) It refers to nominal ratio of country's currency value to average value of a basket of currency.

A. Only A is true.

B. Only B is true.

C. Both A and B are true.

D. Neither A nor B are true.

Q.76 Tax incidence refers to

A. whether a tax is progressive, proportional or regressive

B. how often a tax is collected

C. the person or group who ends up paying a tax

D. how a tax is collected

Q.77 Directions: Read the given statements carefully and choose the correct option accordingly

Assertion (A): A progressive income tax is based on equi-marginal sacrifice.

Reason (R): Higher the income, lower will be the marginal utility of money for the tax payers.

A. Both (A) and (R) are true and (R) is the correct explanation of (A).

B. Both (A) and (R) are true, but (R) is not the correct explanation of (A).

C. (A) is true, but (R) is false.

D. (A) is false, but (R) is true.

Q.78 Which of the following taxes is within the jurisdiction of state governments as enumerated in List - II of the Indian Constitution?

A. Taxes other than stamp duties on transactions in stock exchanges and future markets.

B. Taxes on railway freight and fares

C. Taxes on mineral rights subject to any limitation impost by the Parliament

D. Rate of stamp duty in respect of certain financial documents

Q.79

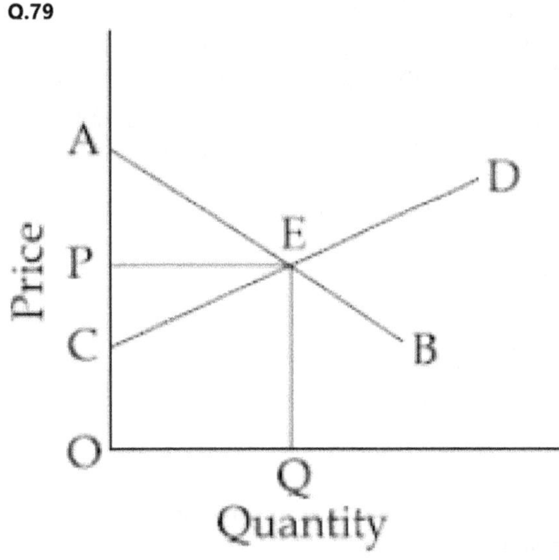

In the above diagram, the consumer surplus is represented by the area of:

A. ΔPCE
B. ΔAPE
C. ΔACE
D. Rectangle OPEQ

Q.80 Simon Hawkins relates to which of the following?

(a) Static Leontief Model

(b) Dynamic Leontief Model

(c) These are necessary and sufficient conditions for the solution of the model.

Choose the correct answer from the given code below.

A. a and b
B. b and c
C. a, b and c
D. a and c

Q.81 Given the production function $Q = 2. K^{\frac{1}{3}} \cdot L^{\frac{2}{3}}$ find the output level when 8 units of capital and 27 units of labour are used.

A. 36
B. 54
C. 18
D. 24

Q.82 A consumer purchases 240 units when the price of the commodity is Rs. 15 and 300 units when the price rises to Rs. 20. The elasticity of demand is

A. $\frac{2}{3}$
B. 1
C. $\frac{3}{4}$
D. $\frac{1}{30}$

Q.83 Match the following lists:

List - I	List - II
(a) Wald test	(i) stationarity
(b) Unit root test	(ii) Errors in variables model
(c) Student's test	(iii) Causality
(d) Granger test	(iv) Significance of Regression Coefficients

A. (ii), (i), (iv), (iii)
B. (i), (ii), (iv), (iii)
C. (iii), (iv), (i), (ii)
D. (iv), (iii), (ii), (i)

Q.84 Which of the following models can be estimated using OLS, following suitable transformations if necessary?

$$(a) Y_t = \alpha + \beta X_t + u_t$$
$$(b) Y_t = \alpha + \beta e^X + u_t$$
$$(c) Y_t = \alpha + \beta In(X_t) + u_t$$
$$(d) Y_t = \alpha + \beta X_t^2 + u_t$$

(Note that 'e' denotes the exponential)

A. a only
B. b and c only
C. a, c and d only
D. a, b, c and d

Q.85 If OLS is applied separately to each equation that is part of a simultaneous interdependent system, then the resulting estimates will be

A. unbiased and consistent
B. biased and consistent
C. biased and inconsistent
D. impossible to apply

Q.86 Which of the following is not a plausible remedy for multicollinearity?

A. Using principal components analysis
B. Dropping one of the collinear variables
C. Using a longer run of data
D. Taking a logarithm of each of the variables

Q.87 Which of the following is not a characteristic of imperfect competition?

A. Perfect knowledge
B. Free transport
C. Free entry of firms
D. Homogeneous product

Q.88 Match the following lists.

List - I	List - II
(a) Compensation Criterion	(i) Williamson
(b) Impossibility Theorem	(ii) F. H. Knight
(c) Managerial Discretion Model	(iii) Kaldor-Hicks
(d) Uncertainty Theory of Profits	(iv) Kenneth Arrow

A. (iv), (i), (iii), (ii)
B. (iii), (iv), (i), (ii)
C. (ii), (iii), (i), (iv)
D. (iii), (ii), (iv), (i)

Q.89 Suppose that at a price of Rs. 300 per month, there are 30,000 subscribers to cable television in Small Town. If Small Town Cablevision raises its price to Rs. 400 per month, the number of subscribers will fall to 20,000. Using the midpoint method for calculating the elasticity, what is the price elasticity of demand for cable TV in Small Town?

A. 1.4
B. 0.66
C. 0.75
D. 2.0

Q.90 Directions: Arrange the following in chronological order.

(i) Relative Income Hypothesis

(ii) Life-cycle Hypothesis

(iii) Absolute Income Hypothesis

(iv) Permanent Income Hypothesis

A. (iii), (i), (iv), (ii)
B. (ii), (iv), (i), (iii)
C. (i), (iii), (ii), (iv)
D. (iv), (ii), (iii), (i)

Q.91 Directions: Arrange the following list in chronological order :

(i) Modernisation

(ii) Rapid and non-inclusive growth

(iii) Removal of poverty and self-reliance

(iv) Rapid and large scale industrialisation

A. (i), (ii), (iv), (iii)   **B.** (ii), (iv), (i), (iii)

C. (iv), (ii), (iii), (i)   **D.** (iv), (iii), (i), (ii)

Q.92 Directions: Arrange the following list in chronological order :

(i) Value and Capital

(ii) Principles of Political Economy and Taxation

(iii) A Revision of Demand Theory

(iv) The General Theory of Employment, Interest and Money

A. (ii), (iv), (i), (iii)   **B.** (iii), (i), (iv), (ii)

C. (iv), (iii), (i), (ii)   **D.** (i), (iv), (iii), (ii)

Q.93 Directions: Arrange the following list in chronological order :

(i) Introduction of MODVAT

(ii) Introduction of Fringe Benefit Tax

(iii) Introduction of Expenditure Tax

(iv) Abolition of Estate Duty

A. (ii), (iii), (i), (iv)   **B.** (i), (iii), (ii), (iv)

C. (iv), (i), (iii), (ii)   **D.** (i), (iv), (ii), (iii)

Q.94 Directions: Read the given statements carefully and choose the correct option accordingly

Assertion (A): Harrod-Domar model assumes fixed technological relationship between capital stock and income flows.

Reason (R): The model assumes flexible capital output ratio.

A. Both (A) and (R) are true and (R) is the correct explanation of (A).

B. Both (A) and (R) are true, but (R) is not the correct explanation of (A).

C. Both (A) and (R) are false.

D. (A) is true, but (R) is false.

Q.95 Directions: Read the given statements carefully and choose the correct option accordingly

Assertion (A): Fisher's index is an ideal index.

Reason (R): Fisher's index satisfies time reversal and factor reversal tests.

A. Both (A) and (R) are true and (R) is the correct explanation of (A).

B. Both (A) and (R) are true, but (R) is not the correct explanation of (A).

C. (A) is true, but (R) is false.

D. (A) is false, but (R) is true.

Q.96 Directions: Refer to the figure below and answer the question:

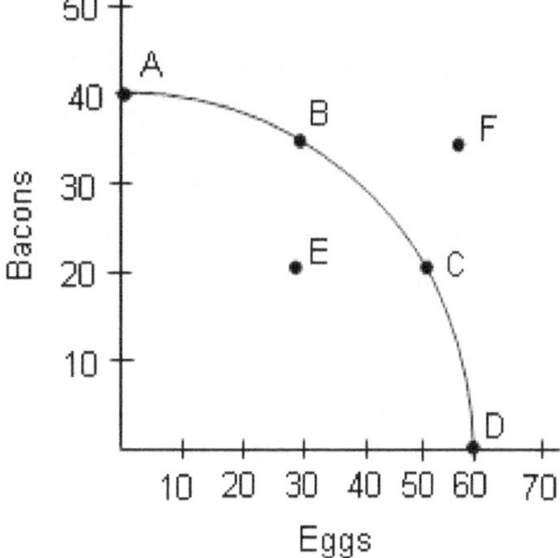

If the economy is operating at E,

A. the opportunity cost of 20 additional units of eggs is 10 units of bacon

B. the opportunity cost of 20 additional units of eggs is 20 units of bacon

C. the opportunity cost of 20 additional units of eggs is 30 units of bacon

D. 20 additional units of eggs can be produced with no impact on bacon production

Q.97 Random sampling implies that the observations are selected

A. purposely

B. in a systemic manner

C. in an adhoc manner

D. in clusters

Q.98 x^2 (chi-square) test is used to test

A. analysis of variance

B. association between the qualitative variables

C. difference between means of two distributions drawn from the same population

D. difference between the means of two distributions drawn from different population

Q.99 If 'r' is the correlation coefficient and byx and bxy are the regression coefficients of the regression lines y on x and x on y, then r is equal to

A. $b_{xy} \times b_{yx}$ **B.** $\sqrt{bxy/byx}$

C. $\sqrt{1 - bxybyx}$ **D.** $\sqrt{bxybyx}$

Q.100 Which of the following is not a form of economic integration in the context of intra-regional trade?

A. Customs Union   **B.** European Union

C. Economic Union   **D.** African Union

// Smart Answer Sheet //

Correct Indicates percentage of students who answered questions correctly.

Skipped Indicates percentage of students who skipped questions.

Q.	Ans.	Correct	Q.	Ans.	Correct	Q.	Ans.	Correct	Q.	Ans.	Correct	Q.	Ans.	Correct
		Skipped			Skipped			Skipped			Skipped			Skipped
1	D	61.22 % / 1.83 %	17	C	69.47 % / 14.19 %	33	D	52.21 % / 17.56 %	49	A	24.12 % / 21.22 %	65	C	53.59 % / 24.88 %
2	A	38.02 % / 7.78 %	18	D	38.93 % / 14.81 %	34	D	38.17 % / 17.71 %	50	D	49.47 % / 21.83 %	66	C	51.45 % / 26.11 %
3	D	53.89 % / 8.71 %	19	D	53.74 % / 14.35 %	35	A	49.31 % / 18.63 %	51	D	29.62 % / 22.29 %	67	B	54.96 % / 25.04 %
4	D	54.35 % / 9.62 %	20	B	41.98 % / 15.42 %	36	B	27.79 % / 19.69 %	52	A	32.37 % / 23.36 %	68	A	45.19 % / 24.58 %
5	C	61.22 % / 10.84 %	21	B	54.2 % / 15.11 %	37	B	40.92 % / 19.54 %	53	A	48.85 % / 23.36 %	69	C	30.08 % / 25.95 %
6	B	18.02 % / 10.53 %	22	B	36.49 % / 15.57 %	38	C	40.46 % / 19.23 %	54	A	55.11 % / 22.91 %	70	D	36.79 % / 26.42 %
7	D	28.55 % / 11.14 %	23	D	53.13 % / 15.42 %	39	B	37.86 % / 20.0 %	55	C	35.57 % / 23.82 %	71	B	54.05 % / 26.1 %
8	A	39.85 % / 11.45 %	24	D	25.8 % / 16.18 %	40	D	51.76 % / 19.84 %	56	B	25.04 % / 25.34 %	72	C	52.82 % / 26.11 %
9	A	43.05 % / 10.69 %	25	D	42.14 % / 17.86 %	41	B	16.79 % / 20.61 %	57	B	30.23 % / 23.97 %	73	C	23.05 % / 28.4 %
10	D	55.42 % / 11.45 %	26	C	58.17 % / 15.88 %	42	A	29.01 % / 20.76 %	58	C	17.86 % / 24.43 %	74	C	53.89 % / 26.26 %
11	D	57.1 % / 10.99 %	27	B	67.94 % / 16.33 %	43	D	32.06 % / 21.53 %	59	D	33.28 % / 25.04 %	75	A	19.69 % / 27.49 %
12	D	19.39 % / 14.96 %	28	C	69.01 % / 15.88 %	44	A	32.52 % / 20.92 %	60	B	38.17 % / 25.65 %	76	C	47.33 % / 25.8 %
13	A	54.2 % / 12.98 %	29	B	21.07 % / 16.64 %	45	A	41.37 % / 20.92 %	61	A	31.6 % / 25.5 %	77	A	37.4 % / 26.42 %
14	C	19.08 % / 16.49 %	30	D	43.66 % / 17.87 %	46	A	49.47 % / 20.76 %	62	B	43.66 % / 24.43 %	78	C	25.95 % / 27.03 %
15	B	57.25 % / 13.9 %	31	A	19.85 % / 18.32 %	47	D	50.08 % / 20.76 %	63	C	16.79 % / 26.57 %	79	B	51.15 % / 26.1 %
16	A	30.69 % / 13.89 %	32	A	54.05 % / 17.4 %	48	A	49.62 % / 20.76 %	64	A	56.03 % / 24.58 %	80	D	17.1 % / 27.17 %

Q.	Ans.	Correct
		Skipped
81	A	31.6 %
		27.94 %
82	C	39.39 %
		28.55 %
83	A	35.27 %
		27.78 %
84	D	17.4 %
		28.4 %

Q.	Ans.	Correct
		Skipped
85	C	23.82 %
		27.48 %
86	D	21.37 %
		28.4 %
87	A	27.02 %
		25.8 %
88	B	51.15 %
		27.63 %

Q.	Ans.	Correct
		Skipped
89	A	17.86 %
		29.01 %
90	A	49.92 %
		26.42 %
91	D	20.46 %
		27.17 %
92	A	25.34 %
		27.79 %

Q.	Ans.	Correct
		Skipped
93	B	21.83 %
		28.09 %
94	D	18.02 %
		27.02 %
95	A	49.31 %
		26.57 %
96	D	17.25 %
		27.33 %

Q.	Ans.	Correct
		Skipped
97	B	31.3 %
		26.1 %
98	B	17.56 %
		26.41 %
99	D	27.94 %
		26.87 %
100	D	31.45 %
		25.5 %

Performance Analysis

Avg. Score (%)	36.5%
Toppers Score (%)	99.0%
Your Score	

//Hints and Solutions//

1. Laws of Returns to Scale are based on the following assumptions:

1. All the factors of production (such as land, labour and capital) are variable but organization is fixed.

2. There is no change in technology.

3. There is perfect competition in the market.

All the options given follow.

Hence, the correct option is (D).

2. Payment of interest as a factor reward is explained by productivity theory. According to productivity theory, interest can be defined as a reward for availing the services of capital for production purposes. Interest is the reward for the productive use of the capital which is equal to the marginal productivity of physical capital. Therefore, those economists who hold classical view have said that "the rate of interest is determined by the supply and demand of capital."

Hence, the correct option is (A).

3. Axioms of Revealed Preference Theory are (a) Rationality (b) Consistency (c) Transitivity.
Revealed preference theory is a method of analyzing choices made by individuals, mostly used for comparing the influence of policies on consumer behavior.

4. Arrangement of concepts in terms of their development in Demand Theory :

(i) Cardinal utility

(ii) Ordinal utility (in form of indifference curve)

(iii) Revealed Preference

(iv) Neumann and Morgenstern Utility Theory.

5. Kinked demand curve is given by Sweezy. Full cost pricing theory is given by Hall And Hitch. Sales maximisation theory is given by Baumol. Limit pricing model is given by Bains.

6. The notion of production function implies technical efficiency. Technical efficiency can be defined around the concept of the reaching the maximum output. Therefore, technical efficiency is defined through a production function.

7. The core is the set of feasible allocations that cannot be improved upon by a subset of the economy's consumers.

8. Demand for consumer durables and human capital forms part of the consumption demand model developed by Milton Friedman.

9. Money multiplier determines total supply of money in the economy. Money multiplier is one of various closely related ratios of commercial bank money to central bank money under a fractional-reserve banking system. It measures an estimate of the maximum amount of commercial bank money that can be created, given a certain amount of central bank money.

10. Fisher's Quantity of Theory of Money establishes relation between money and transactions by the equation: MV = PT Cambridge economists, Marshall linked money to income via quantity theory of money. MV = kPY
The conept of MV = f(r, y, w) was given by Friedman and the last pair is correctly matched.

11. Estate duty was levied on the total property passing to the heirs on the death of a person. Income tax is levied on income of the individuals. Excise duty is levied on production of goods and custom duty is levied on export and import of goods.

12. Training of Rural Youth for Self-Employment (TRYSEM) scheme was launched in 1979. The Rural Landless Employment Guarantee Programme (RLEGP) was launched in 1983. Jawahar Rozgar Yojna (JRY) was launched in 1989. Employment Assurance Scheme (EAS) was launched in 1993.

13. Wealth of nation was published in the year 1776.
Principles of economics was published in the year 1871.
General theory of employment, interest and money was published in the year 1936.
Affluent society was published in the year 1958.

14. Foodgrains Enquiry Committee was formed in the year 1957. State Trading in Foodgrains put its first trial in the year 1959. Commission for Agricultural Costs and Prices was formed in the year 1965. Foodgrain Policy Committee was formed in the year 1966.

15. The Laffer Curve demonstrates the relationship between tax rate and total tax revenue by governments.

16. When government expenditure exceeds total government receipts, the budget deficit is positive.
Budget deficit = Government expenditure - Government receipts

17. Wealth tax is levied on the net worth of the person on the assets mentioned in the act, even if it has been inherited property. Thus, tax on inherited property is wealth tax.

18. A temporary increase in marginal tax rate will lower the output. If tax rate will increase temporarily, production will be low to reduce the tax liability.

19. VAT on a product is imposed at every stage between its production till it reaches a consumer.
VAT is a type of consumption tax that is placed on a product whenever value is added at a stage of production and at its final sale.

20. 'Pump Priming' should be resorted to at a time of deflation. It is a government spending in an attempt to stimulate private spending and the expansion of business and industry.

21. Union excise duties are a part of the Central government's tax revenue because excise duties are considered tax revenue to the Central government.

22. The tenth five year plan aims at reducing poverty by 5%.

23. In the neo classical growth model, an increase in the marginal propensity to save increases steady state output per person and increases steady state capital per person.

24. Capital per person decreases if net investment per person is less than savings per person because if savings made are not being invested, then it will result into decrease in capital.

25. The Harrod–Domar model is a Keynesian model of economic growth. It is used in development economics to explain an economy's growth rate in terms of the level of saving and capital.

Savings = Capital output ratio $\times$ Growth rate of income

= 3 $\times$ 5%

= 15%

Hence, the correct option is (D).

26. The theory of unlimited supply of labour was proposed by A. Lewis.

27. The second five year plan was based on a model developed by P.C. Mahalanobis.

28. Vicious cycle of poverty was proposed by Ragner Nurkse.

29. The trade off between inflation and unemployment remains stable only when the inertial rate of inflation remains unchanged. When the inertial rate of inflation changes, short run Phillips Curve will shift.

30. The money multiplier is the multiplicative inverse of the required reserve ratio as long as currency leakages into circulation and/or foreign market do not occur, banks do not maintain excess reserves, and the required reserve ratio is far in excess of the reserves that banks think are prudent given that they hold.

31. Milton Friedman disagreed that monetary policy has few short run effect on the real economy.

32. A person who left the job to find another job would be classified as fractionally unemployed. It is the unemployment which exists in any economy due to people being in the process of moving from one job to another.

33. High powered money is produced by the Reserve Bank of India.

34. The transaction version of the quantity theory of money was developed by Fisher in 1911 in his book 'Purchasing Power of Money'.

35. Crowding out will emerge in the economy if government spending is on the rise. Crowding out effect is a situation in which government spending is increased and private sector expenditure is decreased due to increased interest rates.

36. AK Model of economic growth is an endogenous growth model used in the theory of economic growth.
Non-operation of diminishing returns to scale and constant endogenous savings rate are not true regarding Y = AK model wherein A is constant on the assumption of constant returns to scale, Y is national output and K is the capital stock. AK models assumes constant exogenous saving rate and fixed level of technology.

37. Value of Marginal Product (VMP) is MPP X AR, the value of marginal product (VMP) is the resource's marginal product multiplied by the product price. The marginal revenue product of a resource is defined as the increase in a firm's total revenue attributable to employing one more unit of that resource.

38. 0 - 6 years is the relevant age group for computation of a child sex ratio.

39. Kelkar Committee recommended abolition of tax rebates under Section 88 of the Income Tax Act.

40. Demographic dividend occurs when the proportion of working people in the total population is high because this indicates that more people have the potential to be productive and contribute to growth of the economy. The phenomenon of 'demographic dividend' of the country relates to an increase in the population in the working age group.

41. An interim audit involves preliminary audit work that is conducted prior to the fiscal year-end of a client.

42. A tax is said to be buoyant if the tax revenues increase more than proportionately in response to a rise in national income or output.

43. A labour market is seen as segmented if it consists of various sub-groups with little or no crossover capability. Segmentation can result in different groups, for example men and women, receiving different wages. Equality of wages of different types of labour in segmented labour markets, is incorrect because there is no equality of wages for different types of labour.

44. In India, farmers who hold land up to 1 hectare are called 'marginal farmers'.

45. If there is balance payments deficit, then in a floating exchange rate system, the external value of the currency would tend to fall as deficit will lead to reduced value of currency.

46. When a country devalues its currency, the domestic prices of its imports are raised and the foreign prices of its exports are reduced. Thus, devaluation helps to improve BOP deficit of a country by increasing its exports and reducing its imports. So, when the sum of price elasticities of demand for exports and imports in absolute terms is greater than unity, devaluation will improve the country's balance of payments.

47. Economic integration is an agreement among countries in a geographic region to reduce and ultimately remove tariff and non-tariff barriers to the free flow of goods or services.
Free Trade Area, Customs Union and Common Market are examples of economic integration.
Cartels are not considered for economic integration because cartels are formed by suppliers to restrict the competition in the market by limiting production.

48. Since 1955, the national income estimates are being prepared by the Central Statistical Organisation (CSO).

49. Savings is that part of income which is not spent on consumption during some given time period. Saving means different things to different people. To some, it means putting money in the bank. To others, it means buying stocks or contributing to a pension plan. But to economists, saving means only one thing - consuming less out of a given amount of resources in the present in order to consume more in the future.

50.

- Trend is depicted by time series.
- Coefficient of variation means (S.D./Mean) x 100.
- Mean = np is a binomial distribution.
- Symmetric distribution is a normal distribution.

51. If the Price Consumption Curve of a commodity is bending backwards, then the commodity must be giffen goods.

52. Liquidity trap is a situation in which prevailing interest rates are low and savings rate is high, which make monetary policy ineffective and fiscal policy becomes more effective. Fiscal policy helps boost spending. Thus, if an economy enters liquidity trap, further increases in the money stock will fail to further lower interest rates and therefore, fail to stimulate. These policy initiatives tried to stimulate the economy through methods other than the reduction of short-term interest rates.

53. The rate at which the Central Bank discounts the bills of commercial banks is called discount rate.

54. It is the correct formula for the measure of price elasticity of demand.
Price elasticity of demand = Change in quantity demanded/Change in price.

55. Green Box subsidies under WTO are allowed because they are confined to agriculture sector.
Green Box subsidies are allowed without limits, provided they comply with relevant criteria. They also include environmental protection and regional development programmes.

56. Its marginal products' functions (mpl and mpk) are of degree 3.

57. The balance of payments of a country on current account is equal to balance of trade plus net invisible exports. B.O.P. of a country is the record of all economic transactions between the residents of the country and the rest of the world in a particular period and includes all external visible and non-visible transactions of a country.

58. Industrial Licensing Policy Inquiry Committee was set up in 1967 under the chairmanship of Mr. Subimal Dutt.

59. The term 'Hindu Rate of Growth' was coined by Raj Krishna. 'Hindu Rate of Growth' is a term referring to the low annual growth rate of the planned economy of India before the liberalisation of 1991, which stagnated around 3.5% from 1950s to 1980s, while per capita income growth averaged 1.3%.

60. If β_2 turns out to be greater than 3, then the curve is called a leptokurtic curve and it is more peaked than the normal curve.

61. The Merchandise Exports from India Scheme (MEIS) was introduced in the Foreign Trade Policy (FTP) 2015 - 20 on April 1, 2015 and is a major export promotion scheme implemented by the Ministry of Commerce and Industry. MEIS aims to incentive export of merchandise which is produced/manufactured in India. Thus, New Trade Policy 2015 - 20 has introduced new scheme called Merchandise Exports from India Scheme.

62.

- Fiscal Deficit is revenue receipts and recovery of loans and other receipts minus total expenditure.
- Revenue Deficit is revenue and interest receipts minus revenue expenditure.
- Budgetary Deficit is total receipts minus total disbursements.
- Capital Deficit is receipts minus disbursements in capital account.

63. Keynesian theory of distribution is given by N. Kaldar. Time preference theory of interest is given by Bohm Bawerk. Sun-Spot theory of trade cycle is given by W.S. Javons. Modern theory of income determination is given by J.M. Keynes.

64. Microeconomics relates to the individual economic agent's (consumer and producer) behaviour and the result of such interactions in determining the price of goods and services. It is, thus, also called price theory.

65. Net national product at market price minus net indirect taxes is equal to net national product at factor cost.

66.

- Reaction of Ho when it is true is called type I error.
- Mean is equal to degrees of freedom is given by chi-square distribution.
- Popular population heterogeneous is in stratified random sampling.
- Mean > mode means positively skewed distribution.

67. The two components of balance of payments account include current account and capital account. One of the components of current account is export and import of services (invisible trade) which includes a large variety of non-factor services (known as invisible items) sold and purchased by the residents of a country, to and from the rest of the world.

68. Personal disposable income is equal to personal income minus personal taxes, which is also equal to consumption plus saving.
Personal income is the sum of all incomes actually received by an individual during a given year (including income received, but not earned) minus all corporate taxes and social contributions.

69. Fisher's index number satisfies both time reversal test and factor reversal test.
Factor reversal test holds that the product of a price index and the quantity index should be equal to the corresponding value index.
Factor reversal test is satisfied by the Fisher's ideal index. This means, of course, that the formula serves equally well for constructing indices of quantities as for constructing indices of prices, the quantity index being derived by interchanging 'p' and 'q' in the ideal formula.

70. According to Keynes, the cause for the unprecedented global depression of the 1930's was lack of sufficient aggregate demand. A falling labour share and rising inequality put downward pressure on aggregate demand for a simple reason: most of GDP consists in consumption expenditures, and workers and middle-income households tend to spend a much higher share of their income on consumption (and to save a correspondingly lower share) compared with recipients of capital income and the very wealthy.

Keynes said the problem was lack of aggregate demand. Keynes argued passionately that governments should intervene in the economy to stimulate demand through public works scheme - higher spending and borrowing.

71. Big push concept was given by R. Rodan. Knife-edge concept was given by Sir Henry Roy Forbes Harrod. Golden age concept was given by Joan Robinson. Golden rule of accumulation concept was given by Michael E. Phelps.

72. Learning by doing concept is advocated by K. J. Arrow. Division of labour concept was advocated by Adam Smith. Stationary state of bliss concept was advocated by John Stuart Mill. Low level equilibrium trap concept was advocated by R.R. Nelson.

73. WTO Ministerial Meeting at Singapore was held in 1996. WTO Ministerial Meeting at Doha was held in 2001. WTO Ministerial Meeting at Cancun was held in 2003. WTO Ministerial Meeting at Hong Kong was held in 2005.

74. Hedging in the foreign exchange market refers to covering a risk of foreign exchange in future. Hedging means dealing with the securities in such a way so that future risks due to changes in exchange rates can be avoided.

75. Only A is true and B is false. Real Effective Exchange Rate (REER) is the weighted average of a country's currency relative to an index or basket of other major currencies, adjusted for the effects of inflation. The weights are determined by comparing the relative trade balance of a country's currency against each country within the index.

76. Tax incidence is a tax burden that falls on a particular person or a group who ends up paying a tax.

Tax incidence is said to "fall" upon the group that ultimately bears the burden of or ultimately has to pay the tax. The key concept is that the tax incidence or tax burden does not depend on where the revenue is collected, but on the price elasticity of demand and price elasticity of supply.

77. Both statements are true and rightly explained.

According to equi-marginal sacrifice, tax burden should be so apportioned among various individuals that marginal sacrifice of utility of each person paying the tax should be the same. Assuming that marginal utility of income falls, the principle of equality of marginal sacrifice implies very high marginal rates of taxation. Thus, both (A) and (R) are true and (R) is the correct explanation of (A).

78. Taxes on mineral rights subject to any limitation impost by the Parliament are levied by state governments.

79. The consumer surplus is represented by the area APE in the given diagram.

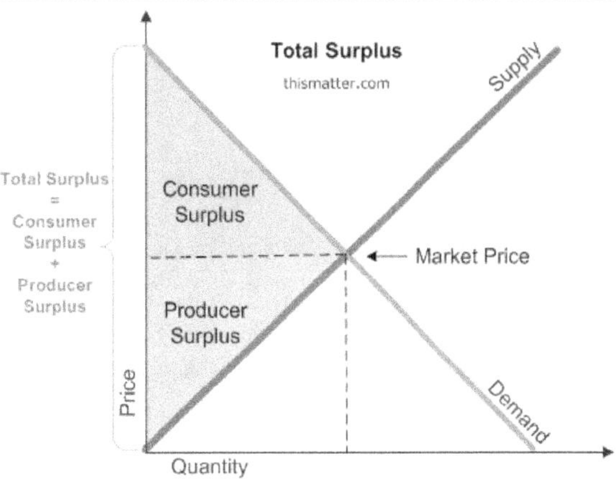

Also, in the given diagram, the area in green colour shows the consumer surplus.

80. Simon Hawkins relates to Static Leontief Model and these are necessary and sufficient conditions for the solution of the model. The Hawkins-Simon condition is a well known method used to determine the existence of a unique positive solution of a static Leontief system. A method that is sometimes easier to apply is the spectral radius condition.

81. $Q = 2 \times (8)^{\frac{1}{3}} \times (27)^{\frac{2}{3}}$

$Q = 2 \times (2 \times 2 \times 2)^{\frac{1}{3}} \times (3 \times 3 \times 3)^{\frac{2}{3}}$

$Q = 2 \times 2 \times (3)^2$

$Q = 36$

82. Price elasticity of demand = % change in demand $\div$ % change in price

% change in demand = 60/240 x 100 = 25%

% change in price = 5/15 x 100 = 33.33%

PED = 25/33.33 = 0.75 = $\dfrac{3}{4}$

83.

- Wald test means error in variable model.

- Unit root test is related to stationarity.

- Student's test is related to significance of regression coefficient.

- Granger test is related to casuality.

84. All of the given models can be estimated using OLS (Ordinary Least Square).

85. If OLS is applied separately to each equation that is part of a simultaneous interdependent system, then the resulting estimates will be biased and inconsistent. Simultaneous equation models are models which consist of several equations where each model has several endogenous variables which are simultaneously related by the interrelated series of equations. These models require additional model building because they often render OLS estimators biased and inconsistent.

86. Multicollinearity is a case of multiple regression in which the predictor variables are themselves highly correlated. It is a situation in which there is an exact linear relation among two or more of the input variables. Taking a logarithm of each of the variables is not a plausible remedy for multicollinearity.

87. Perfect knowledge is not a feature of imperfect competition. It is a feature of perfect competition.

88.

- Compensation Criterion was given by Kaldor-Hicks.
- Impossibility Theorem was given by Kenneth Arrow.
- Managerial Discretion Model was given by Williamson.
- Uncertainty Theory of Profits was given by F. H. Knight.

89. Using the mid-point method, price elasticity of demand $=$
$$\frac{B2-B1}{B2+B1/2} \times \frac{A2+A1/2}{A2-A1}$$

$B =$ Quantity, $A =$ price,
$B2 = 20000, B1 = 30000, A2 = 400, A1 = 300 :$
$$\frac{20000-30000}{20000+30000/2} \times \frac{400+300/2}{400-300} = 1.4$$

90.

- Absolute Income Hypothesis was developed by Keynes in 1936.
- Relative Income Hypothesis was developed in 1949 by Dusenberry.
- Permanent Income Hypothesis was developed in 1957 by Friedman.
- Life-cycle Hypothesis was developed by Ando and Modigliani in 1963.

91. Rapid and large scale industrialisation was the achievement purpose in 2nd Five Year Plan.
Removal of poverty and self-reliance was the achievement purpose in 5th Five Year Plan.
Modernisation was the achievement purpose in 7th Five Year Plan.
Rapid and non-inclusive growth was the achievement purpose in 11th Five Year Plan.

92.

- Principles of Political Economy and Taxation was written by David Ricardo (1817).
- The General Theory of Employment, Interest and Money was written by John Maynard Keynes (1936).
- Value and Capital was written by John Richard Hicks (1939).
- A Revision of Demand Theory was written by Harry Johnson (1956).

93.

1. MODVAT was introduced in 1986.
2. Expenditure Tax was introduced in 1987.
3. Fringe Benefit Tax was introduced in 2005
4. Estate Duty was abolished in 2006.

94. Assertion is true but reason is false because Harrod-Domar model assumes constant capital output ratio.
Harrod-Domar model assumes fixed technological relationship between capital stock and income flows.

95. Fisher's ideal index is the multiplication of Laspeyers's index number and Paasche's index number.
Fisher's ideal index number fulfills both time reversal test and factor reversal test. Therefore, both A and R are correct and rightly explained.

96. If the economy was operating at E, 20 additional units of eggs can be produced with no impact on bacon production because there is under-utilization of resources at point E.

97. Random sampling implies that the observations are selected in a systemic manner and not the biased one. Simple random sampling is the basic sampling technique where we select a group of subjects (a sample) for study from a larger group (a population). Each individual is chosen entirely by chance and each member of the population has an equal chance of being included in the sample. Every possible sample of a given size has the same chance of selection.

98. χ^2 (chi-square) test is used to test association between the qualitative variables. The chi-square test is used to determine if there is a significant difference between the expected frequencies and the observed frequencies in one or more categories.

99. Coefficient correlation is under-root of multiplication of two regression coefficients.

100. Regional Integration is a process in which neighbouring states enter into an agreement in order to upgrade co-operation through common institutions and rules. African Union is not a form of economic integration in the context of intra-regional trade because intra-regional trade in Africa as a share of total foreign trade has traditionally been low compared to other regions.

Q.1 Which of the following taxes is within the jurisdiction of states as enumerated in List - II of the Schedule VII of the Constitution of India?

A. Taxes on railway freights and fares

B. Taxes on sale and purchase of newspaper and on advertisement therein

C. Rate of stamp duty in respect of certain financial documents

D. Taxes on luxuries, including entertainments, betting and gambling

Q.2 Which of the following is tantamount to absence of taxation?

A. Shifting of tax

B. Tax transformation

C. Evasion of tax

D. Tax capitalisation

Q.3 Match the items given in the lists.

List - I	List - II
I. Optimal Income Taxation	1. Charles Tiebout
II. Economic Theory of Politics	2. Peter A. Phyrr
III. Local Public Goods	3. F. Ramsey
IV. Zero-Based Budgeting	4. Anthony Downs

A. 3, 1, 4, 2   **B.** 2, 3, 1, 4   **C.** 3, 2, 1, 4   **D.** 3, 4, 1, 2

Q.4 Which of the following are relevant in Zero-Based Budgeting?

I. Each item of expenditure is challenged in pre-budgeting review.

II. No minimum level of expenditure is allowed to be taken as given.

III. Expenditure of each item is increased marginally.

IV. Most items of expenditure are taken for granted when budget is prepared for the next year.

A. I and III

B. I, II and IV

C. I and II

D. I, III and IV

Q.5 Directions: Arrange the following in chronological order.

I. Indirect Tax Enquiry Committee (Jha Committee)

II. Tax Reforms Committee (Chelliah Committee)

III. Taxation Enquiry Commission (Mathur Commission)

IV. Direct Tax Enquiry Committee (Wanchoo Committee)

A. III, II, IV, I

B. III, I, IV, II

C. II, III, I, IV

D. III, IV, I, II

Q.6 If the international terms of trade settle at a level that is between each country's opportunity cost, then

A. there is no basis of gainful trade for either country

B. both countries gain from trade

C. only one country gains from trade

D. one country gains and the other country loses from trade

Q.7 When a nation imposes an import tariff, the nation's offer curve will

A. shift away from axis measuring its export commodity

B. shift away from the axis measuring import commodity

C. not shift

D. All of these

Q.8 The exchange rate is kept the same in all parts of the markets by which of the following?

A. Exchange arbitrage   **B.** Interest arbitrage

C. Hedging   **D.** Speculation

Q.9 According to the Rybezynski Theorem, the growth of only one factor at constant relative commodity prices leads to an absolute expansion in the output of

A. both commodities

B. the commodity using the growing factor intensively

C. the commodity using the non-growing factor intensively

D. any of the above

Q.10 Which of the following five year plans of India recorded the largest gap in terms of growth rate between the services sector and the industrial sector?

A. Seventh Plan   **B.** Eighth Plan

C. Ninth Plan   **D.** Tenth Plan

Q.11 Match the items in the given lists.

List - I	List - II
I. Critical Minimum Effort Thesis	1. R. F. Kahn
II. Knife-edge Equilibrium	2. Rosentein-Rodan
III. Bastard Golden Age	3. Leibenstein
IV. Big Push Theory	4. Harrod Domar

A. 3, 4, 1, 2   **B.** 1, 3, 4, 2   **C.** 2, 1, 3, 4   **D.** 4, 2, 1, 3

Q.12 Match the items in the given lists.

List - I	List - II
I. Structural view of underdevelopment	1. Classical economists
II. Laissez-faire policy	2. Hollis Chenery
III. Departmental scheme of expanded reproduction	3. Steady state growth
IV. Golden age of accumulation	4. Karl Marx

A. 2, 1, 4, 3   **B.** 4, 2, 3, 1   **C.** 1, 4, 2, 3   **D.** 3, 4, 1, 2

Q.13 Directions: Read the given statements carefully and choose the correct option accordingly.

Assertion (A): In Marxian scheme of things, $M \to C \to M'$, where $M' > M$ and $M' - M$ is surplus value.

Reason (R): The main cause of this surplus value is raw materials, machines etc.

A. (A) is wrong, but (R) is correct.

B. (A) is correct, but (R) is wrong.

C. Both (A) and (R) are correct.

D. Both (A) and (R) are wrong.

Q.14 Arrange the proponents of Classical Theory of Development in a sequential order.
I. David Ricardo
II. Adam Smith
III. J. S. Mill
IV. Robert Malthus

A. II, IV, III, I
B. IV, III, I, II
C. III, II, IV, I
D. I, II, III, Iv

Q.15 Which of the following are components of HDI?
I. Longetivity
II. Infant mortality
III. Educational attainment
IV. Decent standard of living

A. I, II and III
B. II, III and IV
C. II, I and IV
D. I, III and IV

Q.16 Inverted 'U' shaped income distribution hypothesis is associated with

A. J. B. Clark
B. David Ricardo
C. Simon Kuznets
D. Adam Smith

Q.17 The concept of vicious circle of poverty is associated with

A. J. M. Keynes
B. Ragner Nurkse
C. Karl Marx
D. J. S. Mill

Q.18 Which of the following economists has given the model which makes use of the stock adjustment principle to explain business cycles?

A. N. Kaldor
B. J. R. Hicks
C. P. Samuelson
D. J. M. Keynes

Q.19 Which of the following is not specifically mentioned as a determinant of the demand for money?

A. Wealth
B. Nominal yield on alternative assets
C. Inflation rate
D. Real rate of interest

Q.20 The rate of net investment spending per time period depends on steepness of the downward slope of which of the following?

A. Marginal Efficiency of Investment Schedule
B. Marginal Efficiency of Capital Schedule
C. LM-Schedule
D. IS-Schedule

Q.21 **Directions:** Read the given statements carefully and choose the correct option accordingly.
Assertion (A): In liquidity trap, the demand for money is perfectly interest elastic.
Reason (R): Because in this situation, all the investors expects the market rate of interest to rise towards the natural rate of interest

A. (A) and (R) both are correct and (R) is the correct explanation of (A).
B. (A) and (R) both are correct, but (R) is not the correct explanation of (A).
C. (A) is correct, but (R) is incorrect.
D. Both (A) and (R) are incorrect.

Q.22 Match the theory/criterion of investment determination.

List - I	List - II
I. Dale Jorgenson	a. Q-Theory
II. J. M. Keynes	b. Neo-classical Theory
III. James Cohin	c. Accelerator Theory
IV. James Clark	d. Present Value Criterion

A. a, d, b, c
B. b, d, a, c
C. c, d, a, b
D. c, a, d, b

Q.23 Which of the following statements is false?

A. The balanced budget multiplier is unity when taxes are lump sump taxes.
B. The balanced budget multiplier is less than unity when taxes are ad valorem taxes.
C. Tax multiplier is less than government expenditure multiplier.
D. Tax multiplier is more than government expenditure multiplier.

Q.24 In Keynes' equation of absolute income hypothesis, $C = \alpha_0 + by$, where C = Consumption expenditure, α_0 = Consumption expenditure when income (y) is zero and b = Marginal Propensity to Consume (MPC), then which of the following statements is false?

A. MPC is independent of the level of income.
B. MPC is dependent on the level of income.
C. APC falls as income rises.
D. APC > MPC

Q.25 If :
1 = Involuntary unemployment;
2 = Disguised unemployment;
3 = Frictional unemployment;
4 = Structural unemployment; then full employment is consistent with :

A. 1 and 2
B. 2 and 3
C. 3 and 4
D. 1 and 4

Q.26 The equilibrium in the market is incomplete with increasing returns to scale only in the case of

A. imperfectly competitive market
B. monopolistic market
C. perfectly competitive market
D. None of the above

Q.27 At the point of tangency between short-run average total cost and long-run average cost, the short-run marginal cost

A. is greater than long-run marginal cost
B. is less than long-run marginal cost
C. is far above long-run marginal cost
D. equals long-run marginal cost

Q.28 Match the items in the given lists.

List - I	List - II
I. Agency Theory of Firm	1. O. E. Williamson II
II. X-Efficiency	2. M. C. Jensen and W. J. Mecling
III. The Utility Maximisation Model	3. Wilfredo Pareto
IV. Edgeworth box diagram was	4. Harvey Leibenstein

first used by	

A. 3, 2, 1, 4   **B.** 2, 4, 1, 3   **C.** 2, 3, 4, 1   **D.** 3, 4, 1, 2

Q.29 MP_L/MP_K does not change with any proportionate change in labour and capital. The production function is

A. linear
B. non-linear
C. homogeneous
D. homothetic

Q.30 <u>Directions:</u> Read the given statements carefully and choose the correct option accordingly.

Assertion (A): Monopoly is Pareto inefficient.

Reason (R): It would be possible to change the allocation of resources to make the amount of income he would be prepared to pay in exchange of the reduction in price.

A. Both (A) and (R) are correct and (R) is the correct explanation of (A).
B. (A) is correct, but (R) is incorrect.
C. Both (A) and (R) are correct, but (R) is the incorrect explanation of (A).
D. (R) is correct, but (A) is incorrect.

Q.31 The distinguishing characteristics of monopolistic competition are :
I. product differentiation
II. non-price competition
III. large numbers of firms and freedom to enter and exit
IV. firms are independent

A. I and III are correct
B. I, II and IV are correct
C. I, II and III are correct
D. I, III and IV are correct

Q.32 As long as the substitution effect dominates the income effect, the labour supply curve

A. is negatively sloped
B. is positively sloped
C. bends backward
D. shifts towards left

Q.33 Under Cournot Model of Duopoly, each duopolist will produce

A. half the output
B. one-fourth of the output
C. one-sixth of the output
D. one-third of the total output

Q.34 Psychological law of consumption was given by

A. Milton Friedman
B. Pigou
C. Tobin
D. Keynes

Q.35 Which of the following is true?
a. Indifference curves slope downward from left to right.
b. Indifference curves slope downward from right to left.
c. Indifference curves are convex to the point of origin of the two axes.
d. Indifference curves never intersect each other.

A. Only a, b and c
B. Only b, c and d
C. Only a, c and d
D. Only a and d

Q.36 When interest elasticity of demand for money is zero, then the L - M curve is

A. vertically parallel to y-axis
B. horizontally parallel to x-axis
C. positively sloping straight line
D. negatively sloping straight line

Q.37 Natural rate of unemployment is the rate of unemployment at which rate of inflation is

A. stable   **B.** unstable   **C.** falling   **D.** rising

Q.38 Knife-edge problem arises in which of the following models?

A. Slow model
B. Kaldor model
C. Joan Robinson model
D. Harrod-Domar Model

Q.39 If consumption of each additional unit of a commodity is expected to give an increasing marginal utility, then total utility derived by consumer will

A. initially rise, but eventually fall
B. rise at a decreasing rate as long as marginal utility is more than zero
C. rise at an increasing rate as long as marginal utility keeps rising
D. not reflect any increasing trend

Q.40 Endogenous technological change is not caused by

A. FDI
B. Population size
C. Population density
D. Educational level

Q.41 Exclusion principle is not applicable to

A. merit goods
B. social goods
C. private goods
D. all goods

Q.42 To avoid excess burden of tax, we should have

A. low marginal tax rate
B. zero marginal tax rate
C. moderate marginal tax rate
D. reasonable marginal tax rate

Q.43 The law of diminishing returns to scale holds true in the

A. market period
B. short period
C. long period
D. secular period

Q.44 The demand for labour by a firm is a derived demand. It depends upon which of the following factors?

A. The demand for goods and services that labour helps to produce
B. The degree of substitution between labour and other factors of production
C. The elasticity of demand for labour
D. The demand for other factors of production

Q.45 In classical theory, an increase in money supply leads to

A. decrease in price level
B. increase in savings
C. decrease in investment
D. increase in price level

Q.46 Shift in LM curve takes place due to increase in

A. autonomous investment
B. money supply
C. consumption

D. saving rate

Q.47 The Phillips curve shows the relation between
A. income and consumption
B. income and price level
C. income and investment
D. inflation and unemployment

Q.48 The cost incurred by a firm in hiring labour is called
A. explicit cost   B. implicit cost
C. marginal cost   D. total cost

Q.49 The &aposIncremental Capital-Output Ratio&apos is symbolically written as
A. K/L   B. $\Delta K/\ \Delta L$
C. $\Delta K/\ \Delta Y$ D. K/Y

Q.50 If Marginal Propensity to Consume (MPC) is equal to Average Propensity to Consume (APC) for all levels of income (Y), then the correct corresponding consumption (C) function will be
A. $C = a + bY$ B. $C = a\ + \frac{b}{y}$
C. $C = bY$ D. $C = bY^2$

Q.51 Which of the following groups represents the interests of the developing countries?
A. G - 7   B. G - 10   C. G - 77   D. G - 80

Q.52 Funds not belonging to the Government are called
A. contingency funds   B. consolidated funds
C. private accounts   D. public accounts

Q.53 Which of the following is the deficit budget in which the deficits are covered through taxes?
A. Balanced budget   B. Unbalanced budget
C. Surplus budget   D. Zero-base budget

Q.54 Raul Prebisch & aposs argument is concerned with the effects of business cycles on
A. terms of trade
B. balance of payments
C. output
D. consumption

Q.55 The difference between the export and import of services is called balance of
A. trade   B. invisibles
C. current account   D. capital account

Q.56 Public enterprises in India have developed in
A. consumer goods industries
B. key and basic industries
C. service industries
D. all types of industries

Q.57 The statistical technique used to determine the degree of relationship between two variables is called
A. dispersion   B. index numbers
C. association   D. correlation

Q.58 Which of the following index number methods has an upward bias?
A. Laspeyre&aposs method
B. Paasche&aposs method
C. Bowley&aposs method
D. Fisher&aposs method

Q.59 Directions: Read the given statements carefully and choose the correct option accordingly.
Assertion (A): The rate of fall of MR is more than that of AR in the event of their falling.
Reason (R): Both MR and AR curves are linear and negatively sloping.
A. Both (A) and (R) are true, but (R) is not the correct explanation of (A).
B. Both (A) and (R) are true and (R) is the correct explanation of (A).
C. (A) is false, but (R) is true.
D. (A) is true, but (R) is false.

Q.60 Which of the following is the main objective of public distribution system?
A. Export of food   B. Import of food
C. Food security   D. Quality of food

Q.61 The mean absolute deviation is minimized when calculated from
A. mean   B. mode
C. harmonic mean   D. median

Q.62 In a regression, r^2 is the ratio between
A. explained and total variation
B. explained and unexplained variation
C. unexplained and total variation
D. None of the above

Q.63 The main objective of International Monetary Fund (IMF) is to
A. promote international trade
B. help economically backward countries
C. set and enforce rules for international trade
D. promote international liquidity

Q.64 The effect of increase in CRR will be reduced or nullified if
A. bank rate is reduced
B. securities are sold in the open market
C. SLR is increased
D. people do not borrow from non-banking institutions

Q.65 Chamberlin introduced the concept of cost known as
A. fixed cost   B. floating cost
C. selling cost   D. variable cost

Q.66 If commodities are perfect substitutes, then indifference curve becomes a
A. straight line with negative slope
B. download sloping curve
C. right angle
D. rectangular hyperbola

Q.67 Securities and Exchange Board of India (SEBI) monitors which of the following?

- **A.** Companies coming for new public issues
- **B.** Regulation of stock exchanges in India
- **C.** Regulation of insider trading and outsider trading
- **D.** All of the above

Q.68 Arrange the following in the order in which they appeared. Use the codes given below.
(i) International Monetary Fund
(ii) International Finance Corporation
(iii) World Trade Organisation
(iv) General Agreement on Tariffs and Trade

- **A.** (iv), (i), (iii), (ii)
- **B.** (i), (ii), (iv), (iii)
- **C.** (i), (iv), (ii), (iii)
- **D.** (ii), (iii), (i), (iv)

Q.69 Arrange the following in the order in which they appeared. Use the codes given below.
(i) Imperialism
(ii) Mercantalism
(iii) Capitalism
(iv) Feudalism

- **A.** (ii), (iv), (iii), (i)
- **B.** (iv), (iii), (ii), (i)
- **C.** (iii), (iv), (ii), (i)
- **D.** (iv), (ii), (i), (iii)

Q.70 Directions: Read the given statements carefully and choose the correct option accordingly.
Assertion (A): Demand curve is vertical when elasticity of demand is zero.
Reason (R): Marginal utility of a product is increasing.

- **A.** Both (A) and (R) are true and(R) is the correct explanation of (A).
- **B.** Both (A) and (R) are true and(R) is not the correct explanation of (A).
- **C.** (A) is true but (R) is false.
- **D.** (A) is false but (R) is true.

Q.71 Directions: Read the given statements carefully and choose the correct option accordingly.
Assertion (A): Sex ratio is below 1000 in India.
Reason (R): Sex ratio is above 1000 in Kerala.

- **A.** Both (A) and (R) are true and(R) is the correct explanation of (A).
- **B.** Both (A) and (R) are true and (R) is not the correct explanation of (A).
- **C.** (A) is true but (R) is false.
- **D.** (A) is false but (R) is true.

Q.72 Directions: Read the given statements carefully and choose the correct option accordingly.Assertion (A):
Skewness measures regression.
Reason (R): Kurtosis measures flatness at the top of frequency curve.

- **A.** Both (A) and (R) are true and(R) is the correct explanation of (A).
- **B.** Both (A) and (R) are true and(R) is not the correct explanation of (A).
- **C.** (A) is true but (R) is false.
- **D.** (A) is false but (R) is true.

Q.73 Assertion (A): Devaluation will lead to improvement in balance of trade.
Reason (R): Devaluation will lead to increase in price of exports.

- **A.** Both (A) and (R) are true and(R) is the correct explanation of (A).
- **B.** Both (A) and (R) are true and(R) is not the correct explanation of (A).
- **C.** (A) is true but (R) is false.
- **D.** (A) is false but (R) is true.

Q.74 Which of the following committees recommended tax on agriculture holdings in India?

- **A.** Tandon Committee
- **B.** Raj Committee
- **C.** Kelkar Committee
- **D.** Dantwala Committee

Q.75 Choose the correct sequence of Governors of Reserve Bank of India according to their appointment.
(i) Dr. C. Rangarajan
(ii) Dr. I. G. Patel
(iii) Dr. D. Subba Rao
(iv) Dr. Manmohan Singh

- **A.** (iv), (ii), (iii), (i)
- **B.** (ii), (iv), (i), (iii)
- **C.** (iv), (i), (ii), (iii)
- **D.** (ii), (i), (iv), (iii)

Q.76 If an increase in consumer income leads to a decrease in demand for camping equipment, then camping equipment is

- **A.** a normal good
- **B.** a substitute good
- **C.** an inferior good
- **D.** None of the above

Q.77 Which of the following issues was/were not addressed in Uruguay Round?

- **A.** Migration
- **B.** IPRs
- **C.** Services
- **D.** Tariff

Q.78 The consumer is in equilibrium at a point where the budget line

- **A.** is above an indifference curve
- **B.** is below an indifference curve
- **C.** is tangent to an indifference curve
- **D.** cuts an indifference curve

Q.79 A vertical supply curve parallel to Y axis implies that the elasticity of supply is

- **A.** zero
- **B.** infinity
- **C.** equal to one
- **D.** greater than zero but less than infinity

Q.80 Directions: The candidates are required to match List - I against List - II and select the correct answer code.

List - I	List - II
(a) Consumer&aposs surplus	(i) Supply decision
(b) Utility theory	(ii) Art of advertising
(c) Cost analysis	(iii) Progressive taxation
(d) Product differentiation	(iv) Welfare economics

A. (iv), (iii), (i), (ii)   **B.** (iv), (iii), (ii), (i)
C. (iii), (iv), (ii), (i)   **D.** (iii), (iv), (i), (ii)

Q.81 <u>Directions:</u> The candidates are required to match List - I against List - II and select the correct answer code.

List - I Monetary aggregates	List - II
a. M1	i. C + DD + OD + SD
b. M2	ii. C + DD + OD
c. M3	iii. C + DD + OD + TD + TD of post office
d. M4	iv. C + DD + OD + TD

A. (i), (ii), (iii), (iv)   **B.** (ii), (i), (iv), (iii)
C. (iii), (iv), (i), (ii)   **D.** (iv), (i), (ii), (iii)

Q.82 Which of the following is generally referred to as a 'broader measure of money supply'?
A. M_1 **B.** M_2 **C.** M_3 **D.** M_4

Q.83 According to Say's Law, unemployment can be removed by:
A. Rise in wages   **B.** Fall in wages
C. Taxing wages   **D.** Subsiding wages

Q.84 Pareto Optimality can take place at any point on:
A. Laffer Curve   **B.** Engel Curve
C. Contract Curve   **D.** Lorenz Curve

Q.85 A consumer attains his/her equilibrium at the point where:
A. Total Utility = Price
B. Marginal Utility > Price
C. Mariginal Utility < Price
D. Mariginal Utility = Price

Q.86 The Cobb-Douglas Production Function assumes that the elasticity of substitution is:
A. One   **B.** Two   **C.** Three   **D.** Four

Q.87 Match the items in List – I with the items in List – II:

List – I	List – II
a. Principles of Economics	1. Paul Sweezy
b. Kinked Demand Curve	2. Adam Smith
c. Principle of Maximum Social Advantage	3. Marshall
d. Law of Invisible Hand	4. Dalton

A. 3, 1, 4, 2   **B.** 3, 2, 4, 1
C. 2, 1, 3, 4   **D.** 4, 3, 1, 2

Q.88 In the context of different business cycle theories match the nature of cycle/approach given in List – I with the propounders in List – II:

List – I	List – II
i. Constrained Cycles	1. Paul A. Samuelson
ii. Acceleration – Multiplier Interaction Approach	2. J. R. Hicks
iii. Capital – Stock Adjustment Principle	3. Nicholas Kaldor
iv. Real Business Cycles	4. Robert J. Barro

A. i - 2, ii - 1, iii - 3, iv - 4
B. i - 1, ii - 2, iii - 4, iv - 3
C. i - 2, ii - 1, iii - 4, iv - 3
D. i - 1, ii - 3, iii - 2, iv - 4

Q.89 Match items given in List – I with those given in List – II:

List – I	List – II
a. Inventory Theoretic Approach	1. J.M. Keynes
b. Liquidity Preference as Behaviour Towards Risk	2. Milton Friedman
c. Money as a Temporary Abode of Purchasing Power	3. James Tobin
d. A Discontinuous Individual Speculative Demand for Money Function	4. W. Baumol

A. 1,4, 3, 2   **B.** 2, 3, 4, 1
C. 3, 2, 1, 4   **D.** 4, 3, 2, 1

Q.90 According to Mrs. Robinson, the stage of &aposGolden Age&apos =
A. Capital growth rate > Labour growth rate
B. Capital growth rate = Labour growth rate
C. Capital growth rate < Labour growth rate
D. Capital growth rate > 1

Q.91 According to Kuznets, innovation is
A. Application of new knowledge to production process
B. Improvement of efficiency of machines
C. Discovery of new consumption needs
D. Improvement of marketing techniques

Q.92 The case for progressive tax rates exists in terms of
A. Benefits received
B. Cost of service
C. Ability to pay
D. Voluntary exchange approach

Q.93 According to Peacock and Wiseman&aposs analysis, public expenditure increases
A. in a smooth and continuous manner
B. as time passes
C. in jerks or step like fashion
D. both in the short and long runs

Q.94 Which one of the following debt redemption methods is a process by which maturing debts are replaced by new bonds and there is no liquidation of the money burden of debt?
A. Sinking fund   **B.** Refunding
C. Conversion   **D.** Capital levy

Q.95 Fiscal deficit less interest payments is called
A. Net fiscal deficit   **B.** Monetised deficit
C. Primary deficit   **D.** Budgetary deficit

Q.96 Which of the following types of money has no intrinsic value?
A. Bitcoins   **B.** Gold

C. Paper money   **D.** All of the above

Q.97 Match items in List – I with the items in List – II:

List – I	List – II
a. Rajiv Gandhi Udyami Mitra Yojana	1. Jointly set up by Government of India & SIDBI
b. Credit Guarantee Fund Trust of Medium and Small Enterprises	2. Lean Manufacturing
c. National Manufacturing Competitiveness Programme	3. Control of Cartels
d. National Competition Commission of India	4. Promotion of first generation entrepreneurs

A. 4, 1, 2, 3   **B.** 4, 2, 1, 3   **C.** 4, 3, 1, 2   **D.** 3, 4, 1, 2

Q.98 Which of the following is not correct about the micro, small and medium enterprises in India?

A. It covers both registered and informal sectors.

B. Its classification criteria is investment in plant and machinery.

C. The fourth Census of the MSMEs is for the year 2009-10.

D. According to the fourth Census of MSME, total registered MSME sector comprised 67.1 percent manufacturing units and 32.9 percent were service enterprises.

Q.99 Match items of List – I with items of List – II:

List – I	List – II
a. Bharat Nirman Yojana	1. Rural Housing
b. National Food for Work Programme	2. Merged with SGSY
c. Indira Awas Yojana	3. Merged with SGRY
d. Supply of Improved Tool Kits to Rural Artisans	4. Rural Infrastructure

A. 4, 3, 1, 2   **B.** 4, 2, 1, 3

C. 4, 1, 2, 3   **D.** 2, 4, 1, 3

Q.100 Complete the statement with the correct option out of the following given below.

"Basel norms are regulatory stipulations meant for____"

A. Money market

B. Capital market

C. Banks

D. Insurance companies

// Smart Answer Sheet //

Correct   Indicates percentage of students who answered questions correctly.

Skipped   Indicates percentage of students who skipped questions.

Q.	Ans.	Correct / Skipped
1	D	37.28 % / 2.36 %
2	C	53.85 % / 18.34 %
3	D	36.09 % / 23.67 %
4	C	36.09 % / 20.71 %
5	D	35.5 % / 21.9 %
6	B	57.4 % / 20.11 %
7	A	43.2 % / 20.11 %
8	A	48.52 % / 20.71 %
9	B	57.99 % / 22.48 %
10	C	28.4 % / 23.08 %
11	A	65.09 % / 23.08 %
12	A	59.17 % / 23.08 %
13	B	45.56 % / 23.08 %
14	A	59.76 % / 21.9 %
15	D	46.15 % / 21.9 %
16	C	65.68 % / 22.49 %

Q.	Ans.	Correct / Skipped
17	B	71.01 % / 21.89 %
18	A	40.24 % / 22.48 %
19	D	22.49 % / 21.89 %
20	A	30.18 % / 22.48 %
21	A	58.58 % / 22.49 %
22	B	25.44 % / 26.04 %
23	D	36.69 % / 25.44 %
24	A	47.34 % / 23.67 %
25	C	40.83 % / 24.26 %
26	C	34.91 % / 24.26 %
27	D	37.87 % / 24.26 %
28	B	56.8 % / 25.45 %
29	D	23.08 % / 23.67 %
30	A	45.56 % / 24.26 %
31	C	31.36 % / 24.85 %
32	B	33.73 % / 25.44 %

Q.	Ans.	Correct / Skipped
33	D	51.48 % / 25.44 %
34	D	55.62 % / 25.45 %
35	C	60.95 % / 26.03 %
36	B	24.85 % / 25.45 %
37	A	43.79 % / 25.44 %
38	D	59.76 % / 25.45 %
39	C	39.05 % / 26.04 %
40	A	36.09 % / 26.63 %
41	B	50.89 % / 26.03 %
42	C	28.99 % / 25.45 %
43	C	34.32 % / 25.44 %
44	A	39.64 % / 26.04 %
45	D	49.7 % / 25.45 %
46	B	56.8 % / 25.45 %
47	D	66.27 % / 25.45 %
48	A	44.97 % / 26.04 %

Q.	Ans.	Correct / Skipped
49	C	51.48 % / 25.44 %
50	C	48.52 % / 25.44 %
51	C	28.4 % / 26.04 %
52	D	33.14 % / 25.44 %
53	B	31.36 % / 25.44 %
54	A	51.48 % / 26.03 %
55	B	33.73 % / 26.03 %
56	D	47.34 % / 26.62 %
57	D	66.27 % / 25.45 %
58	A	40.83 % / 27.22 %
59	B	30.77 % / 27.22 %
60	C	63.91 % / 26.03 %
61	D	32.54 % / 26.04 %
62	A	43.2 % / 26.03 %
63	A	21.3 % / 26.63 %
64	A	34.91 % / 26.04 %

Q.	Ans.	Correct / Skipped
65	C	44.97 % / 26.04 %
66	A	40.83 % / 26.63 %
67	D	56.21 % / 26.63 %
68	C	29.59 % / 26.62 %
69	D	34.91 % / 27.81 %
70	C	40.83 % / 26.63 %
71	B	46.15 % / 27.22 %
72	D	36.69 % / 26.62 %
73	C	34.32 % / 26.63 %
74	B	37.28 % / 27.81 %
75	B	26.63 % / 27.22 %
76	C	62.72 % / 26.63 %
77	A	45.56 % / 26.63 %
78	C	64.5 % / 26.62 %
79	A	47.34 % / 27.22 %
80	A	24.85 % / 29.0 %

Q.	Ans.	Correct / Skipped
81	B	59.76 %
		28.41 %
82	C	37.87 %
		26.63 %
83	B	39.05 %
		26.63 %
84	C	50.3 %
		26.62 %

Q.	Ans.	Correct / Skipped
85	D	55.03 %
		27.22 %
86	A	67.46 %
		26.62 %
87	A	59.76 %
		27.81 %
88	A	30.18 %
		28.4 %

Q.	Ans.	Correct / Skipped
89	D	38.46 %
		29.59 %
90	B	52.07 %
		27.81 %
91	C	22.49 %
		27.21 %
92	C	60.95 %
		27.22 %

Q.	Ans.	Correct / Skipped
93	C	47.93 %
		27.22 %
94	B	20.71 %
		27.81 %
95	C	57.4 %
		26.62 %
96	D	23.67 %
		27.81 %

Q.	Ans.	Correct / Skipped
97	A	38.46 %
		34.32 %
98	C	25.44 %
		28.41 %
99	A	35.5 %
		30.77 %
100	C	44.38 %
		27.22 %

Performance Analysis

Avg. Score (%)	38.0%
Toppers Score (%)	96.0%
Your Score	

//Hints and Solutions//

1. Taxes on luxuries, including entertainments, betting and gambling are provided under the jurisdiction of the state governments.

2. Evasion of tax is tantamount to absence of taxation because tax evasion is non-payment of tax or underpayment of tax.

3.

1. Optimal Income Taxation concept was given by F. Ramsey.
2. Economic Theory of Politics was given by Anthony Downs.
3. Concept of Local Public Goods was given by Charles Tiebout.
4. Zero-Based Budgeting concept was given by Peter A. Phyrr.

4. Zero-Based Budgeting (ZBB) is a method of budgeting in which all expenses must be justified for each new period. Budgeters review every program and expenditure at the beginning of each budget cycle. Under it, no reference is made or considered of previous years. The budget request has to be evaluated thoroughly with its commencement from the zero-base. Therefore, following statements are relevant.
I. Each item of expenditure is challenged in pre-budgeting review.
II. No minimum level of expenditure is allowed to be taken as given.

5.

1. Taxation Enquiry Commission (Mathur Commission) - 1953
2. Direct Tax Enquiry Committee (Wanchoo Committee) - 1970
3. Indirect Tax Enquiry Committee (Jha Committee) - 1972
4. Tax Reforms Committee (Chelliah Committee) - 1992

6. Comparative advantage is a principle of economics which states that trade between two countries will be mutually beneficial as long as their domestic opportunity costs of production differ.

Comparative advantage occurs when one country can produce a good or service at a lower opportunity cost than another. This means a country can produce a good relatively cheaper than other countries. The theory of comparative advantage states that if countries specialise in producing goods where they have a lower opportunity cost – then there will be an increase in economic welfare.

7. An import tariff is a tax collected on imported goods. Generally speaking, a tariff is any tax or fee collected by a government. Sometimes tariff is used in a non-trade context, as in railroad tariffs. However, the term is much more commonly applied to a tax on imported goods. The nation's offer curve will shift away from axis measuring its export commodity.

8. Arbitrage is the process of a simultaneous sale and purchase of currencies in two or more foreign exchange markets with an objective to make profits by capitalizing on the exchange-rate differentials in various markets. The arbitrage opportunities exist due to the inefficiencies of the market.

9. The Rybczynski theorem was developed in 1955 by the Polish-born English economist Tadeusz Rybczynski (1923–1998). It states that at constant relative goods prices, a rise in the endowment of one factor will lead to a more than proportional expansion of the output in the sector, which uses that factor intensively, and an absolute decline of the output of the other good.

In the context of the Heckscher–Ohlin model of international trade, open trade between two regions often leads to changes in relative factor supplies between the regions. This can lead to an adjustment in the quantities and types of outputs between the two regions. The Rybczynski theorem explains the outcome from an increase in one of these factor's supply as well as the effect on the output of a good which depends on an opposing factor.

10. The main feature of the Ninth Five Year Plan India is that at its onset, our nation crossed the fifty years of independence and this called for a whole new set of development measures. There was a fresh need felt for increasing the social and economic developmental measures. The government felt that the full economic potential of the country, yet to be explored, should be utilized for an overall growth in the next five years. As a result, in the Ninth Five Year Plan India, the emphasis was on human development, increase in the growth rate and adoption of a full scale employment scheme for all. For one such development to promote the social sectors of the nation and to give utmost importance to the eradication of poverty.

11. According to Prof. Harvey Leibenstein, the overpopulated and underdeveloped countries are characterized by the vicious circle of poverty. They have low per capita income. His **'theory of critical minimum effort'** is an attempt to provide a solution to this economic problem. The main idea of the theory is that economic growth in the underdeveloped and overpopulated countries is not possible unless a certain minimum level of investment is injected into the system as a consolidated dose that pulls the system out of doldrums. This minimum level of investment is called 'critical minimum effort'.

Knife-Edge Equilibrium: A condition in which something must either be at a precise equilibrium or else tumble way into catastrophe. In some cases, such as something that is balanced on a knife's edge, it's an accurate description.

Prof. R.F. Kahn originally used the term **'Bastard Golden Age'**. It is the age where unemployment prevails but real wages remain rigid downwards. As a result, the rate of accumulation cannot increase in the absence of technical progress. Therefore, the Bastard Golden Age implies that the stock of capital equipment does not grow faster because of the inflation barrier.

The **theory of big push** is based on the assumption that an industrial economy enjoys a large many external economies. To enjoy these economies, a massive investment is necessary for the development of several industries at the same time.

12. Hollis Chenery's model requires an altering of the existing structures within an underdeveloped economy to pave way for the penetration of new industries and modern structures to attain the status of an industrial nation (Chenery, 1960). It is quite similar to Lewis' model but in its opinion investment and savings although necessary are not enough to drive the degree of growth that is required.

Laissez-faire economics is a theory that restricts government intervention in the economy. It holds that the economy is strongest when all the government does is protect individuals' rights. Laissez-faire is French for "let do" or "leave us alone."

Karl Marx distinguishes between "simple reproduction" and "expanded (or enlarged) reproduction".[4] In the former case, no economic growth occurs, while in the latter case, more is produced than is needed to maintain the economy at the given level, making economic growth possible. In the capitalist mode of production, the difference is that in the former case, the new surplus value created by wage-labour is spent by the employer on consumption (or hoarded), whereas in the latter case, part of it is reinvested in production.

As per Golden Rule of Accumulation, per capital consumption is optimised in a golden age when the thrift rate parities the profit rate. Therefore, it is a specific objective rate of thrift that optimises per capita consumption in a golden age. This is known as the golden rule saving rate or maximum thrift rate.

13. The M-C-M' cycle is the transformation of money (M) into commodities (C), and the change of commodities back again into money (M') of altered value. The emphasis within the paper is on the capital element of the concept and its transactional nature with the aim of avoiding the pitfall of attributing social capital in relation to social behaviours in isolation of context and interaction.

14. The correct sequential order is: Adam Smith, Robert Malthus, J. S. Mill, David Ricardo.

15. Human Development Index (HDI) is a static composite indicator that is used to rank the levels of development among countries. It is classified into three components, namely, life expectancy (years at birth), life expectancy(expected years of schooling), and Standard of living (GDP/GNI per capita). When a country scores a high HDI, it means that the life expectancy and education levels are high, along with the Gross National Income per capita that becomes high as well.

16. According to the Kuznets' Inverted U-hypothesis, as per capita national income of a country increases, in the initial stages of growth, inequality in income distribution rises and after reaching the highest degree in the intermediate level the income inequality falls.

17. According to the principle of vicious circle in UDCs' level of income remains low which leads to low level of saving and investment.

Low investment leads to low productivity which again leads to low income.According to Prof. Nurkse. "It implies circular constellation of forces tending to act and react one another in such a way as to keep a poor country in a state of poverty.

18. According to Kaldor, "The key to the explanation of the trade cycle is to be found in the fact that each of these two positions is stable only in the short period—that as activity continues at either one of these levels, forces gradually accumulate which sooner or later will render that particular position unstable".

19. The demand for money refers to how much assets individuals wish to hold in the form of money (as opposed to illiquid physical assets.) It is sometimes referred to as liquidity preference. The demand for money is related to income, interest rates and whether people prefer to hold cash(money) or illiquid assets like money.

20. The marginal efficiency of investment is the rate of return expected from a given investment on a capital asset after covering all its costs, except the rate of interest. The MEI schedule shows the amount of investment demanded at various rates of interest.

21. A liquidity trap is when monetary policy becomes ineffective due to very low interest rates combined with consumers who prefer to save rather than invest in higher-yielding bonds or other investments.

22. The Neo Classical Theory is the extended version of the classical theory wherein the behavioral sciences gets included into the management. According to this theory, the organization is the social system, and its performance does get affected by the human actions.The classical theory laid emphasis on the physiological and mechanical variables and considered these as the prime factors in determining the efficiency of the organization. But, when the efficiency of the organization was actually checked, it was found out that, despite the positive aspect of these variables the positive response in work behavior was not evoked.

The **accelerator theory** is an economic postulation whereby investment expenditure increases when either demand or income increases. The theory also suggests that when there is excess demand, companies can either decrease demand by raising prices or increase investment to meet the level of demand.

Present value (PV) is the current value of a future sum of money or stream of cash flows given a specified rate of return. Future cash flows are discounted at the discount rate, and the higher the discount rate, the lower the present value of the future cash flows. Determining the appropriate discount rate is the key to properly valuing future cash flows, whether they be earnings or obligations.

James Cohin is aasociated with **Q-Theory**.

23. The size of the increase in GDP depends on the type of fiscal policy. The multiplier on changes in government spending is larger than the multiplier on changes in taxation levels. The taxation multiplier is smaller than the spending multiplier because part of any change in taxes is absorbed by savings.

24. Keynes' consumption function has come to be known as the 'absolute income hypothesis' or theory. His statement of the relationship between income and consumption was based on the 'fundamental psychological law'.

He said that consumption is a stable function of current income (to be more specific, current disposable income—income after tax payment).

Because of the operation of the 'psychological law', his consumption function is such that $0 < MPC < 1$ and $MPC < APC$. Thus, a non- proportional relationship (i.e., $APC > MPC$) between consumption and income exists in the Keynesian absolute income hypothesis. His consumption function may be rewritten here with the form.

25. Involuntary unemployment occurs when a person is willing to work at the prevailing wage yet is unemployed. Involuntary unemployment is distinguished from voluntary unemployment, where workers choose not to work because their reservation wage is higher than the prevailing wage.

Disguised unemployment is a kind of unemployment in which there are people who are visibly employed but are actually unemployed. This situation is also known as 'hidden unemployment'. In such a situation more people are engaged in a work than required.

Frictional Unemployment is the unemployment which exists in any economy due to people being in the process of moving from one job to another.

Structural Unemployment is the unemployment resulting from industrial reorganization, typically due to technological change, rather than fluctuations in supply or demand.

Full employment is an economic situation in which all available labor resources are being used in the most efficient way possible. Full employment embodies the highest amount of skilled and unskilled labor that can be employed within an economy at any given time.

26. A monopolistic market is a theoretical construct that describes a market where only one company may offer products and services to the public. A monopolistic market is the opposite of a perfectly competitive market, in which an infinite number of firms operate.

27. As in the short run, costs in the long run depend on the firm's level of output, the costs of factors, and the quantities of factors needed for each level of output. The chief difference between long- and short-run costs is there are no fixed factors in the long run. There are thus no fixed costs. All costs are variable, so we do not distinguish between total variable cost and total cost in the long run: total cost is total variable cost.

28. Agency theory is a principle that is used to explain and resolve issues in the relationship between business principals and their agents. Most commonly, that relationship is the one between shareholders, as principals, and company executives, as agents.

X-efficiency describes a company's inability to get the maximum output for its inputs due to a lack of competitive pressure.

Utility maximisation refers to the concept that individuals and firms seek to get the highest satisfaction from their economic decisions. For example, when deciding how to spend a fixed some, individuals will purchase the combination of goods/services that give the most satisfaction.

Edgeworth's original two-axis depiction was developed into the now familiar **box diagram** by Pareto in his 1906 book "Manual of Political Economy" and was popularized in a later exposition by Bowley. The modern version of the diagram is commonly referred to as the Edgeworth–Bowley box.

29. The homothetic production function has the same isoquants as those of its underlying homogeneous function, although, generally, with different quantity indexes.

That is why the firm's expansion path and its isoclines would be straight lines from the origin also for a homothetic production function, and along any such straight line with a fixed ratio of the inputs, the firm's MRTS of L for K or the ratio of MP_L to MP_K would be constant.

30. Both the monopolist and the consumers can be made better off. This means that the outcome of a monopoly is Pareto INefficient because either the supplier or the consumers or, in fact, both parties can be made better off without the other being made worse off. Both (A) and (R) are correct and rightly explained.

31. Monopolistically competitive markets have the following characteristics:

1. There are many producers and many consumers in the market, and no business has total control over the market price.
2. Consumers perceive that there are non-price differences among the competitors' products.
3. There are few barriers to entry and exit.[4]
4. Producers have a degree of control over price.
5. The principal goal of the firm is to maximize its profits.
6. Factor prices and technology are given.
7. A firm is assumed to behave as if it knew its demand and cost curves with certainty.
8. The decision regarding price and output of any firm does not affect the behavior of other firms in a group,i.e., impact of the decision made by a single firm is spread sufficiently evenly across the entire group. Thus, there is no conscious rivalry among the firms.
9. Each firm earns only normal profit in the long run.
10. Each firm spends substantial amount on advertisement. The publicity and advertisement costs are known as selling costs.

32. This tends to make workers supply more labour (the "substitution effect"). However, also as the real wage rate rises, workers earn a higher income for a given number of hours. If, beyond a certain wage rate, the income effect is stronger than the substitution effect, then the labour supply curve bends backward.

33. Cournot competition is an economic model used to describe an industry structure in which companies compete on the amount of output they will produce, which they decide on independently of each other. An essential assumption of this model is the "not conjecture" that each firm aims to maximize profits, based on the expectation that its own output decision will not have an effect on the decisions of its rivals. Price is a commonly known decreasing function of total output. The total number of firms in the market, and take the output of the others as given. Each firm has a cost function. Normally the cost functions are treated as common knowledge. The cost functions may be the same or different among firms. The market price is

set at a level such that demand equals the total quantity produced by all firms. Each firm takes the quantity set by its competitors as a given, evaluates its residual demand, and then behaves as a monopoly.

34. Keynes defines psychological law of consumption in terms of "the fundamental psychological law, upon which we are entitled to depend with great confidence both a priori from our knowledge of human nature and from the detailed facts of experience, is that men are disposed, as a rule and on the average, to increase their consumption as their income increases but not by as much as the increase in the income." It simply means that Marginal Propensity to consume is positive but less than unity (>0 but <1).

35. The indifference curves must slope down from left to right. This means that an indifference curve is negatively sloped. It slopes downward because as the consumer increases the consumption of X commodity, he has to give up certain units of Y commodity in order to maintain the same level of satisfaction.

Indifference curves are convex to the origin. As the consumer substitutes commodity X for commodity Y, the marginal rate of substitution diminishes as X for Y along an indifference curve. Thus indifference curve is steeper towards the Y axis and gradual towards the X axis.

The indifference curves cannot intersect each other. It is because at the point of tangency, the higher curve will give as much as of the two commodities as is given by the lower indifference curve. This is absurd and impossible.

36. 1. The LM curve is a schedule that describes the combinations of rate of interest and level of income at which money market is in equilibrium.

2. The LM curve slopes upward to the right.

3. The LM curve is flatter if the interest elasticity of demand for money is high. On the contrary, the LM curve is steep if the interest elasticity demand for money is low.

4. The LM curve shifts to the right when the stock of money supply is increased and it shifts to the left if the stock of money supply is reduced.

5. The LM curve shifts to the left if there is an increase in the money demand function which raises the quantity of money demanded at the given interest rate and income level. On the other hand, the LM curve shifts to the right if there is a decrease in the money demand function which lowers the amount of money demanded at given levels of interest rate and income.

37. Many consider a 4% to 5% unemployment rate to be full employment and not particularly concerning. The natural rate of unemployment represents the lowest unemployment rate whereby inflation is stable or the unemployment rate that exists with non-accelerating inflation.

38. The Harrod–Domar model is a Keynesian model of economic growth. It is used in development economics to explain an economy's growth rate in terms of the level of saving and of capital. It suggests that there is no natural reason for an economy to have balanced growth.According to the Harrod–Domar model there are three kinds of growth: warranted growth, actual growth and natural rate of growth.

39. If consumption of each additional unit of a commodity is expected to give an increasing marginal utility, then total utility derived by consumer will rise at an increasing rate as long as marginal utility keeps rising.

40. Growth in this model is driven by technological change that arises from intentional investment decisions made by profit-maximizing agents. The distinguishing feature of the technology as an input is that it is neither a conventional good nor a public good; it is a nonrival, partially excludable good. Because of the nonconvexity introduced by a nonrival good, price-taking competition cannot be supported. Instead, the equilibrium is one with monopolistic competition. The main conclusions are that the stock of human capital determines the rate of growth, that too little human capital is devoted to research in equilibrium, that integration into world markets will increase growth rates, and that having a large population is not sufficient to generate growth.

41. In economics, the exclusion principle states "the owner of a private good may exclude others from use unless they pay."; it excludes those who are unwilling or unable to pay for the private good, but does not apply to public goods that are known to be indivisible: such goods need only to be available to obtain their benefits rather than purchased.

42. In economics, the excess burden of taxation, also known as the deadweight cost or deadweight loss of taxation, is one of the economic losses that society suffers as the result of taxes or subsidies. Economic theory posits that distortions change the amount and type of economic behavior from that which would occur in a free market without the tax. Excess burdens can be measured using the average cost of funds or the marginal cost of funds (MCF). Excess burdens were first discussed by Adam Smith.

43. The law of diminishing marginal returns states that, at some point, adding an additional factor of production results in smaller increases in output. For example, a factory employs workers to manufacture its products, and, at some point, the company operates at an optimal level. With other production factors constant, adding additional workers beyond this optimal level will result in less efficient operations.

44. The demand for labour (and capital) is thus a derived demand – the value of labour to the employer derives from the value of the end product in the marketplace for goods and services. It is not a final demand. Demand for labour: a derived demand, reflecting the demand for the output of final goods and services.

45. Prices stop falling, as demand equals supply. In the classical model, money is neutral. An increase in the money supply raises the overall price level by the same percentage, with no effect on real variables—real quantities and relative prices.

46. The LM curve, the equilibrium points in the market for money, shifts for two reasons: changes in money demand and changes in the money supply. If the money supply increases (decreases), ceteris paribus, the interest rate is lower (higher) at each level of Y, or in other words, the LM curve shifts right (left). That is because at any given level of output Y, more money (less money) means a lower (higher) interest rate. (Remember, the price level doesn't change in this model.)

47. The Phillips curve is an economic concept developed by A. W. Phillips stating that inflation and unemployment have a stable and inverse relationship. The theory claims that with economic growth comes inflation, which in turn should lead to more jobs and less unemployment.

48. Explicit costs are normal business costs that appear in the general ledger and directly affect a company's profitability. Explicit costs have clearly defined dollar amounts, which flow through to the income statement. Examples of explicit costs include wages, lease payments, utilities, raw materials, and other direct costs.

49. The Incremental Capital-Output Ratio (ICOR) is the ratio of investment to growth which is equal to the reciprocal of the marginal product of capital. The higher the ICOR, the lower the productivity of capital or the marginal efficiency of capital. The ICOR can be thought of as a measure of the inefficiency with which capital is used. In most countries the ICOR is in the neighborhood of 3. It is a topic discussed in economic growth. It can be expressed in the following formula, where K is capital output ratio, Y is output (GDP), and I is net investment.

$$\text{incremental capital output ratio} = \frac{\Delta K}{\Delta Y} = \frac{\frac{\Delta K}{Y}}{\frac{\Delta Y}{Y}} = \frac{\frac{I}{Y}}{\frac{\Delta Y}{Y}}$$

According to this formula the incremental capital output ratio can be computed by dividing the investment share in GDP by the rate of growth of GDP.

50. In economics, the **marginal propensity to consume** (MPC) is a metric that quantifies induced consumption, the concept that the increase in personal consumer spending (consumption) occurs with an increase in disposable income (income after taxes and transfers).

The **average propensity to consume** (APC) measures the percentage of income that is spent rather than saved. This may be calculated by a single individual who wants to know where the money is going or by an economist who wants to track the spending and saving habits of an entire nation.

51. The Group of 77 (G77) at the United Nations is a coalition of 135 developing countries, designed to promote its members' collective economic interests and create an enhanced joint negotiating capacity in the United Nations. There were 77 founding members of the organization, but by November 2019 the organization had since expanded to 135 member countries (including China).[2] Since China participates in the G77 but does not consider itself to be a member, all official statements are issued in the name of The Group of 77 and China.

52. Public accounts fund was constituted under Article 266 (2) of the Constitution. It accounts for flows for those transactions where the government is merely acting as a banker. Examples of those are provident funds, small savings and so on. These funds do not belong to the government.

53. An unbalanced budget is one where the government's estimated receipts are not equal to the proposed expenditure for a given period. An unbalanced budget may be a surplus or deficit budget. When the public are greater than the public expenditure, it is called a surplus budget.

54. They argued that the world economy was divided into the industrial "center" -- the United States and Western Europe -- and the commodity-producing "periphery." The terms of trade would always work against the periphery, meaning that the center would consistently exploit the periphery.

55. The invisible balance or balance of trade on services is that part of the balance of trade that refers to services and other products that do not result in the transfer of physical objects. Examples include consulting services, shipping services, tourism, and patent license revenues. This figure is usually generated by tertiary industry. The term 'invisible balance' is especially common in the United Kingdom.

For countries that rely on service exports or on tourism, the invisible balance is particularly important. For instance the United Kingdom and Saudi Arabia receive significant international income from financial services, while Japan and Germany rely more on exports of manufactured goods.

56. Public enterprise, a business organization wholly or partly owned by the state and controlled through a public authority. Some public enterprises are placed under public ownership because, for social reasons, it is thought the service or product should be provided by a state monopoly.

57. Correlation is a statistical technique that is used to measure and describe the relationship between two variables.Usually the two variables are simply observed as they exist naturally in the environment—there is no attempt to control or manipulate the variables.

58. Laspeyre&aposs Index is a methodology to calculate the consumer price index by measuring the change in the price of the basket of goods to the base year. It was invented by Etienne Laspeyres, an economist from Germany to analyze the changes in the prices as compared to the base year period.

59. When firms can increase their volume of sales only by decreasing the price, then AR falls with increase in sale. It means, revenue from every additional unit (i.e. MR) will be less than AR. As a result, both AR and MR curves slope downwards from left to right. Both (A) and (R) are true and rightly explained.

60. The Indian food security system was established by the Government Of India under the Ministry of Consumer Affairs, Food and Public Distribution to distribute food and non-food items to India's poor at subsidised rates. This scheme was first started in 14 January 1965, during the Second World War, and was launched in the current form in June 1947. Major commodities distributed include staple food grains, such as wheat, rice, sugar and essential fuels like kerosene, through a network of fair price shops (also known as ration shops) established in several states across the country. Food Corporation of India, a Government-owned corporation, procures and maintains the public distribution system (PDS).

61. The mean absolute deviation from the median is always less than or equal to the mean absolute deviation from any other fixed number. The mean absolute deviation from the mean is less

than or equal to the standard deviation; one way of proving this relies on Jensen's inequality.

62. In regression, the R^2 coefficient of determination is a statistical measure of how well the regression predictions approximate the real data points. An R^2 of 1 indicates that the regression predictions perfectly fit the data.

63. Objectives of IMF:

i. To promote international monetary co-operation.

ii. To ensure balanced international trade

iii. To ensure exchange rate stability

iv. To eliminate or to minimize exchange restrictions by promoting the system of multilateral payments.

v. To grant economic assistance to members countries for eliminating the adverse balance of payment

vi. To minimize the imbalances in quantum and duration of international trade.

64. The effect of increased CRR will be reduced or nullified if bank rate is reduced because both are inverse functions. If CRR will increase it contracts credit and if bank rate reduced it expands credit.

65. Advertisement expenditure includes costs incurred for advertising in newspapers and magazines, televisions, radio, cinema slides etc. It was Chamberlin who introduced the analysis of selling costs and distinguished it from the production costs. The production costs include all those expenses which are spent on the manufacturing of the commodity, its transportation cost of handling, storing and delivering of the commodity to actual customers because these add utilities to a commodity.

66. If two goods are perfect substitutes then the indifference curves will have a constant slope since the consumer would be willing to switch between at a fixed ratio. The marginal rate of substitution between perfect substitutes is likewise constant.

67. The functions and powers of SEBI have been listed in the SEBI Act,1992. SEBI caters to the needs of three parties operating in the Indian Capital Market. These three participants are mentioned below:

Issuers of the Securities: Companies that issue securities are listed on the stock exchange. They issue shares to raise funds. SEBI ensures that the issuance of Initial Public Offerings (IPOs) and Follow-up Public Offers (FPOs) can take place in a healthy and transparent way.

Protects the Interests of Traders & Investors: It is a fact that the capital markets are functioning just because the traders exist. SEBI is responsible for safeguarding their interests and ensuring that the investors do not become victims of any stock market fraud or manipulation.

Financial Intermediaries: SEBI acts as a mediator in the stock market to ensure that all the market transactions take place in a secure and smooth manner. It monitors every activity of the financial intermediaries, such as broker, sub-broker, NBFCs, etc.

68. The International Monetary Fund (IMF) is an organization of 189 countries, working to foster global monetary cooperation, secure financial stability, facilitate international trade, promote high employment and sustainable economic growth, and reduce poverty around the world.

The General Agreement on Tariffs and Trade (GATT) is a legal agreement between many countries, whose overall purpose was to promote international trade by reducing or eliminating trade barriers such as tariffs or quotas. According to its preamble, its purpose was the "substantial reduction of tariffs and other trade barriers and the elimination of preferences, on a reciprocal and mutually advantageous basis."

The International Finance Corporation (IFC) is an international financial institution that offers investment, advisory, and asset-management services to encourage private-sector development in less developed countries. The IFC is a member of the World Bank Group and is headquartered in Washington, D.C. in the United States.

The World Trade Organization (WTO) is the only global international organization dealing with the rules of trade between nations. At its heart are the WTO agreements, negotiated and signed by the bulk of the world's trading nations and ratified in their parliaments. The goal is to ensure that trade flows as smoothly, predictably and freely as possible.

69. Feudalism is a system of land ownership and duties. It was used in the Middle Ages. With feudalism, all the land in a kingdom was the king's. However, the king would give some of the land to the lords or nobles who fought for him, called vassals. These gifts of land were called fiefs.

Mercantilism, also called "commercialism," is a system in which a country attempts to amass wealth through trade with other countries, exporting more than it imports and increasing stores of gold and precious metals.

Imperialism is a policy of extending a country's power and influence through colonization, use of military force, or other means.

Capitalism is an economic system. In it the government plays a secondary role. People and companies make most of the decisions, and own most of the property. ... The means of production are largely or entirely privately owned (by individuals or companies) and operated for profit.

70. Zero Elasticity; a perfectly inelastic demand curve. The vertical line shows that at any price, the quantity demanded remains the same. The measured elasticity is zero.

The Law Of Diminishing Marginal Utility states that all else equal as consumption increases the marginal utility derived from each additional unit declines. Marginal utility is the incremental increase in utility that results from consumption of one additional unit.

71. As per the census 2011, Arunachal Pradesh has the highest child sex ratio among the Indian states i.e. 972 while Haryana has the lowest child sex ratio i.e.834 per thousand males. Among the Union Territories of India; Andaman and Nicobar Islands has the highest child sex ratio i.e.968 per thousand males.

Sex Ratio in Kerala is 1084 i.e. for each 1000 male, which is below national average of 940 as per census 2011. In 2001, the sex ratio of female was 1058 per 1000 males in Kerala.

72. The first absolute measure of skewness is based on the difference between mean and mode or mean and median. Symbolicilly i) Absolute Sk = Mean - Mode or ii) Absolute Sk = Mean - Median. If the value of mean is greater than the mode or median, skewness is positive, otherwise it is negative.

Kurtosis. Kurtosis can be defined as the flatness level of a frequency distribution (height of the peak of the curve) in relation to a theoretical distribution that usually corresponds to the normal distribution.

73. Theory such as expenditure switching (also called the absorption analysis) is in favor of devaluation help to improve trade balance: 'by switch expenditure from foreign to domestic goods, raise total production and decrease absorption relative to total production, so improving the trade balance'

The devaluation or depreciation of currency tends to raise the price level in the country and thus increase the rate of inflation. This causes the exports of goods to increase and reduces the supply and availability of goods in the domestic market which tends to raise the domestic price level.

74. The major recommendations of the Raj Committee were:

(i) Imposition of Agricultural Holdings Tax (AHT) on agriculturists.

(ii) In the case of assessees paying non-agricultural tax, income from agriculture should be included in the total income for the purpose of calculating income tax.

(iii) Income from livestock, poultry, dairy farming etc., should be subject to tax.

(iv) An integrated taxation of agricultural property through wealth tax should be introduced.

(v) Capital gains tax on transfer of land should be imposed. According to Raj Committee, there were two basic defects in the present land revenue system.

75. C. Rangarajan or Chakravarthi Rangarajan (born 1932) is an Indian economist, a former Member of Parliament and 19th Governor of the Reserve Bank of India. He is the former Chairman of the Prime Minister's Economic Advisory Council, he resigned the day the UPA lost power. He is also the Chairman of the Madras School of Economics; former President of the Indian Statistical Institute; the Founding Chairman of the CR Rao Advanced Institute of Mathematics, Statistics and Computer Science; former Chancellor of the University of Hyderabad; and a professor in Ahmedabad University.

Indraprasad Gordhanbhai Patel (11 November 1924 – 17 July 2005) popularly known as I. G. Patel, was an Indian economist and a career civil servant who served as the fourteenth Governor of the Reserve Bank of India from 1 December 1977 to 15 September 1982.He served as Director of the London School of Economics, making him the first person of Indian origin to head a higher education institute in the United Kingdom. He also served as Chairperson of the Board of Governors from 1996 to 2001 at Indian Institute of Management Ahmedabad.

Duvvuri Subbarao (born 11 August 1949), is an Indian economist, Central Banker, and retired IAS officer. He was the 22nd Governor of Reserve Bank of India, served under Prime Minister Dr.Manmohan Singh. He lives in Singapore and is a distinguished visiting faculty at National University of Singapore. Dr. D. Subbarao is a 1972 batch Indian Administrative Service (IAS) officer of Andhra Pradesh cadre. He was appointed the 22nd Governor of Reserve Bank of India (RBI) from 5 September 2008, with an extension in 2011 till 4 September 2013.

Manmohan Singh (born 26 September 1932) is an Indian economist, academic, and politician who served as the 13th Prime Minister of India from 2004 to 2014. The first Sikh in office, Singh was also the first prime minister since Jawaharlal Nehru to be re-elected after completing a full five-year term.During the 1970s and 1980s, Singh held several key posts in the Government of India, such as Chief Economic Advisor (1972–76), governor of the Reserve Bank (1982–85) and head of the Planning Commission (1985–87).

76. If an increase in consumer income leads to a decrease in demand for camping equipment, then camping equipment is an inferior good.

77. It took seven and a half years, almost twice the original schedule. By the end, 123 countries were taking part. It covered almost all trade, from toothbrushes to pleasure boats, from banking to telecommunications, from the genes of wild rice to AIDS treatments. It was quite simply the largest trade negotiation ever, and most probably the largest negotiation of any kind in history.

78. The consumer is in equilibrium at a point where the budget line is tangent to an indifference curve. It means that marginal substitution rate between X and Y (MRSXY) should be diminishing.

79. An elasticity of zero indicates that quantity supplied does not respond to a price change: the good is "fixed" in supply. Such goods often have no labor component or are not produced, limiting the short run prospects of expansion. If the elasticity is exactly one, the good is said to be unit-elastic.

80. Consumer surplus is defined as the difference between the consumers' willingness to pay for a commodity and the actual price paid by them, or the equilibrium price. Consumer surplus is infinite when the demand curve is inelastic and zero in case of a perfectly elastic demand curve.

Utility theory. bases its beliefs upon individuals' preferences. It is a theory postulated in economics to explain behavior of individuals based on the premise people can consistently rank order their choices depending upon their preferences. ... Utility theory is a positive theory.

Definition of **cost analysis**. 1 : the act of breaking down a cost summary into its constituents and studying and reporting on each factor. 2 : the comparison of costs (as of standard with actual or for a given period with another) for the purpose of disclosing and reporting on conditions subject to improvement.

Product Differentiation Is Important in Today's Financial Climate. Product differentiation is essential in today's financial climate. It allows the seller to contrast its own product with

competing products in the market and emphasize the unique aspects that make its product superior.

81.

1. M1-C + DD + OD
2. M2- C + DD + OD + SD
3. M3 - C + DD + OD + TD
4. M4- C + DD + OD + TD + TD of post office

82. In the United States, the most common measures of money supply are termed M_0, M_1, M_2, and M_3. These measurements vary according to the liquidity of the accounts included. In most cases, broad money means the same as M_3, while M_0 and M_1 usually refer to narrow money.

83.

1. Say's Law of Markets is theory from classical economics arguing that the ability to purchase something depends on the ability to produce and thereby generate income.

2. Say reasoned that to have the means to buy, a buyer must first have produced something to sell. Thus, the source of demand is production, not money itself.

3. Say's Law implies that production is the key to economic growth and prosperity and the government policy should encourage (but not control) production rather than promoting consumption.

84. Pareto Optimality can take place at any point on Contract Curve. Pareto efficiency or Pareto optimality is a situation that cannot be modified so as to make any one individual or preference criterion better off without making at least one individual or preference criterion worse off.

85. Sufficient condition requires that the indifference curve must be convex to the origin at the point of tangency. Since these two conditions are fulfilled at point E, the consumer is in equilibrium at that point. This is called 'interior solution' where a consumer buys both the goods.

86. Thus the elasticity of substitution of a constant returns to scale production function can be expressed as the elasticity of output per capita with respect to the marginal product of labor. as we announced.Thus,Cobb-Douglas is the only form which a constant returns to scale production function with s = 1 can take.

87. Marshall began writing the **Principles of Economics** in 1881 and he spent much of the next decade at work on the treatise. His plan for the work gradually extended to a two-volume compilation on the whole of economic thought; the first volume was published in 1890 to worldwide acclaim that established him as one of the leading economists of his time. The second volume, which was to address foreign trade, money, trade fluctuations, taxation, and collectivism, was never published at all. Over the next two decades he worked to complete his second volume of the Principles, but his unyielding attention to detail and ambition for completeness prevented him from mastering the work's breadth.

In an oligopolistic market, the kinked demand curve hypothesis states that the firm faces a demand curve with a kink at the prevailing price level.This means that the response to a price increase is less than the response to a price decrease.

The **Principle of Maximum Social Advantage** states that public finance leads to economic welfare when pubic expenditure & taxation are carried out up to that point where the benefits derived from the MU (Marginal Utility) of expenditure is equal to (=) the Marginal Disutility or the sacrifice imposed by taxation.

The unobservable market force that helps the demand and supply of goods in a free market to reach equilibrium automatically is the invisible hand. Description: The phrase **invisible hand** was introduced by Adam Smith in his book 'The Wealth of Nations'.

88. A **constrained cycle**, a cycle with a strong ending, takes place when the interaction between the multiplier and the accelerator is strong enough to lead the economy along the path of expansion until the restraint determined by the production ceiling is reached.

The **multiplier–accelerator** model (also known as Hansen–Samuelson model) is a macroeconomic model which analyzes the business cycle. This model was developed by Paul Samuelson, who credited Alvin Hansen for the inspiration. This model is based on the Keynesian multiplier, which is a consequence of assuming that consumption intentions depend on the level of economic activity, and the accelerator theory of investment, which assumes that investment intentions depend on the pace of growth in economic activity.

A theory of investment based on the capital–output ratio. If at any time actual capital stock is less than is implied by this ratio, the firm invests so as to close part of the gap during the next period. Partial adjustment is assumed, taking account of both uncertainty and costs of adjustment.

 Real business cycle models state that macroeconomic fluctuations in the economy can be largely explained by technological shocks and changes in productivity. These changes in technological growth affect the decisions of firms on investment and workers (labour supply)

89. The i**nventory theoretic approach** enunciated in the Baumol- Tobin Model is to show that an individual will hold a stock of real balances that varies inversely with the interest rate but increases with the level of real income and the cost of transactions.

One of the basic functional relationships in the Keynesian model of the economy is the **liquidity preference** schedule, an inverse relationship between the demand for cash balances and the rate of interest. This aggregative function must be derived from some assumptions regarding the behavior of the decision-making units of the economy, and those assumptions are the concern of this paper.

Money is more basic than the medium of exchange. It is a **temporary abode of purchasing power** and hence an asset or a part of wealth. Friedman treats the demand for money as a part of the wealth theory.

The **speculative or asset demand for money** is the demand for highly liquid financial assets — domestic money or foreign currency — that is not dictated by real transactions such as trade or consumption expenditure. Speculative demand arises from the perception that money is optimally part of a portfolio of assets being held as investments.

90. According to Mrs. Robinson, the stage of &aposGolden Age&apos = Capital growth rate = Labour growth rate.

The rate of growth of surplus which is HC must be able to absorb the rate of growth of labour force which is ON here. This brings up to the 'Golden Age' according to Mrs. Joan Robinson.

After analysing the role of capital accumulation on the growth of an economy, Mrs. Robinson proceeds to analyze the impact of population growth on economic development. An increase in population and labour supply without adequate increase in capital stock would result in a fall in the labour productivity and if the real wages remain constant, it will mean a fall in the rate of profit, which in turn, will adversely affect the rate of capital accumulation.

91. Innovation may be defined as application of discovery of new consumption needs, and a new way of attaining a useful end. All three characteristics are important. It must be a new way. It must be for some positive end. It must be an application, distinct from an idea, or theory, or design. since application implies relation to some positive end, differences among these ends, with inferrable differences in the methods of attaining them, allow us to distinguish economic from other innovations; or technological from social innovations.

92. A progressive tax is a tax in which the tax rate increases as the taxable amount increases. The term "progressive" refers to the way the tax rate progresses from low to high, with the result that a taxpayer's average tax rate is less than the person's marginal tax rate. The term can be applied to individual taxes or to a tax system as a whole; a year, multi-year, or lifetime. Progressive taxes are imposed in an attempt to reduce the tax incidence of people with a lower ability to pay, as such taxes shift the incidence increasingly to those with a higher ability-to-pay. The opposite of a progressive tax is a regressive tax, where the average tax rate or burden decreases as an individual's ability to pay increases.

93. Peacock Wiseman Hypothesis focused on the pattern of public expenditure and stated that public expenditure does not follow a smooth or continuous trend but the increase in public expenditure takes place in jerks or steps. They gave three separate concepts to justify the hypothesis, they are.

1. Displacement Effect
2. Inspection Effect
3. Concentration effect

According to Peacock Wiseman Hypothesis, due to some social or other disturbance in an economy there is a need for increased expenditure as the existing public revenue cannot solve the disturbance.The fiscal activities of the government rise step by step to successive new higher level during the span of decades to meet successive social disturbances.

94. Methods that are adopted for redemption of public debt are: 1. Refunding 2. Conversion 3. Surplus budgets 4. Sinking fund 5. Terminable annuities 6. Additional Taxation 7. Capital Levy 8. Surplus Balance of Payments.

1. **Refunding:**Refunding of debt implies the issue of new bonds and securities by the government in order to repay the matured loans. In the refunding process, usually short-term securities are replaced by issuing long-term securities. Under this method the money burden of public debt is not relinquished but it is accumulated owing to the postponement of debt redemption.

2. **Conversion**: Conversion of public debt implies changing the existing loans, before maturity, into new loans at an advantage in servicing charges. In fact, the process of conversion consists generally, in converting or altering a public debt from a higher to a lower rate of interest.

3. **Surplus budgets:** Quite often, surplus budgets (i.e., by spending less than the public revenue obtained) may be utilised for clearing off public debts. But in recent years due to ever-increasing public expenditures, surplus budget is a rare phenomenon.

4. **Sinking fund:** A sinking fund is a fund created by the government and gradually accumulated every year by setting aside a part of current public revenue in such a way that it would be sufficient to pay off the funded debt at the time of maturity. Perhaps, this is the most systematic and best method of redemption.

5. **Terminable annuities:** This method of debt redemption is similar to that of the sinking fund. Under this method, the fiscal authorities clear off a part of the public debt every year by issuing terminable annuities to the bond-holders which mature annually. Thus, it is the method of redeeming debts in installments. By this method, the burden of debt goes on diminishing annually and by the time of maturity it is fully paid off.

6. **Additional Taxation:** The simplest measure of debt redemption is to impose new taxes and get the required revenue to repay the loan principal as well as the interest.This method causes redistribution of income by transferring the resources from tax-payers to the hands of bond-holders. It may also impose a burden on the future generation if new taxes are levied to repay the long-term debts.

7. **Capital Levy**: Capital levy is strongly recommended by Dalton as a method of debt redemption with the least real burden on the society. Capital levy refers to a very heavy tax on property and wealth. It is once- for-all tax on the capital assets and estates.

8. **Surplus Balance of Payments:** The redemption of external debt, however, is possible only through an accumulation of foreign exchange reserves. This necessitates creation of a favourable balance of payments by the debtor country by augmenting its exports and curbing its imports, thereby improving the position of its trade balance.

95. Primary deficit is defined as fiscal deficit of current year minus interest payments on previous borrowings. In other words whereas fiscal deficit indicates borrowing requirement inclusive of interest payment, primary deficit indicates borrowing requirement exclusive of interest payment (i.e., amount of loan).

96. Intrinsic value is a measure of what an asset is worth. This measure is arrived at by means of an objective calculation or complex financial model, rather than using the currently trading market price of that asset. In financial analysis this term is used in conjunction with the work of identifying, as nearly as possible, the underlying value of a company and its cash flow. In options pricing it refers to the difference between the strike price of the option and the current price of the underlying asset.

97. Rajiv Gandhi Udyami Mitra Yojana to provide handholding support and assistance to the promotion of first generation entrepreneurs, who have already successfully completed or undergoing Entrepreneurship Development Training Programme (EDP) / Skill Development Training Programme (SDP)/ Entrepreneurship cum Skill Development Training Programme (ESDP) /Vocation Training Programmes (VT), through the selected lead agencies i.e. 'Udyami Mitras' , in the establishment and management of the new enterprise, in dealing with various procedural and legal hurdles and in completion of various formalities required for setting up and running of the enterprise.

The Credit Guarantee Fund Scheme for Micro and Small Enterprises (CGS) was launched by the Government of India (GoI) to make available collateral-free credit to the micro and small enterprise sector. ... The extent of guarantee cover is 85% for micro enterprises for credit up to Rs 5 lakh.

The Government has announced formulation of a **National Manufacturing Competitiveness Programme (NMCP)** with an aim to support the Micro, Small and Medium Enterprises (MSMEs) in their endeavor to become competitive. The objective of NMCP is to develop global competitiveness among Indian MSMEs

Competition Commission of India is a statutory body of the Government of India responsible for enforcing The Competition Act, 2002 throughout India and to prevent activities that have an appreciable adverse effect on competition in India. It was established on 14 October 2003.

98. The fourth Census of the MSMEs is for the year 2009-10 is not correct about the micro, small and medium enterprises in India.

99. Bharat Nirman is a business plan for rural infrastructure which was implemented by the Government of India in order to provide some basic amenities to the rural India. Bharat Nirman is an Indian business plan for creating basic rural infrastructure. It comprises projects on irrigation, roads (Pradhan Mantri Gram Sadak Yojana), housing (Pradhan Mantri Awaas Yojana), water supply (National Rural Drinking Water Programme), electrification (Rajiv Gandhi Grameen Vidyutikaran Yojana) and telecommunication connectivity.

The **National Food for Work Programme(NFWP)**, 2004 was launched by minister of rural development, central government on 14 November 2004 in 150 of the most backward districts of India with the objective of generating supplementary wage employment.

Pradhan Mantri Gramin Awaas Yojana, previously **Indira Awaas Yojana**, is a social welfare flagship programme, created by the Indian Government, to provide housing for the rural poor in India. A similar scheme for urban poor was launched in 2015 as Housing for All by 2022.

SITRA was launched in July 1992, as a sub-scheme of IRDP in selected districts; this scheme has since been extended to all the districts of the country. Under the scheme, a variety of crafts persons, except weavers, tailors, needle workers and beedi workers, are supplied with a kit of improved hand tools within a financial ceiling of Rs.2000, of which the artisans have to pay 10 per cent and the remaining 90 per cent is a subsidy from the Government of India. The supply of power driven tools, subject to a ceiling of Rs.4500, is also permitted under this scheme.

100. The set of the agreement by the BCBS, which mainly focuses on risks to banks and the financial system is called Basel accords/Basel Norms. The purpose of the accord is to ensure that financial institutions have enough capital on account to meet obligations and absorbs unexpected losses.

Q.1 Which one of the following is not the basic property of indifference curves ?

A. Negative slope

B. Indifference curves of two imperfect substitutes are concave to the point of origin

C. The indifference curves do not intersect nor are they tangent to one another

D. Upper indifference curves indicate a higher level of satisfaction

Q.2 Match Group - I with Group - II:

Group - I	Group - II
a. Variance	i. Sampling distribution
b. Mode	ii. Normal distribution
c. χ^2 distribution	iii. Measure of dispersion
d. Mesokurtic distribution	iv. Measure of central tendency

A. i, iii, ii, iv   **B.** iii, iv, i, ii

C. ii, iv, iii, i   **D.** iv, ii, i, iii

Q.3 If the mean and variance of a given distribution is 8 and 0.25, then the coefficient of variation will be

A. 4%   **B.** 6.25%   **C.** 12%   **D.** 16%

Q.4 There are 12 white balls, 8 red balls and 5 green balls in a basket. What is the probability that a ball drawn is either red or white?

A. 12/25   **B.** 8/25   **C.** 20/25   **D.** 15/25

Q.5 For testing the equality of population variances the test to be applied is

A. Students t test   **B.** χ^2 test

C. F distribution   **D.** Z distribution

Q.6 The pure monopolist obtains equilibrium level of output when:

A. Marginal Revenue = Marginal Cost

B. Price = Marginal Cost

C. Price is the lowest

D. Price is the highest

Q.7 Marginal Cost is less than the Average Cost when Average Cost falls with:

A. an increase in output

B. a decrease in output

C. constant output

D. an increase in marginal utility

Q.8 Consider the following system of equations, using standard notations:

$$Y_1 = \alpha_0 + \alpha_1 Y_2 + \alpha_3 Y_3 + \alpha_4 X_1 + \alpha_5 X_2 + u_1$$
$$Y_2 = \beta_0 + \beta_1 Y_3 + \beta_2 Y_1 + \beta_3 X_2 + u_2$$
$$Y_3 = \gamma_0 + \gamma_1 X_1 + \gamma_2 X_2 + \gamma_3 X_3 + u_3$$

According to the order condition, the first equation is

A. Unidentified

B. Just identified

C. Over-identified

D. Not possible to tell whether the equation is identified or not because reduced form of the model is not given.

Q.9 Match the following:

List – I	List – II
a. Unit Root Test	1. Durbin- Watson Test
b. Contingency Table	2. Student&aposs t-test
c. Regression Coefficient	3. Stationarity
d. Autocorrelation	4. χ^2-test

A. 2, 3, 1, 4   **B.** 4, 2, 3, 1   **C.** 3, 4, 2, 1   **D.** 3, 2, 1, 4

Q.10 Which of the following statements are true concerning a triangular or recursive system?

(i) The parameters can be validly estimated using separate applications of OLS to each equation.

(ii) The independent variables may be correlated with the error terms in other equations.

(iii) An application of 2 SLS would lead to unbiased but inefficient parameter estimates.

(iv) The independent variables may be correlated with error terms in the equations in which they appear as independent variables.

A. (ii) and (iv) only   **B.** (i) and (iii) only

C. (i), (ii) and (iii) only   **D.** (i), (ii), (iii) and (iv)

Q.11 Verdoorn's & aposs law is about the-

A. Positive relation between the growth of population, employment and output with the growth of production per head.

B. Negative relation between the growth of population, employment and output with the growth of production per head.

C. Positive relation between population growth and employment.

D. Negative relation between population growth and employment.

Q.12 The concept of imperfect competition was developed by whom?

A. Marshall

B. Jevons

C. Joan Robinson

D. Mrs. Lillian Gilbreth

Q.13 Given a production function $Q = AL^{\alpha} K^{\beta}$; $\alpha, \beta > 0$, increasing returns to scale requires that

A. $\alpha + \beta = 1$ **B.** $\alpha + \beta = 0$ **C.** $\alpha + \beta > 0$ **D.** $\alpha + \beta > 1$

Q.14 Which of the following statements is true concerning the optimal solution of linear program with two decision variables?

A. There is only one solution to a linear program.

B. The optimal solution is either an extreme point or is on a line connecting extreme points.

C. All resources must be used up by an optimal solution.

D. All of the above

Q.15 The Linear Cobweb model is given as Supply:

$qt = \alpha + \beta\, pt - 1$

Demand : $pt = \gamma + \delta\, qt$

Where $q(0) = q_0$ is initial condition. For this model stability of market requires the condition

A. $|\delta| < |\beta|$　　　　**B.** $|\delta| < |1/\beta|$

C. $|\delta| > |\beta|$　　　　**D.** $|\delta| = |1/\beta|$

Q.16 Input-Output Technique was invented by

A. Gunnar Myrdal　　　　**B.** Wassily Leontief

C. Hollis B. Chenery　　　　**D.** Robert Solow

Q.17 In a multiple regression with three independent variables, the regression coefficients are to be tested. Which test would be used?

A. Z test　　　**B.** F test　　　**C.** χ^2 test　　　**D.** t test

Q.18 In a two variable regression Y is the dependent variable and X is the independent variable. The correlation coefficient between Y and X is 0.6. For this which of the following results is correct?

A. 36% variations in Y are explained by X.

B. 60% variations in Y are explained by X.

C. 6% variations in Y are explained by X.

D. None of the above.

Q.19 Find out the correct answer from the codes given below: Technique of selective credit control of RBI.

I. Determination of margin requirement for loans against certain securities.

II. Determination of maximum amount of advances or other financial accommodation.

III. Changing of discretionary interest rates on certain type of advances.

IV. Changing the cash reserve requirements of commercial banks.

A. I and II are correct

B. I, II and III are correct

C. I, II and IV are correct

D. I and IV are correct.

Q.20 Find out the correct answer from the code given below: Main features of Regional Rural Banks (RRBs)

I. RRBs have been established by a 'sponsor bank' usually a public sector commercial bank.

II. RRBs grant direct loans and advances only to small and marginal farmers, rural artisans and agricultural labourers.

III. The area of an RRB is limited to a specified region comprising one or more districts of a state.

IV. The lending rates of RRBs are normally not higher than the prevailing lending rates of co-operative societies.

A. II and III are correct.

B. I and III are correct.

C. I, II and IV are correct.

D. I, II, III and IV are correct.

Q.21 High powered money is:

A. Banks&apos reserves at Central Bank

B. Money held by the banks

C. All loans and advances of banks

D. Currency held by the public and cash reserves of the banks

Q.22 Relate the items given in List - I with the List - II with regard to Wage Theory:

List – I	List – II
a. Iron law of wages	1. J.S. Mill
b. Wage-funds theory	2. John R. Hicks
c. Surplus-value theory	3. David Ricardo
d. Marginal productivity theory	4. Karl Marx

A. 1, 3, 4, 2　　**B.** 2, 1, 3, 4　　**C.** 3, 4, 2, 1　　**D.** 3, 1, 4, 2

Q.23 The biggest holder of Government of India dated securities is:

A. Reserve Bank of India

B. Life Insurance Corporation of India

C. Employees Provident Fund

D. Commercial Banks

Q.24 For complementary goods the indifference curve takes the shape of:

A. a straight line

B. a downward sloping line

C. a right angled

D. a negatively sloped curve

Q.25 GDP deflator is a type of which index?

A. Paasche index　　　　**B.** Laspyres index

C. Fisher index　　　　**D.** Divisia index

Q.26 Devaluation will improve the balance of payment deficit, if sum of elasticity of exports and imports of the devaluing country is:

A. greater than one　　　　**B.** less than one

C. equal to zero　　　　**D.** negative

Q.27 Who among the following economists developed the concept of &aposBarriers to Entry&apos of firms?

A. J.S. Bain　　　　**B.** W.J. Baumol

C. Alfred Marshall　　　　**D.** W.S. Jevons

Q.28 Which of the following is a major indivisibility of Rosenstein-Rodan Model of development?

A. Services　　　　**B.** Agriculture

C. Infrastructure　　　　**D.** Supply

Q.29 The concept of Multiplier was introduced for the first time by:

A. F. A. Kahn　　　　**B.** J.M. Keynes

C. R.F. Harrod　　　　**D.** V.K.R.V. Rao

Q.30 According to Milton Friedman, quantity theory of money deals with:

A. Prices　　　　**B.** Income

C. Supply of money　　　　**D.** Demand for money

Q.31 Non-symmetric risk means:

A. A risk that can be eliminated by diversifying.

B. A risk that cannot be eliminated by diversifying.

C. A risk that can be eliminated without diversifying.

D. A risk that cannot be eliminated.

Q.32 The upper portion of kinked demand curve represents

A. low elastic demand   **B.** high elastic demand

C. inelastic demand   **D.** None of these

Q.33 If a monopolist is producing under decreasing cost conditions, increase in demand is beneficial to the society because

A. Goods will be sold in many markets

B. Cost of production falls and hence price

C. Consumers get better quality goods

D. None of the above

Q.34 The firms in the modern world, use reserve capacity to:

A. ensure greater flexibility in operations

B. reduce costs

C. reduce wages

D. reduce taxes

Q.35 If two commodities are good substitutes, indifference curve will:

A. be a straight line

B. approach a right angle

C. approach a straight line

D. slope upwards

Q.36 Which of the following is not correctly matched?

A. Long-run consumption function: Permanent Income Hypothesis

B. Demand for money balances to be held: Fisher's equation

C. Real balance effect: Tobin's portfolio theory

D. Labour theory of value: Ricardo's theory of distribution

Q.37 When the LM curve is vertical, which one of the following is correct?
An increase in money supply will lead to:

A. Fall in the interest rate

B. Fall in the level of income

C. Rise in the rate of interest

D. No change in the level of income.

Q.38 Who among the following economists considered the portfolio approach to demand for money?
(a) J.M. Keynes
(b) M.Friedman
(c) James Tobin
Select the correct answer from the code given below:

A. (a), (b) and (c)   **B.** (b) and (c)

C. Only (b)   **D.** Only (a)

Q.39 A less elastic IS curve means that:

A. Monetary policy is more effective

B. Monetary policy is less effective

C. Fiscal policy is less effective

D. Both (1) and (3)

Q.40 The rate at which a bank lends to the RBI is known as:

A. Bank rate   **B.** Repo Rate

C. Reverse Repo Rate   **D.** Interest Rate

Q.41 The capacity of creating aspect of investment in growth theory was explained by:

A. R.F. Harrod   **B.** E. D. Domar

C. R.M. Solow   **D.** P.A. Samuelson

Q.42 In the short-run, when a simple monopoly firm attains equilibrium and earns only normal profit, its level of output will correspond to:

A. Lowest average cost

B. Average cost above optimum level of output

C. Average cost equals marginal cost

D. Marginal cost much below average cost

Q.43 Wage is determined where:
(a) Demand for labour = supply of labour
(b) MRP of labour = marginal wage
(c) MRP of labour = ARP
(d) MRP of labour = Average wage
Select the correct combination from the above:

A. a and b   **B.** c and d   **C.** a and c   **D.** a and d

Q.44 Match the items of List — I with those of List — II and indicate the correct code from the following:

List — I	List — II
a. Postage stamp pricing	i. Equality of marginal and average cost
b. Loss leader	ii. Constant average and marginal cost
c. Economic capacity	iii. Product line pricing
d. Reserve capacity	iv. Differential pricing

A. iii, iv, ii, i   **B.** iv, iii, i, ii

C. ii, i, iii, iv   **D.** i, ii, iv, iii

Q.45 Which theory assumes that increase in stock of money is directly spent on goods?

A. Quantity theory of money

B. IS-LM theory

C. Keynes

D. None of the above.

Q.46 Which of the following conditions is most likely to benefit a debtor under new classic economic framework?

A. Anticipated deflation

B. Anticipated inflation

C. Unanticipated deflation

D. Unanticipated inflation

Q.47 Concept of scale economics applies in:

A. Long-run with constants technical coefficients

B. Long-run with variable technology

C. Short-run with constant technology

D. Short-run with variable technical coefficient

Q.48 Who among the following economists emphasized the role of non-economic factors in explaining growth?

A. R.M. Solow **B.** Roy Harrod
C. N.Kaldor **D.** E. Domar

Q.49 In imperfect factor and product markets, labor exploitation is represented by:
(A) When ARP is > Average wage
(B) When ARP is > Marginal wage
(C) When ARP is < MRP
(D) When ARP is < Marginal wage
A. A, D **B.** A, C **C.** A, B **D.** D, C

Q.50 Product differentiation is relevant to which set of the following market forms?
A. Monopoly, Monopolistic Competition, Oligopoly
B. Monopoly, Perfect Competition, Oligopoly
C. Oligopsony, Monopolistic Competition, Oligopoly
D. Monopoly, Perfect Competition, Bilateral Monopoly

Q.51 In the given diagram, which of the following segments correctly depicts the supply curve of a producer?

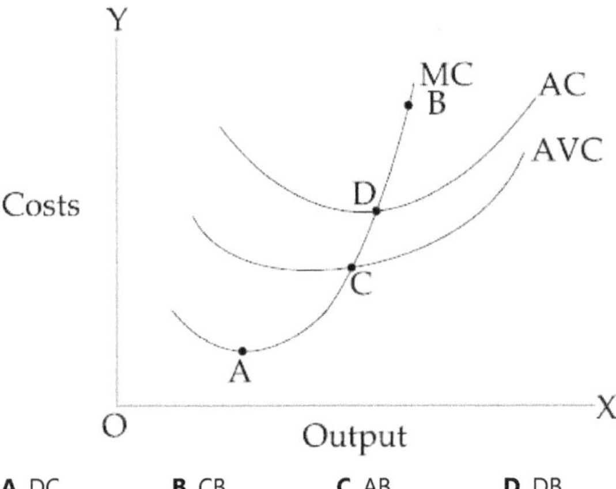

A. DC **B.** CB **C.** AB **D.** DB

Q.52 Neo-classical production function has which of the following characteristics?
(a) Positive and diminishing marginal productivity of the factors
(b) Constant return to scale
(c) Satisfies Inada conditions
A. (a) and (b) **B.** (a) and (c)
C. (b) and (c) **D.** (a), (b) and (c)

Q.53 Between the two situations for a firm profit maximization and sales revenue maximization, the equilibrium for a profit maximiser as compared to sales revenue maximiser takes place at:
A. Larger output and lower price
B. lower output and higher price
C. lower output and lower price
D. larger output and larger price

Q.54 For the linear demand curve, which of the following is true?
A. Elasticity of demand is unity at all points.
B. Elasticity of demand is constant at all points.
C. Elasticity increases as one slides down the demand curve.
D. Elasticity declines as one slides down the demand curve.

Q.55 A discriminating monopolist will charge a lower price in the market in which the price elasticity of:
A. demand is greater **B.** supply is smaller
C. demand is smaller **D.** supply is greater

Q.56 Compute national income when population is 3 cr. and per capita income is Rs. 2,000.
A. Rs. 6,000 cr. **B.** Rs. 2,000 cr.
C. Rs. 3,000 cr. **D.** Rs. 10,000 cr.

Q.57 The imposition of an import tariff by a large nation
A. usually improves the nation&aposs terms of trade and increases the volume of trade
B. worsens the nation&aposs terms of trade but increases the volume of trade
C. worsens the nation&aposs terms of trade and reduces the volume of trade
D. usually improves the nation&aposs terms of trade but reduces the volume of trade

Q.58 According to monetary approach, a revaluation of a nation&aposs currency
A. increases the nation&aposs demand for money
B. increases the nation&aposs supply of money
C. reduces the nation&aposs demand for money
D. reduces the nation&aposs supply of money

Q.59 Which of the following satisfies time reversal test but not factor reversal test?
A. Laspeyre&aposs Index No.
B. Fisher&aposs Index No.
C. Paasche&aposs Index No.
D. Marshall-Edgeworth Index No.

Q.60 Which is a non-probability based sampling method?
A. Systematic Sampling
B. Stratified Random Sampling
C. Quota Sampling
D. Simple Random Sampling

Q.61 The negative relationship between the gap between actual GDP and its trend value and the difference between actual unemployment rate and its equilibrium value is called:
A. The Aggregate Supply Curve
B. The Phillips Curve
C. The Natural Rate of Unemployment Hypothesis
D. Okun&aposs Law

Q.62 Which of the following types of competition lead(s) to exploitation of consumer?
A. Oligopoly
B. Monopolistic competition
C. Monopoly
D. All of the above

Q.63 Efficient allocation of resources is achieved to the greatest extent under which market?
A. Monopoly
B. Perfect competition
C. Oligopoly

D. Monopolistic competition

Q.64 <u>Directions:</u> Consider the following statements and answer accordingly.**Assertion (A):** For normal distribution, Mean = Median = Mode**Reason (R):** Normal distribution is mesokurtic.

A. Both (A) and (R) are correct and (R) is the correct explanation of (A).

B. Both (A) and (R) are correct but (R) is not the correct explanation of (A).

C. (A) is correct, but (R) is incorrect.

D. (A) is incorrect, but (R) is correct.

Q.65 Match the following:

Group - I	Group - II
a. Type II error	1. $P_{01} \times P_{10} = 1$
b. Mean > Mode	2. Probability of not rejecting H0 when it was not true
c. Population is homogenous	3. Positively skewed distribution
d. Time Reversal Test	4. Simple random sampling

A. 2, 3, 4, 1   **B.** 3, 1, 2, 4

C. 4, 2, 3, 1   **D.** 1, 2, 3, 4

Q.66 NAFED is a

A. company

B. non-government organisation

C. government body

D. cooperative organisation

Q.67 In which year was the Kisan Credit Card System introduced?

A. 1978   **B.** 1998   **C.** 1988   **D.** 2008

Q.68 The MRTP Act of 1969 has been

A. replaced by Competition Act 2002

B. merged in Industrial Policy Act of 1978

C. replaced by Trade Union (Amendment) Act 2001

D. merged in Industrial Policy Act of 1991

Q.69 The value of foreign trade multiplier will be high under the condition when

A. marginal propensity to save is high

B. marginal propensity to import is high

C. there is increase in exports

D. marginal propensity to consume domestic goods is high

Q.70 Match the weight of different industry groups in List - I and List - II:

List - I	List - II
a. Basic goods industries	1. 45.7
b. Capital goods industries	2. 8.8
c. Intermedicate goods industries	3. 15.7
d. Consumer goods industries	4. 29.8

A. 1, 2, 3, 4   **B.** 2, 4, 3, 1

C. 3, 2, 1, 4   **D.** 1, 3, 4, 2

Q.71 A proportionate increase in tax revenue to a proportionate increase in the tax base is called:

A. elasticity of a tax   **B.** buoyancy of a tax

C. neutrality of a tax   **D.** None of the above

Q.72 The Bretton Wood System was based on

A. a gold standard

B. a flexible exchange rate system

C. a gold exchange standard

D. None of the above

Q.73 Which one of the following is short period debt meant to meet current needs, that is filling temporary gap in budgets?

A. Funded debt   **B.** Unfunded debt

C. Redeemable debt   **D.** Irredeemable debt

Q.74 Monetised deficit means

A. Fiscal deficit less interest payments

B. Government expenditure which is financed through the sale of adhoc treasury bills

C. Increase in RBI credit to Central Government

D. Fiscal deficit less loans andadvances.

Q.75 Hurdle rate means

A. ARR

B. cost of capital

C. minimum return from investment

D. which is difficult to earn

Q.76 The distribution of the burden of paying a tax is called

A. sharing of tax burden

B. shifting of the tax

C. incidence of a tax

D. tax capitalisation

Q.77 What is a change in economic growth?

A. Structure of economy

B. Mindset of people

C. National income

D. None of these

Q.78 The classical model of economic development emphasises

A. Laissez-Faire Policy

B. Capital Accumulation

C. Both (A) and (B)

D. None of these

Q.79 Which one of the following pairs of "Author - Book" is not correctly matched?

A. Simon Kuznets - Asian Drama

B. J. Robinson - Essays in the Theory of Economic Growth

C. Karl Marx - Das Kapital

D. A. W. Lewis - Theory of Economic Growth

Q.80 Match items given in List - I with those in List - II:

List - I	List - II
a. Equation of Exchange	1. J.M. Keynes

b. Cash Balances Approach	2. Irving Fisher
c. Regressive Expectation model of Demand for Money	3. W.J. Baumol
d. Square Root Formula of Demand for Money	4. A.C. Pigou and Alfred Marshall

A. 2, 4, 1, 3   **B.** 3, 2, 4, 1
C. 4, 3, 1, 2   **D.** 1, 3, 2, 4

Q.81 Which of the following is/are not the assumption(s) of Walter's dividend model?

A. 100% retention/payout assumed
B. Constant EPS and DPS
C. No internal financing
D. Both (1) and (2)

Q.82 It is often true that as the economy begins to recover from a recession, the unemployment rate rises because

A. as the economy initially recovers from a recession, the demand for goods and services falls, so the demand for workers falls

B. as the economy begins to recover from a recession, workers who were previously discouraged about their chances of finding a job begin to look for work again

C. as the economy begins to recover from a recession because of the errors in the way the data is collected

D. as the economy initially recovers from a recession, firms do not immediately increase the number of workers they hire; firms wait to hire more individuals until they are convinced that the recovery is strong

Q.83 When additional government expenditure is financed by selling government securities, then what will be the nature of crowding out effect, given in List - I in the context of the situation given in List - II?

List - I Crowding out effect	List - II Situation
a. Full	1. Keynesian Range
b. Partial	2. Classical Range
c. Nil	3. Intermediate Range

A. 2, 3, 1   **B.** 3, 1, 2   **C.** 1, 3, 2   **D.** 1, 2, 3

Q.84 Consider the following statements:

1). Inflation refers to a general increase in the price of goods and services. This occurs when demand for these items grows faster than the supply. The result is more money chasing fewer goods, and therefore prices increase.

2). Deflation is fall in general price level of goods and services. Deflation is negative inflation.

3). Disinflation is a slow-down in the inflation rate. Disinflation is positive inflation.

4). Stagflation is a situation in which the inflation rate is high, the economic growth rate slows, and unemployment remains steadily high.

Which of the above options are correct:

A. 1 & 2 only   **B.** 2 & 3 only
C. All of the above   **D.** 1,2 & 3 only

Q.85 With reference to demand for money, match List - I with List - II:

List - I	List - II
a. Demand for money is stable	1. J.M. Keynes
b. Liquidity Preference as behaviour towards risk	2. W. Baumol
c. Inventory Theoretic Approach	3. James Tobin
d. No portfolio diversification	4. Milton Friedman

A. 4, 3, 1, 2   **B.** 3, 4, 1, 2
C. 2, 1, 3, 4   **D.** 4, 3, 2, 1

Q.86 The locus of Pareto Optimality in Production and Consumption is given by:

A. Social Welfare Function
B. Utility Possibility Curve
C. Transformation Curve
D. Grand Utility Possibility

Q.87 Match the following:

List-I	List-II
(a) Revealed Preference Hypothesis	(i) A. Bergson
(b) Quasi-rent	(ii) B. S. Minhas
(c) Elasticity of substitution	(iii) A. Marshall
(d) Social welfare function	(iv) P. A. Samuelson

A. (iii), (i), (ii), (iv)   **B.** (iv), (iii), (ii), (i)
C. (iv), (i), (ii), (iii)   **D.** (ii), (iii), (iv), (i)

Q.88 Match the following:

List-I	List-II
(a) Increasing Returns to Scale	(i) $\beta_1, \beta_2 < 1$
(b) Diminishing Returns to Scale	(ii) $\beta_1 + \beta_2 > 1$
(c) Constant Returns to Scale	(iii) $\beta_1 + \beta_2 < 1$
(d) Diminishing Returns to Factors	(iv) $\beta_1 + \beta_2 = 1$

A. (i), (iv), (iii), (ii)   **B.** (iv), (i), (ii), (iii)
C. (ii), (iii), (iv), (i)   **D.** (ii), (iii), (i), (iv)

Q.89 Directions: Read the following statements and answer accordingly.
Assertion (A): Duesenberry hypothesised that consumption-income relationship is irreversible.
Reason (R): Consumption depends not only on current income but also on previous peak income.

A. Both (A) and (R) are true but (R) is not the correct explanation of (A).
B. Both (A) and (R) are true and (R) is the correct explanation of (A).
C. (A) is true, but (R) is false.
D. Both (A) and (R) are false.

Q.90 Which of the following averages is known as 'root-mean square'?

A. Quadratic mean   **B.** Harmonic mean
C. Geometric mean   **D.** Combined mean

Q.91 Quantitative restrictions on imports by a country will lead to

A. decreased demand for imported products
B. increased demand for imported products
C. increased supply of imported products
D. decreased supply of imported products

Q.92 Borrowings from foreigners are known as

A. export of goods
B. unrequited receipts
C. capital receipts
D. current receipts

Q.93 The difference between total revenue and total expenditure is called

A. capital deficit
B. revenue deficit
C. fiscal deficit
D. budgetary deficit

Q.94 Items which are of recurring nature are covered under

A. capital budget
B. revenue budget
C. cash budget
D. unified budget

Q.95 In Nurksian formulation of the thesis of the 'vicious circle of poverty' in the context of an underdeveloped country, the inducement to invest is limited by

A. lack of savings
B. lack of investment opportunities
C. size of the market
D. policy of the government

Q.96 The major difference between Harrod-Domar and Solow models of growth lies in

A. substitutability between labour and capital
B. returns to scale
C. returns to variable factor
D. growth of income

Q.97 In case of proportional relation between consumption and income,

A. APC > MPC
B. APC = MPC
C. APC < MPC
D. APC = MPS

Q.98 Which of the following does not hold correct about the Demsetz view of concentration and monopoly power?

A. Superior efficiency produces both increased concentration and more profits.
B. The causal link is from concentration to profitability.
C. The causal link is from efficiency to concentration.
D. The causal link is from efficiency to profit.

Q.99 For which of the following items of household consumption expenditures in India does NSSO take the reference period as 365 days?

A. Clothing, footwear, bedding, education, etc.
B. Edible oil, fish, meat and egg
C. Vegetables, fruits, spices, beverages and processed food
D. All other food, fuel and light, misc. goods and services

Q.100 Which of the following is real GDP?

A. GDP at base year prices
B. GDP at current year prices
C. GDP at any year prices
D. GDP at future prices

// Smart Answer Sheet //

Correct Indicates percentage of students who answered questions correctly.

Skipped Indicates percentage of students who skipped questions.

Q.	Ans.	Correct / Skipped	Q.	Ans.	Correct / Skipped	Q.	Ans.	Correct / Skipped	Q.	Ans.	Correct / Skipped	Q.	Ans.	Correct / Skipped
1	B	71.92 % / 2.05 %	17	D	34.93 % / 17.81 %	33	B	54.79 % / 21.24 %	49	C	41.78 % / 21.92 %	65	A	64.38 % / 27.4 %
2	B	72.6 % / 14.39 %	18	A	50.68 % / 19.18 %	34	A	57.53 % / 21.92 %	50	C	45.21 % / 22.6 %	66	D	42.47 % / 25.34 %
3	B	43.84 % / 20.54 %	19	B	39.04 % / 19.18 %	35	A	45.21 % / 21.91 %	51	B	43.84 % / 23.28 %	67	B	52.74 % / 23.97 %
4	C	70.55 % / 17.12 %	20	D	45.21 % / 18.49 %	36	B	23.29 % / 21.92 %	52	D	38.36 % / 22.6 %	68	A	54.79 % / 24.66 %
5	C	45.21 % / 16.43 %	21	D	62.33 % / 17.81 %	37	A	34.93 % / 21.92 %	53	B	37.67 % / 24.66 %	69	C	26.03 % / 26.02 %
6	A	60.27 % / 15.76 %	22	D	44.52 % / 20.55 %	38	B	56.16 % / 21.92 %	54	D	34.93 % / 24.66 %	70	A	25.34 % / 30.14 %
7	A	62.33 % / 17.12 %	23	D	25.34 % / 18.5 %	39	B	23.97 % / 21.24 %	55	A	47.95 % / 23.97 %	71	B	54.79 % / 24.66 %
8	A	32.88 % / 17.12 %	24	C	56.16 % / 18.5 %	40	C	52.05 % / 21.24 %	56	A	65.07 % / 26.03 %	72	C	46.58 % / 24.65 %
9	C	60.27 % / 18.5 %	25	A	24.66 % / 19.18 %	41	B	32.19 % / 20.55 %	57	D	46.58 % / 26.02 %	73	B	32.88 % / 26.02 %
10	C	37.67 % / 25.34 %	26	A	67.81 % / 19.18 %	42	D	17.12 % / 22.61 %	58	C	30.14 % / 26.71 %	74	C	35.62 % / 25.34 %
11	A	47.95 % / 19.86 %	27	A	49.32 % / 20.54 %	43	A	49.32 % / 21.23 %	59	D	39.04 % / 24.66 %	75	C	44.52 % / 26.03 %
12	C	49.32 % / 17.8 %	28	D	41.1 % / 19.17 %	44	B	23.97 % / 27.4 %	60	C	60.27 % / 23.98 %	76	C	35.62 % / 23.97 %
13	D	67.12 % / 17.13 %	29	A	57.53 % / 20.55 %	45	A	54.11 % / 22.6 %	61	D	40.41 % / 24.66 %	77	C	56.16 % / 23.98 %
14	B	23.29 % / 21.23 %	30	D	52.74 % / 19.86 %	46	D	33.56 % / 23.97 %	62	D	43.84 % / 24.65 %	78	C	67.81 % / 23.97 %
15	B	35.62 % / 19.86 %	31	A	34.93 % / 21.92 %	47	A	43.15 % / 22.6 %	63	B	58.22 % / 23.97 %	79	A	61.64 % / 24.66 %
16	B	68.49 % / 17.81 %	32	B	60.27 % / 21.92 %	48	C	46.58 % / 21.91 %	64	B	26.03 % / 23.97 %	80	A	43.84 % / 26.71 %

Q.	Ans.	Correct		Q.	Ans.	Correct		Q.	Ans.	Correct		Q.	Ans.	Correct		Q.	Ans.	Correct
		Skipped				Skipped				Skipped				Skipped				Skipped
81	C	16.44 %		85	D	39.04 %		89	A	21.23 %		93	C	18.49 %		97	B	43.84 %
		26.71 %				26.71 %				26.72 %				25.35 %				26.02 %
82	B	32.88 %		86	B	35.62 %		90	A	21.23 %		94	B	41.1 %		98	B	17.81 %
		26.02 %				24.65 %				26.03 %				26.02 %				27.4 %
83	A	39.04 %		87	B	58.9 %		91	D	39.04 %		95	C	18.49 %		99	A	37.67 %
		26.71 %				26.03 %				27.4 %				26.72 %				26.03 %
84	C	41.78 %		88	C	65.07 %		92	C	51.37 %		96	A	52.05 %		100	A	45.21 %
		34.25 %				25.34 %				25.34 %				25.35 %				23.97 %

Performance Analysis

Avg. Score (%)	41.0%
Toppers Score (%)	98.0%
Your Score	

//Hints and Solutions//

1. Indifference curve shows different combinations of two goods which gives an equal level of satisfaction to a consumer at every point.

Properties of IC:

• Negative slope as it slopes left to the rightward gain of one commodity will lead to the loss of others.

• The indifference curves do not intersect nor are they tangent to one another

• Upper indifference curves indicate a higher level of satisfaction

• IC neither touches X-axis or Y-axis.

• IC is convex to the origin in the case of two imperfect substitutes.

2.

1. Variance is a measure of dispersion.
2. Mode is a measure of central tendency.
3. Chi square distribution (χ^2 distribution) is sampling distribution.
4. Mesokurtic distribution is normal distribution.

3. CV = (Standard deviation/mean) x 100

Standard deviation = $\sqrt{0.25}$ = 0.5

CV = (0.5/8) x 100 = 6.25%

4. Probability of getting a white ball = 12/25
Probability of getting a red ball = 8/25
They are mutually exclusive events. Thus, individual probabilities of both colors to be added.
Probability of getting either a white ball or red ball = 12/25 + 8/25 = 20/25

5. An F-test is used to test if the variances of two populations are equal. This test can be a two-tailed test or a one-tailed test. The two-tailed version tests against the alternative that the variances are not equal. The one-tailed version only tests in one direction, that is the variance from the first population is either greater than or less than the second population variance. The choice is determined by the problem. In order to use this test, the following must hold:

• Both populations are normally distributed

• Both samples are drawn independently from each other.

• Within each sample, the observations are sampled randomly and independently of each other.

6. The monopolist's profit maximizing level of output is found by equating its marginal revenue with its marginal cost, which is the same profit maximizing condition that a perfectly competitive firm uses to determine its equilibrium level of output.

7. When average cost is declining as output increases, marginal cost is less than average cost. When average cost is rising, marginal cost is greater than average cost. When average cost is neither rising nor falling (at a minimum or maximum), marginal cost equals average cost.

8. According to the order condition, the first equation is Unidentified.

9.

1. Unit Root Test-Stationarity
2. Contingency Table- χ^2-test
3. Regression Coefficient- Student&aposs t-test
4. Autocorrelation- Durbin- Watson Test

10.

• The parameters can be validly estimated using separate applications of OLS to each equation.

• An application of 2 SLS would lead to unbiased but inefficient parameter estimates.

• The independent variables may be correlated with the error terms in other equations.

11. Verdoorn's law is named after Dutch economist Petrus Johannes Verdoorn (1949). It states that in the long-run productivity generally grows proportionally to the square root of output. In economics, this law pertains to the relationship between the growth of output and the growth of productivity. According to the law, faster growth in output increases productivity due to increasing returns. Verdoorn (1949, p. 59) argued that "in the long run a change in the volume of production, say about 10 percent, tends to be associated with an average increase in labor productivity of 4.5 percent." The Verdoorn coefficient close to 0.5 (0.484) is also found in subsequent estimations of the law.

Hence, the correct option is (A).

12. The concept of Imperfect Competition was initially developed by a prestigious English economist, Roy Harrod. In 1933, Mrs. Joan Robinson of Cambridge University in England and Edward Chamberlin of Harvard University in America, two distinguished economists, complemented this concept with essential contributions.

13. a production function $Q = AL^{\alpha} K^{\beta}$; $\alpha, \beta > 0$, increasing returns to scale requires that $\alpha + \beta > 1$.

14. The optimal solution is either an extreme point or is on a line connecting extreme points concerning the optimal solution of linear program with two decision variables.

15. For this model stability of market requires the condition $|\delta| < |1/\beta|$.

The cobweb model or cobweb theory is an economic model that explains why prices might be subject to periodic fluctuations in certain types of markets. It describes cyclical supply and demand in a market where the amount produced must be chosen before prices are observed.

16. Input-output is a novel technique invented by Professor Wassily W. Leontief in 1951. It is used to analyse inter-industry relationship in order to understand the inter-dependencies and complexities of the economy and thus the conditions for maintaining equilibrium between supply and demand.

17. This section discusses hypothesis tests on the regression coefficients in multiple linear regression. As in the case of simple linear regression, these tests can only be carried out if it can be assumed that the random error terms, $\in_i$, are normally and independently distributed with a mean of zero and variance of σ^2. Three types of hypothesis tests can be carried out for multiple linear regression models:

Test for significance of regression: This test checks the significance of the whole regression model.

t test: This test checks the significance of individual regression coefficients.

F test: This test can be used to simultaneously check the significance of a number of regression coefficients. It can also be used to test individual coefficients.

18. In a two variable regression Y is the dependent variable and X is the independent variable. The correlation coefficient between Y and X is 0.6 which means 36% variations in Y are explained by X.

19. Techniques of selective credit control of RBI are:

1. Directiveness
2. Moral Suasion
3. Fixation of Margin Requirements
4. Rationing of Credit
5. Credit Authorization Scheme

20. Some salient features of regional rural banks are:

1. The area of operation of a rural bank is limited to a specified region which comprises of one or more districts.

2. These banks cannot have a lending rate which is higher than the prevailing lending rate of cooperative credit societies in any particular state.

3. The salary structure of the employees of these banks is fixed in consonance with the salary structure of the employees of the state government, local authorities of comparable level and status in the area.

4. They are public sector banks. The paid-up capital of each bank is Rs. 25 lakhs. 50 percent of the capital is contributed by the Central Government. The concerned state government contributes 15 percent. 35 percent is contributed by the sponsoring public-sector commercial banks.

21. High powered money or powerful money refers to that currency that has been issued by the Government and Reserve Bank of India. Some portion of this currency is kept along with the public while rest is kept as funds in Reserve Bank.

22.

1. Iron law of wages- David Ricardo
2. Wage-funds theory- J.S. Mill
3. Surplus-value theory- Karl Marx
4. Marginal productivity theory- John R. Hicks

23. Commercial banks are the largest holders of government securities with 43.14% share. Insurance companies and Reserve Bank of India (own account) held 21.37% and 13.06% of total outstanding government securities respectively.

24. An indifference curve is the curve at every point of which the utility would remain same. The indifference curve of perfect complementary goods is 'L' shaped.'Left shoe' and 'Right shoe' can be considered as perfect complimentary goods.

25. The GDP deflator, also called implicit price deflator, is a measure of inflation is a Paasche index. It is the ratio of the value of goods and services an economy produces in a particular year at current prices to that of prices that prevailed during the base year.

26. Thus devaluation helps to improve BOP deficit of a country by increasing its exports and reducing its imports. But the extent to which it will succeed depends on the country's price elasticities of domestic demand for imports and foreign demand for exports.

27. In 1956, Joe S. Bain used the definition "an advantage of established sellers in an industry over potential entrant sellers, which is reflected in the extent to which established sellers can persistently raise their prices above competitive levels without attracting new firms to enter the industry." McAfee et al. criticized this as being tautological by putting the "consequences of the definition into the definition itself."

28. To illustrate this, Rosenstein Rodan gives the example of a shoe industry. If a country makes large investments in the shoe industry, all the disguisedly employed labor from the other industries find work and a source of income, leading to a rise in production of shoes and their own incomes. This increased income will not be expended only on buying shoes. It is conceivable that the increased incomes will lead to increased spending on other products too. However, there is no corresponding supply of these products to satisfy this increased demand for the other goods. Following the basic market forces of demand and supply, the prices of these commodities will rise. To avoid such a situation, investment must be spread out amongst different industries.

29. The theory of multiplier occupies an important place in the modern theory of income and employment. The concept of multiplier was first of all developed by F.A. Kahn in the early 1930s. But Keynes later further refined it.

30. In Friedman's modern quantity theory of money, the supply of money is independent of demand for money.The people will spend this excess money partly on consumer goods and partly by purchasing assets. This spending will reduce their cash balances and at the same time there is a rise in the national income.

31. Unsystematic risk, also known as diversifiable risk or non-systematic risk, is the danger that relates to a particular security or a portfolio of securities. Investors construct diversified portfolios in order to allocate the risk over different classes of assets.

32. The upper portion of the kinked demand curve is relatively more elastic. The kinked-demand curve is a demand curve comprised of two segments, one that is relatively more elastic, which results if a firm increases its price, and the other that is relatively less elastic, which results if a firm decreases its price.

33. If a monopolist is producing under decreasing cost conditions, increase in demand is beneficial to the society because cost of production falls and hence price.

34. The reserve capacity makes it possible to have constant SAVC within a certain range of output. It should be clear that this reserve capacity is planned in order to give the maximum flexibility in the operation of the firm.

35. The shape of an indifference curve is convex to the origin and this is based on the principle of diminishing marginal rate of substitution. If two goods X and Y are perfect substitutes, the indifference curve is a straight line with negative slope.

36. In his theory of demand for money Fisher and other classical economists laid stress on the medium of exchange function of money, that is, money as a means of buying goods and services. All transactions involving purchase of goods, services, raw materials, assets require payment of money as value of the transaction made.

37. The LM curve, the equilibrium points in the market for money, shifts for two reasons: changes in money demand and changes in the money supply. If the money supply increases (decreases), ceteris paribus, the interest rate is lower (higher) at each level of Y, or in other words, the LM curve shifts right (left). That is because at any given level of output Y, more money (less money) means a lower (higher) interest rate. (Remember, the price level doesn't change in this model.)

38. It is worth mentioning that Tobin's portfolio approach, according to which liquidity preference (i.e. demand for money) is determined by the individual's attitude towards risk, can be extended to the problem of asset choice when there are several alternative assets, not just two, of money and bonds.

39. The IS curve is a set of points, derived in the Goods Market (see also Keynesian Cross) which are the result of a changing interest rate, holding government spending and net exports constant. A less elastic IS means that monetary policy is less effective.

40. Repo rate is the rate at which the central bank of a country (Reserve Bank of India in case of India) lends money to commercial banks in the event of any shortfall of funds. Repo rate is used by monetary authorities to control inflation.

41. The dominant theme in Domar's theoretical treatment of economic growth is that net investment raises productive capacity and thus causes the economy to grow. Given the capacity creating impact of the net investment, Domar attempts to determine the rate at which income must grow, if full employment is to be maintained.

42. In the short period, the monopolist behaves like any other firm. A monopolist will maximize profit or minimize losses by producing that output for which marginal cost (MC) equals marginal revenue (MR).

43. Wage is determined where: Demand for labour = supply of labour & MRP of labour = marginal wage.

Classical economists argue that wages—the price of labor—are determined (like all prices) by supply and demand. They call this the market theory of wage determination. When workers sell their labor, the price they can charge is influenced by several factors on the supply side and several factors on the demand side.

44.

1. Postage stamp pricing- Differential pricing
2. Loss leader- Product line pricing
3. Economic capacity- Equality of marginal and average cost
4. Reserve capacity- Constant average and marginal cost

45. In monetary economics, the quantity theory of money (QTM) states that the general price level of goods and services is directly proportional to the amount of money in circulation, or money supply.

46. Unanticipated inflation occurs when people do not know inflation is going to occur until after the general price level increases. When this happens, many individuals are left unprotected, such as lenders who get paid back with a money that has a reduced purchasing power.

47. The concept of scale economics applies in long-run with constants technical coefficients. The economies of Scale refer to the cost advantage experienced by a firm when it increases its level of output. The advantage arises due to the inverse relationship between per-unit fixed cost and the quantity produced.

48. Kaldor's Three Laws of Economic Growth (Inductive Approach)

(i) Close relationship between manufacturing and GDP growth (ornon-manufacturing growth).

(ii) Strong relationship between the growth of industrial productivity and industrial output (Verdoorn's law) Increasing returns in other sectors

(iii) Close relationship between aggregate productivity growth and (a) the growth of manufacturing and (b) inversely with the growth non manufacturing employment (consequence of (i) and (ii))

49. Since there is monopoly or imperfect competition in product market, the marginal revenue (MR) is less than the price (AR) of the product. MR < Price (under monopoly both AR (P) and MR slope downward). This is monopolistic exploitation of labour by the firm.

50. Product differentiation is a marketing strategy that strives to distinguish a company's products or services from the competition. Successful product differentiation involves identifying and communicating the unique qualities of a company's offerings while highlighting the distinct differences between those offerings and others on the market. Product differentiation goes hand-in-hand with developing a strong value proposition to make a product or service attractive to a target market or audience.

51. CB segments correctly depicts the supply curve of a producer.

52. Neo-classical production function has following characteristics:

1. Positive and diminishing marginal productivity of the factors.

2. Constant return to scale.

3. Satisfies Inada conditions.

53. Between the two situations for a firm profit maximization and sales revenue maximization, the equilibrium for a profit maximizer as compared to sales revenue maximizer takes place at lower output and higher price.

54.

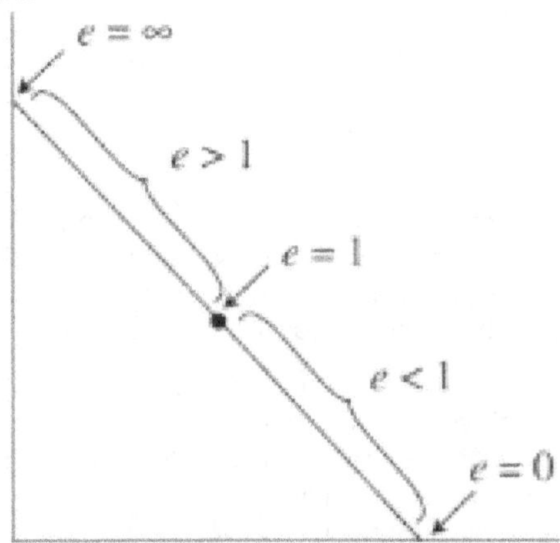

For the linear demand curve the elasticity declines as one slides down the demand curve. A linear demand curve is the graphical representation of the relationship between the price of a good and the quantity of that good consumers are willing to pay at a certain price at a point in time.

55. There must be a different price elasticity of demand for each group of consumers. The firm is then able to charge a higher price to the group with a more price inelastic demand and a lower price to the group with a more elastic demand. By adopting such a strategy, the firm can increase total revenue and profits (i.e. achieve a higher level of producer surplus). To profit maximise, the firm will seek to set marginal revenue = to marginal cost in each separate (segmented) market.

56. $Per\ Capita\ Income = \dfrac{National\ Income}{Population}$

National Income = Per capita income $\times$ Population

$$National\ Income = 3cr \times 2000 = Rs.\,6000cr$$

57. This means that a tariff implemented by a "large" importing country may raise national welfare. Generally speaking, 1) whenever a "large" country implements a small tariff, it will raise national welfare. and 3) there will be a positive optimal tariff that will maximize national welfare.

58. The monetary approach to the balance of payments is associated with the names of R. Mundell and H. Johnson. The other writers who have made contribution to it include R. Dornbusch, M. Mussa, D. Kemp and J. Frankel. The basic premise of the approach is the recognition that the BOP disequilibrium is fundamentally a monetary phenomenon. It attempts to explain the BOP deficits or surpluses through demand for and supply of money.

59. Marshall-Edgeworth Index No. satisfies time reversal test but not factor reversal test.

60. With proportional quota sampling, the aim is to end up with a sample where the strata (groups) being studied (e.g., males vs. females students) are proportional to the population being studied. If we were to examine the differences in male and female students, for example, the number of students from each group that we would include in the sample would be based on the proportion of male and female students amongst the 10,000 university students.

61. When it comes to studying the economy, growth and jobs are two primary factors economists must consider. There is a clear relationship between the two, and many economists have framed the discussion by trying to study the relationship between economic growth and unemployment levels. Economist Arthur Okun first started tackling the discussion in the 1960s, and his research on the subject has since become known as Okun's law.

62. Types of competition lead(s) to exploitation of consumer:

1. Oligopoly

2. Monopolistic competition

3. Monopoly

63. Perfect competition is considered to be efficient because:

1. Supernormal profits are not made by any firm in perfect competition in the long-run.

2. MC = price, so both parties, suppliers and customers, get exactly what they want.

3. No wasteful advertising.

4. Firms are allocatively and productively efficient.

The major assumption behind this analysis and evaluation is that firms cannot produce products cheaper if they were bigger. It assumes that there are no economies of scale available in the market.

64. The mean, median, and mode of a normal distribution are equal. The area under the normal curve is equal to 1.0. Normal distributions are denser in the center and less dense in the tails. Normal distributions are defined by two parameters, the mean (μ) and the standard deviation (σ).

65.

1. Type II error- Probability of not rejecting H0 when it was not true

2. Mean > Mode- Positively skewed distribution

3. Population is homogenous- Simple random sampling

4. Time Reversal Test- $P_{01} \times P_{10} = 1$

66. National Agricultural Cooperative Marketing Federation of India Ltd (NAFED) is an apex organization of marketing cooperatives for agricultural produce in India, under Ministry of Agriculture, Government of India.

67. The Kisan Credit Card (KCC) scheme is a credit scheme introduced in August 1998 by Indian banks. This model scheme was prepared by the National Bank for Agriculture and Rural

Development (NABARD) on the recommendations of R.V.GUPTA committee to provide term loans for agricultural needs.

68. The Ministry of Corporate Affairs, Government of India has issued a Notification dated 28th August 2009, whereby the most controversial the Monopolies and Restrictive Trade Practices Act, 1969 ("the MRTP Act") stands repealed and is replaced by the Competition Act, 2002, with effect from September 1, 2009.

69. But the foreign repercussion will be high in the case of a large country because a change in the national income of such a country will have significant foreign repercussions or backwash effects. Assuming two large countries A and B where A's imports are B's exports and vice versa.

70.

1. Basic goods industries- 45.7
2. Capital goods industries- 8.8
3. Intermedicate goods industries- 15.7
4. Consumer goods industries- 29.8

71. A proportionate increase in tax revenue to a proportionate increase in the tax base is called buoyancy of a tax. Taxes in which the rate of tax increases are called progressive taxes. Thus, in a progressive tax, the amount of tax paid will increase at a higher rate than the increase in tax base or income, for the taxation amount is the product of multiplying the base by the rate and both these increase in a progressive tax.

72. Bretton Woods established a system of payments based on the dollar, which defined all currencies in relation to the dollar, itself convertible into gold, and above all, "as good as gold" for trade. U.S. currency was now effectively the world currency, the standard to which every other currency was pegged.

73. short period debt meant to meet current needs, that is filling temporary gap in budgets is called unfunded debt. Short-term loans are repayable after short interval of time, e.g. Treasury Bills payable after three months, ways and means advances from the Central Bank. They are intended to bridge the gap temporarily between current revenue and current expenditure. It is called floating debt.

74. Monetised deficit is the monetary support the Reserve Bank of India (RBI) extends to the Centre as part of the government's borrowing programme. In other words, the term refers to the purchase of government bonds by the central bank to finance the spending needs of the government.

75. A hurdle rate is the minimum rate of return on a project or investment required by a manager or investor. The hurdle rate describes the appropriate compensation for the level of risk present—riskier projects generally have higher hurdle rates than those with less risk.

76. Incidence of Taxation. Incidence is on the person who ultimately bears the money burden of tax. According to the modern theory, incidence means the changes brought about in income distribution by changes in the budgetary policy.

77. Economic growth is an increase in the the production of economic goods and services, compared from one period of time to another. It can be measured in nominal or real (adjusted for inflation) terms. Traditionally, aggregate economic growth is measured in terms of gross national product (GNP) or gross domestic product (GDP), although alternative metrics are sometimes used.

78. The classical growth theory argues that economic growth will decrease or end because of an increasing population and limited resources. Classical growth theory economists believed that temporary increases in real GDP per person would cause a population explosion that would consequently decrease real GDP.

79. Gunnar Myrdal is the author of Asian Drama.

80.

1. Equation of Exchange- Irving Fisher
2. Cash Balances Approach- A.C. Pigou and Alfred Marshall
3. Regressive Expectation model of Demand for Money- J.M. Keynes
4. Square Root Formula of Demand for Money- W.J. Baumol

81. Walter's model on dividend policy.. Assumptions of Walter's Model Walter's model is based on the following assumptions: Internal Financing All the investments are financed by the firm through retained earnings. In other words, retained earnings are the only source of finance.

82. As unemployment rises, this can worsen the recession. The unemployed will have less income to spend leading to lower consumer spending, lower Aggregate Demand and lower growth rates. This, in turn, can lead to more job losses as firms have to cut back even further on employment levels.

83.

1. Full- Classical Range
2. Partial- Intermediate Range
3. Nil- Keynesian Range

84. Please don't get confused between deflation and disinflation. In disinflation, inflation is still there though its rate is decreasing. However, in deflation, the real prices of goods decline so there is no inflation.

85.

- Demand for money is stable- Milton Friedman
- Liquidity Preference as behaviour towards risk- James Tobin
- Inventory Theoretic Approach- W. Baumol
- No portfolio diversification- J.M. Keynes

86. Utility possibility curve refers to the graph showing the highest amount of utility a person can attain given each utility levels of other persons in the society. It is an upper frontier of a set of various utility possibilities of economic agents for the given amount of production.

87.

- Revealed Preference Hypothesis- P. A. Samuelson
- Quasi-rent- A. Marshall

- Elasticity of substitution- B. S. Minhas
- Social welfare function- A. Bergson

88. Option '3' is the correct answer which is

(a) - (ii), (b) - (iii), (c) - (iv), (d) - (i)

89. According to the relative income hypothesis, consumption standards are irreversible in the short run, but not in the long run because people cannot go on dis-saving or borrowing to maintain their living standards, as it is not sustainable if incomes continue to decrease.

The life-cycle theory of the consumption function was developed by Franco Modigliani, Alberto Ando and Brumberg. An individual's or household's level of consumption depends not just on current income but also, and more importantly, on long-term expected earnings.

90. In mathematics and its applications, the root mean square (RMS or rms) is defined as the square root of the mean square (the arithmetic mean of the squares of a set of numbers). The RMS is also known as the quadratic mean and is a particular case of the generalized mean with exponent 2. RMS can also be defined for a continuously varying function in terms of an integral of the squares of the instantaneous values during a cycle.

91. Restrictions on imports by a country will lead to decreased supply of imported products. Although quantitative restrictions may improve the terms of trade for importing countries, they exacerbate the terms of trade for exporting countries and reduce their economic welfare.

92. Capital receipts refer to those receipts which either create a liability or cause a reduction in the assets of the government. They are non-recurring and non-routine in nature.

93. The difference between total revenue and total expenditure of the government is termed as fiscal deficit. It is an indication of the total borrowings needed by the government. While calculating the total revenue, borrowings are not included.

94. Items which are of recurring nature are covered under revenue budget.

95. This vicious circle of poverty shows that income in underdeveloped countries is low. According to Nurkse "The inducement to invest may be low because of the small buying power of the people, which is due to their small real income, which again is due to low productivity.

96. The main difference between the Harrod-Domar (HD) model and the Solow model is that HD assumes constant marginal returns to capital, while Solow assumes decreasing marginal returns to capital.

97. When income increases, consumption also increases but not to the same extent as the increase in income. It means that increase in income is followed by decrease in marginal and average propensity to consume. Consumption function according to Keynes is non -proportional in the short-run.

98. In a classic 1973 paper, Harold Demsetz argues that the superior efficiency of large firms, rather than market power, explains the typical findings of positive correlations between profitability and concentration in empirical studies. The empirical evidence that he presents to support this assertion indicates that although large firms In more concentrated industries earn supranormal profits, the smaller firms in such industries earn average rates of return. The present work replicates Demsetz with the same 1963 Internal Revenue Service data set, but with a less aggregated version of the data and with more rigorous statistical testing. The results fail to support the Demsetz view of concentration and efficiency.

99. Items of household consumption expenditures in India does NSSO take the reference period as 365 days Clothing, footwear, bedding, education, etc.

100. Real GDP is GDP evaluated at the market prices of some base year. For example, if 1990 were chosen as the base year, then real GDP for 1995 is calculated by taking the quantities of all goods and services purchased in 1995 and multiplying them by their 1990 prices.

Q.1 Grants from the Centre to the States under the recommendations of Finance Commission are known as:

A. Plan grants

B. Development assistance

C. Statutory grants

D. Discretionary grants

Q.2 Which one of the following taxes are within the jurisdiction of the Central Government as enumerated in List I of Seventh Schedule of the Constitution of India?

A. Taxes on mineral rights subject to any limitation imposed by the Parliament

B. Taxes on the consumption and sale of electricity

C. Taxes on sale and purchase of newspapers and on advertisements therein

D. Excise on alcoholic liquors for human consumption, opium, Indian hemp and other narcotics

Q.3 Which of the following is related with optimum currency area?

A. Optimal geographical area for a single currency

B. Optimal geographical area for several currencies whose exchange rates are relatively pegged.

C. Single currency or the pegged currencies fluctuate jointly vis-a-vis other currencies.

D. All of the above

Q.4 Under a managed floating exchange rate system, the Nation&aposs monetary authorities intervene in Foreign Exchange Markets to

A. smooth out short-run fluctuations in exchange rates

B. smooth out long-run fluctuations in exchange rates

C. smooth out short-run and long-run fluctuations in exchange rates

D. keep exchange rates fixed among a group of nations

Q.5 Match the following:

List - I	List - II
(a) Hamilton List	(1) Trade creation and trade diversion effects
(b) Marshall-Lerner	(2) Indian industry
(c) F. Y. Edgeworth	(3) Elasticity approach
(d) Jacob Viner	(4) Impoverishing growth

A. (2), (3), (1), (4) **B.** (2), (3), (4), (1)

C. (3), (2), (4), (1) **D.** (3), (2), (1), (4)

Q.6 Regarding M.F.N. (Most Favoured Nation) clause, find out the correct statement.

A. It guarantees special privilege to the contracting parties.

B. It guarantees only equal treatment.

C. The unconditional M.F.N. clause seems to be more equitable than the conditional one.

D. The conditional M.F.N. clause confers significant rights on the contracting party.

Q.7 A spot Foreign Exchange Transaction refers to

A. the purchase or sale of foreign exchange for delivery within two business days

B. the sale of foreign exchange for delivery

C. the purchase of foreign exchange for delivery

D. None of the above

Q.8 In case of Fixed Exchange Rate regime, adjustment in Balance of Payments takes place through

A. changes in price level

B. changes in exchange rate

C. changes in interest rate

D. None of the above

Q.9 This question consists of two lists; one of Events/Theories/Models/Statements, etc. and the other of Authors. You are required to match an item in List - I with an item in List - II and mark the correct option.

List - I	List - II
(a) Export Pessimism	(i) A. Emmanuel
(b) Un-equal Exchange	(ii) R. Prebisch
(c) Critical Minimum Efforts thesis	(iii) J. Schumpeter
(d) Innovations-Entrepreneurship	(iv) H. Liebenstein

A. (i), (ii), (iii), (iv) **B.** (ii), (i), (iv), (iii)

C. (iii), (iv), (ii), (i) **D.** (iv), (iii), (i), (ii)

Q.10 Put the following in the sequential order of their development:

(i) WTO

(ii) GATT

(iii) Hong Kong Summit

(iv) Dunkel Draft

A. (i), (ii), (iii), (iv) **B.** (ii), (iv), (i), (iii)

C. (iii), (iv), (i), (ii) **D.** (ii), (iii), (iv), (i)

Q.11 Put the following in the sequential order of their development:

(i) Revealed Preference Theory

(ii) Akerlof Lemon's Market

(iii) Ordinal Utility Analysis

(iv) N. M. Utility Analysis

A. (ii), (i), (iii), (iv) **B.** (i), (iv), (ii), (iii)

C. (iii), (i), (iv), (ii) **D.** (iv), (ii), (i), (iii)

Q.12 Put the following in the sequential order of their development:

(i) Multiplier-Accelerator interaction and trace cycle

(ii) Keynes' theory of trade cycle

(iii) Sunspot theory of trade cycle

(iv) Hawtrey's monetary theory of trade cycle

A. (ii), (iii), (iv), (i) **B.** (iii), (iv), (ii), (i)
C. (i), (ii), (iv), (iii) **D.** (iv), (ii), (i), (iii)

Q.13 The regression coefficient is independent of
A. change of origin and scale
B. change of origin only
C. change of scale only
D. neither change of origin nor change of scale

Q.14 Which of the following is not an assumption of Harrod's model of growth?
A. The desired capital output ratio is constant.
B. Savings are a constant proportion of real income in the economy.
C. The labour force grows at some exogenously determined constant exponential rate.
D. Factor prices are flexible in the long run.

Q.15 The probability distribution in which mean and variance are equal is:
A. Poisson **B.** Binomial
C. Normal **D.** Chi-square (x^2)

Q.16 One of the important factors in trade reforms is to
A. increase export duties
B. reduce import duties
C. keep export duties constant
D. keep import duties constant

Q.17 Leontief Paradox on the factor composition of US imports and exports:
A. Supports Heckscher - Ohlin model
B. Refutes Heckscher - Ohlin model
C. Supports Prebish - Singer model
D. Refutes Prebish - Singer model

Q.18 Excess burden of tax means
A. net welfare loss from a tax
B. very heavy burden
C. burden over and above the money burden
D. money burden and real burden

Q.19 Gadgil formula is applicable to
A. grants given by Planning Commission
B. Grants given by Finance Commission
C. grants given by RBI
D. grants given by foreign countries

Q.20 For the first time in India, zero base budgeting was implemented in the finance ministership of
A. P. Chidambaram **B.** Manmohan Singh
C. V. P. Singh **D.** Jaswant Singh

Q.21 In which of the following growth models does human capital play an important role?
A. Neoclassical Model
B. Endogenous Growth Model
C. Marxian Model
D. Harrod-Domar Model

Q.22 Which of the following features is not universally observed in underdeveloped countries?
A. Low per capita income
B. High density of population
C. Higher share of agriculture in GDP
D. Low literacy rate

Q.23 According to Marx, an increase in the organic composition of capital leads to
A. an increase in the rate of growth of economy
B. an increase in employment
C. a decrease in the rate of profit
D. an increase in the rate of profit

Q.24 As per the hypothesis of rational expectations in guessing the future, economic agents
A. are always right
B. are always wrong
C. make systematic errors
D. make random errors

Q.25 According to Milton Friedman, Quantity Theory of Money is the theory of
A. prices **B.** income
C. demand for money **D.** supply of money

Q.26 According to the Phillips curve, when rate of inflation increases, the rate of
A. unemployment also increases
B. unemployment decreases
C. unemployment remains constant
D. full employment prevails

Q.27 Paul M. Sweezy used kinked demand curve to explain
A. price determination in oligopoly
B. price rigidity in oligopoly
C. profit maximisation in oligopoly
D. price and output determination in oligopoly

Q.28 The concept of consumer's surplus was explained by
A. Ricardo **B.** Fisher **C.** Marshall **D.** Pigou

Q.29 A rational consumer choosing between uncertain events will make a choice on the basis of
A. expected monetary benefits
B. expected utility
C. expected prices
D. expected incomes in future

Q.30 Match the following:

List - I	List - II
1. Voluntary exchange approach	(i) Peacock-Wiseman
2. Theory of local public goods	(ii) A. C. Pigou
3. Time-pattern of public expenditure growth	(iii) Wicksell-Lindahl
4. Principle of least aggregate sacrifice	(iv) Charles Tiebout

A. (iii), (iv), (i), (ii) **B.** (iii), (i), (iv), (ii)

C. (iii), (ii), (i), (iv) **D.** (iv), (ii), (iii), (i)

Q.31 Arrange the following options in the right chronological order:
(i) Pradhan Mantri Gramodaya Yojana (PMGY)
(ii) Swarnajayanti Gram Swarojgar Yojana (SGSY)
(iii) Jawahar Rozgar Yojana (JRY)
(iv) Integrated Rural Development Programme (IRDP)

A. (iii) (iv) (ii) (i) **B.** (ii) (iii) (iv) (i)
C. (i) (ii) (iii) (iv) **D.** (iv) (iii) (ii) (i)

Q.32 Which of the following statements would Milton Friedman disagree with?

A. Monetary policy has few short-run effects on the real economy.

B. In the long-run, changes in the money supply primarily affect the price.

C. There is little scope for using monetary policy actively to smooth out business cycles.

D. The Reserve Bank cannot be relied on to effectively smooth out business cycles.

Q.33 Arrange the options having the right chronological order:
(i) Milton Friedman Approach
(ii) Fisher Approach
(iii) Stuck Balance Approach
(iv) Keynes Approach

A. (ii) (iii) (iv) (i) **B.** (i) (ii) (iii) (iv)
C. (iii) (i) (ii) (iv) **D.** (iv) (iii) (i) (ii)

Q.34 Starting with the earliest, arrange the following in the chronological order of development of general theory of equilibrium:
(i) R. Carnillon
(ii) F. Quesnay
(iii) L. Walras
(iv) W. Leontief

A. (iv) (i) (ii) (iii) **B.** (iii) (iv) (i) (ii)
C. (i) (ii) (iii) (iv) **D.** (ii) (iii) (iv) (i)

Q.35 Directions: Read the given statements carefully and choose the correct option accordingly.
Assertion (A): In India, more and more farmers are getting pushed out of agriculture.
Reason (R): Their land base is becoming smaller.

A. (A) is true, but (R) is false.
B. Both (A) and (R) are false.
C. Both (A) and R) are true, and (R) is the correct explanation of (A).
D. Both (A) and (R) are true, but (R) is not the correct explanation of (A).

Q.36 Sustainable development addresses to the needs of the
A. present generation
B. future generation
C. present generation without compromising the needs of the future generations
D. future generations without compromising the needs of the present generation

Q.37 Match the following:

Group - I	Group - II
1. General theory of employment interest and money	(i) David Hume
2. Economics of imperfect competition	(ii) W. W. Rostou
3. Stages of economic growth	(iii) Joan Robinson
4. Specie flow mechanism	(iv) J. M. Keynes

A. (iv), (iii), (ii), (i) **B.** (i), (ii), (iii), (iv)
C. (iii), (i), (iv), (ii) **D.** (ii), (iv), (i), (iii)

Q.38 Let the consumption function be C = Rs. 30 + 0.80Y and investment spending be I = Rs. 70 - 2i, where i is the rate of interest. Then, an increase in autonomous investment by Rs. 30 would shift the IS curve:
A. to the left by Rs. 150
B. to the right by Rs. 150
C. to the right by Rs. 30
D. to the left by Rs. 30

Q.39 `Pump priming` should be resorted to at the time of:
A. Inflation **B.** Deflation
C. Reflation **D.** None of these

Q.40 Which of the following is not a development expenditure of the State?
A. Medical and Health
B. Education
C. Debt Services
D. Development of Agriculture

Q.41 The statement that the compensation principle of welfare economics is capable of giving contradictory results is associated with the name of:
A. T. Scitovsky **B.** A. Pareto
C. A. Bergson **D.** P. A. Samuelson

Q.42 Match the following:

1. Cournot Model of Duopoly	(i) Hypothetical compensation
2. Pareto Optimality	(ii) Limit pricing
3. New Welfare School	(iii) Limited application
4. Bain's Model	(iv) Sub optional solution
	(v) Unlimited application

A. (i), (v), (iv), (iii) **B.** (iv), (iii), (i), (ii)
C. (iii), (i), (v), (iv) **D.** (ii), (v), (iii), (i)

Q.43 Match the following:

1. J. R. Hicks	(i) Differential rent
2. Karl Marx	(ii) Four measures of consumer surplus
3. Francois Quesnay	(iii) Mode of production
4. David Ricardo	(iv) Tableau economique
	(v) Transfer earnings

A. (i), (iv), (ii), (iii) **B.** (ii), (iii), (iv), (i)

C. (iii), (v), (i), (ii)   **D.** (v), (ii), (iii), (iv)

Q.44 Who among the following gave the law of increasing state activities?

A. Musgrave   **B.** Wiseman Peacock

C. Wagner   **D.** Dalton

Q.45 Match the following:

1. Adam Smith	(i) Real Balance effect
2. Heckscher-Ohlin	(ii) Consumer`s surplus
3. E. Von Stackelberg	(iii) Division of labour
4. D. Patinkin	(iv) Factor endowment theory of trade
	(v) Iso-profit curve

A. (i), (iii), (iv), (ii)   **B.** (ii), (iv), (iii), (i)

C. (iv), (v), (i), (ii)   **D.** (iii), (iv), (v), (i)

Q.46 Which index number method has an upward bias?

A. Laspeyres' method   **B.** Paasche's method

C. Bowley`s method    **D.** Fisher`s method

Q.47 Match the following:

Group - I	Group - II
1. Communist Manifesto	(i) Robert Mundell
2. Globalisation and Its Discontents	(ii) Joseph Stiglitz
3. Theory of optimum currency area	(iii) Karl Marx and Engels
4. Essays in Positive Economics	(iv) Milton Friedman

A. (ii), (i), (iii), (iv)   **B.** (i), (ii), (iii), (iv)

C. (iii), (ii), (i), (iv)   **D.** (iii), (i), (iv), (ii)

Q.48 For a price taking firm, average revenue is _____ market price.

A. half   **B.** equal to

C. double of   **D.** less than

Q.49 Random variable is

A. an independent variable

B. an endogenous variable

C. a randomly chosen value

D. a function of states of nature

Q.50 Devaluation will improve the balance of payments deficit if sum of elasticity of exports and imports of the devaluing country is

A. greater than one   **B.** less than one

C. equal to zero   **D.** negative

Q.51 Events A and B are mutually exclusive. Consider the following:

1. $P(A \cup B) = P(A) + P(B)$

2. $P(A \cup B) = P(A) \times P(B)$

3. $P(A \cap B) = 0$

4. A and B are independent events.

Choose the correct code:

A. Only 1 and 2 are true.

B. Only 2 and 3 are true.

C. Only 3 and 4 are true.

D. Only 1 and 3 are true.

Q.52 The Phillips curve shows the relation between

A. income and consumption

B. income and price level

C. income and investment

D. inflation and unemployment

Q.53 Select the correct code of the following statements being correct or incorrect.

Statement (I): The 'law of one price' states that in competitive markets free of transportation costs and barriers to trade, identical products sold in different countries must sell for the same price when their price is expressed in terms of the same currency.

Statement (II): An 'Efficient market' has no impediments to the free flow of goods and services, such as trade barriers.

A. Statement (I) is correct but (II) is incorrect.

B. Statement (II) is correct but (I) is incorrect.

C. Both statements (I) and (II) are correct.

D. Both statements (I) and (II) are incorrect.

Q.54 The goods which people consume more, when their price rises are called ______.

A. Essential goods

B. Capital goods

C. Complementary goods

D. Giffen goods

Q.55 If demand curve assumes the shape of a rectangular hyperbola, price elasticity is

A. zero   **B.** less than one

C. greater than one   **D.** one

Q.56 Insider trading is related to

A. Trade sector   **B.** Share market

C. Credit market   **D.** Horse racing

Q.57 Match the following:

1. Public goods	(i) J. A. Schumpeter
2. Innovations	(ii) W. Leontieff
3. Uncertainty of profit	(iii) W. W. Rostow
4. Input-output analysis	(iv) F. Knight
	(v) Musgrave

A. (ii), (iii), (i), (iv)   **B.** (v), (i), (iv), (ii)

C. (i), (ii), (iii), (v)   **D.** (iii), (iv), (v), (i)

Q.58 In case of proportional relation between consumption and income,

A. APC > MPC   **B.** APC = MPC

C. APC < MPC   **D.** APC = MPS

Q.59 'Galloping Inflation' is also known as ____.

A. Creeping inflation   **B.** Walking Inflation

C. Running Inflation   **D.** Hyper Inflation

Q.60 Match the following:

List - I	List - II
To test for these	We use the following
1. Population mean with known variance	(i) t distribution
2. Population mean with unknown variance	(ii) F distribution
3. Comparison of variance	(iii) X^2 distribution
4. Goodness of a fit accumulation	(iv) Z distribution

A. (i), (ii), (iii), (iv) **B.** (ii), (i), (iv), (iii)

C. (iv), (i), (ii), (iii) **D.** (iii), (i), (ii), (iv)

Q.61 The Bretton Woods system finally collapsed at the global level in the year:

A. 1970 **B.** 1971 **C.** 1972 **D.** 1973

Q.62 If commodities are perfect substitutes, the indifference curve becomes a

A. downward sloping curve

B. right angle

C. straight line with negative slope

D. rectangular hyperbola

Q.63 Psychological law of consumption is given by:

A. Milton Friedman **B.** Pigou

C. Tobin **D.** Keynes

Q.64 A consumer attains his/her equilibrium at the point where:

A. Total Utility = Price

B. Marginal Utility > Price

C. Marginal Utility < Price

D. Marginal Utility = Price

Q.65 Taxes on professions can be levied by :

A. State government only

B. By both state and union government

C. By Panchayats only

D. Union government only

Q.66 Match the following:

List - I	List - II
1. Degree of monopoly theory	(i) T. Scitovsky
2. Double criterion	(ii) Hall and Hitch
3. Behavioural theory of firm	(iii) M. Kalecki
4. Average cost pricing	(iv) Herbert Simon

A. (iii), (i), (iv), (ii) **B.** (ii), (iii), (iv), (i)

C. (iv), (ii), (i), (iii) **D.** (iii), (ii), (iv), (i)

Q.67 According to Say`s Law, unemployment can be removed by:

A. Rise in wages **B.** Fall in wages

C. Taxing wages **D.** Subsidising wages

Q.68 Directions: Read the given statements carefully and choose the correct option accordingly.

Assertion (A): In a bell-shaped distributive curve, the values of Mean, Median and Mode would be identical.

Reason (R): There is no skewness in the series.

A. Both (A) and (R) are true, but (R) is not the correct explanation of (A).

B. (A) is true, but (R) is false.

C. (A) is false, but (R) is true.

D. Both (A) and (R) are true and (R) is the correct explanation of (A).

Q.69 The market equilibrium for a commodity is determined by:

A. The market supply of the commodity.

B. The balancing of the forces of demand and supply for the commodity.

C. The intervention of the government.

D. The market demand for the commodity.

Q.70 If the Rupees per US Dollar exchange rate changes from Rs. 44 to Rs. 46 in a year by the market forces, it implies:

A. Appreciation of the Rupee

B. Depreciation of the Rupee

C. Devaluation of the Rupee

D. Exchange rate remains more or less the same

Q.71 Capital per person decreases if net investment per person

A. is less than the population growth rate

B. exceeds the population growth rate

C. exceeds savings per person

D. is less than savings per person

Q.72 Rolling Plan Concept was propounded by

A. Gunnar Myrdal **B.** J. K. Galbraith

C. Paul A. Samuelson **D.** A. K. Sen

Q.73 The Tenth Five Year Plan aims at reducing poverty by:

A. 2% **B.** 5% **C.** 8% **D.** 9%

Q.74 Ramesh spends some rupees on flour, rice, tuition fee, etc., then which index will be used to calculate the average of this whole expenditure?

A. Wholesale Price Index

B. Productive Price Index

C. Consumer Price Index

D. Producer Price Index

Q.75 Consider the following distributions:

1. Z distribution
2. t distribution
3. Binomial distribution
4. F distribution

Which among the above is/are not sampling distribution(s)?

A. Only 1 **B.** Only 3

C. Both 1 and 3 **D.** Both1 and 4

Q.76 Match the following:

Group - I	Group - II
1. Rejection of Ho when it is true	(i) Stratified random sampling
2. Mean is equal to degrees of freedom	(ii) Type-I error

| 3. Population is heterogeneous | (iii) Positively skewed distribution |
| 4. Mean > Mode | (iv) x^2 distribution |

A. (ii), (iv), (iii), (i)   **B.** (i), (ii), (iii), (iv)
C. (ii), (iv), (i), (iii)   **D.** (iv), (i), (ii), (iii)

Q.77 Based on a sample of 100 observations, correlation coefficient between x and y is found to be nearly zero. Then,
A. x and y are definitely unrelated
B. x and y are linearly related to each other
C. x and y may be non-linearly related to each other
D. there is spurious correlation between x and y

Q.78 In a regression equation of X on Y, b_{yx} is equal to:

A. b_{xy} **B.** $\sqrt{y}$ **C.** r   **D.** $\frac{r^2}{b_{xy}}$

Q.79 According to Friedman, the consumption of a household depends on:
A. Transitory income
B. Permanent income
C. Both permanent and transitory incomes
D. Relative income

Q.80 In a binomial distribution, the sum of mean and variance is 15 and the product of mean and variance is 54, then the number of observations (n) is equal to
A. 27   **B.** 30   **C.** 24   **D.** 33

Q.81 Which one of the following is not reserved for the public sector?
A. Atomic energy   **B.** Railways
C. Insurance   **D.** Port Trust of India

Q.82 Match the items given in List - I with those in List - II:

List - I	List - II
a. Committee on Taxation of Agricultural Wealth and Income, 1972	1. Raja J. Chelliah
b. Direct Taxes Enquiry Committee, 1970	2. L. K. Jha
c. Tax Reform Committee, 1991	3. K. N. Wanchoo
d. Indirect Tax Enquiry Committee, 1976	4. K. N. Raj

A. 4, 1, 2, 3   **B.** 4, 3, 1, 2
C. 3, 2, 1, 4   **D.** 2, 3, 1, 4

Q.83 What is the impact of decreasing margin requirements on credit creation?
A. Increase   **B.** Decrease
C. No change   **D.** None of these

Q.84 Which of the following is a private sector bank?
A. Canara Bank
B. Vijaya Bank
C. IndusInd Bank
D. Bank of Maharashtra

Q.85 What is the other name of the long run average cost curve?
A. Profit curve   **B.** Planning curve

C. Demand curve   **D.** Indifference curve

Q.86 Open market purchases of securities by the Central Bank on behalf of the Govt. _____ the credit in the economy.
A. expands   **B.** contracts
C. stabilises   **D.** fluctuates

Q.87 Which of the following is a qualitative measure of credit control?
A. Rationing of credit
B. CRR
C. SLR
D. Open market operations

Q.88 Which of the following was the first bank to be established in India?
A. RBI
B. Imperial Bank of India
C. Bank of Rajasthan
D. Bank of Hindustan

Q.89 Which of the following is true?
A. GDP at factor cost = GDP at market price + Net indirect taxes
B. GDP at factor cost = GDP at market price - Indirect taxes
C. GDP at factor cost = GDP at market price - Subsidy
D. GDP at factor cost = GDP at market price - Net factor income from abroad

Q.90 Arrange the introduction of the following taxes in India in chronological order:
I. Service tax
II. Income tax
III. Banking cash transaction tax
IV. Gift tax
A. II, IV, I, III   **B.** II, I, III, IV
C. II, III, I, IV   **D.** IV, II, I, III

Q.91 Match the items of List - I and with items of List - II from the given codes:

List - I	List - II
I. Adam Smith	1. Opportunity cost
II. David Ricardo	2. Factor endowment
III. Ohlin	3. Absolute advantage
IV. Haberler	4. Comparative advantage

A. 3, 4, 2, 1   **B.** 4, 2, 1, 3   **C.** 2, 3, 4, 1   **D.** 1, 2, 3, 4

Q.92 If demand for goods and services is more than their supply, the resultant inflation is
A. cost push inflation
B. stagflation
C. deflation
D. demand pull inflation

Q.93 If consumers always spend 15 percent of their income on food, then the income elasticity of demand for food is
A. 1.50   **B.** 1.15   **C.** 1.00   **D.** 0.15

Q.94 Directions: Arrange the following in chronological order.
(i) Formation of WTO
(ii) Uruguay Round of GATT
(iii) Formation of GATT
(iv) Formation of UNCTAD

A. (i), (iii), (ii), (iv)   **B.** (iv), (iii), (ii), (i)
C. (iii), (iv), (ii), (i)   **D.** (ii), (iv), (i), (iii)

Q.95 Consider the following system of equations, using standard notations.

$$Y_1 = \alpha_0 + \alpha_4 Y_2 + \alpha_3 Y_3 + \alpha_4 X_1 + \alpha_5 X_2 + u_1$$
$$Y_2 = \beta_0 + \beta_1 Y_3 + \beta_2 Y_1 + \beta_3 X_2 + u_2$$
$$Y_3 = \gamma_0 + v_1 X_1 + \gamma_2 X_2 + \gamma_3 X_3 + u_3$$

According to order condition, the second equation is

A. unidentified
B. just identified
C. over identified
D. not possible to infer identification due to incomplete information

Q.96 Consider the following statements and select the correct code:

Assertion (A): A rise in income terms of trade only indicates that the country can obtain a larger volume of imports from the sale of exports.
Reason (R): A change in income terms of trade index cannot be interpreted as a measure of gain from trade.

A. Both (A) and (R) are true, and (R) is the correct explanation of (A).
B. Both (A) and (R) are true, but (R) is not the correct explanation of (A).
C. Statement (A) is true but (R) is false.
D. Statement (A) is false, but (R) is true.

Q.97 An overvalued Indian rupee in the foreign exchange market will have which of the following consequences?

A. Make imports cheaper and exports costlier
B. Make imports costlier and exports cheaper
C. Give protection to domestic industry against foreign competition
D. Will improve balance of payments

Q.98 Arrange the following in the order in which they appeared. Use the codes given below.
(i) Friedman's Quantity Theory of Money
(ii) Fisher's Equation of Exchange
(iii) Cambridge Equation of Exchange
(iv) Don Patinkins Theory of Money

A. (ii), (iii), (iv), (i)   **B.** (i), (ii), (iii), (iv)
C. (ii), (iii), (i), (iv)   **D.** (iii), (iv), (ii), (i)

Q.99 Chalapathi Rao Committee was meant for the restructuring of

A. state financial corporations in India
B. commercial banks in India
C. co-operative banks in India
D. regional rural banks in India

Q.100 The net value added method of measuring national income is also known as

A. net output method
B. production method
C. industry of origin method
D. All of the above

// Smart Answer Sheet //

Correct Indicates percentage of students who answered questions correctly.

Skipped Indicates percentage of students who skipped questions.

Q.	Ans.	Correct / Skipped	Q.	Ans.	Correct / Skipped	Q.	Ans.	Correct / Skipped	Q.	Ans.	Correct / Skipped	Q.	Ans.	Correct / Skipped
1	C	52.89 % / 3.31 %	17	B	50.41 % / 15.71 %	33	A	42.98 % / 22.31 %	49	A	45.45 % / 23.15 %	65	A	49.59 % / 22.31 %
2	C	47.11 % / 13.22 %	18	A	48.76 % / 15.7 %	34	C	23.97 % / 23.14 %	50	A	68.6 % / 22.31 %	66	A	53.72 % / 23.14 %
3	D	45.45 % / 16.53 %	19	A	43.8 % / 17.36 %	35	C	52.89 % / 21.49 %	51	D	47.11 % / 23.14 %	67	B	57.85 % / 22.32 %
4	A	38.02 % / 16.53 %	20	C	38.02 % / 19.0 %	36	C	61.98 % / 21.49 %	52	D	74.38 % / 22.31 %	68	D	52.07 % / 22.31 %
5	B	60.33 % / 14.88 %	21	A	19.01 % / 18.18 %	37	A	75.21 % / 20.66 %	53	C	42.15 % / 22.31 %	69	B	48.76 % / 23.97 %
6	B	34.71 % / 16.53 %	22	A	10.74 % / 17.36 %	38	C	31.4 % / 27.28 %	54	D	40.5 % / 28.92 %	70	B	52.07 % / 23.96 %
7	A	74.38 % / 15.7 %	23	C	33.06 % / 18.18 %	39	B	64.46 % / 20.66 %	55	D	51.24 % / 23.14 %	71	A	30.58 % / 23.14 %
8	A	36.36 % / 16.53 %	24	D	33.06 % / 18.18 %	40	C	69.42 % / 20.66 %	56	B	50.41 % / 23.14 %	72	A	55.37 % / 23.97 %
9	B	78.51 % / 14.05 %	25	C	72.73 % / 18.18 %	41	A	55.37 % / 23.14 %	57	B	73.55 % / 22.32 %	73	B	51.24 % / 23.14 %
10	B	35.54 % / 15.7 %	26	B	66.12 % / 19.0 %	42	B	61.98 % / 21.49 %	58	B	55.37 % / 22.32 %	74	C	50.41 % / 22.32 %
11	C	66.94 % / 14.88 %	27	B	47.93 % / 18.19 %	43	B	63.64 % / 22.31 %	59	D	35.54 % / 23.96 %	75	B	65.29 % / 23.97 %
12	B	30.58 % / 18.18 %	28	C	75.21 % / 19.0 %	44	C	46.28 % / 21.49 %	60	C	47.93 % / 23.14 %	76	C	66.94 % / 22.32 %
13	B	35.54 % / 15.7 %	29	B	52.07 % / 19.83 %	45	D	72.73 % / 21.48 %	61	B	38.02 % / 22.31 %	77	C	19.83 % / 24.8 %
14	D	45.45 % / 16.53 %	30	A	52.89 % / 20.66 %	46	A	42.15 % / 21.49 %	62	C	46.28 % / 22.32 %	78	D	48.76 % / 23.14 %
15	A	44.63 % / 15.7 %	31	D	39.67 % / 22.31 %	47	C	52.89 % / 23.97 %	63	D	70.25 % / 22.31 %	79	C	35.54 % / 23.14 %
16	B	43.8 % / 16.53 %	32	C	30.58 % / 23.14 %	48	B	52.89 % / 28.1 %	64	D	70.25 % / 22.31 %	80	A	29.75 % / 28.1 %

Q.	Ans.	Correct		Q.	Ans.	Correct		Q.	Ans.	Correct		Q.	Ans.	Correct		Q.	Ans.	Correct
		Skipped				Skipped				Skipped				Skipped				Skipped
81	C	49.59 %		85	B	57.85 %		89	B	45.45 %		93	C	26.45 %		97	A	52.89 %
		22.31 %				22.32 %				23.15 %				25.62 %				22.32 %
82	B	40.5 %		86	A	47.93 %		90	A	33.88 %		94	C	41.32 %		98	C	47.93 %
		23.96 %				22.32 %				22.32 %				22.32 %				22.32 %
83	A	52.07 %		87	A	55.37 %		91	A	73.55 %		95	B	31.4 %		99	D	30.58 %
		23.14 %				23.14 %				22.32 %				21.49 %				22.31 %
84	C	51.24 %		88	D	33.06 %		92	D	68.6 %		96	A	35.54 %		100	D	43.8 %
		22.31 %				22.31 %				22.31 %				23.14 %				20.66 %

Performance Analysis

Avg. Score (%)	45.0%
Toppers Score (%)	97.0%
Your Score	

//Hints and Solutions//

1. Grants from the Centre to the States under the recommendations of Finance Commission are known as statutory grants.

2. Taxes on sale and purchase of newspapers and on advertisements therein falls under the jurisdiction of the Central Government.

3. Optimum currency area is s geographic area in which a single currency would create the greatest economic benefit to have the entire region share. All of the given options are related to optimum currency area.

4. Under a managed floating exchange rate system, the Nation's monetary authorities intervene in Foreign Exchange Markets to smooth out short-run fluctuations in exchange rates without attempting to effect long-run trend in exchange rates.

5.

1.	Hamilton List describes the Indian industry.
2.	Marshall-Lerner has given the elasticity approach.
3.	F. Y. Edgeworth has given the view on impoverishing growth.
4.	Jacob Viner has given the views on trade creation and trade diversion effects.

6. Most-favoured-nation (MFN): treating other people equally Under the WTO agreements, countries cannot normally discriminate between their trading partners. Grant someone a special favour (such as a lower customs duty rate for one of their products) and you have to do the same for all other WTO members.

7. A foreign exchange spot transaction, also known as FX spot, is an agreement between two parties to buy one currency against selling another currency at an agreed price for settlement on the spot date. The exchange rate at which the transaction is done is called the spot exchange rate.

8. Under the gold standard, the exchange rate between currencies is fixed and the BOP adjustment is effected through the changing price levels between the countries. But under the paper currency standard, the adjustment of disequilibrium in BOP is bought about by the changes in exchange rates between currencies.

9.

1.	Export Pessimism- R. Prebisch
2.	Un-equal Exchange- A. Emmanuel
3.	Critical Minimum Efforts thesis- H. Liebenstein
4.	Innovations-Entrepreneurship- J. Schumpeter

10. The correct sequential order is: GATT, Dunkel Draft, WTO, Hong Kong Summit.

11. The correct sequential order is: Ordinal Utility Analysis, Revealed Preference Theory, N. M. Utility Analysis, Akerlof Lemon's Market.

12. The correct sequential order is: Sunspot theory of trade cycle, Hawtrey's monetary theory of trade cycle, Keynes' theory of trade cycle, Multiplier-Accelerator interaction and trace cycle.

13. The regression coefficients are independent of the change of origin, but not of the scale. By origin, we mean that there will be no effect on the regression coefficients if any constant is subtracted from the value of X and Y.

14. The Harrod–Domar model is a Keynesian model of economic growth. It is used in development economics to explain an economy's growth rate in terms of the level of saving and of capital. It suggests that there is no natural reason for an economy to have balanced growth. The Harrod–Domar model makes the following a priori assumptions.

15. For the Poisson distribution the mean and variance are always equal.

mean = variance = λ where λ is the parameter of the Poisson distribution.

In other distributions, you can have the mean and variance parameters equal to each other but it may not be necessary for the mean and variance to be equal for all possible distributions with that particular distribution family.

16. This describes the impact of trade liberalization on efficiency and growth. 1. The author authorities. An important switch in policy came in June 1966, when India undertook. Two factors paved the way for a return to liberalization in the late 1970s,. Trade reform programs have two main objectives. The first is to help raise economic growth and employment generation by improving resource allocation. Unemployment doesn't last long, especially where workers' pay was not substantial in the original job. Normal labor turnover often exceeds job displacement from trade liberalization. Inter industry shifts occur after trade liberalization, which minimizes the dislocation of factors of production.

17. Leontief paradox. Leontief's paradox in economics is that a country with a higher capital per worker has a lower capital/labor ratio in exports than in imports. This econometric find was the result of Wassily W.

18. The excess burden of taxation, also known as the deadweight cost or deadweight loss of taxation, is one of the economic losses that society suffers as the result of taxes or subsidies. Economic theory posits that distortions change the amount and type of economic behavior from that which would occur in a free market without the tax. Excess burdens can be measured using the average cost of funds or the marginal cost of funds (MCF). Excess burdens were first discussed by Adam Smith.

An equivalent kind of inefficiency can also be caused by subsidies (which technically can be viewed as taxes with negative rates).[citation needed]

Economic losses due to taxes were evaluated to be as low as 2.5 cents per dollar of revenue, and as high as 30 cents per dollar of revenue (on average), and even much higher at the margins.

19. The Gadgil formula was formulated with the formulation of the third five-year plan for the distribution of plan transfers amongst the states.

20. Zero-based budgeting (ZBB) is a method of budgeting in which all expenses must be justified. the federal government for the first time implemented zero-base budgeting in The Government Economy and Spending Reform act of 1976.

21. An important branch of empirical macroeconomic literature examines international income differences and the trend of convergence by including human capital in the Solow growth model, and clearly establishes that human capital plays a very important role in the growth process.

22. The following points highlight the fourteen basic characteristics of underdeveloped ... Underdeveloped countries are maintaining a very low level of income in Existence of chronic mass poverty is another characteristic of underdeveloped economies. This problem of poverty arises not due to any temporary economic.

23. Marx argues that a rising organic composition of capital is a necessary effect of capital accumulation and competition in the sphere of production, at least in the long term. This means that the share of constant capital in the total capital outlay increases, and that labor input per product unit declines.

24. Definition of Rational expectations – an economic theory that states – when making decisions, individual agents will base their decisions on the best information available and learn from past trends. Rational expectations are the best guess for the future. But as per the hypothesis of rational expectations in guessing the future, economic agents make random errors.

25. First of all Friedman says that his quantity theory is a theory of demand for money and not a theory of output, income or prices. Money is more basic than the medium of exchange. It is a temporary abode of purchasing power and hence an asset or a part of wealth.

26. The Phillips curve relates the rate of inflation with the rate of unemployment. The Phillips curve argues that unemployment and inflation are inversely related: as levels of unemployment decrease, inflation increases.

27. The kinked demand curve of oligopoly was developed by Paul M. Sweezy in 1939. Instead of laying emphasis on price-output determination, the model explains the behavior of oligopolistic organizations. The kinked demand curve model seeks to explain the reason of price rigidity under oligopolistic market situations.

28. Definition of Consumer Surplus:

1. Regarding this Prof. Marshall has said that "The excess of price which he (consumer) would be willing to pay rather than go without. The thing over that which he actually does pay, is the economic measure of this surplus satisfaction. It may be called "Consumer's Surplus".

29. Value of Information: The decision a consumer makes when outcomes are uncertain is based on limited information. If more information were available, the consumer could reduce risk. Since information is a valuable commodity, people will be prepared to pay for it.

30.

1. Voluntary exchange approach- Wicksell-Lindahl
2. Theory of local public goods- Charles Tiebout
3. Time-pattern of public expenditure growth- Peacock-Wiseman
4. Principle of least aggregate sacrifice- A. C. Pigou

31. The chronological order is : Integrated Rural Development Programme (IRDP), Jawahar Rozgar Yojana (JRY), Swarnajayanti Gram Swarojgar Yojana (SGSY), Pradhan Mantri Gramodaya Yojana (PMGY).

32. Milton Friedman was an American economist who received the 1976 Nobel Memorial Prize. Friedman would work for the University of Chicago for the next 30 years.. These challenged a prevailing, but largely untested, view on their relative. Political scientist C.B. Macpherson disagreed with the statement that there is little scope for using monetary policy actively to smooth out business cycles.

33.

1. Fisher Approach
2. Stuck Balance Approach
3. Keynes Approach
4. Milton Friedman Approach

34. The chronological order of development of general theory of equilibrium:

(i) R. Carnillon

(ii) F. Quesnay

(iii) L. Walras

(iv) W. Leontief

35. In India, more and more farmers are getting pushed out of agriculture, one of the reason for this is Their land base is becoming smaller.

36. Sustainability is development that satisfies the needs of the present without compromising the capacity of future generations, guaranteeing the balance between economic growth, care for the environment and social well-being.

37.

1. General theory of employment interest and money- J. M. Keynes
2. Economics of imperfect competition- Joan Robinson
3. Stages of economic growth- W. W. Rostou
4. Specie flow mechanism- David Hume

38. An increase in autonomous investment by Rs. 30 would shift the IS curve to the right by Rs. 30.

39. Pump priming should be resorted to at a time of deflation. Option 2 i.e Deflation is the correct answer. Pump Priming in economics and financial terms refers to the injection of money by the government when the economy of the country is depressed or during the time of deflation.

40. Development expenditure is the money spent by government on developmental and welfare programmes. Expenditure on

economic service, expenditure on social and communist services, grant to states are examples of developmental expenditures.

41. According to Scitovsky, Kaldor- Hicks criterion involves such contradictory and inconsistent results. Since Scitovsky was the first to point out this paradoxical result in Kaldor-Hicks criterion, it is known as 'Scitovsky Paradox'.

42.

1. Cournot Model of Duopoly- Sub optional solution
2. Pareto Optimality- Limited application
3. New Welfare School- Hypothetical compensation
4. Bain's Model- Limit pricing

43.

1. J. R. Hicks- Four measures of consumer surplus
2. Karl Marx- Mode of production
3. Francois Quesnay- Tableau economique
4. David Ricardo- Differential rent

44. Law of Increasing State Activities – Adolph Wagner. Adolph Wagner a German economist propounded the Law of increasing State activities. He gave a relationship between level of development and public expenditure.

45.

1. Adam Smith- Division of labour.
2. Heckscher-Ohlin- Factor endowment theory of trade.
3. Von Stackelberg- Iso-profit curve.
4. Patinkin- Real Balance effect.

46. The Laspeyres index, the CPI level, the price level, the inflation level, is therefore biased upward, it overstates the increase in price levels the consumer pays.

47.

1. Communist Manifesto- Karl Marx and Engels
2. Globalisation and Its Discontents- Joseph Stiglitz
3. Theory of optimum currency area- Robert Mundell
4. Essays in Positive Economics- Milton Friedman

48. For a price taking firm ,average revenue is equal to market price.Because the firm can sell as much as it can produce at the market price,the marginal revenue for each unit sold is equal to the price, and the average revenue is equal to the price,as every unit costs the same, so when you divide the total revenue by the number of unit sold, you get the price.

49. A random variable is a variable whose value is unknown or a function that assigns values to each of an experiment's outcomes. Random variables are often used in econometric or regression analysis to determine statistical relationships among one another.

50. The Theory:

Thus devaluation helps to improve BOP deficit of a country by increasing its exports and reducing its imports. But the extent to which it will succeed depends on the country's price elasticities of domestic demand for imports and foreign demand for exports. With low prices, exports increase.

51. Mutually Exclusive Events

Two events are mutually exclusive if they cannot occur at the same time. Another word that means mutually exclusive is disjoint. If two events are disjoint, then the probability of them both occurring at the same time is 0.

52. The Phillips curve given by A.W. Phillips shows that there exist an inverse relationship between the rate of unemployment and the rate of increase in nominal wages. A lower rate of unemployment is associated with higher wage rate or inflation, and vice versa.

53. Assuming that there is free competition in the market and prices are flexible and there is no trade frictions, in two different places with the same currency, two identical goods will be having same prices as per the law of one price.

Efficient markets are those markets where all the information is available to everyone at the same time and the prices respond at real time or immediately, goods are free to trade and there is no great barrier in the market.

54.

- Giffen good is a good that people consume more as its price rises and vice versa, thus violating the basic law of demand.

- They are inferior products that does not have easily available substitutes, as a result of which the income effect dominates the substitution effect and demand increases as the price rises. Few example Giffen goods are grocery items such as rice and butter in which if your income rises you would like to use branded grocery item.

55. When percentage change in the quantity demanded is equal to percentage change in price, then demand for such a commodity is said to be unitary elastic. In this case, $Ed = 1$ and the demand curve is a rectangular hyperbola. Rectangular hyperbola is a curve under which the total area at all points will be the same.

56. Insider trading is the trading of a public company's stock or other securities (such as bonds or stock options) by individuals with access to nonpublic information about the company.

57.

1. Public goods- Musgrave
2. Innovations- J. A. Schumpeter
3. Uncertainty of profit- F. Knight
4. Input-output analysis- W. Leontieff

58. It states that, when income increases, consumption also increases but not to the same extent as the increase in income. It means that increase in income is followed by decrease in marginal and average propensity to consume. Consumption function according to Keynes is non -proportional in the short-run.

59. Galloping inflation is also known as **Hyper Inflation** or **jumping inflation**.

Gallopin Inflation is a type of inflation that occurs when the prices of goods and services increase at the two-digit or three-digit rate per annum.

Hyperinflation occurs when the prices go out of control and the monetary authorities are unable to impose any check on it. Germany had witnessed hyperinflation in 1920's. Hyperinflation is a stage of very high rate of inflation. While economies seem to survive under galloping inflation, a third and deadly strain takes hold when the cancer of hyperinflation strikes. Nothing good can be said about a market economy in which prices are rising a million or even a trillion percent per year .

60. Population mean with known variance- Z distribution.

Population mean with unknown variance- t distribution.

Comparison of variance- F distribution.

Goodness of a fit accumulation- X^2 distribution.

61. The problem of the US deficit remained and intensified. Finally in **August 1971**, President Nixon announced that the US would end on-demand convertibility of the dollar into gold for the central banks of other nations. The Bretton Woods system collapsed and gold traded freely on the world's markets.

62. The shape of an indifference curve is convex to the origin and this is based on the principle of diminishing marginal rate of substitution. If two goods X and Y are perfect substitutes, the indifference curve is a straight line with negative slope.

63. Keynes's Psychological Law of Consumption: Further, Keynes put forward a psychological law of consumption, according to which, as income increases consumption increases but not by as much as the increase in income. In other words, marginal propensity to consume is less than one.

64. Sufficient condition requires that the indifference curve must be convex to the origin at the point of tangency. Since these two conditions are fulfilled at point E, the consumer is in equilibrium at that point. This is called 'interior solution' where a consumer buys both the goods.

65. Profession tax is the tax levied and collected by the state governments in India. It is an indirect tax. A person earning an income from salary or anyone practising a profession such as chartered accountant, company secretary, lawyer, doctor etc. are required to pay this professional tax. Different states have different rates and methods of collection. However, not all states impose this tax.

66. Degree of monopoly theory- M. Kalecki.

Double criterion- T. Scitovsky.

Behavioural theory of firm- Herbert Simon.

Average cost pricing- Hall and Hitch.

67. According to Say`s Law, unemployment can be removed by Fall in wages. But unemployment can be removed by increase in the rate of investment. Money is not Neutral: Say's law of markets is based on a barter system and ignores the role of money in the system.

68. In a bell-shaped distributive curve, the values of Mean, Median and Mode would be identical because There is no skewness in the series. Both (A) and (R) are true and rightly explained.

69. Market Equilibrium is determined when the quantity demanded of a commodity becomes equal to the quantity supplied. The price deter mined corresponding to market equilibrium is known as equilibrium price and the corresponding quantity is known as equilibrium quantity.

70. Influenced by market forces and economic conditions of the respective. Calculate Gain/ Loss due to change in exchange rate and calculate tax/ tax ... In the spot market USD 1 = Rs.40, if in the forward market (1 Year). 3-months forward rate is presently quoted as 3.3 yen per Rupee. FR of 3 Mont $1=Rs.46–46.50.

71. While depreciation reduces k by wearing out the existing stock of capital, population. In the steady state the favourable effect of investment on the capital stock. In the presence of population growth, capital per worker and output per will have lower level of capital per worker and, thus, lower level of GDP per capita.

72. The Janata Party government rejected the fifth five-year plan and introduced a new Sixth five-year plan(1978-1983). This plan was again rejected by the Indian National Congress government when it came to power in 1980 and a new sixth plan was made. The earlier one was subsequently referred to as a rolling plan. Rolling plan concept was coined by Gunnar Myrdal.

73. The tenth five year plan aimed at achieving an average GDP growth rate of 8% of the overall economy which included all the sectors that is the social, economical and environmental sectors. The plan also included reduction in poverty ratio by 5% by 2007.

74. Consumer Price Index (CPI) will be used to calculate the average of this whole expenditure. It calculates the average price paid by the consumer to the shopkeepers. The CPI measures the expenses like education, communication, transportation, recreation, apparel, foods and beverages, housing and medical care.

Hence, the correct option is (C).

75. Student's t distribution is a continuous probability distribution. sampling distribution of a statistic (like a sample mean) will follow a normal distribution, where x is the sample mean, μ is the population mean, s is the standard deviation of certain data sets that are not appropriate for analysis, using the normal distribution.

76. Rejection of Ho when it is true- Type-I error.

Mean is equal to degrees of freedom- X^2 distribution.

Population is heterogeneous- Stratified random sampling.

Mean > Mode- Positively skewed distribution.

77. Based on a sample of 100 observations, correlation coefficient between x and y is found to be nearly zero. Then, x and y may be non-linearly related to each other.

78. The regression equation X on Y is X = c + dy is used to estimate value of X when Y is given and a, b, c and d are constant.

Y = a + bx can also be interpreted as 'a' is the average value of Y when X is zero. X = c + dy, value c is the average value of X, when Y is zero.

79. Under the relative income hypothesis, current consumption depends on current income relative to previous peak income. Consequently, current consumption depends on more than current income. According to Friedman, permanent income is the amount a household can consume while keeping its wealth intact.

80. In a binomial distribution, the sum of mean and variance is 15 and the product of mean and variance is 54, then the number of observations (n) is equal to 27.

81. The three industries of Railways, Atomic Energy and Defense are reserved for operation and management by the public sector or Government only. This is because of the need for security and secrecy to be maintained especially in the functioning of the Atomic Energy sector and Defense of the country. Also, Railways is basic service available at a low rate to all and thus handled by the Government.

82. Committee on Taxation of Agricultural Wealth and Income, 1972- K. N. Raj.

Direct Taxes Enquiry Committee, 1970- K. N. Wanchoo.

Tax Reform Committee, 1991, Raja J. Chelliah.

Indirect Tax Enquiry Committee, 1976, L. K. Jha.

83. During deficient demand or deflation, the central bank decreases the margin in order to increase the credit creation capacity of the commercial bank and as a result, the money supply in an economy gets increased and the deficient demand is combated.

84. Accordingly, nine banks were set-up in private sector including some by development financial institutions. Prominent among them are ICICI Bank, GTB, HDFC and IDBI bank.

85. A long run average cost curve is known as a planning curve. This is because a firm plans to produce an output in the long run by choosing a plant on the long run average cost curve corresponding to the output.

86. Open market operations is the sale and purchase of government securities and treasury bills by RBI or the central bank of the country. OMO is one of the tools that RBI uses to smoothen the liquidity conditions through the year and minimise its impact on the interest rate and inflation rate levels.

87. Quantitative or traditional methods of credit control include banks rate policy, open market operations and variable reserve ratio. Qualitative or selective methods of credit control include regulation of margin requirement, credit rationing, regulation of consumer credit and direct action.

88. Bank of Hindustan, a now defunct bank, is considered as among the first modern banks in colonial India. It was established by the agency house of Alexander and Company. In India, the paper currency was first issued during British East India Company rule.

89. GDP at Market Prices and **GDP at Factor Cost**. The First Thing we could understand from the above discussion is

that **GDP** (FC) is **GDP** (MP) minus **indirect taxes** plus subsidies. Here we can figure out that the more is the subsidy, the more is difference between the **GDP**(FC) & **GDP** (MP).

90. The correct chronological order is:

- Income tax,
- Gift tax,
- Service tax,
- Banking cash transaction tax.

91. Adam Smith- Absolute advantage.

David Ricardo- Comparative advantage.

Ohlin- Factor endowment.

Haberler- Opportunity cost.

92. When the aggregate supply of goods and services decreases because of an increase in production costs, it results in cost-push inflation. If demand for goods and services is more than their supply, the resultant inflation is demand pull inflation.

93. Income elasticity of demand for food will be decreased, because as the consumer spends 15% from their income for food alone then. Individual income demand decreases and market supply increases. Then the income elasticity of demand for food is 1.00.

94. The correct chronological order is: Formation of GATT, Formation of UNCTAD, Uruguay Round of GATT, Formation of WTO.

95. According to order condition, the second equation is just identified.

96. A rise in income terms of trade only indicates that the country can obtain a larger volume of imports from the sale of exports because a change in income terms of trade index cannot be interpreted as a measure of gain from trade.

97. An overvalued Indian rupee in the foreign exchange market will make imports cheaper and exports costlier.

98. The correct order is: Fisher's Equation of Exchange, Cambridge Equation of Exchange, Friedman's Quantity Theory of Money, Don Patinkins Theory of Money.

99. The Chalapathi Rao Committee set up for the revival of regional rural banks (RRB) has recently submitted its report to the Centre. The report has recommended a complete makeover in the RRB structure.

100. This total is called Net Domestic Product at FC or Domestic Income. Then by adding net factor income from abroad to Domestic Income (NDP at FC), we get National Income (NNP at FC). Mind, in value added method, national income is measured at the stage of production (or addition of value).

Mock Test 06

Q.1 Foreign Trade Policy 2015-20 contains specific measures for trade facilitation and ease of doing business. These measures include : (I) Online filing of documents/ applications and Paperless trade in 24x7 environment

(II) Online inter-ministerial consultations

(III) Simplification of procedures/processes, digitisation and e-governance

(IV) Tax holidays in SEZs (special Economic Zones)

A. I and II
B. II and III
C. I, II and III
D. I, II, III and IV

Q.2 Budget 2017-18 contains some major reforms.These include :

(I) presentation of Budget advanced to 1st February

(II) merger of Railways Budget with General Budget

(III) removal of plan and non plan classification of expenditure

(IV) presentation of railway Budget advanced to 15th February

Select the correct answer using the codes given below.

A. I, II and III
B. I, III and IV
C. II, III and IV
D. I, II and IV

Q.3 Assertion (1): Goods and Services Tax (GST) is a proposed system of indirect taxation in India merging most of the existing taxes into single system of taxation. Reason (R): Amalgamating several Central and State taxes into a single tax would mitigate cascading or double taxation, facilitating a common national market.

Codes:

A. Both (1) and (R) are correct
B. Both (1) and (R) are incorrect
C. (1) is correct, but (R) is incorrect.
D. (1) is incorrect, but (R) is correct.

Q.4 Agenda for 2017-18 , according to budget 2017-18 is :

A. Transform, Energise and Clean India
B. Make in India
C. All round development and poverty alleviation.
D. corruption free India.

Q.5 Examine the following statements and choose the correct answer :

Statement - I: The current account deals with short-term transactions known as actual transactions, as they have a real impact on income, output and employment levels of a country Statement - II: The capital account is a record of the inflows and outflows of capital that directly affect a country's foreign assets and liabilities Codes :

A. Both the Statements are wrong
B. Both the statements are correct
C. Statement - I is correct but the statement - II is wrong
D. Statement - I is wrong but the statement - II is correct

Q.6 With reference to demonetization, examine the following statements and choose the correct code :Statement - (I) Demonetization is the act of stripping a currency unit of its status as legal tenderStatement - (II) reasons of demonetization include combating inflation, corruption and crime(counterfeiting,tax evasion) and discouraging cash-dependent economy.Statement - (III) : On 8 November 2016, the Government of India announced the demonetisation of all Rs.500 and Rs.1,000 banknotes of the Mahatma Gandhi Series Codes :

A. (I) and (II) are correct but (III) is wrong
B. (I) and (II) are wrong but (III) is correct
C. (I), (II) and (III) are correct
D. II and III are correct

Q.7 Assertion (1): Counter trade is a system of international trading that helps governments reduce imbalances in trade between them and other countries

Reason (R): Countertrade is often used when a foreign currency is in short supplyCodes:

A. Both (1) and (R) are correct
B. Both (1) and (R) are incorrect
C. (1) is correct, but (R) is incorrect.
D. (1) is incorrect, but (R) is correct.

Q.8 Which of the following statements is not true ?

A. Microeconomics is the study of economic tendencies, or what is likely to happen when individuals make certain choices

B. Macro economics is a branch of the economics field that studies how the aggregate economy behaves

C. In microeconomics, individual actors are often broken down into microeconomic subgroups, such as buyers, sellers and business owners.

D. Those working in the field of microeconomics study aggregated indicators such as unemployment rates, GDP and price indices.

Q.9 Assertion (1): Pareto critrion states simply that an economic change which harms no one and makes someone better off indicates an increase in social welfareReason (R): This criterion does not apply to those economic changes which harm some and benefit others.Codes:

A. Both (1) and (R) are correct
B. Both (1) and (R) are incorrect
C. (1) is correct, but (R) is incorrect.
D. (1) is incorrect, but (R) is correct.

Q.10 Inclusive growth is an important objective of the development process. In this context, which of the following would amount to inclusive growth?(I). poverty reduction.

(II). disinvestment.

(III). Inequality

(IV). productive economic opportunity.

Select the correct answer using the codes given below.

A. I, II and III
B. I, III and IV
C. II, III and IV
D. I, II and IV

Q.11 Consider the following economy traits

(I) Prolonged increase in demand

(II) Heating up of economy

(III) Demand-supply lag

They are the characteristic feature of which phase of business/economy cycle?

A. Recession
B. Depression
C. Recovery
D. Boom

Q.12 In India, which of the following is/are a mechanism of deficit financing?

(I) borrowing from RBI.

(II) borrowing from commercial banks.

(III) issuing fresh currency notes.

Select the correct answer using the codes given below.

A. I, II
B. I, III
C. II and III
D. I, II and III

Q.13 With reference to narrow money, consider the following statements :

I. They are highly liquid.

II. Banks run their lending programme mainly with this money.

Which of the statements given above is/are correct ?

A. I only
B. II only
C. I, II
D. Neither I nor II

Q.14 Match the following:

List-I
(1) Fiscal deficit
(2) Revenue deficit
(3) Budgets of deficit
(4) Capital deficit

List-II
(i) Revenue and interest receipt minus revenue expenditure(ii) Revenue receipts and recovery of loans and other receipt minus total expenditure plus total borrowings
(iii) Receipts minus disbursement in capital account
(iv) Total receipts and total disbursements

A. (i), (ii), (iii), (iv)
B. (ii), (i), (iv), (iii)
C. (iii), (ii), (iv), (i)
D. (iv), (iii), (i), (ii)

Q.15 The Law of Demand shows the functional relationship between

A. Price and Supply
B. Price and Demand
C. Income and Demand
D. Supply and Demand

Q.16 Marginal Utility Theory was conceptualized by

A. Keynes
B. Alfred Marshall
C. J.R. Hicks
D. Samuelson

Q.17 Marshall assumes that utility is

A. Cardinal
B. Ordinal
C. Not Quantifiable
D. None of the above

Q.18 According to Keynesian theory of determination of output and employment, effective demand results in

A. Employment
B. Output
C. Rise in Price
D. Increase in Supply

Q.19 High Powered Money is equal to

A. $H = C + RR$
B. $H = C + RR + ER$
C. $H = RR + ER$
D. $H = C + ER + D$

Q.20 Which of the following indicators is included in measuring Economic Growth?

A. Health Facility
B. Literacy
C. Less Growth of Population
D. All of the above

Q.21 Which one of the following receipts is included in Revenue Budget

A. Receipts from Market Loans
B. Receipts from Borrowing from RBI
C. Interest Receipts
D. None of these

Q.22 Which of the following is a measure of economic development?

A. increase in national income
B. increase in per capita income
C. increase in human development
D. All of the above

Q.23 If the Government levies tax on sugar and collects the amount from the Manufacturer of sugar, but the manufacturer transfer the money burden on another person, say, the wholesale dealer by raising the price of sugar and if the process of shifting continues from wholesaler of final consumer, the incidence is said to be on final consumer. This is known as :

A. The Direct money burden
B. The Indirect money burden
C. The Direct real burden
D. The Indirect real burden

Q.24 The policy which aims at compensating the economy to meet chronical situation of inflation and deflation by manipulating taxes and public expenditures is

A. Monetary policy
B. Compensatory fiscal policy
C. Compensatory monetary policy
D. Fiscal policy

Q.25 The other term for National Income is

A. NNP_{FC}
B. NNP_{MP}
C. GNP_{FC}
D. GNP_{MP}

Q.26 For Maximization of Profit in the short-run, the condition is

A. $AR = AC$
B. $MR = MC$
C. $MR = AR$
D. $MC = AC$

Q.27 The Kinked demand curve explains

A. Price Rigidity
B. Price Flexibility

C. Demand Rigidity   **D.** Demand Flexibility

Q.28 Fiscal deficit in the Union Budget means :

A. The difference between current expenditure and current revenue

B. The sum of budgetary deficit and net increase in internal and external borrowings

C. Net increase in Union Government borrowings from the Reserve Bank of India

D. The sum of monetised deficit and budgetary deficit

Q.29 The Debit side (-) of the balance sheet includes

A. Imports of Goods and Services

B. Exports of Goods and Services

C. Borrowing from abroad

D. Receipts in the form of gifts, grants etc

Q.30 Imposition of Tariff leads to

A. Decrease in Prices of Exports

B. Decrease in Prices of Imports

C. Increase in Prices of Exports

D. Increase in Prices of Imports

Q.31 Anti - Poverty Programme for Self Employment was

A. IRDP   **B.** NREP

C. RLEGP   **D.** None of the above

Q.32 Monetary policy is formulated by

A. State Bank

B. Central Bank

C. Commercial Bank

D. Reserve Bank of India

Q.33 Keynesians favor

A. Fiscal policy   **B.** Monetary policy

C. Credit policy   **D.** Income policy

Q.34 Which one of the following is not the source of Tax Revenue?

A. Corporation duty

B. Life Insurance Corporation

C. Income - Tax Custom Duty

D. Excise Duty on Property and Wealth

Q.35 Which item is Non-Developmental expenditure of state government?

A. Medical and Health

B. Old Age Pension Programme

C. Education

D. Irrigation Work

Q.36 Unit Test is satisfied by

A. Laspeyre's Index   **B.** Paasche's Method

C. Fischer Method   **D.** All of the above

Q.37 $P_{01} = p_1q_1/p_0q_1 \times 100$ is the formula of?

A. Laspeyre's Method   **B.** Paasche's Method

C. Bowley Method   **D.** Fischer Method

Q.38 Consider the following statements-

(1) Money is a stock whereas spending is a flow.

(2) Wealth is a stock while income is a flow

(3) The government debt is a stock but interest payments is a flow

(4) The lending by bank is a flow and its out standing loan is a stock

Which of the statements given above are correct?

Codes:

A. Only 1 and 2   **B.** 1, 2 and 3

C. 2, 3 and 4   **D.** All of the above

Q.39 A change in money supply is no case be able to alter the rate of interest. This view is held by-

A. Liquidity Preference Theory of Interest

B. Classical Theory of Interest

C. Loanable Fund Theory of Interest

D. None of the above

Q.40 The UNDP publishes Human development report ____.

A. In every two years   **B.** Annually

C. In every five years   **D.** Monthly

Q.41 Budget 2017-18 proposes certain reforms in tax administration. These reforms include :

(I) Cash transactions above Rs. 5 lakh banned.

(II) Maximum amount of cash donation that can be received by a political party is Rs. 2,000.

(III) MSMEs' (annual turnover less than Rs.50crore) rate reduced to 25%.

(IV) Personal income tax: Rate reduced to 5% for income bracket of Rs. 2.5-5 lakh

Which of the above statements are correct?

A. I , II and III   **B.** II, III and IV

C. I, II and IV   **D.** I, II, III, IV

Q.42 Second Generation Reforms refer to

A. major changes in economic policies.

B. economic reforms by second generation.

C. political reforms

D. political and legal reforms

Q.43 Consider the following statements in respect of 'stand up India'

(I) It was launched on 5 April 2016

(II) to support entrepreneurship among women and SC & ST communities

(III) to support young entrepreneurs

(IV) It is a scheme to help industrial development"

Which of the above statements are correct ?

A. I and II only.   **B.** II and III only.

C. II and III.   **D.** I, II and IV

Q.44 Key elements of ASEAN 2025 are :

(I) Political-Security Community Blueprint 2025

(II) Economic Community Blueprint 2025

(III) Socio-Cultural Community Blueprint 2025

(IV) Military community

A. I, II and III   **B.** I, II and IV

C. II, III and IV   **D.** All of the above

Q.45 With reference to 'Digi Dhan Vyapar Yojana' , consider the following statements:

(I) This is a State sponsored scheme for the merchants across the country.

(II) Under it, merchants doing business using POS are eligible to win Rs.50000 per week

(III) 3 Mega Prizes for merchants will be of Rs 50 lakhs, 25 lakh, 12 lakh for digital transactions between 8 November 2016 to 13 April 2017Which of the above statements are correct?

A. I and II   **B.** II and III   **C.** I and III   **D.** I, II, III

Q.46 The two largest denomination notes, Rs 500 and Rs 1000 were "demonetised". The aim of this action was to curb :I) corruption,

(II) counterfeiting

(III) the use of high denomination notes for terrorist activities

(IV) the accumulation of "black money",

Select the correct answer using the code given below.

A. I only   **B.** I and II only
C. II and III only   **D.** I, II, III and IV

Q.47 With reference to Black Money (Undisclosed Foreign Income and Assets) and Imposition of Tax Act, 2015 , consider the following statements :(I) Black Money (Undisclosed Foreign Income and Assets) and Imposition of Tax Act, 2015 (popularly Black Money Act) is an Act of the Parliament of India(II) It aims to curb black money, or undisclosed foreign assets and income and imposes tax and penalty on such income.(III) the total undisclosed foreign income and asset of any previous year of an assessee shall be the income from a source located outside India,(IV) the undisclosed asset shall be chargeable to tax at the rate of thirty per cent of value of such undisclosed assetWhich of the following statements are correct ?

A. I , II and III   **B.** I, II and IV
C. II, III and IV   **D.** I, II, III and IV

Q.48 Both Foreign Direct Investment (FDI) and Foreign Institutional Investor (FII) are related to investment in a country. Which one of the following statements best represents an important difference between the two ?

A. FII helps bring better management skills and technology, while FDI only brings in capital

B. FII helps in increasing capital availability in general, while FDI only targets specific sectors

C. FDI flows only into the secondary market, while FII targets primary market

D. FII is considered to be more stable than FDI

Q.49 The Balance of payment comprises of :

(I) Current account. (II) Capital account

(III) Financial account (IV) Revenue account

A. I , II and III   **B.** I, II and IV.
C. II, III and IV   **D.** I, II , III and IV

Q.50 Which of the following is part of capital account of a country ?

A. Export and import of goods

B. Export and import of services

C. unilateral transfers from one country to another

D. NRI deposits

Q.51 Which of the following is not an industrial development bank in India ?

A. NABARD   **B.** IDBI
C. IFCI   **D.** SIDBI

Q.52 Match the items in List - I with those in List - II and select the correct code for the answer:

List - I
(1) Monopoly
(2) Monopolistic competition
(3) Perfect competition
(4) Oligopoly
List - II
(i) Price Taker
(ii) Homogeneous product's price maker
(iii) Heterogeneous product
(iv) Price Rigidity
Codes: (1) (2) (3) (4)

A. (ii) (iii) (i) (iv)   **B.** (i) (ii) (iv) (iii)
C. (iii) (iv) (ii) (i)   **D.** (iv) (i) (iii) (ii)

Q.53 Structural changes in economy refers to

A. major changes in economic policies.

B. shift or change in the basic ways a market or economy functions or operates

C. industrial reforms

D. growth of economy

Q.54 In the context of Indian economy, 'Open Market Operations' refers to

A. Borrowing by scheduled banks from the RBI

B. Lending by commercial banks to industry and trade

C. Purchase and sale of government securities by the RBI

D. None of the above

Q.55 National treatment (NT) is an important policy of WTO. NT means

A. All countries must not discriminate between imported and domestic product

B. WTO members must not discriminate between imported and domestic product

C. Exported products of a WTO member state must not be discriminate by other members via-a-vis domestic products

D. Both (2) & (3)

Q.56 A rapid increase in the rate of inflation is sometimes attributed to the "base effect". What is "base effect"?

A. It is the impact of drastic deficiency in supply due to failure of crops

B. It is the impact of the surge in demand due to rapid economic growth

C. It is the impact of the price levels of previous year on the calculation of inflation rate

D. None of the statements (1), (2) and (3) given above is correct in this context

Q.57 The concept of carbon credit originated from which one of the following?

A. Earth Summit, Rio de Janeiro

B. Kyoto Protocol

C. Montreal Protocol

D. G-8 Summit, Heiligendamm

Q.58 When the Reserve Bank of India announces an increase of the Cash Reserve Ratio, what does it mean?

A. The commercial banks will have less money to lend.

B. The Reserve Bank of India will have less money to lend.

C. The Union Government will have less money to lend.

D. The commercial banks will have more money to lend.

Q.59 The national income of a country for a given period is equal to the

A. total value of goods and services produced by the nationals

B. sum of total consumption and investment expenditure

C. sum of personal income of all individuals

D. money value of final goods and services produced

Q.60 In the context of Indian economy; which of the following is/are the purpose/ purposes of 'Statutory Reserve Requirements'?(I) To enable the Central Bank to control the amount of advances the banks can create(II) To make the people's deposits with banks safe and liquid(III) To prevent the commercial banks from making excessive profits(IV) To force the banks to have sufficient vault cash to meet their day-to-day requirementsSelect the correct answer using the code given below.

A. I only

B. I and II only

C. II and III only

D. I, II, III and IV

Q.61 Which of the following is/are used as an indicator in calculating Multidimensional Poverty Index (MPI)?(I). maternal mortality (II). nutrition

(III) access to electricity (IV) access to telephone

Select the correct answer using the codes given below.

A. I, II, III

B. I, III, IV

C. II, III

D. I, II and IV

Q.62 Assertion (1) : The World Trade Organization (WTO) is the only international organization that deals with the global rules of trade between nationsReasoning (R) : The WTO provides a platform that allows member governments to try to sort out any trade problems they face with other members.Codes:

A. Both (1) and (R) are correct

B. Both (1) and (R) are incorrect

C. (1) is correct, but (R) is incorrect.

D. (1) is incorrect, but (R) is correct.

Q.63 Match the items of list - I with the items of List - II and select the correct answer with the codes given below :

List - I
(1) SAARC
(2) ASEAN
(3) EU
(4) NAFTA
List - II

(I) Philippines
(ii) Canada
(iii) Afghanistan
(iv) Hungary
Codes : (1) (2) (3) (4)

A. (ii) (iv) (i) (iii)

B. (iv) (ii) (i) (iii)

C. (iii) (i) (iv) (ii)

D. (iii) (iv) (ii) (i)

Q.64 India's central bank, RBI performs various functions. Which of these functions are according to the RBI Act, 1934 managing inflation?

I. acting as banker's bank

II. managing India's Forex

III. handling government's borrowing program

Select the correct answer using the codes given below.

A. II and III

B. I, II and III

C. II, III

D. I and II

Q.65 Consider the following statements about Index of Industrial Production (IIP)

I. It is released monthly by Central Statistical Organisation (CSO)

II. It shows the volume of industrial activity.

Which of the statements given above is/are correct ?

A. I only

B. II only

C. Both I and II

D. Neither I nor II

Q.66 Which of the following also acts as a mechanism for government lending.

I. CRR

II. Repo rate

III. Reverse repo rate

IV. SLR

Select the correct answer using the codes given below.

A. 1 and 3 only

B. 1, 2 and 4 only

C. 1 and 4 only

D. 4 only

Q.67 Match the items of List - I with List - II :

List - I
(1) Exchange Pegging
(2) Clearing Agreement
(3) Foreign Exchange Rationing
(4) Moratorium Application
List - II
(i) fixing the exchange value
(ii) fixing quota of amount and rate of foreign exchange.(iii) predetermined or specified rate of exchange
(iv) stoppage of payments for imports
Codes : (1) (2) (3) (4)

A. (i) (iii) (ii) (iv)

B. (iv) (iii) (ii) (i)

C. (iv) (i) (ii) (iii)

D. (iv) (ii) (i) (iii)

Q.68 Liquidity preference is a theory of

A. Supply of money

B. Saving

C. Investment

D. Demand for money

Q.69 According to Keynes consumption is a function of

A. Investment

B. Capital

C. Saving   **D.** Income

Q.70 The problem why rational people are unwilling to participate in a fair game, refers to

A. Leontiff paradox

B. St. Petersburg Paradox

C. Bernoulli's Paradox

D. Neumann's Paradox

Q.71 The economist who popularized indifference curve approach is

A. Simon Kuznets   **B.** Paul Samuel son

C. J.R. Hicks   **D.** Sweezy

Q.72 Public debt implies loans raised by government

A. Within the country

B. Outside the country

C. Within and outside the country

D. Not applicable

Q.73 The term sustainable development was first used by

A. World conservation strategy

B. The world development Report 1999

C. The world development Report 2000

D. None of these

Q.74 The effect of population growth on per capita income is

A. Favourable   **B.** Unfavourable

C. No effect   **D.** Very low

Q.75 Selling a product in a foreign market at a lower price than in home market is called

A. Cartel   **B.** Dumping

C. Subsidy   **D.** Import Quota

Q.76 Which protective device aims at restricting and regulating imports?

A. Dumping   **B.** Subsidy

C. Import Quota   **D.** Tariff quota

Q.77 The function that shows the functional relationship between utility and quantity of goods is known as

A. General utility function

B. Specific utility function

C. Total utility function

D. Marginal utility function

Q.78 What is the first order condition of consumer's equilibrium?

A. Bordered Hessian Determinant > 0

B. $f_2\, p_1/f_1\, p_2$

C. Bordered Hessian Determinant < 0

D. $f_2\, p_1/f_1\, p_3$

Q.79 Consider the following statements :

I. The Life Cycle Hypothesis(LCH) of consumption emphasises that income follows a regular pattern over a person's lifetimeII. The Permanent Income Hypothesis(PIH) emphasises that people experience random and temporary changes in their incomes from year to year Which of the statements given above is/are correct ?

Codes :

A. I only   **B.** II only

C. Both I and II   **D.** Neither I nor II

Q.80 Who is the exponent of the principle of correlation?

A. Bowleg   **B.** Spearman

C. Connor   **D.** Karl Pearson

Q.81 r XY/N_{xy} refers to

A. Price index

B. Karl Pearson's coefficient of correlation

C. Spearman's rank Differences methods

D. Mean Deviation

Q.82 Agricultural Development banks are sponsored by

A. RBI   **B.** Nationalized Banks

C. SBI   **D.** Cooperative Banks

Q.83 Most of the disguised unemployed persons in India are found in

A. Transport   **B.** Industry

C. Agriculture   **D.** Trade

Q.84 Keynes defined Money demand as

A. Cash + Time deposit

B. Cash + Demand deposit

C. Cash + High powered money

D. Cash + Saving with post office

Q.85 Horizontal equity refers to

A. Equal treatment of equals

B. Unequal treatment of unequals

C. Equal treatment of unequals

D. Unequal treatment of equals

Q.86 Age is given on the vertical axis so that the youngest age group is ....and the oldest age group is ....

A. At the bottom; at the top

B. At the top; at the bottom

C. On the left side; on the right side

D. On the right side,; on the left side

Q.87 Who is known as the father of input output analysis?

A. W.W Leontiff   **B.** Hicks

C. Samuelson   **D.** Trance is Quesnay

Q.88 Between income and consumption there is generally

A. No correlation

B. Positive correlation

C. Negative correlation

D. Partial correlation

Q.89 Blue revolution is related to

A. Poultry   **B.** Fisheries

C. Drinking water   **D.** Space research

Q.90 Narrow definition of money is

A. M_4 **B.** M_3 **C.** M_2 **D.** M_1

Q.91 In case of inferior goods, the income effect is

A. Positive   **B.** Negative   **C.** Zero   **D.** Infinite

Q.92 Which bank meets the long-term credit needs of agriculturists?

A. Primary agricultural credit societies
B. Central cooperative bank
C. Land Development bank
D. State cooperative banks

Q.93 Globalization signifies a process of

A. Internationalization
B. Liberalisation
C. Internationalization and liberalization
D. Privatization

Q.94 According to Harrod-Domar Growth Model, Growth is directly related to

A. k/o ratio and inversely related to savings
B. Savings and inversely related to k/o ratio
C. Savings and k/o ratio
D. Savings and k/o ratio directly

Q.95 Euro-currency market is a means of transferring

A. Long -term and medium term funds with in the country
B. Short - term and medium term funds with in the country
C. Short - term and medium term funds from one country to another country.
D. Long -term funds from one country to another

Q.96 According to the minimum wage Act, 1948

A. Wages for agricultural labourers are to be fixed by the state governments
B. Wages for agricultural labourers are to be fixed by the central governments
C. Wages for industrial labours are to be fixed by the entrepreneurs
D. Wages for industrial labours are to be fixed by the central governments

Q.97 Bretton woods led to formation of

A. GATT   **B.** IBRO
C. IMF   **D.** All of the above

Q.98 The LPG model of development was introduced by

A. Vijay kelkar
B. V. K. R. V Rao
C. Jagdish Bhagwati
D. Dr. Manmohan singh

Q.99 In new economic policy of 1991

A. Government has restricted foreign investment policy
B. Government has liberalized foreign
C. Several concessions and facilities have been given on foreign direct investment
D. Both (2) and (3)

Q.100 The new endogeneous growth theory was developed as a reaction to missions and deficiencies in

A. Hicks - Samuelson model
B. Jargenson's neo - classical model
C. Solow - swan neo - classical growth model
D. Meade's Neo - classical Model of economic growth

// Smart Answer Sheet //

Correct Indicates percentage of students who answered questions correctly.

Skipped Indicates percentage of students who skipped questions.

Q.	Ans.	Correct / Skipped
1	C	23.64 % / 14.54 %
2	A	48.18 % / 10.91 %
3	A	60.91 % / 20.0 %
4	A	30.91 % / 14.54 %
5	B	60.0 % / 25.45 %
6	C	44.55 % / 28.18 %
7	A	49.09 % / 23.64 %
8	D	60.91 % / 27.27 %
9	A	53.64 % / 21.81 %
10	B	40.0 % / 26.36 %
11	D	29.09 % / 20.91 %
12	B	21.82 % / 17.27 %
13	A	28.18 % / 22.73 %
14	B	35.45 % / 15.46 %
15	B	70.91 % / 20.91 %
16	B	73.64 % / 16.36 %

Q.	Ans.	Correct / Skipped
17	A	76.36 % / 15.46 %
18	B	24.55 % / 24.54 %
19	B	53.64 % / 18.18 %
20	C	56.36 % / 8.19 %
21	C	52.73 % / 13.63 %
22	B	13.64 % / 10.91 %
23	B	50.91 % / 20.91 %
24	B	48.18 % / 9.09 %
25	A	45.45 % / 22.73 %
26	B	59.09 % / 24.55 %
27	A	64.55 % / 20.9 %
28	B	54.55 % / 10.0 %
29	A	48.18 % / 26.37 %
30	D	43.64 % / 10.91 %
31	A	19.09 % / 20.91 %
32	B	19.09 % / 18.18 %

Q.	Ans.	Correct / Skipped
33	A	60.0 % / 14.55 %
34	B	79.09 % / 10.0 %
35	B	67.27 % / 21.82 %
36	D	49.09 % / 16.36 %
37	B	54.55 % / 16.36 %
38	D	40.0 % / 28.18 %
39	A	43.64 % / 19.09 %
40	B	51.82 % / 24.54 %
41	B	26.36 % / 28.19 %
42	A	60.0 % / 12.73 %
43	A	19.09 % / 26.36 %
44	A	40.0 % / 17.27 %
45	B	20.91 % / 28.18 %
46	D	73.64 % / 12.72 %
47	D	35.45 % / 30.0 %
48	B	39.09 % / 17.27 %

Q.	Ans.	Correct / Skipped
49	A	37.27 % / 23.64 %
50	D	35.45 % / 25.46 %
51	A	59.09 % / 19.09 %
52	A	71.82 % / 14.54 %
53	B	60.91 % / 14.54 %
54	C	69.09 % / 25.46 %
55	D	59.09 % / 20.91 %
56	C	46.36 % / 18.19 %
57	B	40.0 % / 23.64 %
58	A	58.18 % / 25.46 %
59	D	30.91 % / 19.09 %
60	B	18.18 % / 18.18 %
61	C	28.18 % / 15.46 %
62	A	52.73 % / 25.45 %
63	C	48.18 % / 20.91 %
64	B	55.45 % / 16.37 %

Q.	Ans.	Correct / Skipped
65	A	10.91 % / 25.45 %
66	D	19.09 % / 22.73 %
67	A	38.18 % / 26.37 %
68	D	60.0 % / 23.64 %
69	D	63.64 % / 23.63 %
70	B	25.45 % / 24.55 %
71	C	64.55 % / 22.72 %
72	C	54.55 % / 8.18 %
73	A	30.0 % / 13.64 %
74	B	57.27 % / 24.55 %
75	B	72.73 % / 20.0 %
76	C	49.09 % / 23.64 %
77	A	20.91 % / 17.27 %
78	B	34.55 % / 28.18 %
79	C	50.91 % / 21.82 %
80	D	62.73 % / 11.82 %

Q.	Ans.	Correct / Skipped
81	B	56.36 %
		14.55 %
82	C	14.55 %
		12.72 %
83	C	74.55 %
		17.27 %
84	C	26.36 %
		24.55 %

Q.	Ans.	Correct / Skipped
85	A	50.91 %
		18.18 %
86	A	49.09 %
		24.55 %
87	A	60.91 %
		20.91 %
88	B	60.91 %
		23.64 %

Q.	Ans.	Correct / Skipped
89	B	70.0 %
		22.73 %
90	D	59.09 %
		24.55 %
91	B	67.27 %
		22.73 %
92	C	24.55 %
		24.54 %

Q.	Ans.	Correct / Skipped
93	C	47.27 %
		23.64 %
94	B	44.55 %
		15.45 %
95	C	50.0 %
		22.73 %
96	A	31.82 %
		19.09 %

Q.	Ans.	Correct / Skipped
97	D	36.36 %
		18.19 %
98	D	62.73 %
		25.45 %
99	D	69.09 %
		21.82 %
100	C	54.55 %
		20.0 %

Performance Analysis

Avg. Score (%)	43.0%
Toppers Score (%)	100.0%
Your Score	

//Hints and Solutions//

1. It has been decided to develop an online procedure to upload digitally signed documents by Chartered Accountant / Company Secretary / Cost Accountant. In the new system, it will be possible to upload online documents like annexure attached to ANF 3B, ANF 3C and ANF 3D, which are at present signed by these signatories and submitted physically.Henceforth, hardcopies of applications and specified documents would not be required to be submitted to RA, saving paper as well as cost and time for the exporters.As a measure of ease of doing business, landing documents of export consignment as proofs for notified market can be digitally uploaded. It is proposed to have Online inter-ministerial consultations for approval of export of SCOMET items, Norms fixation, Import Authorisations, Export Authorisation, in a phased manner, with the objective to reduce time for approval. Under EPCG scheme, obtaining and submitting a certificate from an independent Chartered Engineer, confirming the use of spares, tools, refractory and catalysts imported for final redemption of EPCG authorizations has been dispensed with.

2. Budget 2017-18 contains 3 major reforms.

First, presentation of Budget advanced to 1st February to enable the Ministries to operationalise all activities from the commencement of the financial year.Second, merger of Railways Budget with General Budget to bring Railways to the centre stage of Government's Fiscal Policy and Third, removal of plan and nonplan classification of expenditure to facilitate a holistic view of allocations for sectors and ministries.

3. Goods and Services Tax (GST) is a proposed system of indirect taxation in India merging most of the existing taxes into single system of taxation. It was introduced as The Constitution (One Hundred and First Amendment) Act 2016.GST would be a comprehensive indirect tax on manufacture, sale and consumption of goods and services throughout India, to replace taxes levied by the central and state governments.The introduction of Goods and Services Tax (GST) would be a significant step in the reform of indirect taxation in India.Amalgamating several Central and State taxes into a single tax would mitigate cascading or double taxation, facilitating a common national market. The simplicity of the tax should lead to easier administration and enforcement. From the consumer point of view, the biggest advantage would be in terms of a reduction in the overall tax burden on goods, which is currently estimated at 25%-30%, free movement of goods from one state to another without stopping at state borders for hours for payment of state tax or entry tax and reduction in paperwork to a large extent.

4. Agenda for 2017-18 is : "Transform, Energise and Clean India" - TEC India TEC India seeks to Transform the quality of governance and quality of life of our people; Energise various sections of society, especially the youth and the vulnerable, and enable them to unleash their true potential; and Clean the country from the evils of corruption, black money and non-transparent political funding Ten distinct themes to foster this broad agenda: Farmers : committed to double the income in 5 years; Rural Population : providing employment & basic infrastructure; Youth : energising them through education, skills and jobs; The Poor and the Underprivileged : strengthening the systems of social security, health care and affordable housing; Infrastructure: for

efficiency, productivity and quality of life; Financial Sector : growth & stability by stronger institutions; Digital Economy : for speed, accountability and transparency; Public Service : effective governance and efficient service delivery through people's participation; Prudent Fiscal Management: to ensure optimal deployment of resources and preserve fiscal stability; Tax Administration: honouring the honest.

5. The balance of payments contains two accounts: current and capital.
The current account deals with short-term transactions known as actual transactions, as they have a real impact on income, output and employment levels of a country through the movement of goods and services in the economy.It is comprised of visible trade (export and import of goods), invisible trade (export and import of services), unilateral transfers and investment income (income from factors such as land or foreign shares). The resulting balance of the current account is approximated as the sum total of balance of trade.The capital account is a record of the inflows and outflows of capital that directly affect a country's foreign assets and liabilities.It is concerned with all international trade transactions between citizens of a given country and citizens in other countries. The components of the capital account include foreign investment and loans, banking capital and other forms of capital, as well as monetary movements or changes in foreign exchange reserve.

6. Demonetization is the act of stripping a currency unit of its status as legal tender.
The current form or forms of money is pulled from circulation and retired, often to be replaced with new notes or coins.There are multiple reasons why nations demonetize their local units of currency: to combat inflation, to combat corruption and crime (counterfeiting, tax evasion), to discourage a cash-dependent economy and to facilitate trade.On 8 November 2016, the Government of India announced the demonetisation of all Rs.500 and Rs.1,000 banknotes of the Mahatma Gandhi Series. The government claimed that the action would curtail the shadow economy and crack down on the use of illicit and counterfeit cash to fund illegal activity and terrorism.

7. Countertrade is a system of international trading that helps governments reduce imbalances in trade between them and other countries. It involves the direct or indirect exchange of goods for other goods instead of currency. Countertrade is often used when a foreign currency is in short supply or when a country applies foreign exchange controls, which are limits imposed on the availability of foreign currencies to importers for the purchase of foreign products. Countertrade is often used by developing countries to control trade and as a development technique.it is a sort of bilateral trade where one set of goods is exchanged for another set of goods and a seller provides a buyer with deliveries.

8. Microeconomics is the study of economic tendencies, or what is likely to happen when individuals make certain choices or when the factors of production change. Macroeconomics is a branch of the economics field that studies how the aggregate economy behaves. Those working in the field of macroeconomics study aggregated indicators such as unemployment rates, GDP and price indices, and then analyze how different sectors of the economy relate to one another to understand how the

economy functions. Macroeconomists develop models explaining relationships between a variety of factors such as consumption, inflation, savings, investments, international trade and finance, national income and output. Contrarily, microeconomics analyzes how individual agents act, namely consumers and corporations, and studies how these agents' behavior affects quantities and prices in certain markets.

9. Pareto laid the foundation of the modern welfare economics by formulating the concept of social optimum which is based on the concept of ordinal utility and is free from interpersonal comparisons of utilities and value judgements.He aimed at formulating a value-free objective criterion designed to test whether a proposed policy change increases social welfare or not.Pareto critrion states simply that an economic change which harms no one and makes someone better off indicates an increase in social welfare. Thus, this criterion does not apply to those economic changes which harm some and benefit others.

10. Inclusive growth is a concept that advances equitable opportunities for economic participants during economic growth with benefits incurred by every section of society. Growth is inclusive when it creates economic opportunities along with ensuring equal access to them. Apart from addressing the issue of inequality, the inclusive growth may also make the poverty reduction efforts more effective by explicitly creating productive economic opportunities for the poor and vulnerable sections of the society. Inclusive growth is a concept that advances equitable opportunities for economic participants during economic growth with benefits incurred by every section of society.This concept expands upon traditional economic growth models to include focus on the equity of health, human capital, environmental quality, social protection, and food security.

11. All these are features of a boom phase of business cycle. During boom phase, the demand goes on increasing and the economy heats up. The supply is limited and hence there develops a demand-supply lag. Disinvestment is reducing the government ownership in public sector enterprises. It is not in any way related to inclusive growth. The rest three helps in inclusive growth.

12. Deficit financing is a method of meeting government deficits through the creation of new money.The deficit is the gap caused by the excess of government expenditure over its receipts.Deficit financing in India is done by -1. Withdrawal of past accumulated cash balances

2. Borrowing from RBI

3. Issuing fresh currency notes.

Borrowing from commercial banks is not a part of deficit banking.

13. Narrow money = currency with public + demand deposit with banks + "other' deposits with RBI.It is denoted by M_1. It is highly liquid. Now, banks cannot carry their lending progam with such highly liquid money as they have to return it pay when required by depositor.For eg. demand deposit is a part of M_1 . Banks have to return the demand deposit immediately if the depositor demands it. But if bank had lent that money to others, it cannot return it. So, the lending program is mainly carried by

such money which is less liquid, like broad money (M_3). So, statement II is incorrect.

14. Fiscal deficit refers to the excess of total expenditure over total receipts (excluding borrowings) during the given fiscal year. Fiscal Deficit = Total Expenditure - Total Receipts excluding borrowings. The extent of fiscal deficit is an indication of how far the government is spending beyond its means.Revenue Deficit (RD) denotes the difference between revenue receipts and revenue Expenditure. The excess of expenditure on revenue account over receipts on revenue account measures revenue deficit. Receipts on revenue account include both tax and non-tax revenue and also grants. A budget deficit occurs when an individual, business or government budgets more spending than there is revenue available to pay for the spending, over a specific period of time. Debt is the aggregate value of deficits accumulated over time. Capital Deficit denotes the difference between capital receipts and capital disbursements.The excess of capital disbursements over capital receipts measures the capital deficit.

15. This law expresses that when price increases, demand decrease and vice versa.

16. Marginal utility theory was conceptualized by Alfred Marshall. According to this theory, the consumer is in equilibrium when the marginal utilities of various goods are proportional to their prices.

17. Cardinal means utility is measurable and quantifiable and can be measured in terms of utils.

18. According to Keynesian theory of determination of output and employment, effective demand results in Output. Output creates income and income provides employment.

19. High powered money is equal to H = C + RR + ER Where, C = Currency RR = Required reserves ER = Excess reserves.

20. Indicators is included in measuring Economic Growth are: (1) Health Facility (2) Literacy (3) Less Growth of Population

21. Revenue Budget consist both tax revenue and non tax revenue. Interest receipt is non-tax revenue.

22. Increase in per capita income is a measure of economic development . Economic development may be defined as increase in per capita output and institutional transformation.

23. This Burden is known as The Indirect money burden Because it indirectly falls on consumer and ultimately he has to pay it.

24. During inflation, government should take steps to reduce its expenditure by having surplus budget & raising taxes while during deflation government should raise expenditures through reducing taxes.

25. Net national Product at factor cost (NNPFC) is also called National Income.

26. When marginal revenue is equal to marginal cost then the firm earns profit in short run.

27. The Kinked demand curve explains Price Rigidity. This kind of demand curve is found in oligopoly market. In this firms follow other firms when price decreases but doesn't follow when price increases.

28. Fiscal deficit in the union budget is the sum of budgetary deficit and net increase in internal and external borrowings.

29. The debit side (-) of the balance sheet includes Imports of Goods and Services, Because debit side includes all the payments.

30. When tariff is imposed on any good then the price of Imports increases because tariff raises the price of good.

31. IRDP - Integrated rural Development Programme

32. Monetary policy is formulated by Central Bank. Monetary policy is formulated to regulate liquidity in the economy through various instruments available with it.

33. Keynesians favour Fiscal policy. In economics and political science, fiscal policy is the use of government revenue collection (taxes or tax cuts) and expenditure (spending) to influence a country's economy. The use of government revenues and expenditures to influence macroeconomic variables developed as a result of the Great Depression, when the previous laissez-faire approach to economic management became unpopular. Fiscal policy is based on the theories of the British economist John Maynard Keynes, whose Keynesian economics theorized that government changes in the levels of taxation and government spending influences aggregate demand and the level of economic activity. Fiscal and monetary policy are the key strategies used by a country's government and central bank to advance its economic objectives. The combination of these policies enables these authorities to target inflation (which is considered "healthy" at the level in the range 2%–3%) and to increase employment. Additionally, it is designed to try to keep GDP growth at 2%–3% and the unemployment rate near the natural unemployment rate of 4%–5%. This implies that fiscal policy is used to stabilize the economy over the course of the business cycle.

34. Life insurance corporation is non - tax revenue.

35. Medical and Health Education Irrigation Work All are developmental expenditure's item.

36. Unit test requires that the formula for constructing an index should be interdependent of the units in which variables are specified.

37. P_o = index for current period based on base period.p_0 = index for base period.q_1 = Quantity index for current yearp_1 = Price index for current year.

38. Money, wealth, government debt and loan are stocks whereas spending, income, interest payments and lending by bank are flow.

39. On liquidity trap where rate of interest becomes perfectly elastic, rise in money supply does not affect the interest rate, as clear from diagram.

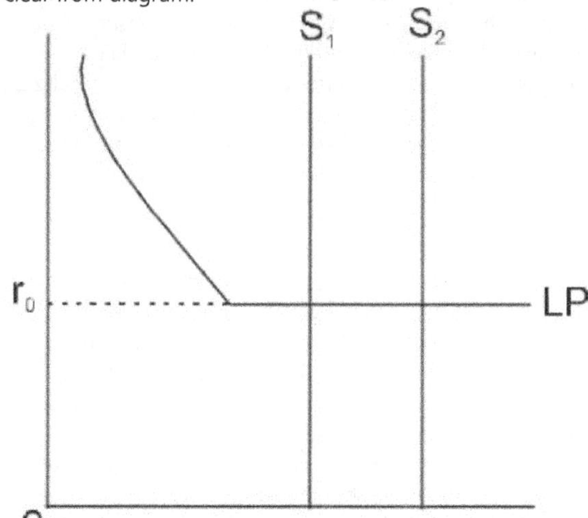

40. The united nations development programme (UNDP) Publishes Human development report (HDR) annually. HDR is like a 'report card' of each country in the field of human development. HDR ranks countries on the basis of value of HDI.

41. Proposals regarding tax administration include : Cash transactions above Rs. 3 lakh banned. Transparency in political funding: Parties continue to receive anonymous donations; propose system of cleaning up. Political funding: Maximum amount of cash donation that can be received is Rs. 2,000. Political parties can receive donations by cheques or digitally. Every party has to file returns within specified time. Amendment proposed to RBI Act to issue electoral bonds. Personal income tax: Rate reduced to 5% for income bracket of Rs. 2.5-5 lakh; All other categories to get uniform benefit of Rs. 12,500 per person;Surcharge on income bracket Rs. 50 lakh-Rs. 1 crore will be levied Personal income tax: Simple one-page form for taxable income up to Rs. 5 lakh will be implemented.GST: Preparedness of IT system on schedule. Not many changes to excise duties in GST regime. FPI category 1 and 2 investors exempted from indirect transfer provisions. Time period of revising tax returns reduced to 12 months Real estate: Changes will be made in capital gains tax. Corporate tax rate: MSMEs' (annual turnover less than Rs.50crore) rate reduced to 25%. LNG: customs duty reduced to 2.5% Limit of cash donation for charitable trusts reduced to Rs. 2,000.

42. There is no specific definition for Second Generation Reforms. Broadly, it means the major changes in Economic policy, tax reforms, privatization, private participation, change in the implementation of schemes, reduction in subsidies, market driven pricing, etc.Economic Reforms means changing the economic policy of the country in order to improve the living standards of the people. When the government believes that the current policy is not sufficient to improve the quality of life, they will introduce a wide range of policy changes which will help to augment the growth. All reforms will promote competitiveness among people.

43. Start up India was launched on 5 April 2016 to support entrepreneurship among women and SC & ST communities The scheme offers bank loans of between Rs.10 lakh (US$15,000) and Rs.1 crore (US$150,000) for scheduled castes and scheduled tribes and women setting up new enterprises outside of the farm sector. Startup India is an initiative of the Government of India. The campaign was first announced by Indian Prime Minister, Narendra Modi during his 15 August 2015 address from the Red Fort, in New Delhi.

44. The ASEAN 2025 Document is the outcome of a year of planning and intense discussions, and reflects the determination of Member States to forge ahead with the next phase of ASEAN's evolvement.ASEAN 2025 consists of specific action lines and strategic measures to realise the targets identified.The key aspirations across the three pillars are: Political-Security Community. Economic Community and Socio-Cultural Community.It is a forward looking roadmap that articulates ASEAN goals and aspirations to realise further consolidation, integration and stronger cohesiveness as a Community.ASEAN is working towards a Community that is "politically cohesive, economically integrated, and socially responsible".

45. This is the central Government sponsored scheme for the merchants across the country. Under it, merchants doing business using POS are eligible to win Rs.50000 per week. 3 Mega Prizes for merchants will be of Rs 50 lakhs, 25 lakh, 12 lakh for digital transactions between 8 November 2016 to 13 April 2017. It will be announced on 14 April 2017.

46. A radical governance-cum-social engineering measure was enacted on November 8, 2016.The two largest denomination notes, Rs 500 and Rs 1000-together comprising 86 percent of all the cash in circulation-were "demonetised" with immediate effect, ceasing to be legal tender except for a few specified purposes.These notes were to be deposited in the banks by December 30, while restrictions were placed on cash withdrawals. In other words, restrictions were placed on the convertibility of domestic money and bank deposits.The aim of the action was fourfold: to curb corruption, counterfeiting, the use of high denomination notes for terrorist activities, and especially the accumulation of "black money", generated by income that has not been declared to the tax authorities.

47. Black Money (Undisclosed Foreign Income and Assets) and Imposition of Tax Act, 2015 (popularly Black Money Act) is an Act of the Parliament of India.It aims to curb black money, or undisclosed foreign assets and income and imposes tax and penalty on such income. It came into effect from 1 April, 2016.Section 3. (1) There shall be charged on every assessee for every assessment year commencing on or after the 1st day of April, 2016, subject to the provisions of this Act, a tax in respect of his total undisclosed foreign income and asset of the previous year at the rate of thirty per cent of such undisclosed income and asset.Section 4. (1) Subject to the provisions of this Act, the total undisclosed foreign income and asset of any previous year of an assessee shall be,-(1) the income from a source located outside India, which has not been disclosed in the return of income furnished within the time specified (2) the income, from a source located outside India, in respect of which a return is required to be furnished under section 139 of the Income-tax Act but no return of income has been furnished within the time specified and (3) the value of an undisclosed asset located outside India.

48. Direct investment targets a specific enterprise, with the aim of increasing its capacity/productivity or changing its management

control. Direct investment to create or augment capacity ensures that the capital inflow translates into additional production. In the case of FII investment that flows into the secondary market, the effect is to increase capital availability in general , rather than availability of capital to a particular enterprise. FDI is preferred over FII investments since it is considered to be the most beneficial form of foreign investment for the economy as a whole.

49. A 'Balance Of Payments (BOP)' is a statement that summarizes an economy's transactions with the rest of the world for a specified time period. The balance of payments, also known as balance of international payments, encompasses all transactions between a country's residents and its nonresidents involving goods, services and income; financial claims on and liabilities to the rest of the world; and transfers such as gifts.The BOP is divided into three main categories: the current account, the capital account and the financial account. Within these three categories are subdivisions, each of which accounts for a different type of international monetary transaction. The current account includes transactions in goods, services, investment income and current transfers, while the capital account mainly includes transactions in financial instruments.An economy's balance of payments transactions and international investment position (IIP) together constitute its set of international accounts.

50. The capital account is where all international capital transfers are recorded. This refers to the acquisition or disposal of non-financial assets (for example, a physical asset such as land) and non-produced assets, which are needed for production but have not been produced, like a mine used for the extraction of diamonds.The capital account is broken down into the monetary flows branching from debt forgiveness, the transfer of goods, and financial assets by migrants leaving or entering a country, the transfer of ownership on fixed assets (assets such as equipment used in the production process to generate income), the transfer of funds received to the sale or acquisition of fixed assets, gift and inheritance taxes, death levies and, finally, uninsured damage to fixed assets. The current account, on the other hand, is used to mark the inflow and outflow of goods and services into a country. Earnings on investments, both public and private, are also put into the current account.

51. At present, at the all-India level, there are five industrial development banks, one agricultural development bank and one export-import bank.The development banks for the industry are the Industrial Development Bank of India (IDBI), the Industrial Finance Corporation of India (IFCI), the Industrial Credit and Investment Corporation of India (ICICI), and the Industrial Reconstruction Corporation of India (IRCI) for large industries and the National Small Industries Development Bank of India (SIDBI) for small-scale industries. For agriculture, it is the National Bank for Agriculture and Rural Development (NABARD).

52. 'Monopoly' is a market structure characterized by a single seller, selling a unique product in the market. In a monopoly market, the seller faces no competition, as he is the sole seller of goods with no close substitute.Characteristics associated with a monopoly market make the single seller the market controller as well as the price maker. He enjoys the power of setting the price for his goods. The term monopolistic competition represents the combination of monopoly and perfect competition. Monopolistic competition refers to a market situation in which there are a large number of buyers and sellers of products. However, the product of each seller is different in one aspect or the other.The perfect competition is characterized by the presence of many firms. The all sell identical products. The seller is a price taker, not price maker. The term oligopoly has been derived from two Greek words, oligoi means few and poly means control. Therefore, oligopoly refers to a market form in which there are few sellers dealing either in homogenous or differentiated products.

53. It is now a well known phenomenon that as an economy moves ahead on the path of economic development, structural changes are inevitable. Developing countries like India are experiencing major structural changes in the recent decades. All developed countries have gone through a process of structural change which implied movement from agricultural sector to the industrial sector and then finally to the services.

54. Open market operations (OMO) refers to the buying and selling of government securities in the open market in order to expand or contract the amount of money in the banking system, facilitated by the RBI. Purchases inject money into the banking system and stimulate growth, while sales of securities do the opposite and contract the economy.When RBI sells government security in the markets, the banks purchase them. When the banks purchase Government securities, they have a reduced ability to lend to the industrial houses or other commercial sectors. This reduced surplus cash, contracts the rupee liquidity and consequently credit creation / credit supply. When RBI purchases the securities, the commercial banks find them with more surplus cash and this would create more credit in the system.

55. National treatment: Treating foreigners and locals equally - Imported and locallyproduced goods should be treated equally - at least after the foreign goods have entered the market.The same should apply to foreign and domestic services, and to foreign and local trademarks, copyrights and patents. National treatment only applies once a product, service or item of intellectual property has entered the market. Therefore, charging customs duty on an import is not a violation of national treatment even if locally-produced products are not charged an equivalent tax.

56. The Base effect relates to inflation in the corresponding period of the previous year. If the inflation rate was too low in the corresponding period of the previous year, even a smaller rise in the Price Index will arithmetically give a high rate of inflation now.On the other hand, if the price index had risen at a high rate in the corresponding period of the previous year and recorded high inflation rate, a similar absolute increase in the Price index now will show a lower inflation rate now.

57. The concept of carbon credit originated from Kyoto Protocol. The Kyoto Protocol is an international treaty which extends the 1992 United Nations Framework Convention on Climate Change (UNFCCC) that commits State Parties to reduce greenhouse gas emissions, based on the premise that(1) global warming exists and (2) human-made CO_2 emissions have caused it. A carbon credit is a generic term for any tradable certificate or permit representing the right to emit one tonne of carbon dioxide or the mass of another greenhouse gas with a carbon dioxide equivalent (CO_2) equivalent to one tonne of carbon dioxide.

58. When the Reserve Bank of India announces an increase of the Cash Reserve Ratio the commercial banks will have less money to lend.Cash Reserve Ratio (CRR) is a specified minimum fraction of the total deposits of customers, which commercial banks have to hold as reserves either in cash or as deposits with the central bank. CRR is set according to the guidelines of the central bank of a country.The amount specified as the CRR is held in cash and cash equivalents, is stored in bank vaults or parked with the Reserve Bank of India.The aim here is to ensure that banks do not run out of cash to meet the payment demands of their depositors. CRR is a crucial monetary policy tool and is used for controlling money supply in an economy.

59. National income is the total value a country's final output of all new goods and services produced in one year There are various concepts of National Income. The main concepts of NI are:GDP, GNP and NNP.These different concepts explain about the phenomenon of economic activities of the various sectors of the various sectors of the economy. National income= NNP (Net National Product) at Market price minus indirect tax plus subsidies. Net National Product is the market value of all final goods and services after allowing for depreciation. It is also called National Income at market price.Gross National Product, GNP, is the total market value of all final goods and services produced annually in a country plus net factor income from abroad. Thus, GNP is the total measure of the flow of goods and services at market value resulting from current production during a year in a country including net factor income from abroad.

60. The ratio of liquid assets to demand and time liabilities is known as Statutory Liquidity Ratio (SLR).In simple words, it is the percentage of total deposits banks have to invest in government bonds and other approved securities.A SLR bond also qualifies for the portfolio maintained by banks to meet the liquidity requirement.The main objectives for maintaining the Statutory Liquidity Ratio are the following:(i) Statutory Liquidity Ratio is maintained in order to control the expansion of Bank Credit. By changing the level of Statutory Liquidity Ratio, Reserve bank of India can increase or decrease bank credit expansion.(ii) Statutory Liquidity Ratio in a way ensures the solvency of commercial banks.(iii) By determining Statutory Liquidity Ratio, Reserve Bank of India, in a way, compels the commercial banks to invest in government securities like government bonds. If any Indian Bank fails to maintain the required level of Statutory Liquidity Ratio, then it becomes liable to pay penalty to Reserve Bank of India. The defaulter bank pays penal interest at the rate of 3% per annum above the Bank Rate, on the shortfall amount for that particular day. The RBI can increase the Statutory Liquidity Ratio to contain inflation, suck liquidity in the market, to tighten the measure to safeguard the customers money.

61. Nutrition and access to electricity are included, while maternal mortality is not. Access to telephone comes under assets and is thus included. The global Multidimensional Poverty Index (MPI) is an international measure of acute poverty covering over 100 developing countries.It complements traditional income-based poverty measures by capturing the severe deprivations that each person faces at the same time with respect to education, health and living standards. The MPI assesses poverty at the individual level. If someone is deprived in a third or more of ten (weighted) indicators, the global index identifies them as 'MPI poor', and the extent - or intensity - of their poverty is measured by the number of deprivations they are experiencing.The MPI can be used to create a comprehensive picture of people living in poverty, and permits comparisons both across countries, regions and the world and within countries by ethnic group, urban/rural location, as well as other key household and community characteristics.

62. The World Trade Organization (WTO) is the only international organization that deals with the global rules of trade between nations.The WTO is built on WTO agreements signed by the majority of the world's trading nations; its main function is to help producers of goods and services, exporters and importers better protect and manage their businesses. The WTO provides a platform that allows member governments to try to sort out any trade problems they face with other members. The WTO itself was born out of a negotiation, and its main focus is to provide open lines of communication between its members as it relates to international trade.

63. The South Asian Association for Regional Cooperation (SAARC) is an economic and geopolitical organisation of eight countries that are primarily located in South Asia or the Indian subcontinent.The organisation was established by the governments of Bangladesh, Bhutan, India, Maldives, Nepal, Pakistan, and Sri Lanka. Since then the organisation has expanded by accepting one new full member, Afghanistan, and several observer members.The Association of Southeast Asian Nations (ASEAN) is a political and economic organisation of ten South east Asian countries. It was formed on 8 August 1967 by Indonesia, Malaysia, the Philippines, Singapore, and Thailand. The European Union (EU) is a politico-economic union of 28 member states that are located primarily in Europe. Hungry is a member of EU.The North American Free Trade Agreement (NAFTA) is an agreement signed by Canada, Mexico, and the United States, creating a trilateral rules-based trade bloc in North America.

64. RBI's functions - acting as banker's bank, managing India's Forex and handling govt's borrowing programme Before march 2015, the Reserve Bank was not formally an inflation targeting central bank. The defining features of an inflation targeting central bank are a precise mandate, a single instrument (the policy interest rate) in its armoury, a single minded devotion to achieving this target and a principal-agent relationship with the Government.So, even though RBI was informally helping manage inflation, it was not it's function as defined by the RBI Acvt, 1934 However, in March 2015 it was formally decided that from now, RBI will have the official mandate to manage inflation.For this the RBI Act, 1934 has been amended.

65. IIP or the index of industrial production is the number denoting the condition of industrial production during a certain period (month for eg.).It does not show the volume of industrial activity but only its growth with respect to a reference period. As IIP shows the status of industrial activity, one can find out if the industrial activity has increased, decreased or remained same.

66. SLR, statutory liquidity ratio is the amount of money that is invested in certain specified securities predominantly central government and state government securities. Investing in government securities by bank is one way of fulfilling the requirement of SLR. In this way, SLR acts as a lending mechanism to government. Repo rate is a rate at which banks borrow from RBI for short periods up to 7 or 14 days but predominantly overnight.

67. Above are methods of exchange control. Exchange control refers to the policy of the government through which it controls or intervenes in the foreign exchange market.In other simple words, government puts restrictions on the sale and purchase of foreign currencies and refers a measure which influences the foreign exchange rate and closing free movements of foreign exchange in the country. Exchange Pegging : It is the method of exchange control. Exchange pegging refers to the policy of fixing the exchange value of the current according to some desired rate. When it is fixed higher than market rate, it is "Pegging up". but if fixed lower than market rate, it is known as "pegging down". Clearing Agreement : Another method of exchange control is clearing agreement. It is an undertaking between two countries to exchange goods and services in accordance with a predetermined or specified rate of exchange. This method is applied to check fluctuation in exchange rate and to maintain equilibrium in balance of payments. Foreign Exchange Rationing : Government has the right to direct all the exports and other investors to surrender all foreign exchange with the central banks. Foreign exchange, so collected can be rationed by fixing quota of amount and rate of foreign exchange. Moratorium Application : A legal authorization to debtor to stop payment is known as Moratorium. To solve temporary problems of payment, a country can stop to make payment for imports and interest on capital.

68. Keynes formulated the theory of liquidity preference in which he suggested three motives of money1. Transactions demand 2. Precautionary demand 3. Speculative demand

69. When income rises, consumption also rises but not as much as income.

70. According to Bernoulli's paradox, a rational individual will take decision under risky and uncertain situations on the basis of expected utility rather then expected monetary value.

71. The economist J.R. Hicks popularized indifference curve approach.
According to this approach, a higher indifference curve shows higher utility.

72. Public authorities can raise loans within or outside the country to fulfill their requirements.

73. The term was first used by the 'world conservation strategy' presented by international union for the conservation of Nature and natural rescores in 1980.

74. The effect of population growth on per capita income is Unfavourable. Population growth increases the pressure of population on land, it leads to rise in costs of consumption goods and increase in family members, increase expenses, which adversely affects per capital income.

75. Selling a product in a foreign market at a lower price than in home market is called dumping. It is also one of the methods of protection.

76. In order to protect domestic industries from foreign competition and to correct disequilibrium in the balance of payments, import quota aims.

77. The function that shows the functional relationship between utility and quantity of goods is known as :General utility function $U = f(q_1 , q_2)$.

78. The first order condition of consumer's equilibrium is f_2 p_1 f_1/f_1 p_2 f_2 is slop ofindifference curve, p_1/p_2 is slope of budget line. It means when the indifference curve touches the price line or budget line, this is the first order condition of consumers equilibrium.

79. Milton Friedman's permanent income hypothesis (PIH) presented in 1957, complements Modigliani's LCH. Both the hypotheses argue that consumption should not depend on current income alone.But there is a difference of insight between the two hypotheses while the LCH emphasises that income follows a regular pattern over a person's lifetime, the PIH emphasises that people experience random and temporary changes in their incomes from year to year.The LCH states that the main reason that an individual's income varies is retirement.Since most people do not want their current living standard (as measured by consumption) to fall after retirement they save a portion of their income every year. The PIH, on the other hand, states that current consumption is not dependent solely on current disposable income but also on whether or not that income is expected to be permanent or transitory. The PIH argues that both income and consumption are split into two parts - permanent and transitory.According to Friedman consumption depends primarily on permanent income, because consumers use saving and borrowing to smooth consumption in response to transitory changes in income. The reason is that consumers spend their permanent income, but they save rather than spend most of their transitory income.

80. Karl Pearson is the exponent of the principle of correlation Correction helps us in determining the degree of relationship between two or more variables.

81. R XY/N_{xy} refers to Karl Pearson's coefficient of correlation

x = standard deviation of series x

y = standard deviation of series y

N = Number of pairs of observations

r = correlation coefficient.

82. Agricultural Development banks are sponsored by SBI - State bank of India.

83. Most of the disguised unemployed persons in India are found in Agriculture. In agricultural sector, the population is which is working is more than it is needed.

84. Keynes defined Money demand as Cash + High powered money. High powered money is sum of commercial bank reserves and currency (notes and coins) held by the public.

85. Horizontal equity refers to equal treatment of equals. Horizontal inequality meant that people of equal economic position are not treated equally.

86. Age is given on the vertical axis so that the youngest age group is at the bottom and the oldest age group is at the top. Youngest age group (eg. 0 to 4 years olds) Oldest age group (eg. Over 100 years olds).

87. W.W Leontiff is known as the father of input output analysis. Leontiff published his work in 1941.

88. Between income and consumption there is generally a positive correlation. As income increases, consumption also increases, that's why they are positively correlated.

89. As green revolution is related to agricultural strategies, blue revolution is related to fisheries.

90. Narrow definition of money is M_1 . M_1 includes currency with public, demand deposits in banks, other deposits with RBI.

91. In case of inferior goods, the income effect is negative. As consumer's income increases, the consumption of inferior goods decreases.

92. Land Development bank meets the long-term credit needs of agriculturists. These banks earlier known as Land Mortgage banks.

93. Globalization is the process of integrating various economics of the world without creating any hindrances in the free flow of goods and services, technology, capital and even labour or human capital.

94. According to Harrod-Domar Growth Model, Growth is directly related to savings and inversely related to k/o ratio. Harrod Domar concentrates in his growth model that how can steady growth rate be achieved with a fixed capital output ratio i.e. capital co-efficient and the fixed saving income ratio i.e. propensity to save.

95. Euro-currency market is a means of transferring short - term and medium term funds from one country to another country.Euro-currency market is a means of transferring short term and medium term funds from one country to another country.

96. According to the minimum wage Act, 1948, Wages for agricultural laborers are to be fixed by the state governments.The measure taken up by the government for the benefit and welfare of the agricultural laborers is the minimum wages Act, 1948.

97. GATT - General Agreement on Tariff and Trade. IBRO - International bank for reconstruction and development IMF - International monetary fund.

98. Liberalization, privatization and globalization (LPG) model was introduced in 1991 by the finance Minister Dr. Man Mohan Singh with a big bang was intended to charter a new strategy with emphasis on LPG.

99. In new economic policy of 1991 Government has liberalized foreign and Several concessions and facilities have been given on foreign direct investment.

100. The new endogenous growth theory was developed as a reaction to missions and deficiencies in Solow - swan neo - classical growth model.

Q.1 The capital that is consumed by an economy or a firm in the production process is known as:

A. Capital loss
B. Production cost
C. Dead-weight loss
D. Depreciation

Q.2 Who propounded the opportunity cost theory of international trade?

A. Ricardo
B. Marshall
C. Heckscher & Ohlin
D. Haberler

Q.3 Which among the following statement is INCORRECT?

A. On a linear demand curve, all the five forms of elasticity can be depicted
B. If two demand curves are linear and intersecting each other, then, coefficient of elasticity would be same on different demand curves at the point of intersection.
C. If two demand curves are linear and parallel to each other, then, at a particular price, the coefficient of elasticity would be different on different demand curves.
D. The price elasticity of demand is expressed in terms of relaive not absolute changes in Price and Quantity demanded.

Q.4 If the demand for a good is inelastic, an increase in its price will cause the total expenditure of the consumers of the good to

A. Increase
B. Decrease
C. Remain the same
D. Become zero

Q.5 The horizontal demand curve parallel to x-axis implies that the elasticity of demand is

A. Zero
B. Infinite
C. Equal to 1
D. Greater than zero but less than infinity

Q.6 An individual demand curve slopes downward to the right because of the

A. Working of the law of diminishing marginal utility
B. Substitution effect of decrease in price
C. Income effect of fall in price
D. All of the above

Q.7 Income elasticity of demand is defined as the responsiveness of

A. Quantity demanded to a change in income
B. Quantity demanded to a change in price
C. Price to a change in income
D. Income to a change in quantity demanded

Q.8 The supply of a good refers to

A. Stock available for sale
B. Total stock in the warehouse
C. Actual production of the good
D. Quantity of the good offered for sale at a particular price per unit of time

Q.9 For the success of the penetration price policy, which one of the following is not desirable?

A. Short-run demand for the product to have elasticity greater than unity.
B. Availability of economies of large scale production.
C. Product to have very low cross-elasticity of demand.
D. Easy acceptance and adoption of the product by the consumers.

Q.10 Assume that consumer's income and the number of sellers in the market for good X both falls. Based on this information, we can conclude with certaintty that the equilibrium.

A. Price will decrease
B. Price will increase
C. Quantity will decrease
D. Quantity will increase

Q.11 The economist's objections to monopoly rest on which of the following grounds?

A. There is a transfer of income from consumers to the monopolist
B. There is welfare loss as resources tend to be misallocated under monopoly
C. Both A and B are incorrect
D. Both A and B are correct

Q.12 In which of the following market structure is the degree of control over the price of its product by a firm very large?

A. Imperfect competition
B. Perfect competition
C. Monopoly
D. In A and B both

Q.13 The offer curves introduced by Alfred Marshall, helps us to understand how the _______ is established in international trade.

A. Terms of trade
B. Equilibrium price ratio
C. Exchange rate
D. Satisfaction level

Q.14 Demand for factors of production is

A. Derived demand
B. Joint demand
C. Composite demand
D. None of the above

Q.15 The producer's demand for a factor of production is governed by the _______ of the factor.

A. Price will decrease
B. Marginal productivity
C. Availability
D. Profitability

Q.16 Under conditions of perfect competition in the product market

A. MRP = VMP
B. MRP > VMP
C. VMP > MRP
D. None of the above

Q.17 Which statistical measure helps in measuring the purchasing power of money?

A. Arithmetic average
B. Index numbers
C. Harmonic mean
D. Time series

Q.18 Fisher's ideal index number is

A. Arithmetic mean of Laspeyre's and Paasche's index
B. Harmonic mean of Laspeyre's and Paasche's index
C. Geometric mean of Laspeyre's and Paasche's index
D. None of the above

Q.19 Which among the following statement is INCORRECT?

A. Floating exchange rate system works on the market mechanism
B. Floating exchange rate breeds uncertainties and speculation
C. Economic and political factors and value judgement influence the choice of the exchange rate system
D. The system of floating exchange rate requires comprehensive government intervention

Q.20 Which among the following statement is INCORRECT?

A. Welfare economics is based on value judgements
B. Welfare economics is also called 'economics with a heart'
C. Welfare economics focuses on questions about equity as well as efficiency
D. The founder of Welfare economics was Alfred Marshall

Q.21 Who is the 'lender of the last resort' in the banking structure of India?

A. State bank of India
B. Reserve bank of India
C. EXIM bank of India
D. Union bank of India

Q.22 _______ is the official minimum rate at which the Central Bank of a country is prepared to re-discount approved bills held by the commercial banks:

A. Repo rate
B. Bank rate
C. Prime lending rate
D. Reverse repo rate

Q.23 In order to control credit, Reserve Bank of India should

A. Increase CRR and decrease Bank rate
B. Decrease CRR and reduce Bank rate
C. Increase CRR and increase Bank rate
D. Reduce CRR and increase Bank rate

Q.24 Which among the following is a function of the Reserve Bank of India?

A. Bank issues the letters of credit to their customers certifying their credibility
B. Collecting and compilation of statistical information relating to banking & other financial sector
C. Banks underwrite the securities issued by public or private organizations

D. Accepting deposits from the public

Q.25 Credit creation power of the commercial banks gets limited by which of the following?

A. Banking habits of the people
B. Cash Reserve Ratio
C. Credit policy of the central bank
D. All of the above

Q.26 Number of times a unit of money changes hands in the course of a year is called

A. Supply of money
B. Purchasing power of money
C. Velocity of money
D. Value of money

Q.27 What is meant by Autarky in international trade?

A. Monopoly in international trade
B. Imposition of restrictions in international trade
C. Removal of all restrictions from international trade
D. The idea of self sufficiency and no international trade by a country

Q.28 Normally a demand curve will have the shape

A. Horizontal
B. Vertical
C. Downward sloping
D. Upward sloping

Q.29 Who defined Economics as a 'science which studies human behaviour as a relationship betweeen ends and means which have alternative uses'?

A. L. Robbins
B. Alfred Marshall
C. Joan Robinson
D. Paul A. Samuelson

Q.30 Law of demand shows relation between

A. Income and price of commodity
B. Price and quantity of commodity
C. Income and quantity demanded
D. Quantity demanded and quantity supplied

Q.31 A mixed economy is characterized by the co-existence of

A. Modern and traditional industries
B. Public and private sectors
C. Foreign and domestic investments
D. Commercial and subsistence farming

Q.32 Which of the following is NOT a feature of iso-product curve?

A. Are downward sloping to the right
B. Show different input combination producing the same output
C. Intersect each other
D. Are convex to the origin

Q.33 This is an assumption of law of demand

A. Price of the commodity should not change
B. Quantity should not change
C. Supply should not change
D. Income of consumer should not change

Q.34 Microeconomics deals with the

A. Allocation of resources of the economy as between production of different goods and services
B. Determination of prices of goods and services
C. Behavior of industrial decision makers
D. All of the above

Q.35 Some economists refer to iso-product curves as

A. Engels curve
B. Production indifference curve
C. Budget line
D. Ridge line

Q.36 According to Joseph Schumpeter, profit is the reward for

A. Innovation
B. Uncertainty-bearing
C. Risk-taking
D. Management

Q.37 If quantity demanded is completely unresponsive to changes in price, demand is

A. Inelastic
B. Unit elastic
C. Elastic
D. Perfectly inelastic

Q.38 Which of the following is Microeconomics concerned with?

A. The size of national output
B. The level of employment
C. Changes in general level of prices
D. None of the above

Q.39 Which of the following is also known as plant curves?

A. Long-run average cost (LAC) curves
B. Short-run average cost (SAC) curves
C. Average variable cost (AVC) curves
D. Average total cost (ATC) curves

Q.40 Other things equal, if a good has more substitutes, its price elasticity of demand is

A. Larger
B. Smaller
C. Zero
D. Unity

Q.41 An economic theory is

A. An axiom
B. A proposition
C. A hypothesis
D. A tested hypothesis

Q.42 What is the shape of the average fixed cost (AFC) curve?

A. U-shape
B. Horizontal up to a point and then rising
C. Sloping down towards the right
D. Rectangular hyperbola

Q.43 A decrease in demand causes the equilibrium price to

A. Rise
B. Fall
C. Remain constant
D. Indeterminate

Q.44 Price of a product falls by 10% and its demand rises by 30%. The elasticity of demand is

A. 10%
B. 30%
C. 3
D. 1

Q.45 Identify the aspect of taxation which is related to normative economics

A. Incidence of tax
B. Effect of tax on the capacity willingness to work
C. Equity of tax
D. None of the above

Q.46 If elasticity of demand is very low, it shows that the commodity is

A. A necessity
B. A luxury
C. Has little importance in total budget
D. 'a' and 'c' above

Q.47 An increase in the supply of a commodity is caused by

A. Improvements in technology
B. Fall in the prices of other commodities
C. Fall in the prices of factors of production
D. All of the above

Q.48 When price is below equilibrium level, there will be

A. Surplus commodity in the market
B. Shortage of commodity in the market
C. Supply curve will shift
D. Demand curve will shift

Q.49 The following are causes of shift in demand EXCEPT

A. Change in income
B. Change in price
C. Change in fashion
D. Change in prices of substitutes

Q.50 Demand for a commodity refers to a

A. Desire for the commodity
B. Need for the commodity
C. Quantity demanded of that commodity
D. Quantity of the commodity demanded at a certain price during any particular period of time

Q.51 Elasticity of supply refers to the degree of responsiveness of supply of a commodity to changes in its

A. Demand
B. Price
C. Cost of production
D. State of technology

Q.52 When demand is perfectly inelastic, an increase in price will result in

A. A decrease in total revenue
B. An increase in total revenue
C. No change in total revenue
D. A decrease in quantity demanded

Q.53 The cost on one thing in terms of the alternative given up is known as

A. Production cost
B. Physical cost
C. Real cost
D. Opportunity cost

Q.54 When equilibrium price rises but equilibrium quantity remains unchanged, the cause is

A. Supply and demand both increase equally
B. Supply and demand both decrease equally
C. Supply decreases and demand increases
D. Supply increases and demand decreases

Q.55 If demand is unitary elastic, a 25% increase in price will result in

A. 25% change in total revenue
B. No change in quantity demanded
C. 1% decrease in quantity demanded
D. 25% decrease in quantity demanded

Q.56 Contraction of demand is the result of

A. Decrease in the number of consumers
B. Increase in the price of the commodity concerned
C. Increase in the prices of other goods
D. Decrease in the income of purchasers

Q.57 According to M. Kalecki, the true measure of the degree of monopoly power is the

A. Ratio between price and marginal cost
B. Extent of monopolistic profit enjoyed by the monopolist
C. Cross-elasticity of demand for the product of the monopolist
D. Price charged by the monopolist minus marginal cost of production

Q.58 Price of a product is determined in a free market by

A. Demand for the product
B. Supply of the product
C. Both demand and supply
D. The government

Q.59 When cross elasticity of demand is a large positive number, one can conclude that

A. The good is normal
B. The good is inferior
C. The good is a substitute
D. The good is complement

Q.60 All but one of the following are assumed to remain the same while drawing an individual's demand curve for a commodity. Which one is it?

A. The preferences of the individual
B. His monetary income
C. The price of the commodity under consideration
D. The prices of other goods

Q.61 Which of the following is not an essential condition of pure competition?

A. Large number of buyers and sellers
B. Homogeneous product
C. Freedom of entry
D. Absence of transport cost

Q.62 In market equilibrium, supply is vertical line. The downward sloping demand curve shifts to the right. Then

A. Price will fall
B. Price remains same
C. Price will rise
D. Quantity rises

Q.63 If demand is inelastic, a change in the price

A. Will change the quantity in same direction
B. Will change total revenue in same direction
C. Will change total revenue in the opposite direction
D. Will not change total revenue

Q.64 Which one of the following pairs of commodities is an example of substitutes?

A. Tea and sugar
B. Tea and coffee
C. Pen and ink
D. Shirt and trousers

Q.65 Which one is the assumption of law of demand

A. Price of the commodity should not change
B. Quantity demanded should not change
C. Prices of substitutes should not change
D. Demand curve must be linear

Q.66 What is the shape of the demand curve faced by a firm under perfect competition?

A. Horizontal
B. Vertical
C. Positively sloped
D. Negatively sloped

Q.67 Ten rupees is the equilibrium price for good X. If government fixes the price at Rs.5, there is

A. A shortage
B. A surplus
C. Excess supply
D. Loss

Q.68 A rise in supply and demand in equal proportion will result in

A. Increase in equilibrium price and equilibrium quantity
B. Decrease in equilibrium price and increase in equilibrium quantity
C. No change in equilibrium price and increase in equilibrium quantity
D. Increase in equilibrium price and no change in equilibrium quantity

Q.69 Zubair has a special taste for college canteen's hotdogs. The owner of the canteen doubles the prices of hotdogs. Zubair did not respond to the increase in prices and kept on demanding the same quantity of hotdogs. His demand for hotdogs is

A. Perfectly elastic
B. Perfectly inelastic
C. Elastic
D. Less elastic

Q.70 In the case of a straight-line demand curve meeting the two axes, the price-elasticity of demand at the mid-point of the line would be

A. 0
B. 1
C. 1.5
D. 2

Q.71 Which is the first-order condition for the profit of a firm to be maximum?

A. AC=MR
B. MC=MR
C. MR=AR
D. AC=AR

Q.72 Which of the following is one of the assumptions of perfect competition?

A. Few buyers and few sellers
B. Many buyers and few sellers
C. Many buyers and many sellers
D. All sellers and buyers are honest

Q.73 Price and demand are positively correlated in case of

A. Normal goods
B. Comforts
C. Giffen goods
D. Luxuries

Q.74 Identify the coefficient of price-elasticity of demand when the percentage increase in the quantity of a commodity demanded is smaller than the percentage fall in its price

A. Equal to one
B. Greater than one
C. Smaller than one
D. Zero

Q.75 In which form of the market structure is the degree of control over the price of its product by a firm very large?

A. Monopoly
B. Imperfect condition
C. Oligopoly
D. Perfect competition

Q.76 A firm under perfect competition is

A. Price maker
B. Price breaker
C. Price taker
D. Price shaker

Q.77 The elasticity of demand of durable goods is

A. Less than unity
B. Greater than unity
C. Equal to unity
D. Zero

Q.78 In the case of an inferior good, the income elasticity of demand is

A. Positive
B. Zero
C. Negative
D. Infinite

Q.79 Which is the other name that is given to the average revenue curve?

A. Profit curve
B. Demand curve
C. Average cost curve
D. Indifference curve

Q.80 Which of the following markets comes closest to perfect market?

A. Wheat market
B. Cigarette market
C. Cold drinks market
D. Stock market

Q.81 Mr. Raees Ahamd bought 50 litres of petrol when his monthly income was Rs.25000. Now his monthly income has risen to Rs.50,000 and he purchases 100 litres of petrol. His income elasticity of demand for petrol is:

A. 1
B. 100%
C. Less than 1
D. More than 1

Q.82 Total utility is maximum when

A. Marginal utility is zero
B. Marginal utility is at its highest point
C. Marginal utility is equal to average
D. Average utility is maximum

Q.83 Under which of the following forms of market structure does a firm have no control over the price of its product?

A. Monopoly
B. Monopolistic competition
C. Oligopoly
D. Perfect competition

Q.84 Which is a condition for existence of monopoly?

A. Big size
B. Identical product
C. Absence of government taxes
D. No close substitute

Q.85 When price elasticity of demand for normal goods is calculated, the value is always

A. Positive
B. Negative
C. Constant
D. Greater than

Q.86 If the demand for a commodity is inelastic, an increase in its pice will cause the total expenditure of the consumers of the commodity to

A. Remain the same
B. Increase
C. Decrease
D. Any of the above

Q.87 In case of monopoly

A. Marginal revenue curve always slopes upward
B. Total revenue curve always slopes upward
C. Marginal revenue is always equal to average revenue
D. Marginal revenue is always less than average revenue

Q.88 Income elasticity of demand for normal goods is always

A. 1
B. Negative
C. More than 1
D. Positive

Q.89 The situation of monopolistic competition is created by

A. Small number of producers of a commodity
B. Lack of homogeneity of the product produced by different firms
C. Imperfection of the market for that product
D. All of the above

Q.90 In case of perfect competition in the market

A. Marginal revenue curve always slopes upward
B. Marginal revenue curve always slopes downwards
C. Marginal revenue is always equal to average revenue
D. Marginal revenue is always less than average revenue

Q.91 Demand is a function of

A. Price
B. Quantity
C. Supply
D. None of the above

Q.92 The budget line is also known as the

A. Iso-utility curve
B. Production possibility line
C. Isoquant
D. Consumption possibility line

Q.93 Discriminating monopoly implies that the monopolist charges different prices for its commodity

A. From different groups of consumers
B. For different uses
C. At different places
D. All of the above

Q.94 The major difference between perfect competition and monopolistic competition is

A. Number of firms
B. Differentiated product
C. Rate of profit
D. Free exit and entry

Q.95 Which one is not a assumption of the theory of demand based on analysis of indifference curves?

A. Given scale of preferences as between different combinations of two goods

B. Diminishing marginal rate of substitution

C. Constant marginal utility of money

D. Consumers would always prefer more of a particular good to less of it, other things remaining the same

Q.96 Price discrimination will be profitable only if the elasticity of demand in different markets into which the total market has been divided is

A. Uniform   **B.** Different   **C.** Less   **D.** Zero

Q.97 Marginal revenue is always less than price at all levels of output in

A. Perfect competition   **B.** Monopoly

C. Both 'a' and 'b'   **D.** None of the above

Q.98 What does price elasticity of demand measure?

A. Change in price caused by changes in demand

B. The rate of change of sales

C. The responsiveness of demand to price changes

D. The value of sales at a given price

Q.99 The elasticity of substitution between two perfect substitutions is

A. Zero   **B.** Greater than zero

C. Less than infinity   **D.** Infinity

Q.100 Which of the following is NOT a characteristic of perfect competition?

A. Free entry and exit of the firms

B. The demand curve of firm is horizontal

C. The marginal revenue curve is horizontal

D. An individual firm can influence the price

// Smart Answer Sheet //

Correct — Indicates percentage of students who answered questions correctly.

Skipped — Indicates percentage of students who skipped questions.

Q.	Ans.	Correct / Skipped	Q.	Ans.	Correct / Skipped	Q.	Ans.	Correct / Skipped	Q.	Ans.	Correct / Skipped	Q.	Ans.	Correct / Skipped
1	D	43.21 % / 11.11 %	17	B	50.62 % / 22.22 %	33	D	61.73 % / 13.58 %	49	B	41.98 % / 25.92 %	65	C	37.04 % / 24.69 %
2	D	67.9 % / 16.05 %	18	C	49.38 % / 22.22 %	34	D	67.9 % / 16.05 %	50	D	67.9 % / 20.99 %	66	A	59.26 % / 19.75 %
3	B	35.8 % / 17.29 %	19	D	43.21 % / 17.28 %	35	B	56.79 % / 19.75 %	51	B	66.67 % / 16.05 %	67	A	38.27 % / 24.69 %
4	A	43.21 % / 18.52 %	20	D	48.15 % / 8.64 %	36	A	76.54 % / 14.82 %	52	B	44.44 % / 14.82 %	68	C	48.15 % / 25.92 %
5	B	55.56 % / 24.69 %	21	B	80.25 % / 13.58 %	37	D	48.15 % / 22.22 %	53	D	76.54 % / 20.99 %	69	B	54.32 % / 25.93 %
6	D	43.21 % / 20.99 %	22	B	29.63 % / 19.75 %	38	D	34.57 % / 19.75 %	54	C	45.68 % / 20.99 %	70	B	61.73 % / 24.69 %
7	A	59.26 % / 23.46 %	23	C	60.49 % / 18.52 %	39	B	20.99 % / 22.22 %	55	D	62.96 % / 20.99 %	71	B	66.67 % / 17.28 %
8	D	72.84 % / 20.99 %	24	B	55.56 % / 14.81 %	40	A	54.32 % / 22.22 %	56	B	55.56 % / 20.98 %	72	C	80.25 % / 9.87 %
9	C	44.44 % / 23.46 %	25	D	51.85 % / 24.69 %	41	D	40.74 % / 18.52 %	57	A	29.63 % / 24.69 %	73	C	45.68 % / 20.99 %
10	C	35.8 % / 20.99 %	26	C	59.26 % / 24.69 %	42	D	55.56 % / 18.51 %	58	C	70.37 % / 19.75 %	74	C	54.32 % / 24.69 %
11	D	62.96 % / 18.52 %	27	D	45.68 % / 19.75 %	43	B	48.15 % / 17.28 %	59	D	22.22 % / 18.52 %	75	A	62.96 % / 24.69 %
12	C	60.49 % / 19.76 %	28	C	75.31 % / 22.22 %	44	C	69.14 % / 20.98 %	60	C	29.63 % / 17.28 %	76	C	72.84 % / 20.99 %
13	A	60.49 % / 16.05 %	29	A	38.27 % / 18.52 %	45	C	34.57 % / 17.28 %	61	D	59.26 % / 22.22 %	77	B	41.98 % / 23.45 %
14	A	66.67 % / 17.28 %	30	B	75.31 % / 16.05 %	46	D	29.63 % / 18.52 %	62	C	61.73 % / 22.22 %	78	C	64.2 % / 22.22 %
15	B	64.2 % / 19.75 %	31	B	76.54 % / 17.29 %	47	D	65.43 % / 19.76 %	63	B	38.27 % / 18.52 %	79	B	56.79 % / 16.05 %
16	A	67.9 % / 14.82 %	32	C	71.6 % / 14.82 %	48	B	41.98 % / 19.75 %	64	B	74.07 % / 22.23 %	80	A	55.56 % / 12.34 %

Q.	Ans.	Correct / Skipped
81	A	54.32 %
		19.75 %
82	A	71.6 %
		17.29 %
83	D	64.2 %
		23.45 %
84	D	65.43 %
		20.99 %

Q.	Ans.	Correct / Skipped
85	B	19.75 %
		22.23 %
86	B	45.68 %
		24.69 %
87	D	46.91 %
		23.46 %
88	D	56.79 %
		23.46 %

Q.	Ans.	Correct / Skipped
89	D	56.79 %
		25.93 %
90	C	64.2 %
		24.69 %
91	A	66.67 %
		24.69 %
92	D	50.62 %
		24.69 %

Q.	Ans.	Correct / Skipped
93	D	53.09 %
		17.28 %
94	B	54.32 %
		19.75 %
95	C	37.04 %
		19.75 %
96	B	55.56 %
		18.51 %

Q.	Ans.	Correct / Skipped
97	B	48.15 %
		23.45 %
98	C	61.73 %
		22.22 %
99	D	34.57 %
		18.52 %
100	D	72.84 %
		16.05 %

Performance Analysis

Avg. Score (%)	51.5%
Toppers Score (%)	94.0%
Your Score	

//Hints and Solutions//

1. The capital that is consumed by an economy or a firm in the production process is known as Depreciation. In economics, depreciation is the gradual decrease in the economic value of the capital stock of a firm, nation or other entity, either through physical depreciation, obsolescence or changes in the demand for the services of the capital in question.

2. Haberler propounded the opportunity cost theory of international trade. Gottfried Haberler has attempted to restate the comparative costs in terms of opportunity cost. He demonstrates that the doctrine of comparative costs can hold valid even if the labour theory of value is discarded. The theory determines the cost of producing a commodity in terms of the alternative production that has to be foregone for producing the commodity in question.

3. If two demand curves are linear and intersecting each other, then, coefficient of elasticity would be different on different demand curves at the point of intersection.

4. If the demand for a good is inelastic, an increase in its price will cause the total expenditure of the consumers of the good to increase. Raising prices will always cause total revenue to increase.

5. The horizontal demand curve parallel to x-axis implies that the elasticity of demand is infinite.It is zero when the demand curve is parallel to the y-axis.

6. An individual demand curve slopes downward to the right because of the Working of the law of diminishing marginal utility, Substitution effect of decrease in price and Income effect of fall in price.

7. Income Elasticity of Demand (YED) is defined as the responsiveness of demand when a consumer's income changes. It is defined as the ratio of the change in quantity demand over the change in income. The higher the income elasticity, the more sensitive demand for a good is to changes in income.

8. The supply of a good refers to quantity of the good offered for sale at a particular price per unit of time. The term supply refers to the entire relationship between the quantity supplied and the price of a good.

9. Conditions for market penetration pricing strategy:

• Short-run demand for the product to have elasticity more than unity.

• Availability of economies of large scale production.

• The market is highly price-sensitive and low prices stimulate market growth.

• Low price reduces actual and potential competition

• Easy acceptance and adoption of the product by the consumers.

10. We can conclude with certainty that the equilibrium quantity will decrease.

11. The economist's objections to monopoly rest on the following grounds that there is a transfer of income from consumers to the monopolist and there is welfare loss as resources tend to be misallocated under monopoly.

12. In Monopoly market structure the degree of control over the price of its product by a firm very large. In a monopoly type of market structure, there is only one seller, so a single firm will control the entire market. It can set any price it wishes since it has all the market power. Consumers do not have any alternative and must pay the price set by the seller.

13. The offer curves introduced by Alfred Marshall, helps us to understand how the terms of trade is established in international trade. An offer curve shows how the volumes traded change when the terms of change.

14. Demand for factors of production is derived demand. The demand for any factor of production, such as labor, physical capital or land is a derived demand because it arises not from the intrinsic utility provided by the factor but because of the value placed on the production it produces by consumers.

15. The producer's demand for a factor of production is governed by the marginal productivity of the factor.

16. Under conditions of perfect competition in the product market MRP = VMP. Under the assumption of perfect competition a firm employs a factor up to that number at which the price of the factor is just equal to the value of the marginal product (=MRP of the factor).

17. Index numbers statistical measure helps in measuring the purchasing power of money. Index numbers possess much practical importance in measuring changes in the cost of living, production trends, trade, income variations, etc.

18. Fisher's Ideal volume index is the geometric mean of the Laspeyre's and Paasche's volume indices. A measure of change in volume from period to period. It is calculated as the geometric mean of a chain Paasche's volume index and a chain Laspeyres volume index.

19. A floating exchange rate is one that is determined by supply and demand on the open market. A floating exchange rate doesn't mean countries don't try to intervene and manipulate their currency's price, since governments and central banks regularly attempt to keep their currency price favorable for international trade.

20. Arthur Cecil Pigou succeeded Prof. Marshall as the Professor of Economics at the University of Cambridge. After Marshall, he became the leading neo classical economist. He is the founder of "Welfare Economics" His leading ideas on welfare economics are found in his "Economics of Welfare" (1920).

21. Reserve bank of India is the 'lender of the last resort' in the banking structure of India. A lender of last resort is an institution, usually a country's central bank, that offers loans to banks or other eligible institutions that are experiencing financial difficulty or are considered highly risky or near collapse.

22. Bank rate is the official minimum rate at which the Central Bank of a country is prepared to rediscount approved bills held by the commercial banks.

23. In order to control credit, Reserve Bank of India should Increase CRR and increase Bank rate. During high inflation in the economy, RBI raises the CRR to lower the bank's loanable funds.

24. Collecting and compilation of statistical information relating to banking & other financial sector is a function of the Reserve Bank of India.

25. Credit creation power of the commercial banks gets limited by Banking habits of the people, Cash Reserve Ratio and Credit policy of the central bank.

26. Number of times a unit of money changes hands in the course of a year is called Velocity of money. The velocity of money is the number of times a unit of money changes hands during exchanges in a year.

27. Autarky in international trade means the idea of self sufficiency and no international trade by a country. A country is said to be in a complete state of autarky if it has a closed economy, which means that it does not engage in international trade with any other country.

28. Normally a demand curve will have downward sloping shape. The demand curve is downward sloping, indicating the negative relationship between the price of a product and the quantity demanded.

29. L. Robbins defined economics: "Economics is the science which studies human behaviour as a relationship between ends and scarce means which have alternative uses."

30. Law of demand shows relation between Price and quantity of commodity. Quantity demanded of a commodity is inversely related to the price of the commodity.

31. A mixed economy is characterized by the co-existence of Public and private sectors. Mixed economies, with state-supervised markets, are most related to fascism (in the economic sense) and have several common features.

32. Iso-product curves does not intersect each other that's a significant feature of Iso-product curves.

33. Income of consumer should not change is an assumption of law of demand. The first assumption regarding the law of demand to operate is that the income of the consumer must remain same or should not change (i.e. neither rise nor fall).

34. Microeconomics deals with the Allocation of resources of the economy as between production of different goods and services, Determination of prices of goods and services and Behavior of industrial decision makers.

35. Some economists refer to iso-product curves as Production indifference curve. A given quantity of output may be produced with different combinations of factors. Iso-quant curves are also known as Equal-product or Iso-product or Production Indifference curves.

36. According to Joseph Schumpeter, profit is the reward for Innovation. He believed that an entrepreneur can earn economic profits by introducing successful innovations.

37. If quantity demanded is completely unresponsive to changes in price, demand is Perfectly inelastic. Perfectly inelastic demand means that quantity demanded remains the same when price increases or decreases. Consumers are completely unresponsive to changes in price.

38. Microeconomics is primarily concerned with the factors that affect individual economic choices, the effect of changes in these factors on the individual decision makers, how their choices are coordinated by markets, and how prices and demand are determined in individual markets.

39. Short-run average cost (SAC) curves is also known as plant curves. These SACs are also called plant curves. In the short run, a firm can operate on any SAC, given the size of the plant.

40. Other things equal, if a good has more substitutes, its price elasticity of demand is larger.

41. An economic theory is a tested hypothesis. Hypothesis testing is an act in statistics whereby an analyst tests an assumption regarding a population parameter. The methodology employed by the analyst depends on the nature of the data used and the reason for the analysis. Hypothesis testing is used to infer the result of a hypothesis performed on sample data from a larger population.

42. Rectangular hyperbola is the shape of the average fixed cost (AFC) curve. The AFC curve is a rectangular hyperbola in the sense that all rectangles formed by AFC are of equal sizes.

43. A decrease in demand causes the equilibrium price to Fall. A decrease in demand and an increase in supply will cause a fall in equilibrium price, but the effect on equilibrium quantity cannot be determined.

44. Price of a product falls by 10% and its demand rises by 30%. The elasticity of demand is 3.

45. The aspect of taxation which is related to normative economics is Equity of tax.

46. If elasticity of demand is very low, it shows that the commodity is necessity and has little importance in total budget.

47. An increase in the supply of a commodity is caused by Improvements in technology, Fall in the prices of other commodities and Fall in the prices of factors of production.

48. When price is below equilibrium level, there will be Shortage of commodity in the market.

49. The following are causes of shift in demand except Change in price. A shift in the demand curve is when a determinant of demand, other than price, changes. A shift to the left means demand drops, and vice-versa.

50. Demand for a commodity refers to a quantity of the commodity demanded at a certain price during any particular period of time.

51. Elasticity of supply refers to the degree of responsiveness of supply of a commodity to changes in its Price. Elasticity of supply measures the degree of responsiveness of quantity supplied to a change in own price of the commodity. It is also defined as the percentage change in quantity supplied divided by percentage change in price.

52. When demand is perfectly inelastic, an increase in price will result in an increase in total revenue.

53. The cost on one thing in terms of the alternative given up is known as Opportunity cost. Opportunity cost is an economics term that refers to the value of what you have to give up in order to choose something else.

54. When equilibrium price rises but equilibrium quantity remains unchanged, the cause is supply decreases and demand increases. As price increases, it serves as an incentive for suppliers to increase supply and also leads to a fall in demand. It is important to realize that these processes continue to operate until a new equilibrium is established.

55. If demand is unitary elastic, a 25% increase in price will result in 25% decrease in quantity demanded.

56. Contraction of demand is the result of Increase in the price of the commodity concerned. The demand for a commodity changes due to a change in price. It is called extension and contraction of demand. When there is decrease in price of commodity there is in increase in demand of that commodity.

57. According to M. Kalecki, the true measure of the degree of monopoly power is the Ratio between price and marginal cost. Monopoly is the form of market organisation in which there is a single firm selling a commodity for which there are no close substitutes.

58. Price of a product is determined in a free market by both demand and supply. In microeconomics, supply and demand is an economic model of price determination in a market. It postulates that, holding all else equal, in a competitive market, the unit price for a particular good, or other traded item such as labor or liquid financial assets, will vary until it settles at a point where the quantity demanded (at the current price) will equal the quantity supplied (at the current price), resulting in an economic equilibrium for price and quantity transacted.

59. When cross elasticity of demand is a large positive number, one can conclude that the good is complement. Two goods that complement each other have a negative cross elasticity of demand: as the price of good Y rises, the demand for good X falls.

60. The price of the commodity under consideration are assumed to remain the same while drawing an individual's demand curve for a commodity.

61. Absence of transport cost is not an essential condition of pure competition. If the two conditions of pure competition are fulfilled, there can be no question of monopolistic control. In perfect competition, apart from the absence of monopoly, some other conditions are also essential, e.g., free entry and exit, the absence of transport cost, perfect knowledge.

62. In market equilibrium, supply is vertical line. The downward sloping demand curve shifts to the right, then Price will rise.

63. If demand is inelastic, a change in the price will change total revenue in same direction. When demand is price inelastic, a given percentage change in price results in a smaller percentage change in quantity demanded. That implies that total revenue will

move in the direction of the price change: an increase in price will increase total revenue, and a reduction in price will reduce it.

64. Tea and coffee pairs of commodities is an example of substitutes. This is a negative relationship, as is true for all pairs of goods that are complements.

65. Prices of substitutes should not change is the assumption of law of demand. For example if the price of Coke is decreased then it will lead to fall in the demand for Pepsi even when the price of Pepsi has remain constant as Pepsi is close substitute of Coke, in the same way if the price of Coke is increased than it will lead to rise in demand for Pepsi.

66. The shape of the demand curve faced by a firm under perfect competition is Horizontal. The demand curve faced by a firm in a perfectly competitive market is infinitely elastic. Graphically, this means that it is a horizontal line at the market price.

67. Ten rupees is the equilibrium price for good X. If government fixes the price at Rs.5, there is a shortage.

68. A rise in supply and demand in equal proportion will result in no change in equilibrium price and increase in equilibrium quantity.

69. Zubair has a special taste for college canteen's hotdogs. The owner of the canteen doubles the prices of hotdogs. Zubair did not respond to the increase in prices and kept on demanding the same quantity of hotdogs. His demand for hotdogs is perfectly inelastic.

70. In the case of a straight-line demand curve meeting the two axes, the price-elasticity of demand at the mid-point of the line would be 1.

71. MC=MR is the first-order condition for the profit of a firm to be maximum. The Profit Maximization Rule states that if a firm chooses to maximize its profits, it must choose that level of output where Marginal Cost (MC) is equal to Marginal Revenue (MR) and the Marginal Cost curve is rising. In other words, it must produce at a level where MC = MR.

72. Many buyers and many sellers is one of the assumptions of perfect competition. Yes, in a perfectly competitive market, there are many buyers and many sellers. As a consequence, they have no market power and cannot influence the market price. This is an assumption of the model of perfect competition.

73. Price and demand are positively correlated in case of Giffen goods. A Giffen good is a product for which demand increases as the price increases and falls when the price decreases.

74. The coefficient of price-elasticity of demand is smaller than one when the percentage increase in the quantity of a commodity demanded is smaller than the percentage fall in its price.

75. In Monopoly market structure the degree of control over the price of its product by a firm very large. In a monopoly type of market structure, there is only one seller, so a single firm will control the entire market. It can set any price it wishes since it has all the market power.

76. A firm under perfect competition is Price taker. In perfect market conditions (also called perfect competition) a firm is a price taker because other firms can enter the market easily and produce a product that is indistinguishable from every other firm's product. This makes it impossible for any firm to set its own prices.

77. The elasticity of demand of durable goods is greater than unity. Price elasticity of demand for durable goods is generally more elastic in short run than in long run. That is, quantity demanded is more sensitive to price changes of such durable goods in short run and not so much in the long run.

78. In the case of an inferior good, the income elasticity of demand is Negative. A negative income elasticity of demand is associated with inferior goods; an increase in income will lead to a fall in the demand and may lead to changes to more luxurious substitutes.

79. Demand curve is the other name that is given to the average revenue curve. Average revenue curve is often called the demand curve due to its representation of the product's demand in the market.

80. Wheat market comes closest to perfect market. A perfectly competitive firm is called a price taker, because the pressure of competing firms forces them to accept the prevailing equilibrium price in the market. When a wheat grower wants to know what the going price of wheat is, he or she has to go to the computer or listen to the radio to check.

81. Mr. Raees Ahamd bought 50 litres of petrol when his monthly income was Rs.25000. Now his monthly income has risen to Rs.50,000 and he purchases 100 litres of petrol. His income elasticity of demand for petrol is 1.

82. Total utility is maximum when Marginal utility is zero. It is based in the law of diminishing marginal utility which says 'as more and more units of a good are consumed, MU i.e level of satisfaction derived from each successive unit goes on falling because desire for that commodity tend to fall.

83. Under Perfect competition forms of market structure does a firm have no control over the price of its product. All goods in a perfectly competitive market are considered perfect substitutes, and the demand curve is perfectly elastic for each of the small, individual firms that participate in the market. These firms are price takers–if one firm tries to raise its price, there would be no demand for that firm's product.

84. No close substitute is a condition for existence of monopoly. If a close substitute exists, then the monopoly cannot exist. Remember, a monopoly can only exist when the cross-elasticity of the product that the monopolist produces is zero.

85. When price elasticity of demand for normal goods is calculated, the value is always Negative. The PED is the percentage change in quantity demanded in response to a one percent change in price. The PED coefficient is usually negative, although economists often ignore the sign. Demand for a good is relatively inelastic if the PED coefficient is less than one (in absolute value).

86. If the demand for a commodity is inelastic, an increase in its price will cause the total expenditure of the consumers of the commodity to Increase. When demand is inelastic, a fall in the price of a commodity leads to fall in total expenditure on it. On the other hand, when price increases, total expenditure also increases.

87. In case of monopoly, Marginal revenue is always less than average revenue. A monopolist's marginal revenue is always less than or equal to the price of the good. Marginal revenue is the amount of revenue the firm receives for each additional unit of output.

88. Income elasticity of demand for normal goods is always Positive. A positive income elasticity of demand is associated with normal goods; an increase in income will lead to a rise in demand.

89. The situation of monopolistic competition is created by Small number of producers of a commodity, Lack of homogeneity of the product produced by different firms and Imperfection of the market for that product.

90. In case of perfect competition in the market marginal revenue is always equal to average revenue. They coincide because marginal revenue is equal to average revenue at every output quantity. The equality between marginal revenue and average revenue is the result of perfect competition.

91. Demand is a function of Price. An increase in the price of the commodity decrease the demand for that commodity, while the decrease in price increases its demand.

92. The budget line is also known as the Consumption possibility line. The CPF, or consumption–possibility frontier, is the budget constraint where participants in international trade can consume.

93. Discriminating monopoly implies that the monopolist charges different prices for its commodity From different groups of consumers, for different uses and at different places.

94. The major difference between perfect competition and monopolistic competition is differentiated product. Product differentiation (or simply differentiation) is the process of distinguishing a product or service from others, to make it more attractive to a particular target market. This involves differentiating it from competitors' products as well as a firm's own products.

95. Constant marginal utility of money is not a assumption of the theory of demand based on analysis of indifference curves. An indifference curve is a graph that shows a combination of two goods that give a consumer equal satisfaction and utility, thereby making the consumer indifferent.

96. Price discrimination will be profitable only if the elasticity of demand in different markets into which the total market has been divided is different.

97. Marginal revenue is always less than price at all levels of output in Monopoly. A monopolist's marginal revenue is always less than or equal to the price of the good. Marginal revenue is the amount of revenue the firm receives for each additional unit of output.

98. The price elasticity of demand measures the responsiveness of the quantity demanded to changes in the price. Demand is inelastic if it does not respond much to price changes, and elastic if demand changes a lot when the price changes. Necessities tend to have inelastic demand.

99. The elasticity of substitution between two perfect substitutions is Infinity. Elasticity of factor substitution can take any value from zero to infinity, always being positive.

100. An individual firm can influence the price is not a characteristic of perfect competition. All goods in a perfectly competitive market are considered perfect substitutes, and the demand curve is perfectly elastic for each of the small, individual firms that participate in the market. These firms are price takers–if one firm tries to raise its price, there would be no demand for that firm's product.

Q.1 ADB has forecasted India's current economic growth forecast for this fiscal by 0.3% to ___.

A. 6.6 percent   **B.** 6.7 percent

C. 6.8 percent   **D.** 6.9 percent

Q.2 Which scheme is working for creating digital inclusion and equitable growth in the BPO sector?

A. India BPO Development Scheme

B. India BPO Growth Scheme

C. India BPO Promotion Scheme

D. India BPO Advancement Scheme

Q.3 India's first electronic manufacturing cluster will come up in which state?

A. Andhra Pradesh   **B.** Madhya Pradesh

C. Chhattisgarh   **D.** Karnataka

Q.4 Fed Reserve raised interest rates by what percent on Dec 13, 2017 ?

A. Quarter of a percentage point

B. Half of a percentage point

C. Single percentage point

D. Double percentage point

Q.5 What is the MSME Public Procurement Portal called?

A. MSME Samjhauta   **B.** MSME Sambandh

C. MSME Sandesh   **D.** MSME Sampark

Q.6 India is the _____ largest fish producer in the world.

A. Third   **B.** Fifth

C. Eighth   **D.** None of the above

Q.7 According to IEA, Indians without access to electricity fell to what number in 2016 from 1.7 bn in 2000?

A. 1.4 bn   **B.** 1.3 bn   **C.** 1.2 bn   **D.** 1.1 bn

Q.8 Monetary policy committee of RBI decided to keep repo rate _____ at 6% on 6th Dec, 2017.

A. Unchanged   **B.** High

C. Low   **D.** Moderate

Q.9 The third edition of the DRC-NITI Aayog Dialogue was held in _____.

A. Bengaluru   **B.** Beijing

C. Shenzen   **D.** New Delhi

Q.10 Multilateral funding agency Asian Development Bank (ADB) on 29th Nov said it will provide a loan to improve rural road connectivity in five states, including Assam and West Bengal. How much is the amount?

A. $500 million   **B.** $250 million

C. $400 million   **D.** Rs 1 lac crore

Q.11 India has recorded one of the highest growth rate in the world in which aspect in last six years?

A. Number of hospitals

B. Number of jails

C. Number of petrol pumps

D. Number of malls

Q.12 The government has set up the National Anti-Profiteering Authority amid reports that some companies, particularly restaurants, are not passing on the benefit of ________ to consumers.

A. Interest Rate Cuts

B. GST Rate Cuts

C. VAT Rate Cuts

D. Income Tax Refunds

Q.13 Commerce and Industry Minister Suresh Prabhu announced the new industrial policy that will seek to promote emerging sectors. When will it be released?

A. 2019   **B.** 2018   **C.** 2017   **D.** 2020

Q.14 The Union Ministry of Housing & Urban Affairs has announced that 30.76 lakh houses for the urban poor have been sanctioned so far since the launch of which scheme in June 2015?

A. Pradhan Mantri Awas Yojana (Rural) Scheme

B. Pradhan Mantri Awas Yojana (Urban) Scheme

C. Pradhan Mantri Jevan Bhima Yojana (Urban) Scheme

D. Pradhan Mantri Rozgar Yojana (Urban) Scheme

Q.15 The Union Cabinet chaired by the Prime Minister Narendra Modi has approved setting up of 15th Finance Commission (FC) under which article?

A. Article 280 (1)   **B.** Article 290 (1)

C. Article 300 (1)   **D.** Article 100 (1)

Q.16 India's food processing sector has the potential to attract $33 billion investment by 2024, according to a study by which trade body?

A. ASSOCHAM   **B.** Nasscom

C. FICCI   **D.** IMC

Q.17 India was at what rank among 63 countries on the IMD Talent Rankings in terms of ability to attract, develop and retain talent?

A. 25   **B.** 50   **C.** 51   **D.** 54

Q.18 Which is India's first mega coastal economic zone (CEZ)?

A. Vizag Port

B. Chennai Port

C. Jawaharlal Nehru Port

D. Indira Gandhi Port

Q.19 The Union Government has signed a guarantee agreement for IBRD/CTF loan for Solar Parks Project with which international body?

A. International Monetary Fund

B. United States Government
C. World Bank
D. Global Bank

Q.20 The Union Cabinet approved setting up of which apex body under Goods and Services Tax (GST) regime so as to ensure the benefit of tax reaches consumers?
A. National Good and Services Authority
B. National GST Tax Authority
C. National Anti-profiteering Authority
D. National Anti-laundering Authority

Q.21 The Cabinet Committee on Economic Affairs gave its approval for removing the prohibition on the export of what type of items?
A. Steel Ingots   **B.** Textiles
C. Pulses   **D.** Onions

Q.22 CBDT reported a rise in PAN applications post demonetisation. What was the number?
A. 300%   **B.** 200%   **C.** 500%   **D.** 100%

Q.23 Commerce Ministry closed down its nearly 100-year-old public procurement arm called __________.
A. DGS&B   **B.** DGS&D   **C.** DGC&A   **D.** DGP&T

Q.24 Bharti Airtel has offloaded 83 million shares of which subsidiary on Nov 14, 2017?
A. Bharti Televentures
B. Bharti Infratel
C. Bharti-AXA Life Insurance
D. Tikona Infinet Limited

Q.25 Which trade body released the report "Ideate, Innovate, Implement" in Nov 2017 on impact of GST?
A. ASSOCHAM
B. FICCI
C. PhD Chambers of Commerce
D. CRISIL

Q.26 Minister of State for Power and New & Renewable Energy launched which portal for the power sector?
A. Indian Power Portal   **B.** Garv
C. Urja   **D.** Tarang

Q.27 GST Council took a slew of decisions during the 23rd meeting including which of the following:
A. Rate cuts for consumers
B. Reduction of tax on restaurants
C. Businesses to benefit from compliance norm easing
D. All of the above

Q.28 GST Council is set to liberalise which scheme for small business owners to pay flat tax on turnover?
A. Composition scheme
B. Operation scheme
C. Tax liability scheme
D. Both a and c

Q.29 Government has doubled import duty on which crop to 20 percent to curb cheap shipments in Nov 2017?

A. Bajra   **B.** Rice   **C.** Jowar   **D.** Wheat

Q.30 Two MoUs have been signed between Haryana Vishwakarma Skill University and which two other organizations to create skill development and entrepreneurship on 8th Nov 2017?
A. Indian Institute of Corporate Affairs, Atal Innovation Mission- Niti Aayog
B. FICCI, Atal Innovation Mission- Niti Aayog
C. ASSOCHAM, Atal Innovation Mission- Niti Aayog
D. PHD Chambers of Commerce, Atal Innovation Mission- Niti Aayog

Q.31 Indian engineering exports are benefitting from a turnaround from the US which accounted for what percent of the demand?
A. 90%   **B.** 91%   **C.** 92%   **D.** 93%

Q.32 During Jan-Sept 2017, which state emerged as the top investment destination in India?
A. Gujarat   **B.** Karnataka
C. Kerala   **D.** Delhi

Q.33 India is set to become the third largest aviation market in the world in terms of _____ by 2026.
A. Passengers   **B.** Routes traversed
C. Airplanes   **D.** Airports

Q.34 Government has constituted a ministerial panel to oversee merger proposals of which banks in Nov 2017?
A. State owned banks   **B.** PSB
C. PSU banks   **D.** All of the above

Q.35 India will be the third largest economy within a span of how many years, according to HSBC estimates?
A. 5   **B.** 7   **C.** 8   **D.** 10

Q.36 According to an IATA report, India is the _____ largest aviation market in 2025.
A. Fourth   **B.** Fifth
C. Sixth   **D.** None of the above

Q.37 Bharatmala Pariyojana seeks to provide _______ outlay of road construction in the Modi government.
A. Largest   **B.** Smallest
C. Around 5.35 trillion   **D.** Both a and c

Q.38 ADB and GOI have signed a USD 300m loan to improve quality of public service delivery in which state?
A. West Bengal   **B.** Odisha
C. Bihar   **D.** Jharkhand

Q.39 MP is the ___ highest in milk production in the country, according to its animal husbandry department.
A. First   **B.** Second   **C.** Third   **D.** Fifth

Q.40 Payments Council of India estimates PPIs will rise to what percent in half a decade from less than 10 percent now?
A. 30-40 percent   **B.** 40-50 percent
C. 50-60 percent   **D.** 60-70 percent

Q.41 According to World Bank, India's GDP may lower from 8.6% in 2015 to what percent in 2017?

A. 6   **B.** 6.5   **C.** 7   **D.** 7.5

Q.42 Who heads the GoM of Finance Ministers of state to look into the GST composition scheme?

A. Amar Agarwal
B. Haseeb Drabu
C. Himant Biswa Sarma
D. Parminder Singh Dhindsa

Q.43 What is the repo rate?

A. Rate at which central bank lends short term money to banks
B. Rate at which central bank lends long term funds to banks
C. Rate at which central bank borrows short term money from banks
D. Rate at which central bank borrows long term funds from banks

Q.44 Global cotton output is set to rise by what percent in 2017-2018 according to ICAC?

A. 15 percent   **B.** 12 percent
C. 13 percent   **D.** 10 percent

Q.45 IBBI has registered which company as the first Information Utility?

A. NeSL   **B.** NSL   **C.** NEL   **D.** NLSE

Q.46 Web Portal of Warehousing Development and Regulatory Authority was launched with which system by Ministry of Consumer Affairs, Food and Public Distribution?

A. Electronic Negotiable Warehouse Receipt System
B. e-NWR system
C. Electronic Navigation Warehouse Receipt System
D. Both a and b are the same

Q.47 RBI has relaxed norms for which of the following bonds?

A. Masala bonds
B. Rupee denominated overseas bonds
C. Green bonds
D. Both a and b

Q.48 Which platforms will be treated as NBFCs and regulated by RBI?

A. peer to peer lending   **B.** P2P
C. B2C   **D.** Only a and b

Q.49 REIT and InVITS have been allowed to raise capital by which means?

A. Issuing debt securities
B. Initiating IPO
C. Making investments in stock market
D. Raising loans

Q.50 India has ranked at which position on the WEF Global Human Capital Index?

A. 103   **B.** 104   **C.** 105   **D.** 106

Q.51 GoI has pledged to double farmer income by which year?

A. 2019   **B.** 2020   **C.** 2021   **D.** 2022

Q.52 How many districts grew pulses in 2016-2017 as against 2012-2013 according to the 4th Estimates?

A. 638 districts of 29 states
B. 538 districts of 29 states
C. 438 districts of 29 states
D. 338 districts of 29 states

Q.53 ECB had initiated Ogden rate changes which ____ the earnings of UK insurers.

A. Slashed   **B.** Lowered
C. Raised   **D.** a and b are the same

Q.54 What is Project Insight?

A. Project for monitoring high value transactions to curb circulation of black money
B. Data mining, collation, collection and processing of such information
C. Effective risk management to widen tax base
D. All of the above

Q.55 What are the 4 indices under the framework of the National Nutrition Strategy?

A. uptake of contraceptive services, food, drinking water & sanitation and income & livelihoods
B. uptake of health services, food, drinking water & sanitation and income & livelihoods
C. uptake of mental health services, food, drinking water & sanitation and income & livelihoods
D. uptake of emergency services, food, drinking water & sanitation and income & livelihoods

Q.56 According to the Quarterly Public Debt Management Report Apr-June 2017, the weighted average yield maturity was ______.

A. 14.72 years   **B.** 14.82 years
C. 14.92 years   **D.** 14.52 years

Q.57 Which premium aromatic variety of rice cultivated by farmers in West Bengal got GI tag?

A. Gobindo Bhog   **B.** Chappan Bhog
C. Samriddhi Bhog   **D.** Krishna Bhog

Q.58 SNLP has illuminated ______ km of Indian roads in Aug 2017.

A. 50 thousand   **B.** 55 thousand
C. 60 thousand   **D.** 65 thousand

Q.59 Union Cabinet gave approval for expediting strategic disinvestment of which companies?

A. State owned   **B.** Public
C. Private   **D.** Both a and b

Q.60 What is the nationwide policy for general health launched in 2017 called?

A. National Health Programme 2017
B. National Health Policy 2017
C. National Health Plan 2017
D. National Health Yojana 2017

Q.61 What is the percentage growth of the real economy in 2016-2017?

A. 7%   **B.** 7.1%   **C.** 7.2%   **D.** 7.3%

Q.62 India has ratified the ___ commitment period of the Kyoto protocol in Aug 2017.

A. First   **B.** Second   **C.** Third   **D.** Fourth

Q.63 Which project unveiled in July 2016 to make India's logistics sector efficient through IT, will now expand to South India?

A.   Logistics Data Bank
B.   Logistics Development Bank
C.   Logistics Dual Bank
D.   Logistics Deceleration Bank

Q.64 What is the NABARD pilot project for digitisation of SHGs called?

A. e-Shakti   **B.** e-Samriddhi
C. e-Shanti   **D.** e-Samraksha

Q.65 Under Pradhan Mantri Paridhan Rojgar Protsahan Yojana, how much of the share of employee's contribution of EPF will the Ministry of Textiles bear, in addition to 8.33%?

A. 3.47 percent   **B.** 3.57 percent
C. 3.67 percent   **D.** 3.77 percent

Q.66 Indian telecom industry indicated India has which rank in terms of total internet users?

A. 2nd   **B.** 3rd   **C.** 4th   **D.** 5th

Q.67 What is the name of first digital banking branch of Canara Bank, located in Bengaluru?

A. CANDI   **B.** CANTI   **C.** CANKI   **D.** CANM

Q.68 How many broadband connections does the National Telecom Policy envisage by 2020?

A. 500 million   **B.** 600 million
C. 800 million   **D.** 1 billion

Q.69 SIDBI has started which operations to benefit MSMEs w.e.f 27th July 2017?

A.   Rural banking
B.   Issue of participatory notes
C.   MF management
D.   Merchant banking

Q.70 Case Study on birth of which tax system in India was launched by the FM on 25th July 2017?

A. Indirect Tax   **B.** Direct Tax
C. Sales Tax   **D.** None of the above

Q.71 What does NTFAP stand for in the context of trade?

A.   National Trade Facilitation Action Programme
B.   National Trading Facilitation Action Programme
C.   National Trade Facilitation Action Plan
D.   National Trading Facilitation Action Plan

Q.72 World Bank's latest edition of Global Economic Prospects says India is ____ fastest growing economy in the world.

A. 2nd   **B.** 3rd   **C.** 4th   **D.** 5th

Q.73 IBBI stands for which of the following?

A.   Insolvency and Banking Board of India
B.   Insolvency and Bankruptcy Board of India
C.   Insolvency and Board of Bankruptcy of India
D.   Insufficiency and Bankruptcy Board of India

Q.74 According to GoI, allowing more deposits of old INR 500 and 1000 notes will lead to?

A.   Benami transactions
B.   Defeat the purpose of demonetisation
C.   Both a and b
D.   None of the above

Q.75 India has topped which OECD report?

A.   Government at a Glance 2017
B.   Government Factsheet 2017
C.   Government Index 2017
D.   None of the above

Q.76 Which is the world's third largest oil importer?

A. Bangladesh   **B.** Pakistan
C. Nepal   **D.** India

Q.77 A new tax payer service module was compiled by the IT dept called __________.

A. Aaykar Setu   **B.** Aaykar Jyoti
C. Aaykar Yojana   **D.** Aaykar Rupee

Q.78 President of India promulgated two ordinances for which state to join GST?

A. Mizoram   **B.** Manipur   **C.** J&K   **D.** HP

Q.79 When are traders exempt from GST registration?

A.   When annual turnover is more than 20 lakhs and does not involve interstate supply
B.   When annual turnover is less than 20 lakhs and does not involve interstate supply
C.   When annual turnover is more than 15 lakhs and does involve interstate supply
D.   When annual turnover is more than 13 lakhs and does involve interstate supply

Q.80 World Bank has cleared a loan to aid which Indian mission?

A. Start up India   **B.** Stand up India
C. Skill India   **D.** None of the above

Q.81 Which publication was released by RBI in June 2017 on gross fiscal deficits of states?

A.   Handbook of Statistics on States 2016-2017
B.   Handbook of Statistics on States 2015-2016
C.   Handbook of Statistics on States Second Edition
D.   Both a and c are same

Q.82 Which number has been made essential for opening bank accounts and for transactions exceeding INR 50,000?

A. TIN   **B.** TAN   **C.** PAN   **D.** Aadhaar

Q.83 RBI has indicated that India's CAD has narrowed due to contraction in the ____ deficit.

A. Fiscal
B. Monetary
C. Trade
D. None of the above

Q.84 Match the following:

(A) *Principles of Economics*   1. *Gunnar Myrdal*
(B) *Diamond water paradox*   2. *J. K. Galbraith*
(C) *Value and Capital*   3. *Alfred Marshall*
(D) *Asian Drama*   4. *J. R. Hicks*
(E) *Language of Economics*   5. *Adam Smith*

A.

(A)	(B)	(C)	(D)	(E)
5	2	3	1	4

B.

(A)	(B)	(C)	(D)	(E)
2	4	3	5	1

C.

(A)	(B)	(C)	(D)	(E)
1	2	3	5	4

D.

(A)	(B)	(C)	(D)	(E)
3	5	4	1	2

Q.85 What is the aim of the Financial Resolution and Deposit Insurance Bill, 2017?

A. Provide the resolution framework for specified financial sector to deal with bankruptcy situations in banks, insurance companies and financial sector entities.
B. Pave the way for Resolution Corporation
C. Repeal or amendment of resolution related provisions in sectoral Acts as listed in Bill schedules
D. All of the above

Q.86 The concept of supply curve as used in economic theory is relevant only for the case of

A. Oligopoly competition
B. Perfect or pure competition
C. Monopolistic competition
D. Monopoly

Q.87 Which government insurance body is taking over Sahara India Life Insurance Company?

A. LIC
B. GIC
C. IRDAI
D. None of the above

Q.88 RBI forex reserves have touched a lifetime high on June 2 at ____________.

A. USD 381.167 billion
B. USD 391.167 billion
C. USD 401.167 billion
D. None of the above

Q.89 Ministries will now have to decide on FDI proposals within ______ days of application, w.e.f 6th June 2017?

A. 60 days   **B.** 65 days   **C.** 70 days   **D.** 75 days

Q.90 Match the following:

(A) *Increasing cost industry*   1. *Horizontal long run supply curve*
(B) *Decreasing cost industry*   2. *Positively sloped long run supply curve*
(C) *Constant cost industry*   3. *Negatively sloped long run supply curve*

A.

(A)	(B)	(C)
3	2	1

B.

(A)	(B)	(C)
1	2	3

C.

(A)	(B)	(C)
2	3	1

D.

(A)	(B)	(C)
2	1	3

Q.91 Fitch group BMI research has indicated India is one of __ top consumers in Asia.

A. 4   **B.** 5   **C.** 6   **D.** 7

Q.92 India has ranked at which place in the IMD World Competitiveness List?

A. 40
B. 44
C. 47
D. None of the above

Q.93 Which is the first railway station of the country to be redeveloped using PPP mode?

A. Habibganj
B. Hazratganj
C. Hafeezganj
D. None of the above

Q.94 Who chairs the SEBI committee on Corporate Governance?

A. Uday Kotak
B. Adi Godrej
C. Ratan Tata
D. None of the above

Q.95 India lost its fastest growing major economy tag in _____ of FY 2016-2017.

A. Q1   **B.** Q2   **C.** Q3   **D.** Q4

Q.96 Which is the third largest aviation market in the world?

A. China
B. UK
C. US
D. None of the above

Q.97 IOC has overtaken which PSU to become India's most profitable state owned company?

A. ONGC
B. BSNL
C. MTNL
D. None of the above

Q.98 DIPP has amended the startup definition to include which of the following?

A. A startup has a turnover not less than 25 crores
B. It has not completed 7 years from day of incorporation
C. Both of the above
D. Neither of the above

Q.99 Cochin Port Trust has received performance awards for which feat(s) from Ministry of Shipping?

A. Highest growth in operating surplus
B. Third highest growth in cargo traffic among major ports in 2016-2017
C. Both of the above
D. Neither of the above

Q.100 What rates are the 4 slab service tax structures proposed by the GST council?

A. 5,12,18,28
B. 6,13,19, 29
C. 7, 14, 20, 30
D. None of the above

// Smart Answer Sheet //

Correct   Indicates percentage of students who answered questions correctly.

Skipped   Indicates percentage of students who skipped questions.

Q.	Ans.	Correct / Skipped	Q.	Ans.	Correct / Skipped	Q.	Ans.	Correct / Skipped	Q.	Ans.	Correct / Skipped	Q.	Ans.	Correct / Skipped
1	B	30.77 % / 27.69 %	17	C	24.62 % / 38.46 %	33	A	33.85 % / 30.77 %	49	A	10.77 % / 38.46 %	65	C	24.62 % / 40.0 %
2	C	20.0 % / 32.31 %	18	C	24.62 % / 38.46 %	34	D	36.92 % / 30.77 %	50	A	27.69 % / 36.93 %	66	A	26.15 % / 32.31 %
3	A	30.77 % / 35.38 %	19	C	52.31 % / 26.15 %	35	D	27.69 % / 36.93 %	51	D	44.62 % / 33.84 %	67	A	36.92 % / 38.46 %
4	A	29.23 % / 33.85 %	20	C	20.0 % / 18.46 %	36	D	12.31 % / 35.38 %	52	A	23.08 % / 32.3 %	68	B	20.0 % / 43.08 %
5	B	29.23 % / 40.0 %	21	C	24.62 % / 27.69 %	37	D	36.92 % / 35.39 %	53	D	27.69 % / 36.93 %	69	D	24.62 % / 38.46 %
6	D	16.92 % / 40.0 %	22	A	20.0 % / 33.85 %	38	A	21.54 % / 40.0 %	54	D	44.62 % / 38.46 %	70	D	16.92 % / 40.0 %
7	D	23.08 % / 36.92 %	23	B	26.15 % / 27.7 %	39	C	20.0 % / 36.92 %	55	B	43.08 % / 33.84 %	71	C	33.85 % / 30.77 %
8	A	35.38 % / 38.47 %	24	B	26.15 % / 29.23 %	40	A	29.23 % / 40.0 %	56	C	21.54 % / 36.92 %	72	C	20.0 % / 29.23 %
9	B	13.85 % / 38.46 %	25	A	26.15 % / 40.0 %	41	C	24.62 % / 35.38 %	57	A	27.69 % / 40.0 %	73	B	47.69 % / 36.93 %
10	A	18.46 % / 40.0 %	26	A	23.08 % / 40.0 %	42	C	35.38 % / 33.85 %	58	A	24.62 % / 40.0 %	74	C	38.46 % / 38.46 %
11	C	20.0 % / 35.38 %	27	D	53.85 % / 32.3 %	43	A	36.92 % / 33.85 %	59	D	46.15 % / 32.31 %	75	A	24.62 % / 36.92 %
12	B	41.54 % / 33.84 %	28	D	49.23 % / 30.77 %	44	D	18.46 % / 33.85 %	60	B	32.31 % / 32.31 %	76	D	50.77 % / 36.92 %
13	B	15.38 % / 33.85 %	29	D	30.77 % / 33.85 %	45	A	18.46 % / 35.39 %	61	B	24.62 % / 33.84 %	77	A	30.77 % / 33.85 %
14	B	41.54 % / 32.31 %	30	A	35.38 % / 32.31 %	46	D	40.0 % / 35.38 %	62	B	32.31 % / 38.46 %	78	C	49.23 % / 38.46 %
15	A	46.15 % / 33.85 %	31	B	27.69 % / 35.39 %	47	D	41.54 % / 33.84 %	63	A	15.38 % / 35.39 %	79	B	36.92 % / 30.77 %
16	A	24.62 % / 33.84 %	32	B	15.38 % / 33.85 %	48	D	36.92 % / 36.93 %	64	A	29.23 % / 35.39 %	80	C	29.23 % / 27.69 %

Q.	Ans.	Correct		Q.	Ans.	Correct		Q.	Ans.	Correct		Q.	Ans.	Correct		Q.	Ans.	Correct
		Skipped				Skipped				Skipped				Skipped				Skipped
81	D	40.0 %		85	D	47.69 %		89	A	33.85 %		93	A	29.23 %		97	A	40.0 %
		33.85 %				36.93 %				38.46 %				35.39 %				36.92 %
82	D	15.38 %		86	B	35.38 %		90	C	38.46 %		94	A	33.85 %		98	C	46.15 %
		35.39 %				36.93 %				40.0 %				33.84 %				36.93 %
83	C	24.62 %		87	C	26.15 %		91	B	32.31 %		95	D	20.0 %		99	D	9.23 %
		35.38 %				36.93 %				40.0 %				36.92 %				35.39 %
84	D	53.85 %		88	A	18.46 %		92	D	12.31 %		96	D	18.46 %		100	A	55.38 %
		35.38 %				40.0 %				40.0 %				33.85 %				33.85 %

Performance Analysis

Avg. Score (%)	23.0%
Toppers Score (%)	100.0%
Your Score	

//Hints and Solutions//

1. The Asian Development Bank (ADB) in its Asian Development Outlook Supplement has lowered India's economic growth forecast for current fiscal i.e. FY 2017-18 by 0.3% to 6.7% from earlier 7%.

The reasons cited for this downward revision of growth forecast of largest economy South Asia are lingering effect of demonetisation, transitory challenges to Goods and Services Tax (GST) and weather-related risks to agriculture.

ADB Forecast:

- ADB has also revised downwards India's gross domestic product (GDP) outlook for next fiscal beginning from March 2018 to 7.3% from 7.4% mainly due to rising global crude oil prices and soft growth in private sector investment.

- However, it expects growth to pick up in remaining two quarters of FY 2017-18 as Government is implementing measures to ease compliance with new GST as well as bank recapitalisation.

- Inflation in India has remained subdued in first seven months of 2017-18, averaging 2.7%, with low food prices and demand still not out of woods because of demonetisation.

2.

- Schemes such as BPO Promotion and Common Services Centres have helped us create digital inclusion and equitable growth.

- Growth of IT sector in India has traditionally remained confined to a few select urban clusters.

- The India BPO Promotion Scheme was conceived t change this.

- Given the special focus of the Government to develop the North East regions of India, the North East BPO Promotion Scheme was also conceived simultaneously.

- The schemes provide special incentives of upto Rs. 1 lakh per seat in the form of Viability Gap Funding (VGF).

- Disbursement of financial support under these schemes is directly linked with employment generation.

- These schemes provide special incentives for employment to women and Divyang, setting up operations in towns other than capital towns, generating employment beyond target and promoting local entrepreneurship.

3.

- India's first Electronic Manufacturing Cluster (EMC) will be coming to Andhra Pradesh.

- EMC has been designed and developed for providing facilities and amenities for manufacturing mobiles and allied products.

- The Union Government, through Ministry of Electronics and Information Technology (MeiTY) in 2012 had announced about setting up EMC in India, with grant-in-aid for establishing such clusters.

- In 2015, Andhra Pradesh Government had announced first exclusive mobile and electronic manufacturing cluster in the new capital city Amaravati.

- State Government had allotted 113.27 acres of land for new cluster, through Andhra Pradesh Industrial Infrastructure Corporation (APIIC).

- For this purpose, a Special Purpose Vehicle (SPV) called Sri Venkateswara Mobiles and Electronics Manufacturing Hub Private Limited was formed.

4. The Federal Reserve raised interest rates by a quarter of a percentage point on December 13, as anticipated, but left its rate outlook for the coming years unchanged even as policymakers projected a short-term acceleration in US economic growth.

Having raised its benchmark overnight lending rate three times this year, the Fed projected three more hikes in each of 2018 and 2019 before a long-run level of 2.8% is reached. That is unchanged from the last round of forecasts in September.

Gross domestic product is expected to grow 2.5% in 2018, up from the 2.1% forecast in September, while the unemployment rate is seen falling to 3.9% next year, compared to 4.1% in the last set of projections.

But inflation is projected to remain shy of the Fed's 2% goal for another year, with weakness on that front remaining enough of a concern that policymakers saw no reason to accelerate the expected pace of rate increases.

Policymakers do see the federal funds rate rising to 3.1% in 2020, slightly above the 2.8% "neutral" rate they expect to maintain in the long run. That indicates possible concerns about a rise in inflation pressures over time.

5.

- The Ministry of Micro, Small and Medium Enterprises (MSME) launched Public Procurement Portal '**MSME Sambandh**' for Public Procurement Portal for MSMEs.

- The objective of the portal is to monitor the implementation of the Public Procurement from MSEs by Central Public Sector Enterprises (CPSEs).

- It will help MSMEs in participating in the procurement process. Besides, it will help Ministries and the CPSEs can assess their performance in procurement process as stipulated in Procurement Policy, 2012.

- The Procurement Policy launched in 2012 mandates the Central Government Departments, CPSEs to procure necessarily from MSEs.

- It means that every Central Ministry, Department, PSU shall set an annual goal for procurement from MSE sector at beginning of year.

- Its objective is to achieve overall procurement goal of minimum of 20% of the total annual purchases of the products or services produced or rendered by MSEs.

6. The agriculture ministry has announced India is second largest fish producer in the world.

Overall fish production has increased from 0.75 million tonne of 1950-51 to 11.41 million tonne in 2016-17.

Besides, this sector provides employment and livelihood support to more than 15 million people of in the country.

The announcement was at the Aqua Goa Mega Fish Festival, 2017, organized at SAG Campal Ground, Panaji, Goa.

Fisheries is a fast growing sector in India, which provides nutrition and food security to a large population of the country as well as providing income and employment to fishermen and fish farmers.

Fisheries development in India is not only meeting the protein requirements of the country, but it is also making significant contribution of about 6.2 percent in the fish production of the world.

7. Half a billion people have gained access to electricity in India since 2000, almost doubling the country's electrification rate, according to the World Energy Access report released on Dec 6, 2017 by the International Energy Agency (IEA).

This "remarkable" growth puts India on course to achieving access to electricity for all in the early 2020s, the report added.

The number of people without access to electricity fell to 1.1 billion in 2016 from 1.7 billion in 2000.

It is on track to decline to 674 million by 2030, with India reaching universal access well before then. Since 2012, more than 100 million people per year have gained electricity access, an acceleration from the rate of 62 million people per year seen between 2000 and 2012.

Our analysis in the World Energy Outlook confirms that India is emerging as a major driving force in global energy trends, with all modern fuels and technologies playing a part.

Half a billion people have gained access to electricity in India since 2000, almost doubling the country's electrification rate.

This remarkable growth puts India on course to achieving access to electricity for all in the early 2020s - a colossal achievement.

Rate of Electrification:

- Coal has fuelled about 75% of the new electricity access since 2000, with renewable sources accounting for around 20%, according to the report.

- However, 239 million people remained without electricity access in 2016, about a quarter of the worldwide total.

- The report added that India is expected to reach universal electricity access in the early-2020s. Progress has also been made on clean cooking, although 830 million people in India still lack access.

- There are clear indications however that government policy efforts targeting LPG have begun to take hold.

- The share of the population relying primarily on biomass for cooking fell to 59% in 2015 from 66% in 2011.

- By 2030, the promotion of LPG and improved biomass cookstoves by the government means that more than 300 million people gain access to clean cooking facilities, but still more than one-in-three people remain without.

8. The monetary policy committee of the Reserve Bank of India on Dec 6 2017 decided to keep the repo rate unchanged at 6%, for the second consecutive meeting.

RBI did so while maintaining its neutral stance. This means banks are unlikely to revise their home or car loan rates anytime soon.

While observing that moderation in inflation (excluding food and fuel) observed in Q1 of 2017-18 had, 'by and large', 'reversed', the six-member committee said inflation may continue to accelerate in the near term.

The RBI revised its inflation projection to the range of 4.3-4.7% for the last two quarters of the current financial year.

The central bank had projected an inflation range of 4.2-4.6% in the last policy meeting held in October.

On growth, while observing that Q2 growth for the quarter ended September was lower than that projected in its October resolution, the central bank has retained the full-year GVA growth projection at 6.7%.

9. The 3rd edition of the Dialogue between the NITI Aayog and the Development Research Council of China, the DRC- NITI Aayog Dialogue was held in Beijing on Dec 5, 2017.

The meeting was co-chaired by Vice Chairman NITI Aayog, Dr. Rajiv Kumar, and Mr Li Wei, President (Minister), DRC.

The Indian delegation led by Vice Chairman, NITI Aayog included senior officials from NITI Aayog as well as Ministries of New & Renewable Energy and Food Processing.

The Chinese delegation comprised of researchers and officials from DRC as well as the Chinese Ministries of Finance, Commerce, Foreign Affairs, and the National Development & Reform Commission.

The DRC-NITI Dialogue provides an important platform for both sides to discuss key macro- economic issues impacting both countries and areas of mutual interest.

The 3rd Dialogue enabled an in-depth interaction between the two delegations on the world economic prospects, India-China economic cooperation and practices for sustainable growth.

Both sides exchanged views on policies and measures to address the challenges for attaining sustainable growth. In-depth discussions were held on sharing of experiences and best practices in the areas of Electric mobility, Clean energy, Higher education and Special Economic Zones (SEZs).

The two sides agreed that the 4th NITI Aayog - DRC Dialogue will be convened in India in 2018.

10. Multilateral funding agency Asian Development Bank (ADB) on 29th Nov, 2017 said it will provide a $500 million loan to improve rural road connectivity in five states, including Assam and West Bengal.

The board of directors of ADB has approved the multi-tranche financing facility (MFF) for the 'Second Rural Connectivity

Investment Programme' to improve rural roads in five states of India, ADB said in a statement.

Under this project, ADB will invest to construct and upgrade over 12,000 kilometre rural roads in Assam, Madhya Pradesh, Chhattisgarh, Odisha and West Bengal. It will also support state governments to improve rural road maintenance and safety.

ADB is building on the success of previous assistance for rural roads in India. The agency will work closely with the government to improve connectivity for the rural people to access markets, health centres, education and other opportunities.

In the first tranche, ADB is expected to invest USD 250 million in December for construction of initial 6,254 km all weather rural roads in these states. While the second tranche of the loan of same amount is expected to come by the third quarter of 2019.

This leg of the ADB loan assistance for rural roads builds on the first 'Rural Connectivity Investment Programme in 2012' financing USD 800 million MFF to add about 9,000 km all-weather rural roads in these five states.

Apart from this MFF, the Manila-headquartered agency will provide a USD 500,000 technical assistance (TA) grant from its Technical Assistance Special Fund to strengthen sustainability of rural road assets, disaster resilience and innovation in rural road development.

The TA is due for completion in December 2021, with the investment programme expected to be completed by the end of 2023, ADB said.

Rural roads comprise nearly 80 per cent of India's overall paved road network connecting them to major district roads, state roads and national highways.

11. India has recorded 45 per cent jump in the number of petrol pumps in the last six years, possibly the highest growth rate in the world, as public and private sector firms jostled to capture retailing sites.

With 60,799 outlets dispensing petrol and diesel at the end of October, India is behind only US and China in number of petrol pumps, data available from Petroleum Planning & Analysis Cell of the Oil Ministry.

In 2011, the country had 41,947 outlets, of which 2,983 or 7.1 per cent, were owned or operated by private retailers like Reliance Industries and Essar oil.

Today, private firms own 5,474, or 9 per cent of the total outlets, with Essar being the leader with 3,980 stations.

Several countries around the globe have seen the number of petrol pumps drop as they moved towards Electric Vehicles (EVs) and alternate forms of energy but they have grown in India, which is the world's fastest growing oil consumer.

India had in 2015 overtaken Japan as the world's third- largest oil consuming country behind US and China. Fuel consumption grew by 9.5 per cent in the April-October period of the current fiscal.

Oil ministry data showed that 18,852 outlets were added between 2011 and 2017. Of the 60,799 petrol pumps in the country, 55,325 are owned by state-owned fuel retailers.

India Oil Corp (IOC) owns and operates 26,489 petrol stations, of which 7,232 are rural outlets. Hindustan Petroleum Corp Ltd (HPCL) is the second biggest fuel retailer with 14,675 outlets, 3,159 being rural sites.

Bharat Petroleum Corp Ltd (BPCL) owns 14,161 outlets, of which 2,548 are rural outlets.

Private Company Growth In Petrol Sector

- In the private sector, Reliance Industries owns 1,400 outlets while Royal Dutch Shell has 90 stations.

- Besides, there are 1,273 outlets dispensing CNG to automobiles, the most number of 423 being in Delhi, the data showed.

- Industry officials said public sector oil companies will continue to add at least 2,000 petrol pumps per annum over the next few years.

- In the private sector, Essar, which was recently taken over by Russia's Rosneft, had been the most aggressive. It had 1,382 outlets in 2011 and now has 3,980, which it plans to take up to 5,600 by March 2019.

- With deregulation of petrol in June 2010 and diesel in 2014, private players have once again become active on fuel retailing expansion.

12. The government has set up the National Anti-Profiteering Authority amid reports that some companies, particularly restaurants, are not passing on the benefit of the goods and services tax (GST) rate cuts to consumers.

B N Sharma, additional secretary in the department of revenue, was on 28th Nov 2017 appointed chairman of the authority.

According to the Appointments Committee of the Cabinet (ACC), Sharma is an IAS officer of the Rajasthan cadre of the 1985 batch. He will have the rank and pay of a Secretary in the government.

The authority under the GST regime has been constituted to ensure that the benefit of lower indirect tax rates are passed on to consumers.

The anti-profiteering measures were recently approved by the Union Cabinet and have been designed to ensure that the full benefits of input tax credits and reduced GST rates on supply of goods or services flow to the consumers.

13. Commerce and Industry Minister Suresh Prabhu announced the new industrial policy that will seek to promote emerging sectors will be released in year 2018.

The proposed policy, the draft of which has been prepared by the Commerce and Industry Ministry, will completely revamp the Industrial Policy of 1991.

The draft policy is ready and the ministry is now planning to organise 8-9 roadshows to discuss it with all the stakeholders.

Among other things, the policy would endeavour to reduce regulations and bring in new industries currently in focus.

The Department of Industrial Policy and Promotion (DIPP) in August floated a draft industrial policy with the aim to create jobs for the next two decades, promote foreign technology transfer and attract USD 100 billion FDI annually.

The department is working to formulate an outcome oriented actionable policy that provides direction and charts a course of action for a globally competitive Indian industry that leverages skill, scale and technology.

14. The Union Ministry of Housing & Urban Affairs has announced that 30.76 lakh houses for the urban poor have been sanctioned so far since the launch of Pradhan Mantri Awas Yojana (Urban) Scheme in June 2015.

Currently, 15.65 lakh houses are at various stages of construction and about 4.13 lakh houses have been constructed since launch of PMAY (Urban).

15. The Union Cabinet chaired by the Prime Minister Narendra Modi has approved setting up of 15th Finance Commission (FC). It is a constitutional obligation to set up FC under Article 280 (1) of the Constitution.

The Terms of Reference for 15th FC will be notified in due course of time. In terms of constitutional provisions, setting up 15th FC, its recommendations will cover five years commencing on April 1, 2020.

15th Finance Commission

- The recommendations of the 15th Finance Commission will be implemented in the period 1 April 2020 to 31 March 2025.

- The 14th Finance Commission is considered to have fundamentally reset the centre-state fiscal relationship by raising the untied share of states in net central taxes to 42% from 32% after ending discretionary resource transfers from the centre to the states.

- Economist Indira Rajaraman, who was a member of the 13th Finance Commission opined the 15th Finance Commission will change considerably after GST was implemented.

16. India's food processing sector has the potential to attract $33 billion investment by 2024, according to a study released here on 20th Nov 2017 by ASSOCHAM.

The country's food and retail market is expected to touch $482 billion by 2020, up from $258 billion in 2015, with recent reforms making the sector more competitive and marke-oriented, it said.

ASSOCHAM:

- The Associated Chambers of Commerce and Industry of India (ASSOCHAM) is one of the apex trade associations of India.

- The organisation represents the interests of trade and commerce in India, and acts as an interface between industry, government and other relevant stakeholders on policy issues and initiatives.

- The goal of this organisation is to promote both domestic and international trade, and reduce trade barriers while fostering conducive environment for the growth of trade and industry of India.

17. India ranked 51st among 63 countries on the IMD Talent Rankings in terms of ability to attract, develop and retain talent. In previous rankings, India was ranked 54th.

The annual IMD World Talent Ranking covers 63 countries and assessed methods countries adopted to attract and retain talent. The rankings of countries are based on their performance in three main categories - investment and development, appeal, and readiness.

18. The Union Government has given go-ahead for setting up India's first mega coastal economic zone (CEZ) at Jawaharlal Nehru Port (JNPT) in Maharashtra.

The first of its kind mega CEZ will stretch along north Konkan region spread across Mumbai, Thane, Pune, Nashik and Raigarh.

About 45 companies across auto, telecom and IT sectors will soon bid for 200 hectares of land to set up manufacturing units in zone.

JNPT:

- The Jawaharlal Nehru Port Trust (JNPT) at Navi Mumbai (formerly known as the Nhava Sheva Port) located within the Mumbai harbour on the west coast of India, was commissioned on 26th May 1989.

- It occupies a place of prominence among the major Indian ports.

- It is the second youngest and one of the most modern major ports of the country. Though it was initially planned to be a "satellite port" to the Mumbai Port with the purpose of decongesting traffic at the latter, eventually it was developed as an independent port on its own right and it became the country's largest container port.

- Being one of the oldest ports in India, the Mumbai port was proving to be structurally inadequate to meet the requirements of modern cargo handling.

- There was an urgent need for a new port in the Mumbai region, which eventually led to the birth of JNPT in 1989.

19. The Union Government has signed a guarantee agreement for IBRD/CTF loan of US $98 million and Grant Agreement for US $2 million for Shared Infrastructure for Solar Parks Project with World Bank.

The objective Shared Infrastructure for Solar Parks Project is to increase solar generation capacity through establishment of large-scale parks in the country.

20. The Union Cabinet approved setting up of National Anti-Profiteering Authority (NAA), an apex body with an overarching mandate under Goods and Services Tax (GST) regime so as to ensure the benefit of tax reaches consumers.

It also approved creation of posts of Chairman and Technical Members of National Anti-profiteering Authority (NAA) under GST regime.

NAA:

- The establishment of the NAA, to be headed by a senior officer of the level of Secretary to the Government of India with four Technical Members from the Centre and/or the States.

- It is one more measure aimed at reassuring consumers that Government is fully committed to take all possible steps to ensure the benefits of implementation of GST in terms of lower prices of the goods and services reach them.

- It may be recalled that effective from midnight of 14th November, 2017 the GST rate has been slashed from 28% to 18% on goods falling under 178 headings.

- There are now only 50 items which attract the GST rate of 28%.

- Likewise, a large number of items have witnessed a reduction in GST rates from 18% to 12% and so on and some goods have been completely exempt from GST.

- The "anti-profiteering" measures enshrined in the GST law provide an institutional mechanism to ensure that the full benefits of input tax credits and reduced GST rates on supply of goods or services flow to the consumers.

- This institutional framework comprises the NAA, a Standing Committee, Screening Committees in every State and the Directorate General of Safeguards in the Central Board of Excise & Customs (CBEC).

21. The Cabinet Committee on Economic Affairs on 16th Nov, 2017 gave its approval for removing the prohibition on the export of all types of pulses to give the farmers greater choice in marketing their produce for improved incomes.

The CCEA (Cabinet Committee on Economic Affairs) has approved the removal of prohibition on export of all types of pulses.

CCEA:

- CCEA has a mandate to review economic trends on a continuous basis, as also the problems and prospects, with a view to evolving a consistent and integrated economic policy framework for the country.

- It also directs and coordinates all policies and activities in the economic field including foreign investment that require policy decisions at the highest level.

- Price controls of industrial raw materials and products, industrial licensing policies is undertaken by CCEA

- The CCEA also lays down priorities for public sector investment and considers specific proposals for investment of not less than specific levels (Rs. 3 Billion at present) as revised from time to time.

- CCEA facilitates finalization of factual reports on the accomplishments of the Ministries, Agencies and Public Sector Undertakings involved in implementation of prioritized schemes or projects for evaluation by the Prime Minister.

- The CCEA also considers cases of increase in the firmed up cost estimates/revised cost estimates for projects etc. in respect of the business allocated to the CCEA.

- On 2 January 2013, Cabinet Committee on Infrastructure was merged with CCEA.

22. CBDT Chairman Sushil Chandra announced while there were around 2.5 lakh PAN applications per month earlier, after the Centre announced to scrap high value currency notes in November last year, the number rose to 7.5 lakh.

Additionally, the department was taking a number of measures to curb black money and that steps such as no cash transaction of above INR 2 lakh was a move in that direction.

CBDT:

The Central Board of Direct Taxes (CBDT) provides essential inputs for policy and planning of direct taxes in India and is also responsible for administration of the direct tax laws through Income Tax Department. The CBDT is a statutory authority functioning under the Central Board of Revenue Act, 1963. It is India's official FATF unit.

Organisational Structure

The CBDT is headed by CBDT Chairman and also comprises six members. The Chairperson holds the rank of Special Secretary to Government of India while the members rank of Additional Secretary to Government of India.

23. The commerce ministry closed down its nearly 100-year-old public procurement arm–the Directorate General of Supplies and Disposals (DGS&D)-on October 31.

The closure of the DGS&D, which traces its origin to London during the British raj, follows setting up of the government e-market (GeM) platform last year for public procurement of goods and services.

About 1,100 of its employees are being shifted to different departments, including income tax, while the senior officers are likely to be accommodated in other branches of the government. DGS&D assets, which were present across the country, are transferred to the Land and Development Office of the urban development ministry.

The directorate has four regional offices, including Mumbai, Kolkata and Chennai. It has 12 Purchase Directorates.

24. Bharti Airtel on Nov 14, 2017 offloaded 83 million shares of its subsidiary Bharti Infratel for ₹ 3,325 crore through a secondary share sale in the stock market.

Bharti Airtel will primarily use the proceeds to reduce its debt, the company said in a statement. The firm's net debt stood at ₹ 91,480 crore at the end of September 2017.

The sale was for a consideration of more than ₹ 3,325 crore or about $510 million and was executed at a price of ₹ 400.6 a share.

Following the transaction, Bharti Airtel and its wholly-owned subsidiaries hold 53.51% in Bharti Infratel. Promoters held 58% as of September 2017, as per BSE data.

The allocation was done to global investors, fund managers and long only funds, including many repeat investors.

Led by healthy investor appetite, the deal was upsized by over 25%.

J.P. Morgan, UBS and Goldman Sachs were joint placement agents for the transaction.

25. Despite a temporary economic slowdown after the implementation of the Goods and Services Tax (GST) in July 2017, India is on the threshold of sustainable growth, according to an ASSOCHAM report.

In its study, titled: "Ideate, Innovate, Implement: the apex industry body held that despite slowdown in growth after GST implementation, India is on the path to growth.

It said that faster GST implementation, removal of check gates between states that have smoothened inter-state movements and central sales tax (CST) no longer being a cost will help improve the situation.

The report maintained that GST will have a significant impact on all aspects of the businesses operating in the country including-supply chain, logistics, cash flows and transactions.

The study said that GST will have an impact on prices agreed for contracts entered under the pre-GST regime and proposed to be executed either partly or completely under the post-GST regime.

Also, the introduction of GST should entail a reduction in overall process on account of reduced tax costs.

The Assocham-EY report also suggested central and state governments need to work in tandem by executing investor-friendly policies to further strengthen investment prospects.

26. Shri R.K. Singh, Minister of State (IC) for Power and New & Renewable Energy, launched the National Power Portal (NPP) on 14th Nov, 2017. The portal may be accessed at http://npp.gov.in.

NPP is a centralised system for Indian Power Sector which facilitates online data capture/ input (daily, monthly, annually) from generation, transmission and distribution utilities in the country and disseminate Power Sector Information (operational, capacity, demand, supply, consumption etc.).

It works through various analysed reports, graphs, statistics for generation, transmission and distribution at all India, region, state level for central, state and private sector.

The NPP Dashboard has been designed and developed to disseminate analyzed information about the sector through GIS enabled navigation and visualization chart windows on capacity, generation, transmission, distribution at national, state, DISCOM, town, feeder level and scheme based funding to states.

The system also facilitates various types of statutory reports required to be published regularly.

This Dashboard would also act as the single point interface for all Power Sector Apps launched previously by the Ministry, like TARANG, UJALA, VIDYUT PRAVAH, GARV, URJA, MERIT.

NPP is integrated with associated systems of Central Electricity Authority (CEA), Power Finance Corporation (PFC), Rural Electrification Corporation (REC) and other major utilities and would serve as single authentic source of power sector

information to apex bodies, utilities for the purpose of analysis, planning, monitoring as well as for public users.

The system is available 24×7 and ensures effective and timely collection of data. It standardized data parameters and formats for seamless exchange of data between NPP and respective systems at utilities.

NPP Stakeholders

- The stakeholders of NPP are Ministry of Power (MoP), CEA, PFC for Integrated Power Development Scheme (IPDS), REC for Deen Dayal Upadhyaya Gram Jyoti Yojana (DDUGJY), other power sector utilities in government as well as private sector, Apex Bodies, other government organizations and public users.
- The Nodal Agency for implementation of NPP and its operational control is CEA.
- The system has been conceptualized, designed and developed by National Informatics Centre (NIC).

27. The Goods and Services Tax Council took a slew of decisions during its 23rd meeting in Guwahati on Friday to benefit consumers and businesses alike.

While consumers will stand to benefit from a number of rate cuts, including the tax on restaurants, businesses stand to benefit from a significant easing of compliance norms to do with filing returns.

Up to November 15, when the decisions take effect, the GST system requires businesses to submit at least three forms to file their returns.

The GSTR-1 dealt with the invoice-wise details of supply, GSTR-2 dealt with the receipts of goods, and GSTR-3 was an overall summary derived from the two previous forms.

Now, the GST Council has decided that, in order to ease the compliance burden on businesses, companies would be allowed to only file the GSTR-1 form, up to March 31, 2018.

The Council has set up a committee to look into how to make the GSTR-2 form easier, following which it will be brought back into the system.

The Council also decided to extend the usage of the summary GSTR-3B form, meant to make life easier for those unfamiliar with the filing process, till March 31 from the earlier December 31 deadline.

Companies with a turnover of up to ₹1.5 crore a year will now be able to file their GSTR-1 forms for each month in a quarterly manner.

Companies earning ₹1.5 crore or more a year can file their July to October forms by December 31.

Not only did the latest Council meeting ease the deadlines, but it also slashed the penalties for filing late.

For companies with nil tax liability for a particular month, the penalty for delays has been cut to ₹20 per day from ₹200 per day. All other companies will have to file a penalty of ₹50 per day, down from ₹200 per day.

The GST Council - the apex body for decision making headed by finance minister Arun Jaitley - also decided to impose a uniform GST rate of 5 percent across all categories of standalone restaurants - air-conditioned and non-air-conditioned - but withdraw the benefits of input tax credit (ITC) from such businesses.

Restaurants in starred hotels and outdoor catering services will attract a GST of 18 percent along with ITC benefits.

Composition Scheme

- The annual turnover threshold on the composition scheme will be raised from Rs 1 crore to Rs 1.5 crore.

- This will be done after the law is amended to raise the turnover ceiling for eligibility of composition.

- The law will be amended to raise the ceiling to Rs 2 crore. The limit will be raised immediately after the law amended to Rs 1.5 crore

- Under the scheme, traders, manufacturers and restaurants can pay tax at 1, 2 and 5 percent, respectively.

- The council has also decided to fix a uniform rate of 1 percent for traders and manufacturers.

- The move to widen the turnover threshold is aimed at easing the compliance burden for taxpayers as they will have to file returns only once in a quarter as against monthly returns that needs to be filed by other normal taxpayers.

- However, dealers cannot avail input tax credit, unlike a normal taxpayer.

- Also, traders availing the composition scheme on goods, who also provide small services upto Rs 5 lakh annually, will not be considered ineligible for the scheme.

- GST, billed as the country's biggest indirect tax overhaul, has consolidated a dozen of state and central duties into one single levy.

- ll goods and services have been fitted into four broad slab structure - 5, 12, 18 and 28 percent -along with a cess on luxury and demerit goods such as tobacco, pan masala and aerated drinks.

28. The twenty-third meeting of the Goods and Services Tax (GST) Council in Guwahati on Friday is set to tighten the noose on players who, authorities believe, have started splitting their business operations into smaller entities to avoid higher tax liabilities.

The Council is also set to cut tax rates on a large number of product lines.

The Council is expected to further liberalise the Composition Scheme for small businesses and traders to pay a flat and low tax on their turnover.

The annual turnover eligibility threshold is likely to be raised to ₹1.5 crore from the ₹1 crore limit, imposed at the Council's October meeting.

However, the government is concerned about the emergence of a parallel economy despite the restrictions on the Composition Scheme, whose original threshold limit was just ₹75 lakh a year.

Small States may have legitimate concerns, but the restriction on inter-State supplies by businesses under the Composition Scheme could also fuel the prospects for more informal trade outside the tax net.

The GoM has not been able to arrive at a consensus on the question of whether supplies from small firms that are part of the Composition Scheme should translate into input tax credits for larger firms who buy from them.

29. The government on Nov 8, 2017 doubled the import duty on wheat to 20 per cent to curb cheap shipments and give positive price signal to farmers in the ongoing Rabi season.

It also imposed import duty of 50 percent on peas to check cheaper shipments from countries like Canada.

The Central Board of Excise and Customs (CBEC) in a notification said that it seeks to (i) increase rate of basic customs duty on Peas, (Pisum sativum) from present Nil rate to 50%. (ii) increase rate of basic customs duty on wheat from 10% to 20%.

In March, the government had imposed 10 percent import duty on wheat to contain sharp fall in local prices in view of bumper crop of 98.38 million tonnes in 2016-17 crop year (July-June).

As farmers have started planting of rabi (winter) wheat crop, the government wants to give positive price signal and encourage farmers to grow wheat in more area.

The government does not want wheat growers to follow the way of pulses farmers who shifted to other crops this kharif season as prices remained low just before the sowing period owing to bumper crop last year.

India produced a record 22 million tonnes of pulses in 2016-17 crop year which led to a fall in domestic prices, even below the MSP.

Moreover, the country also imported about 5 million tonnes of pulses last fiscal.

The import duty on peas has been imposed to curb shipments and boost domestic prices.

Recently, the government had also imposed quantitative restrictions on import of other pulses like tur.

30. Two Memorandum of Understanding (MoUs) have been signed between Indian Institute of Corporate Affairs, Atal Innovation Mission - Niti Ayog and Haryana Vishwakarma Skill University in Delhi on Nov 8, 2017.

The partnerships on skill development and entrepreneurship seek to align with the National Priority Areas.

Therefore, quality deliverables under these collaborations will go a long way in initiating and sustaining innovative approaches towards strengthening the enterprise movement in the country.

With an aim of enabling millions and millions of Indian youth acquire necessary skills and contribute towards making India a modern country, India has launched 'Skilling India' as a multi-skill development programme on mission mode for job creation and entrepreneurship skill development for all socio-economic classes.

To realise this dream, upgrading skills to international standards through significant industry involvement and developing necessary frameworks for standards, curriculum and quality assurance are the prerequisites.

Along with impetus on Skilling India, promotion of Entrepreneurship is being pursued by Government through 'Start-up India'.

Incubators plays a vital role as the incubation process not only provided the start-up with an inspiring environment, quality mentoring and a support structure, it also helped them refine their business model and get access to an economical, yet professional working space.

IICA has explored ways to collaborate and undertake various activities to promote incubation/ entrepreneurship and innovation.

To facilitate activities such as capacity building programmes/ workshops/ seminar, research in area of incubation, innovation, skill development etc., IICA has inked the Statement of Intent with Atal Innovation Mission-Niti Aayog and the Memorandum of Understanding with Haryana Vishwakarma Skill University.

These collaborations are likely to provide the opportunities for all stakeholders to participate and contribute to larger cause of incubation and skill creation.

31. Indian engineering exports are benefiting from an impressive turnaround in demand in most of the developed economies especially the U.S., which accounted for an annual growth of 91% in shipments in September this fiscal, according to an analysis by EEPC India, the apex body for Indian engineering exporters.

The U.S. continued to be the topmost exporting destination for India's engineering products in September 2017, registering a huge expansion both on monthly as well as on cumulative basis during April-September 2017-18 over the same period last fiscal.

While the shipments of engineering exports to the US went up by a whopping 91% to $1.53 billion in September, 2017 from $551 million in the same month last fiscal, the April-September exports had gone up over by 47% to $4.79 billion from $3.25 billion in the first half of the previous fiscal.

Since the demand pick up, particularly in iron and steel, all ferrous and non-ferrous metals, is evident in the global market, the exports are expected to remain buoyant.

All European nations falling under the top 25 engineering export destinations like Germany, Italy, Belgium, Netherland, France and Poland also recorded considerable growth.

Engineering exports to Germany saw a jump of over 67% to $288 million in September, 2017 over $172 million in the same month last fiscal.

Likewise, the shipments to Italy rose by 30% to $209 million from $161 million.

32. Poll-bound Gujarat, with 'investment intentions' worth INR 65,741 crore obtained during the period January-September this year, is behind the national topper Karnataka that bagged 'investment intentions' worth INR 147,625 crore in the period.

Karnataka, with investment intentions of INR 154,173 crore had last year (January-December) wrested the numero uno spot from Gujarat that got investment proposals of INR 56,156 crore.

In 2015, Gujarat was the state with the maximum 'investment intentions' in value terms with INR 64,733 crore, while Karnataka was only the fourth with INR 31,668 crore.

Other States leading in 'investment intentions' during January-September 2017 were Maharashtra (INR 25,018 crore), Andhra Pradesh (INR 24,031 crore), Jharkhand (INR 13,002 crore), Telangana (INR 12,567 crore) and Uttar Pradesh (INR 9,443).

India received investment proposals of INR 332,266 crore till September this year. In all of 2016, the country had received intentions worth INR 414,086 crore, while it received only INR 311,031 crore in 2015.

A state-wise assessment of implementation of the 340 reform recommendations in 2016 had seen Gujarat ranked third behind Andhra Pradesh and Telengana, while Karnataka was 13th in the list. The business reforms action plan in 2017 includes 405 reform recommendations, and the latest implementation scorecard shows Telengana topping the list, followed by Haryana and West Bengal, while Karnataka is eighth and Gujarat ninth.

33. India is witnessing a high-growth trajectory and set to become the third-largest aviation market in the world in terms of passengers by 2026.

The announcement was made at the 2nd India aero expo 2017 inaugurated by Vice President Shri Venkaaih Naidu.

The aviation sector not only plays a key role in promoting connectivity and creating jobs but is also an important driver of the economy.

Aviation is the backbone of the global transport system. It indeed is the most vital sector for linking businesses, bringing people together and promoting tourism worldwide.

India became the world's fastest growing domestic travel market for the 22nd time in a row recording a 26.6 per cent year-on-year growth in January 2017, according to IATA.

India's Aviation Sector:

- India is witnessing a high-growth trajectory and set to become the third-largest aviation market in the world in terms of passengers by 2026.

- India's air cargo is estimated to grow at 9 per cent over the next few years.

- IATA also expects the air passengers to double from 3.8 billion air passengers in 2016 to 7.2 billion by 2035.

- India replaced Japan to become the largest domestic aviation market globally.

- India recorded a total of 100 million domestic flyers in 2016 as compared to 97 million people who travelled by air in Japan during the same period.

Government Measures to Promote Aviation

- Recognizing the growing importance of the aviation sector, the Government has taken a series of measures to improve infrastructure and regional air connectivity in the country.

- UDAN scheme seeks to promote regional connectivity by serving the un-served and under-served airports. Connecting Tier-II cities, pilgrim towns and historic places with the wider air routes is important for boosting tourism and business travel.

- Among others, developing no frills and Greenfield airports, augmenting existing capacities, creating synergy between scheduled and non-scheduled airlines for better penetration and connectivity through collaborative efforts of the State and Central Governments is needed.

34. Moving ahead with reforms in the public sector banking space, the government has constituted a ministerial panel headed by Finance Minister Arun Jaitley that will oversee merger proposals of state-owned banks.

The other members of the panel include Railway and Coal Minister Piyush Goyal and Defence Minister Nirmala Sitharaman.

While announcing the unprecedented INR 2.11 lakh crore capital infusion roadmap for the public sector banks (PSBs) last week, Jaitley indicated this will be accompanied by series of banking reforms over the next few months.

The constitution of Alternative Mechanism (AM) is a movement in that direction.

The Cabinet in August had decided to set up an Alternative Mechanism to fast-track consolidation among public sector banks to create strong lenders.

The move to create large banks aims at meeting the credit needs of the growing Indian economy and building capacity in the PSB space to raise resources without dependence on the state exchequer.

The mechanism will oversee the proposals coming from boards of PSBs for consolidation.

The decision to set up such a mechanism follows State Bank of India merging its five associate banks, as also the Bharatiya Mahila Bank, with itself.

35. India is likely to overtake Japan and Germany to become the third largest economy in the next 10 years, HSBC Holdings Plc said in a September report.

According to HSBC's estimates, India will be a $7 trillion economy in 2028.

This is compared to less than $6 trillion and $5 trillion for Germany and Japan, respectively.

Presently, India's gross domestic product (GDP) is around $2.3 trillion (fiscal 2016-17).

HSBC:

HSBC Holdings plc is a British multinational banking and financial services holding company, tracing its origin to a hong in Hong Kong.

- It is the world's seventh largest bank by total assets and the largest in Europe with total assets of US$2.374 trillion (as of December 2016).

- It was established in its present form in London in 1991 by The Hongkong and Shanghai Banking Corporation to act as a new group holding company.

- The HSBC name is derived from the initials of the Hongkong and Shanghai Banking Corporation.

- The company was first formally incorporated in 1866.

- The company continues to see both the United Kingdom and Hong Kong as its "home markets".

36. India is set to become the third largest aviation market the International Air Transport Association (IATA) said in a report on Tuesday.

IATA, which represents about 85% of the global airline traffic, projects India to overtake the UK to become the third largest air passenger market by 2025.

China will be the top market, followed by the US.

In a similar report last year, IATA had projected India to overtake the UK by 2026.

The biggest driver of demand will be the Asia-Pacific region.

The region will be the source of more than half the new passengers over the next two decades.

The point at which China will displace the US as the world's largest aviation market (defined as traffic to, from and within the country) has also moved two years closer since last year's forecast.

By 2036, India will have about 478 million airline passenger traffic, which will be more than that of Japan (just under 225 million) and Germany (just over 200 million) combined.

India's current passenger traffic is about 141 million.

The most critical number will, however, be the doubling of overall passenger traffic globally from 4 billion to nearly 7.8 billion passengers in 2036 on a 3.6% compound annual growth rate (CAGR).

All indicators lead to growing demand for global connectivity. The world needs to prepare for a doubling of passengers in the next 20 years.

Indian airlines have over 800 planes on order and in the next five years alone are set to add 350-400 aircraft. All Indian airlines put together have a fleet of around 500 aircraft currently.

37. As much as 418 km of national highway and State highway stretches in Kerala figures in the 6,005-km economic corridors, inter-corridors, feeder routes, and national corridors being developed to improve the efficiency of freight movement under the Bharatmala Pariyojana.

According to the NHAI, these corridors are proposed for development to at least four-lane access controlled (fully access control for economic corridors).

However, the DPR for access controlled six-laning and eight-laning may be required on certain stretches, depending on the traffic.

Keeping in view a futuristic approach, it has been decided that the land for any 4/6-lane highway road will be acquired with a right of way (RoW) of 60 m irrespective of the width of the carriageway.

INR 6.92 trillion has been allocated for building an 83,677 km road network over the next five years.

The largest ever outlay for road construction comes in the backdrop of the National Democratic Alliance (NDA) government implementing the goods and services tax (GST).

The road construction push includes the Bharatmala Pariyojana with a INR 5.35 trillion investment to construct 34,800km of roads.

In addition, INR 1.57 trillion will be spent on the construction of 48,877km of roads by the state-run National Highway Authority of India (NHAI) and the ministry of road transport and highways.

To expedite the Bharatmala projects, apart from ministry of road transport and highways and state-run firms-NHAI and National Highways and Infrastructure Development Corporation Ltd (NHIDCL)-even respective state public works departments (PWDs) will be roped in for timely execution.

This in turn will generate 142 million man-days of jobs, the government said.

Measures today will boost infra spending in a big way.

Funding Bharatmala

- To fund the marquee Bharatmala scheme, INR 2.09 trillion will be raised as debt from the market, while iNR 1.06 trillion in private investments is being targeted through public private partnerships.

- In addition, INR 2.19 trillion will be provided from Central Road Fund (CRF), Toll-Operate-Maintain-Transfer (TOT) projects and toll collections of NHAI.

- Projects such as Sagarmala and Bharatmala will prepare a strong base for infrastructure development, enabling a person to travel across the country on a single road.

38. The Asian Development Bank and the Government of India signed a $300 million loan to continue a series of fiscal reforms in the State of West Bengal to improve the quality of public service delivery.

The Second West Bengal Development Finance Program targets a further increase in public investment through reduction of unproductive expenditure, and savings from efficiencies in revenue collections.

The Program will build on earlier intervention under Phase I of the project through the $400 million Program that targeted a comprehensive fiscal consolidation program in the state.

The new Program will create the fiscal space necessary to sustain higher public investment in the State which could put the state's finances on a balanced and sustainable path.

The program agreement was signed by Mr. Parwez Ahmad Siddiqui, Secretary, Finance Department, Government of West Bengal.

ADB's first Program focused on augmenting public investments that reached almost 1.3%, as a percentage of gross state domestic product, in FY2016 from 0.5% in FY2012 while the fiscal deficit reduced to 2.2% from 3.4% in the same period.

The new Program will not only target public investment but would also support private investments more directly by creating an infrastructure facility to support project preparation, development, and appraisal, with emphasis on public-private partnerships in health and education.

It also seeks to simplify the registration and licensing procedure for micro, small and medium enterprises.

Spread over two years, the Program will also carry forward reforms such as linking medium term expenditure plans to actual budgets, supported by strengthening internal audit system, and enhancements in the integrated financial management system (IFMS).

Other activities under the program include improved tax monitoring and continued support for information technology systems in strengthening tax and land administration.

39. Madhya Pradesh has achieved third position in milk production in the country, the state's animal husbandry ministry said.

Due to sustained efforts, the state has achieved third position in milk production in the country.

It was at sixth or seventh place 10 to 12 years back and last year it was at the fourth place,

Moreover for products, the new packaging is totally safe, leak-proof, made from food-grade plastic and there is no scope of any adulteration in it as its seal cannot be tampered with.

The state government is committed to doubling the farmers' income by 2022 and in it the state's veterinary department has a major role to play.

Milk producers were this year paid INR 200 crore, which is maximum by the state government so far.

40. The contribution of Prepaid Payment Instruments (PPI) will rise to 30-40 percent over 5 years from less than 10 percent now on the Reserve Bank push, as per PCI.

RBI came out with the third set of reforms in PPI yesterday to make it interoperable with all existing payment instruments, on par with acceptance of debit/credit cards in a phased manner.

This would ensure that PPIs contribution to digital payments from current share of less than 10 percent can move to 30-40 percent in the next 5 years.

The Council praised the regulator for a progressive and positive set of guidelines.

It however said a concern is that even the low usage wallets with limited merchant transaction functionality are required to do a KYC beyond 12 months.

"This adds friction to customers and costs to issuer. In line with international guidelines, a framework of proportional KYC could have been adopted," it said.

PCI is the representative body of PPI issuers.

RBI guidelines mark the 10 year anniversary to the industry and seem to be a true reflection of a collaborate approach for the industry.

41. India's GDP may slow from 8.6% in 2015 to 7.0% in 2017 because of disruptions by demonetisation and the GST, the World Bank has forecast and warned that subdued private investment due to internal bottlenecks could put downside pressures on the country's potential growth.

The International Monetary Fund also lowered India's growth projection to 6.7 % in 2017, 0.5 percentage points less than its previous two forecasts and slower than China's 6.8%.

India's economic momentum has been affected by disruptions from the withdrawal of banknotes and uncertainties around the Goods and Services Tax (GST), the World Bank said in its South Asia Economic Focus, a biannual economic update.

As a result, growth is expected to slow from 8.6% in 2015 to 7.0% in 2017. Sound policies around balancing public spending with private investment could accelerate growth to 7.3% by 2018, it said.

While sustained growth is expected to translate to continued poverty reduction, more focus could be made to help benefit the informal economy more, said the report released here ahead of the annual meeting of the International Monetary Fund and the World Bank.

A slowdown in India's growth rate, the bank said, has also affected the growth rate of South Asia. As a result, South Asia has fallen to second place after East Asia and the Pacific.

Real GDP growth slowed to 7.1 % in 2016, from 8 % in 15/16, and further to 5.7 % in Q1 FY2017.

On the one hand, public and private consumption gained pace: after implementation of the 7th central pay commission recommendations; and due to the revival in rural demand after normal monsoon and agricultural impetus.

However, overall demand slowed as public investments started to wane.

According to the bank, the GST is expected to disrupt economic activity in early 2018, but the momentum may pick-up.

Evidence suggests that post-GST, manufacturing and services contracted sharply.

The growth activity is expected to stabilise within a quarter - maintaining the annual GDP growth at 7.0 % in 2018.

Growth is projected to increase gradually to 7.4 % by 2020, underpinned by a recovery in private investments, which are expected to be crowded-in by the recent increase in public capex and an improvement.

This is in the present investment climate (partly due to the passage of the GST and Bankruptcy Code, and measures to attract the FDI).

The most substantial medium-term risks are associated with private investment recovery, which continues to face several domestic impediments such as corporate debt overhang, regulatory and policy challenges, along with the risk of an imminent increase in US interest rates.

If the internal bottlenecks are not alleviated, subdued private investment would put downside pressures on India's potential growth.

Downside risks to the global economy - and accordingly to export growth and capital flows - are also substantial given the possibility of monetary policy normalisation in the USA and risks of protectionism.

42. Assam Finance Minister Himanta Biswa Sarma heads the group of ministers (GoM) of state finance ministers that have been set up to look into various issues pertaining to a scheme for small taxpayers under the Goods and Services tax (GST), also known as the composition scheme.

The GoM will also look into the proposal to reducing GST rates on air-conditioned restaurants from 18 percent to 12 percent.

Deputy Chief Minister of Bihar Sushil Modi, Jammu & Kashmir Finance Minister Haseeb Drabu, Punjab Finance Minister Parminder Singh Dhindsa and Chattisgarh's Commercial Taxes Minister Amar Agarwal will be a part of the GoM.

Composition scheme is an alternate method of taxation, which allows small businesses with annual turnover up to INR 75 lakhs, to pay tax at a concessional rate, as well as reduce the compliance cost.

The revenue threshold is INR 50 lakhs for dealers across nine states such as Arunachal Pradesh, Nagaland, Tripura, among others.

The enrolment into the plan is however, optional.

On Friday, the GST Council headed by Finance Minister Arun Jaitley decided to raise the annual turnover threshold on the scheme to INR 1 crore and reopen its registration for the third time till March 31, 2018.

Under the scheme, traders, manufacturers and restaurants can pay tax at 1, 2 and 5 percent, respectively.

The move to widen the turnover threshold is aimed at easing the compliance burden for taxpayers as they will have to file returns only once in a quarter as against monthly returns that needs to be filed by other normal taxpayers.

However, dealers cannot avail input tax credit, unlike a normal taxpayer.

Input credit means at the time of paying tax on output, a producer, trader or service provider can reduce the tax already paid on inputs.

The committee of GoM will take crucial decisions related to the scheme such as if the plan can be extended to taxpayers making inter-state supplies of goods, which was earlier not allowed.

The officials will examine whether turnover of exempted goods under GST can be excluded from the total turnover threshold for levying tax under composition scheme.

Apart of rationalising tax structure of different categories of restaurants, the committee will also examine if input tax credit (ITC) can be made available to registered taxpayers under GST from dealers who have opted for composition scheme.

Initially, the response for the composition scheme was lukewarm, with only 10.24 lakh dealers opting for it over a span of one and half months, starting July 1. Last month, the Council decided to reopen registration for the scheme from September 17.

This time, however, more than 5 lakh dealers opted for the scheme over just 13 days, taking the total number of assessess to 15.43 lakhs.

43. The Reserve Bank of India (RBI) on Oct 4 kept the key interest rates unchanged, as was widely expected.

Repo rate - the rate at the which the central bank lends short-term money to banks- thus continues to stay at 6 per cent. The RBI had cut repo rate by 25 basis points (bps) in August.

RBI has also cut the economic growth forecast for the current fiscal to 6.7 per cent from earlier projections of 7.3 per cent.

The decision of the Monetary Policy Committee (MPC) is consistent with a neutral stance of monetary policy in consonance with the objective of achieving the medium-term target for consumer price index (CPI) inflation of 4 per cent within a band of +/- 2 per cent, while supporting growth.

SLR or statutory liquidity ratio was, however, cut by 50 basis points to 19.5 per cent with effect from October 14.

Banks are required to invest certain percentage of their deposits in specified financial securities like Central Government or State Government securities.

This percentage is known as SLR. However, with adequate liquidity in the system, the SLR cut is unlikely to have much impact on banks.

The announcement which came at the end of a two-day meeting of the MPC of the RBI, is in sync with what the experts had predicted.

Inflation, which in August reached a five-month high of 3.36 per cent, is being billed as the reason behind RBI's decision to maintain status quo.

The RBI decision of increasing inflation forecast from 4 per cent to a range of 4.2 to 4.6 per cent for the October to March half backs this proposition.

Analysts expect inflation could continue to quicken, given food prices tend to rise during the winter.

Reverse repo rate - the rate at which the central bank borrows money from commercial banks- was also left unchanged at 5.75 per cent.

Industry body CII (Confederation of Indian Industry) had pitched for a rate cut of 100 bps while Assocham too had written to the MPC.

The slowing down of private investments being one of the major reasons behind the slump in growth, industry was hopeful of a rate cut, in order to provide a booster shot to the economy.

The central bank said it is imperative to reinvigorate investment activity which, in turn, would revive the demand for bank credit by industry as existing capacities get utilised and the requirements of new capacity open up to be financed.

44. Global cotton output is likely to rise 10 per cent to 25.4 million tonnes in 2017-18 marketing year on expected production increase in India and the US, a global body has said.

The production may go up mainly because of expansion in acreage by 3 million hectares to over 32 million hectares across the world, according to International Cotton Advisory Committee (ICAC).

The worldwide output of the cash crop stood at 23.05 million tonnes(MT) last year.

India's marketing year runs from October to September.

The acreage has increased due to better cotton prices in 2016-17 and higher cotton price ratio to other competing crops during this year, ICAC said in a report.

China, India and the US are the world's top three cotton producing countries.

As per ICAC, the global cotton consumption is projected to increase 2.7 per cent to 25.22 MT this year from 24.56 MT last year.

Mill use in China is projected to grow 1.5 per cent to 8.1 MT. Cotton mill use is also projected to grow moderately in India, Pakistan, Turkey, Bangladesh, Vietnam and Brazil.

As far as cotton trade is concerned, it is likely to be stable at 8 MT in 2017-18 marketing year.

The US will remain the largest exporter accounting for 40 per cent, or 3.1 MT of the world's shipments.

Bangladesh will remain the largest importer in 2017-18 accounting for 18 per cent, or 1.4 MT of the global imports.

Since global production is projected to edge over mill use during 2017-18, ending stocks could increase moderately and reach 18.7 MT with stocks to use ratio remaining little changed at 75 per cent.

"However, ending stocks in China are projected to decline by 1.7 MT during 2017-18, while outside China stocks are projected to increase by 1.85 MT," the report noted.

ICAC is an association of governments of cotton producing and consuming countries.

45. The Insolvency and Bankruptcy Board of India (IBBI) registered National E-Governance Services Limited (NeSL) as an Information Utility (IU) under the IBBI (Information Utilities) Regulations, 2017.

This registration is valid for five years from the date of registration.

IU stores financial information that helps to establish defaults as well as verify claims expeditiously and thereby facilitates completion of transactions under the Insolvency and Bankruptcy Code, 2016 in a time bound manner.

It constitutes a key pillar of the insolvency and bankruptcy ecosystem, the other three being the Adjudicating Authority (National Company Law Tribunal and Debt Recovery Tribunal), the IBBI and Insolvency Professionals.

NeSL becomes the first IU registered by the IBBI.

46. Shri Ram Vilas Paswan, Union Minister of Consumer Affairs, Food and Public Distribution today launched the Web Portal of Warehousing Development and Regulatory Authority (WDRA) & "Electronic Negotiable Warehouse Receipt (e-NWR) System" in New Delhi.

Addressing the gathering on the occasion Shri Paswan lauded the initiatives taken by the WDRA in simplifying the Warehouse Registration Rules, digitizing the entire process of registration, monitoring and surveillance as well as creation and management of Negotiable Warehouse Receipts (NWRs) in electronic form through two repositories.

The e-NWRs would have no chances of any tempering, mutilation, fudging, loss or damage and with no possibility of any multiple financing.

Hence, these NWRs will not only facilitate an easy pledge financing by banks and other financial institutions but also smooth trading on various trading centres like commodity exchanges, electronic National Agriculture Markets (e-NAM) and other electronic platforms.

The e-NWRs will save expenditure in logistics as the stocks could be traded through multiple buyers without physical movement and can be even split for partial transfer or withdrawal.

These initiatives would revolutionise the marketing of agricultural commodities and help farmers realize better price for their produce which will be a step towards doubling the farmers' income by 2022 as well as Digital India mission as envisaged by India's PM.

47. The Reserve Bank today relaxed norms for issuance of rupee-denominated overseas bonds, popularly known as masala bonds.

They will be treated as external commercial borrowings from October 3, thereby freeing up more investments by FPIs.

Currently, the limit for investment by foreign portfolio investors (FPIs) in corporate bonds is INR 2,44,323 crore.

This covers issuance of masala bonds by resident entities of INR 44,001 crore, including the ones in pipeline.

After a review, the RBI said that from October 3, masala bonds will no longer form part of the limit for FPI investments in corporate bonds.

They will form part of the ECBs and will be monitored accordingly.

As a result, INR 44,001 crore arising out of shifting of masala bonds will be released for foreign portfolio investor (FPI) investment in corporate bonds over the next two quarters.

Now, FPI investment limit for corporate bonds will increase to INR 2,44,323 crore from January 1.

Further, an amount of INR 9,500 crore in each quarter will be available only for investment in the infrastructure sector by long-term FPIs - sovereign wealth funds, multilateral agencies, endowment, insurance and pension funds and foreign central banks.

With surge in inflows in Indian debt markets, the cumulative utilisation of FPI limit in corporate bonds stood at 99.07 per cent as on September 21, 2017, reflecting limited scope of further FPI investments.

The Reserve Bank of India (RBI) changed the rules pertaining to the calculation of the foreign investment limit in so-called masala bonds, potentially opening up space for Indian companies to sell more such securities.

"Such a shift will allow companies to issue masala bonds as they are currently barred by Sebi (Securities and Exchange Board of India).

This will also lead to better monitoring of issuances by RBI as the external commercial borrowings framework is restrictive in terms of end-use of funds.

In a 20 July circular, market regulator Sebi had said that issuance of masala bonds would be temporarily stopped until the total foreign holding of corporate bonds falls below 92% of the limit.

As of 21st Sept 2017, foreign investors had exhausted over 99% of the available cap.

In June, the Reserve Bank of India had tightened the rules on the issuance of masala bonds.

The central bank mandated a minimum maturity of three years for sales of up to $50 million. Issuances above $50 million must be of five years or above maturity.

48. All peer-to-peer lending (P2P) platforms would be treated as non-banking financial companies (NBFCs) and will be regulated by the Reserve Bank of India (RBI), according to a government of India notification released on 20th Sept 2017.

The notification is a precursor to the much-delayed final guidelines that the RBI, the banking regulator, will soon be released for regulation of P2P lending in India.

As per RBI, P2P lending is a form of crowd-funding used to raise loans which are paid back with interest.

It can be defined as the use of an online platform that matches lenders with borrowers in order to provide unsecured loans.

The borrower can either be an individual or a legal person requiring a loan.

If you want to invest money in it, you go to a P2P marketplace and register as a lender.

Interest rates or fees are paid to the platform by both the lender as well as the borrower. Borrowers pay an origination fee–either a flat rate fee or as a percentage of the loan amount raised—according to their risk category.

Background

- The RBI had floated a consultation paper in April 2016.

- The proposed regulatory framework would encompass the permitted activity, regulations on capital, governance, business continuity plan and customer interface, apart from regulatory reporting.

- P2P lending is one such business model that has gathered momentum globally and is taking root in India.

- Although nascent in India and not significant in value yet, potential benefits that P2P lending promises to various stakeholders (to borrowers, lenders, agencies etc) and its associated risks to the financial system are too important to be ignored.

- The regulator had argued in favour of regulating the P2P lending entities in the consultation paper, stating that the sector has the potential to "disrupt the financial sector and throw surprises".

- The paper further stated that the importance of an alternative lending channel which the P2P platforms are offering also needs to be acknowledged.

- P2P lending promotes alternative forms of finance, where formal finance is unable to reach and also has the potential to soften the lending rates as a result of lower operational costs and enhanced competition with the traditional lending channels.

- If properly regulated, the P2P lending platforms can do this more effectively.

- This RBI regulation will bring much-needed legal clarity in the system, and lenders/platform will get legal rights to take adequate steps against defaulters.

- Also, regulation will mean wide acceptability of this concept among lenders as well as borrowers.

- This will fulfil RBI's expectation of taking P2P lending to the masses of this country.

49. Capital market regulator Securities and Exchange Board of India (Sebi) on 18th Sept 2017 allowed infrastructure investment trusts (InvITs) and real estate investment trusts (REITs) raise capital by issuing debt securities.

The Sebi board, at its meeting on 18th Sept 2017, also made several other relaxations to the InvIT and REIT framework to give a boost to the stalled infrastructure projects in the country.

InvITs and REITs are investment vehicles that allow investors take exposure to an income-generating infrastructure project or real estate property.

Prior to this development, the framework only allowed launch of equity-oriented REITs and InvITs, which offer only indicative yields, not fixed yields.

Issue of debt-oriented REITs and InvITs will offer a fixed-return to investors, which could give a fillip to these instruments, said bankers.

Further, Sebi has extended the concept of 'strategic investor' for REIT. Currently, it was only allowed for InvITs, which has seen two issues in the domestic market.

It also allowed single-asset REIT on the lines of InvIT.

It also allowed a REIT to lend to the underlying holding company (Hodco) or special purpose vehicle (SPV).

Sebi had notified the regulations for REITs and InvITs in 2014. However, fund raising through these instruments has failed to take off.

So far, only two InvITs - IRB InvIT Fund and Indiagrid Trust - have been listed on the stock exchanges. While several realty players have shown interest in launching a REIT, there hasn't been a single issuance under this route.

SEBI Proposals for REIT, InVIT:

- The regulator has also proposed to amend definition of valuer for both the trusts. Currently, the valuer should not be an investor in InvITs or the assets being valued.

- The valuer should have minimum experience five years in undertaking valuation of the infrastructure assets.

- The changes approved by Sebi is yet another attempt to push the REIT and InvIT regime, which till date has practically been a non-starter despite the regime being notified several years back (with an exception of just a few such vehicles being set-up).

- Allowing such vehicles to raise debt capital by way of issuance of bonds is unique for a Sebi fund regulatory vehicle as its not permitted for other Sebi regulated fund vehicles like alternative investment funds (AIFs) and mutual funds.

- This brings the investment trust regime more at par with the RBI's NBFC regime which typically raises private capital by issuance of NCDs

- Besides, the market regulator has apprised the board on the action taken against the 331 suspected shell companies which were barred to trade since August 7.

- So far, the regulator has asked for a forensic audit of about 12 firms. While stock exchanges are looking into the credentials of about 90 firms, in some cases, the Securities Appellate Tribunal (SAT) had put a stay order on the trading ban.

- Sebi has learnt to have also reviewed the cases that are pending before various courts and appellate tribunals.

- In a first, Sebi has also appointed a chief economic adviser who may assist the regulator on various policy issues.

50. India has been placed at a low 103 rank, the lowest among BRICS economies, on the World Economic Forum's (WEF's) Global Human Capital Index, which has been topped by Norway.

India also ranks "among the lowest in the world" when it comes to the employment gender gap, but has fared well when it comes to development of skills needed for the future with a rank of 65 out of total 130 countries surveyed.

The list compiled by Geneva-based World Economic Forum (WEF) takes into account "the knowledge and skills people possess that enable them to create value in the global economic system" to measure the 'human capital' rank of a country.

India was ranked 105th on this list last year, while Finland was on the top which has pushed by Norway to second place this year.

The WEF said India is ranked lower than its BRICS peers, with Russian Federation placed as high as 16th place, followed by China at 34th, Brazil at 77th and South Africa at 87th place.

Among the South Asian countries also, India was ranked lower than Sri Lanka and Nepal, although higher than neighbouring Bangladesh and Pakistan.

Low Ranking by India:

- India is held back by a number of factors, including low educational attainment (primary education attainment among 25 -54 year olds is 110th for example) and low deployment of its human capital, meaning the skills available are not getting put to good use.

- WEF said India ranks 118 for labour force participation among the key 35-54 year old demographic, suggesting far too many Indians are engaged in informal or subsistent employment.

- However there is a modern India rising. When it comes to development of skills needed for the future, the country fares strongly, ranking 65 out of 130.

- The country also performed well in the know-how parameter that measures the use of specialised skills at work

- The overall list was topped by Norway, followed by Finland and Switzerland in the second and third place respectively.

- Other countries in the top 10 include, the United States (4th), Denmark (5th), Germany (6th), New Zealand (7th), Sweden (8th), Slovenia (9th) and Austria (10th).

- The report measures 130 countries against four key areas of human capital development; Capacity (determined by past investment in formal education), Deployment (accumulation of skills through work), Development (continued upskilling and reskilling of existing workers) and Know-how (specialised skills-use at work).

- According to the report, 62 per cent of human capital has now been developed globally.

51. In order to improve the economic condition of the farmers, Prime Minister, Shri Narendra Modi has set up an ambitious target in front of the nation.

The goal is to double the income of the farmers by 2022. It has been for the first time, a Prime Minister has put such a target in front of the compatriots for the welfare of the farmers.

Under the able guidance of Prime Minister, Shri Narendra Modi, the Agriculture and Farmers Welfare Ministry has to achieve this target by 2022.

The Ministry is committed to making his dreams come true. Farmers and officers are implementing schemes to increase the income of the farmers.

Krishi Vigyan Kendras (KVKs) organised pledge taking ceremonies in 562 districts of the country between August 19 to September 11, 2017, as a clarion call to farmers to double their income by 2022 and a total of 47,08,47 farmers and agricultural workers participated in it.

- KVKs organised this program in the 562 districts of the country. The program saw the participation of the State Government and the Central Government officers, Agricultural Officers, Students and a large number of farmers in each district.

- 49 Central Ministers participated in pledge taking ceremonies at 79 locations (Districts).

- In 284 places (Districts), Members of Parliament attended the program.

- In 111 locations (Districts), State Ministers attended the program.

- In 350 locations (Districts), the MLAs attended the program.

- In 398 places (Districts), Chairman of District Panchayat attended the program.

52. The fourth Estimates has revealed record food grain production at 275.68 million tonnes comprising of 110.15 mn tonnes paddy, 98.38 mn tonnes wheat, 22.95 mn tonnes pulses and 44.19 mn tonnes coarse cereal.

Activities of NFSM, which are as follows, were also covered:

- In 2016-17, 638 districts of 29 states grew pulses against 468 districts of 16 states in 2012-13.

- Coarse cereals were included in 12th scheme. NFSM-coarse cereal is being implemented in 265 districts of 28 states since 2014-15

The council took following decisions at the NFSM meeting:

- Allocation of additional funds to target pulse cultivation in the rice fallow areas of Eastern States; and allocate additional funds for the pulses & oilseeds cultivation to tackle wheat blast disease in the West Bengal.

- Allocation of funds by the Indian Council of Agricultural Research (ICAR) institutes for Frontline Demonstration of rice, wheat, pulses and coarse cereals by various Krishi Vigyan Kendras.

- Distribution of seeds mini kits and assistance to the central agencies for the production of certified seeds of pulses.

- Experiment of TL seeds developed by the ICAR, under seed hub program during 2016-17 and their implementation during Frontline Demonstration in 2017-18.

- Under NFSM pulse program, promotion of beekeeping with arhar dal during Frontline Demonstration.

- Approval for extension of all the projects approved under NFSM till 2016-17.

- Additional fund allocation for production of breeder seeds of pulses and creation of seed hubs.

- Funds approved for the year 2015-16 agricultural awards.

- Presentations by states like Andhra Pradesh, Maharashtra, Odisha and Uttar Pradesh.

- Increased expenditure has led to increase in production of the food grains.

53. Plans by the government to backtrack on the controversial Ogden rate changes, which have slashed the earnings of UK insurers, lifted heavily-exposed Direct Line on the FTSE 100.

The government said yesterday that if the rate, which concerns personal injury claims, were set today it would "fall within the range of 0pc to 1pc".

This means smaller compensation claims for insurers to pay and higher earnings.

Insurers' shares tumbled when the Government announced in February that the Ogden rate would drop to -0.75pc from 2.5pc with the fall forcing Direct Line to report significantly smaller profits and halve its dividend.

A broad-based rebound helped the wider FTSE 100 finish in positive territory for the first time this week, closing 42.85 points higher at 7396.98.

On the currency markets the pound's stumble towards parity with the euro took further impetus after European Central Bank president Mario Draghi revealed that the Governing Council will make the "bulk" of its decisions on tapering its €60bn-a-month quantitative easing programme in October.

Despite Mr Draghi calling the euro's recent volatility and strength a "source of uncertainty", the currency pushed past $1.20 against the dollar.

The pound, meanwhile, retreated to back below €1.09, as it took another knock on its drift towards parity with the euro.

Elsewhere, the FTSE 100 snapped its losing streak and rose higher for the first time this week.

54. The Income Tax department is planning to implement the first phase of 'Project Insight' from May 2017 to monitor high value transactions, with a view to curbing the circulation of black money.

This project has been initiated for data mining, collection, collation and processing of such information for effective risk management with a view to widening and deepening tax base.

Project Insight will use big data analytics to match information from social media sites to deduce mismatches between spending pattern and income declaration.

The tax department will analyse mismatches in income declarations and spending patterns to trace tax evasions and black money, an official said.

The government has also made linking of PAN with Aadhaar mandatory to get a 360 degree view of a person's income and assets.

The tax department had last year signed a pact with L&T Infotech for implementation of Project Insight, which is designed to strengthen the non-intrusive information driven approach for improving tax compliance.

This is part of the steps the government has taken to unearth and tax undeclared or illegal wealth.

The steps include launch of 'Operation Clean Money' after demonetisation of old higher denomination currency for collection, collation and analysis of information on cash transactions, extensive use of information technology and data analytics tools for identification of high risk cases, expeditious e-verification of suspect cases and enforcement actions.

The information technology-based Project Insight will strengthen the information driven approach for improving tax compliance.

The project will use technology to allow the government collate databases of IT returns, IT forms, TDS/TCS statements and Statement of Financial Transactions received from financial institutions. As part of Project Insight, a new Compliance Management Centralised Processing Centre (CMCPC) would also be set up for handling preliminary verification, campaign management, generation of bulk letters/notices and follow-up.

Key Issues

- 'Project Insight' is an integrated platform that will utilize vast amount of information easily available on social media to conduct raids online rather than traditional way of conducting random searches, known as tax raids.

- It will use data mining, big data and analytics to scoop out tax evaders from social media platforms like Facebook, Twitter and Instagram.

- The Permanent Account Number (PAN) will be the unique identifier is used by the Income Tax department to link and analyse various transactions relating to the tax payers.

- This will enhance the department's ability to monitor the flow of funds and will provide an audit trail of high value transactions and curb circulation of black money

- The 'Project Insight' will be implemented in phased manner during the period 2016-2018. For its implementation, the IT department has signed a contract with L&T Infotech Ltd.

- It will also be leveraged for implementation of Foreign Account Tax Compliance Act Inter Governmental Agreement (FATCA IGA) and Common Reporting Standard (CRS).

Significance of 'Project Insight'

- It will help in catching tax evaders in a non-intrusive manner using technology and without traditional intrusive methods like search and seizure.

- The integrated platform will play a key role in widening of tax base and data mining to track tax evaders.

- The reporting compliance management system of project will ensure that third party reporting by entities like banks and other financial institutions is timely and accurate.

- It will also set up a streamlined data exchange mechanism for other government departments.

55. Leader of the Green Revolution Dr. M.S Swaminathan and Padma Shri Dr. H Sudarshan, on Sept 5 2017, launched the National Nutrition Strategy, along with Vice Chairman Dr. Rajiv Kumar and Member Dr. Vinod Paul.

With a benefit to cost ratio of 16:1 for 40 low and middle-income countries, there is a well recognized rationale, globally, for investing in Nutrition.

The recently published NFHS-4 results reflect some progress, with a decline in the overall levels of under nutrition in both women and children.

However, the pace of decline is far below what numerous countries with similar growth trajectories to India have achieved.

Moreover, India pays an income penalty of 9% to 10% due to a workforce that was stunted during their childhood.

To address this and to bring nutrition to the centre-stage of the National DevelopmentAgenda, NITI Aayog has drafted the National Nutrition Strategy.

Formulated through an extensive consultative process, the Strategy lays down a roadmap for effective action, among both implementers and practitioners, in achieving our nutrition objectives.

The nutrition strategy envisages a framework wherein the four proximate determinants of nutrition - uptake of health services, food, drinking water & sanitation and income & livelihoods - work together to accelerate decline of under nutrition in India.

National Nutrition Strategy:

- The Nutrition Strategy framework envisages a Kuposhan Mukt Bharat - linked to Swachh Bharat and Swasth Bharat.

- The aim is to ensure that States create customized State/ District Action Plans to address local needs and challenges.

- This is especially relevant in view of enhanced resources available with the States, to prioritise focussed interventions with a greater role for panchayats and urban local bodies.

- The strategy enables states to make strategic choices, through decentralized planning and local innovation, with accountability for nutrition outcomes.

56. Since April-June (Q1) 2010-11, Public Debt Management Office (PDMC) (earlier Middle Office), Budget Division, Department of Economic Affairs, Ministry of Finance, is bringing-out a Quarterly Report on Public Debt Management on regular basis.

The Current Quarterly Report pertains to the quarter April-June 2017 (Q 1 FY 18).

The liquidity in the economy remained in surplus, after the demonetization, during the quarter, which kept the yield environment low.

However, the cash position of the Government of India (GoI) was somewhat stressed during the quarter, due to mismatch in receipt and payment which is generally seen during the first half of the financial year.

The weighted average maturity (WAM) and weighted average yield (WAY) of the G-Sec issuance made during Q1 FY18 was 14.92 years and 7.01 per cent respectively.

During Q1 FY18, Government issued dated securities worth Rs.1,68,000 crore (29.0 per cent of BE), higher than Rs. 1,65,000 crore (28.4 per cent of BE) in Q1 of FY 17.

Auctions of both, Government dated securities and Treasury Bills during Q1 of FY18 were held smoothly.

The Public Debt (excluding liabilities under the 'Public Account') of the Central Government provisionally increased by 3.6 per cent (provisional) in Q1 of FY 18 on Q-o-Q basis.

Internal debt constituted 93.0 per cent of Public Debt as at end-June 2017 while marketable securities accounted for 83.2 per cent of Public Debt.

About 26.6 per cent of outstanding stock has a residual maturity of up to 5 years at end - June 2017 or 5.3 per cent of outstanding stock will mature every year over the next five years, which implies that rollover risk in the debt portfolio continues to be low.

57. The premium aromatic variety Gobindo Bhog rice has received the GI tag.

More farmers are taking up its cultivation since its gives higher productivity and remuneration.

Some 600 farmers have sown the rice for the first time this crop season (August-November).

This has increased the number of farmers opting for the aromatic rice to over 1,800.

The Bidhan Chandra Kishi Viswavidyalaya (BCKV), through a programme, launched since 2009, has extended cultivation of the rice to new areas and promoted it among a larger number of farmers.

According to a study by the BCKV, 80 per cent of the rice produced is consumed locally, while 20 per cent is exported.

The area under cultivation for this variety is expected to go up further by over 50 per cent this crop year compared with last year.

Having started the programme with less than 100 farmers in Nadia district in 2009, BCKV has brought in 1,800 farmers across 18 blocks of the South Bengal districts of Murshidabad, Burdwan, Hooghly, Nadia, North 24 Parganas and South 24 Parganas.

The area under cultivation has increased 10-fold in 2012 from a mere 45 acres four years ago.

Paddy productivity of this premium variety has gone up by more than 40 per cent to about 1.3 tonnes an acre, he said.

Currently, this variety fetches a price of Rs 2,800-3,000 for a 60-kg bag.

58. The Government of India's Street Lighting National programme (SLNP) has illuminated 50,000 KM of Indian roads.

This is with installation of 30 lakh LED street lights across the country.

With this milestone Energy Efficiency Services Limited under Ministry of Power, has become the world's largest street light management company.

The installation of 30 lakh LED street lights has resulted in 39 crore kWh of annual energy savings.

This is with avoided capacity of over 104.19 MW to the Urban Local Bodies (ULBs).

Further it has also helped in reduction of 3.29 lakh tonnes of CO2 annually.

SNLP:

- Under SLNP, Rajasthan is leading the country with an installation of 7.85 lakh LED street lights.

- This is followed by Andhra Pradesh and Gujarat with 6.03 lakhs and 5.4 lakhs respectively.

- Presently, EESL is retrofitting 15,000 conventional lights with LED street lights every day. Project is near completion in the states of Himachal Pradesh, Tripura and Gujarat.

- EESL is also implementing a special heritage lighting project in Kashi region of Uttar Pradesh where 4,000 lights are being installed.

- The programme has also recently commenced in the cities of Chandigarh and Port Blair, Andaman and Nicobar Islands.

- Further, the procurement price of the LED Street Lights has been reduced from Rs. 135/watt to Rs. 80/watt due to mass procurement of the lights.

59. The Cabinet on Aug 16, 2017 decided to set up a high-powered committee of Union ministers, including Finance Minister Arun Jaitley, to expedite strategic disinvestment of state-owned companies.

The Cabinet gave its nod for setting up an Alternative Mechanism (AM) consisting of Finance Minister, Road Transport and Highways Minister, and Minister of Administrative Department, to decide on the matters relating to strategic disinvestment.

The government has budgeted to raise INR 72,500 crore through stake sale in PSUs.

This includes INR 46,500 crore from minority stake sale, INR 15,000 crore from strategic disinvestment and INR 11,000 crore from listing of PSU insurance companies.

60. The Indian Constitution makes the provision of healthcare in India the responsibility of the state governments, rather than the central federal government. It makes every state responsible for

"raising the level of nutrition and the standard of living of its people and the improvement of public health as among its primary duties".

The National Health Policy was endorsed by the Parliament of India in 1983 and updated in 2002, and then again updated in 2017 called the **National Health Policy 2017**. The recent four main updates in 2017 mentions the need to focus on the growing burden of non-communicable diseases, on the emergence of the robust healthcare industry, on growing incidences of unsustainable expenditure due to health care costs and on rising economic growth enabling enhanced fiscal capacity. In practice however, the private healthcare sector is responsible for the majority of healthcare in India, and most healthcare expenses are paid directly out of pocket by patients and their families, rather than through health insurance. Government health policy has thus far largely encouraged private-sector expansion in conjunction with well designed but limited public health programmes.

A government-funded health insurance project was launched in 2018 by the Government of India, called **Ayushman Bharat**.

According to the World Bank, the total expenditure on health care as a proportion of GDP in 2015 was 3.89%. Out of 3.89%, the governmental health expenditure as a proportion of GDP is just 1%, and the out-of-pocket expenditure as a proportion of the current health expenditure was 65.06% in 2015.

61. The Survey notices a rekindled optimism on structural reforms in Indian economy.

Various factors such as launch of the GST; Positive impacts of demonetization; decision in principle to privatize Air India; further rationalization of energy subsidies and Actions to address the Twin Balance Sheet (TBS) challenge contribute to this optimism.

The document also adds that a growing confidence that macro-economic stability has become entrenched is evident because of a series of government and RBI actions and because of structural changes in the oil market have reduced the risk of sustained price increases.

However the Survey cautions that anxiety reigns because a series of deflationary impulses are weighing on an economy, yet to gather its full momentum and still away from its potential.

These include: stressed farm revenues, as non-cereal food prices have declined; farm loan waivers and the fiscal tightening they will entail; and declining profitability in the power and telecommunication sectors, further exacerbating the TBS problem.

Examining if India is undergoing a structural shift in the inflationary process toward low inflation, the Survey notes that the oil market is very different today than a few years ago in a way that imparts a downward bias to oil prices, or at least has capped the upside risks to oil prices.

Also Farm loan waivers could reduce aggregate demand by as much as 0.7 percent of GDP, imparting a significant deflationary shock to an economy.

Spurt in New Tax Payers and Reported Income After Demonetization; 5.4 lakh New Tax Payers Post-Demonetization.

Demonetisation's impact on the informal economy increased demand for social insurance, particularly in less developed states.

MGNREGS and its implementation by the Government have met the programme's stated role of being a social safety net during times of need.

It also adds that sustaining current growth trajectory will require action on more normal drivers of growth such as investment and exports and cleaning up of balance sheets to facilitate credit growth.

The ratio of stressed companies in the power sector (defined as the share of debt owed by companies with an interest coverage (IC) ratio of less than 1) has been steadily rising this year, reaching 70 percent, with an associated vulnerable debt of over INR 3.6 lakh crore.

The telecommunications sector has experienced its own version of the "renewables shock" in the form of a new entrant that has dramatically reduced prices for, and increased access to, data, thereby benefitting - at least in the short run - consumers.

After launching of services by the new entrant in September 2016, the average revenue per user (ARPU) for the industry on aggregate has come down by 22 percent vis-à-vis the long term (December 2009-June 2016) ARPU, and by about 32 percent since September 2016.

As regards Outlook for Growth 2017-18, Survey (Volume I) had forecast a range for real GDP growth of 6.75 percent to 7.5 percent for FY 2018.

For Outlook for Prices & Inflation 2017-18, the Survey notes the outlook for inflation in the near-term will be determined by a number of proximate factors, including:

The outlook for capital flows and exchange rate which in turn will be influenced by the outlook and policy in advanced economies, especially the US;

- the recent nominal exchange rate appreciation;

- the monsoon;

- the introduction of the GST;

- the 7th Pay Commission awards;

- likely farm loan waivers; and

- the output gap

The document says that the fact that current inflation is running well below the 4 percent target, suggests that inflation by March 2018 is likely to be below the RBI's medium term target of 4 percent.

Review of Economic Developments: Economic Survey 2016-2017

- Real economy grew by 7.1 per cent in 2016-17 compared with 8 percent the previous year. This performance was higher than the range predicted in the Economic Survey (Volume I) in February.

- This growth suggested that the economy was relatively resilient to the large liquidity shock of demonetization which reduced cash in circulation by 22.6 percent in the second half of 2016-17.

- The apparent resilience was even more marked in nominal growth magnitudes because both nominal GVA and GDP growth accelerated by over 1 percentage point in 2016-17 compared with 2015-16.

- Annual inflation averaged 5.9 per cent in 2014-15 and has since declined to 4.5 per cent in FY 2017. More dramatic have been developments during 2016-17- inflation declined sharply from 6.1 percent in July 2016 to 1.5 percent in June 2017.

- The sharp dip in WPI inflation in late FY 2015 and throughout FY 2016 owed to the deceleration in global commodities prices, especially crude oil prices.

- With global commodity prices recovering and the 'base effect' (low inflation in the previous year) giving an upward push, wholesale inflation perked up during FY 2017

- With the green shoots slowly becoming visible in merchandise trade, and robust capital flows, the external position appears robust, reflected inter alia in rising reserves and a strengthening exchange rate.

- The current account deficit narrowed in 2016-17 to 0.7 percent of GDP, down from 1.1 percent of GDP the previous year, led by the sharp contraction in trade deficit which more than outweighed the decline in net invisibles

- Export growth turned positive after a gap of two years and imports contracted marginally, so that India's trade deficit narrowed to 5.0 per cent of GDP (US$ billion) in FY 2017 as compared to 6.2 per cent (US$ 130.1 billion) in the previous year.

62. India has ratified the second commitment period of the Kyoto Protocol that commits countries to contain the emission of greenhouse gases, reaffirming its stand on climate action.

India's Permanent Mission to the UN said that India deposited its Instrument of Acceptance of the Doha Amendment to the Kyoto Protocol under the UN Convention on Climate Change.

With this, India became the 80th country to accept the amendment relating to the second commitment period of the Kyoto Protocol, the international emissions reduction treaty.

India's acceptance reaffirms our continued commitment to climate action,.

India's Permanent Representative to the UN Ambassador Syed Akbaruddin, who handed over India's Instrument, tweeted "maintaining momentum on Climate Change. India submits instrument of acceptance of Doha Amendment to Kyoto Protocol".

Kyoto Protocol:

- The Kyoto Protocol is an international agreement linked to the United Nations Framework Convention on Climate Change (UNFCCC).

- This commits its Parties by setting internationally binding emission reduction targets.

- The Kyoto Protocol was adopted in Kyoto, Japan, in December 1997 and entered into force in February 2005.

- The first commitment period under the Kyoto Protocol was from 2008-2012.

- The Doha Amendment to the Kyoto Protocol was adopted in Qatar in December 2012.

- The amendment includes new commitments for parties to the Kyoto Protocol who agreed to take on commitments in a second commitment period from January 2013 to December 2020 and a revised list of greenhouse gases to be reported on by Parties in the second commitment period, according to the UNFCCC website.

63. The Logistics Data Bank (LDB) project, unveiled in July 2016 to make India's logistics sector more efficient through the use of Information Technology, will soon expand operations to the country's southern region.

So far, it had covered only the western logistics corridor.

The facility - where every container is attached to a Radio Frequency Identification Tag (RFID) tag and then tracked through RFID readers - aids importers and exporters in tracking their goods in transit.

This has, in turn, cut the overall lead time of container movement as well as reduced transaction costs that consignees and shippers incur.

It is billed as a major 'ease of doing business' initiative aimed at boosting India's foreign trade and ensuring greater transparency.

The project covers "the entire movement (of containers) through rail or road till the Inland Container Depot and Container Freight Station.

The service integrates information available with the agencies across the supply chain to provide detailed, real-time information within a single window.

The LDB is being implemented through a Special Purpose Vehicle called Delhi Mumbai Industrial Corridor Development Corporation Logistics Data Services Ltd. (DLDSL).

This is jointly (50:50) owned by the Delhi Mumbai Industrial Corridor (DMIC) Trust and Japanese IT services major NEC Corporation.

On July 1, 2016, the LDB project was launched at the Jawaharlal Nehru Port, Mumbai.

From May this year, its operations expanded to the container terminals at Adani Port Special Economic Zone, Mundra and Adani Hazira Port — both in Gujarat.

So far, in all, the DLDSL provides container tracking services to around 70% of the container traffic in India.

The services include providing users the 'average delivery time' as well as notifications through SMS and email.

About 3.88 million containers (1.87 million import containers and 2.01 million export containers) have been tagged and de-tagged under the project until now.

Initial discussions on the LDB project were held in May 2012.

Talks were held on a regulatory framework from the Directorate General of Foreign Trade (DGFT) to ensure that all logistics players share data to make the project viable.

Later on, meetings were held between the DGFT, the shipping ministry and other stakeholders including the Tariff Authority for Major Ports regarding the regulatory framework on Mandatory User Charges (MUC) as well.

In November 2014, TAMP passed an order for levy of MUC for the project.

64. e-Shakti is a pilot project of National Bank for Agriculture and Rural Development (NABARD) for digitisation of Self Help Groups (SHGs).

It was initiated to address certain concerns like improving the quality of book keeping of SHGs and to enable banks to take informed credit decisions about the group through a Management Information System (MIS).

The project covers 25 districts and 1,30,176 SHGs have been digitised as on 31st March, 2017.

As per information compiled by NABARD, about 69,696 SHGs of the SHGs which have been digitised are credit linked as on 31st July, 2017.

No SHG has been de-recognised on account of, or, after digitisation.

The digitisation project does not impact the profit/ loss position of the SHGs.

65. Under Pradhan Mantri Paridhan Rojgar Protsahan Yojana (PMPRPY), Ministry of Textiles will bear additional 3.67% share of the employer's contribution of the Employers Provident Fund Scheme in addition to the 8.33% already covered under Pradhan Mantri Rojgar Protsahan Yojana (PMRPY).

This is for all new employees of apparel and made-up units enrolling in EPFO, for the first three years of their employment.

The Government has allotted INR 30 crores to the Ministry of Labour for FY 2016-17 and has made a provision of INR 200 crores for FY 2017-18.

As on 19.05.2017, 492 units have been registered under PMPRPY, which is reported to cover 1,82,400 new workers.

66. The Indian telecom industry has seen a paradigm shift from a voice centric market to a data-centric market.

While voice business still contributes a large chunk towards operator revenues, data revenues have shown an exponential growth trajectory over the last few years.

Towards the close of 2016 the number of internet subscribers in India was 391.50 million making India globally the 2nd highest in terms of internet users.

Mobile data traffic also grew by 76 per cent in India in 2016 primarily attributed to increased smart phone penetration.

This growing usage of smart phones, especially in urban areas, has increased the usage of internet on hand-held devices.

In 2016, 559 megabytes of mobile data was generated per month by an average smart phone, up from 430megabytes per month in 2015.

Consumption of video content is also forecasted to be 75 percent of India's mobile data traffic by 2021, compared to 49 percent in 2016.

Advancements in innovative IoT technologies, like health monitors, smart transport, smart meters among others, is projected to result in 21 per cent increase in M2M services.

These advances will result in a significant growth of mobile data, and as the telecom sector moves to newer technologies, TSPs will need to identify innovative avenues to monetise this data opportunity.

The Indian Telecom Market is expected to cross the INR 6.6 trillion revenue mark by the year 2020.

The Minister said that Indian Government had launched the 'Digital India' initiative in July 2015 which had three broad targets -

- Digital Infrastructure as a core utility to every citizen,
- Governance and Services on Demand
- Digital empowerment of citizens.

One of the projects under the 'Digital India' initiative was 'BharatNet', launched to deploy high-speed optical fibre cables to connect 2.5 lakh Gram Panchayat across the country by 2018.

This project would also help in increasing the fiberized sites in India which currently stands at less than 20 per cent as compared to other developed countries.

The project is being implemented in Phases, with more than 100,000 gram panchayats connected under Phase-I as of July 2017 and states like Kerala, Karnataka, Chhattisgarh, Haryana, Uttar Pradesh and Madhya Pradesh neared 100 per cent completion.

Major Achievements of the Indian Telecom Ministry

- Over 400 million internet users
- FDI quadrupled in FY2016-17 recording inflow of approximately USD 5.6 billion
- Greater than 20 per cent tower sites now diesel free
- Rural Tele density increased by 30 per cent over the last five years
- More than 3/4th of the data consumption was from 3G/4G
- Telecom industry generates over 4 million jobs direct and indirect
- LTE device ecosystem grew by 270 per cent from 2015
- 38 new mobile manufacturing units set up since September 2015
- 30 new locations added to 'Smart City' mission in June 2017, total count reaches 90 smart cities

- The government, is also working aggressive to connect 54,000 unconnected villages and would speed up its efforts after getting due reports from all states.
- There is the inter-ministerial group to look into the financial health of the sector.
- The new Telecom Policy will be a key building block for achieving the growth target of 10 percent from the current 7.6 percent as Telecom and IT are the two sectors contributing to 16.5 percent to the GDP, and there are immense possibilities for it to go up to 25 percent.

67. Canara Bank, which has set an ambitious target of moving to 'paperless' futuristic banking, launched its first 'Digital Banking Branch' at Spencer Towers in MG Road, Bengaluru.

Titled 'CANDI', the branch will provide an end-to-end digital experience to customers.

The bank, as part of the run-up to its digital foray, has introduced customer-friendly mobile apps which help customers get most of the information related to their accounts from the app without the need to visit the branch.

The most attractive feature of the Digital Branch is a humanoid robot that addresses basic queries of customers on banking products and services.

This is a first-of-its kind initiative by a public sector bank in the country.

The bank is in the process of re-inventing branch strategy and moving towards more digitisation and self-service channels.

The bank, to push its digital agenda, has equipped itself with a suite of next-generation banking tools which use advanced technology to streamline services and improve efficiency,.

The tools and devices include Customer On-Board Application which facilitates instant opening of Savings Bank account by the customer himself using fingerprint/ IRIS authentication.

Also on the anvil are printing of personalised debit card, cheque book, mobile/ Internet banking registration, generation of e-Passheet and issuance of virtual welcome kit.

There is an app-based token and queue management system to facilitate paperless appointment system using cloud technology and Digital Challan to facilitate filling up challans digitally by customers at their own convenience for services like cash deposit, fund transfer and cheque clearing.

There is a Digital Feedback System to get feedback from customers on the services availed by them and video banking to facilitate interaction with remote-site Subject Matter Experts on various categories of retail loans and corporate advances.

The branch works from 8 am to 8 pm on business working days.

There is also an interactive touchscreen-based 'Touch Banking' to enable the customers understand banking products like car loan, home loan, education loan, mutual fund, life/health insurance and apply online for the products.

68. The Minister for Communications Shri Manoj Sinha said that as per information provided by Telecom Regulatory Authority of

India (TRAI), there were 422.19 million broadband subscribers and the internet penetration (internet subscriber per 100 populations) was 32.86% in the country as on 31st March 2017.

National Telecom Policy-2012 envisages 600 million broadband connections by the year 2020.

Government has planned the BharatNet project to provide 100 Mbps broadband connectivity to all Gram Panchayats (approx. 2.5 lakh) in the country.

Under first phase of the project, 1 lakh Gram Panchayats (GPs) are to be connected by laying underground Optical Fibre Cable(OFC) which is under implementation.

Under Phase-II, targeted to be completed by March 2019, connectivity will be provided to remaining 1.5 lakh GPs in the country using an optimal mix of underground fibre, fibre over power lines, radio and satellite media.

Provision of last mile access to the network and broadband service provisioning shall be through Wi-Fi or any other broadband access technologies in all 2,50,000 GPs in the country.

As on 23.07.2017, the status of implementation of BharatNet is as under:-

No. of GPs where OFC laying is completed : 100,299 GPs

Optical Fibre Cable laid : 221,925 Kms

Broadband Connectivity provided in GPs : 25,426 GPs

69. Small Industries Development Bank of India (SIDBI) has started full-fledged merchant banking operations to benefit the expanding number of growth-oriented micro, small and medium enterprises (MSMEs).

This is especially those with a strong technology and innovation quotient.

The initiative is aimed at enhancing the access of MSMEs to the capital markets, including the SME Trading Platform and Institutional Trading Platform.

SIDBI has supported over 125 venture capital funds and thus can provide support for listing the investee companies on SME exchanges through its merchant banking operations.

SIDBI, by virtue of direct credit assistance for nearly two decades, also has a good number of such MSMEs that would like to list in the SME exchanges.

It is this strength that SIDBI would like to utilise by connecting the right investment opportunity to the funds and also would like to help these funds with exit opportunities at attractive valuations.

A significant increase in the number of venture funds active in the start-up/ MSME space in the past two years will create a large pipe of fast growing companies seeking public markets.

This will prove beneficial to the SME exchange as well as investors seeking liquidity or exit.

70. A Case Study on the birth of the Goods and Services Tax (GST) in India – "The GST Saga: A Story of Extraordinary National Ambition" was released on 25th July 2017 by the Union Finance Minister, Shri Arun Jaitley in his office in North Block in the national capital.

In view of the successful roll-out of the GST on 1 July 2017, it was felt that there was a need for the public to know of the story of how GST evolved, its timeline, the different stakeholders involved and how it eventually culminated in its inauguration in the Central Hall of the Parliament of India on the midnight of 30th June,2017 and 1st July, 2017 by the President and Prime Minister of India.

This case study accordingly captures the entire journey of GST right from its ideation in the Kelkar Task Force Report in 2003.

Other salient features such as the dates on which the SGST Laws were enacted in the 31 States, peculiarity of the Indian GST model, how the fitment of rates was done and the IT backbone of GST have also been addressed in the case study.

This makes it a concise yet comprehensive repository of the GST story.

71. National Trade Facilitation Action Plan (NTFAP) aims to align border procedures with international best practices and improve Ease of Doing Business.

It would not only ensure compliance with the Trade Facilitation Agreement (TFA) but would also give impetus to trade facilitation.

Action Plan gives a time bound map, not only for implementing TFA, but also for India's initiatives for trade facilitation and Ease of doing Business which goes beyond TFA.

The Action Plan was released by the Finance Minister Shri Jaitley on 21st July 2017.

WCO appreciated the various initiatives taken by the Indian Customs to facilitate trade particularly the release of the National Trade Facilitation Action Plan (NTFAP).

While praising the massive reforms undertaken by the present Government in the Indian Taxation System including implementation of GST, WCO indicated that the efforts made with regard to outreach and capacity building before implementation of GST in India can be emulated by many other countries.

WCO is working with G-20 on illicit financial flows.

72. India is the world's fourth fastest growing economy in the world thus far in 2017.

That's according to the World Bank's latest edition of Global Economic Prospects. For 2017, India's economy is expected to advance 7.2%. That's slightly above the country's long-term growth.

GDP Annual Growth Rate in India averaged 6.12% from 1951 until 2017, reaching an all time high of 11.40% in the first quarter of 2010 and a record low of -5.20% in the fourth quarter of 1979.

The Indian economy has benefited from a stable macroeconomic environment of low inflation and interest rates. This has helped shake off a temporary slow-down in consumer spending and a drop in investment that followed the demonetization program back in November 2016 - which took 86% of the country's currency out of circulation. India's economy has also benefited from ongoing market reforms that have improved competitiveness.

For 2016-17, India scored 4.52 points out of 7, according to Global Competitiveness Report published by the World Economic Forum, slightly above its ten year average of 4.33 points. That helped the country climb to rise to the position as the 39th most competitive nation in the world out of 138 countries ranked in the report.

The Competitiveness Rank in India averaged 52.73 from 2007 until 2017, reaching an all time high of 71.00 in 2015 and a record low of 39.00 in 2017. Improved competitiveness, in turn, has helped narrow the country's current account deficit to 0.70% of the country's Gross Domestic Product in 2016. Current Account to GDP in India averaged -1.40 percent from 1980 until 2016, reaching an all time high of 2.28% in 2003 and a record low of -4.80% in 2012. Financial markets have taken note. The iShares S&P India have gained 20.76 percent over the last twelve months.

73. The Insolvency and Bankruptcy Board of India (IBBI) has powers to start probe against service providers registered with it without intimating them, according to new regulations.

IBBI, which is implementing the Insolvency and Bankruptcy Code (IBC), has notified the regulations for inspection and investigation of service providers registered with it.

Insolvency professional agencies, professionals, entities and information utility are considered as service providers under the Code.

The Code, which provides for a market-determined and time-bound resolution of insolvency proceedings, became operational in December 2016.

As per the regulations, the investigation authority has to serve a notice intimating the entity concerned about the probe at least ten days in advance.

However, the requirement could be done away with on grounds such as apprehensions that the records of the particular service provider might be destroyed before the probe starts.

74. One last opportunity to deposit the 500- and 1,000-rupee notes that were banned in November will defeat the whole point of demonetisation as well as the battle against black money, according to the government of India.

The top court had asked the centre to consider a final window to benefit those with a genuine reason for not turning in the outlawed notes by the end of last year.

The deadline that was set by the RBI after Prime Minister Narendra Modi's shock announcement on demonetisation.

Different citizens' appeals were clubbed together by the Supreme Court.

But the government complained today of "the gross misuse or abuse" of previous extensions or exceptions that allowed old notes to be used to book railway tickets or at petrol pumps among others.

Allowing a new opportunity to deposit the banned notes would result in "any number of benami transactions" and make it difficult for departments to distinguish "genuine cases from bogus ones", the centre warned.

The PM said the short notice was vital to ensure that black money holders were deprived of the opportunity to launder their money.

However, the RBI says it has still not determined the exact figure of the returned notes. By the end of December, banks had received virtually all the currency notes that had been banned - which implied that no black money had been destroyed.

INR 15.5 lakh crore was the value of the outlawed currency - about INR 15 lakh crore was accounted for in deposits by the end of 2016, said several reports.

The last official estimate from the RBI, shared in mid-December, pegged the returned notes at Rs. 12.5 lakh crore.

75. India has topped in the Organisation for Economic Co-operation and Development's (OECD) Government at a Glance 2017 report.

It states that Narendra Modi led NDA coalition has secured 73% trust of people, highest in the world. OECD's Government at a Glance report presents an index of countries that trust their governments the most.

It determines government's trust levels by whether or not people consider their government stable and reliable, if it's able to protect its citizens from risk and whether it can effectively deliver public services.

The Canadian government headed by Prime Minister Justin Trudeau was ranked second with confidence of 62% citizens.

Turkey was in third place with 58% of the populace placing its trust in the Reciep Erdogan government.

Russia and Germany were ranked fourth and fifth with confidence levels at 58% and 55% respectively.

US government led by President Donald Trump secured only 30% of the peoples' confidence.

United Kingdom led by PM Theresa May secured 41% of the peoples' confidence.

Greece was placed at the bottom of the list with a mere 13% of the people's confidence.

The report states that government spending averaged 40.9% of GDP in OECD countries in 2015, up from 38.8% in 2007. In 2016, government spending as a share of GDP was highest in France with 56.5% followed by Finland (56.1%) and Denmark (53.6%).

It was lowest Mexico (24.5%), Ireland (29.5%) and South Korea (32.4%).

Organisation for Economic Co-operation and Development (OECD)

- OCED is an international economic organisation of 34 countries to stimulate economic progress and world trade Founded: 1961.

- It defines itself as a forum of countries committed to democracy and the market economy.

- It provides common platform for members to compare policy experiences, seek answers to common problems, identify good practices etc.

- Most OECD members are regarded as developed countries i.e. high-income economies with very high Human Development Index (HDI).

- Its headquarter is in Paris, France.

76. India, the world's third-largest oil importer, will import crude oil from the United States for the first time after Indian Oil Corp bought a cargo that will be delivered in October.

The purchase comes after Prime Minister Narendra Modi's visit to the US in June when President Donald Trump said his country looked forward to exporting more energy products to India.

IOC bought 1.6 million barrels of US Mars crude, a heavy, high-sulphur grade, and 400,000 barrels of Western Canadian Select that will be delivered onboard a Very Large Crude Carrier.

PetroChina was awarded the tender to sell the cargoes and is expected to load the oil off the US Gulf Coast, said a trading source with direct knowledge of the sale.

The cargo was priced on a delivered ex-ship basis, which is "very competitive" to that of Basra Light,

India is the latest Asian country to buy US crude after South Korea, Japan, China, Thailand, Australia and Taiwan.

Countries seek to diversify oil imports from other regions after the OPEC cuts drove up prices of Middle East heavy-sour crude, or grades with a high sulphur content.

Indian refiners are seeking these heavy, high-sulphur grades as feedstocks after modifications at their plants make it easier to process these types of crudes, which typically sell at a lower cost relative to other oil types.

The US could become an alternative source for the Indian companies for these grades.

A second Indian refiner Bharat Petroleum Corp Ltd also planned to buy its first ever US crude oil cargo and has issued a purchase tender.

BPCL:

- Headquarters: Mumbai

- CEO: S. Varadarajan (30 Sep 2013)

- Owner: Government of India (54.93%)

- Revenue: 2.404 trillion INR (2015, US $36 billion)

- Founded: 1976

77. The Finance Ministry launches a new tax payer service module 'Aaykar Setu' that compiles various tax tools, live chat facility, dynamic updates, and important links to various processes within the Income Tax Department in a single module.

This e-initiative would not only provide better taxpayer services but would also help in reducing the direct physical interface between assesses and tax assessing authorities.

To enhance mobile access experience, a mobile responsive android version was also released along with the desktop version.

This highlights the Government's commitment towards continuously upgrading tax payer services.

This initiative will be minimizing the chances of any tax harassment.

The new step is an effort by the Income Tax Department (ITD) to directly communicate with the taxpayers, on a range of multiple informative and useful tax services aimed at providing tax information at their fingertips.

The module compiles various tax tools, live chat facility, dynamic updates, and important links to various processes within the Income Tax Department in a single module.

The tax payers will also be able to receive regular updates regarding important tax dates, forms and notifications on mobile numbers registered with the ITD.

All taxpayers who wish to receive such SMS alerts are advised to register their mobile numbers in the Aaykar Setu module.

The Central Board of Direct Taxes (CBDT) constantly endeavours to provide better taxpayer services and reduce taxpayer grievances.

New schemes and e-initiatives to educate the taxpayers and deliver tax payer services in an effective manner are key to this effort.

78. The President of India has promulgated today two ordinances, namely, the Central Goods and Services Tax (Extension to Jammu and Kashmir) Ordinance, 2017 and the Integrated Goods and Services Tax (Extension to Jammu and Kashmir) Ordinance, 2017.

This was for extending the domain of Central GST Act and the Integrated GST Act to the State of Jammu and Kashmir, with effect from 8th July, 2017.

With this, the State of Jammu and Kashmir has become part of the GST regime, making GST truly a "one nation, one tax" regime.

Earlier, the Goods and Services Tax was launched in the country from the midnight of 1st July, 2017.

However, because of the special provisions applicable to the State of Jammu and Kashmir extra steps had to be taken before the State could join the GST fold.

On 6th July 2017, the State of Jammu and Kashmir had taken the first step towards adopting the GST regime with the President of India giving assent to the Constitution (Application to Jammu and Kashmir) Amendment Order, 2017.

Resultantly, the One Hundred and First Amendment Act, 2016 to the Constitution of India that paved the way for introduction of GST in the country, became applicable to the State of Jammu and Kashmir also.

Following this, on 7th July, 2017, the Jammu and Kashmir Goods and Services Tax Bill, 2017 was passed by the State Legislature, empowering the State to levy State GST on intra-state supplies with effect from 8th July, 2017.

Concomitantly, the President of India has promulgated two ordinances, namely, the Central Goods and Services Tax (Extension to Jammu and Kashmir) Ordinance, 2017 and the Integrated Goods and Services Tax (Extension to Jammu and Kashmir) Ordinance, 2017.

79. The government on July 6, 2017 conducted the first GST "masterclass" for all stakeholders including citizens.

These "masterclasses" are in the form of hour-long programs and will be held for six days.

Here are key takeaways from the first GST masterclass:

1) Registration on GST portal:

The government clarified that it is mandatory for the traders and dealers to complete the Part-B of their GST registration within the period of 90 days.

If an individual is not hands-on with online registration, then she/he can visit any excise, VAT or Service Tax office of state and central government where officials will get the job done.

There is no charge involved in this process.

Responding to a query on problems regarding registration of names bearing special characters (e.g. D'Souza or L&T), the government said that the software of the GST portal has been fixed to overcome the hiccup.

2) Updating details after registration:

The GST masterclass also discussed the updation of details of a business in the GST portal.

The government said that for minor details like bank account number, phone number, e-mail ID, updation can be done by the trader herself/ himself by visiting the GST registration portal.

However, modification like change in legal name of business, address of place of business, addition or deletion of partners or directors etc. can be done only by tax officials.

3) Exemption on turnover of INR 20 lakh

Trader class by now are well-versed with the fact that they are exempt from GST registration if their annual turnover is less than Rs 20 lakh.

However, the GST Council officials clarified that if a business involves inter-state supply, then GST registration is mandatory even if the turnover is below the threshold.

However, it was pointed out that if a business has a turnover below INR 20 lakh currently and happens to cross the threshold over time, then it needs to get itself registered within 30 days of it.

4) Items outside GST purview:

The Revenue Secretary on Wednesday reiterated the items which are outside the ambit of GST.

Following is the list of such products and the competent authority which can charge tax on them:

- 5 petroleum commodities- VAT can be levied by state government while excise duty by the centre government

- Stamp duty and registration charges- By state government

- Vehicle Tax- By state government

- Electricity Duty- By state government

- Potable alcohol- By state government

- Entertainment Tax- By state government in order to benefit local bodies

5) Miscellaneous

- The provisional ID number received at the time of registration will be the same as the ID number received at the completion of registration.

- All registered dealers will have to furnish their GSTN registration numbers on signboards.

- In case, a dealer is facing problems in uploading Digital Signature Certificate (DSC), he/she can also opt to authenticate using an OTP (One Time Password) sent to his/her mobile number and e-mail ID.

80. The World Bank has cleared a USD 250-million loan to aid the Skill India mission.

The loan amount would be used for making Indian youth more employable through reskilling.

The USD 250 million Skill India Mission Operation (SIMO) is set to increase the market relevance of short-term skill development programmes (3-12 months or up to 600 hours) both at the national and state levels.

It will help the government of India to better equip the young workforce with employable skills.

SIMO will be a six- year programme in support of National Policy for Skill Development and Entrepreneurship (2017-23).

Under the programme, persons in the age group of 15-59 will acquire skill training irrespective of their employment status.

This will benefit 1.2 crore youngsters in the age bracket of 15 and 29 years who are entering the labour market every year.

The programme is expected to benefit approximately 15,000 trainers and 3,000 assessors.

The programme has also a mandate to offer placement and entrepreneurship opportunities to women and increase their exposure to skill training.

Need for Programme:

- As per the official estimates, India is in need of additional 109 million skilled workers to work in 24 key sectors by 2022.

- SIMO will support the government's vision of increasing women's participation in the labour force and increase greater off-farm employment.

- Higher skilled labour force will have an improved employment opportunity to raise their earnings.

World Bank:

- World Bank World Bank is one of five institutions created at the Breton Woods Conference in 1944. World Bank is part of the United Nations system, but its governance structure is different.

- World Bank's headquarter is situated at Washington DC. World Bank provides loans to developing countries for capital programmes.

- World Bank comprises only two institutions viz. the International Bank for Reconstruction and Development (IBRD) and the International Development Association (IDA).

- In contrast, World Bank Group comprises three more viz. International Finance Corporation (IFC), Multilateral Investment Guarantee Agency (MIGA), and International Centre for Settlement of Investment Disputes (ICSID).

81. According to 'Handbook of Statistics on States 2016-17', the gross fiscal deficits of all the states have soared to Rs 4,93,360 crore in fiscal 2016 from Rs 18,790 crore in FY1991.

This is the second edition of RBI's statistical publication.

'Handbook of Statistics on States 2016-17 follows a 'one-indicator-one table' approach. It covers all sub-national statistics on socio- demographics, state domestic product, agriculture, industry, infrastructure, banking and other fiscal indicators across the states during the period 1950-51 to 2016-17.

The handbook also provides data on the state-wise availability of power, per capita availability of power, installed capacity of power, and power requirement, the length of national highways, roads and state highways, and railheads.

Uttar Pradesh had a fiscal deficit of INR 3,070 crore in FY91, which has soared to INR 64,320 crore in FY16.

It is projected to improve to INR 49,960 crore in FY17.

Rajasthan had a fiscal deficit of INR 540 crore in FY91, which has soared to INR 67,350 crore in FY16.

Maharashtra has a fiscal deficit of INR 37,950 crore in FY16 which is projected to soar to INR 35,030 crore in FY17.

Gujarat which has seen rapid industrialisation in the period of data analysis has got its fiscal deficit increased from INR 1,800 crore in FY91 to 22,170 crore in FY16 and the deficit is projected to further deteriorate in FY17 to INR 24,610 crore.

Andhra Pradesh has a deficit of INR 17,000 crore in FY16 which is set to increase to INR 20,500 crore in FY17.

Tamil Nadu is also projected to have a higher deficit at INR 40,530 crore in FY17. Karnataka is also estimated to post higher deficit in FY17 at INR 25,660 crore.

Bihar which has a fiscal deficit of INR 28,510 crore in FY16 is slated to improve its finances with the fiscal deficit of INR 16,010 crore in FY17.

Similarly, West Bengal is also slated to improve its fiscal deficit to INR 19,360 crore in FY17 .

However, the gross fiscal deficit is projected to decline to INR 40,530 crore in FY17.

82. Stepping up its fight against tax evasion, the Centre has made it mandatory to quote the Aadhaar number for opening bank accounts and for transactions exceeding INR 50,000.

With the amendments to the Prevention of Money Laundering (Maintenance of Records) Rules, 2005 notified earlier this month, banks will have to demand both Aadhaar and the Permanent Account Number (PAN) for verification of identity, starting June 1.

By the Finance Act, 2017, the Government had made it mandatory to seed PAN with Aadhaar and quote it in income-tax returns.

However, the Supreme Court had held that only those individuals who possess an Aadhaar card need to link it with PAN.

The new rules mandate existing bank account-holders to provide their Aadhaar details by December 31, while new applicants will be expected to quote either the 12-digit number or offer proof that they have applied for Aadhaar enrolment.

Small accounts - those with a limit of INR 50,000 - can be opened without Aadhaar, but only at bank branches that are core-banking enabled, or where it is "possible to manually monitor" such accounts.

Banks are expected to ensure that foreign remittances are not credited to such accounts, and that the stipulated limits on monthly and annual transactions and balance are not breached.

According to the new rules, "The small account shall initially remain operational for 12 months, and thereafter for a further period of 12 months if the holder of such an account provides evidence before the banking company of having applied for any of the officially valid documents within 12 months."

The small account will be monitored, and in case of suspicion of money laundering, or financing of terrorism or such other high-risk activities, the identity of the account-holder will be verified by Aadhaar, or proof of having enrolled for it.

It is a step forward in promoting transparency and curbing benami holdings in financial institutions, including banks.

83. According to Reserve Bank of India (RBI), India's current account deficit (CAD) narrowed during 2016-17 fiscal owing to a contraction in the country's trade deficit.

The CAD for the last fiscal narrowed down to 0.7% of the GDP from that of 1.1% in 2015-16 due to contraction in the trade deficit.

Country's trade deficit narrowed down to $112.4 billion in 2016-17 from $130.1 billion in 2015-16.

Further, the net FDI (Foreign Direct Investment) inflows in 2016-17 also got narrowed to $35.6 billion from $36 billion during 2015-16.

Current Account:

- The current account is the net difference between inflows and outflows of foreign currencies.

- Current Account transactions increase or decrease national income.

- It includes all transactions of export and import of goods and services, investment income, and unilateral transfers.

- It consists of two major items (a) merchandise exports (credit to home country) and imports (debit to home country) (b) invisible exports (sale of services) and imports (purchase of services).

- If the sum of all these transactions is negative then it is called as current account deficit.

84.

(A) *Principles of Economics*	3. *Alfred Marshall*
(B) *Diamond water paradox*	5. *Adam Smith*
(C) *Value and Capital*	4. *J. R. Hicks*
(D) *Asian Drama*	1. *Gunnar Myrdal*
(E) *Language of Economics*	2. *J. K. Galbraith*

85. The Union Cabinet chaired by the Prime Minister Shri Narendra Modi has approved the proposal to introduce a Financial Resolution and Deposit Insurance Bill, 2017.

The Bill would provide for a comprehensive resolution framework for specified financial sector entities to deal with bankruptcy situation in banks, insurance companies and financial sector entities.

The Financial Resolution and Deposit Insurance, Bill 2017 when enacted, will pave the way for setting up of the Resolution Corporation.

It would lead to repeal or amendment of resolution-related provisions in sectoral Acts as listed in Schedules of the Bill.

It will also result in the repealing of the Deposit Insurance and Credit Guarantee Corporation Act, 1961 to transfer the deposit insurance powers and responsibilities to the Resolution Corporation.

The Resolution Corporation would protect the stability and resilience of the financial system; protecting the consumers of covered obligations up to a reasonable limit; and protecting public funds, to the extent possible.

The Government has recently enacted the Insolvency and Bankruptcy Code, 2016 ("Code") for the insolvency resolution of non- financial entities.

The proposed Bill complements the Code by providing a resolution framework for the financial sector. Once implemented, this Bill together with the Code will provide a comprehensive resolution framework for the economy.

Financial Resolution and Deposit Insurance Bill:

- The Financial Resolution and Deposit Insurance Bill, 2017 seeks to give comfort to the consumers of financial service providers in financial distress.

- It also aims to inculcate discipline among financial service providers in the event of financial crises by

limiting the use of public money to bail out distressed entities.

- It would help in maintaining financial stability in the economy by ensuring adequate preventive measures, while at the same time providing the necessary instruments for dealing with an event of crisis.

- The Bill aims to strengthen and streamline the current framework of deposit insurance for the benefit of a large number of retail depositors. Further, this Bill seeks to decrease the time and costs involved in resolving distressed financial entities.

86. As 'demand' is defined as a schedule of the quantities of a good that will be purchased at different prices, the supply similarly, refers to a schedule of the quantities of a good that will be offered for sale at different prices. Supply curve is therefore, a graphic representation of what quantities of a good will are offered for sale at all possible prices. Supply curve depicts the sellers' quantity reactions to various prices. Thus the quantity supplied, like the quantity demanded, is a function of price.

There is, however, an important difference between the reaction of quantity supplied and that of quantity demanded to changes in price of a good. Whereas the quantity demanded of a good generally increases with the fall in price of the good and decreases with the rise in its price, the quantity supplied decreases with the fall in price of a good and increases with the rise in its price.

In other words, while the quantity demanded has a negative or inverse relation with the price, the quantity supplied bears generally a direct relation with the price. The positive relation between quantity- supplied and price lies in the nature of the costs of production which generally rise as more quantity of a good is produced.

This is because of positive relation between price and quantity supplied that supply curve slopes upward from left to right. While the short-run supply curve always slopes upward to right, the long-run supply curve may slope either upward or downward, or it may be of a horizontal straight line depending upon whether the industry is working under increasing cost or decreasing cost or constant cost conditions. However, the upward-sloping supply curve showing increasing cost is a more typical case even in the long run.

It is worth nothing here that the concept of supply curve, as it is used in **economic theory, is relevant only for the case of perfect or pure competition** and it is quite inapplicable to the cases of imperfect competition—monopolistic competition, monopoly and oligopoly.

This is because the notion of supply curve refers to the question as to how much quantity of a commodity a firm will supply at various given prices. In other words, notion of supply curve refers to the quantity reactions of a firm when the firm itself exercises no influence over the determination of price and takes price as given datum for it and adjusts its quantity produced or supplied.

Since only in perfect or pure competition a firm exercises no influence over the price which is determined by impersonal market mechanism of demand and supply and is beyond the control of individual firms, the concept of supply curve is relevant only for perfect or pure competition. So far as short-run supply curve of the industry under perfect competition is concerned, it is a mere lateral summation of the supply curves of the firms.

Under various forms of imperfect competition, an individual firm does not take the price as given and is not a mere quantity adjuster. In fact, under various forms of imperfect competition, a firm sets its own price. For a firm under imperfect competition it is not a question of adjusting output or supply at a given price but of choosing price-output combination which maximises its profits.

Commenting on the relevance of supply curve, Prof. Baumol writes, "The supply curve is, strictly speaking, a concept which is usually relevant only for the case of pure (or perfect) competition. The reason for this lies in its definition-the supply curve is designed to answer question of the form, 'How much will firm A supply if it encounters a price which is fixed at P dollars". But such a question is most relevant to the behaviour of firms that actually face prices over whose determination they exercise no influence.

87. The Insurance Regulatory and Development Authority of India (IRDAI) has announced taking over the management of the Sahara India Life Insurance Company.

Insurance regulator, IRDAI in an order issued in New Delhi on 12 June 2017 said that Subrata Roy run insurer was "acting in a manner" prejudicial to the interest of subscribers.

IRDAI appointed one of its general managers, RK Sharma, as administrator to manage the affairs of the insurer with "immediate effect".

IRDAI appointed RK Sharma (GM (F&A-NL)) the administrator of Sahara India Life Insurance Company by exercising the powers granted under section 52 A of the Insurance Act, 1938.

The Administrator shall conduct the management of the business of the insurer as per applicable provisions of the Insurance Act, 1938.

The regulator said it has "reasons" to believe that Sahara India Life Insurance Company "is acting in a manner likely to be prejudicial to the interest of holders of life insurance policies".

IRDAI further said it will be the endeavour of the administrator to ensure the servicing of the policyholders and managing the affairs of the insurer in a smooth manner as far as feasible.

IRDAI:

- Website: irdai.gov.in
- Founded: 1999
- Sector: Insurance
- Headquarters: Hyderabad
- Agency executive: T.S.Vijayan (Chairman)
- Type: Statutory corporation

88. According to RBI, India's foreign exchange (Forex) reserves have increased by $2.404 billion to touch a lifetime high of $381.167 billion in the week that ended on June 2.

The increase was due to increase in foreign currency assets (FCAs). Components The components of India's Foreign Exchange Reserves include: Foreign currency assets (FCAs), Gold, Special

Drawing Rights (SDRs) and RBI's Reserve position with International Monetary Fund (IMF).

Out of all the components, FCAs constitute the largest component of the Forex Reserves.

FCA rose by $2.748 billion to $357.290 billion in the reporting week.

FCA:

- FCAs consist of US dollar and other major non-US global currencies.
- It also comprises of investments in US Treasury bonds, bonds of other selected governments, deposits with foreign central and commercial banks.
- FCAs include with them the effects of appreciation or depreciation of non-US currencies like the euro, pound, and the yen and is expressed in terms of dollars.
- The gold reserves declined by $343.2 million to $20.095 billion in the reporting week.
- SDRs' value decreased marginally by $0.2 million to $1.472 billion.
- RBI's reserve position with the IMF declined by $0.4 million to $2.309 billion.

89. The Union Government on 6 June 2017 said that Ministries will have to decide on FDI proposals within 60 days of the application and any rejection will need concurrence of the Department of Industrial Policy and Promotion (DIPP).

Earlier in May 2017, India had scrapped the 25-year old foreign investment advisory body named Foreign Investment Promotion Board (FIPB). It was scrapped with an aim to attract more FDI by providing quick approvals.

In an office memorandum, the Finance Ministry said subsequent to the abolition of FIPB, concerned administrative ministries have been allotted the work of granting approval for foreign investment in the specific sector.

The Industry Ministry, in consultation with the administrative ministry, will come out with a detailed guideline for processing of the FDI proposals and ensure a "consistency of treatment and uniformity of approach".

The Standard Operating Procedure will involve the process of inter-ministerial consultation for the examination of FDI proposals, wherever necessary.

FDI approval decisions in majority of the sectors have been relegated to concerned ministry and those relating to private security agencies would be decided by the Home Ministry.

While DEA will be responsible for clearing the proposals of financial services or there is a doubt about the regulator.

The memorandum also says that any FDI proposal related to banks will be approved by the Department of Financial Services.

The memorandum says that FDI proposals by NRIs/EoUs requiring approval of the government will be dealt with by the Department of Industrial Policy and Promotion (DIPP).

In this case, the DIPP will continue to be the administrative ministry for this purpose. DIPP will also be responsible for handling the applications seeking import of capital goods or machinery.

Applications of investments from countries of concern will require security clearance as per the FEMA guidelines and FDI policy. These applications will be processed by the Home Ministry. In this case, the Home Ministry will only process those applications that reach them via automatic route but requiring security clearances, cases pertaining to approval route sectors requiring security clearance will be processed by the concerned administrative ministry.

In cases of FDI application where there will be a doubt about the administrative ministry, DIPP will also be responsible for identifying the ministry where application will be processed.

(A) $Increasing\ cost\ industry$	2. $Positively\ sloped\ long\ run\ supply\ curve$
(B) $Decreasing\ cost\ industry$	3. $Negatively\ sloped\ long\ run\ supply\ curve$
(C) $Constant\ cost\ industry$	1. $Horizontal\ long\ run\ supply\ curve$

90.

91. According to BMI Research, a Fitch group company, India is among the **top five** consumer markets in Asia offering retailers the strongest consumer spending growth of an average of 6.1% over the next five years.

The other four countries are China, Sri Lanka, Vietnam and Indonesia. BMI Research was founded in 1984 Business Monitor International and later in 2014 was acquired by Fitch Group.

The firm performs industry and financial market analysis in 24 industries and 200 global markets.

According to the report, the real consumer spending growth in 2017 will be 6.2%. The factors responsible for increase in consumer spending in India include increase in access to consumer credit, lower inflation and favourable regulatory environment for foreign owned retailers.

These factors will continue to enhance India's consumer sectors in the coming years. India's thriving e-commerce segment is expected to grow at double-digit rates in the forecast period up to 2021.

The report has found that due to the limitations of activities for overseas retailers, e-commerce has been dominated by local firms like Flipkart and Snapdeal.

In India, bricks-and-mortar retailers have also began to foray into the e-commerce segment supported by the high mobile penetration in the country.

92. India has been ranked 45th, down four notches from last year, in terms of competitiveness in the annual rankings compiled by IMD which saw Hong Kong topping the list.

US was "pushed out" of the top three slots while Hong Kong consolidated its dominance of the annual rankings for the second year.

The list is compiled by the International Institute for Management Development's (IMD) World Competitiveness Centre. Switzerland and Singapore were ranked second and third respectively, with the USA at the fourth spot - its lowest position in five years and down from third last year.

The Netherlands completed the top five, jumping up from eighth last year.

Others in the top 10 list include Ireland at 6th, Denmark 7th, Luxembourg (8th), Sweden (9th) and UAE at 10th.

As India slid, China improved its position by seven places to 18th, thanks to its dedication to international trade. "If you look at China, its improvement of seven places to 18th can be traced to its dedication to international trade. This continues to drive the economy and the improvement in government and business efficiency,"

Professor Arturo Bris, Director of the IMD World Competitiveness Centre said. The bottom of the table, meanwhile, is largely occupied by countries experiencing political and economic upheaval.

Ukraine was ranked 60th, while Brazil was placed at the 61st position and Venezuela at 63rd.

IMD:

- The IMD World Competitiveness Centre is a research group at IMD business school in Switzerland.

- It has been publishing the rankings every year since 1989.

- This year's list comprises 63 countries with Cyprus and Saudi Arabia making their first appearance. Meanwhile, for the first time this year, the IMD World Competitiveness Centre also published a separate report ranking countries' digital competitiveness.

- At the top of the digital ranking is Singapore, followed by Sweden, the USA, Finland and Denmark, while the bottom five are Indonesia, Ukraine, Mongolia, Peru and Venezuela.

93. Habibganj railway station in the suburbs of Bhopal will become country's first railway station to be redeveloped in a public-private partnership (PPP) mode.

On June 9, station redevelopment work in the railway station will be launched by Railway Minister Suresh Prabhu.

The idea is to develop Habibganj railway station as a world-class transit hub equipped with all amenities.

The operation and maintenance of the railway station has been given to Bhopal-based Bansal Group for a period of eight years.

The group has managed to win the bid in 2016. Bansal Group plans to completely overhaul the station and develop four commercial land parcels to make Habibganj a commercial hub with shops, offices and hotels, all in a span of three years.

The environment-friendly railway station will be powered by solar energy. The station will have facilities for disabled, in addition, to lifts, escalators and travelators, underpasses.

In case of emergency, the station will be redesigned in such a way that the premises can be evacuated in four minutes and passengers can reach designated points of safety in six minutes.

Bansal Group will be responsible for all the facilities at the station like food stalls, retiring rooms, power, platform maintenance, parking etc.

IRSDC will oversee the Habibganj project. IRSDC is formed by railway unit Ircon International Ltd (IRCON) and Rail Land Development Authority (RLDA) to undertake station redevelopment projects.

WB's First PPP Mode Station:

- The idea to set up world-class railway stations was mooted by former railways minister Mamata Banerjee in 2009-10.

- It was only in 2015, the project was revived by the railway minister Suresh Prabhu.

- The Habibganj project is a part of the Indian Railways' ambitious plan to re-develop 400 A1 and A category railway stations.

- Indian Railways' ambition to redevelop 400 stations into world-class facilities is completely based upon its idea of land monetization.

- It aims to modernize and upgrade passenger amenities at stations by raising money through commercial development of railway land.

- Avenues such as land monetization, catering and parking will be utilized to boost overall revenue.

94. Market Regulator SEBI has formed a Committee on Corporate Governance under the chairmanship of Uday Kotak, the executive vice chairman and managing director of Kotak Mahindra Bank.

The move is aimed at improving the standards of corporate governance of listed companies.

The panel which is headed by Uday Kotak will also include representatives of Corporate India, stock exchanges, professional bodies, investor groups, chambers of commerce, law firms, academicians and research professionals and SEBI.

The panel has been mandated to submit the report within a period of four months.

The mandate of the committee is to make recommendations on: Ensuring independence in spirit of independent directors and their active participation in functioning of the company.

The steps that are need to be taken for improving safeguards and disclosures pertaining to related party transactions.

To suggest measures for addressing issues faced by investors on voting and participation in general meetings.

The steps required for improving effectiveness of board evaluation practices. Suggest on issues pertaining to disclosure and transparency.

Corporate Governance Norms:

- In April, SEBI unveiled the detailed corporate governance norms for listed companies.

- The new norms which are in alignment with the new Companies Act would be effective from October 1.

- The new norms are aimed at encouraging companies to adopt best practices on corporate governance. SEBI's new norms provides for stricter disclosures and protection of investor rights including equitable treatment for minority and foreign shareholders.

SEBI:

- SEBI is the statutory regulator for the securities market in India established in 1988.

- It was given statutory powers through the SEBI Act, 1992.

- SEBI's headquarters is in Mumbai, Maharashtra. SEBI's mandate is to protect the interests of investors in securities, promote the development of securities market and to regulate the securities market.

95. India lost its fastest-growing major economy tag in the January-March period, which was the fourth quarter of the financial year (FY) 2016-17, with the Gross Domestic Product (GDP) growth coming down to 6.1 per cent compared with a provisional 7 per cent in the previous quarter.

The growth of 6.1 per cent was also lower than China's growth in the same period which was 6.9 per cent.

The data released by the Ministry of Statistics on 31 May 2017 showed that the GDP grew 7.1 per cent in the FY 2016-17, which was slower than 8 per cent growth registered during FY 2015-16.

The GDP numbers for the FY 2016-17 was based on the new 2011-12 base year, which was adopted in recent past. The changes in the new base year also include Index of Industrial Production (IIP) and Wholesale Price Index (WPI).

India's economic growth unexpectedly slowed to its lowest in more than two years and reports suggest that it was dragged down by construction, manufacturing and trade services.

Report on contraction in these fields are given below. It contracted 3.7 per cent year-on-year in the March quarter compared with a 3.4 per cent growth in the prior quarter.

It grew 5.3 per cent in the last quarter from a year ago, slower than an annual rise of 8.2 per cent in the December quarter.

The annual growth in these areas slowed to 6.5 per cent in the January-March period from 8.3 per cent a quarter ago.

The second reason for this unexpected slump in GDP growth in March quarter can also be attributed to Prime Minister Narendra Modi's decision on 8 November 2016, in which he scrapped two high-value banknotes of the country, i.e. INR 1000 and 500 notes.

96. The civil aviation industry in India has emerged as one of the fastest growing industries in the country during the last three years.

With a 19 percent growth in domestic passenger traffic from about 6.1 crore in 2014 to 10 crore in 2016-17, India is now the third largest aviation market in the world, with the promise to grow even further.

What is most impressive about this growth is its inclusive nature defined by the Regional Connectivity Scheme - UDAN, that has made air travel possible for even the common man in remote areas.

The average or median airfares fell by 18 percent during 2016-17, making flying more affordable for the common man.

Scheduled domestic flight movements also rose from 7 lakh in 2014 to 8.2 lakh in 2016, an 8.2 percent CAGR growth.

As against 395 aircrafts in the fleet of Indian carriers, there are 496 aircrafts in operation today, and another 654 are under purchase.

Route Dispersal Guidelines have been rationalized, multiple provisions have been made for MRO service providers and a slew of initiatives like the AirSewa portal, enhanced compensation for cancellation and boarding denial have been taken for improving passenger convenience

The Regional Connectivity Scheme UDAN has been by far the most path-breaking achievement of the Ministry.

31 currently served, 12 under-served and 27 unserved airports are now connecting 128 RCS routes across the country.

50 airports are being revived and 13 lakh new UDAN seats are being added annually under the first round of UDAN for a Viability Gap Funding of INR 205 crore.

The Ease of Doing Business by allowing 100 % FDI in domestic scheduled air transport, Open Skies Service Agreements offers to 49 countries and 5 SAARC nations etc, developing a robust security architecture by complying with ICAO requirements, Anti Hijacking Act etc, promoting innovative technology like GAGAN, India's first navigation based system to improve accuracy of air navigation services and focusing on skill development in the aviation sector has been benefiting India.

The first Executive Aviation Course was launched by India's first Aviation University in February 2017. 800 ATCs were recruited by AAI in the last 2 years and more than 400 are planned to be recruited in 2017.

Aerospace and Aviation Skill Sector Council has been formed to monitor growth of skill development.

The civil aviation sector in India has undergone a complete transformation in the last three years with India emerging as the world's third largest aviation market.

As against 70-75 airports in the country in all these years, India has more than 100 airports with the implementation of UDAN.

97. Indian Oil Corp (IOC) has overtaken Oil and Natural Gas Corp (ONGC) to become India's most profitable state-owned company.

IOC, which has for decades been India's biggest company by turnover, posted a 70 per cent jump in net profit to INR 19,106.40 crore in the financial year ended March 31, 2017.

This was more than the INR 17,900 crore net profit ONGC posted in the 2016-17 fiscal, making IOC the most profitable PSU, according to earning statements of the companies.

Billionaire Mukesh Ambani-led Reliance Industries retained the crown of being India's most profitable company for the third year in a row, posting a net INR 29,901 crore in financial year 2016-17.

Tata Consultancy Services, India's largest software services exporter, with a net profit of INR 26,357 crore was the second most profitable company in the country.

ONGC was long India's most profitable company but lost the crown to private sector Reliance and TCS a couple of years back. It has now been unseated as the most profitable PSU by IOC.

In the previous 2015-16 fiscal, IOC had a net profit of INR 11,242.23 crore as compared to ONGC's INR 16,140 crore.

While IOC Chairman B Ashok attributed the profit growth to higher refining margins, inventory gains and operational efficiencies, ONGC Chairman and Managing Director Dinesh K Sarraf said the company lost INR 3,000 crore in net profit due to government's natural gas pricing policy that has made the business economically unviable.

The BJP-led government had in October 2014 evolved a new pricing formula using rates prevalent in gas surplus nations like the US, Canada and Russia to determine rates in a net importing country.

Prices have halved to $2.48 per million British thermal unit since the formula was implemented.

Sarraf said the company lost INR 5,010 crore in revenue on natural gas business from 35 per cent drop in gas prices in last one year.

98. The Department of Industrial Policy and Promotion (DIPP), which is the nodal body for Start-up India, has amended the definition of a start-up.

As per the new definition, an entity will be considered as a Start-Up if its turn over is less than INR 25 crore and has not completed seven years from the date of its incorporation/registration.

In the definition, the change is with respect to the time period which is currently five years. The new definition has increased it to 7 years taking into the consideration the long gestation period involved in establishing start-ups.

The scope of definition of start-up will also be widened to include scalability of business model with potential of employment generation or wealth creation.

An entity that has completed 7 years from the date of its incorporation or if its turnover exceeds INR 25 crore, it will cease to be a start-up.

The process of recognition of an entity as a start-up will be through an online application made over the mobile app/portal set up by the DIPP.

For the Start-Ups in the biotechnology sector, they will be considered as start-ups for a period of up to 10 years from the date of incorporation/registration.

Start-ups will not require a letter of recommendation from an incubator or an industry association to get tax benefits under the Start-up India action plan.

However, the entities should obtain a certificate of an eligible business from an inter- ministerial board of certification as constituted by the DIPP to claim tax benefit

An entity will be deemed as a start-up if it is working towards innovation, development or improvement of products/processes/services, or if it is a scalable business model with potential for employment generation or wealth creation.

99. Cochin Port Trust has received two Best Performance Awards from Ministry of Shipping for the highest growth in operating surplus and also for achieving third highest growth in cargo traffic among the major ports in the year 2016-17.

Cochin Port Trust has registered an operating profit of INR 127.72 crore during 2016-17 as against INR 70.89 crore during 2015-16 recording a growth of 80 per cent.

Operating profit during 2014-15 was INR 19.55 crore.

The Port handled 25.01 MMT cargo during 2016-17 with a growth of 13.2 per cent over 22.10 MMT handled in 2015-16.

The containers handled during 2016-17 is 4.91 lakh TEUs with a growth of 17.0 per cent over 4.20 lakh TEUs in 2015-16.

100. The GST Council headed by finance Minister Arun Jaitley has finalised a 4-slab service tax structure at the rates of 5, 12, 18 and 28 per cent as against the single rate of 15% levied on all taxable services. GST regime is scheduled to be implemented from July 1.

In the next GST Council meeting, tax rates on gold and other precious metals will be taken up for discussion. Luxury hotels, gambling, race club betting and cinema services will attract a tax rate of 28%. Education, healthcare and non-AC rail travel will remain exempted from the GST tax regime.

However, the states will be given the option to levy additional taxes on cinema to compensate for the revenue losses entailed due to merging of entertainment tax with GST. At present, the total tax incidence on cinema including entertainment and 4-slab service tax is in the range of 55%.

The states need to use the legislative route if it wants to levy additional tax on cinema. States will also be permitted to levy any new tax as the taxation powers of the states have only been restricted and not abolished after the rollout of GST. Telecom and financial services will be taxed at a rate of 18%. Transport services will be taxed at the rate of 5%.

Cab aggregators like Ola and Uber will have to pay 5% under GST in place of 6%. AC rail travel will attract 5% tax. Economy class air travel will attract 5% GST while business class will attract 12%. Travelling on metro, local train and religious travel such as Haj Yatra would be exempted from GST.

The e-commerce players like Flipkart and Snapdeal would be required to shell out 1% Tax Collected at Source (TCS). Non-AC restaurants and AC restaurants will attract a GST of 12% and 18% respectively. Advertisements published in newspapers will attract 5% GST. At present it is exempt from 4-slab service tax.

GST Council:

- ST Council is a federal forum with both centre and states in India on board formed in September 2016.

- It is made of: The Union Finance Minister (as Chairman), The Union Minister of State in charge of Revenue or Finance, and The Minister in charge of Finance or Taxation or any other Minister, nominated by each state government.

- The decisions of the GST Council are made by three-fourth majority of the votes cast. The centre has one-third of the votes cast, and the states together have two-third of the votes cast.

- Each state has one vote, irrespective of its size or population.

- The Secretary (Revenue) will be appointed as the Ex-officio Secretary to the GST Council. The Chairperson, Central Board of Excise and Customs (CBEC), will be included as a permanent invitee (non-voting) to all proceedings of the GST Council.

- One post of Additional Secretary to the GST Council in the GST Council Secretariat (at the level of Additional Secretary to the Government of India) will be created.

- Four posts of Commissioner in the GST Council Secretariat (at the level of Joint Secretary to the Government of India) will also be created.

Q.1 GST council has finalised tax rates and approved _____ rules of the GST regime.

A. 5   **B.** 6   **C.** 7   **D.** 8

Q.2 Which new portal has ITD launched in May 2017?

A. Operation Clear Money
B. Operation Clean Money
C. Operation Constant Money
D. Operation Circulation Money

Q.3 Which sector's revenue from exports touched an all time high of INR 2282 crore this fiscal?

A. Jute   **B.** Coir   **C.** Rubber   **D.** Cotton

Q.4 Organisations with turnover of how much will have to specify PAN while filing the Udyog Aadhaar Memo for registration?

A. INR 20 lakhs   **B.** INR 50 lakhs
C. INR 75 lakhs   **D.** None of the above

Q.5 India has jumped _____ spots to be 26th on World Bank's electricity accessibility index.

A. 13   **B.** 33   **C.** 73   **D.** 93

Q.6 What is the new base year for IIP and the WPI?

A. 2011-2012   **B.** 2004-2005
C. 2007-2008   **D.** None of the above

Q.7 NITI Aayog has set up a task force to _______.

A. Generate timely employment data
B. Generate reliable employment information
C. Both of the above
D. Neither of the above

Q.8 In its economic outlook report for Asia-Pacific, IMF has cautioned against _______ population.

A. Ageing   **B.** Young
C. Working   **D.** None of the above

Q.9 How many core parameters will the Liveability Index rank Indian cities on?

A. 13   **B.** 14
C. 17   **D.** None of the above

Q.10 What value will India grow to this fiscal (2017) as bankruptcy and GST laws help, according to ADB?

A. 7.3   **B.** 7.4   **C.** 7.5   **D.** 7.6

Q.11 Which base year will the new IIP follow to map economic activities more accurately?

A. 2011-2012   **B.** 2012-2013
C. 2013-2014   **D.** 2014-2015

Q.12 India is the world's _______ largest LPG importer, according to Petroleum Planning & Analysis cell.

A. First   **B.** Second   **C.** Third   **D.** Fourth

Q.13 How much can GST boost India's GDP growth by, according to the US Fed Reserve?

A. 4.4 percent   **B.** 4.3 percent
C. 4.2 percent   **D.** 4.1 percent

Q.14 Where is the largest Indian engineering sourcing show opening?

A. Chennai   **B.** Kolkata
C. Delhi   **D.** None of the above

Q.15 What is the issue prize for the Sovereign Gold Bond Scheme 2017-2018 series I?

A. INR 2901 per gram of gold
B. INR 2801 per gram of gold
C. INR 2901 per gram of silver
D. INR 2801 per gram of silver

Q.16 Which digitally developed economy has topped the Huawei Global Connectivity Index 2017?

A. US   **B.** UK
C. EU   **D.** Germany

Q.17 Which new World Bank report was released on 16th April 2017?

A. Gloablization March
B. Globalization Fallout
C. Globalization Backlash
D. None of the above

Q.18 Which year did humanity harvest its largest cereal crop according to FAO?

A. 2015-2016   **B.** 2016-2017
C. 2014-2015   **D.** None of the above

Q.19 What rank does India have in terms of GDP as a tourist economy?

A. 7th largest tourist economy
B. 8th largest tourist economy
C. 9th largest tourist economy
D. 10th largest tourist economy

Q.20 What low did growth of 8 core sectors of the country slip to in Feb 2017?

A. 1%   **B.** 2%   **C.** 3%   **D.** 4%

Q.21 For which state's development has India signed its first loan agreement with NDB?

A. MP   **B.** UP   **C.** HP   **D.** AP

Q.22 Which country became the net exporter of electricity during April - February 2017 for the first time?

A. India   **B.** Pakistan
C. Afghanistan   **D.** Nepal

Q.23 Which bank is offering "Unnati" credit cards to holders with balance of INR 20 to 25 thousand, without considering credit history?

A. State Bank of India
B. State Bank of Mysore
C. State Bank of Travancore
D. None of the above

Q.24 Which fair was inaugurated in Motihari Bihar to promote cashless transactions?

A. Digidhan
B. DigiFair
C. DigiCash
D. DigiMobi

Q.25 Which of the following is the apex policy making body for indirect taxes?

A. CBEC
B. CBAC
C. CBUC
D. CBIC

Q.26 What is the criteria for an Insolvency Professional according to IBBI?

A. The IP must not engage in any employment
B. IP cannot play two roles - profession and employment - at once
C. Both a and b
D. Neither of the above

Q.27 Which firms will have to deduct tax collected at source up to 1 percent while making a payment?

A. E-commerce
B. M-commerce
C. MSME
D. Financial

Q.28 Which coal ministry outfit has been tasked with grading and notifying Coal India Ltd mines?

A. Coal Controller's Organisation
B. Coal Controller's Association
C. Coal Controller's Agency
D. None of the above

Q.29 Indian exports soared by 17% in Feb 2017, led by ______.

A. Petroleum, engineering and chemicals
B. Manufacturing, services and IT
C. All of the above
D. Neither of the above

Q.30 India's retail inflation grew to what percent in February?

A. 3.65
B. 3.64
C. 3.63
D. 3.62

Q.31 Country's industrial production grew by what percent Y-O-Y in Jan 2017?

A. 2.4
B. 2.5
C. 2.7
D. 2.9

Q.32 RBI has prohibited NBFCs from lending how much in cash against gold?

A. INR 20,000
B. INR 25,000
C. INR 26,000
D. INR 21,000

Q.33 Match the following:

(A) Various combinations of two commodities   1.
Indifference map
    that a consumer can purchase

(B) Various combinations of two commodities   2.
Indifference curve
    that give consumer equal satisfaction

(C) A set of indifference curves   3.
Budget line

(D) Point of tangency of a budget   4.
Consumer's equilibrium
    line and an indifference curve

A.
(A)	(B)	(C)	(D)
2	3	4	1

B.
(A)	(B)	(C)	(D)
4	3	2	1

C.
(A)	(B)	(C)	(D)
1	2	4	3

D.
(A)	(B)	(C)	(D)
3	2	1	4

Q.34 Which country has the highest bribery rate in the Asia Pacific region?

A. Japan
B. China
C. Pakistan
D. None of the above

Q.35 OALP in the context of oil and gas stands for?

A. Open Acreage Licensing Policy
B. Open Association Licensing Policy
C. Open Acreage Licensing Programme
D. None of the above

Q.36 What is Udan?

A. Civil aviation/regional connectivity scheme
B. Defence procurement scheme
C. IAF scheme
D. None of the above

Q.37 GST Council has approved the draft versions of which bills?

A. CGST
B. IGST
C. SGST
D. Both a and b

Q.38 Number of ODF districts in India has now crossed?

A. 50
B. 75
C. 90
D. 100

Q.39 NASSCOM indicated the software services sector will grow at what percent in 2017-2018?

A. 8-10 percent
B. 6-8 percent
C. 4-10 percent
D. 6-10 percent

Q.40 Which of the following is the correct statement?

(1) The slope of the Isoquants represents the MRTS

(2) The MRTS of the inputs x and y = MPx/MPy

(3) The elasticity of substitution between two inputs x and y is proportionate change in the ratio of two inputs divided by proportionate change in the MRTS.

(4) If degree of homogeneity is greater than one, the production function is increasing returns to fixed factor

A. 2, 3 and 4
B. 2, 3 and 4
C. 1, 2, 3
D. 1, 2 and 3

Q.41 SEBI announced plans to tighten regulations for which type of trading?

A. Spot trading   **B.** Investor trading
C. Algorithmic trading   **D.** None of the above

Q.42 Which economy will be the fastest growing among G-20 nations, as per Moodys?
A. Japan   **B.** UK   **C.** China   **D.** India

Q.43 SBI Research has pegged Q3 GDP of India at ______.
A. 5.7%   **B.** 5.8%   **C.** 5.9%   **D.** 6%

Q.44 IMF has pegged Indian GDP at which figure post demonetisation?
A. 6.5%   **B.** 6.6%   **C.** 6.7%   **D.** 6.8%

Q.45 To promote a cashless economy, government is developing ________.
A. Digital matrix to evaluate states for cashless economy
B. Online platform for regulating cashless payments
C. Mobile app for regulating online transactions
D. All of the above

Q.46 Which state released a digital roadmap?
A. Punjab   **B.** Haryana
C. Delhi   **D.** None of the above

Q.47 What is Momentum Jharkhand?
A. Scheme
B. Social welfare programme
C. Global investors summit
D. None of the above

Q.48 India ranked at which position in the Index of Economic Freedom?
A. 142   **B.** 143   **C.** 144   **D.** 145

Q.49 Banks need how much capital to sustain 8-9% growth?
A. INR 90,000 crore   **B.** INR 91,000 crore
C. INR 92,000 crore   **D.** INR 93,000 crore

Q.50 Which of the following became the first cashless township in India?
A. GNFC   **B.** GIFT-TECH
C. Both of the above   **D.** None of the above

Q.51 Indian economy, according to India Ratings and Research, will grow at ____ in the next fiscal.
A. 7.2%   **B.** 7.3%   **C.** 7.4%   **D.** 7.5%

Q.52 India Inc's FDI overseas declined by what percent in Jan 2017?
A. 56%   **B.** 57%   **C.** 58%   **D.** 59%

Q.53 In Monetary Review on 8th Feb 2017, RBI has kept repo rate ________.
A. Unchanged   **B.** Changed to 7.25%
C. Changed to 8.25%   **D.** None of the above

Q.54 Indian economy will overtake the US in PPP by what year?
A. 2020   **B.** 2030   **C.** 2040   **D.** 2050

Q.55 Which Indian UT got approval for its first railway line?
A. Daman and Diu
B. Lakshadweep
C. Andaman and Nicobar Islands
D. None of the above

Q.56 India Innovation Index ranks states on ____________.
A. Innovation
B. Economic development
C. Economic growth
D. None of the above

Q.57 What is the share of nuclear power in the total electricity generation in the country in 2015-2016?
A. 3.4%   **B.** 3.5%   **C.** 3.6%   **D.** 3.7%

Q.58 Union Government is to contribute to which new dedicated railway safety fund?
A. Rashtriya Rail Sanraksha Kosh
B. Rashtriya Rail Sammelan Kosh
C. Rashtriya Rail Sahyog Kosh
D. None of the above

Q.59 Gyan Sangam is slated for March 2017 and is a retreat for __________.
A. PSBs
B. Government owned Financial Institutions
C. Government controlled insurance companies
D. All of the above

Q.60 Karang, a small lake island in Manipur reached which important milestone?
A. First cashless island
B. First ODF island
C. First island to have wireless technology
D. None of the above

Q.61 Post demonetisation, IMF has cut down the Indian growth rate to what percent?
A. 6.3   **B.** 6.4   **C.** 6.5   **D.** 6.6

Q.62 Central government plans to set up how many electronic manufacturing clusters in 400 towns and cities?
A. 18   **B.** 19   **C.** 20   **D.** 21

Q.63 BIS has revised Indian standards on hallmarking ________.
A. Gold ingots   **B.** Gold biscuits
C. Gold coins   **D.** Gold jewellery

Q.64 Which state has registered India's second highest per capita income in 2016?
A. Delhi   **B.** Chandigarh
C. Sikkim   **D.** None of the above

Q.65 According to latest data, over 26 crore accounts have been opened under PMJDY. How many of these are in rural areas, approximately?
A. 10 crore   **B.** 12 crore
C. 16 crore   **D.** None of the above

Q.66 How many tourists visited India in Dec 2016?
A. 8.91 lakh   **B.** 8.90 lakh
C. 7.91 lakh   **D.** 7.90 lakh

Q.67 RBI has opposed which move of the Watal Committee?
A. Digital payments
B. Separate entity to regulate payments and settlements
C. Cashless transactions
D. None of the above

Q.68 Which scheme provides for 50% tax and surcharge on declarations of unaccounted cash deposited in banks?
A. Pradhan Mantri Jan Dhan Yojana
B. Pradhan Mantri Garib Kalyan Yojana
C. Pradhan Mantri Jan Kalyan Yojana
D. None of the above

Q.69 RBI kept repo rate unchanged at 6.25 percent. What did it abolish?
A. Temporary 100 percent CRR
B. 30 percent CRR
C. 40 percent CRR
D. None of the above

Q.70 India has crossed which milestone between April 2000 and Sept 2016?
A. 300 billion FDI
B. 400 billion FDI
C. 300 billion GDP
D. 400 billion GDP

Q.71 Which district in Assam became the first to pay wages to tea garden workers through bank accounts?
A. Hailakandi
B. Jorhat
C. Sylhet
D. None of the above

Q.72 CSO has announced that India's GDP has accelerated in Q2 (2016-2017) to what percent?
A. 7.1   **B.** 7.2   **C.** 7.3   **D.** 7.4

Q.73 Which state is aiming to be the first to operate cashless from 31st Dec?
A. Maharashtra
B. Odisha
C. Tamil Nadu
D. Goa

Q.74 What does IDS stand for?
A. Income Declaration Scheme
B. Informal Declaration of Resources
C. Identified Disclosure Scheme
D. None of the above

Q.75 RBI asked banks to maintain additional average daily balance through incremental CRR of what percent?
A. 80   **B.** 90   **C.** 100   **D.** 110

Q.76 To protect domestic manufacturers from cheap imports, Union Government slapped duty on import of which products?
A. All steel products
B. Certain steel products
C. Hot rolled flat sheets and plates
D. Both b and c

Q.77 ASSOCHAM study has pegged Indian m-wallet growth at CAGR of how much by 2021-22?
A. 131%
B. 141%
C. 151%
D. None of the above

Q.78 Which is the longest expressway in India?
A. Mumbai-Pune
B. Agra-Lucknow
C. Both a and b
D. Neither of the above

Q.79 Which state was the first to adopt a resolution welcoming demonetisation?
A. MP   **B.** UP
C. AP   **D.** Chhattisgarh

Q.80 The new high security INR 500 note has which of the following features?
A. Bleed Lines
B. Circle with 500 in the right
C. Ashoka Pillar emblem
D. All of the above

Q.81 Who will be named mascot of GoI's Incredible India Campaign?
A. Amitabh Bachchan   **B.** Priyanka Chopra
C. Aamir Khan   **D.** None of the above

Q.82 RBI has given banks the right to issue masala bonds in foreign markets, also known as ________.
A. Rupee denominated bonds
B. Green bonds
C. Tea bonds
D. None of the above

Q.83 India took a step forward rolling out GST with the Centre and states agreeing in a 4 slab structure- 5,12,18 and 28 percent along with a cess on luxury and which other type of goods?
A. Green   **B.** Sin
C. Bond   **D.** None of the above

Q.84 Union Government in Nov 2016 decided to launch a USD 2 billion dollar clean energy equity fund. What is its target for renewable energy generation capacity by 2022?
A. 175 GW   **B.** 185 GW   **C.** 176 GW   **D.** 186 GW

Q.85 Centre has decided to launch how many mandis across the country for setting up waste management plans?
A. 587   **B.** 586   **C.** 585   **D.** 584

Q.86 The Union Government on 31st Oct notified rules for the Real Estate (Regulation and Development)(General) Rules 2016 that seeks to regulate which sector?
A. Housing
B. Commercial complexes
C. Residential houses
D. Both a and c

Q.87 Andhra and Telangana have topped the ease of doing business ranking. Which state slipped to third position in the list prepared by World Bank and DIPP?
A. Rajasthan   **B.** Uttar Pradesh
C. Haryana   **D.** None of the above

Q.88 Odisha government has set up a fitment committee for implementation of which pay commission recommendations for employees and pensioners?

A. 6th   **B.** 7th   **C.** 8th   **D.** 9th

Q.89 World Bank has appointed its first adviser to promote which issues in development work?

A. Women   **B.** African American
C. LGBT   **D.** Disabled

Q.90 GSTN has inked a pact for sharing forex realisation data with which trade body?

A. DEA   **B.** DGFT
C. ASSOCHAM   **D.** FICCI

Q.91 The RBI relaxed guidelines on domestic interest rate for which category of instruments for banks?

A. Futures   **B.** Stocks
C. Shares   **D.** Debentures

Q.92 WEF/World Economic Forum on 25th Oct 2016 released which report on gender gap?

A. International Gender Gap Report 2016
B. Global Gender Gap Report 2016
C. World Gender Gap Report 2016
D. None of the above

Q.93 RBI asks banks to change debit cards in a fraud that was detected in what way?

A. Use of the debit cards in PoS without authorisation
B. Use of the debit cards at ATMs without authorisation
C. Use of the debit card at stores without authorisation
D. None of the above

Q.94 India has received which rank in the protection of minority investors?

A. 12   **B.** 13   **C.** 14   **D.** 15

Q.95 RBI on 20th Oct 2016 notified the amended norms for foreign investment in startups. Which act has been amended as part of this move?

A. Foreign Exchange Management (Issue of Security by Person Resident Outside India) Regulations 2000
B. Foreign Exchange Management (Transfer of Security by a Person Resident Outside India) Regulations 2000
C. Foreign Exchange Management (Issue and Transfer of Security by a Person Resident Outside India) Regulations 2000
D. Foreign Exchange Management (Transfer or Issue of Security By a Person Resident Outside India) Regulations 2000

Q.96 India on 21st Oct signed a USD 650 million loan agreement with which organisation for the Eastern Dedicated Freight Corridor III?

A. World Bank
B. Asian Development Bank
C. New Development Bank
D. None of the above

Q.97 SEBI has put in place disclosure norms for InvITs on 20th Oct, 2016. What does InvITs stand for?

A. Infrastructure Investment Trusts
B. Investment infrastructure trusts
C. Investment India trust
D. India infrastructure trust

Q.98 SIBDI has launched an INR 60 crore fund to promote innovation, rural entrepreneurship and agricultural industry. What is it called?

A. INSPIRE   **B.** ASPIRE
C. IGNITE   **D.** None of the above

Q.99 RBI has released a framework for penalising on payment issues. Fines have been fixed up to which amount?

A. INR 50 lakhs   **B.** INR 75 lakhs
C. INR 1 crore   **D.** INR 1.5 crore

Q.100 RBI has permitted 100% FDI in which services under the automatic route?

A. Personal Financial Services
B. Other Financial Services
C. Key Financial Services
D. None of the above

// Smart Answer Sheet //

Correct Indicates percentage of students who answered questions correctly.

Skipped Indicates percentage of students who skipped questions.

Q.	Ans.	Correct / Skipped
1	C	23.91 % / 26.09 %
2	B	36.96 % / 28.26 %
3	B	17.39 % / 30.44 %
4	A	19.57 % / 36.95 %
5	C	15.22 % / 41.3 %
6	A	60.87 % / 30.43 %
7	C	47.83 % / 34.78 %
8	A	34.78 % / 34.79 %
9	D	6.52 % / 36.96 %
10	B	30.43 % / 32.61 %
11	A	34.78 % / 32.61 %
12	B	21.74 % / 34.78 %
13	C	21.74 % / 30.43 %
14	A	41.3 % / 34.79 %
15	A	32.61 % / 32.61 %
16	A	30.43 % / 34.79 %

Q.	Ans.	Correct / Skipped
17	C	26.09 % / 41.3 %
18	B	32.61 % / 34.78 %
19	A	45.65 % / 26.09 %
20	A	26.09 % / 23.91 %
21	A	23.91 % / 23.92 %
22	A	41.3 % / 34.79 %
23	A	58.7 % / 23.91 %
24	A	34.78 % / 28.26 %
25	D	34.78 % / 32.61 %
26	C	45.65 % / 39.13 %
27	A	47.83 % / 23.91 %
28	A	23.91 % / 36.96 %
29	A	13.04 % / 26.09 %
30	A	32.61 % / 30.43 %
31	C	21.74 % / 32.61 %
32	A	21.74 % / 30.43 %

Q.	Ans.	Correct / Skipped
33	D	63.04 % / 28.26 %
34	D	17.39 % / 28.26 %
35	A	36.96 % / 30.43 %
36	A	50.0 % / 28.26 %
37	D	45.65 % / 36.96 %
38	D	21.74 % / 32.61 %
39	A	21.74 % / 39.13 %
40	C	28.26 % / 36.96 %
41	C	26.09 % / 26.08 %
42	D	32.61 % / 34.78 %
43	B	17.39 % / 32.61 %
44	B	26.09 % / 36.95 %
45	A	8.7 % / 28.26 %
46	B	23.91 % / 32.61 %
47	C	41.3 % / 28.27 %
48	B	21.74 % / 36.96 %

Q.	Ans.	Correct / Skipped
49	B	26.09 % / 41.3 %
50	A	15.22 % / 34.78 %
51	C	17.39 % / 32.61 %
52	B	28.26 % / 32.61 %
53	A	41.3 % / 39.13 %
54	C	21.74 % / 30.43 %
55	C	30.43 % / 30.44 %
56	A	28.26 % / 34.78 %
57	A	21.74 % / 41.3 %
58	A	43.48 % / 30.43 %
59	D	47.83 % / 30.43 %
60	A	34.78 % / 30.44 %
61	D	10.87 % / 36.96 %
62	A	19.57 % / 32.6 %
63	D	45.65 % / 30.44 %
64	B	23.91 % / 36.96 %

Q.	Ans.	Correct / Skipped
65	C	26.09 % / 36.95 %
66	A	19.57 % / 30.43 %
67	B	47.83 % / 36.95 %
68	B	10.87 % / 36.96 %
69	A	23.91 % / 39.13 %
70	A	26.09 % / 36.95 %
71	A	32.61 % / 26.09 %
72	C	26.09 % / 26.08 %
73	D	26.09 % / 39.13 %
74	A	43.48 % / 30.43 %
75	C	26.09 % / 36.95 %
76	D	56.52 % / 30.44 %
77	B	39.13 % / 39.13 %
78	B	28.26 % / 30.44 %
79	D	17.39 % / 23.91 %
80	D	65.22 % / 23.91 %

Q.	Ans.	Correct	Skipped
81	D	19.57 %	28.26 %
82	A	36.96 %	26.08 %
83	B	23.91 %	36.96 %
84	A	32.61 %	32.61 %

Q.	Ans.	Correct	Skipped
85	C	30.43 %	39.14 %
86	D	56.52 %	30.44 %
87	D	13.04 %	36.96 %
88	B	36.96 %	34.78 %

Q.	Ans.	Correct	Skipped
89	C	30.43 %	36.96 %
90	B	26.09 %	36.95 %
91	A	15.22 %	34.78 %
92	B	43.48 %	36.95 %

Q.	Ans.	Correct	Skipped
93	B	39.13 %	28.26 %
94	B	17.39 %	36.96 %
95	D	21.74 %	32.61 %
96	A	23.91 %	30.44 %

Q.	Ans.	Correct	Skipped
97	A	30.43 %	36.96 %
98	B	32.61 %	34.78 %
99	C	34.78 %	30.44 %
100	B	17.39 %	30.44 %

Performance Analysis

Avg. Score (%)	21.5%
Toppers Score (%)	91.0%
Your Score	

//Hints and Solutions//

1. The GST Council headed by finance Minister Arun Jaitley has finalised tax rates and has approved all the seven rules for the GST regime that is scheduled to be implemented from July 1.

The remaining two rules of the GST pertaining to transition and return is under the examination of the legal committee.

In total, the council has fixed the rates of 1211 items. It will decide rates of some other items and services in the coming days.

Out of 1211 items, 81% of the items will attract tax of 18% or less. Only the remaining 19% of items will attract a highest rate of 28%.

Household items like Sugar, Tea, Coffee and edible oil will attract 5% levy. Cereals and milk will be exempted from the tax.

Manufactured goods will attract 18% levy. Luxury cars will attract 28% GST in addition to a cess of 15%.

Small petrol cars will attract 28% GST plus a 1% cess, and diesel cars will be taxed at 28% plus 3% cess.

Capital goods, a key asset for the manufacturing sector, will be taxed at 28%. Aerated drinks will fall under the 28% tax bracket.

GST Council Overall Tax:

- The GST Council has not increased the overall tax in any of the 1211 items but have reduced tax on many items.

- For example, Soap, which is now taxed at the rate of 22-24%, will be taxed at 18%. The present tax incidence in excess of 28% on luxury items will be treated as cess and will be deposited in the corpus for compensating states if they suffer any revenue loss.

- Food items are expected to become cheaper. Daily use items like hair oil, toothpaste, and soap are kept in the 18% tax slab instead of 28%.

- The cost of energy generation is expected to become less as tax incidence on coal has been reduced from 11% to 5%.

- GST regime is expected to unify the whole of the country into a common market eliminating both Central and State levies.

- GST is also expected to increase state and federal tax revenues, ease inflation and boost economic growth by 1-2% points in the medium term.

2. Income Tax Department (ITD) has initiated Operation Clean Money to investigate tax evaders. As a part of the operation, the government has launched a website on 'Operation Clean Money' operation.

The Operation Clean Money' portal has been designed by the Central Board of Direct Taxes (CBDT). Initial phase of the operation involves identification of around 18 lakh persons who have made large deposits or purchases between 9th November to 30th December 2016, which do not appear to be in line with the tax payer's profile.

The provision of online verification of these transactions is aimed at reducing the compliance cost for the taxpayers while optimising the resources of the Income Tax department.

The PAN holders can view the information in the portal. The taxpayers would be allowed to submit online explanation without the need to visit the Income Tax Office.

As a reminder, e-mail and SMS will also be sent to the taxpayers for submission of online response on the portal. The IT department will make use of the data analytics to select cases for verification.

After selection of cases, additional information requested would be communicated electronically. On getting the information, the portal will get dynamically updated.

The taxpayers covered under this phase are required to submit their responses within 10 days in order to avoid further notice and enforcement actions under the Income Tax Act. The response provided by the tax payer would be analyzed against available information with the department.

If response found justified, the verification would be closed. The verification will also be closed if the cash deposit has been declared under Pradhan Mantri Garib Kalyan Yojna (PMGKY).

Operation Clean Money:

- Operation Clean Money was launched immediately after government's demonetisation drive in order to bring the tax evaders with undeclared incomes under the tax net.

- The income tax department has so far identified about 1.8 million persons and asked them to explain their deposits, pay tax or disclose past undisclosed income through the Pradhan Mantri Garib Kalyan Yojana.

3. The Indian Coir sector's revenue from exports touched an all time high of INR 2282 Cr by value and 9.57 Metric Tonnes in quantity in the 2016-17 financial year.

The Coir Board Chairman is C P Radhakrishnan.

The coir sector had fetched export revenue of Rs 1630 Cr in the financial year 2015-16 against INR 1,476 Cr achieved in fiscal year 2014-15.

Indian coir sector has tremendous potential to grow and provide employment to a large number of people.

Coir Board is going ahead with a project to fabricate a versatile spinning machine capable of producing yarn with uniform thickness in large quantity.

The government is considering to introduce a scheme that would extend financial support upto INR 2.50 Cr to the sector in order to promote larger investments by entrepreneurs.

4. Organisations with over Rs 20 lakh turnover will have to specify the PAN while filling the Udyog Aadhaar Memorandum for registration.

These organisations include companies, limited liability partnerships, cooperative societies, societies and trusts.

The decision, taken at a meeting chaired by the MSME Secretary K K Jalan recently.

This will be implemented after two months of the Goods and Services Tax coming into operation.

The GST regime is likely to come into force on July 1.

Presently, it is not mandatory for these organisations to mention the PAN number in the Udyog Aadhaar Memorandum.

However, since it will be compulsory for firms with turnover above INR 20 lakh to have a PAN number under the GST, this decision has been taken.

Apart from the Permanent Account Number (PAN) and Aadhaar, micro, small and medium enterprises (MSMEs) will also have to attach a chartered accountant's certificate for participating in public tenders.

Udyog Aadhaar is for existing firms. The upcoming units do not need to apply for its registration.

The meeting of the Advisory Committee under the MSMED Act decided that there could be a ministry sponsored MSME specific M Tech course, which will focus mainly on practical shop-floor training, the business model that can be worked out among the MSME Associations present in the meeting, a suggestion mooted by the All India Council for Technical Education.

In the course curriculum, 20-30 specific activities can be listed after due deliberations.

The MSME ministry had earlier issued a one-page Udyog Aadhaar Memorandum, which must be filled online by all micro, small and medium enterprises (MSMEs), for simplifying the registration procedure for entrepreneurs and promoting ease of doing business.

5. India has jumped 73 spots to be ranked 26th in World Bank's electricity accessibility list. The country was ranked 99th in 2014.

Out of the 18,452 villages which lacked electricity, over 13,000 has been provided access to electricity.

In addition, a person applying for new electricity connection would be able to get the connection within 24 hours in areas where power infrastructure is available and in areas where there is no power infrastructure, electricity connection would be given in a week.

The government's rural electrification programme is on track for completion within the targeted 1,000 days.

The flagship scheme Deendayal Upadhyaya Gram Jyoti Yojana (DDUGJY) was launched by Prime Minister Narendra Modi with an aim to provide 24/7 uninterrupted electricity supply to each rural household across the country by 2022.

It aims to strengthen sub-transmission and distribution network to prevent power losses.

It focuses on feeder separation for rural households and agricultural purpose.

The Ministry of Power has also launched a new app, GARV-II to provide real-time data of all six lakh villages of the country.

Ministry of Power

- Formed: 2 July 1992
- Preceding Ministry: Ministry of Energy Sources
- Jurisdiction: Government of India
- Headquarters: Shram Shakti Bhawan, Rafi Marg, New Delhi, India
- Annual budget: INR 13,881.14 crore (US$2.2 billion) (2017-18 est.)
- Minister responsible: Piyush Goyal, Minister of State (Independent Charge)
- Website: www.powermin.nic.in

6. The government has released new-look index of industrial production (IIP) and the wholesale price index (WPI) , which have been built on the new series of data.

The new IIP and WPI series has been released by Chief Statistician of India and Secretary, Ministry of Statistics & Programme Implementation, and Secretary, Department of Industrial Policy and Promotion to usher in greater accuracy and improved synchronisation leading to better policies.

Instead of the earlier 2004-05, base year for the IIP and the WPI will be 2011-12.

Already, the Consumer Price Index (CPI), the Gross Domestic Product (GDP) and gross value addition etc., have 2011-12 as the base year.

The common base year of 2011-12 is aimed at reducing discrepancies.

WPI

The number of items covered in the new series of the WPI has increased from 676 to 697.

Overall, 199 new items have been added and 146 old items have been dropped.

Under the primary articles, new vegetables and fruits like radish, carrot, cucumber, bitter gourd, mosambi (sweet lime), pomegranate, jackfruit, and pear have been added.

Under the mineral group, new items like copper concentrate, lead concentrate and garnet have been added and other items like copper ore, gypsum, kaolin, dolomite, and magnesite have been dropped.

Under the manufacturing items, 173 new items including conveyer belt, rubber tread, steel cables, tissue paper, and wooden splint have been added, while 135 items like khandsari, poppadom, and video CD players have been taken out.

Under the new series of WPI, weight of manufactured items has decreased to 64.2 per cent from 64.9 per cent in old series.

Similarly, the weight of fuel and power has decreased to 13.1 per cent from 14.9 per cent. On the other hand, the weight of primary items have increased to 22.6 per cent from 20.1 per cent.

IIP :

The IIP has been revised after a gap of 13 years and the obsolete items which are no longer in production in the index have been replaced with contemporary products in the new index making it to be more comprehensive in nature.

Introduction of the new series would make all the key macroeconomic indicators such as IIP, WPI, CPI and national accounts to have a common base of 2011-12, paving way for easier comparisons among them. The new series indices have painted a healthier picture of the Indian economy in 2016-17 than that of the old series.

The new series of IIP will include 809 manufacturing products and 55 mining products that are re-grouped into 521 item groups.

The new series of IIP will include technology items like smart phones, tablets, LED television etc.

A technical review committee has also been established to identify new items by ensuring that the series remains relevant.

The committee is slated to meet at least once a year.

7. The government has set up a task force headed by NITI Aayog vice-chairman Arvind Panagariya to come up with a methodology to generate timely and reliable employment data.

The Prime Minister Narendra Modi himself has initiated the process and has asked the task force to submit its recommendations at the earliest.

The other members of the task force are labour secretary M. Sathiyavathy, secretary of the statistics department T.C.A. Ananth, NITI Aayog's Pulak Ghosh and Manish Sabharwal, chairman and co-founder of staffing firm Teamlease Services Ltd.

India lacks reliable data on jobs. The available data is currently outdated.

The data on jobs in the informal sector which employs country's majority of the workforce is not easily available.

Also, the data released by the Labour Bureau is restricted to the organized sector. National Sample Survey Office (NSSO) data which is the most comprehensive data available on jobs is generated with a time lag.

Better data on jobs data will help policy planners assess the impact of policies on jobs and will shed light on the actual size of the informal economy

India's Labour Market

- India's labour market constitutes of over 470 million people.

- According to CRISIL, around 18 million people enter the workforce every year.

- As per the data with the NSSO, India had created around 59.9 million jobs between 1999-2000 and 2004-05 and created nearly two million jobs between 2004-05 and 2009-10.

- Between 2009-10 and 2011-12, 13.9 million jobs were created in the country.

8. The International Monetary Fund (IMF) called on Asian economies to learn from Japan's experience and act early to cope with rapidly ageing populations, warning that parts of the region risk getting old before becoming rich.

Asia has enjoyed substantial demographic dividends in the past decades, but the growing number of elderly is set to create a demographic "tax" on growth, according to the IMF.

Adapting to ageing could be especially challenging for Asia, as populations living at relatively low per capita income levels in many parts of the region are rapidly becoming old.

Some countries in Asia are getting old before becoming rich.

The population growth rate is projected to fall to zero for Asia by 2050 and the share of working-age people, now at its peak, will decline over the coming decades, the report said.

The share of the population aged 65 and older will increase rapidly and reach close to two-and-a-half times the current level by 2050, it said.

That means demographics could subtract 0.1 percentage point from annual global growth over the next three decades, it said.

The challenges are particularly huge for Japan, which faces both an ageing and shrinking population. Its labour force shrank by more than 7 per cent in the past two decades.

The high percentage of its citizens living on pensions may be behind Japan's excess savings and low investment, which are weighing on growth and blamed in part for keeping inflation below the Bank of Japan's 2 per cent target.

Japan's experience highlights how demographic headwinds can adversely impact growth, inflation dynamics and the effectiveness of monetary policy.

The IMF called on Asian nations to make changes like introducing credible fiscal consolidation plans, boosting female and elderly labour force participation, and revamping social safety nets.

9. Ministry of Urban Development will launch measuring of Liveability Index of cities in the next month. The index will be based on indigenously evolved methodology.

The Ministry of Urban Development has already released a detailed document on "Methodology for Collection and Computation of Liveability Standards in Cities".

The index will measure the Liveability Standards of 140 cities including 53 cities with population of 1 million and above.

To carry out the assessment, the Ministry has invited bids for selecting the agency. The aim of the assessment will be to instil a sense of healthy competition among cities and towns in the country and to help them focus their attention on improving governance and infrastructure availability.

Cities will be assessed on 15 core parameters relating to Governance, social infrastructure pertaining to education, health and safety and security, economic aspects and physical infrastructure like housing, open spaces, land use, energy and water availability, solid waste management, pollution etc.

Totally, based on 79 aspects, the Cities would be ranked on the Liveability Index.

A sense of healthy competition is being promoted among cities and towns in the country to focus their attention on improving governance and infrastructure availability.

Government officials and experts from India, Indonesia, Sri Lanka and Bangladesh are participating in the workshop for sharing respective experiences on decentralization and empowerment of local bodies.

Ministry of Urban Development

- Minister responsible : Shri Venkaiah Naidu
- Headquarters : Nirman Bhawan, New Delhi
- Formed : 1952
- Jurisdiction : Republic of India

10. The Indian economy will grow 7.4 per cent this fiscal and 7.6 per cent in the next as the bankruptcy and GST laws will help create a better business friendly environment.

This is as per the Asian Development Bank (ADB).

Ahead of its 50th annual meeting to be attended by finance minister and central bank governors of member nations, ADB indicated new bankruptcy law will make it easier to do business in India.

The growth rate compares to 7.1 per cent of the previous fiscal.

Over 7 per cent growth rate is high if one compares it to other emerging market economies and also China.

Behind this is cyclical factor, improved terms of trade. The Indian government adopted new bankruptcy law that improved the business enabling environment.

That is the a short-term and medium-term factor behind the gross acceleration in India.

On the impact of demonetisation of old 500 and 1,000 rupee notes that took out 86 per cent of the currency in circulation, it obviously generated short-term decline in cash-based transactions and consumer sentiment.

ADB has not studied if the demonetisation had any consequences on black money.

The GST, the biggest indirect tax reform since independence, together with the new bankruptcy law are big positives for India.

The bankruptcy law and the GST will help in creating a better business enabling environment, which seems to be a factor behind this gross acceleration of India,.

The rupee strengthened to 64.2 against the US dollar and has been gaining strength as compared to other emerging economy currencies.

The rupee has appreciated by over 5 per cent against the US dollar since January.

ADB:

- Headquarters: Mandaluyong, Philippines
- President: Takehiko Nakao
- Founded: 19 December 1966

- Membership: 67 countries
- Staff: 2997 employees
- Purpose: Economic development
- Motto: Fighting poverty in Asia and the Pacific

11. India will unveil a new series of Index of Industrial Production with a base year 2011-12 on May 9 with an aim to map economic activities more accurately.

The new series for Index of Industrial Production (IIP), which captures industrial activities on monthly basis, will be launched by Chief Statistician and MOSPI Secretary TCA Anant.

A high-level panel had firmed up the methodology for the IIP with new base year of 2011-12.

Currently, the IIP is calculated on base year of 2004-05.

The change in baseline for the IIP is expected to bring in more accuracy in mapping the level of economic activity and calculating other numbers like national accounts.

Work is also in progress to change the base year for the wholesale price index (WPI) to 2011-12 year.

The Central Statistics Office (CSO) has already changed the base year for the country's national accounts, including the gross domestic product (GDP) and the gross value addition (GVA).

The retail inflation based on the consumer price index (CPI) is also calculated on the base year of 2011-12.

For long, economists and think tanks have been pitching for release of new time series of the IIP and the WPI so that GDP numbers can be based on more accurate and realistic data.

What is the Base Year and IIP?

- The base year is revised periodically to capture the changes in the structure and composition of the industry.
- This is over time due to technological changes, economic reforms and consumption pattern of the people.
- The IIP gives a broad outlook on output of various types of goods like basic, consumer and capital ones, which helps in gauging the level of economic progress and investments in the economy.
- India will unveil a new series of Index of Industrial Production with a base year 2011-12 on May 9 with an aim to map economic activities more accurately.

12. India has become world's second largest LPG importer, a position that was previously occupied by Japan.

China remains as the world's top importer.

According to Petroleum Planning & Analysis Cell, LPG imports in the country has increased 23% during the financial year 2016-2017 to about 11 million tonnes.

The main reason behind the increase in the consumption of LPG in India is due to the two government schemes coupled with free gas connections.

From May 2016, the government is providing free cooking gas connections to women from extremely poor households, to reduce the use of polluting fuels such as wood and dried cow dung.

This has increased India's active LPG users to about 200 million, which is 60% more than Japan's entire population.

According to the World Health Organization, polluting fuels used for cooking purposes results in 1.3 million premature deaths in India every year.

India has set an ambitious target of increasing LPG usage to cover 80% of the households by March 2019.

As per the present estimates of the oil ministry, demand for fuel will touch 35 million tonnes by 2031-32 in India.

Pradhan Mantri Ujjwala Yojana (PMUY)

- PMUY was launched by Prime Minister Narendra Modi in May 2016 with the tagline of Swachh Indhan, Behtar Jeevan.

- The scheme's motive is to provide free of cost LPG (cooking gas) connections to women from BPL Households.

- The scheme seeks to empower women and protect their health by shifting them from traditional cooking based on unclean cooking fuels or on fossil fuels to clean cooking gas.

- It is being implemented by Union Ministry of Petroleum and Natural Gas.

- The scheme will be implemented over three years' time period until the financial year 2018-19.

13. The goods and services tax (GST) can boost India's GDP growth by up to 4.2 per cent – double the previous estimate – as lower taxes on manufactured goods will bump up output and make products cheaper, according to the US Fed Reserve.

GST could reduce inefficiencies in the production process while eliminating the current compounding effect of different central and state levies.

Termed the biggest tax reform since Independence, GST will unify at least 10 indirect taxes into one to be collected at state and central levels.

In the International Finance Discussion Paper (IFDP), the US Fed researchers said GST is an inclusive policy that is also expected to bring down overall domestic and international trade barriers.

GST is expected to raise overall Indian welfare and is projected to be an inclusive policy in that it would be welfare improving for all Indian states.

The Fed research note stated that assuming the aggregate weighted GST rate is 16 per cent, there would be positive impact on real GDP of 4.2 per cent.

The model suggests that GST would lead to real GDP gains of 4.2 per cent under the baseline assumptions, driven by a surge in manufacturing output.

GST would raise overall welfare by 5.3 per cent in India.

Under the existing structure, at each point of sale, additional taxes are applied to the after-tax value of each goods and services.

The main purpose for GST is to eliminate this compounding effect by fixing the final tax rate, where goods will fall into one of the four rate categories of 5, 12, 18, and 28 per cent.

The unified structure is currently expected to be rolled out in July.

GST's impact on GDP growth as estimated by Fed economists is much higher than the 1-2 per cent as expected by the Indian government.

IMF, World Bank Views on GST

- The International Monetary Fund (IMF) had earlier this year said GST could help raise India's medium-term GDP growth to over 8 per cent.

- This could create a single national market for enhancing efficiency of movement of goods and services.

- Even the World Bank has said a smooth implementation of GST could prove to be a significant push to economic activity as growth could pick up to 7.2 per cent in 2017-18.

- It will move further to 7.5 per cent in 2018-19.

14. According to EEPC India, Russia coming forward as the Partner Country in this event is a testimony to the stature achieved by IESS. India has a long standing partnership with Russia in engineering sector.

A large 120 member delegation from Russia is exhibiting their technology and products at the IESS 2017.

As many as 400 top global exhibitors and over 500 foreign delegates are participating in this flagship engineering event which is built around the theme – "Smart Tech for Smart Engineering".

Besides Russia, delegates from USA, UK, Germany, UAE, Brazil, South Africa, Algeria, Benin, Botswana, Egypt, Ethiopia, Ghana, Kenya, Namibia, Uganda, Vietnam, Bangladesh, Sri Lanka, Ukraine, Uzbekistan and Nepal are also visiting IESS, which has emerged as one of the most prestigious engineering sourcing shows in the country.

This edition of IESS has exclusive Technology and Innovation Pavilions with representations from BARC, IIT Mumbai, IIT Madras, FCRI (Fluid Control Research Institute), ARCI (International Advanced Research Centre for Powder Metallurgy and New Materials), CMTI (Central Manufacturing Technology Institute) and MSME Tools Room.

IESS, across its five previous editions, has left an indelible footprint of success.

India's engineering exports are likely to reach USD 60+ billion in the fiscal 2016-17, on the back of revival of demand in the USA and for select products like iron.

For the April-January period of ten months of the current fiscal, the engineering exports have touched a figure of USD 50.87

billion, exceeding the total shipments of USD 49 billion in the entire financial year of 2015-16.

For January, 2017 engineering exports aggregated USD 5.29 billion, showing an increase of over 12 % over the same month last fiscal.

15. The Sovereign Gold Bond Scheme 2017-18--Series I will be opened for subscription from 24 to 28 April, 2017. The bonds will be issued on 12 May.

The issue price of the bond is based on the simple average closing price (published by the India Bullion and Jewellers Association) for gold of 999 purity of the week preceding the subscription period.

It works out to be INR 2,951 per gram.

However, the government, in consultation with the RBI, has decided to offer a discount of INR 50 per gram on the nominal value of the Sovereign Gold Bond.

Hence, the issue price of gold bond for this tranche has been fixed at INR 2,901 per gram of gold.

The bonds would earn an interest of 2.75% per annum, payable every six months on initial investment.

The tenor of the bond will be for a period of 8 years with exit option from fifth year to be exercised on the interest payment dates.

The minimum investment limit into these bonds is one gram of gold, while the maximum amount subscribed by an entity cannot be more than 500 grams per person per fiscal year

The bonds will be sold through banks, post offices, Stock Holding Corporation of India (SHCIL), and recognised stock exchanges—National Stock Exchange (NSE) and BSE.

Given that the short-term outlook for gold looks promising, investors can hope to make tidy gains on the interim rally as well.

Investors who are looking for investing in gold can go for sovereign gold bonds.

These bonds are issued by the Government of India and offer returns linked to gold price.

Investors will also get a coupon of 2.5 per cent per annum.

The capital gains you make by investing in these bonds is tax exempt, provided you hold them till the end of the tenure of eight years.

Exit, though, is allowed from the fifth year through the secondary market. But this will result in capital gains tax of 20 per cent (with indexation benefit).

Interest on these bonds - a promised 2.5 per cent rate - will be paid semi-annually.

The other paper form of gold - Gold ETFs - has the disadvantage of higher costs.

16. Digitally-developed economies around the globe are continuing to progress due to larger investments and adoptions in Information Communication Technology, says the newly released Huawei Global Connectivity Index (GCI) 2017.

The study also finds developing economies have started to accelerate their growth by investing strategically in ICT capabilities, yet the gap between them and continues to grow.

This is the fourth annual GCI study that shows how countries are progressing with digital transformation based on 40 unique indicators that cover five technology enablers: broadband, data centres, cloud, big data and Internet of Things.

US tops the list with Singapore and Sweden a close second and third.

India performs well on the key indicators of a knowledge economy but falls behind in its broadband assessments–giving it an overall rank of 43–between Venezuela and Morocco.

For India which has climbed one rank from last year, the government is planning to provide high-speed internet connectivity to 250,000 communities.

The citizens will be provided with a digital identity which will be unique, lifelong, online, and valid.

Government departments will be seamlessly integrated with high-speed optical fibre, which will improve inter operability of these organizations and will result in real-time service delivery from online or mobile platform.

This would stimulate the development of cloud for easy and portable connections for citizens.

It is encouraging to note that over the past 3 years, India has grown faster in ICT infrastructure compared to its global peers including 1.4 times faster growth in investment in cloud, 2.3 times growth in computer households and 1.1 times in Analytics Data Creation per capita.

GCI 2017 study reported the relationship between ICT investment and GDP growth is generally accepted in government and industry.

Examining the GCI 2017 data with numerous economic forecasting models, the report says a nation which increased investment in ICT investment in infrastructure by additional 10% annually from 2017 to 2025 can benefit from a multiplier effect.

Using this economic impact model, the report finds that every additional US$1 of ICT infrastructure investment could bring a return of US$3 in GDP at present, US$3.70 in 2020 and the potential return increases to US$5 in 2025.

17. India's gross domestic product is expected to spike to 7.2% in the 2017-'18 financial year from 6.8% the previous fiscal.

This is according to a new World Bank report titled "Globalization Backlash", which was released on April 16, 2017.

The international agency forecast that India's economic growth will rise gradually to 7.7% in 2019-'20, "underpinned by a recovery in private investments".

The World Bank analysis, however, has warned against significant risks to India's favorable growth outlook.

Among them, there are uncertainties in the global environment, an unclear picture of the impact demonetisation has had on small and informal firms, hindrances to private investment and rapid hikes in the prices of oil and other commodities.

A timely and smooth implementation of the GST could prove to be a significant upside risk to economic activity in FY17/18.

The World Bank's "Globalization Backlash" report focuses on the gross domestic product climate in South Asia, predicting that growth in the region will maintain momentum.

South Asia remains the fastest growing region in the world and the strong performance in the eastern part of the region, in particular in India, Bhutan and Bangladesh, defied disappointing world growth in 2016.

The current globalization backlash should thus not dissuade South Asian countries from having a stronger outward orientation.

18. Humanity harvested the largest ever cereal crop in its history in 2016-17 - a staggering 2.6 billion metric tonnes, according to the latest estimates of the UN-affiliated Food and Agriculture Organisation (FAO).

The year is ending with the largest ever global stock of foodgrains in history, some 682 million tonnes.

India too is heading for a record cereal crop as the previous year's final wheat is harvested and counted in.

According to reports, the second advance estimate of the government put cereal production for 2016-17 at nearly 250 million tonnes, crossing the record of about 246 million tonnes set in 2013-14.

While the world celebrates this plentiful harvest, over 20 million people are facing starvation in Africa and Yemen in the worst drought in 60 years.

Globally, some 795 million people go to bed hungry every day, according to the World Food Programme. This includes about 15% of India's population, some 20 million people.

The global output was fuelled by increased wheat output in North America — by more than 10 million tonnes year on year - and increases in the Russian Federation and India.

All these offset the European Union decline by 16.5 million tonnes caused by bad weather.

Rice output increased in China, India, and Southeast Asia. Coarse cereal production jumped by 22.7 million tonnes, led by US, EU, India and Ukraine, offsetting El Nino-caused declines in Brazil and policy-driven dip in China.

FAO is now forecasting a slight dip in world cereal production in 2017, mainly due to a fall in wheat output in Australia, Canada and the US after farmers planted less seeing lower prices.

Elsewhere there is famine in Africa. According to aid agencies and the UN, the food crisis in East Africa and Northern Nigeria is mostly because of continued war and consequent disruption of economy and connectivity.

19. India ranks 7th in tourism economy in terms of GDP according to the WTTC (World Travel and Tourism Council).

According to data, the travel and tourism sector generated INR 14.1 trillion (USD208.9 billion) in 2016.

This makes it the world's 7th largest in terms of absolute size; the sum is equivalent to 9.6% of India's GDP.

Additionally, the sector created 40.3 million jobs in 2016, which ranks India 2nd in the world in terms of total employment generated.

The sector accounts for 9.3% of the country's total jobs.

India's Travel and Tourism sector was also the fastest growing amongst the G20 countries, growing by 8.5% in 2016.

A further 6.7% growth is forecast for 2017.

India's figures are predominantly generated by domestic travel, which accounts for 88% of the sector's contribution to GDP in 2016.

Visitor exports, money spent by foreign travellers in India, only represents 12% of tourism revenues and in 2016 totalled Rs 1.5 trillion (USD22.8bn).

This is 5.4% of the country's total exports, compared to a global average of 6.6%.

Data from the UN World Tourism Organisation (UNWTO) shows that India received only 9 million international arrivals in 2016, placing it at 40th place in the world; a tenth of those received by top-ranking France.

However, there is a lot of potential for India to grow their visitor exports.

WTTC data suggests that visitor exports will grow by 5.4% in 2017.

WTTC:

- Headquarters: London, United Kingdom
- Founded: 1990
- Industry: Travel & Tourism
- Chairman: Gerald Lawless

20. Growth of the country's eight core sectors slipped to an over one-year low of 1% in February 2017.

This was mainly due to a fall in output of crude oil, natural gas, refinery products, fertiliser and cement.

The eight core sectors had expanded 9.4% in February 2016, and 3.4% in January 2016.

In February 2016, crude oil output contracted 3.4%, natural gas output by 1.7%, refinery products output fell 2.3%, fertiliser output declined 5.3%, and cement output dropped 15.8%.

But coal and steel production recorded positive growth during the month.

The eight core industries comprise close to 37.9% of the weight of items included in the Index of Industrial Production (IIP).

The electricity has the maximum weight (of 10.32%) among the eight sectors followed by Steel (6.68%), Petroleum Refinery (5.94%), Crude Oil production (5.22 %), Coal production (4.38 %),

Cement (2.41%), Natural Gas production (1.71 %) and Fertilizer production (1.25%).

21. India signed its first loan agreement with the New Development Bank (NDB) for $350 million to be used in the development and upgradation of district roads in Madhya Pradesh.

"he objective of the project is the upgradation of major district roads in the state of Madhya Pradesh to improve connectivity of the interior areas of the state with the national and state highway networks.

The project would include upgradation, rehabilitation or reconstruction of approximately 1,500 km of district roads to intermediate lane, all-weather standards, with road safety features and improved road asset maintenance and management.

The project is to be implemented over five years with the Government of Madhya Pradesh and the Madhya Pradesh Road Development Corporation acting as the implementing agencies.

The loan agreement was signed by Raj Kumar, Joint Secretary, Department of Economic Affairs and Xian Zhu, Vice President & Chief Operating Officer of the New Development Bank.

New Development Bank:

- Headquarters: Shanghai, China
- President: K. V. Kamath
- Founder: BRICS
- Founded: 15 July 2014, Fortaleza, Ceará, Brazil
- Type of business: International Financial Institution
- First president: K. V. Kamath

22. India has become a net exporter of electricity during the April-February 2017 period this fiscal for the first time.

This is as per the Central Electricity Authority, the designated authority of the government of India for cross border trade of electricity.

This is the first time India has turned from net importer of electricity to net exporter.

According to the statement, during the current year 2016-17 (April-February), India has exported around 5,798 million units to Nepal, Bangladesh and Myanmar.

This is 213 million units more than the import of around 5,585 million units from Bhutan.

Export to Nepal and Bangladesh increased 2.5 and 2.8 times respectively in the last three years. Ever since the cross border trade of electricity started in mid-80s, India has been importing power from Bhutan and marginally exporting to Nepal in radial mode at 33 kV and 132 kV from Bihar and Uttar Pradesh respectively.

On an average, Bhutan has been supplying around 5,000-5,500 million units to India.

India had also been exporting around 190 MW power to Nepal over 12 cross border interconnections at 11kV, 33kV and 132 kV level.

The export of power to Nepal further increased by around 145 MW with commissioning of Muzaffarpur (India)– Dhalkhebar (Nepal) 400kV line (being operated at 132 kV) in 2016.

The export of power to Bangladesh from India got further boost with commissioning of the first cross border interconnection between Baharampur in India and Bheramara in Bangladesh at 400kV in September 2013.

It was further augmented by commissioning of second cross border Interconnection between Surjyamaninagar (Tripura) in India and South Comilla in Bangladesh.

At present, around 600 MW power is being exported to Bangladesh.

The export of power to Nepal is expected to increase by around 145 MW shortly over 132 kV Katiya (Bihar) - Kusaha (Nepal) and 132 kV Raxaul (Bihar) - Parwanipur (Nepal).

Bhutan:

- Capital: Thimphu
- King: Jigme Khesar Namgyel Wangchuck
- Prime minister: Tshering Tobgay
- Currencies: Indian rupee, Bhutanese ngultrum
- Official language: Dzongkha

23. State Bank of India on 28th March 2017 announced offering credit cards to account holders with a balance of INR 20,000-25,000.

The card called Unnati will be offered through a network of 20 thousand plus SBI branches.

SBI will not consider the customer's credit history. Card called Unnati will be issued free for first four years.

Lack of credit history will be the challenge in increasing card penetration in the country. Card will facilitate generation of credit history for fresh users which will bring them into the organised financial stream.

To encourage adoption of credit cards and facilitate expansion in the reach of digital payments, the SBI Card Unnati will be offered free, at zero annual fee, for four years.

SBI has close to 30 crore customer accounts, including Jan Dhan Yojana. Post-demonetisation the balance amount in these accounts increased significantly.

Many customers do not have credit history and are not eligible for cards. SBI wants to bring about financial inclusion in terms of credit facility with this new product.

The Bank is also in the process of increasing its stake in SBI Card to 74 per cent.

SBI currently holds 60 per cent stake in SBICPSL and 40 per cent in GECBPMSL.

The balance being held by GE Capital in both the ventures.

The SBI has approval to infuse Rs 1,160 crore in the two JVs - SBI Cards and Payment Services Pvt Ltd (SBICPSL) and GE Capital Business Processes Management Services Ltd (GECBPMSL)-through purchase of equity shares from GE Capital.

This is to increase the bank's stake in both the companies to 74 per cent.

The nation's largest lender SBI entered credit card business in 1998 by roping GE Capital India, the consumer finance arm of US-based GE Capital.

SBI Card, having 4.3 million user, said its latest offering 'Unnati' targeted at all SBI customers, including Jan Dhan account holders throughout the country.

SBI:

- Founded: 2 June 1806, Bank of Calcutta/ 27 January 1921, Imperial Bank of India/ 1 July 1955, State Bank of India/ 2 June 1956, nationalization

- Headquarters: Mumbai, Maharashtra, India

- Area served: Worldwide

- Chairperson: Arundhati Bhattacharya

- Products: Consumer banking, corporate banking, finance and insurance, investment banking, mortgage loans, private banking, private equity, savings, securities, asset management, wealth management, credit cards.

24. Promotion of Digidhan and cashless transactions are part of the mission to bring digital transactions to the fore.

Keeping this in mind, a Digidhan Fair was held in Motihari, Bihar.

The fair involved banks, Common Service Centres (CSC), private digital payment service providers etc. informing the consumers as well as traders about the new technology.

Government has taken several initiatives to promote cashless transactions. Keeping cashless transaction and increasing population of educated youth under consideration, the government has launched Bheem App, which is quite popular.

So far 1.25 crore people have been linked to the App and a transaction of Rs. 361 crore has been made.

More than 100 crore phones are there in India and out of them 30-40 crore is smartphones.

There are about 50 crore internet users.

If used properly, credit cards won't be required.

Banks have devised UPI cards under which if the mobile app is downloaded, people can do the transaction through any bank on the basis of their phone numbers.

2.15 crore railway tickets are booked out of which 1.30 crore tickets are booked online. He informed that there is 144 crore bank accounts by and large, out of them 117 are the savings account.

A total number of Jandhan account is 28.02 crore.

So far 40 crore bank accounts are linked to Aadhaar Cards.

Total number of Aadhaar cards is 113 crore and there is 20.13 crore POS machines in the country and by the end of this month 10 lakh new machines will be added.

Apart from this, there is 5.7 crore e-wallet users and 110.6 crore credit/debit cards.

So far 21.9 crore consumers have got Rupay cards and its usage has increased up to 40% in the recent time.

Steps to Curb Black Money:

- Special Investigation Team (SIT) was constituted.

- A law was made to tackle undeclared foreign assets and deposits.

- India revised the Double Taxation Avoidance Agreement (DTAA) with Mauritius and Cyprus

- A treaty was signed with Switzerland to obtain information about the bank accounts of Indians in HSBC bank.

- Cashless and digital payments have to be promoted

- Benami Transaction act will be modified.

- Income declaration scheme 2016

25. Apex policy making body for indirect taxes, CBEC is now to be known as Central Board of Indirect Taxes & Customers in the run up to the GST regime from July 1.

CBEC is being renamed as the Central Board of Indirect Taxes and Customers after getting legislative approval.

CBIC will supervise the work of all field formations and directorates and assist the government in policy making in relation to GST, continuing central excise levy and custom functions.

The existing formations of central excise and service tax under the CBEC have been re-organised to implement and enforce the provisions of the proposed GST Laws, it added.

The renamed Directorate General of Goods & Service Tax Intelligence is also being strengthened and expanded to become an important wing of the government in its fight against tax evasion and black money.

The existing training establishment, to be renamed as National Academy of Customs, Indirect Taxes and Narcotics will have an all-India presence.

This will enable capacity building to the employees of the indirect tax administration of the Centre as well as of the State Governments and to members of Trade and Industry.

GST:

- Indirect tax reform GST is expected to curb tax evasion.

- It will make commodities cheaper and add up to 2 per cent to India's GDP growth.

- GST will subsume excise, service tax, VAT and other local levies.

CBIC

- The CBIC will have 21 zones.

- It will have 101 GST Tax payer Services Commissionerates comprising 15 sub-Commissionerates,

- 768 Divisions, 3,969 Ranges, 49 Audit Commissionerates and 50 Appeals Commissionerates are also included.

26. The first order issued by the recently-established Insolvency and Bankruptcy Board of India (IBBI) is expected to influence many firms, including well-known consultancies that are eyeing the huge market for stressed assets and debt resolution.

In its March 2 order, IBBI rejected an application for registration as an Insolvency Professional (IP) by an individual who works with one of the so-called Big Four consultancy firms.

It held that "… an IP must not 'engage in any employment', repeat 'any employment'.

It envisages that a person must not play two roles — profession and employment - simultaneously," according to the order.

IBBI is not going to grant registration to individuals in such a scenario and so entities that want to be registered will have to form a separate subsidiary with dedicated resources related to insolvency and bankruptcy work.

The law does allow insolvency professional entities or IPEs wherein the majority of partners are registered IPs."

This segment is going to be extremely large in the future. There is around ?6.6 lakh crore worth of recognised NPAs in the banking sector as of today.

Legal experts say that the first order from IBBI has set a tone on how it is going to interpret the provisions of its regulations and is in line with the views of other regulators.

IBBI:

- IBBI seeks to consolidate and amend laws relating to reorganisation as well as insolvency resolution of corporate persons, partnership firms and individuals in a time-bound manner.

- It has been set up by the code to regulate professionals, information utilities (IUs) and agencies engaged in the resolution of insolvencies of companies.

- It has chairman and 10 members.

- Current chairman is M S Sahoo.

- There four government-nominated members.

27. eCommerce firms like Snapdeal and Amazon will have to deduct 1 percent tax collected at source while making payments to suppliers under the GST regime which is expected to come in from July 1.

Model Goods and Services Tax law, finalised by the GST Council, provides 1 percent TCS to be deducted by e-commerce operators.

Model law provides electronic commerce operators who are not agents should collect one percent TCS as notified on the recommendation of the Council of net value of taxable supplies made by other suppliers where the consideration with respect to the supplies should be collected by the operator.

Experts have expressed concern that a similar amount will be levied on inter-state movement of goods taking TCS deduction to 2 percent.

"We have included the word 'up to' in the final model GST law. This would mean that TCS would not exceed 1 per cent of the sale proceeds.

Industry has been expressing concern over the TCS provisions saying it would mean a lock-in of capital and also dissuades companies from selling through online aggregators.

E-commerce companies will also have to file returns on the TCS deductions, but in case of return of goods by the consumer, these companies will not have to deduct TCS as there is no actual sale.

The model law had defined 'electronic commerce' as supply of goods or services, including digital products, over electronic network.

'Electronic commerce operator' would mean those persons who own, operate or manage digital or electronic facility or platform for electronic commerce.

28. Coal Controller's Organisation, a coal ministry outfit has been tasked with grading and notifying the mines of Coal India Ltd from April 2017.

This makes a significant change of internal grading by Coal India.

This could lead to a change in existing grades as per the mines. Grading until now was done by coal producing subsidiaries of CIL and vetted by the CCO.

This change has been triggered by a fresh thrust on quality following recurring complaints on coal quality and grade mismatch by coal consumers in power and non-power sectors.

CIL has geared up to produce coal as per demand, but quality remains an issue.

In between coal seams, the presence of layers of stone and extraneous materials have led to variation in grades.

29. Noting positive growth for 6 months in a row, Indian exports soared 17.48 percent to USD 24.5 billion in Feb 2017 led by petroleum, engineering and chemicals.

But trade deficit also widened to USD 8.89 bn as imports grew.

Exports during Feb 2017 showed a double digit positive growth for the first time.

Imports were up 21.76% to USD 33.38b leaving a trade deficit of USD 8.89b as against USD 6.57 bn in Feb 2016.

During the April-Feb period of the current fiscal, exports have expanded by 2.52 percent to USD 245.4 bn.

Imports dipped 3.67 percent to USD 340.7 bn.

Trade deficit during the 11 month period stood at USD 95.28 bn as against USD 114.3 bn in the same period of the previous fiscal.

Oil imports rose by 60% to USD 7.68bn in Feb. Non-oil imports rose by 13.65% to USD 25.7 bn.

Gold imports too jumped manifold to USD 3.48 bn in February as against USD 1.4 bn in the same month last fiscal.

Trade Deficit:

- Trade deficit is an economic measure of a negative balance of trade.
- In this, a country's imports exceeds its exports.
- A trade deficit represents an outflow of domestic currency to foreign markets.

30. India's retail inflation rate grew by 3.65 percent in February, up from January's 3.17 percent.

This mirrors flat demand as companies and households hit by note-ban induced cash crunch raised spending on goods and services.

In February 2016, consumer price index inflation grew 5.18 percent, indicating a more expansionary economy a year back.

Retail inflation information, measured by CPI, is the broadest metric to measure cost of living in India.

The recent price data released by CSO represents a pick up in pace of remonetisation, led by food price increase.

Consumer food price inflation is a metric to measure changes in monthly kitchen costs. It grew 2.01 percent as against 0.53 percent in January and 5.30 percent in February 2016.

Fruit prices have risen 8.33 percent in February, up from 5.81 percent in January. The price of prepared meals and snacks saw a negligible change at 5.45 percent growth in February and 5.54 percent in January.

The scrapping of high value notes led to less spending, decreasing the demand for perishable products, when the sudden currency recall exercise commenced.

Prices of veggies and pulses remained tepid. The growth in CPI for vegetables contracted to -8.29 percent in February from 0.70 percent in 2016.

Index for fuel and light witnessed a small growth at 3.90 percent in February from 3.42 percent in January.

Housing inflation remained almost flat and grew at 4.90 percent in February, compared with 5.02 percent in January.

31. India's industrial production grew 2.7 percent Y-O-Y in Jan 2017 despite demonetisation, according to CSO.

Growth was due to the base effect as output had shrunk 1.59% in Jan 2016

Performance was better than 0.38 percent contraction in Dec 2016 but lagged the 5.65 percent growth posted in Nov 2016.

Manufacturing sector accounted for 75% of the total IIP grew 2.3% in January from -2.94 in January 2016 and -1.97% in Dec 2016, but slower than Nov's 5.47 percent pace.

Mining sector recorded a 5.3% growth in January, compared with 1.54% in January 2016 and 5.24% in December 2016.

Electricity production registered a 3.9% growth in January, lower than 6.56% in January 2016 and 6.28% in December 2016.

Capital goods output - a crucial pointer to investment demand in the economy - rose 10.7% from a low base of a contraction of (-) 21.55% in January 2016 as well as from (-) 3.01% in December 2016.

Consumer goods output contracted (-) 1% in January indicating weak consumer demand.

Consumer durables output grew 2.9%.

Only nine out of the 22 industry groups in the manufacturing sector have shown positive growth in the month of January 2017 as compared with the corresponding month of the previous year.

'Electrical machinery & apparatus' recorded the highest positive growth of 42.4%, followed by 21.8% growth in 'radio, TV & communication equipment' and 12.4% in 'basic metals'.

'Office, accounting and computing machinery' registered the highest negative growth of -16%, followed by -14.8% in 'food products & beverages' and -13.4% in 'Other transport equipment'.

Though retail inflation was below the target of 5%, IIP growth for April-January 2016-17 over the corresponding period of the previous year stood at 0.6%.

32. In a fresh move towards a cashless economy, the RBI prohibited the NBFCs of all kinds from lending more than INR 20,000 in cash against gold.

NBFCs have issued cheques for numerous loan amounts above prescribed limits. NBFCS have been directed earlier to disburse only high value loans of INR 1 lakh or more against gold by cheque.

The decision to limit the loan on gold to INR 20,000 from INR 1 lakh is in line with the IT act.

NBFCs:

- A Non-Banking Financial Company (NBFC) is a company registered under the Companies Act, 1956.
- It is engaged in the business of loans and advances, acquisition of shares/ stocks/ bonds/ debentures/ securities.
- It is issued by Government or local authority or other marketable securities of a like nature, leasing, hire-purchase, insurance business, chit business.
- It does not include any institution whose principal business is that of agriculture activity, industrial activity, purchase or sale of any goods (other than securities) or providing any services and sale/purchase/construction of immovable property.
- A non-banking institution which is a company and has principal business of receiving deposits under any scheme or arrangement in one lump sum or in instalments by way of contributions or in any other manner, is also a non-banking financial company.

33. (A) Various combinations of two commodities   3. Budget line

    that a consumer can purchase

(B) Various combinations of two commodities — 2. Indifference curve

   that give consumer equal satisfaction

(C) A set of indifference curves — 1. Indifference map

(D) Point of tangency of a budget — 4. Consumer's equilibrium

   line and an indifference curve

34. India has been given the dubious distinction of the highest bribery rate among 16 Asia Pacific countries surveyed by Transparency International/TI

Nearly 7 in 10 Indians accessing public services paid a bribe.

This is in contrast to the least corrupt country, Japan where only 0.2% of respondents bribed individuals.

Close to half of the respondents from India were positive about the government's efforts to combat bribery.

Even as the government's efforts to tackle bribery were appreciated, slightly more than 40% of the respondents viewed that corruption had increased over the past twelve months.

63% of the respondents in India also felt that they as individuals had the power to fight corruption.

The Global Corruption Barometer for the Asia Pacific Region was released by TI on March 7, in Berlin.

Approximately 90 crore people, or just over one in four, across 16 countries in Asia Pacific, including some of its biggest economies like India and China, are estimated to have paid a bribe to access public services.

For its report - People and Corruption: Asia Pacific, part of the Global Corruption Barometer series, TI surveyed nearly 22,000 people in these countries about their recent experiences with corruption.

India was followed closely by Vietnam where around two thirds (65%) had paid a bribe when accessing public services.

Across the Asia Pacific region, just 22% of the respondents thought that corruption had decreased while 40% of the respondents (41% in India) were of the option that it was on the rise.

In mainland China, 73% of the respondents felt that the level of corruption had worsened. This was the highest of any country surveyed.

Nearly 73% of those who paid a bribe in India were from the poorer section of society, in Pakistan and Thailand this percentage was 64% and 46% respectively.

Surprisingly a reverse trend was found in some countries like China, where the richer sections were more likely to pay a bribe.

In India, respondents reported the highest bribery incident in procuring government healthcare services and even identification related documents.

Nearly 59% of the respondents had paid a bribe for such services.

Bribes paid for education were next on the list with 58% having reported doing so.

TI:

- Headquarters: Berlin
- Founded: 4 May 1993
- Type of business: International non-governmental organization
- Founders: Peter Eigen, George Moody Stuart, Fritz Heimann, more
- Leaders: Cobus de Swardt, José Ugaz

35. India on March 8, 2017 announced an open acreage licensing policy for oil and gas exploration.

This is allowing bidders to carve out areas where they want to drill as the energy- hungry country looks at greater foreign investment to boost output.

The world's third-largest oil consumer will conduct auction of oil and gas blocks under the Open Acreage Licensing Policy (OALP) twice a year, with the first round being held in July this year.

OALP auction will be held under the overhauled exploration licensing policy allows pricing and marketing freedom to operators and shifts to a revenue sharing model.

The July auction will be India's first major exploration licensing round since 2010, although it had recently awarded 31 small discovered fields mainly to state-owned and local firms under the liberalised Hydrocarbon Exploration Licensing Policy (HELP).

Crude Oil and Natural Gas & OALP:

- India's domestic crude oil production of 36.95 million tons in 2015-16 barely met 20 per cent of its oil needs.
- Natural gas output at 32.249 billion cubic metres meets less than half of its needs.
- OALP will be a departure from the current licensing policy of government identifying the oil and gas blocks and then putting them on auction.
- It gives an option to a company looking for exploring hydrocarbons to select the exploration areas on its own.
- This selection can be done based on the seismic and well data that the Directorate-General of Hydrocarbons has put in a National Data Repository.
- NDR offers a total of 160 terabyte data of India's 26 sedimentary basins.

36. Government of India has approved INR 4500 crore project to revive 50 unserved and under-served airports as well as airstrips.

With the plan, the government is looking to enhance air connectivity to small cities and towns while the revival of such airports and airstrips would be "demand driven".

The proposal was agreed to by the Cabinet Committee on Economic Affairs, chaired by Prime Minister Narendra Modi.

The total cost of the project is estimated to be INR 4,500 crore. 15 airports/airstrips each would be revived during 2017-18 and

2018-19 each while 20 airports/airstrips would be revived during 2019-20.

As many as 50 unserved and under-served airports and airstrips of state governments, Airports Authority of India (AAI) and civil enclaves would be under the project.

Small cities/towns will be connected on commencement of operation of flights to under-served/unserved airports.

It will moreover boost the economic development in these areas as well as surrounding areas in terms of job creation and related infrastructure development.

Revival plan is demand driven. It would depend on firm commitment from airline operators as well as the state governments in terms of providing various concessions.

The unserved and under-served airports are to be developed without insisting on financial viability.

In the Union Budget, Finance Minister Arun Jaitley had announced plans for making adequate provisions for revival of unserved and under-served airports.

To make flying more affordable, the government has already unveiled the ambitious regional connectivity scheme UDAN ('Ude Desh Ka Aam Naagrik') under which fares are to be capped at INR 2,500 for one-hour flights.

37. The Goods and Services Tax (GST) Council, in its meeting held in Vigyan Bhawan in New Delhi under the Chairmanship of the Union Minister for Finance & Corporate Affairs, Shri Arun Jaitley has approved the draft CGST Bill and the draft IGST Bill as vetted by the Union Law Ministry.

This clears the deck for the Central Government to take these two Bills to the Parliament for their passage in the ongoing Budget Session.

i. A State-wise single registration for a taxpayer forfiling returns, paying taxes,and to fulfil other compliance requirements. Most of the compliance requirements would be fulfilled online, thus leaving very little room for physical interface between the taxpayer and the tax official.

ii. A taxpayer has to file one single return state-wise to report all his supplies, whether made within or outside the State or exported out of the country and pay the applicable taxes on them. Such taxes can be Central Goods and Services Tax (CGST), State Goods and Services Tax (SGST), Union Territory Goods and Services Tax (UTGST) and Integrated Goods and Services Tax (IGST).

iii. A business entity with an annual turnover of upto Rs. 20 lakhs would not be required to take registration in the GST regime, unless he voluntarily chooses to do so to be a part of the input tax credit (ITC) chain. The annual turnover threshold in the Special Category States (as enumerated in Article 279A of the Constitution such as Arunachal Pradesh, Sikkim, Uttarakhand, Himachal Pradesh, Assam and the other States of the North-East) for not taking registration is Rs. 10 lakhs.

iv. A business entity with turnover upto Rs. 50 lakhs can avail the benefit of a composition scheme under which it has to pay a much lower rate of tax and has to fulfil very minimal compliance requirements. The Composition Scheme is available for all traders, select manufacturing sectors and for restaurants in the services sector.

v. In order to prevent cascading of taxes, ITC would be admissible on all goods and services used in the course or furtherance of business, except on a few items listed in the Law.

vi. In order to ensure that ITC can be used seamlessly for payment of taxes under the Central and the State Law, it has been provided that the ITC entitlement arising out of taxes paid under the Central Law can be cross-utilised for payment of taxes under the laws of the States or Union Territories. For example, a taxpayer can use the ITC accruing to him due to payment of IGST to discharge his tax liability of CGST / SGST / UTGST. Conversely, a taxpayer can use the ITC accruing to him on account of payment of CGST / SGST / UTGST, for payment of IGST. Such payments are to be made in a pre-defined order.

vii. In the Services sector, the existing mechanism of Input Service Distributor (ISD) under the Service Tax law has been retained to allow the flow of ITC in respect of input services within a legal entity.

viii. To prevent lock-in of capital of exporters, a provision has been made to refund, within seven days of filing the application for refund by an exporter, ninety percent of the claimed amount on a provisional basis.

ix. In order to ensure a single administrative interface for taxpayers, a provision has been made to authorise officers of the tax administrations of the Centre and the States to exercise the powers conferred under all Acts.

x. An agriculturist, to the extent of supply of produce out of cultivation of land, would not be liable to take registration in the GST regime.

xi. To provide certainty in tax matters, a provision has been made for an Advance Ruling Authority.

xii. Exhaustive provisions for Appellate mechanism have been made.

xiii. Detailed transitional provisions have been provided to ensure migration of existing taxpayers and seamless transfer of underutilised ITC in the GST regime.

xiv. An anti-profiteering provision has been incorporated to ensure that the reduction of tax incidence is passed on to the consumers.

xv. In order to mitigate any financial hardship being suffered by a taxpayer, Commissioner has been empowered to allow payment of taxes in instalments.

Source: Press Information Bureau

The Council has also included a revised peak rate of 20 per cent under GST, instead from the earlier 18 per cent.

This would mean that the total incidence of the tax could go as high as 40 per cent.

But smoothening concerns, Revenue Secretary Hasmukh Adhia said that it would not impact the four-tier rate structure of 5, 12, 18 and 28 per cent.

The UT-GST Bill would be for levying of the new tax in Union Territories that do not have a legislature (excluding Delhi and Puducherry).

The four laws will be approved by the Union Cabinet and taken to the Parliament in the coming session,.

Finance Ministry officials said that the proposed anti-profiteering agency under GST would not send out inspectors to check on prices but will look at applications made consumers.

The remaining two Bills namely, State Goods and Services Tax (SGST) Bill and the Union territory Goods and Services Tax (UTGST) Bill, which would be almost a replica of the CGST Act, would be taken-up for approval after their legal vetting in the next meeting of GST Council scheduled on 16 March 2017.

38. Ministry of Drinking Water and Sanitation launched Swachh Shakti Saptah, a week-long programme of activities across the country to highlight the role of women in Swachh Bharat Mission and to recognize their leadership.

Union Minister of Drinking Water and Sanitation, Shri Narendra Singh Tomar, made the national launch of Swachh Shakti Saptaah in Gurugram, Haryana, at a joint event with the Government of Haryana.

Over 1000 women swachhta champions from grassroots in Haryana attended the event.

Deputy Commissioners of 11 ODF districts of Haryana were honoured on the occasion.

Event will culminate in Gujarat with function named Swachh Shakti 2017 where the Prime Minister, Shri Narendra Modi, will address 6000 women sarpanches and honour them for their contribution to Swachh Bharat.

The Minister also announced that the number of ODF (Open Defecation Free) districts in the country has now crossed 100.

Over 1.7 lakh villages have become ODF.

Haryana will become an ODF State by November 2017.

39. Software services industry lobby NASSCOM indicated it expects the sector to grow 8-10 percent in 2017-2018.

NASSCOM revised down its fiscal 2017 revenue growth target to 8-10 percent from 10-12 percent as US headwinds emerged.

The United States is the largest revenue source for the industry.

Many domestic IT companies may change their business strategies and regroup themselves owing to newer trends such as increasing automation artificial intelligence, digital data and digital disruption.

At the same time, there is a feeling within Nasscom that the industry is going to change. It is going to change because of automation, artificial intelligence, digital data and digital disruption. So, many companies will regroup themselves and re-architect their journey forward.

Current trend also suggest that job accretion will be at best half of its growth in recent years.

NASSCOM:

- Chairperson: C. P. Gurnani
- Founded: 1 March 1988
- Motto: Transform Business, Transform India
- Headquarters: Chanakyapuri, New Delhi
- Founders: Dewang Mehta, Nandan Nilekani

40. (1) The slope of the Isoquants represents the MRTS.

(2) The MRTS of the inputs x and y = MPx/MPy.

(3) The elasticity of substitution between two inputs x and y is proportionate change in the ratio of two inputs divided by proportionate change in the MRTS.

41. The **Securities and Exchange Board of India (SEBI)** plans to further tighten the regulations for **algorithmic trading**.

This aims to minimise instances of misuse of such systems that can be used to execute complex trading strategies at a very high speed.

SEBI chairman U.K. Sinha said that while India was one of the few countries in the world to regulate algorithmic trading - popularly called algo trading - the market regulator is looking to further strengthen the norms.

The aim is for instances of flash crashes that have happened overseas, and also in India a few times, could be minimised.

Algorithmic trading refers to the use of software programmes to execute trading strategies at a much faster pace.

On the National Stock Exchange (NSE), algo trades accounted for close to 16% of all trades.

On the BSE, it was 8.56% in January.

The SEBI chairman also said that while many countries and regulators, including the International Organization of Securities Commissions (IOSCO), have been debating on this issue for many years, only India had been able to come out with proper regulations.

SEBI:

1. Formed : 12 April 1992.
2. Agency executive : Ajay Tyagi, Chairman.
3. Headquarters : Mumbai, Maharashtra.

42. Moody has predicted India will be the fastest growing economy among G-20 countries clocking a 7.1 per cent growth in 2017.

The Indian economy had slowed in the fourth quarter of 2016 due to the withdrawal of 86 per cent of the currency in circulation, without an immediate replacement.

India is forecast to have the fastest growing economy among all G-20 countries with growth put at 7.1 per cent for 2017, down from a previous expectation of 7.5 per cent because of the effects of demonetisation.

With regard to global growth, Moody's said continuing cyclical recovery in global economic activity with growth in G-20 countries picking up modestly to 3 per cent in 2017 and 2018 from 2.6 per cent in 2016.

The potential shifts in US policy add uncertainty to this forecast.

There is unusually high uncertainty around our global forecasts due to the wide range of outcomes that could arise from significant shifts in US policy on a number of domestic and international issues, including trade and immigration.

The systemic risks to this forecast may stem from shifts in US trade policies, risks to global financial markets and emerging market economies if American interest rates were to rise faster than anticipated and/or the US dollar were to appreciate sharply.

Also there could be risks of a sudden and sharp deceleration in China and political and fragmentation risks in the EU and the euro area, Moody's indicated.

In the report titled 'Modest Acceleration in the Global Economy, but Shifting US Policies Inject Uncertainty', Moody's said there is a high risk of a significant protectionist shift in US trade policy and could inflict lasting damage to the global economy.

Regarding Asia, Moody's said China's economy stabilised around the official growth target of 6.7 per cent in 2016. It will likely continue to decelerate to 6.3 per cent and 6 per cent in 2017 and 2018.

Moody's expects that the US economy will get additional lift from a stimulative fiscal policy stance pushing growth above potential.

Accordingly, Moody's has revised its real GDP growth forecast to 2.4 per cent in 2017 and 2.5 per cent in 2018, from 2.2 per cent and 2.1 per cent, respectively.

Moody's forecast assumes the US Federal Reserve will raise the federal funds rate by 75-100 basis points in three to four rate hikes in 2017.

US Federal Reserve:

- Chairperson: Janet Yellen.
- Founder: United States Congress.
- Founded: 23 December 1913.
- Headquarters: Washington, D.C.
- Central bank of: United States of America.

43. The economy would have grown under-6 per cent in the third quarter, destroyed by the note ban, according to SBI Research.

The government will release the December quarter GDP print on February 28.

SBI research holds GDP growth to be decisively lower than 6 per cent in Q3 at 5.8 per cent and 6.4 per cent in Q4.

Overall, the estimate for H2 is 6.1 per cent with a downward bias against CSO's 7 per cent and the fiscal 2017 growth at 6.6 per cent.

In the next year growth could move up faster if demand comes back faster post-remonetisation, it added.

The report said growth will be pulled down by the poor show by sectors like construction, real estate, cement and FMCG, which are likely to witness a decline in sales in Q3 and will recover thereafter.

With the CSO (Central Statistics Organisation) estimate of 7.1 per cent for fiscal 2017, the Q3 and Q4 GDP growth would be around 6.1 per cent and 7.8 per cent.

This is improbable given the extent of liquidity shock that has led to a drastic consumer spending shock.

The 7.1 per cent GDP estimate by CSO implies a 7.8 per cent GDP growth in Q4, which looks highly unlikely.

As per the CSO, GDP is likely to grow by 7.1 per cent in fiscal 2017 compared to 7.9 per cent a year ago.

RBI, on the other hand, estimated GVA growth at 6.9 per cent as against its earlier estimate of 7.6 per cent. Of this 70 bps reduction, 35 bps are attributed to demonetisation and the rest to base effect.

CSO:

- The Central Statistics Organisation (CSO) of India is responsible for co-ordination of statistical activities in India.
- It also oversees evolving and maintaining statistical standards.
- It has a well-equipped Graphical Unit.
- The CSO is located in Delhi.
- Some portion of Industrial Statistics work pertaining to Annual Survey of industries is carried out in Calcutta.

44. IMF says India's growth is projected to slow to 6.6 per cent in 2016-17 fiscal due to the strains that have emerged in the economy as a result of "temporary disruptions" caused by demonetisation.

In its annual report, however, the International Monetary Fund (IMF) said demonetisation would have only short term impact on the economy and it would bounce back to its expected growth of more than eight per cent in the next few years.

The post-November 8, 2016 cash shortages and payment disruptions caused by the currency exchange initiative have undermined consumption and business activity, posing a new challenge to sustaining the growth momentum.

Growth is projected to slow to 6.6 per cent in FY2016/17, then rebound to 7.2 per cent in FY2017/18, due to temporary disruptions, primarily to private consumption, caused by cash shortages.

India's economy grew at 7.6 per cent in 2015-16 due to a favourable monsoon, low oil prices and continued progress in resolving supply-side bottlenecks, as well as robust consumer confidence.

The investment recovery is expected to remain modest and uneven across sectors, as deleveraging takes place and industrial capacity utilization picks up, the report said.

IMF Directors supported the Indian efforts to clamp down on illicit financial flows, but noted "the strains that have emerged" from the currency exchange initiative.

IMF EDs commended New Delhi for its strong policy actions, including continued fiscal consolidation and an anti-inflationary monetary policy, which have underpinned macroeconomic stability.

As such, the IMF recommended continued vigilance to potential domestic and external shocks and urged the authorities to further advance economic and structural reforms to address supply bottlenecks, raise potential output, create jobs, and ensure inclusive growth.

All About the IMF

- Headquarters: Washington, D.C., United States
- CEO: Christine Lagarde (since 2011)
- Founded: 27 December 1945, Bretton Woods, New Hampshire, United States
- Leader: Christine Lagarde
- Staff: 2700
- Founders: John Maynard Keynes, Harry Dexter White
- Parent organization: United Nations

45. Amitabh Kant, Chief Executive Officer of the government's policy think-tank NITI Aayog, said on 21st Feb 2017 that the government is developing a digital matrix.

The matrix to evaluate states in the push for a less-cash economy.

States are playing a critical role in getting citizens to opt for digital payments.

Stating that the government was taking steps to promote digital payments and bring digital on par with cash, Kant said that the Budget had announced a number of incentives including cash back and referral bonuses.

Kant said the government was also pushing for an Aadhaar app and a reduction in the Merchant Discount Rate.

RBI had proposed to drastically cut MDR charges on debit card payments from April 1 with a view to maintain momentum of digital transactions post note ban, especially among small merchants.

Kant said the ultimate aim was to enable to market to take over and drive the digital payment movement in a big way.

Continuing the digital push, the Reserve Bank of India had on 20th Feb 2017 launched the BharatQR platform.

This is a platform where scanning a QR code through a mobile phone will allow a customer to transfer money from one source to another.

46. Digital Haryana Roadmap will promote increased use of IT tools in the state and aid in a hassle-free delivery of citizen-centric services.

The Chief Minister, who was presiding over a meeting of CM Digital Haryana Cell here, said that not just delivery of services, but also the working of offices would undergo a complete change.

This is under the Digital Haryana Roadmap 2017-19.

The roadmap has been designed to convert governance into "Saral Shashan" which has been defined as "simple, all-inclusive, real-time, action-oriented and long lasting governance."

Under this, all departments where Information Technology-related projects are being implemented, would be connected.

The coordination would be established among them for proper monitoring of projects and policies.

Emphasis would be laid on curbing corruption and promoting digital literacy.

Service delivery to citizens would include immunisation updates through voice bursts, online calls with doctors, direct scholarship debit to bank accounts, real-time attendance updates to parents through SMS.

Other services include information on local voter registration via SMS, new service updates through Atal Seva Kendras, auto authentication for marriage registration and online registration of new apartments.

The government offices would be transformed to facilitate, among other things, daily feedback on school enrolment and bulk SMS to parents of children to improve attendance in schools.

It will also be promoting paperless governance.

Playing the enablers for various IT initiatives facilitating transformation across the state will be Atal Seva Kendras, online mobiles, and government offices.

Digital Haryana Roadmap 2017-19 was reaffirmation of the state government's resolute resolve to serve the people well.

It will make life easy by 'cutting down interface between the people and the administration' through increased use of IT tools.

185 IT projects are being implemented or are under process of implementation in the state, of which ten per cent are being implemented by the Central Government.

20 per cent projects have budget provision of more than Rs one crore, 50 per cent projects were launched in the last two years, and 70 per cent are being implemented through government agencies.

Haryana:

- Area: 44,212 km²
- Capital: Chandigarh
- Population: 27.76 million (2016)
- Chief minister: Manohar Lal Khattar

47. Around 209 MoUs were signed between different companies at the Momentum Jharkhand, a two-day global investors summit held in Ranchi, state capital.

Due to these MoUs, investment worth 3 lakhs, 39 thousands and 87 crores rupees will come in the state.

These investments will create direct job for two lakhs nine thousands and 176 people while indirectly create about four lakhs employment opportunities.

Out of total 209, the maximum numbers of MoUs were signed in mining sector which is 121. It was followed by IT and e-governance, with 30 MoUs while Urban development and housing with 17 MoUs.

Jharkhand:

- Founded: 15 November 2000
- Area: 79,714 km^2
- Capital: Ranchi
- Population: 31.9 million (2012)

48. India has ranked a dismal 143rd in an annual index of economic freedom by a top American think-tank, behind its several South Asian neighbours including Pakistan.

The progress on market-oriented reforms has been "uneven" as per the index.

The Heritage Foundation in its Index of Economic Freedom report said despite India sustaining an average annual growth of about 7 per cent over the past five years, growth is not deeply rooted in policies that preserve economic freedom.

Putting India in the category of "mostly unfree" economies, the conservative political think-tank said progress on market-oriented reforms has been "uneven".

Also, India's overall score of 52.6 points is 3.6 points less than that of last year, when India was ranked 123rd.

Hong Kong, Singapore and New Zealand topped the index.

Among South Asian countries, only Afghanistan (163) and Maldives (157) were ranked below India. Nepal (125), Sri Lanka (112), Pakistan (141), Bhutan (107), and Bangladesh (128) surpassed India in economic freedom.

The think-tank, however, credited Prime Minister Narendra Modi with "reinvigorating" India's foreign policy

India is a significant force in world trade, the report noted, but corruption, underdeveloped infrastructure, and poor management of public finance undermine overall development.

China with a score of 57.4 points - an increase of 5.4 points compared to previous year - was placed at 111 position. The United States was ranked 17 with 75.1 points.

The world average score of 60.9 is the highest recorded in the 23-year history of the index. Forty-nine countries - the majority of which are developing countries, but also including countries such as Norway and Sweden - achieved their highest-ever index scores.

49. Indian banks will require INR 91,000 crore in tier-1 capital till March 2019 to sustain a minimum annual growth rate of 8-9 percent, according to a report by India Ratings and Research (Ind-Ra).

This includes INR 20,000 crore of residual tranches from the government's capital infusion in public sector banks under the under 'Indradhanush' programme.

There is an increasing divide between the large and smaller PSBs, with the former having some access to growth capital, better market valuation, and also some non-core assets to divest.

The latter would only receive bailout capital if required.

The long tail of credit costs is expected to subdue profitability of domestic banks despite plateauing their stressed assets.

Ind-Ra has maintained a stable rating and sector outlook on private sector banks and large PSBs while it has retained the negative sector outlook for small, mid-sized state-owned banks for 2017-18.

It expects large PSBs with better access to capital and private sector banks with their robust capitalisation to navigate another year of low growth and rising credit costs with a stable outlook.

The agency had retained its negative outlook on mid-sized and smaller PSBs with weak capitalisation and large stock of ageing non-performing loans (NPLs).

These banks will find it increasingly difficult to grow given increasing capital requirements and large funding gaps impeding their ability to compete on spreads as per Ind-Ra.

According to Ind-Ra's sector-wise stress analysis, sectors such as iron and steel and textiles have seen recognition but provisioning might still not be enough to protect against eventual loss given defaults.

Significant proportion of unrecognised stress pertains to sectors such as infrastructure, realty and capital goods which potentially have long-term viable assets.

These would increasingly need cash flow restructuring to avoid slippages.

NPLs:

- A nonperforming loan (NPL) refers to a sum of borrowed money upon which the debtor has not made his scheduled payments for at least 90 days.
- A nonperforming loan is either in default/close to being in default.
- Once a loan is nonperforming, the odds that it will be repaid in full are considered to be low.

50. Gujarat Narmada Valley Fertilizers (GNFC) township, the state owned company's township at Bharuch, is 100% cashless and probably the first such township in India.

It has a population of around 5,000 and floating population of around 10,000 every day.

It has facilities like a big shopping centre, restaurants, eateries, schools and colleges, hospital, stadium, guest house, etc.

The GNFC township shall be launched by Gujarat chief minister Vijay Rupani on February 13 at Bharuch.

The GNFC is the first integrated industrial township in the country to go 100% digital in all financial transactions.

All the shops in the Gujarat Narmada Valley Fertilizers township, which include paan shops, laundries, vegetable shops, barber shops, provision stores, cycle repairing shops, flour mills, conduct their business only through cashless transactions.

Transactions are done using PoS machines, e-wallets like BHIM, UPI, SBI Buddy, etc.

51. The Indian economy is likely to grow by 7.4% in the next fiscal, according t India Ratings and Research.

GDP growth estimate for 2016-2017 has been revised from 6.8 to 7.9 percent, lower than the CSO advanced estimate of 7.1%.

Gross value added of three production sectors, namely agriculture, industry and services would grow at 3%, 6.1% and 9.1% Y-O-Y in this fiscal.

The current account deficit will come at 1% of the GDP in 2017-2018 as against 0.9 percent in 2016-2017.

This will help the rupee trade at an average 69.18/USD in FY18.

India is likely to face continued headwinds on the exports front due to the play out of Brexit and the anti-globalisation stance of US President Donald Trump and imports are unlikely to pick up so long as the domestic investment cycle does not revive.

As against the popular perception, Ind-Ra said the main setback to investment growth came from the negative 2.2 percent growth in the gross fixed capital formation (GFCF) of household sector.

Ind-Ra expects GFCF to grow at 4.9 percent in 2017-18.

India's economic growth forecast of 7.4 percent by Ind-Ra in 2017-18 is on the upper end of the 6.75 to 7.5 percent band estimated in the Economic Survey.

Ind-Ra:

- India Ratings & Research (India Ratings) is a rating agency committed to providing the India's credit markets with accurate, timely and prospective credit opinions.

- India Ratings has grown rapidly during the past decade gaining significant market presence in India's fixed income market.

- India Ratings is a wholly owned subsidiary of the Fitch Group.

- India Ratings currently maintains coverage of corporate issuers, financial institutions.

- India Ratings is headquartered in Mumbai and has six branch offices located at Ahmedabad, Bengaluru, Chennai, Delhi, Hyderabad and Kolkata.

- India Ratings is recognised by the Securities and Exchange Board of India, the Reserve Bank of India and NHB.

52. Corporate India FDI overseas fell by 57% to USD 1.82 billion, in Jan 2017 according to RBI data.

Investments made in Jan 2016 amounted to USD 4.25 billion in contrast.

Of the total overseas direct investment of USD 1.82 billion, USD 246.37 million came in the form of equity money; USD 483.78 million through loans.

While the rest of USD 1.09 billion was the guarantee issued by the Indian firms in their foreign units.

Among a few major investors, Bharat Petrosources invested USD 721.42 million in four tranches in joint venture and wholly owned subsidiary in Australia and Singapore.

Intas Pharmaceuticals invested USD 344.35 million in its fully owned unit in the UK, while ONGC Videsh put in a total of USD 52.59 million in four different joint ventures in Myanmar, Russia and Vietnam.

Reliance Industries invested USD 40 million in its wholly owned energy services unit in Singapore.

53. The Reserve Bank of India (RBI) has kept the repo rate unchanged at 6.25% in its monetary policy review on 8th Feb 2017.

It was citing inflation concerns after the first quarter of the next financial year, once the base effect vanishes.

The RBI said all the six members of the monetary policy committee voted in favour of the decision.

" Favourable base effects and lagged effects of demand compression may mute headline inflation in Q1 of 2017-18," the central bank said in a statement.

"Thereafter, it is expected to pick up momentum, especially as growth picks up and the output gap narrows. Moreover, base effects will reverse and turn adverse during Q3 and Q4 of 2017-18," the RBI added.

Now, the RBI has projected inflation in the range of 4.0 to 4.5% in the first half of the financial year and in the range of 4.5 to 5.0% in the second half.

The central bank cited 'three significant upside risks' that impart some uncertainty to the baseline inflation path -

- The hardening profile of international crude prices;

- Volatility in the exchange rate on account of global financial market developments, and the

- Fuller effects of the house rent allowances under the 7th Central Pay Commission (CPC) award.

At the same time, the RBI lauded the Central government for its effort in maintaining fiscal discipline that could have a favourable impact on inflation.

Monetary Policy Review

1. Repo rate under the liquidity adjustment facility (LAF): Unchanged at 6.25 percent.

2. Reverse repo rate under the LAF: Unchanged at 5.75 per cent.

3. Marginal standing facility (MSF): Unchanged at 6.75 per cent.

4. Bank Rate: Unchanged at 6.75 per cent.

5. Reserve Ratios Cash Reserve Ratio (CRR) of scheduled banks: Unchanged at 4.0 per cent of net demand and time liability (NDTL).

6. Statutory Liquidity Ratio (SLR): Unchanged 20.75 per cent.

54. The Indian economy is expected to overtake the US by 2040 in PPP terms.

The global economic order is expected to shift from advanced to emerging economies over the next few decades.

By 2040, India could edge past the US to become the world's second largest economy in purchasing power parity (PPP) terms, as per a PwC report.

According to PwC, E7 economies comprising Brazil, China, India, Indonesia, Mexico, Russia and Turkey would grow at an annual average rate of almost 3.5 per cent over the next 34 years.

This is compared to just 1.6 per cent for the advanced G7 nations of Canada, France, Germany, Italy, Japan, the UK and the US.

In fact, China has already overtaken the US to become the world's largest economy in PPP terms, while India currently stands in third place and is projected to overtake the US by 2040 in PPP terms.

PwC believes Vietnam, India and Bangladesh would be three of the world's fastest growing economies over this period.

We will continue to see shift in global economic power away from established advanced economies towards emerging economies in Asia and elsewhere.

The E7 could comprise almost 50 per cent of world GDP by 2050, while the G7's share declines to only just over 20 per cent.

To realise this growth potential, emerging market governments need to implement structural reforms to improve macroeconomic stability, diversify their economies away from undue reliance on natural resources (where this is currently the case), and develop more effective political and legal institutions.

Challenges include falling global trade growth, rising income inequality within many countries and increasing global geopolitical uncertainties are intensifying the need to create diversified economies.

This create opportunities for everyone in a broad variety of industries.

55. The Union Railway Ministry has approved a 240-KM broad-gauge railway line project in Andaman and Nicobar islands.

The first railway line on Andaman and Nicobar Islands will connect Port Blair (capital) in the south with Diglipur, the biggest town on the north Andaman Island.

Presently both destinations are linked by a 350-km bus service that takes over 14 hours and a ship that takes around 24 hours and there is no air connectivity.

Following completion, it will give fillip to tourism from the current 4.5 lakh visitors a year to around 6 lakh a year.

About A & N Islands:

- Andaman and Nicobar Islands are a group of islands at the juncture of the Bay of Bengal and Andaman Sea.
- It is one of the seven UTs of India.
- It comprises two island groups, the Andaman Islands and the Nicobar Islands, separated by the 10°N parallel.

- The islands host the Andaman and Nicobar Command, the only tri-service geographical command of the Indian Armed Forces.
- The islands are home to the only known Paleolithic people, the Sentinelese people.

56. To make India an innovation-driven economy, NITI Aayog, Department of Industrial Policy & Promotion (DIPP) and Confederation of Indian Industry (CII) together launched a mega initiative "India Innovation Index" on Feb 2nd 2017.

This will rank states on Innovations through country's first online innovation index portal that will capture data on innovation from all Indian states on innovation and regularly update it in real time.

The India Innovation Index Framework will be structured based on the best practices followed in Global Innovation Index (GII) indicators.

Additionally it will function by adding India-centric parameters those truly reflect the Indian innovation ecosystem.

Inaugurating the India Innovation portal, Mr Amitabh Kant, CEO NITI Aayog said, "This portal will be a first-of-its-kind online platform where Global Innovation Index indicators and India–centric data from various states will be coalesced."

Data collated on this portal will not only be used to ameliorate current data gaps w.r.t the GII, but be the prime source for the India Innovation Index, which will be jointly developed by NITI Aayog, DIPP and CII.

This is in consultation with World Economic Forum, the World Intellectual Property Organization, Cornell University, OECD, UNIDO, ILO, UNESCO, ITU and others.

The aim is to rank Indian states as per their innovation prowess.

It will also provide impetus to them to build their respective innovation ecosystems and spur the innovation spirit among institutions and people.

Global Innovation Index:

- The Global Innovation Index (GII), co-published by World-Intellectual Property Organization (WIPO), Cornell University and INSEAD with CII as a Knowledge Partner since inception.
- It has been ranking world economies including India since 2007 according to their innovation capabilities and outcomes.
- It uses 82 indicators among a host of other important parameters.
- It has established itself as both a leading reference on innovation and a 'tool for action' for policy makers.
- India currently ranks 66th out of 128 countries on the Global innovation Index (GII) 2016.

57. The share of nuclear power in the total electricity generation in the country was about 3.4% in the year 2015-16.

It will be progressively increased by addition of nuclear power capacity.

The present capacity of 5780 MW will reach 6780 MW by the end of this financial year, with the commercial operation of Kudankulam Unit-2, which is already generating infirm power at the rated capacity.

The capacity is expected to reach 9580 MW by 2020 on progressive completion of projects under construction and about 12980 MW by 2024 on completion of new projects accorded sanction.

A large expansion programme based on both Indian technologies and with foreign technical cooperation is planned ahead.

GoI has also given 'in principle' approval for the site at Kovvada in Srikakulam district of Andhra Pradesh.

This is for setting up six Light Water Reactors in cooperation with the USA.

Pre-project activities including land acquisition, obtaining statutory clearances and detailed site investigations are continuing at the site.

In parallel, discussions on the techno-commercial aspects with M/s Westinghouse Electric Company (WEC) to arrive at a project proposal have also started.

58. The Union Finance Ministry has agreed to contribute partially to a new dedicated railway safety fund.

It is named as 'Rashtriya Rail Sanraksha Kosh' and presented in the upcoming Union Budget 2017-18.

The proposed safety fund will be utilised for track improvement, bridge rehabilitation, rolling stock replacement, human resource development, improved inspection system and safety work at level crossing.

The Finance Ministry is likely to grant a fresh infusion of only INR. 5,000 crore in the upcoming financial year out of the initial proposed corpus of INR. 20,000 crore.

About INR. 10,000 crore will be earmarked from the Central Road Fund (CRF).

This is collected by levying a cess on diesel and petrol at present for safety-related work.

Railways may now be asked to fund the remaining INR. 5,000 crore for the initial corpus from its own resources.

For this, Indian Railways may either have to bring back a cess on rail tickets to finance its share of Rail Safety Fund or look to fund it from non-budgetary resources.

About the Rashtriya Rail Sanraksha Kosh

- Railways requested Union Finance Ministry to create 'Rashtriya Rail Sanraksha Kosh.

- This is a 'non-lapsable' safety fund of INR. 20,000 crore over five years.

- Its request was based on the recommendations of a high-level safety review committee.

- This was headed by Dr. Anil Kakodkar, former Chairman Atomic Energy Commission.

- The Committee, in its report submitted in 2012, had projected an investment requirement of INR. 1 lakh crore on safety over five years.

59. The push for digitisation in the wake of demonetisation and the proposal for public sector bank (PSB) consolidation are to top the agenda for Gyan Sangam.

This is the retreat for PSBs, government-owned Financial Institutions (FI) and insurance companies, slated for March.

The sessions on digitisation will include presentations on increasing the use of Artificial Intelligence (AI) systems. It will also study big data analytics in the banking & financial services industry in India.

The major slowdown in credit growth – to a more than six-decade low of 5.1% for the fortnight ended December 23 – and ways to revitalise it, as well as measures to effectively tackle bad loans will also be discussed.

The retreat would have discussions on automating many of these functions to ensure productivity improvement.

Strategies for strengthening the 'banking correspondent'-network and increasing the usage of micro ATMs and Point of Sale machines will also be discussed.

The high-profile meeting will also deliberate upon the need for the autonomous Banks Board Bureau (BBB) to expedite banking reforms including PSB consolidation.

The BBB was set up to help select heads of public sector banks and financial institutions as well as assist banks with strategies and capital-raising plans.

Also on the agenda for discussion is the proposed National Asset Management Company (or a 'bad bank').

This is a special category asset reconstruction company with stakeholders including the government and the private sector for takeover and turnaround of bad loans, stressed assets and restructured assets.

60. Karang, a small lake island in Manipur has become the first cashless island.

The Union Ministry of Electronics and Information Technology under the Digital India programme declared this is the first cashless island in India.

The island has fulfilled the necessary criteria of the Centre.

Karang is located in the middle of Loktak, the largest freshwater lake in NE India.

Akodara was the first digital village in India in 2015.

61. IMF has cut down India's growth rate for the current fiscal year to 6.6 percent. The previous estimate was 7.6%.

The slowing of the growth rate is on account of temporary negative consumption shock of demonetisation after the WB decelerated India's growth estimates.

Growth forecast for the current and next fiscal year were trimmed by one percentage and 0.4 percentage points, due to temporary negative consumption shock .

This has been caused by cash shortage and payment disruption noted with recent currency note withdrawal and exchange, as per World Economic Outlook released by the IMF.

IMF also said after a lackluster outturn in 2016, economic activity will pick up in the next 2 years. This is more so for the emerging market and developing economies.

Global growth for 2016 is now 3.1 percent in line with the Oct 2016 forecast.

The economic activities in emerging markets and developing economies/EMDEs is to accelerate in 2017-2018 with global growth at 3.4 and 3.6 percent respectively.

India's growth in 2017 is projected at growth rate of 7.2% as against previous growth forecast of 7.6 percent.

Indian economy is expected to revive with 7.7% growth in 2018.

Cut in the growth rate comes after WB decelerated India's GDP growth for 2016-2017 fiscal to 7 percent from previous estimate of 7.6 percent citing impact of demonetisation.

India would regain momentum in coming years. India continues to be among the fastest growing countries in the emerging economies.

In 2016, China with a growth percentage of 6.7% has outperformed India. IMF has forecasted China's growth rate to 6.5% for 2017 based on continued policy support.

In 2018, China is projected to grow at 6 percent against India's 7.7%.

IMF:

- Abbreviation stands for: International Monetary Fund.
- Formation: 27 December 1945.
- Type: International financial institution.
- Headquarters: Washington, D.C., United States.
- Membership: 189 countries.
- Official language: English.
- Managing Director: Christine Lagarde.
- Main organ: Board of governors.
- Parent organization: United Nations.
- Staff: 2,700.

62. Centre plans to set up 18 electronics manufacturing clusters in 400 towns and cities. India's electronic manufacturing market will be worth USD 400 billion by 2020 according to some estimates.

Government is focusing on domestic production of technology products, according to Union Minister for Communications, Ravi Shankar Prasad at the Pravasi Haryana Divas 2017.

Digital payment infrastructure and service is set to be a rising industry. Haryana has a lot of potential and possibilities for innovation in the field of digital payment, internet, AI, digital education and cybersecurity.

Considerable potential is there for small and medium level enterprises to grow.

About 42 mobile phone manufacturing companies and 30 component factories have been established in the country.

India has close to 105 crore mobile phones , 10 crore Aadhaar cards, 500 billion internet connections and 350 billion smartphones.

63. Bureau of Indian Standards (BIS) on 10th Jan said it has revised Indian Standard on gold hallmarking, which is effective from January 1 this year.

Indian standard on gold hallmarking has been revised and has been made effective for implementation with effect from January 1, 2017.

The hallmarked gold jewellery will now be available in three grades of 14 carat, 18 carat and 22 carat.

The caratage will also be marked on jewellery in addition to fineness for convenience of consumers,

For 22 carat jewellery 22K will be marked in addition to 916 (22K916), for 18 carat jewellery 18K will be marked in addition to 750 (18K750) and for 14 carat jewellery, 14K will be marked in addition to 585 (14K585).

Hallmark on gold jewellery will now have four marks.

These are the BIS Mark, the purity in carat and fineness (22K916 for 22 carat), assaying centre's identification mark and jeweller's identification mark.

Know More About BIS

- The Bureau of Indian Standards (BIS) is the national Standards Body of India.
- It working under the aegis of Ministry of Consumer Affairs, Food & Public Distribution.
- Headquarters?: ?Manak Bhawan
- Agency executive?: ?: Alka Panda, Director General
- Formed?: ?23 December 1986

64. National capital Delhi has registered the highest per capita income among all states and union territories of the country with INR 2,80,000 during 2015-2016, according to the National Statistical handbook.

Delhi's per capita income is three times the national average INR 93,293.

It was followed by Chandigarh and Sikkim with per capital incomes of INR 2,42,386 and INR 2,27,465.

Data released by Oxford Economics in Nov 2016 found Delhi has emerged as the economic capital of India.

It has overtaken Mumbai as per GDP in terms of purchasing power parity.

Chandigarh registered the second highest per capita income at 2.5 times the national average.

Chandigarh's current figure of INR 2,42,386 is a meagre increase of over INR 1,699, or 0.7 per cent, compared to the previous year when it was INR 2,40,687, a statistical handbook released in Delhi showed.

Delhi's current figure increased by over INR 28,000, or 13 per cent, compared to the previous year when it was INR 2,52,011.

The per capita income at the national level was found to be INR 93,293 during 2015-16.

65. According to the fresh data released by the Finance Ministry, over 26 crore accounts have been opened under the Pradhan Mantri Jan Dan Yojana across the country till date.

Nearly 16 crore accounts have been opened in rural areas and more than 10 crore in the urban.

Over 71,5000 crore rupees has been deposited in these accounts.

Zero balance accounts have come down by nearly 24%.

Around 20 crore RuPay debit cards have also been issued under the scheme.

The PMJDY was launched in Aug 2014 by PM Narendra Modi to ensure financial inclusion for covering all households with at least one bank account.

More About PMJDY

- Government scheme launched by government of India.
- Aims to provide easy access to financial services such as Remittance, Credit, Insurance, Savings, Deposit and Pension.
- Financial inclusion scheme officially launched on 15th August 2014.
- East financial access ensured to everyone at national level.

66. Demonetisation did not impact the tourist footfall adversely this year, with 8.91 lakh foreign tourists visited India in Nov 2016.

This marks the growth of 9.3 % over the same month last year.

Foreign tourist arrivals (FTAs) during December 2015 was 8.16 lakh, while it was 7.65 lakh in December 2014.

Foreign Exchange Earnings (FEEs) from tourism during the month of December were INR 14,474 crore as compared to INR 12,649 crore in the same month last year, recording a growth of 14.4 %.

The US accounted for highest share of tourist arrivals followed by the UK and Bangladesh in December 2016, according to an official release.

FTAs during January-December, 2016 were 78.53 lakh, recording a growth of 10.4 % as compared to 71.14 lakh during the corresponding period last year.

FEEs from tourism in January-December were Rs 1,38,845 crore, witnessing an increase of 14.7 % as compared to the INR 1,21,041 crore during the corresponding period last year.

67. The Reserve Bank of India (RBI) has opposed a move to establish a separate entity to regulate payments and settlements as recommended by Ratan Watal Committee for Digital Payments.

The 11-member committee was formed in September 2016 by the Union Finance Ministry to review existing payment systems in country and recommend appropriate measures for encouraging Digital Payments.

One of the committee's terms of reference was to study and recommend changes in the regulatory mechanism under various acts such as the RBI Act, Payments and Settlement Act, and the Information Technology Act among others.

Based on this, the committee had recommended making regulation of retail payments independent from the function of RBI to give digital payments boost.

It called for establishing separate Payments Regulatory Board (PRB) as an independent body for retail payments and suggested that RBI's regulation must be kept only for SIPS (systemically important payment system).

According to RBI, the global practice is that both the SIPS and retail payment systems are under the central bank for a variety of reasons including issues of inter-connectivity between the systems and the role of the central bank as the lender of last resort (LOLR).

RBI has suggested a monetary-policy-committee-style structure for the PRB, where outcomes are decided independently, but implementation remains with the banking regulator.

68. GoI has urged people to take advantage of the last window for disclosing black money and make declarations under the Pradhan Mantri Garib Kalyan Yojana that opens on 17th Dec, 2016.

The Pradhan Mantri Garib Kalyan Yojana provides for 50 percent tax and surcharge on declarations of unaccounted cash deposited in banks.

Declarants also have to park a quarter of the total sum in a non-interest bearing deposit for 4 years.

The government also released an email id blackmoneyinfo@incometax.gov.in and urged people to mail any information about people who have black money.

PMGKY will close on March 31, 2017.

Disclosure under the scheme will attract 50% tax and penalty. Declarations under the black money disclosure scheme will be kept confidential. Information will not be used for prosecution.

Receipt of tax paid on deposited will have to be shown to avail disclosure scheme benefits including immunity from prosecution.

Currently, INR 393 crore of cash and jewellery has been seized of which INR 316 crore is cash and the rest is bullion and jewellery. Of the total INR 316 crore, INR 80 crore is in new currency.

Raids have revealed INR 2600 crore of concealed income.

69. Reserve Bank of India (RBI) on 7th Dec 2016 kept its key lending - the repo rate - unchanged at 6.25 percent.

This move ended hopes of lower borrowing costs to arrest the demonetisation-induced slide in spending and investment.

The Monetary Policy Committee felt that the assessment is clouded by the still unfolding effects of the withdrawal of specified bank notes (SBNs).

It also lowered its growth forecast for 2016-17 to 7.1 percent from 7.6 percent earlier.

The MPC also decided to restore the cash reserve ratio (CRR) - the proportion of deposits banks are required to park with the RBI - at 4 percent.

The surge in post-demonetisation liquidity had prompted the RBI to temporarily ask banks to park the entire mountain of additional cash as 100 percent cash reserve ratio (CRR) with the central bank.

RBI revised the ceiling on issuance of securities under the market tabilization scheme (MSS) to INR 6 lakh crore, from the previous limit of INR 30,000 crore for financial year 2016-17.

Banks were not in favour of a higher CRR, as parking funds with the RBI in this window does not fetch any returns, and works against lowering lending rates for final individual and corporate borrowers.

India's Repo Rate

- Stands for: Repurchase Option.

- Since January 2015, the RBI has cut the repo rate six times. India's retail inflation has touched 4.20 percent in October, triggering hopes of a rate cut.

- The RBI and the government have set a retail inflation target of 4 per cent for the next five years with an upper tolerance level of 6 percent and lower limit of 2 per cent.

- Household spending accounts for more than half of India's GDP.

- The slowdown in household spending could push back investment growth.

70. India crossed the $300 billion foreign direct investment (FDI) milestone between April 2000 and September 2016.

It has succeeded in firmly establishing its credentials as a safe investment destination in the world. Thirty-three per cent of the FDI came through the Mauritius route.

This is because the investors wanted to take advantage of India's double taxation avoidance treaty with the island nation.

India received $101.76 billion from Mauritius between April 2000 and September 2016.

The cumulative FDI inflows during the period amounted to $310.26 billion.

The inflows in the first half of the current financial year were $21.62 billion, according to data compiled by the Department of Industrial Policy and Promotion.

- The other big investors have been from Singapore, the US, UK and the Netherlands.

- According to the World Investment Report 2016, global FDI flows rose by 38 per cent to $1.76 trillion, the highest level since the global economic and financial crisis began in 2008.

About Indian economy FDI Flows

- Liberalisation of the FDI policy framework has benefitted India.

Major national development programmes that made India the destination for foreign funds include:

- Start Up India

- Stand Up India

- Make in India

- Digital India

- Skill India

- Besides increasing competitiveness, it has boosted investment.

- India last crossed the $300 billion mark at a time when the global economic slowdown has had a dampening impact on FDI flows.

71. The move follows Assam government's directive of making cashless transactions to the plantation workers. 5 correspondents from the Assam Grameen Vikash Bank assisted the payment process.

504 plantation workers who are employed at the Burnie Braes tea estate received their wages through their individual bank accounts.

This move supports Prime Minister Narendra Modi's Cashless India drive, following the demonetisation of old ?500 and ?1000 currency notes on 9 November 2016.

Other states which have districts that have gone cashless include Goa and Maharashtra.

72. Central Statistical Office on 30th Nov 2016 announced India's GDP accelerated to 7.3 percent in the second quarter of 2016-2017. This is up from a provisional 7.1 percent expansion in Q1.

Gross Value Added rose to 7.1 percent.

GDP growth accelerated in the second quarter from 7.1 percent, but GVA growth slowed 7.3 percent in that period.

Both GDP and GVA growth were slower in this Q2 compared to 2015-2016's Q2. The Q2 of 2015-2016 showed a GDP growth of 7.6 percent and GVA growth of 7.3 percent.

The agriculture sector maintained the overall growth by registering a 3.3 percent GVA growth rate in Q2 of this financial year in comparison with 2 percent in Q2 of 2015-16.

The manufacturing sector saw considerable slowdown as it registered GVA growth of 7.1 percent in Q2 of this financial year as against 9.2 percent in 2015-2016's Q2.

The mining and quarrying sector growth fell by 1.5 percent in Q2 compared with the contraction of 0.4 percent in the first quarter and a growth of 5 percent in Q2 of 2015-16.

Sectors like manufacturing, electricity, mining, services and others show a fall in the September quarter because they are not supported by demand.

Except for agriculture, public administration and construction, drop in outputs across all sectors took place.

Gross fixed capital formation equalled 29 percent of GDP in this Q2 compared to 32.9 percent in the previous year's Q2.

Government final consumption expenditure was 13 percent of GDP in this Q2 compared to 12.1 percent in the earlier year. GFCE grew 18.8 percent in this Q1 and 15.2 percent in this Q2.

Government's Capital Expenditure (Plan and Non Plan) fell 12.81 percent to INR 129459 crore as against INR 143329 crore a year back.

What is GDP?

GDP: Monetary value of all finished goods and services produced in a country in a certain time period. It is generally calculated on annual basis; it can be computed on quarterly basis as well.

It is a broad measurement of nation's overall economic activity.

GDP = Private consumption+ Public consumption+ Government outlays+ Investments + Exports - Imports.

Where, GDP = C + G + I + NX

- C = all private consumption, or consumer spending
- G = sum of government spending,
- I = sum of all the country's investment, including businesses capital expenditures and
- NX is the nation's total net exports, calculated as total exports minus total imports (NX = Exports - Imports).

73. Around the confusion created by demonetisation, the Indian state of Goa is the first state to operate cashless in the country from 31st Dec 2016.

The announcement was made by Defence Minister Manohar Parrikar who is the former CM of the state.

The plan includes making small vendors sell perishable goods as per mobile payment.

Vendors will be given Mobile Money Identifier codes when they register at a bank.

Customers will be able to make the transactions by dialling 99# and following instructions that appear on the screen.

The smartphone can be used to make the payment.

There is no limit on the cashless transfer of money and these transactions will be immune from any sort of fees.

Goa Goes Cashless

Goa has benefits due to its small size.

- Population: 15 lakh
- It has 17 lakh registered mobile connections.
- It has 22 lakh bank accounts.
- Most Goans use debit or credit cards

74. With the last date for paying first instalment of due taxes and penalties under one time black money window IDS nearing, banks have been asked to not look for source.

This is to ensure that payments are accepted without any hassle.

The directive comes after a recent CBDT communication to RBI which cited a CBDT communication to RBI saying a declarant had complained about the bank branch refusing to accept tax and penalty as part of IDS.

Scheme stipulates that minimum of 25 percent of tax, surcharge and penalty must be paid by Nov 30, 2016.

The CBDT has also appended the scheme of the IDS which stipulates that a minimum amount of 25 per cent of the tax, surcharge and penalty is to be paid by November 30, 2016.

A further amount of 25 per cent of the tax, surcharge and penalty to be paid by March, 31 next year;

Balance amount to be paid on or before September 30, 2017.

About Income Declaration Scheme/IDS

- IDS is four months in duration
- It was a one-time window beginning in June 2016
- It gave black money holders a chance to come clean by declaring their stash and paying 45 percent tax and penalty
- 64,275 declarants disclosed an amount of INR 65,250 under IDS
- This will yield INR 30,000 crore to the government

75. RBI has asked banks to temporarily maintain additional average daily balance to drain out surplus liquidity with them.

This follows the banking system being flooded with liquidity triggered by heavy inflow of deposits, due to ongoing demonetisation exercise.

CRR or slice of deposits that banks have to maintain with the central bank remains at 4 percent of the deposits.

Surfeit of liquidity is on account of the fact that they altogether parked INR 2,27,242 crore in 3 reverse repo auction conducted by the RBI on Nov 26, 2016.

In a circular to banks, RBI said increase in deposits between Sept 16 and Nov 11, scheduled banks will have to maintain incremental CRR of 100 percent beginning Nov 26.

This measure will absorb a part of the surplus liquidity arising from the return of INR 500 and 1000 bank notes, while leaving adequate liquidity with banks to meet credit needs of numerous sectors.

RBI has observed that with the demonetisation decision, there has been an increase in deposits relative to expansion in bank credit leading to large excess liquidity in the system.

It assessed the magnitude of surplus liquidity with the banking system is expected to rise further in coming weeks.

This surplus liquidity will be partly absorbed by applying incremental CRR.

76. To protect domestic manufacturers from cheap imports, the Centre on 24th Nov 2016 slapped safeguard duty on import of certain steel products.

Steel products on which safeguard duty was slapped included hot rolled flat sheets and plates (Excluding hot rolled flat products in coil form) of alloy or non-alloy steel.

As per the Revenue Department notification, the effective duty rate will be calculated after deduction of the value of goods.

Anti dumping duty will become payable when import price is below USD 504 per tonne on CIF basis.

CIF means Cost Insurance Freight basis.

Notification has said the duty arrived will be 10 percent and gradually lower to 8 percent in 2018 and 6 in 2019.

10 percent ad-valorem minus anti dumping duty payable will be imposed on imports up to 22nd Nov 2017.

The same will be lowered to 8 percent between 23rd Nov 2017 and 22nd Nov 2018. It will be reduced to 6 percent between 23rd November 2018 and 22nd May 2019

The safeguard duty on import of cheap steel was slapped after steel makers approached the DG of anti dumping and allied duties.

The DG was requested to come up with safeguard measures against imports of cheap steel. Steel makers who approached the DG include JSW, SAIL and Essar.

About Safeguard Duty

- Safeguard duty is imposed on products imported into the country in increased quantities, injuring the domestic industry

- Ad Valorem tax is a tax whose amount is based on value of transaction or property- tax is imposed at the time of transaction in the form of sales or VAT tax.

- Earlier in Nov 2016, government imposed anti-dumping duty on few cold rolled flat steel products from 4 nations including China and South Korea.

77. The Indian m-wallet market is expected to grow at a compounded annual growth rate (CAGR) of 141% to reach Rs 30,000 crore by the end of 2021-22, a study by ASSOCHAM and RNCOS indicated.

The growth, during 2015-16 to 2021-22, would be driven by growing usage of smartphones, robust mobile internet penetration, growth of e-commerce sector together with increasing disposable incomes.

The Indian m-wallet market in 2015-16 was around Rs 154 crore. It is also anticipated that the market value of m-wallet transactions in India will grow at a CAGR of 154% during FY16 to FY22, and reach Rs 55 lakh crore from Rs 20,600 crore.

The study was titled 'Indian m-wallet market: Forecast 2022'.

While mobile wallet service contributed to 21% share in mobile payment volume transactions in FY16, its share is expected to increase to 79% by FY22, the study said.

78. Agra-Lucknow expressway, India's longest expressway till date was inaugurated on Nov 20.

- The 302 km long six greenfield expressway is special on multiple counts from record time under which it has been completed to the fact that it will reduce travel time between the two UP cities

- The expressway will cut down travel time between Agra and Lucknow to just 3.5 hours from the current 7 hours

- The Agra-Lucknow expressway has a design speed of up to 120 km/hour

- The six lane expressway is expanded to 8 lanes- this includes 4 rail over bridges, 13 major bridges, 57 minor bridges, 148 pedestrian underpasses, 74 vehicular underpasses and 9 flyovers.

- The total expressway is planned to be lined with a metal beam crash barrier on both sides and wire fencing state-of-the-art advance traffic management system for safe and secure transit

- The expressway has been built in a record time of 23 months by the UPEIDA/ Uttar Pradesh Expressways Industrial Development Authority

- The Agra-Lucknow expressway boasts of development centres, agricultural madness, schools, rest houses, petrol pumps, service centres and public amenities among other prominent features

- The expressway spans 10 districts, 236 villages and 3500 ha of land

- It will start in the village of **Etmadpur Madra near Agra and end in Sarosa Bharosa** near Mohan Road, Lucknow

- The Agra- Lucknow expressway will also be connected to the famous Yamuna expressway through the Agra ring road, boosting connectivity to Delhi and NCR areas such as Noida.

- Objective of the expressway is to ensure development of closely areas, providing a fast moving corridor that permits seamless travel, reduces the carbon footprint of vehicles and helps farmers to reach their products to larger cities and attract investors in the state.

- As per **UPEIDA**, a green belt is being developed on the sides of the Agra Lucknow expressway by planting trees on either sides and in the median.

79. Chhattisgarh became the first state of India to adopt a resolution welcoming demonetisation scheme of the Union government

- The resolution was moved in the state assembly by CM Raman Singh.

- Resolution passed on 16th November 2016 saw 41 votes in favour and 25 against.

- On Nov 8, at 8:00 pm , PM Modi had announced the demonetisation of high value currency notes of India and that INR 1000 and 500 notes will cease to be legal tender from 8-9 Nov midnight.

- The decision aims to **remove black money** from the system.

- It will **usher in clean transactions and clean up the money system and impact contentious issues plaguing** the system.

- The Chhattisgarh government has also pledged to take steps to encourage people in small businesses to switch over to e-payment system and places with swipe machines would be exempt from VAT.

- The state government has also made arrangements to make online payments to farmers for their paddy procured under the support price system.

80. The new high-security INR **500 notes have been released** to banks for distribution on 14th Nov

- As per the central bank statement, the new INR 500 notes bear the signature of **RBI governor Urijit Patel**

- The note is stone grey coloured and bears year of printing 2016 and the **Swach Bharat logo printed on the reverse**

- The new 500 note differs from the earlier in size, theme, colour, location of security features and design elements.

- It has The **Red Fort as an image** of the Indian heritage site with the Indian flag on the reverse of it.

- The banknote also has other features enabling visually impaired persons to identify the denomination: Intaglio printing of the Mahatma Gandhi portrait, Ashoka Pillar emblem, bleed lines, circle with 500 in the right and the identification mark.

81. The **Union Tourism Ministry** is set to name Prime Minister Narendra Modi as the mascot of the Incredible India campaign.

- This position was vacant following **Aamir Khan's** removal as the brand ambassador of the campaign in **January 2016** for his remarks on Indian Intolerance.

- Bollywood superstars **Amitabh Bachchan** and **Priyanka Chopra** were also said to have been considered for the role.

- Video footage of PM Modi speaking on tourism in India and abroad will form part of the campaign.

- Incredible India campaign was conceptualised in **2002 by V Sunit and Amitabh Kant, Joint Secretary, Ministry of Tourism.**

- It is the first tourism marketing initiative of its kind.

- The main objective is the creation of a distinctive identity for tourism from India.

- Campaign has established India as a high-end destination for tourists, generating 16 percent increase in tourist traffic in the first year itself.

82. The Reserve Bank of India has permitted banks to issue rupee denominated bonds in the overseas market.

- These are also called **masala bonds.**

- The aim is to shore up the capital base and financing as well as affordable housing infrastructure.

- Banks can raise perpetual debt instruments which can be considered for calculating the bank's additional tier

1 capital or debt capital instrument that can calculate the bank's tier 2 capital.

- Bonds will be issued under **Basel III norms.**

- They will therefore have the loss absorption clause.

- As per the clause, the bank can opt for not honouring coupon payment in the event of financial stress.

- For financing infrastructure, and reasonable housing, banks can issue long term bonds which don't have the loss absorption clause.

- Central bank first announced the notion of masala bonds on Aug 25, when a slew of measures were announced to develop the bond and currencies market.

- Additional funds generated from the rupee bond route will help develop the market of masala bonds overseas.

83. India took a step forwards rolling a unified Goods and Services Tax with the Centre and states agreeing on a 4 slab structure– 5,12,18 and 28 percent–along with a cess on luxury and sin goods such as tobacco.

- The Centre had proposed a 4 tier system- 6,12,18 and 26 percent along with a 4 percent levy on gold.

- The final rate structure had brought down the lowest slab by one percentage point to 5 percent while raising the highest rate by 2 percentage points to 28 percent.

- Around 50 percent of the items in the retail inflation basket primarily food items will be kept out of GST.

- There will be zero tax on such items.

- A lower tax slab of 6 percent is proposed for those essential commodities on which no excise duty is levied at present by the Centre but a 5 percent VAT is levied by the states.

- There will be two standard rates of 12 and 18 percent which will be applicable to many taxable goods.

- Effective tax on most white goods such as refrigerators is between 30 to 31 percent including 12.5 percent central excise duty, state value added tax of 14.5 percent and cascading effect of about 4 percentage points.

- Following GSTm the effective tax rate on most of the goods will come down to 28 percent.

- Additional revenue generated by raising the peak rate from the earlier proposed 28 to 28 percent will be set off against the revenue loss from slashing the lowest rate to 5 percent from 6 percent.

- The number of goods were transferred from the 28 percent to the 18 percent category.

- A decision on tax on gold has been left aside for now.

84. Union Government in Nov 2016 has taken the decision to launch **USD 2 billion dollar** clean energy equity fund.

- The fund is being created to support the ambitious target of adding **175 GW renewable energy generation** capacity by 2022.

- Government has decided to launch the fund jointly with state power entities namely National Thermal

Power Corporation Limited, Rural Electrification Corporation and Power Finance Corporation Limited.

- The New and Renewable Energy Ministry has initiated this project.

- Report also indicated that seed funding will be done by the Union government for this fund.

- The funding will be from the National Investment and Infrastructure Fund.

- Government of India will also collect **4 billion USD** per year in the next 3-4 years for the clean energy fund.

- Government of India is also planning a **USD 1 billion dollar PE fund** for the renewable energy sector.

85. As part of the Centre's cleanliness mission, agricultural ministry has made the decision to set up a fund of INR 10 lakh each for 585 mandis across the nation for waste management plans to treat both biodegradable and non-biodegradable wastes.

- Besides, the ministry has also decided to earmark 1 percent fund of the flagship Rashtriya Krishi Vikas Yojana for the cleanliness drive.

- INR 5000 crore was allocated to RKVY in the budget for the current financial year 2016-2017.

- Swachchta or cleanliness action plans have been prepared.

- The money to the marketplaces will be provided under the eNAM scheme.

- The eNam scheme is an electronic trading platform where all 585 marketplaces will be connected in a way to act as a common market for buyers and sellers of farm produce.

- Government has integrated 250 of these mandi in 10 states with eNam in the first phase.

- Numerous technologies making the best use of agricultural waste such as preparation of bio-compost, vermin-composting, whey utilisation, straw enrichment and water recycling of waste, cotton waste management,waste management for fisheries and engineering technologies will be considered as part of the waste disposal plants in mandi across the nation.

86. This seeks to regulate the housing sector besides ensuring transparency and timely completion of projects in the UTs.

- Rules notified by the Housing Ministry will be applicable to Andaman and Nicobar islands, Dadra and Nagra Haveli, Daman and Diu, Lakshwadeep and Chandigarh.

- Real Estate Regulation and Development Act 2016 is a major reform measure to regulate the vast real estate sector, requiring the registration of all projects with state level Real Estate Regulatory Authorities to ensure protection of buyers and developers.

- The rules will also be framed for the NCR of Delhi while other states and UTs will come out with their own rules.

87. Andhra, Telangana have topped the ease of doing business ranking. They have jointly topped the ease of doing business ranking while Gujarat has slipped to third position in the list prepared by the World Bank and DIPP.

- Chattisgarh, MP, and Haryana have occupied fourth, fifth and sixth slots respectively in an index based on degree of implementation of DIPP's 340 point Business Reform Action Plan.

- The Action Plan includes reforms on 58 regulatory processes, policies, practices or procedures spread across 10 reform areas spanning the lifecycle of a typical business.

- Many single window clearance, tax reforms, labor and environment reforms, dispute resolution and construction permit were the tax reform areas considered.

- In 2015, Gujarat featured at the top with AP at second place and Telangana at 13th.

- As per the latest 2016 index, those in the list of top 10 states in India providing a better climate for business including Jharkhand (7th), Rajasthan (8th), Uttarakhand (9th) and Maharashtra (10th).

- Among leading states, Odisha occupied the 11 slot followed by Punjab, Karnataka, UP, WB, Bihar and HP.

- These rankings were provided in a report titled Assessment of State Implementation of Business Reforms 2016 which was prepared by World Bank in association with the Department of Industrial Policy and Promotion.

- The exercise is aimed at promoting competition among states to improve business climate to attract domestic as well as foreign investments.

- In the World Bank's latest Doing Business report, India's place has remained unchanged from previous year's original ranking of 130 among 190 economies assessed on various parameters.

- Last year's ranking has been revised to 131 from which the country has improved its place by one spot.

88. Odisha government has set up a fitment committee for implementation of 7th Pay Commission recommendations for employees and pensioners.

- State government will implement the 7th Pay commission recommendations to benefit state government workers and pensioners.

- The 7th Pay Commission is headed by Justice AK Mathur has recommended a 23.55 percent overall hike in pay, allowances, and pensions for central government employees w.e.f January 1, 2016.

- An official estimation has pegged the pay revision requirement at INR 5500 crore per year.

- Currently, the state government has granted INR 29,836 crore per year over salaries and pensions.

89. The World Bank has appointed its first adviser tasked with promoting the lesbian, gay, bisexual, transgender and intersex issues in its development work.

- This newly created senior position is part of the bank's efforts to solidify commitments for researching and curbing discrimination against LGBTI persons across the 136 nations where it has offices.

- The initiative by the poverty-fighting institution comes at a time when discrimination against LGBTI people is facing increased scrutiny internationally.

- The bank, which makes loans in developing countries and conducts research has named Clifton Cortez to fill the position.

- Following two decades of experience in development, Cortez has managed partnerships for the United Nations program on HIV-AIDS, UNAIDS.

- In recent years, the bank's research has increasingly turned to economic impact of discrimination on LGBTI persons.

- This year, the Washington DC based organisation has been collecting data on the economic and social status of LGBTI persons worldwide and launch several research projects on LGBTI persons.

- The World Bank's announcement came after USAID publicised a new rule barring foreign aid contractors from discrimination against LGBTI persons in the service it funds.

- The UN appointed its first independent investigator to help protect the community worldwide from discrimination and violence.

- An UN report in 2015 indicated many LGBTI people have been killed in thousands in recent times and violence included rape, abuse, knife attacks and mutilation.

90. GSTN has inked a pact with DGFT for sharing forex realisation data with the aim to strengthen processing of exports transactions of GST taxpayers.

- The Goods and Services Network has signed an MoU with the commerce ministry for sharing of foreign exchange realisation and import-export code data.

- The move can strengthen processing of export transactions of taxpayers under GST, lower human interface and increase accountability.

- GSTN is a not-for-profit non-government private limited company promoted by the central and state government with specific mandate to create the IT infrastructure and the services required for implementing GST.

- MoU was signed whereby the electronic bank realisation certificate captures transaction level detail of the foreign exchange realisation in India.

- The electronic Bank Realisation Certificate project implemented by DGFT created an integrated platform for receipt, processing and use of all bank realisation related information by banks, central and state government departments and exporters.

- The project enabled banks to upload foreign exchange realisation information subject to exports on the DGFT server under a secured protocol.

91. The Reserve Bank of India relaxed guidelines on what the domestic interest rate futures can be offered on 28th Oct, 2016.

- This permits banks to hedge their short-term interest exposure.

- Till now, the banks could not hedge their interest rate risk on active government bond benchmarks other than 91-day treasury bills.

- Registered exchanges can select the underlying instrument or interest rate of new contracts subject to RBI approval, according to the central bank circular.

92. World Economic Forum on 25th October 2016 released the Global Gender Gap Report 2016 which provides scores for 144 nations compared to 145 countries included in the 2015 report.

- More than a decade of data has revealed that progress is too little for realising the complete potential of humanity within the lifetimes.

- Iceland topped the Gender Gap Index in the 8th consecutive year in a row.

- India stood at 87th position from the 108th position in 2015.

- As per the report, the global gender gap across health, education, economic opportunity and politics will take 83 years across 107 nations covered since the report was first released to close the gap completely.

Top 10 countries with high gender equality are as follows:

1. Iceland

2. Finland

3. Norway

4. Sweden

5. Rwanda

6. Ireland

7. The Philippines

8. Slovenia

9. New Zealand

10. Nicaragua

- Five countries with the least gender equality are Yemen, Pakistan, Syria. Saudi Arabia and Chad.

- Non European nations in the top 10 included Rwanda, The Philippines, New Zealand and Nicaragua.

- Of the 142 countries covered by the Index both this and last year, 68 nations have increased their overall gender gap score compared to 2015 while 74 have seen it decrease.

- No country in the world has closed the gender gap, but 4 out of 5 Nordic countries and Rwanda have closed more than 80 percent of theirs Yemen, the lowest

ranking country has closed slightly less than 52 percent of its gender gap

- The Global Gender Gap Index reveals that all countries can do more to close the gender gap.

- Across the index, there are 5 countries that have closed 80 percent of the gap or more.

- Additionally, 64 countries have closed between 60 to 70 percent while 10 countries have closed between 50 to 60 percent.

- India has ranked at 87th position and succeeded in closing the gender gap with regard to wage equality and all indicators of Educational Attainment sub-index completely closing primary and secondary education enrolment gender gaps.

- It sees some regression on women estimated earned income and continues to rank third lowest in the world on health and survival.

- It is the world's least improved country on this sub index over the past 10 years.

- Economic participation and opportunity was a field where India ranked in 136th position with 0.408 score.

- In the segment, India's performance was one of the lowest among surveyed countries.

- In 2015, India was placed at 139th position while India was ranked at 113rd position with 0.408 score.

- In this segment, India's performance was one of the lowest among the surveyed countries.

- In 2015, India was placed at 139th position.

- With an average remaining gender gap of 33 percent, the South Asia region is the second lowest scoring on this year's Global Gender Gap Index ahead to the MENA and behind the Sub-Saharan Africa region.

- Bangladesh and India are top ranked nations in the region, having closed just over 70 percent and 68 percent of their overall gender gap, while the lowest ranked countries are Bhutan and Pakistan, having closed 64 percent and 56 percent of their overall gender gap respectively.

- No country in the region has fully closed its Educational Attainment gender gap and only one country Sri Lanka has completely closed its Health and Survival Gap.

- The region is home to one of top 5 climbers over the past decade on the overall Index and on Educational Attainment: Nepal.

- The ranks of BRICS countries in ascending order are South Africa, Russia, Brazil, China and India.

- Three basic concepts underlying the Global Gender Gap report include focuses on measuring gaps rather than levels, capturing gaps in outcome variables rather than input variables and ranking countries according to gender equality rather than women's empowerment.

93. The RBI has requested that banks should change debit cards whose security is suspected to have been bargained in the wake of being utilised as part of ATMs.

- The issue was initially suspected by some payment gateways For example VISA, Mastercard and Rupay by the National Payments Corporation of India when it was noticed security could be ruptured in a few occasions.

- Credit and debit cards confront security issues when unapproved parties get access to classified details inserted in the card- such access may happen even as the card is being utilised as part of an ATM.

- Cards falling in the suspicious activities and requires substitution is estimated around 17.5 lakh.

- Total aggregate debit card base in the nation was 697 million starting July 2016.

- Banks for instance SBI, HDFC and BoB has began supplanting the cards.

- SBI, the nation's biggest bank has begun the way towards supplanting 0.6 million check cards.

- A few banks such as Axis Bank, HDFC and ICICI Bank have conceded being hit by comparative digital assault driving Indian banks to either change or ask for clients to change their ATM pins around 3.2 million debit cards.

- In Sept 1st week, some banks witnessed fraudulent exchanges in which debit cards were utilised in China and the US whereas card holders are in India.

- Cardholders found many activities and filed complaints with banks.

- Banks held that NPCI which has regulation over retail payment frameworks in India should intervene.

- Test by NPCI found a malware prompted security break in the frameworks of Hitachi PaymentServices which gives ATMs, PoS and other different services in India.

- After the test found that ATM security could have been breached in May 2016, all there service suppliers asked banks to tell their customers who could be at hazard to change their PIN or issue them new cards.

- Many banks requested that clients change their ATM pins and issued new cards by making old ones null and void.

- This is one of the biggest information breaches in the nation with around 3.2 million cards issued by Indian banks could possibly be replaced.

- Holders were also requested that their PINS could be changed to avoid frauds.

- As per NPCI, 90 ATMs have been compromised and no less than 641 card holders of 19 banks have lost 1.3 crore as consequence of deceitful transactions on their debit cards.

- Malware is noxious programming including infections, worms, trojans, ransomware, spyware and different programs that harm PC frameworks at ATMs, bank

servers and permit cybercriminals to get private debit card information.

94. India has ranked 13th in the protection of minority investors. Global ranking in terms of protection of minority investors has slipped three notches to 13, but is much higher than the 130th rank attained by India for ease of doing business.

- Sub-ranking for the protection of minority investors is topped jointly by New Zealand and Singapore

- Others that ranked higher than India are Hong Kong, Malaysia, Kazakhstan, the UK, Georgia, Canada, Norway the UAE, Slovenia and Israel

- In World Bank's Doing Business report, India just moved one place from last year to 130

- Others that ranked higher than India are Hong Kong, Malaysia, Kazakhstan, the UK, Georgia, Canada, Norway, the UAE, Israel and Slovenia

- In the latest World Bank Doing Business report, New Zealand topped the list while Singapore was ranked second

- The report said protection of minority investors indicator measures the protection of shareholders in corporate governance

- According to the report, India carried out an ambitious, multi-year overhaul of its Companies Act, bringing Indian firms in line with global standards

- This is more so in respect of accountability and corporate governance practices while ensuring businesses contribute more to shared prosperity through a quantified and legislated CSR requirement

- Corporate regulation is an ongoing process, as per the new actions taken by the NDA government

- Two sets of amendments were released in August 2014 and May 2015

- A committee has been tasked with identifying more amendments to the Act and involving recommendations and concerns from private sector stakeholders and regulatory bodies

- India's score increased in 3 of 6 indices of the protecting minority investors indicator set

- To simplify administrative requirements, the minimum paid in capital was abolished

- For instilling greater transparency, disclosure requirements especially in relation to related party transactions were initiated

- Bringing Indian firms in line with global standards, the Act increased disclosure requirements, particularly related party transactions

- India also became the first economy in the world with a quantified and legislated corporate social responsibility requirement

- Full fledged reforms can give policymakers the opportunity to innovate and sends a strong signal to the business community, the report said.

95. RBI has made changes to the Foreign Exchange Management (Transfer or Issue of Security By a Person Resident Outside India) Regulations 2000 to notify amended norms for foreign investment in startups

- The notification states any FVCI/ Foreign Venture Capital Investors registered with SEBI will not acquire approval from the RBI and can invest in unlisted companies

- FVCI can invest in sectors such as infrastructure, biotechnology and seed research

- They can also invest in equity or equity linked instrument or debt instrument issued by an Indian startup regardless of the sector in which the startup is engaged.

- They can invest in VCV registered with SEBI or units of scheme of a fund set up by VCF or Category 1 Alternative Investment Fund.

- Downstream investments by a VCF or Cat-1 AIF which has received investment from FVCI will have to comply with provisions for downstream investment laid down in schedule 11 of the Principal Regulations.

96. India on 21st Oct 2016 signed a USD 650 million dollar loan agreement with World Bank for the Eastern Dedicated Freight Corridor III project

- This project will benefit industries of Eastern and Northern India which rely on railway network for transportation of material inputs and exports.

- Industries will depend on railway network for transportation for the distribution of bulk processed and semi-processed commodities and consumer goods.

- Railway passengers will be benefited through decongestion of existing passenger lines.

- The EDFC-III project was set to augment rail transport capacity, improve service quality and enhance freight carriage through a 401 km Ludhiana Khurja section of the Eastern Dedicated Freight Corridor.

97. SEBI has placed disclosure norms in position for InvITs on 20th Oct 2016. The offer document will now contain financial information, related party transactions and past performances

- SEBI in the previous month decided to further relax InvITs norms in a bid to make the instrument more efficient for raising capital

- SEBI had notified InvIT regulations in 2014, permitting the setting up and listing of such trusts which are very popular in advanced markets

- No single trust has been set up yet as investors want further measures such as tax breaks to ensure instruments are more attractive

- SEBI said the official document will now contain financial information of past 3 financial years including balance sheet, profit and loss statement, income and expenditure and net assets and total returns.

- InvITs will also have to disclose commitments, contingent liabilities, earnings per unit, total debt, net worth and debt equity ratios before and after completion of issue

- Trust will have to make a statement about the history of interest and principal payments of InvIT and operating cash flow from the project for the past three years and interim period

- In the event of related party transactions involving acquisition or disposal of an InvIT asset, trust will have to part with information about the summer of the valuation report along with material obligations pertaining to the transaction and commissions got by any associates of the related party in relation to transaction.

98. SIBDI has launched an INR 60 crore corpus ASPIRE Fund on 20th Oct 2016 to promote innovation, agricultural industry and rural entrepreneurship. SIDBI will focus on numerous angel/venture capital funds that will invest in start ups or early stage enterprises, based on value addition in the rural economy and job creation through social impact funding

- The INR 60 crore funds of funds falls under ASPIRE or A Scheme for Promotion of Innovation and Rural Entrepreneurship and Agro Industry.

- This supports various venture capital funds registered with the market regulator SEBI for investing in startups in the agro and rural space.

- Government initiatives such as ASPIRE are one of many steps for providing support to various venture capital for unleashing the potential of MSME.

- ASPIRE has an aggregate corpus of INR 200 crore and SIDBI is also launching the India Aspiration Fund under which 35 funds have been extended aggregate support of INT 1211.75 crore.

99. RBI came out with a framework for penalising banks and payment systems operators for offences under the Payment and Settlement Systems Act with fines of up to INR 1 crore

- A framework has been put up for imposition of penalty/fine under section 30 of the PSS Act and compounding contraventions or offences under section 31 of the PSS Act

- Contravention of the provisions of the PSS act, non compliance of directions or orders made thereunder and violation of terms and conditions of authorisation will result in fines.

- Fines will be based on nature of offences or contraventions and there will be minimum penalty of INR 5 lakh which can go to INR 1 crore

- Entities which have been made to pay the fine will disclose the same in their annual financial statement.

- RBI will also make the penalty public.

- RBI will directly debit the current account while those not having the facility with the central bank will have to deposit the amount into designated RBI account within one week of the issue of written order.

- Non payment will be dealt as per provisions of the PSS Act.

100. In a move to attract foreign capital in the country, RBI has permitted 100 percent FDI in other financial services carried out by NBFCs.

- In consultation with the government of India, it has been decided to permit foreign investment up to 100 percent under the automatic routes in Other Financial Services

- These financial services include activities regulated by any financial sector regulator namely RBI, SEBI, IRDA, PFRDA, NHB or any financial sector regulatory body

- Such foreign investment would be subject to conditionality including minimum capitalisation norms

- Other salient features of the revised regulatory framework include downstream investment by any entity engaged in Other Financial Services and will be subject to extant sectoral regulations.

- In the Budget 2016-2017 Speech, FM Arun Jaitley had announced about this liberation.

- Currently 100 percent FDI is allowed in 18 NBFC activities such as merchant banking, underwriting, portfolio management services, stock broking and financial consultancy

- In 2015-2016, FDI in India grew by 29 percent Y-O-Y to USD 40 billion.

Q.1 Which one is increasing function of price?

A. Demand   **B.** Utility

C. Supply   **D.** Consumption

Q.2 The consumer is in equilibrium at a point where the budget line

A. Is above an indifference curve

B. Is below an indifference curve

C. Is tangent to an indifference curve

D. Cuts an indifference curve

Q.3 Which of the following oligopoly models is concerned with the maximization of joint profits?

A. Price leadership model

B. Bertrand's model

C. Collusive model

D. Edgeworth's model

Q.4 A firm decides to exit the industry when

A. AC starts rising

B. MC starts rising

C. Price is less than LAC

D. TC starts rising

Q.5 It describes the law of supply

A. Supply curve   **B.** Supply schedule

C. Supply equation   **D.** All of the above

Q.6 An indifference curve slopes down towards right since more of one commodity and less of another result in

A. Same satisfaction

B. Greater satisfaction

C. Maximum satisfaction

D. Decreasing expenditure

Q.7 In the context of oligopoly, the kinked demand curve hypothesis is designed to explain

A. Price and output determination

B. Price rigidity

C. Price leadership

D. Collusion among rivals

Q.8 Profit is maximum when

A. TC and TR curves are parallel

B. MC and MR curves are parallel

C. TC and TR curves cross each other

D. AC and AR curves cross each other

Q.9 Supply curve will shift when

A. Price falls   **B.** Price rises

C. Demand shots   **D.** Technology changes

Q.10 The Revealed Preference Theory deduces the inverse price-quantity relationship from

A. Assumption of indifference

B. Postulate of utility maximization

C. Observed behavior of the consumer

D. Introspection

Q.11 Which form of market structure is characterised by interdependence in decision-making as between the different competing firms?

A. Oligopoly

B. Perfect competition

C. Imperfect competition

D. None of the above

Q.12 In monopoly and perfect competition, the cost curves are

A. Same   **B.** Different

C. Opposite   **D.** None of the above

Q.13 If price changes by 1% and supply changes by 2%, then supply is

A. Elastic   **B.** Inelastic

C. Indeterminate   **D.** Static

Q.14 An ISO-product slopes

A. Downward to the left

B. Downward to the right

C. Upward to the left

D. Upward to the right

Q.15 Which of the following is NOT the assumption of the Marginal Productivity Theory of Distribution?

A. Homogenity of a factor

B. Perfect competition in the factor market

C. All factors, except one, are variable

D. Given stock of each factor and full employment

Q.16 Normal profit is called normal because

A. It is neither very high nor very low

B. It is minimum acceptable to the producer

C. It is minimum which buyer wants to pay

D. It is the maximum allowed by government

Q.17 Supply curve is

A. Vertical in long run

B. Flatter in long run

C. Same in long and short run

D. Horizontal in both short and long run

Q.18 A vertical supply curve parallel to the price axis implies that the elasticity of supply is

A. Zero

B. Infinity

C. Equal to one

D. Greater than zero but less than infinity

Q.19 With which of the theories of wages, is the name of John Stuart Mill associated?

A. Marginal productivity theory of wages

B. Wages-fund theory

C. Subsistence theory of wages

D. Iron aw of wages

Q.20 If a firm shuts down temporarily, it will incur loss equal to

A. AFC   **B.** AVC   **C.** TFC   **D.** TVC

Q.21 During a particular year, farmers experienced a dry weather. If all the other factors remain constant, farmers supply curve for wheat will shift

A. Rightward   **B.** Leftward

C. Upward   **D.** None of the above

Q.22 The supply of a commodity refers to

A. Actual production of the commodity

B. Total existing stock of the commodity

C. Stock available for sale

D. Amount of the commodity offered for sale at a particular price per unit of time

Q.23 Economic rent can accrue to

A. Land only

B. Capital only

C. Specialized technical personnel only

D. Any of the factors of production

Q.24 When supply of a commodity increases without change in price, it is called

A. Fall in supply

B. Expansion in supply

C. Contraction in supply

D. Rise in supply

Q.25 Which cost increases continuously with the increase in production?

A. Avearge cost   **B.** Marginal cost

C. Fixed cost   **D.** Variable cost

Q.26 A factor of production, whose supply is fixed in the short run, may get additional earnings. These earnings are generally referred to as

A. Surplus value

B. Quasi-rent

C. Transfer earnings

D. Super normal profits

Q.27 The necessary condition for equilibrium position of a firm is

A. MR>MC   **B.** MC>Price

C. MC=MR   **D.** MC=AC

Q.28 In May 2013, firm was supplying 500kg of sugar at market price of Rs.30/- per kg. During June 2013, firm's supply of sugar had decreased to 450kg at price of Rs.20/- per kg. These changes show that supply of sugar is

A. Oerfectly elastic   **B.** Perfectly inelastic

C. Less elastic   **D.** More elastic

Q.29 Which of the following cost curves is never U-shaped?

A. Average cost curve

B. Marginal cost curve

C. Average variable cost curve

D. Average fixed cost curve

Q.30 The classical theory explained interest as a reward for

A. Parting with liquidity

B. Abstinence

C. Saving

D. Inconvenience

Q.31 When a competitive firm achieves long run equilibrium, then,

A. P=MC   **B.** MR=MC

C. P=ATC   **D.** All of the above

Q.32 What best explains a shift in market supply curve to the right?

A. An advertising campaign is successful in promoting the good

B. A new technique makes it cheaper to produce the good

C. The government introduces a tax on the good

D. The price of raw materials increases

Q.33 Total costs in the short-term are classified into fixed costs and variable costs. Which one of the following is a variable cost?

A. Cost of raw material

B. Cost of equipment

C. Interest payment on past borrowing

D. Payment of rent on buildings

Q.34 The most efficient scale of production of a firm is where

A. LAC is minimum   **B.** SAC is minimum

C. LMC is minimum   **D.** SMC is minimum

Q.35 In the short run, when the output of a firm increases, its average fixed cost

A. Increases

B. Decreases

C. Remains constant

D. First declines and then rises

Q.36 Elinor Ostrom and Oliver Williamson are the Nobel Prize Laureates in Economics in 2009. Do you know in which year was Francois Quesnay's Tableu Economique published?

A. 1767   **B.** 1764   **C.** 1761   **D.** 1758

Q.37 Identify the author of "The principles of Political Economy and Taxation"

A. Alfred Marshall   **B.** J.S.Mill

C. David Ricardo   **D.** A. Turgot

Q.38 Which is not a central problem of an economy?

A. What to produce

B. How to produce

C. How to maximize private profit

D. For whom to produce

Q.39 A significant property of the Cobb-Douglas production function is that the elasticity of substitution between inputs is

A. Equal to 1   **B.** More than 1
C. Less than 1   **D.** 0

Q.40 Who is generally regarded as the founder of the 'Classical School'?

A. David Ricardo   **B.** Adam Smith
C. T.R.Malthus   **D.** J.S.Mill

Q.41 Union leaders are in better position to bargain for higher wages if demand for labour is

A. Elastic   **B.** Inelastic
C. Very large   **D.** Permanent

Q.42 Economies of scale are of two kinds

A. Temporary and permanent
B. Internal and external
C. Managerial and industrial
D. Natural and artificial

Q.43 Which statement is true

A. ATC + AVC = AFC   **B.** ATC + MC = AFC
C. ATC + AFC = AVC   **D.** AFC + AVC = ATC

Q.44 Identify the economist who had little formal education and started working in the money market at an early age of fourteen.

A. David Ricardo   **B.** Adam Smith
C. V.F.D. Pareto   **D.** A.A. Cournot

Q.45 In which form, the largest percentage of national income is earned?

A. Interest income   **B.** Proprietor's income
C. Employee' wages   **D.** Rental income

Q.46 Law of return applies to firms working in

A. Perfect competition
B. Monopoly
C. Small firm
D. All kinds of market situations

Q.47 Which is NOT a cause of shift in cost curves of a firm?

A. Excise tax
B. Prices of inputs
C. Increase in productivity
D. Price of product

Q.48 Who first raised the fear of a world food shortage?

A. David Ricardo   **B.** T.R.Malthus
C. J.S.Mill   **D.** J.B.Say

Q.49 The minimum wage is an example of

A. Price floor   **B.** Price ceiling
C. Equilibrium wage   **D.** Efficiency of labour

Q.50 During short period, diminishing returns may follow because

A. Quantity of labour is fixed
B. Quantity of output is fixed

C. Quantity of capital is fixed
D. Quantity of any one factor is fixed

Q.51 MC is given by

A. Slope of TFC   **B.** Slope of TC
C. Slope of AC   **D.** None of the above

Q.52 When was Adam Smith's major work "An enquiry into the Nature and Causes of Wealth of Nations" published?

A. 1756   **B.** 1766   **C.** 1776   **D.** 1786

Q.53 The standard of living of workers depends upon their

A. Nominal wages   **B.** Real wages
C. Average product   **D.** Government policy

Q.54 Which of the following is example of external economies of scale?

A. Discount on purchases of raw materials
B. Technical progress leads to development of machine at low price
C. Hiring of specialized staff due to increase in scale of production
D. A firm starts producing by-products

Q.55 TC curve

A. Starts from origin
B. Does not start from origin
C. Is parallel to Y-axis
D. None of the above

Q.56 "The real price of everything, what every thing really costs to the man who wants to require it, is the toil and trouble of acquiring it. Who made this statement?

A. Karl Marx   **B.** Adam Smith
C. David Ricardo   **D.** J.S.Mill

Q.57 As for the cost of production of an individual farmer, the rent paid by him

A. Enters into the price of his product
B. Does not enter into price of his product
C. Is unjustified
D. None of the above

Q.58 Human wants are

A. One thousand   **B.** Few
C. Innumerable   **D.** Countable

Q.59 TVC curve

A. Starts from origin
B. Does not start from origin
C. Is parallel to Y-axis
D. None of the above

Q.60 "Rent is a creation of value, not of wealth". Who made this observation?

A. Adam Smith   **B.** David Ricardo
C. Alfred Marshall   **D.** A.C.Pigou

Q.61 These are kinds of rent EXCEPT

A. Differential rent   **B.** Scarcity rent
C. Mobility rent   **D.** Location rent

Q.62 A consumer is in equilibrium when marginal utilities are

A. Minimum　　　　　**B.** Highest
C. Equal　　　　　　**D.** Increasing

Q.63 TC curve
A. Rises continously
B. Falls after reaching a maximum
C. Is horizontal
D. None of the above

Q.64 In which year, was the first volume of Das Capital by Karl Marx published?
A. 1848　　**B.** 1859　　**C.** 1867　　**D.** 1873

Q.65 According to Keynes, interest is a payment for
A. Consumer's preference
B. Producer's preference
C. Liquidity preference
D. State Bank's preference

Q.66 When marginal is negative, it must be true that
A. The average is negative
B. The average is decreasing
C. The total is negative
D. The total is decreasing

Q.67 All the following curves are U-shaped except
A. AVC　　**B.** AFC　　**C.** AC　　**D.** MC

Q.68 Interest is paid because
A. Capital is scarce
B. Capital is productive
C. Capital is attractive
D. Capital is surplus

Q.69 The term 'marginal' in economics means
A. Unimportant　　　　**B.** Additional
C. The minimum unit　　**D.** Just barely passing

Q.70 The cost which a firm incurs for purchasing or hiring factors is called
A. Implicit　　**B.** Explicit　　**C.** Real　　**D.** Nominal

Q.71 The Communist Manifesto, written jointly by Marx and Engels's was published in
A. 1843　　**B.** 1848　　**C.** 1853　　**D.** 1859

Q.72 Every factor of production gets rewarded equal to its
A. Cost　　　　　**B.** Marginal product
C. Price　　　　**D.** Increasing return

Q.73 Utility is more closely related to the term
A. Useful　　　　**B.** Useless
C. Necessary　　**D.** Satisfaction

Q.74 The short run
A. Is less than one year
B. Requires that at least one input is fixed
C. Requires that all inputs are fixed
D. Is just long enough to permit entry and exit

Q.75 Who stated explicitly for the first time, the Law of Comparative Costs?
A. David Ricardo　　**B.** Adam Smith
C. James Mill　　　**D.** Thomas Mun

Q.76 According to Keynes, interest is a payment for
A. Use of durable goods
B. Use of capital
C. Use of money
D. Use of land

Q.77 Demand curve slopes downward because of the law of
A. Consumer equilibrium
B. Utility maximization
C. Utility minimization
D. Diminishing marginal utility

Q.78 The long run is a
A. Period of three years or longer
B. Period long enough to allow firms to change plant size and capacity
C. Period long enough to allow firm to make economic decisions
D. A period which affects larger than smaller firms

Q.79 The Purchasing Power Parity Theory' came into prominence in 1916 through the writings of
A. J.M.Keynes　　　**B.** L.E.Von Miser
C. Gustav Cassel　　**D.** F.A.von Hayek

Q.80 If rate of interest is 10%, the PV (present value) of Rs.100 received in 1 year's time is
A. 90　　**B.** 90.9　　**C.** 95　　**D.** 110

Q.81 Law of substitution is another name for law of
A. Law of diminishing MU
B. Law of Equi-MU
C. Law of demand
D. Satisfaction

Q.82 As output increases, AC curve
A. Falls　　　　　　　**B.** Rises
C. Remains constant　　**D.** All of the above

Q.83 Identify the work of Irving Fisher
A. A Treatese on Money
B. Policy against Inflation
C. The Making of Index numbers
D. Monetary Theory

Q.84 Professor Knight is famous for his theory of
A. Rent　　　　　**B.** Profit
C. Population　　**D.** Wages

Q.85 When Marginal Utility is positive, Total Utility
A. Increases　　　　　**B.** Decreases
C. Remains constant　　**D.** Is highest

Q.86 The three broad types of productive resources are
A. Money, profit and interest

B. Capital, labour and natural resources
C. Bond, stock shares and deposits
D. Technology, human capital and markets

Q.87 Economic development of a country requires
A. Skilled labour
B. Diplomacy
C. Abundant natural resources
D. a' and 'c' both

Q.88 Profits are
A. Residual payment
B. Pre-determined
C. Fixed contract
D. Always higher than wages

Q.89 Diminishing marginal utility is the basis of
A. Law of supply   **B.** Law of demand
C. Law of returns   **D.** None of the above

Q.90 Productivity of land can be raised by
A. Extensive cultivation
B. Intensive cultivation
C. Better marketing
D. a' and 'b' both

Q.91 Land only
A. Is a free gift of nature
B. Lacks geographical mobility
C. Is not hirable
D. a' and 'b' both

Q.92 Profits
A. Are lower in the long run than in the short run
B. Can be negative
C. Are less in perfect competition than in monopoly
D. All of the above

Q.93 When Marginal Utility is zero, Total Utility is
A. Minimum   **B.** Maximum
C. Law of return   **D.** None of the above

Q.94 Which of the following is NOT an input?
A. Labour   **B.** Entrepreneurship
C. Natural resources   **D.** Production

Q.95 Which of the following input factor takes risk, innovates and coordinates
A. Capital   **B.** Labour
C. Productivity   **D.** Entrepreneur

Q.96 Some economists say that profit earner is a kind of
A. Rent receiver   **B.** Interest receiver
C. Wage earner   **D.** Government officer

Q.97 Quality of a commodity that satisfies some human want or need is called
A. Service   **B.** Demand
C. Utility   **D.** Efficiency

Q.98 Which of the following is CORRECT with respect to resources?
A. Money is a capital good
B. Human skills are a labour input
C. Entrepreneur is part of the labour input
D. Natural resources include human input

Q.99 The transformation of resources into economic goods and services is called
A. Technical efficiency   **B.** Input
C. Production   **D.** Increasing returns

Q.100 Operating Surplus arises in the-
A. Government Sector
B. Production for self-consumption
C. Subsistence farming
D. Enterprise Sector

// Smart Answer Sheet //

Correct Indicates percentage of students who answered questions correctly.

Skipped Indicates percentage of students who skipped questions.

Q.	Ans.	Correct / Skipped
1	C	53.7 % / 14.82 %
2	C	72.22 % / 22.22 %
3	C	61.11 % / 25.93 %
4	C	66.67 % / 24.07 %
5	D	51.85 % / 25.93 %
6	A	57.41 % / 27.78 %
7	B	62.96 % / 25.93 %
8	A	31.48 % / 27.78 %
9	D	50.0 % / 25.93 %
10	C	46.3 % / 25.92 %
11	A	61.11 % / 25.93 %
12	A	50.0 % / 24.07 %
13	A	68.52 % / 24.07 %
14	B	51.85 % / 22.22 %
15	C	50.0 % / 27.78 %
16	B	48.15 % / 24.07 %

Q.	Ans.	Correct / Skipped
17	B	35.19 % / 22.22 %
18	A	51.85 % / 27.78 %
19	B	46.3 % / 22.22 %
20	C	29.63 % / 14.81 %
21	B	59.26 % / 22.22 %
22	D	75.93 % / 22.22 %
23	D	55.56 % / 20.37 %
24	D	42.59 % / 18.52 %
25	D	53.7 % / 27.78 %
26	B	48.15 % / 25.92 %
27	C	68.52 % / 24.07 %
28	C	51.85 % / 25.93 %
29	D	66.67 % / 24.07 %
30	C	50.0 % / 22.22 %
31	D	57.41 % / 25.92 %
32	B	50.0 % / 27.78 %

Q.	Ans.	Correct / Skipped
33	A	57.41 % / 22.22 %
34	A	53.7 % / 22.23 %
35	B	48.15 % / 27.78 %
36	D	24.07 % / 29.63 %
37	C	46.3 % / 22.22 %
38	C	70.37 % / 25.93 %
39	A	68.52 % / 25.92 %
40	B	61.11 % / 27.78 %
41	B	25.93 % / 24.07 %
42	B	64.81 % / 22.23 %
43	D	66.67 % / 25.92 %
44	A	27.78 % / 25.92 %
45	C	27.78 % / 24.07 %
46	D	50.0 % / 22.22 %
47	D	46.3 % / 25.92 %
48	B	64.81 % / 27.78 %

Q.	Ans.	Correct / Skipped
49	A	31.48 % / 25.93 %
50	D	53.7 % / 27.78 %
51	B	59.26 % / 27.78 %
52	C	59.26 % / 22.22 %
53	B	61.11 % / 22.22 %
54	B	33.33 % / 27.78 %
55	B	51.85 % / 25.93 %
56	C	18.52 % / 29.63 %
57	A	51.85 % / 27.78 %
58	C	72.22 % / 25.93 %
59	A	50.0 % / 27.78 %
60	B	51.85 % / 25.93 %
61	C	38.89 % / 24.07 %
62	C	42.59 % / 27.78 %
63	A	27.78 % / 27.78 %
64	C	27.78 % / 31.48 %

Q.	Ans.	Correct / Skipped
65	C	59.26 % / 24.07 %
66	D	57.41 % / 24.07 %
67	B	62.96 % / 25.93 %
68	A	29.63 % / 25.93 %
69	B	64.81 % / 27.78 %
70	B	57.41 % / 25.92 %
71	B	33.33 % / 27.78 %
72	B	64.81 % / 16.67 %
73	D	70.37 % / 22.22 %
74	B	48.15 % / 27.78 %
75	A	66.67 % / 25.92 %
76	C	37.04 % / 27.77 %
77	D	70.37 % / 27.78 %
78	B	57.41 % / 27.78 %
79	C	53.7 % / 24.08 %
80	B	24.07 % / 22.23 %

Q.	Ans.	Correct		Q.	Ans.	Correct		Q.	Ans.	Correct		Q.	Ans.	Correct		Q.	Ans.	Correct
		Skipped				Skipped				Skipped				Skipped				Skipped
81	B	40.74 %		85	B	25.93 %		89	B	57.41 %		93	B	66.67 %		97	C	64.81 %
		20.37 %				25.92 %				25.92 %				24.07 %				25.93 %
82	D	35.19 %		86	B	59.26 %		90	B	16.67 %		94	D	61.11 %		98	B	38.89 %
		24.07 %				25.93 %				25.92 %				22.22 %				27.78 %
83	C	50.0 %		87	D	62.96 %		91	D	61.11 %		95	D	62.96 %		99	C	53.7 %
		27.78 %				25.93 %				25.93 %				25.93 %				25.93 %
84	B	48.15 %		88	A	50.0 %		92	D	53.7 %		96	C	31.48 %		100	D	35.19 %
		25.92 %				27.78 %				27.78 %				25.93 %				27.77 %

Performance Analysis

Avg. Score (%)	39.5%
Toppers Score (%)	96.0%
Your Score	

//Hints and Solutions//

1. Supply is increasing function of price. The higher the price of a good, the more a firm is willing to produce and offer, hence, the supply function is upward sloping. In fact, in the perfect competition market, the supply curve is the marginal cost curve. Increasing production is only profitable if the good can be sold at a higher price.

2. The consumer is in equilibrium at a point where the budget line is tangent to an indifference curve. It means that marginal substitution rate between X and Y (MRSXY) should be diminishing.

3. Collusive models is concerned with the maximization of joint profits. Firms join together and work for the joint profit maximization.

4. A firm decides to exit the industry when Price is less than LAC. LAC at the efficient scale of production is thus the minimum average cost.

5. Supply curve, Supply schedule and Supply equation all of them describes the law of supply.

6. An indifference curve slopes down towards right since more of one commodity and less of another result in Same satisfaction.

7. In the context of oligopoly, the kinked demand curve hypothesis is designed to explain Price rigidity. The curve is more elastic above the kink and less elastic below it. This means that the response to a price increase is less than the response to a price decrease.

8. Profit is maximum when TC and TR curves are parallel. Profit becomes maximum irrespective of the market situation, when the difference between total revenue (TR) and total cost (TC) becomes the greatest.

9. Supply curve will shift when Technology changes. Factors that can shift a supply curve either to the left or the right are changes in input prices, number of sellers, technology, social concerns and expectations.

10. The Revealed Preference Theory deduces the inverse price-quantity relationship from observed behavior of the consumer. Revealed preference theory asserts that the best way to measure consumer preferences is to observe their purchasing behavior.

11. Oligopoly form of market structure is characterised by interdependence in decision-making as between the different competing firms. An oligopoly is a market form wherein a market or industry is dominated by a small number of large sellers (oligopolists). Oligopolies can result from various forms of collusion which reduce competition and lead to higher prices for consumers. Oligopolies have their own market structure.

12. In monopoly and perfect competition, the cost curves are same. In a monopoly, the price is set above marginal cost and the firm earns a positive economic profit. Perfect competition produces an equilibrium in which the price and quantity of a good is economically efficient.

13. If price changes by 1% and supply changes by 2%, then supply is Elastic. The Price Elasticity of Supply (PES) for elastic and inelastic supply would be different. The PES for elastic supply would be greater than 1. This tells us that if prices were to increase (or decrease) by 1%, the quantity supplied would increase (or decrease) in a number greater than 1%.

14. An ISO-product slopes downward to the right. They slope downward because MTRS of labour for capital diminishes. When we increase labour, we have to decrease capital to produce a given level of output.

15. All factors, except one, are variable is NOT the assumption of the Marginal Productivity Theory of Distribution.

16. Normal profit is called normal because It is minimum acceptable to the producer. Normal profit is a situation where a firm makes sufficient revenue to cover its total costs and remain competitive in an industry.

17. Supply curve is Flatter in long run. All firms have identical cost conditions. Hence, in the case of a constant cost industry, the long-run supply curve LSC is a horizontal straight line (i.e., perfectly elastic) at the price OP, which is equal to the minimum average cost. This means that whatever the output supplied, the price would remain the same.

18. A vertical supply curve parallel to the price axis implies that the elasticity of supply is Zero.

19. With Wages-fund theory, the name of John Stuart Mill associated. Mill said that wages mainly depend upon demand for and supply of labour or the proportion between population and capital available.

20. If a firm shuts down temporarily, it will incur loss equal to TFC. The intersection of the average variable cost curve and the marginal cost curve, which shows the price where the firm would lack enough revenue to cover its variable costs, is called the shutdown point. If the perfectly competitive firm can charge a price above the shutdown point, then the firm is at least covering its average variable costs. It is also making enough revenue to cover at least a portion of fixed costs, so it should limp ahead even if it is making losses in the short run, since at least those losses will be smaller than if the firm shuts down immediately and incurs a loss equal to total fixed costs.

21. During a particular year, farmers experienced a dry weather. If all the other factors remain constant, farmers supply curve for wheat will shift Leftward.

22. The supply of a commodity refers to amount of the commodity offered for sale at a particular price per unit of time. Price of a commodity is determined by the demand for and supply of a commodity.

23. Economic rent can accrue to any of the factors of production. Economic rent is any payment to an owner or factor of production in excess of the costs needed to bring that factor into production.

24. When supply of a commodity increases without change in price, it is called rise in supply.

25. Variable cost increases continuously with the increase in production. Variable cost varies at different level of output, this implies that when the output of a particular firm is at zero, the variable cost will be zero and when there is increase in

production of output, there will also be a corresponding increase in the variable cost.

26. A factor of production, whose supply is fixed in the short run, may get additional earnings. These earnings are generally referred to as Quasi-rent. The earnings from machines and instruments are termed as quasi-rent. The quasi-rent refers to the income produced when the demand for products increases suddenly.

27. The necessary condition for equilibrium position of a firm is MC=MR. A firm is in equilibrium when it has no tendency to change its level of output. It needs neither expansion nor contraction. It wants to earn maximum profits in by equating its marginal cost with its marginal revenue, i.e. MC = MR.

28. In May 2013, firm was supplying 500kg of sugar at market price of Rs.30/- per kg. During June 2013, firm's supply of sugar had decreased to 450kg at price of Rs.20/- per kg. These changes show that supply of sugar is less elastic.

29. Average fixed cost curve is never U-shaped. The average fixed costs AFC curve is downward sloping because fixed costs are distributed over a larger volume when the quantity produced increases.

30. The classical theory explained interest as a reward for Saving. According to the classical theory, interest is the price paid for saving of capital. Like the value of other things, the price of saving is determined by its demand for and supply of savings.

31. When a competitive firm achieves long run equilibrium, then, P=MC, MR=MC and P=ATC.

32. A new technique makes it cheaper to produce the good best explains a shift in market supply curve to the right. A rightward shift in the supply curve, say from a new production technology, leads to a lower equilibrium price and a greater quantity.

33. Total costs in the short-term are classified into fixed costs and variable costs. Cost of raw material is a variable cost. Variable costs vary based on the amount of output, while fixed costs are the same regardless of production output.

34. The most efficient scale of production of a firm is where LAC is minimum. LAC at the efficient scale of production is thus the minimum average cost.

35. In the short run, when the output of a firm increases, its average fixed cost decreases.

36. Elinor Ostrom and Oliver Williamson are the Nobel Prize Laureates in Economics in 2009. In the year 1758, Francois Quesnay's Tableu Economique was published.

37. The Principles of Political Economy and Taxation (19 April 1817) is a book by David Ricardo on economics. Ricardo claims in the preface that Turgot, Stuart, Adam Smith, Jean-Baptiste Say, Sismondi, and others had not written enough "satisfactory information" on the topics of rent, profit, and wages.

38. How to maximize private profit is not a central problem of an economy. Some of the central problems that are faced by every economy of a country are as follows: Production, distribution and disposition of goods and services are the basic economic activities of life. In the course of these activities, every society has to face scarcity of resources.

39. A significant property of the Cobb-Douglas production function is that the elasticity of substitution between inputs is Equal to 1.

40. Adam Smith is generally regarded as the founder of the 'Classical School'.

41. Union leaders are in better position to bargain for higher wages if demand for labour is Inelastic. The capacity of trade unions to raise wages in a particular industry depends on the elasticity of demand for labour.

42. Economies of scale are of two kinds Internal and external. Internal economies of scale are firm-specific or caused internally while external economies of scale occur based on larger changes outside the firm. Both result in declining marginal costs of production, yet the net effect is the same.

43. AFC + AVC = ATC is true.

44. David Ricardo the economist had little formal education and started working in the money market at an early age of fourteen. At the age of 14 he entered into business with his father, who had made a fortune on the London Stock Exchange.

45. In the form of Employee' wages, the largest percentage of national income is earned.

46. Law of return applies to firms working in all kinds of market situations. A firm's production function could exhibit different types of returns to scale in different ranges of output.

47. Price of product is not a cause of shift in cost curves of a firm. Cost curves shift in response to changes in two factors: If a technological change results in the firm using more capital, the average fixed cost curve shifts upward and at low levels of output, the average total cost curve may shift upward. At large output levels, average total cost decreases.

48. T.R.Malthus first raised the fear of a world food shortage. In 1798 Thomas Robert Malthus famously predicted that short-term gains in living standards would inevitably be undermined as human population growth outstripped food production, and thereby drive living standards back toward subsistence.

49. The minimum wage is an example of Price floor. A price floor is the absolute minimum price at which a good or service (labor in this case) can be sold and it is usually set by the government. Price floors are set above the market equilibrium price of a good or service.

50. During short period, diminishing returns may follow because quantity of any one factor is fixed.

51. MC is given by Slope of TC. Slope tells us how (total) costs change when we change output/quantity produced.

52. In 1776, Adam Smith's major work "An enquiry into the Nature and Causes of Wealth of Nations" was published.

53. The amount of goods and services which the labourer actually gets is called his real wages. The standard of living and the prosperity of a labourer depend not on his money wages but on his real wages.

54. Technical progress leads to development of machine at low price is example of external economies of scale.

55. TC curve does not start from origin. The shape of the total cost curve is based on short-run production returns, especially the law of diminishing marginal returns. Another observation is that the total cost curve does not go through the origin, but rather begins at a positive value on the vertical axis. This vertical intercept indicates fixed cost.

56. "The real price of everything, what every thing really costs to the man who wants to require it, is the toil and trouble of acquiring it. David Ricardo made this statement.

57. As for the cost of production of an individual farmer, the rent paid by him enters into the price of his product. The classical political economists found value to be determined in production; since most of the cost of production could be reduced to labor, this approach was refined into the Labor Theory of Value.

58. Human wants are Innumerable. With the passage of time and human progress, we find a marked growth in the number and variety of wants. Modern man has countless wants.

59. TVC curve starts from origin. TVC starts from origin which shows TVC is zero when output is zero. TC curve is derived by adding the TFC and TVC curve.

60. "Rent is a creation of value, not of wealth". David Ricardo made this observation.

61. There are kinds of rent except mobility rent. Created by the Elan law, the mobility lease is a short-team lease agreement for a furnished property. It gives more the landlord flexibility and eases access to housing, particularly for students or people who move around for work. The landlord cannot demand any security deposit from the tenant.

62. A consumer is in equilibrium when marginal utilities are equal. A consumer is in equilibrium when he derives maximum satisfaction from the goods and is in no position to rearrange his purchases.

63. TC curve rises continously. Total cost (TC) is the total economic cost of production and is made up of variable cost, which varies according to the quantity of a good produced and includes inputs such as labour and raw materials, plus fixed cost, which is independent of the quantity of a good produced and includes inputs that cannot be varied in the short term: fixed costs such as buildings and machinery, including sunk costs if any. Since cost is measured per unit of time, it is a flow variable.

64. The first of three volumes of Das Kapital was published on 14 September 1867, dedicated to Wilhelm Wolff and was the sole volume published in Marx's lifetime.

65. According to Keynes, interest is a payment for Liquidity preference. The Liquidity Preference Theory says that the demand for money is not to borrow money but the desire to remain liquid. In other words, the interest rate is the 'price' for money.

66. When marginal is negative, it must be true that the total is decreasing. Marginal utility may decrease into negative utility, as it may become entirely unfavorable to consume another unit of any product.

67. All the following curves are U-shaped except AFC. The AFC curve is a rectangular hyperbola in the sense that all rectangles formed by AFC are of equal sizes. The AFC curve is asymptotic to both the axes. This means that it touches neither the horizontal axis nor the vertical axis.

68. Interest is paid because Capital is scarce. The borrower can get additional income from borrowed capital and in easily afford to pay interest. Hence it is scarcity.

69. The term 'marginal' in economics means Additional. In economics, the term marginal is used to indicate the change in some benefit or cost. when an additional unit is produced. For instance, the marginal revenue is the change in. total revenue when an additional unit is produced.

70. The cost that a firm incurs in hiring or purchasing any factor of production is referred to as Explicit cost. An explicit cost is a direct payment made to others in the course of running a business, such as wage, rent and materials, as opposed to implicit costs, where no actual payment is made.

71. The Communist Manifesto, written jointly by Marx and Engels's was published in 1848.

72. Every factor of production gets rewarded equal to its Marginal product. No single firm can influence the market price of a factor of production. Therefore, in order to get the equilibrium position, a firm will employ labourers up to a point where their respective marginal revenue productivity is equal to their wage rate.

73. Utility is more closely related to the term Satisfaction. The term was introduced initially as a measure of pleasure or satisfaction within the theory of utilitarianism by moral philosophers such as Jeremy Bentham and John Stuart Mill.

74. The short run Requires that at least one input is fixed. The short run is a concept that states that, within a certain period in the future, at least one input is fixed while others are variable.

75. David Ricardo stated explicitly for the first time, the Law of Comparative Costs. Absolute advantage refers to the uncontested superiority of a country to produce a particular good better. Comparative advantage introduces opportunity cost as a factor for analysis in choosing between different options for production.

76. According to Keynes, the rate of interest is purely "a monetary phenomenon." Interest is the price paid for borrowed funds. People like to keep cash with them rather than investing cash in assets. Thus, there is a preference for liquid cash.

77. Demand curve slopes downward because of the law of Diminishing marginal utility. The law of diminishing marginal utility states that with each increasing quantity of the commodity, its marginal utility declines.

78. The period is long enough to allow firms to change plant size and capacity. The long run is a period of time in which all factors of production and costs are variable. In the long run, firms are able to adjust all costs.

79. The Purchasing Power Parity Theory' came into prominence in 1916 through the writings of Gustav Cassel.

80. If rate of interest is 10%, the PV (present value) of Rs.100 received in 1 year's time is 90.9. "Present value" of a rupee received a year from now, is equal to only 90.9 paise [100/(1.1)].

81. Law of substitution is another name for law of Law of Equi-MU. The Law of equimarginal Utility is another fundamental principle of Economics. This law is also known as the Law of substitution or the Law of Maximum Satisfaction.

82. The average cost is U-shaped because an increase in output increases the returns and reduces the total cost. As the curve continues to slope downwards, it enters a phase of constant returns where the returns and output are at their optimum level. After the constant level, continued increase in output stops yielding any further increments in the returns (diminishing returns) and the costs begin to rise, forcing the curve to start sloping upwards.

83. The Making of Index numbers is the work of Irving Fisher. Index numbers played an important role in his monetary theory, and his book The Making of Index Numbers has remained influential down to the present day. Fisher's main intellectual rival was the Swedish economist Knut Wicksell.

84. Professor Knight is famous for his theory of Profit. He is best known for his Risk, Uncertainty and Profit, a monumental study of the role of the entrepreneur in economic life.

85. When Marginal Utility is positive, Total Utility Decreases. When we say that the total utility is increasing at a diminishing rate, we mean that amount of change in total utility is decreasing with the consumption of every extra unit which is nothing but marginal utility.

86. The three broad types of productive resources are Capital, labour and natural resources.

87. Economic development of a country requires Skilled labour and Abundant natural resources.

88. Profits are Residual payment. Residual payments are most often associated with the entertainment industry, since movies and music can generate revenues long after they are originally released.

89. Diminishing marginal utility is the basis of Law of demand. When the price of a goods falls, downward sloping marginal utility curve implies that the consumers must buy more of the good so that its marginal utility falls and becomes equal to the new price.

90. Productivity of land can be raised by Intensive cultivation. Intensive Farming is a farming method that uses higher inputs and advanced agricultural techniques to increase the overall yield.

91. Land only Is a free gift of nature and it lacks geographical mobility.

92. Profits are lower in the long run than in the short run, it can be negative and are less in perfect competition than in monopoly.

93. When Marginal Utility is zero, Total Utility is maximum. It is based in the law of diminishing marginal utility which says 'as more and more units of a good are consumed, MU i.e level of satisfaction derived from each successive unit goes on falling because desire for that commodity tend to fall.

94. Production is not an input. It is an output. Production is the method of turning raw materials or inputs into finished goods or products in a manufacturing process.

95. Entrepreneur input factor takes risk, innovates and coordinates. An entrepreneur is an individual who creates a new business, bearing most of the risks and enjoying most of the rewards. The entrepreneur is commonly seen as an innovator, a source of new ideas, goods, services, and business/or procedures.

96. Some economists say that profit earner is a kind of Wage earner. Wage earner is a person who works for wages or salary.

97. Quality of a commodity that satisfies some human want or need is called Utility. Within economics the concept of utility is used to model worth or value, but its usage has evolved significantly over time. The term was introduced initially as a measure of pleasure or satisfaction within the theory of utilitarianism by moral philosophers such as Jeremy Bentham and John Stuart Mill.

98. Human skills are a labour input is correct with respect to resources. The human or the interpersonal skills are the skills that present the managers' ability to interact, work or relate effectively with people. These skills enable the managers to make use of human potential in the company and motivate the employees for better results.

99. The transformation of resources into economic goods and services is called Production. Production is the method of turning raw materials or inputs into finished goods or products in a manufacturing process.

100. The operating surplus of an enterprise measures the difference between revenue and expenditure – i.e. the surplus or deficit – accruing from production.

Q.1 PM Narendra Modi has dedicated three hydropower projects in HP. This includes Koldam, Parbati and which other project?

A. Rampur
B. Rangpur
C. Revapur
D. None of the above

Q.2 The base year for calculating the revenue structure of the state according to the GST Council is:

A. 2014-2015
B. 2015-2016
C. 2016-2017
D. 2017-2018

Q.3 GST rate of what percent has been suggested by the GST Council for single GST rate?

A. 18-19   **B.** 19-20   **C.** 16-17   **D.** 17-18

Q.4 Indian banks are staring at deposit erosion of what amount between Sept and Nov 2016?

A. INR 1.5-2 lakh
B. INR 2-2.5 lakh
C. INR 2.5-3 lakh
D. None of the above

Q.5 Who has been appointed as a whole-time member of market regulatory authority SEBI on Oct 7, 2016?

A. RBI Governor
B. RBI ED
C. Niti Aayog Chairman
D. Niti Aayog Member

Q.6 As part of implementing the bankruptcy code, government of India has constituted the IBBI. What does IBBI stand for?

A. Insolvency and Bankruptcy Board of India
B. International Bankruptcy Board of India
C. Insolvency and Banking Regulations Board of India
D. None of the above

Q.7 Fix term employment was introduced in which sector by the Labour Ministry?

A. Apparel manufacturing
B. Apparel retail
C. Both of the above
D. Neither of the above

Q.8 Remittances to India have declined by what percent in 2016, according to World Bank India?

A. 4%   **B.** 5%   **C.** 6%   **D.** 7%

Q.9 A public debt management cell was formed on Oct 4 2016 by the Union Finance Ministry. Who is the person in charge of the cell?

A. Joint Secretary, DEA
B. Secretary, DEA
C. Additional Secretary, DEA
D. None of the above

Q.10 World Bank has indicated GDP growth in 2016 will be 7.6. What will it be in 2017?

A. 7.8   **B.** 7.7   **C.** 7.9   **D.** 8.0

Q.11 To boost trade among BRICS nations, India has planned to organise the trade fair for the bloc at which venue?

A. Goa
B. Delhi
C. Mumbai
D. None of the above

Q.12 How much untaxed money has been disclosed under IDS?

A. INR 62,350 crore
B. INR 65,650 crore
C. INR 67,350 crore
D. None of the above

Q.13 RBI has been amended by which act to provide for a Monetary Policy Committee for the maintenance of price stability?

A. Finance Act 2016
B. Treasuries Act 2016
C. Financial Policy Act 2016
D. None of the above

Q.14 Niti Aayog is aiming for India to exploit its long coastline to become what kind of an economy?

A. Marine   **B.** Sea   **C.** Ocean   **D.** Blue

Q.15 A Niti Aayog masterplan has selected how many islands in India as tourism growth zones?

A. 5   **B.** 6   **C.** 7   **D.** 9

Q.16 India slipped by how many positions to 112th in the World Economic Freedom Index?

A. 10   **B.** 11   **C.** 12   **D.** 13

Q.17 To meet local development guidelines, flexi funds have been increased in CSS to 25 percent for states and what value for UTs?

A. 25   **B.** 26   **C.** 28   **D.** 30

Q.18 Union Cabinet approved the formation of the GST Council as per which article of the amended Constitution?

A. 279A   **B.** 279B   **C.** 279C   **D.** 279D

Q.19 G-20 leaders have pledged to roll back protectionist measures by the close of 2018. This includes which nations?

A. US
B. China
C. India
D. All of the above

Q.20 FICCI Economic Survey pegged India's economy at which figure during the current financial year?

A. 7.6 percent
B. 7.7 percent
C. 7.8 percent
D. 7.9 percent

Q.21 According to ASSOCHAM, which city has the largest share of technology drive startups?

A. Bengaluru
B. Mysuru
C. Chennai
D. Hyderabad

Q.22 India has become one of the fastest growing economies in the world. Template for Scheme of Star Rating of Mines has been developed for this sector by whom?
A. Indian Bureau of Mines
B. Indian Mine Bureau
C. Minister of Mines
D. None of the above

Q.23 IRDA has proposed outsourcing norms for insurance companies. In what areas can they take services of individuals?
A. Medical Examination
B. Claim Investigation
C. Recovery
D. All of the above

Q.24 India has been ranked at which place in the list of innovative economies according to UN WIPO Global Innovation Index 2016?
A. 65th   **B.** 66th   **C.** 67th   **D.** 68th

Q.25 FRBM disclosure statements should be transparent, according to the CAG. What does FRBM stand for?
A. Fiscal Responsibility and Business Management
B. Fiscal Responsibility and Management
C. Financial Responsibility and Business Management
D. Financial Responsibility and Management

Q.26 RBI has eased priority sector norms to boost cash flow to which sector?
A. Agriculture   **B.** Manufacturing
C. MSME   **D.** IT

Q.27 No separate railway budget will be available from which year?
A. 2017   **B.** 2018   **C.** 2019   **D.** 2020

Q.28 The 15th report on the rules of e-waste management was released on 11th August 2016. Who headed the committee submitting the report?
A. R. Gandhi   **B.** V. Gandhi
C. D. Gandhi   **D.** None of the above

Q.29 Cabinet has approved signing and ratification between which country and India on economic cooperation on 10th August 2016?
A. Bosnia   **B.** Belgium   **C.** Bulgaria   **D.** Croatia

Q.30 Cabinet provided ex post facto approval for amendment of which sections of the Factories Act in August 2016?
A. Section 64   **B.** Section 65
C. Section 115   **D.** All of the above

Q.31 CCEA has approved one time grant of INR 900 crores for R&D for the development of AUSC technology for thermal power plants. What does AUSC stand for?
A. Advanced Ultra Super Critical
B. Anterior Ultra Super Critical
C. Advancing Ultra Super Critical
D. Atomic Ultra Super Critical

Q.32 Cabinet has approved the proposal to amend foreign investment rules in which sector?
A. E-commerce   **B.** NBFC
C. Mobile commerce   **D.** None of the above

Q.33 LS approved the Taxation laws (Amendment) Bill 2016. What does it seek to do?
A. Provide tax incentives to the garment sector
B. Raise customs duty on marble and granite from 10 to 40 percent
C. Both of the above
D. Neither of the above

Q.34 Parliamentary Committee chaired by whom suggested removal of 2.5 percent duty on import of coking coal as well as scrapping of clean energy cess of INR 400 per tonne?
A. Rakesh Singh
B. Rakesh Kumar
C. Rakesh Kumar Singh
D. None of the above

Q.35 TRAI's new portal will give information on calls across locations. What information will it provide to consumers?
A. Call drops
B. Coverage or call quality
C. Quality of Service parameters
D. All of the above

Q.36 Government has allowed which class of employees to work from home or a place outside the zone provided they meet certain conditions?
A. NIMZ   **B.** IT SEZ
C. ITeS SEZ   **D.** Only b and c

Q.37 How many lakh tonnes of e-waste were generated in the country in 2014 according to UN University?
A. 14   **B.** 15   **C.** 16   **D.** 17

Q.38 How many households in rural India use electricity as a main source of lighting as per census 2011?
A. 55%   **B.** 56%   **C.** 57%   **D.** 58%

Q.39 GIPCL has entered into PPA with Solar Energy Corporation of India for solar power projects in which state?
A. Rajasthan   **B.** Gujarat
C. West Bengal   **D.** Odisha

Q.40 RBI has launched a portal to curb illegal money pooling by firms called __________.
A. Sanchet.rbi.org.in   **B.** Sachet.rbi.org.in
C. Sanket.rbi.org.in   **D.** None of the above

Q.41 Which stock exchange signed an agreement with IIT-K for collaboration in areas including cyber security in August 2016?
A. NSE
B. BSE
C. Madras Stock Exchange
D. Kolkata Stock Exchange

Q.42 Government has imposed a penalty of what amount on telecom operators for violating subscriber verification norms till May 31?

A. INR 2616 crore
B. INR 2515 crore
C. INR 2414 crore
D. INR 2313 crore

Q.43 Directorate General of Anti Dumping recommended duties on steel products from which country/countries?

A. South Korea
B. Russia
C. Brazil
D. All of the above

Q.44 India's trade deficit with China has jumped to which amount in 2015-2016?

A. USD 53 billion
B. USD 54 billion
C. USD 55 billion
D. USD 56 billion

Q.45 RBI has released the on tap universal banking license excluding which group as eligible entities from the purview?

A. Small industrial houses
B. Medium industrial houses
C. Large industrial houses
D. None of the above

Q.46 How many textile parks have been approved in Uttarakhand on August 1, 2016?

A. 2 **B.** 3 **C.** 4 **D.** 5

Q.47 Report on the roadmap to double farmers income by 2020 incorporates e-NAM. What does e-NAM stand for?

A. Electronic National Agrarian Market
B. Electronic National Agricultural Market
C. Electronic New Agricultural Market
D. None of the above

Q.48 Foreign direct investment in the country grew by what percent to USD 10.55 billion during Q1, 2016?

A. 6 **B.** 7 **C.** 8 **D.** 9

Q.49 SBI has engaged which corporation's Kisan Seva Kendras as banking correspondents to extend banking facilities to farmers across the nation?

A. IOC **B.** GAIL **C.** SAIL **D.** ONGC

Q.50 How many infrastructure projects have led to cost overrun of INR 1.59 lakh crore according to official data?

A. 241 **B.** 242 **C.** 243 **D.** 244

Q.51 Government has raised FDI level in brownfield pharma to what percent under the automatic route to attract capital and technologies in the pharmaceutical sector?

A. 74 **B.** 49 **C.** 50 **D.** 56

Q.52 GoI has notified pay revisions as per 7th Pay Commission providing a hike of how many times to government employees?

A. 2.53 **B.** 2.54 **C.** 2.55 **D.** 2.57

Q.53 What was the overall power deficit during April-June quarter this fiscal, according to Central Electricity Authority?

A. 0.9 **B.** 0.8 **C.** 0.7 **D.** 0.6

Q.54 India has received how much in FDI in the first two months of the current fiscal (2016-2017)?

A. USD 5.34 billion
B. USD 5.44 billion
C. USD 5.45 billion
D. None of the above

Q.55 RBI has received a proposal for providing long term loans at low interest rates to which public sector bank?

A. SBI
B. OCI
C. PNB
D. EXIM Bank

Q.56 SIT on black money has recommended a ban on cash transactions of more than what amount?

A. INR 2 lakhs
B. INR 3 lakhs
C. INR 4 lakhs
D. INR 5 lakhs

Q.57 According to a CRISIL report, urban inflation fell from 9 percent to 5.3 percent in the past 24 months. According to this report, in the same period rural inflation fell from 10.1 percent to what percent?

A. 6.1 **B.** 6.2 **C.** 6.3 **D.** 6.4

Q.58 The Wholesale Price Index rose to a 20 month high of 1.6 percent in June from what figure in May?

A. 0.6 **B.** 0.7 **C.** 0.8 **D.** 0.9

Q.59 Government has released INR 100 crore towards which yojana for 2015-2016?

A. Atal Pension Yojana
B. Sukanya Samriddhi Yojana
C. Nai Roshni Scheme
D. None of the above

Q.60 Pension Fund Regulatory and Development Authority introduces new feature for NPS subscribers called ______.

A. NPS by NSDL e-Gov
B. NDS by NSFL e-Gov
C. NPS by NSGL e-Gov
D. None of the above

Q.61 Ministry of Railways has signed an agreement with which corporate group for modernisation of Habibganj station in MP?

A. Bansal Group
B. Tata Group
C. Birla Group
D. Reliance

Q.62 Cabinet Committee on Economic Affairs approved the proposal of DoT regarding the transfer of shares by ITI to the SNIF. What does SNIF stand for?

A. Special National Investment Fund
B. Special National Incentive Fund
C. Special National Interactive Fund
D. None of the above

Q.63 Government has permitted disinvestment of 15 percent paid up equity of National Buildings Construction Corporation Ltd. What percent of shareholding does it own in NBCC?

A. 90 percent
B. 95 percent
C. 80 percent
D. 85 percent

Q.64 What does GAAR stand for in the context of foreign portfolio investors on redemption and maturity of participatory notes?

A. General Anti Avoidance Rules
B. General Anti Action Rules
C. General Anti Affirmative Rules
D. None of the above

Q.65 Fertiliser industry overall volumes rose by what percent to 58.2 MT in 2015-2016 despite back to back droughts in the previous two years, according to rating agency ICRA?
A. 7   **B.** 6   **C.** 5   **D.** 4

Q.66 Index of Industrial Production for May was at the upside of what percent against a decline of -0.8 percent in April?
A. 1.3   **B.** 1.4   **C.** 1.5   **D.** 1.2

Q.67 MoU has been signed between SIDBI and which other bank?
A. Axis Bank   **B.** HDFC
C. IDBI   **D.** None of the above

Q.68 SaaS market in India will triple to what amount by 2020, according to a research report by NASSCOM?
A. 700 million   **B.** 500 million
C. 1 billion   **D.** None of the above

Q.69 Indian sugar production could decline by what percent as a result of likely drop in sugarcane output on account of poor rains in Karnataka and Maharashtra?
A. 7   **B.** 6   **C.** 5   **D.** 4

Q.70 RBI on July 7, 2016 notified interest rates for different small saving schemes for quarter ending September. What is the interest rate on savings deposits?
A. 3   **B.** 4   **C.** 3.5   **D.** 4.5

Q.71 Rajasthan has become the first state in the country to introduce minimum wages for whom?
A. Full time workers   **B.** Casual labour
C. Part time workers   **D.** None of the above

Q.72 Regulator FSSAI has joined hands with which organisation to check misleading ads in the foods and beverages sector?
A. ASCI   **B.** ASDI   **C.** ASOI   **D.** ASBI

Q.73 According to the textile ministry, India's textiles and apparels exports will touch which mark in FY2016?
A. 50 billion   **B.** 38 billion
C. 45 billion   **D.** 40 billion

Q.74 India has jumped how many places in the global logistics performance ranking of the WB?
A. 18   **B.** 19   **C.** 20   **D.** 21

Q.75 WB approved a loan for TEQIP III. What does this stand for?
A. Technical Education Quantity Improvement Project III
B. Technical Education Quality Improvement Project III
C. Technical Education Improvement Quality Project III
D. None of the above

Q.76 National Mineral Exploration Policy was given Cabinet approval paving the auction for how many mineral blocks and boost the country's mining potential?

A. 100   **B.** 150   **C.** 140   **D.** 130

Q.77 Cotton area in Punjab and Haryana declines by what percent in the 2016-2017 crop year?
A. 27   **B.** 26   **C.** 25   **D.** 24

Q.78 Which public sector bank was named in the Hall of Shame List of 158 banking institutions investing billions of dollars in companies creating cluster bombs, according to Dutch campaign group PAX Worldwide Investments in Cluster Munitions report?
A. SBI   **B.** OCI   **C.** PNB   **D.** IDBI

Q.79 India has retained its ranking as the 10th highest recipient of FDI in 2015, according to which UNCTAD report?
A. World Investment Report 2016
B. World Investment Report 2015
C. World Investing Report 2016
D. World Investing Report 2015

Q.80 Union government on 20th June 2016 changed the FDI policy with the aim of providing major impetus to employment and job creation. FDI beyond 49 percent in Defence Sector was allowed through which route?
A. Approval   **B.** Automatic
C. Both of the above   **D.** None of the above

Q.81 Apple Store will open its first outlet following revision of FDI norms. What percentage of FDI has been announced in existing brownfield pharmaceutical companies through automatic route?
A. 71 percent   **B.** 72 percent
C. 73 percent   **D.** 74 percent

Q.82 SBI on 16th June 2016 floated INR 200 crore rupee start up find to assist startups in which space?
A. IT   **B.** Fintech
C. Social media   **D.** None of the above

Q.83 India Ratings and Research has revised FY17 estimates of CAD from 1.2 percent to how much?
A. 1.3-1.4   **B.** 1.4-1.5   **C.** 1.3-1.5   **D.** 1.3-1.6

Q.84 India will see marginal 3.1 percent uptick in the IT spend at what figure in 2016?
A. USD 4 billion   **B.** USD 5 billion
C. USD 6 billion   **D.** USD 7 billion

Q.85 CAD is set to widen to what percent of GDP in FY 2017, according to Nomura India?
A. 1.4 percent   **B.** 1.5 percent
C. 1.6 percent   **D.** 1.7 percent

Q.86 India's overall trade balance improved in May with what nature of trade deficit?
A. US $6.24 billion   **B.** US $6.37 billion
C. US $6.27 billion   **D.** None of the above

Q.87 RBI's new debt recast norms are credit positive for banks and will reduce gross NPA by how many basis points following one year?

A. 30-100   B. 40-100   C. 50-100   D. 60-100

Q.88 RBI has launched which initiative following the rise of CPI and WPI based inflation?
A. Inflation Expectations Survey of Householder
B. Inflation Expectations Survey of Households
C. Inflation Expectation Schedule of Homes
D. None of the above

Q.89 RBI has released a paper on stressed assets known as ____________.

A. Scheme for Sustainable Structuring of Stressed Assets
B. Scheme for Sustainable Structure of Distressed Assets
C. Scheme for Sustaining Structure of Stressed Assets
D. None of the above

Q.90 Which country has become the world's third largest oil consumer according to BP Statistical Review of World Energy released on 8th June, 2016?
A. China   B. Japan   C. India   D. Pakistan

Q.91 Cotton exports from India have come down on account of what factor?
A. Local prices have rallied
B. Tight supplies because of drought
C. Both a and b
D. Neither a nor b

Q.92 What does fintech stand for?
A. Financial Techniques
B. Financial Technology
C. Fiscal Technology
D. None of the above

Q.93 Telecom Commission has stuck to what percent of spectrum usage charge rate?
A. 2   B. 4   C. 5   D. 6

Q.94 India's mobile data traffic will grow by what percent by 2021?
A. 14   B. 15   C. 16   D. 17

Q.95 India's international air traffic has logged CAGR of what percent in the period between 2006 and 2016?
A. 10.2   B. 10.3   C. 10.5   D. 10.9

Q.96 What percent of the budget estimate did the fiscal deficit come to in April?
A. 25.4   B. 25.6   C. 25.7   D. 25.8

Q.97 Telecom industry's revenue has grown by what percent in 2015?
A. 6.3%   B. 6.4%   C. 6.5%   D. 6.6%

Q.98 Fresh capacity addition by wind power may decline to 2500 MW against 3415 MW in the previous fiscal due to challenges in which two states, ICRA reported?
A. Madhya Pradesh and Chattisgarh
B. Madhya Pradesh and Maharashtra
C. Madhya Pradesh and Rajasthan
D. Madhya Pradesh and Uttar Pradesh

Q.99 Indian economy will grow by what percent according to FICCI's Economic Outlook Survey?
A. 7.7%   B. 7.8%   C. 7.9%   D. 7.10%

Q.100 Government of India has approved the establishment of India's third NIMZ in which state?
A. UP   B. HP
C. Rajasthan   D. Odisha

// Smart Answer Sheet //

Correct   Indicates percentage of students who answered questions correctly.

Skipped   Indicates percentage of students who skipped questions.

Q.	Ans.	Correct / Skipped
1	A	42.11 % / 31.57 %
2	B	15.79 % / 42.1 %
3	D	21.05 % / 42.11 %
4	A	13.16 % / 50.0 %
5	B	15.79 % / 50.0 %
6	A	34.21 % / 47.37 %
7	A	10.53 % / 50.0 %
8	B	13.16 % / 52.63 %
9	A	23.68 % / 50.0 %
10	B	10.53 % / 50.0 %
11	B	28.95 % / 42.1 %
12	D	7.89 % / 47.37 %
13	A	18.42 % / 42.11 %
14	D	28.95 % / 42.1 %
15	D	7.89 % / 47.37 %
16	A	10.53 % / 44.73 %
17	D	18.42 % / 50.0 %
18	A	18.42 % / 55.26 %
19	D	44.74 % / 34.21 %
20	C	21.05 % / 28.95 %
21	A	34.21 % / 36.84 %
22	A	34.21 % / 42.11 %
23	D	44.74 % / 36.84 %
24	B	18.42 % / 39.47 %
25	B	7.89 % / 50.0 %
26	C	21.05 % / 55.27 %
27	A	21.05 % / 39.48 %
28	C	21.05 % / 47.37 %
29	D	13.16 % / 50.0 %
30	D	21.05 % / 42.11 %
31	A	23.68 % / 42.11 %
32	B	26.32 % / 39.47 %
33	C	42.11 % / 39.47 %
34	A	10.53 % / 39.47 %
35	D	44.74 % / 44.73 %
36	D	28.95 % / 44.73 %
37	D	10.53 % / 50.0 %
38	A	18.42 % / 50.0 %
39	B	15.79 % / 47.37 %
40	A	15.79 % / 55.26 %
41	B	26.32 % / 44.73 %
42	D	13.16 % / 50.0 %
43	D	26.32 % / 44.73 %
44	A	13.16 % / 50.0 %
45	C	13.16 % / 47.37 %
46	A	10.53 % / 44.73 %
47	B	28.95 % / 47.37 %
48	B	23.68 % / 50.0 %
49	A	18.42 % / 55.26 %
50	A	10.53 % / 50.0 %
51	A	18.42 % / 42.11 %
52	D	7.89 % / 42.11 %
53	A	13.16 % / 50.0 %
54	A	10.53 % / 50.0 %
55	D	23.68 % / 42.11 %
56	B	5.26 % / 47.37 %
57	B	13.16 % / 55.26 %
58	C	15.79 % / 50.0 %
59	A	28.95 % / 44.73 %
60	A	28.95 % / 39.47 %
61	A	13.16 % / 47.37 %
62	A	31.58 % / 50.0 %
63	A	10.53 % / 44.73 %
64	A	23.68 % / 47.37 %
65	A	13.16 % / 55.26 %
66	D	13.16 % / 44.73 %
67	D	7.89 % / 47.37 %
68	C	13.16 % / 55.26 %
69	A	13.16 % / 57.89 %
70	B	13.16 % / 55.26 %
71	C	15.79 % / 39.47 %
72	A	39.47 % / 31.58 %
73	A	13.16 % / 50.0 %
74	B	18.42 % / 52.63 %
75	B	36.84 % / 47.37 %
76	A	10.53 % / 50.0 %
77	A	15.79 % / 50.0 %
78	A	15.79 % / 52.63 %
79	A	23.68 % / 42.11 %
80	A	26.32 % / 36.84 %

Q.	Ans.	Correct		Q.	Ans.	Correct		Q.	Ans.	Correct		Q.	Ans.	Correct		Q.	Ans.	Correct
		Skipped				Skipped				Skipped				Skipped				Skipped
81	D	15.79 %		85	A	15.79 %		89	A	21.05 %		93	D	5.26 %		97	C	28.95 %
		42.1 %				50.0 %				55.27 %				47.37 %				50.0 %
82	B	21.05 %		86	C	15.79 %		90	C	28.95 %		94	B	15.79 %		98	B	15.79 %
		44.74 %				52.63 %				55.26 %				47.37 %				50.0 %
83	C	21.05 %		87	A	7.89 %		91	C	28.95 %		95	C	10.53 %		99	A	7.89 %
		50.0 %				52.64 %				55.26 %				50.0 %				47.37 %
84	D	10.53 %		88	A	13.16 %		92	B	34.21 %		96	C	18.42 %		100	D	13.16 %
		50.0 %				52.63 %				52.63 %				44.74 %				44.73 %

Performance Analysis

Avg. Score (%)	14.0%
Toppers Score (%)	50.0%
Your Score	

//Hints and Solutions//

1. PM Narendra Modi visited Mandi in Himachal Pradesh where he dedicated three hydropower projects to the nation namely Koldam, Parbati and Rampur

- PM Modi on 18th Oct inaugurated the three hydropower projects of 1752 MW capacities in HP
- Inauguration of the new hydropower projects will change economic horizon of the hilly state
- The three hydropower projects are:
  540 MW generation capacity third phase of Parbati hydropower project of NHPC in Kullu
  800 MW Koldam power project in Bilaspur district
  412 MW Rampur Project of SJVN Ltd in Shimla.
- This was the PM's Maiden visit to the hill state after becoming PM

2. The Goods and Services Council on 18th October 2016 reached a consensus on the way in which states would be compensated for loss of revenue with a four slab structure of 6, 12, 18 and 26 along with lower rates for essential items and highest band for luxury goods

- Base year for calculating the revenue of the state would be 2015-2016
- Secular growth rate of 14% would be taken for calculating the likely revenue of each state in the first 5 years of implementation of the GST
- A consensus was reached on definition of revenue to compensate the state for revenue loss due to GST implementation
- Rate structure should be such that it does not lead to further inflation and both States and Centre have adequate funds to discharge their duty.
- The rate is to be revenue neutral so that there is no need to burden consumers with additional tax
- To ensure inflation remains under control, food items along with other 50 percent items of common usage are proposed for tax exemption
- Lower rates would be levied on essential items and the highest for luxury and demerit goods.

3. India's plan to implement a nation-wide GST entered the final stage with the GST Council coming up with a formula to compensate states in the event of revenue loss after the new system is adopted

- On 18th Oct 2016, the council decided 2015-2016 will be taken as the base year for calculating revenue assuming secular and long term growth rate of 14 percent.
- States will be fully compensated for potential revenue loss up to 5 years
- GST Council has also finalised area based exemptions and 1 states including 8 NE states and three hilly states will be treated under the new tax regime.

- The tax exemption provided by the states as incentives to the industry will be counted in the definition of revenue for calculation of revenue loss.
- Objective is to ensure rates will not be inflationary.
- There could be four slabs of GST rates namely 6,12,18 and 26 percent.
- The cess on the highest band could be for ultra luxury items and demerit items such as tobacco.
- The panel under CEA has recommended a revenue neutral rate of 15- 15.5 percent with a standard rate of 17-18 percent levied on most goods and all services.

4. Indian banks are staring at deposit erosion of INR 1.5-2 lakh between Sept and Nov 2016 as Foreign Currency Non Resident deposits mobilised in 2013 mature around that period

- This could result in acute liquidity shortage and possible de-growth of balance sheets
- At the deposit growth rate currently, mobilisation by banks is to the tune of INR 2.4 lakh crore deposits in three months
- To maintain the same growth, banks will need to raise INR 4 lakh crore in three months
- Liquidity impact is to be felt by banks around maturity time
- RBI is also planning liquidity support and special measures to nullify shortage
- Central Bank also has build up a long forwards position in dollars amounting to USD 21.15 billion in more than three months and up to one year segment that can be used for honouring the pay-outs
- Central Bank's social position will be around USD 24.67 billion indicating RBI will infuse dollars to prevent exchange rate volatility

5. RBI's Executive Director Gurumoorthi Mahalingam has been appointed as the whole-time member of market regulatory SEBI

- His appointment was approved by the Union Finance Ministry for 5 years or till he attains the age of 65, whichever is earlier.
- Mahalingam succeeds Prashant Saran as whole-time member
- Saran retired from the post in June 2016
- Aside from the Chairman, SEBI has three more Whole-Time members / WTMs
- Mahalingam is an ED and former regional director of the RBI
- In his current role in RBI, Mahalingam was involved in monitoring and surveillance of money, forex, government securities and derivative market intervention operations
- Associated with the RBI for the past 3 decades, he has held various posts in the organisation
- He has been associated with NISM or National Institute of Securities Markets, an educational initiative of the SEBI as its visiting faculty

- He holds an MSc in Statistics and Operations Research from IIT-K and an MBA in International Banking and Finance from Birmingham Business School in the United Kingdom

6. Government of India has come out with another set of draft rules including liquidation of insolvent corporate persons under the Insolvency and Bankruptcy code

- As part of implementing the code, government of India has constituted the Insolvency and Bankruptcy Board of India

- Draft norms will be finalised after taking the stakeholder views into account

- Notified by the government in May, code seeks consolidation and amendment of laws relating to reorganisation and insolvency resolution of corporate persons, partnership firms and individuals in a timely manner

- Latest set of draft regulations relate to liquidation of insolvent corporate persons, insolvency resolution processes for corporate persons and application to the judicial authority

- Ministry has also issued draft regulations for registration of insolvency professionals, agencies and model bye-laws

- The IBBI chaired by MS Sahoo will have 10 members

- Apart from the chairman currently there are 4 government nominated members and the rest will be appointed in the coming months.

7. GoI has introduced fixed term employment in the apparel sector. The Labour Ministry notified the amendments in the Industrial Employment (Standing Orders) paving the way for fixed term employment in the apparel manufacturing sector

- Decision would facilitate employment of workers in the apparel manufacturing sector on a fixed term basis against the backdrop of the seasonal character of the sector

- It would also ensure sam working conditions, wages and other benefits for fixed term employees in the sector as a regular employee

- Following the termination of fixed term employment, workers will not be entitled to notice or pay

- This move has been critiqued by many labour unions including BMS which have termed it anti worker

- Fixed term employment in the apparel manufacturing sector was introduced as part of the Industrial Employment(Standing Order) Act vide notification dates Oct 7, 2016

- The working conditions in terms of hours, wages, allowances and statutory dues of the fixed term employee would be at par with a permanent one

- FIxed term workers will also be eligible for statutory benefits available to permanent workers in proportion to the period of service rendered by them though the period of employment does not extend to the

- qualifying period of the employment required in the statue

- This is one of the measures approved in an INR 6000 crore package for textile sectors announced in June in 2016

- Measures assume significance due to massive potential for social transformation through women empowerment

- Close to 70 percent of the workforce in the garment industry are women

- Therefore, a majority of the new jobs created are more likely to go to women

8. World Bank India, the world's largest remittance recipient in 2015 may receive a remittance of USD 65.5 billion this year, a drop of 5 percent according to the World Bank.

- The reason for this is weak economic growth in remittance source countries and cyclic low oil prices

- In 2016, remittance flows are expected to decline by 5% in India and 3.5% in Bangladesh while they will grow by 5.1% in Pakistan and 1.6 percent in Sri Lanka, the latest report on remittances said

- Despite the drop, India is topping the countries receiving remittance this year, according to most estimates

- The World Bank indicated in 2016, India is expected to receive a remittance of USD 65.5 billion followed by China (USD 65.2 billion)

- Pakistan is positioned at number 5 and estimated to receive USD 20.3 billion in 2016

- Remittances to South Asia are expected to decline by 2.3 percent in 2016 following a 1.6 percent decline in 2015

- This is due to weak economic growth in remittances source countries and cyclic low oil prices

- India retained its top spot in 2015, attracting close to USD 69 billion in remittances according to the World Bank

- Remittances from GCC countries continued to decline on account of lower oil prices and about market nationalisation policies in Saudi Arabia

- Gulf Cooperation Council is an alliance of 6 Middle Eastern companies- Kuwait, Saudi arabia, UAE, Oman, Bahrain and Qatar

- This is set against the backdrop of tepid global growth, remittance flows to low and middle income countries to low and middle income countries

- New normal of slow growth has been entered and in 2016, remittance flows to LMIC are projected to reach USD 442 billion, marking an increase of 0.8percent over 2015

- Modest recovery in 2016 is largely driven by an increase in remittance flows to Latin America and the Caribbean on the basis of a stronger economy in the US

- By contrast, the remittance flows to other developing regions either fell or recorded a deceleration in growth

- Low prices continued to be a factor in reduced remittance flows from Russia and the GCC countries

- Additionally, structural factors have also played a role in dampening remittances growth

- Anti-money laundering efforts have prompted banks to shit accounts of money transfer operators, diverting activity to informal channels

- Remittances continue to be an important component of the global economy, surpassing international aid

- This new normal of weak growth in remittances can impact economies across the globe and create a new set of challenges for economic growth.

9. Union Finance Ministry on Oct 4, constituted the Public Debt Management Cell. The cell has been created to streamline public borrowing and ensure better cash management with the objective of deepening bond markets. Currently, the overall in charge of the PDMC will be the Joint secretary (Budget) Department of Economic Affairs, Ministry of Finance.

- In two years, the PDMC is scheduled to be upgraded to a statutory Public Debt Management Agency

- The interim arrangement will permit separation of debt management functions from RBI to PDMA in a seamless and gradual manner without market disruptions

- The PDMA will have only advisory functions to avoid conflict with RBI's statutory functions

- It will also advise government of India on matters pertaining to investment, capital market operations, administration of interest rates on small savings among others

- Middle office of the Budget Division will be subsumed into PDMC with immediate effect

- Transition from PDMC to PDMA will be implemented by JIC or Joint Implementation Committee chaired by the Joint Secretary Budget

- Other members of the JIC will be from the RBI and the government

- According to a circular issued by the ministry, the JIC would operate under the supervision of the Monitoring Group on Cash and Debt Management with Secretary Economic Affairs and D-G, RBI as co-chairpersons.

- PDMC will be staffed by debt managers from the RBI budget division, current Middle Office and other government units

- The PDMA seeks to bring India's external borrowings and domestic debt under one roof.

10. Following the MPC, the World Bank has indicated that the GDP growth of India will remain robust in 2016 at 7.6 percent and 2017 at 7.7. percent

- As per the World Bank, Indian economic growth will remain robust and poverty eradication will top the agenda

- South Asia remains a global growth hotspot and resilient to headwinds such as slowdown in China

- Even in South Asian countries like Pakistan growth is expected to reach 5.4 percent in 2018 and Bangladesh will sustain growth at 6.8 percent

- The main challenges remain domestic, and include policy uncertainty as well as fiscal and fiscal vulnerabilities.

11. To boost trade among the BRICS nations, India will, for the first time, organise a trade fair for the bloc including BRICS

- Intra BRICS trade in 2014 was USD 297 billion- less than 5 % of the USD 6.5 trillion worth trade that the five countries had with the world that year

- Goods imports from the world onto the BRICS countries amounted to USD 3.03 trillion in 2014 while global goods exports of BRICS nations were USD 3.47 trillion that year

- The first BRICS Trade Fair and Exhibition will be held from Oct 12=14 in the NCT ahead of the BRICS political summit in Goa (Oct 15-16 2016)

- Initiative was proposed by PM Modi in 2015

- The focus of the fair is Building BRICS- Innovation for Collaboration

- The fair will promote intra BRICS economic engagement and showcase 20 key sectors including aerospace, auto, agro processing, chemicals, green energy, healthcare, railways and textile

- Startups and innovators will also showcase technology to solution providers in areas such as healthcare, education,waste management and energy efficiency

- Leaders from Bangladesh, Myanmar, Bhutan, Nepal and Thailand have also been invited to the fair.

12. Finance Minister Arun Jaitley said that INR 65,250 crore in black or untaxed money has been disclosed under the Government's Income Declaration Scheme (IDS).

- The one-time compliance window closed .

- As per the scheme, launched on June 1, those who evaded taxes were allowed to avoid punishment by paying tax, penalty and cess totalling 45% of the declared income.

- Reiterating that the one-time window was not an amnesty scheme like the 1997 one, Jaitley said the tax collected in the 1997 Voluntary Disclosure of Income Scheme (VDIS) was Rs 9,760 crore with an average declaration of Rs 7 lakh.

- The tax collected from the Income Declaration Scheme (IDS) 2016 will go into the Consolidated Fund of India and will be used for larger welfare of people, he added.

- Scheme was operational from June 1 till the midnight of September 30, the finance minister said the tax authorities were still tabulating the declarations, both in physical and electronic form.

- Roughly, the declarations work out to INR 1 crore per declarant.

13. The Reserve Bank of India Act 1934 has been amended by the Finance Act 2016 to provide for an institutionalised and statutory framework for price stability through the Monetary Policy Committee

- As per the provisions of the RBI Act, of the six members of the Monetary Policy Committee, three are from the RBI
- Other three members of the MPC will be appointed by the Central Government
- In exercise of the powers given by section 45ZB of the Reserve Bank of India Act 1934, the Union Government has constituted the Monetary Policy Committee of the RBI with the composition:
- The Governor of the Bank: Ex Officio Chairperson
- Deputy Governor of the Bank, in charge of Monetary Policy: Member,ex officio
- One officer of the Bank to be nominated from the Central Board: Member, ex officio
- Chetan Ghate, Professor ISI: Member
- Pami Dua, Director, DSE: Member
- Ravindra Dholakia, Professor, IIM-A: Member
- Members of the Monetary Policy Committee will hold office for 4 years
- Monetary Policy Committee has been appointed with the aim of fixing the benchmark policy rate or repo rate required to combat inflation within a specified target level.
- Committee based approach for determining Monetary Policy adds value and transparency to the monetary policy decisions.
- Meetings of the Committee will be held 4 times in a year and decisions will be published after each such meeting.

14. Niti Aayog has started a consultation process for the integration of defence and internal security with a 15 year vision.

- The planning body has initiated a discussion to leverage India's status as a major maritime nation with a long coastline and a potential to become a key blue economy
- BJP government, for the first time, has taken the decision to include these subjects in the plan process to create long term planning element for better preparation
- India has a naturally maritime strength with:
- coastline of 7500 km
- Above 2 million square km of EEZ
- More than 1300 islands and networks of the river
- India has a natural and strategic benefit
- Maritime trade accounts for 75 percent of the value of total trade and more than 90 percent of the volume of Indian trade

- Indian ship building industry is 17th in the world with South Korea, Japan and China way ahead
- It currently faces constraints such as inefficient tax structure and access related restrictions
- Deep sea fishing is another area where growth is possible.

15. Lakshadweep and Andaman & Nicobar Islands have been identified as tourism growth zones as part of a Niti Aayog masterplan.

- Nine islands have been selected as the part of the masterplan
- The islands are being seen as drivers of tourism and sustainable economic growth on the lines of countries like Singapore
- Water parks and natural resource will be used to promote tourist initiatives, overcoming limited land areas while being mindful of conservation
- Ecological sensitivity of the islands will also be taken into account while improving options for tourists
- Options in Lakshadweep which sees high end tourism are limited compared to A&N islands
- Andaman and Nicobar islands identified as part of the masterplan were Smith Island, Avis Island and Long Island
- Slotted for development in Lakshadweep are Bangaram, Thinnakara, Suheli, Cheriyam and Minicoy
- Tourist facilities in Lakshadweep are currently limited to Bangaram and a few other islands
- Inclusion of Little Andaman, the biggest island in the chain with area of 734.34 square km was discussed in detail
- It is roughly the size of Singapore
- Singapore has earmarked 10 percent of its area for parks/natural resources and ranks fourth globally in the environment performance index
- 90 percent of Andaman and Nicobar islands are notified as reserved or deemed forest; only 6 percent of the land is available for development.
- Plan gained momentum after the islands were selected for tourism, agriculture and infrastructure as well as renewable energy development

16. India slipped by 10 ranks to 112th in a list of 159 countries and territories.

- It fared badly in all categories including legal system and regulation according to the Economic Freedom of the World; 2016 Annual Report
- THe report say China, Bangladesh and Pakistan ranking back at 113, 121 and 133
- Bhutan, Nepal and Sri Lanka fared better
- India fared badly in legal system and property rights (86) sound money policies (130) freedom for global trade (144) and regulation(132)

- Except for size of government where it fared better (8) a negative performance was evident across the index

- Report is based on 2014 data and measures economic freedom by analysing policies and institutions of the countries and territories studied

- The report uses 42 distinct variables, from for example the World Bank, to measure this. Some examples: tax rates, degree of juridical independence, inflation rates, costs of importing, and regulated prices.

- Each of the 5 areas above is given equal weight in the final score.

The cornerstones of economic freedom are:

- Personal choice rather than collective choice;

- Voluntary exchange coordinated by markets rather than allocation via the political process;

- Freedom to enter and compete in markets; and

- Protection of persons and their property from aggression by others

In practice, the index measures:

- Size of Government;

- Expenditures, Taxes, and Enterprises;

- Legal Structure and Security of Property Rights;

- Access to Sound Money;

- Freedom to Trade Internationally; and

- Regulation of Credit, Labor, and Business.

17. Government has issued fresh flexi fund guidelines that provide more freedom to states for spending money under the Centrally Sponsored Schemes to meet local developmental requirements.

- As per the new norms, flexi funds in each CSS has been increased from 10 to 25 percent for states and 30 percent for UTs

- States can use the fund to undertake mitigation or restoration activities in case of natural calamities or to satisfy local requirements in areas affected by internal security disturbances.

- State governments will constitute state level sanctioning committee to avail of this fund

- This fund facility is not for CSS which emanate from legislation like MNREGA

- Subgroup of CMs in consultation with the stakeholders had earlier supported rationalisation of CSS

18. Union Cabinet on 12th September 2016 approved the process, formation and functioning of the Goods and Services Tax Council

- Council will comprise FM and state Finance Ministers making recommendations on important issues pertaining to GST including items and rates

- Creation of the GST Council is as per A279A of the amended Constitution

- Creation of the GST Council Secretariat took place with its office in New Delhi

- Appointment of the Secretary (Revenue) as the Ex Officio Secretary to the GST Council also took place

- Chairpersons were included while CBEC was a permanent invitee (non-voting) on all proceedings of the GST Council

- A post of additional secretary to the GST Council in the GST Council Secretariat and 4 posts of Commissioner in the GST Council Secretariat was also approved

- As per Article 279A of the amended Constitution, GST Council shall comprise the following members:

- Union Finance Minister- Chairperson

- Member: Union Minister of State in Charge of Revenue of Finance

- Members: Minister in charge of finance or taxation or any other minister nominated by the state government

- On September 8, 2016 President Pranab Mukherjee have assent to the 122nd Constitutional Amendment Bill paving the way for the rollout of GST

- The new tax regime will do away with indirect taxes ushering in one tax for the entire country

- Around 18 states have ratified the bill

- GST is a single indirect tax which will subsume most of the central and state taxes as VAT, excise duty, service tax and CST

19. G-20 nations pledged to roll back protectionist measures by end of 2018 and ensure rule based, transparent multilateral trading system with WTO for global growth.

- The group of 20 nations also reaffirmed to continue to support the world of WTO, UNCTAD and OECD in monitoring protectionism

- Emphasising the benefits trade and open markets must be communicated to the wider public more effectively and accompanied by domestic policies to ensure benefits are widely distributed.

- Leaders also committed to ratify the Trade Facilitation Agreement towards the close of 2016 and called for other WTO members to do the same.

- They also reiterated advancing negotiations on remaining Doha Development Agenda issue as a matter of priority including three pillars of agriculture-market access, domestic support and export competition, non agricultural market access and services among others.

- The nations also recognised the need to ensure consistency with WTO rules.

- Leaders also endorsed the strategy for global trade growth under which the G20 will lead by example to lower trade costs, harness trade and investment policy coherence boost trade in service, enhance trade finance and promote e-commerce development and address trade and development .

- It also added that the G-20 will continue to prioritise the work on food security, nutrition, sustainable agricultural growth and rural development as a significant contribution to implementing the 2030 Agenda for Sustainable Development

- The G-20 also reaffirmed its commitment to promoting investment with focus on infrastructure in terms of both quantity and quality

- It would also support policies that encourage firms of all sizes in particular women and young entrepreneurs, women led firms and SMEs to take advantage of global value chains.

- Further it said generating quality employment is indispensable for sustainable development and is at the centre of the domestic and global agenda of the G-20.

- The communique also stressed it will further develop G-20 employment plans in 2017 to address these commitments and monitor progress in a systematic and transparent manner in attaining the G-20 goals especially on youth employment and female labour participation

20. As per a FICCI survey, India's economy is likely to expand by 7.8 percent during the current financial year.

- There has been marginal improvement in growth estimate for 2016-2017

- RBI also pegged the growth rate at 7.6 percent in 2016-2017

- FICCI's Economic Outlook survey put median GDP growth forecast of 7.8 percent for the current fiscal year. Further, the estimated median GVA (gross value added) growth for Q1 FY17 has been put at 7.6 percent.

- The survey was conducted during July-August among leading economists belonging to the industry, banking and financial services sector.

- The trade body also said the median growth forecast for IIP has been put at 3.5 percent for the year 2016-17, with a minimum and maximum range of 2 percent and 4.3 percent, respectively. Median inflation forecast for 2016-17 has noted a marginal increase in comparison to the previous round.

- The median forecast for Wholesale Price Index based inflation rate for 2016-17 has been put at 2.4 percent while for Consumer Price Index it is 5.2 percent.

21. Bengaluru is host to the largest share of technology driven start-ups followed by Delhi-NCR and Mumbai while Hyderabad and Chennai are quite popular among techies who are budding entrepreneurs.

- Study was conducted in association with Thought Arbitrage.

- It found that technology driven startups growth was such that India moved up to third position with the US occupying the top position with more than 47,000 and UK with over 4,500.

- India's tech startups number around 4200 up to 2015.

- In terms of total number of start ups, comprising tech and non tech areas, India figured among the five largest hosts in the world along with China.

- Number of startups in both India and China were 10,000 each.

- US is at world number one position among the overall list of 83,000 budding entrepreneurs.

- Of the Indian startups, riding on the technology, the IT hub Bengaluru was host to 26 percent.

- NCR had 23 percent and Mumbai 17 percent.

- In the catching up category Hyderabad had around 8 percent and Chennai and Pune at 6 percent each.

- Disruptive innovation in technology and process is creating new Indian startups and foreign investors including some of the well known venture capital funds showing interest in these startups.

- Synergizing Start Up India with Make in India and Digital India has the potential to expand Indian eco system for the new entrepreneurs.

- Paper suggested tax exemption for research and experimentation to encourage ideas without fear of failure.

- Courses on creation of small businesses need to be encouraged in the learning campus too.

22. India has become one of the fastest growing and developing economies in the world.

- Enriched with numerous minerals, there has been a growing need to balance mining activities with protection of the ecology.

- Ministry of Mines, Government of India has focused on Sustainable Development Framework for the Indian Mining Sector as a guiding principle for Indian mining industry encompassing well being and inclusive growth with environmental protection.

- Ministry of Mines has developed a credible system of evaluation of mining footprints first launched at Odisha's Sukinda Chromite mine.

- Ministry through the Indian Bureau of Mines has developed a template for the scheme of Star Rating of Mines.

- The aim is to bring the mines to a minimum standard of star rating in the shortest time to adopt sustainable practice.

- A two layered system providing self-evaluation templates to be filled in by the mine operator followed by validation through Indian Bureau of Mines. Templates have been notified vide notification dated 23.05.2016. The star rating will be based on the following parameters:
  Scientific and systematic mining to mitigate environmental impact, addressing the social impact of resettlement and rehab of mining affected people Local community engagement and development of

social economic nature for the local community Progressive and final mine closure to ensure for restoration of mined out land in better conditions than the original and international standards for mining operations and reporting

- A web enabled online system for evaluation of measures has been developed by the National Institute of Smart Governance Hyderabad.

- Schema of Star rating will be a vital step for the compliance of ecological protection and social responsibility by the mining sector.

- PIB has listed the following benefits of this system:

- Comprehensive mitigation of environmental impacts on land, air and water by mining activities.

- Collation of various technical, environmental and social data of the mining sector at one platform by IBM, which would be utilised to enable better management and monitoring of the compliance of various conditions laid down by statutory authorities for mining.

- Formulation of Comprehensive Regional Plans'- a robust Environment &Social Management framework.

- Availability of the information on mining as well as the conservation activities in public domain to enable greater transparency to enable effective participation of stakeholder and speedy resolution of conflicts.

- Reduced delays in obtaining various clearances (environmental, forest, mining plan, etc.) for mines. Self-certification to be allowed for the approvals for scheme of mining.

- Mine monitoring and high standards adoption for evaluation.

23. Regulator Insurance Regulatory and Development Authority of India on 18th August 2016 proposed outsourcing norms for insurance companies under which service of individuals can be taken for medical examination, claim investigation and recovery.

- Every insurer should also have in place a comprehensive board approved outsourcing policy

- In considering or renewing an outsourcing arrangement insurer should subject the agency to due diligence according to the proposed proposed IRDAI (Outsourcing of Activities by Indian Insurers) Regulations, 2016.

- The insurer shall satisfy itself that the outsourcing agency's security policies, procedures and controls will enable the insurer to protect confidentiality and security of policyholder information," according to the draft.

- Meanwhile, in other banking and insurance news, SBI market share rose from 17 to 23 percent.

- Board of State Bank of India approved a swap ratio for merger of three listed associate banks and Bharathiya Mahila Bank

- Deal involves allowing 28 SBI shares of INR 1 each for every 10 shares in the State Bank of Bikaner and Jaipur

(INR 10 each) and 22 shares of SBI for every 10 shares held in State Bank of Mysore and State Bank of Travancore.

- The other two associate banks, that is, State Bank of Hyderabad and State Bank of Patiala, are unlisted entities, which are fully owned by the SBI.

- For Bharathiya Mahila Bank, which is also an unlisted entity but owned by the government, SBI fixed the swap ratio at 4.42 crore shares of SBI for every 100 crore share of BMB.

- Barring State Bank of Mysore shareholders, the share allotment ratio is broadly even for all the holders. In our view, even if the allotment ratio is favourable / unfavourable for shareholders of associate banks, it is unlikely to make any difference since SBI holds 75-90% in these banks

- The merged entity will have a business of around Rs.40 lakh crore, and SBI will aspire to be in the top 50 global banks, going ahead.

- Meanwhile India Post Payments Bank has received the certificate of incorporation from the Registrar of Companies, paving the way for the postal department's bank to begin operations in 2017 as announced.

- This will be the first public sector undertaking under the Department of Posts.

- The Department of Posts is expected to complete the roll out of its branches all over the country by September 2017. The government said this could be the fastest roll out for a bank anywhere in the world.

- The Union Cabinet, chaired by Prime Minister Narendra Modi, had in January approved the proposal to set up IPPB with total project cost of Rs.800 crore.

- The new bank is expected to commence operations by March 2017 and will set up 650 branches and 5000 ATMs across the country.

24. India has been ranked 66th in the list of world's most innovative economies.

- It has moved 15 places from the year 2015 as per a new UN report that calls for more more transparent policies if the country aims to be a global innovator.

- In a report by the UN World Intellectual Property Organisation, India moved up from 81 to 66 in the overall global rankings.

- Global Innovation Index 2016 released by the WIPO, Cornell University and INSEAD business school has ranked India among the top 50 economies overall in two pillars namely market sophistication (33) and knowledge and technology outputs (43).

- India maintained a stable or improved ranking across all pillars with the most significant improvement in human capital and research up by 40 spots and business sophistication up 59 spots.

- Within human capital and research, India's data coverage increased with respect of graduates in science and engineering stream ranked eighth overall this year.

- India's ranking in the business sophistication pillar is impacted by substantial improvement in knowledge workers up 46 spots and knowledge absorption up 33 spots

- India also improved in ranking of firms offering formal training by as much as 56 spots to reach rank 42.

- India improved access across all indicators within the knowledge absorption pillar and metamorphosed it into a solid ranking in the Global Innovation Index's newly incorporated research talent in business enterprise where it is ranked 31st.

- India ranked 117th in business environment and 118th in education , indicating it can improve the ease of starting business and pupil teacher ratio.

25. FRBM disclosure statements should be transparent and complete, according to the Comptroller and Auditor General. Centre should take steps to ensure that FRBM disclosure statements are transparent and complete with respect to all aspects.

- In its first report relating to review of the Fiscal Responsibility and Management Act, CAG said the government should carry out suitable amendments to the Act as well as Rules to address inconsistency.

- Government will strengthen the process of making underlying assumptions for projection of receipt and expenditure in various fiscal policy statements to insulate them from frequently changing and integrating the projections in the disclosure statements tabled for the Parliament in 2014-2015.

- Report said a refund of INR 1.17 lakh crore (including interest on refund of taxes) was made from gross direct tax collection in 2014-2015 but was not disclosed in government accounts.

- CAG also regretted that 12th Finance Commission recommendations pertaining to inclusion of 8 additional statements in the Union government accounts for more transparency were not implemented despite in-principle acceptance.

26. RBI eased priority sector norms to boost cash flow to MSMEs including factoring transactions under priority sector lending with the aim to increase cash flow to small and medium sized enterprises.

- For increasing liquidity support for the MSME sector, the decision has been taken to factor transactions with on recourse basis eligible for priority sector classification by banks which are carrying out the business of factoring on a departmental basis.

- Factoring refers to a kind of financial transaction and debtor finance in which the business sells its invoices to a third party referred to as factor, at a discount.

- Companies often factor receivable assets to meet immediate cash requirements.

- Factoring transactions occurring through TReDS shall also be eligible for classification under priority sector lending upon operationalisation of the platform.

- TReDS is an exchange based trading platform to facilitate financing bills by small entities to corporate and other buyers including the government department and PSUs.

27. There will be no separate railway budget from the next financial year, putting an end to a practice that began in 1924, with the finance ministry acquiescing to the proposal to merge the transporter's annual exercise with the general budget.

- Finance ministry has constituted a 5 member committee of officers to work out the modalities for the exercise which will end the annual budget speech being followed by the rail budget.

- Move to discard the British era practice of a separate rail budget by the Modi government was after a 2 member committee comprising Niti Aayog member Bibek Debroy and Kishore Desai recommended the exercise to be scrapped.

- Finance minister Arun Jaitley has been asked to merge the rail budget with the general budget in the long term interest of the national transporter as well as the economy of the nation.

- Once the rail budget is merged with the general budget, Indian Railways will be like any other government department receiving budgetary support under the supervision of the finance minister.

- Once the overall funds are allocated, railways will then segregate them for various reasons with sources suggesting that the model will be akin to the one of the postal department.

28. Parliamentary panel has asked the government to evolve mechanisms for e-waste management rules to be implemented

- Referring to the CPCB estimate that India generated 16.4 lakh MT of e-waste in 2014, the committee noted that merely notifying rules is not enough without strong and effective implementation

- Committee of Subordinate Legislation chaired by Dilipkumar Mansukhlal Gandhi tabled its 15th report on e-waste management in the LS

- Committee expressed serious concern over handling of environmentally sensitive issue of e-waste management

- As per the provisions of the E-waste (management and handling) Rules 2016 the environment ministry amended the rules by notifying e-waste management rules 2016 in March.

- Committee has notified that there has been an exponential increase in the generation of e-waste across the world including India

- According to CPCB estimates, 1,46,800 MT of e-waste was generated in India in 2005; it rose to 8,00,000 MT in 2012 and 16.4 lakh MT by 2014

29. Cabinet gave approval for the signing and ratification of an agreement between India and Croatia on economic cooperation

- An earlier agreement had been signed in 1994 to develop bilateral trade and economic relations.

- Average bilateral trade growth was 17.44 percent during the past three years and stood at USD 205.04 million in 2014-2015.

30. Cabinet provided ex-post facto approval for the amendment of Sections 64, 65 and 115 of the Factories Act 1948 via the Factories (Amendment) Bill, 2016 in Parliament.

- Amendments relate to increase in over time hours from 50 hours per quarter to 100 hours (Section 64) and 75 hours per quarter to 125 hours (Section 65).

31. Cabinet Committee on Economic Affairs approved the one time grant of INR 900 crores over three years for R&D projects for the development of Advanced Ultra Super Critical Technology for thermal power plants

- Estimated cost of the project is INR 1554 crore.

- INR 900 crore will be provided as plan gross budgetary support to BHEL for implementation of the research and development project.

- Project was proposed by a consortium of three government entities: BHEL, NTPC and IGCAR.

32. Cabinet has approved a proposal to amend rules for foreign investment in non banking finance companies

- Amendments in existing FEMA regulations on NBFCs will enable flow of foreign investment in other financial services on automatic route provided such services are regulated by financial sector authorities like SEBI, RBI and PFRDA

- Foreign investment in other financial services that are not under regulators or government agency can be made by the approval route.

- Minimum capitalisation norms under FDI policy have been eliminated as most regulators have fixed maximum capitalisation norms.

- Present regulations on NBFCS holds that FDI will be permitted only for 18 specified NBFC activities.

33. A bill to provide tax incentives to the garment sector and enable the government to raise customs duty on marble and granite from 10 to 40 percent was approved by the LS after FM Arun Jaitley said these measures would help in creating jobs and protecting the domestic industry from import surge

- The Bill also seeks to expand the definition of demerger with a view to facilitate splitting or modification of PSY companies.

- Changes in income tax act will give effect to conditions attached to transfer of shares by the government.

34. A Parliamentary committee suggested the removal of 2.5 percent duty on import of coking coal and scrapping of clean energy cess of INR 400 a tonne as measures stand in the way of competitiveness of domestic steel firms

- Standing Committee on Coal and Steel chaired by Rakesh Singh pointed that expenditure by Indian steel companies on research and development remained 0.05-0.5 percent of their sales turnover lower than 1-2 percent by those in China, South Korea and Japan.

- Committee also found at rate of per KWH in power in India, domestic steel producers are at a disadvantage of INR 800-900 per tonne as compared to steel producers in China, Japan and South Korea.

- Certain levies and duties in the form of District Mineral Fund, National Mineral Expansion Trust, import on raw material such as coking coal and levy on clean energy cess are imposed on Indian steel producers.

- Investments in R&D, works of companies like SAIL and TATA Steel were lauded. Committee recommended that Indian steel companies should benchmark R&D spending with internationally prevalent best practices in the sector.

35. TRAI's new portal has provided information on call drops, network coverage and call quality of telecom operators across India

- This is a transparency portal where consumers will get information on all parameters of Quality of Service or QoS

- The information is available on the URL http://analytics.trai.gov.in.

- Consumers in a particular location can see the number of towers across the area, the call drop rate and the performance of ISPs on different parameters in the area

- This will bring about transparency in the network performance.

- Portal also provides information on network performance.

- It provides information on network utilisation trends, BTS density and call drop trends.

- Data is being received digitally and electronically from service providers so there is less delay.

- It is now being put up in visual form on the portal to provide a clear idea on quality of service parameters for service providers.

36. Government has allowed employees working in IT and ITeS special economic zones/SEZ to work from home or a place outside the zone provided that they meet certain conditions and demands of the industry

- Government has extended this flexibility subject to conditions such that the person would be a regular SEZ employee and authorised by the unit to undertake work pertaining to it

- Work performed by the home based employee should be as per services approved by the SEZ unit and the work is related to a project of the unit

- This comes in wake of reports that exports from IT and ITeS SEZ clocked marginal growth of 0.77% to INR 4.76 lakh crore in 2015-2016

- Government is looking to revive investor interest in such export hubs

- SEZ units should provide laptop/desktop and secured connectivity to establish a connection between employee and work related to the project of the SEZ unit

37. Government noted that 17 lakh tonnes of e-waste was generated in 2014 and it notified rules in March in 2016 regarding better management of this waste

- A survey by Central Pollution Control Board in 2005 found the generation of e-waste in the country was assessed at 1.46 lakh tonnes and estimated to exceed 8 lakh tonne by 2012.

- As per the UN University report, 17 lakh tonnes of e-waste was generated in 2014.

- Currently, there are 151 registered e-waste dismantlers and recyclers in the private sector in 13 states having the combined capacity of 4.46 lakh metric tonne per annum.

- Power Ministry has also comprehensively reviewed the e-waste (Management & Handling) Rules 2011 and notified e-waste (management) rules in March 2016.

38. According to the Power Ministry, 55 percent of total rural households and 92.67 percent of urban households use electricity as a main source of lighting as per census 2011

- Power Minister Piyush Goyal also said the government aims to install feeder metres in every feeder to provide accurate figures pertaining to the demand and supply of electricity.

- Based on 2011 census, 16,78,26,730 total households were using electricity of which 9,28,08,038 were in the rural areas and 7,88,65,937 were in urban areas.

- Government aims to provide 24/7 electricity by 2022.

39. Gujarat Industries Power Company has entered into a PPA with Solar Energy Corporation of India for solar power projects in Gujarat

- Last month, GIPCL said it has received letters of intent (LoIs) from Solar Energy Corporation of India (SECI) for execution of a solar power project in Gujarat.

- GIPCL had emerged as a successful bidder in the e-reverse auction for 40 MW solar power project in Gujarat Solar Park.

40. To prevent illegal and unauthorised pooling of funds by firms, RBI launched a website called sanchet.rbi.org.in which alerts people regarding entities allowed to collect deposits.

- Portal will facilitate filing, tracking of complaints besides providing information about whether any particular entity is permitted to accept deposits and registered with the regulatory authority for the same.

- Sachet means the Hindi word for later and will help regulators to assist members of the public.

41. Leading stock exchange BSE on 3rd August 2016 signed an agreement with Indian Institute of Technology Kanpur for collaboration in areas including cyber security.

- Leading stock exchange BSE will be assisted in testing vulnerabilities in IT system and network and help form guidelines and audit security operations.

- Key highlights of the MoU include cooperation for cyber security research in financial marks developing an environment to deal with cyber security challenges and tools to strengthen cyber security and advise BSE in cyber related issues.

42. GoI has imposed a penalty of INR 2313 crore on telecom operators for violation of subscriber verification norms till May 31, telecom Minister Manoj Sinha has informed the Parliament.

- For non compliant CAFs, TERM cells have taken actions which include imposition of penalty on non compliant CAFs and filing of FIRs against allegedly forged cases as per guidelines issued from time to time.

- As per data state run BSNL tops the chart with INR 583.09 crore followed by Reliance Communications (INR 377.51 crore), Tata Teleservices (INR 328.15 crore), Airtel (INR 300.34 crore).

- Other top companies caught in the net include Vodafone, Idea Cellular, Aircel and MTS.

43. An Indian government body has suggested the provisional anti-dumping duty on imports of hot rolled steel products to reduce overseas purchase of alloy and shield local mills.

- Directorate General of Anti Dumping recommended the duties on steel products from China, Japan, South Korea, Russia, Brazil and Indonesia.

- Indian steelmakers such as SAIL, TATA Steel and JSW Steel have lobbied for protectionist measures to block cheap overseas purchases undercutting local mills and squeezing margins.

44. India's trade deficit with China jumped to USD 53 billion in 2015-2016 from USD 48.48 billion in the previous fiscal.

- Increasing trade deficit with China will be attributed to the relative demands for imports in India and China for each other's goods.

- Efforts are on to increase overall exports by diversifying trade basket with emphasis on manufactured goods, services, resolution of market access issues and other non tariff barriers.

- Major imports from China include telecom instruments, computer hardware and peripheral, fertiliser, electronic component, project goods, chemical and drug intermediaries.

- Exports to China include ore, slag, ash, iron and steel, tin, raw hides, leather, plastics and cotton.

- Bilateral trade between the countries stood at USD 70.73 billion in 2015-2016, from USD 72.34 billion in the earlier fiscal.

45. While releasing on tap universal banking license and excluding large industrial houses as eligible entities from the purview, RBI said investment in banks up to 10 percent is permitted.

- According to Guidelines for on tao Licensing of Universal Banks in the private sector, the initial minimum paid up voting equity capital for a bank should be INR 500 crore and thereafter, the bank should have minimum net worth of INR 500 crore at all times.

- Individuals and professionals that are residents at senior level and existing non banking financial companies that are controlled by residents and have a successful track record for atlas 10 years in banking and finance at senior level and NBFCs controlled by residents with a good track record of 10 years can apply for the license.

- Entities/groups in the private sector owned and controlled by entities and a successful track record for 10 years with total assets of INR 5000 crore or more such that non financial business of the group does not account for more than 40 percent or so in terms of total assets/gross income are also eligible promoters.

- Applicants have to meet the Fit and Proper criteria.

- Promoter/promoting entity/promoter group should have good track record of sound financial, credentials, integrity an at least 10 years of successful track record; foreign shareholding in the bank will be as per existing FDI.

- Currently, the aggregate foreign investment limit is 74 percent and the licensing window will b open on tap and applications could be submitted to RBI at any time.

- Applications will be referred to Standing External Advisory Committee to be set up by RBI is 10 months from the date when in principle approval was granted and lapse automatically.

46. Two textile parks have been approved for Uttarakhand and the state government has to now decide where they will be set up.

- In these parks, the weavers will be provided hi-tech infrastructure facilities, modern technology raw materials and training.

- The parks aim to improve the condition of weavers in remote areas and hilly areas along the Sino Indian border.

- This park will also help skilled youth get new work opportunities.

47. An inter-ministerial panel mandated to recommend a roadmap to double farmer's income by 2020 is set to be released in September. Highlighting measures to boost farm output and farmers income, more funds have been allocated under numerous schemes such as PMKSY and hence there are no provisions for a separate and distinct agriculture budget.

- As regards e-NAM or electronic national agriculture market, 23 mandis in 8 states have been integrated and

a total 200 mandis will be brought to online platform by September.

- By 2020, the move is to double farmer's income. An inter-ministerial committee was set up in April to study and recommend the doubling of income for farmers.

- Broad mandate of the panel is to examine the current income level of farmers/agri labourers and measure the historical rate of the growth of current income level as well as assess the required growth rate to double the income of farmers.

- The panel will recommend various strategies to be adopted to attain the target and also suggest an institutional mechanism to review and monitor the implementation of the realised goal.

- Committee is a dynamic one and will be making recommendations from 2016 Kharif itself.

- Ministry has held that to double farmers income from 2016-2017 to 2021-2022 in real terms, the desired compound annual growth rate will be much higher than attained so far

- Government is also aiming to reorient the agricultural sector by shifting from pure production based to income based considerations for farmers.

48. FDI in India grew by 7 percent to USD 10.55 billion during Q1 of 2016-2017. Foreign investment inflows were at USD 9.88 billion in January-March 2015 according to Department of Industrial Policy and Promotion.

- Sectors which attracted maximum FDI during this period included computer hardware and software, services, telecommunications, power, pharmaceuticals and trading business.

- In terms of nations, India received the maximum overseas inflows from the US, Singapore, Japan, Mauritius and the Netherlands.

- Further liberalisation of the foreign investment policies for services sector in the budget means more inflows will come.

- Government has recently relaxed FDI norms in 8 sectors namely defence, civil aviation, food processing, private security agencies and pharmaceuticals.

- Foreign investment is critical for India which needs USD 1 trillion for overhauling infrastructure such as ports, airports and highways for boosting growth.

- Strong inflow of foreign investments will help improve the country's BOP situation and strengthen the rupee value against other global currencies including the US dollar.

49. SBI has engaged Indian Oil Corporation's Kisan Seva Kendras as banking correspondents to extend banking facilities to farmers across the nation.

- SBI signed an MoU with IOC as part of the financial inclusion programme lending further services to the farming community.

- Indian Oil Corporation has set up 6,500 Kisan Seva Kendras in rural and remote areas providing access to numerous agricultural inputs like seeds, fertilisers and pesticides to farmers.

- Tie up will enable farmers to avail various products and services by SBI customer service points such as saving account, recurring deposit and more.

- IOC with net profit of INR 103.99 billion for 2015-2016 is India's largest commercial enterprise.

50. Around 241 infrastructure projects including those delayed due to land acquisition, forest clearances and other reasons led to cost overrun of INR 1.59 lakh crore according to official data.

- Statistics Ministry monitored around 1076 infrastructure projects an addition INR 150 crore or more across sectors like roads, railways and power in May 2016.

- Out of 1076 projects, 4 are ahead of schedule, 252 are on schedule, 330 are delayed and 241 projects reported cost overrun while 70 projects reported time and cost overrun.

51. Government of India has raised FDI limit in pharmaceutical companies to attract and retain latest technologies, capital and follow international best practices.

- FDI cap in brownfield pharma was recently raised to 74 percent under the automatic route from 49 percent earlier.

- Beyond 74 percent, foreign investment is permitted under the approval route for attracting capital and technological advancement.

- Government has also put in place necessary safeguards by providing non-compete clause will not be permitted.

- Indian promoters will operate in the same line of business in new ventures.

- Close to 3088 Industrial Entrepreneurs Memorandum were signed between January 2015 and July 2016 envisaging an investment of INR 4.8 lakh crore.

- Close to 427 IEMs were signed in the electrical equipment sector followed by textiles and food processing.

- Maximum IEMs were inked in Maharashtra followed by Gujarat, Karnataka and Telangana.

52. Government of India has notified revised pay grades for implementation of the recommendations of the 7th Pay Commission.

- This provided nearly 10 lakh employees with 2.57 times hike in basic pay.

- Minimum pay in central government effective from January 1, 2016 will be INR 18,000 per month and at the highest level, it will be 2.5 lakhs.

- Existing pay (Pay in Pay Band plus Grade Pay) in the pre-revised structure on December 31, 2015 shall be multiplied by a factor of 2.57.

- Two dates should be there for the grant of increment namely January and July 1 each year, instead of July 1 only.

- Employees will be entitled to only one annual increment on either of these two dates depending upon the date of appointment, promotion or grant of financial upgradation.

- Cabinet has also provided a pay increase for central government employees and pensioners which is estimated to cost the exchequer INR 1.02 lakh crore each year.

53. Overall power deficit during the April-June quarter this fiscal was 0.9 percent while peak deficit was 2 percent.

- Central Electricity Authority said the demand-supply gap of electricity had been brought to the lowest ever since 2.1 percent during 2015-2016.

- It has further reduced to 0.9 percent during April-June 2016-2017.

- As against an overall demand of 295.34 billion units in April-June, 292.82 billion units were supplied, a deficit of 0.9 percent.

- Close to 149.97 billion units were supplied against the peak demand of 152.97 billion units.

- This recorded a deficit of 2 percent in the time under review.

54. India has received USD 5.34 billion FDI in the current two months of the present financial year

- During April-May, country attracted USD 4.76 billion FDI under automatic route.

- Around USD 582 million came through the approval route.

- The aim is to ensure that India is one of the most attractive and investment friendly investment destinations in the world.

- Government has relaxed FDI policy in sectors such as pharma, defence, food retailing and broadcast.

- During the two months, defence received no FDI and pharma attracted USD 452.86 million foreign inflows.

- The other sectors include air transport, information and broadcasting and retail trading.

- In Q1 April-June of 2016-2017, FPI investors pumped in INR 10,4561 crore.

- For attracting the international investor, numerous reforms were taken in the FDI and FPI policy.

55. RBI has received a proposal from the Commerce and Industry Ministry to use part of the forex reserves to provide long term loans at low interest rates to the Export Import Bank of India

- A portion of the forex reserves have been asked to be set aside for project export finance for the EXIM Bank.

- RBI offered the un-utilised amount under its limit of USD 5 billion to the India Infrastructure Finance Company as a long term loan to EXIM Bank.

- IIFCL indicated RBI committed the entire quantum of USD 5 billion to borrowers and there would not be any residual or un-utilised amount offered to EXIM bank.

- EXIM Bank has been able to command competitive pricing in its foreign currency debt issues.

- Amount of INR 1300 crore was released to the EXIM Bank by the government as capital in 2015-2016.

56. Special Investigation Team on black money has recommended a ban on cash transactions of more than INR 3 lakh and restricting cash holding with individuals to not more than INR 15 lakh to curb illegal wealth in the economy.

- SIT headed by Justice MB Shah submitted its 5th report to the SC on methods for curbing black money in the economy.

- SIT recommended a total ban on cash transactions above INR 3 lakhs and an Act to be framed to declare such transactions as illegal/punishable by law.

57. A report released by CRISIL shows that for the past 5 years, 69 percent of India's population residing in its rural areas has experienced a higher degree of inflation as against urban counterparts.

- Report indicates in the past 24 months to June 2016, while urban inflation fell from 9 percent to 5.3 percent (compared with the two years prior)rural inflation fell from 10.1 percent to 6.2 percent.

- Gap has remained around 100 basis points in the recent past and is in the recent past and is caused by higher core and fuel inflation in rural areas.

- In fiscal 2016, rural core inflation was 6.7 percent as against 4.8 percent in urban.

- Sub-categories such as health, education, household goods and services as well as recreation and amusement recorded higher inflation in hinterland in the previous fiscal.

- NSSO household consumption expenditure data for 2011-2012 offers data in support of this.

- Schemes to improve access to infrastructure such as Pradhan Mantri Gram Sadak Yojana have yet to near completion.

58. Wholesale Price Index rose to 20 month high of 1.6 percent in June from 0.8 percent in May will work well for toll road projects revenues for the fiscal 2017-2018, according to ICRA.

- The toll rates are expected to increase in the range of 3.0-3.7 percent during FY2018, marking the highest growth after FY2015.

- Average increase in WPI for 2017 is around 3 percent and a report also indicated that toll fees are revised annually to adjust for inflation as determined by movements in WPI.

- The report also indicated that toll fees are annually revised to adjust for inflation as determined by WPI movements.

- Projects for which toll rates are linked fully with WPI, the toll rates are revised downwards whereas for other

projects, increase has been 2.7 percent in FY2016 and 1.9 in FY2017.

- Traffic growth has been robust during FY2016 which is likely to continue during the current fiscal.

- According to the report, in a low inflation scenario. when there is no commensurate fall in interest rates, profitability of toll road projects is negatively impacted.

59. Government of India has released INR 100 crore towards co-contribution for Atal Pension Yojana for 2015-2016.

- As per the scheme, those who have registered before March 31, 2016 will get co-contribution from the government which will be 50 percent of the subscriber contribution up to a total of INR 1000.

- Co-contribution will be for 5 years from 2015-2016 to 2019-2020.

- Government of India through PFRDA has released co-contribution for 2015-2016 for 16.96 lakh eligible APY subscribers amounting to INR 99.57 crore.

- Subscribers lacking pending contribution in accounts till March 2016 won't be paid with co-contribution

- Government is implementing Atal Pension Yojana through banks and Department of Post.

- Total number of subscribers registered under this yojana has crossed 30 lakh as on June 30,2016.

60. Pension Fund Regulatory and Development Authority introduced new features for the benefits of National Pension System subscribers including a mobile app "NPS by NSDL e-Gov."

- Subscribers can raise a request for transaction statement for a particular financial year.

- Subscribers can also view their NPS account as well as latest details of scheme wise units along with the latest NAV and total value of the schemes, details of the five contributions credited and change contact details or modify password and set security question through Mobile App.

- Subscribers can now update or modify their address on their own using Aadhaar based authentication.

61. An agreement was signed between Indian Railway Stations Development Corporation Limited and Bansal Group for the redevelopment and modernisation of Habibganj Railway Station located in Bhopal, M.P.

- The Habibganj station would now be the first station to be redevelopment and this station is one of the eight such railway stations which have been allocated to IRSDC by the Ministry of Railways.

- IRSDC has been entrusted with the task of railway development.

62. Cabinet Committee on Economic Affairs approves the proposal of the Department of Telecommunications regarding the transfer of shares by ITI Limited to the Special National Investment Fund to meet SEBI's minimum public shareholding requirement.

- ITI Limited will be allowed to meet SEBI's requirements of minimum 25 percent public shareholding by August 2017.

- Cabinet also approved the revised cost estimate of INR 7290.62 crore for the ongoing Puntsangchhu-II Hydroelectric Project in Bhutan.

- Total escalation of the project at this stage is INR 3512.82 crore as per the government.

63. Government expects to earn INR 56,000 crore through the sale of its stake in PSUs this financial year. This will result in estimated receipts of INR 1706 crore to the government.

- Actual realisation amount will be based on market conditions and investor interest prevailing at the time of actual disinvestment.

- To create a belongingness among employees of NBCC, the decision has been made to allot additional shares to eligible and willing employees at discount of 5 percent to the issue/discovered (lowest cut off) price of the offer for sale.

- Government expects to earn INR 56,000 crore through the sale of its stake in PSUs this financial year.

- Around INR 36,000 crore of this comes from minority stake sales and the remaining INR 20,000 crore from strategic stake sales.

64. General Anti Avoidance Rules/GAAR should not apply to foreign portfolio investor on redemption and maturity of participatory notes, according to industry body ASSOCHAM.

- The chamber said it was common for investors to gain economic exposure to Indian securities through P-notes

- ASSOCHAM holds that existence of a P-Note arrangement or status of underlying Indian position referencing P-notes or passing economic benefits or status of underlying Indian position referencing P-notes or passing of economic benefits to P-note holders should not be the criteria for evaluation commercial substance at the FPI level.

- The body also said GAAR provisions should not apply to FPI on redemption or maturity of P-notes.

65. Fertiliser industry's overall volume rose 7 percent to 58.2 million tonnes in 2015-2016 despite back to back droughts in the previous two years, according to rating agency ICRA

- Overall volume for fertiliser industry during 2014-2015 stood at 54.1 MT

- ICRA fertiliser industry report "Fertiliser Volumes, Price Trends and Green Vision" made this announcement.

- Volume growth during FY16 has been driven by low opening inventory levels compared with the previous years and low base effect was supported by moderate growth in the domestic production of urea and higher import for non urea fertilisers.

- Higher volume growth has led to rising systemic inventory levels on March 2016

- Domestic production of urea witnessed 8 percent growth during FY2016 driven by positive change initiatives at policy level by the government.

- This includes the New Urea Policy 2015 and the Gas Pooling Policy.

66. Index of Industrial Production for May rose on an upside coming at 1.2 percent against a decline of -0.8 percent in April.

- This has been the best figure since February 2016.

- Four of the previous six months have seen a contraction.

- Contraction declined to 2.2 percent for the month in question.

- Consumer Price Index for June was flat at 5.77 percent as against 5.76 percent in May.

- Food inflation rose to 7.79 percent in the previous month.

67. An MoU was signed between SIDBI and YES Bank under the partial risk sharing facility for financial energy efficient projects.

- SIBDI will guarantee 75 percent of the loans up to INR 15 crore extending to energy efficiency projects.

- SIDBI is the project execution agency while the bank is the first Indian lender to be empaneled in the program.

68. Software-as-a-Service market in India is expected to grow by as much as three times to USD 1 billion by 2020, as per NASSCOM research.

- Demand will be driven by businesses aiming to zero in on core operations.

- Market for SaaS was pegged at USD 300 million in 2014-2015 as against USD 407 million in 2015-2016.

- SaaS is a pay-as-you-go software distribution model.

- Research points that there are differences in over 150 firms offering solutions in SaaS segment with start ups powering the segment.

- Close to 40-45 percent of the companies within the segment are startups.

- Investors are showing keen interest in the number of startups.

- India SaaS based products have received close to USD 450 million in the first two quarters of the previous year.

- Close to 170 million was invested in such start-ups in 2014 across 22 deals.

- Number of such deals have grown by 2 times to 22 in 2014 from 11 in 2011.

- With 60 percent of the funding, in post 2012, more startups are being able to access funding in the past 5 years.

- The US and EU account for more than 80 percent of the demand for Indian SaaS Solutions as per the report.

- Internationally, the SaaS market was pegged at USD 31 billion in 2015; it is expected to grow at 18 percent annually to USD 72 billion by 2020.

- Players like SAP, Oracle, IBM and Microsoft have cornered close to 50 percent of the global SaaS market.

69. Indian sugar production could fall by 7 percent to 23.26 MT in the next marketing year commencing in October with a decrease in sugar output on account of rainfall deficit in Maharashtra and Karnataka.

- Sugar output is estimated to fall for the second straight year in 2016-2017 marketing year on account of drought in major sugar producing states.

- Sugar production in India, the world's second largest sugar producer after Brazil is estimated as having fallen to 25.1 MT in 2015-2016 marketing year ending September from 28.3 MT in the previous year.

- ISMA has released the preliminary estimate indicating sugar output was pegged at 23.26 million tonnes in 2016-2017.

- This is around 1.8 to 1.9 MT less than current production of 25.1 MT.

- This is in concordance with the government's estimate of 23-23.5 MT for the next year- ISMA attributed the likely fall in sugar output to a decline of 5.5 percent in sugarcane acreage to 4.99 million ha in 2016-2017 as against 5.28 million ha in the previous year

- This results in lower sugar cane output.

- ISMA data indicates sugar production in Maharashtra- the biggest producer in India- is estimated to decline to around 6.15 MT in 2016-2017 from 8.40 MT in the present year.

- The area under cane cultivation in 2016-2017 fell due to a drought like situation whereby there was poor rainfall and lesser water availability for irrigation.

- Cane area in the state is currently 7,80K ha as against 1.05 million ha in 2015-2016.

- UP is the second largest sugar producing state. Here the production is estimated to rise to 7.54 MT in 2016-2017 marketing year from 6.82 MT in the present year.

70. RBI on July 7, 2016 has notified the interest rate for different small savings scheme for the quarter closing September.

- Interest rates have been retained as they were for the previous April-June quarter

- Internet rates for small savings schemes like Kisan Vikas Patra and Public Provident Fund Scheme are notified on a quarterly basis.

- Interest rate on savings deposit is 4 percent while for the 5 year recurring deposit and 5 year senior citizen's scheme is 7.4 percent and 8.6 percent respectively.

- Public Provident Fund Scheme earns interest rate of 8.1 percent and Kisan Vikas Patra of 7.8 percent.

- 110 months maturity period is stipulated for these schemes.

- Interest rate on Sukanya Samriddhi Account Scheme is 8.6 percent and in another notification, there has been a review of reporting requirements with an aim to reduce the burden of compliance. Banks have been told to discontinue submission of such reports with immediate effect.

71. Rajasthan has become the first state in the country to introduce minimum wages for part time workers

- Labour department has issued a notification and now part time workers come under the Minimum Wages Act 1948

- State government has also increased minimum wages in all categories of scheduled employment by INR 104 per month.

- Rajasthan is called the Land of the Kings; it has several colour coordinated cities like Jaipur (Pink City) and Udaipur (White City).

72. Regulatory authority FSSAI has partnered ASCI to check misleading ads in the food and beverages sector.

- ASCI will monitor ads across numerous media and the council has been provided suo moto monitoring mandate by FSSAI to process complaints against misleading food and beverages ads.

- Agreement also requires ASCI to report FSSAI's non compliance of ASCI's decisions for further action as per the FSSAI act.

- The MoU was signed between FSSAI CEO Pawan Agarwal and ASCI chairman Benoy Roychoudhury.

- FSSAI is an agency of the Ministry of Health and Family Welfare, GoI.

73. Aided by the special package and marketing plans, India's textiles and apparel exports are expected to touch USD 50 billion mark this fiscal from USD 38 billion in FY2016

- Union Cabinet approved INR 6000 crore package for the sector aiming to create one crore new jobs in 3 years and attract investments of USD 11 billion while eyeing USD 30 billion in exports

- Key markets like EU and US are expected to grow and new markets such as Iran, Russia and S. America will also be explored

- Country is ready to capitalise on falling share of China in textile exports in the global market and the nation's market share has fallen to 38 percent from 40 percent on account of high wage rate and entry into high tech end products.

- Cotton Textile Export Promotion Council also released an Ernst and Young report titled "Textile Industry as a Vehicle of Job Creation for Inclusive Growth."

- It is also important to finalise FTAs with EU, Australia and Canada in addition to negotiating concessional tariff with China to protect domestic suppliers.

- Labour intensive home textiles segment suffered on account of tariff disadvantage of 9.6 to 16 percent in markets like EU and Canada

74. India has jumped 19 places in the latest World Bank ranking in the global logistics performance, reflecting the improvement in movement of goods inside the country thus facilitating better trade.

- The World Bank in its latest once-in-two-year Logistics Performance Index (LPI) said India is now ranked 35th as against the 54th spot it occupied in the previous 2014 report.

- In the 2014 report, India had a LPI score of 3.08, which increased to 3.42 in 2016. For the third time, Germany with 4.23 points tops the ranking, followed by Luxembourg (4.22), Sweden (4.20), Netherlands (4.19) and Singapore(4.14).

- Other countries in top 10 are Belgium, Austria, United Kingdom, Hong Kong and the United States.Japan is ranked 11. C

- China has jumped one spot to be ranked 27th while Pakistan is at 68th. Syria ranked lowest.

- According to the report, over the past six years, the world's top-10 performers have remained consistent and include dominant players in the supply chain industry.

75. World Bank's Board of Executive Directors on 24th June 2016 approved USD 201.50 million for Technical Education Quality Improvement Project III in India to improve the quality of engineering education in certain Indian states

- Objective of the project is enhancing quality and equity in participating engineering education institutes and enhancing the efficiency of the engineering education system in focus states.

- Maturity period for the project of 25 years was extended with an additional 5 years grace period.

- There are two components of the projects - improving quality and equity in engineering institutes in focus states.

76. The National Mineral Exploration Policy has been given Cabinet approval for the auction of 100 prospective mineral blocks and boost the country's mining potential. Cabinet cleared NMEP so that the government can auction 100 blocks that have been identified by the Geological Survey of India for exploration. Mines Ministry has notified the National Mineral Exploration Trust

- Via the NMEP, government wants to attract private sector in exploration besides involving state operated GSI, MECL and other key agencies.

- States will also play a greater role by referring exploration projects which can be taken up through NMET.

- From India's entire Obvious Geological Potential area, identified by GSI currently 10 percent has been explored and mining is undertaken in 1.5-2 percent of the area.

77. Cotton area in Punjab and Haryana has declined 27 percent to 7.56 ha in the 2016-2017 as farmers shifted to other crops after incurring huge losses due to whitefly pest attack earlier this year. Two states planted cotton in 10.3 lakh ha in the 2015-2016 crop year (July-June)

- Sowing of cotton in Punjab and Haryana has been completed and total area is down as farmers were scared to grow cotton due to whitefly pest attack that has damaged the crop massively in these two states in the previous year.

- Farmers have shifted to pulses, paddy and other crops in the states.

- As per the latest data, area planted to cotton in Punjab was lower by 43.11 percent at 2.56 lakh ha in 2016-2017 crop year from 4.5 lakh ha in the earlier year.

- Cotton area coverage in neighbouring Haryana fell 14 percent to 5 lakh ha this year as against 5.8 lakh ha in 2015-2016.

- More than 90 percent of farmers have sown Bt cotton seeds which is the maximum retail price of which is being fixed by the central government from this year onwards.

78. SBI is the only Indian entity in the list. It includes global giants like Barclays, JP Morgan, Credit Suisse and BoA.

- Report looks at investments into companies involved in production of cluster munitions

- 158 financial institutions invested over 28 billion US dollars in the seven companies researched in the report between June 2012 and April 2016.

- These 7 companies are China Aerospace Science and Industry, China Aerospace Science and Technology, Hanwha (South Korea), Norinco (China), Orbital ATK (US), Poongsan (South Korea) and Textron (US).

- Maximum number of banks are from the US.

79. India has retained the ranking as the tenth highest recipient of FDI in 2015 receiving USD 44 billion in investment that year compared to US $35 billion in 2014, as per the UN

- World Investment Report 2016 released by UNCTAD found India also jumped a place in terms of attractiveness as a business destination in 2015 to sixth place with 14 percent of respondents naming it as destination of their choice.

80. Changes introduced in the policy include increase in sectoral caps, bringing more activities under automatic route and easing of conditionality for foreign investment. These amendments seek to further simplify the regulations governing FDI in India.

- To permit 100 percent FDI under government approval route for trading in respect of food products manufactured in India.

- FDI beyond 49% has been permitted through government approval route, in cases resulting in access to modern technology. FDI limit for defence sector has also been made applicable to Manufacturing of Small Arms and Ammunitions covered under Arms Act

- 100 percent FDI allowed under automatic route for Teleports, Direct to Home, Cable Networks and Mobile TV.

- Moreover, infusion of FDI beyond 49% in a company not seeking permission from Ministry will result in change in the ownership pattern.

- To permit 100% FDI under automatic route in Brownfield Airport projects. In Scheduled Air Transport

Service and regional Air Transport Service, it has now been decided to raise FDI limit to 100%. For NRIs, 100% FDI will continue to be allowed under automatic route.

- FDI up to 49% is now permitted under automatic route in this sector and FDI beyond 49% and up to 74% would be permitted with government approval route.

81. FDI in brownfield pharma under automatic route was up to 74 percent. Government on June 20 allowed up to 74 percent FDI in existing pharmaceutical companies via automatic route with the aim to promote the sector.

- Earlier 100 percent FDI was permitted through the government approval route.

- It has been decided to permit up to 74 percent FDI in automatic route for brownfield pharma and the government approval route beyond 74 percent will continue.

- 100 percent FDI under automatic route in greenfield pharma is permitted while. approval route for 100 percent FDI in brownfield pharma is under the approval route.

- FDI in brownfield projects has been an issue impacting accessibility and growth of the generic industry in the nation.

- Market size of India's pharma company is USD 20 billion. Acquisitions in this field include Daiichi Sankyo's purchase of Ranbaxy, Abbot Lab's acquisition of Piramal Health Care domestic business. Mylan purchased Matrix Lab while Dabur Pharma was acquired by Fresenius and Sanofi Aventis recently purchased Shanta Biotech.

82. SBI on 16th June 2016 floated a 200 crore rupee fund for startups in the fintech space. Fund will consider assistance of INR 3 crore rupees to a firm registered for promoting business innovation using technology in financial services

- Traditional banks around the world are working with fintech firms to promote business innovations using technology in financial services.

- Suitable regulatory framework will also be set up to address the associated risks like cyber security risk, data theft risk and technology risk.

83. Ind-Ra lowered FY2017 CAD estimate to 1.3-1.5 percent from 1.2 percent due to lower remittances and software earnings in forth quarter for current fiscal. India's CAD narrowed sharply to USD 0.3 billion/o/1 percent of GDP in Q4, FY2016 from USD 7.1 billion or 1.3 percent in Q3 on account of lower trade gap.

- For the 2015-2016 fiscal, CAD or the difference in the in and outflow of foreign exchange fell to 1.1 percent of the GDP.

- Low CAD indicates stability on the external front. On the one hand, low crude prices and collapse in global prices of commodities have resulted in lower trade deficit.

- Low oil prices have caused Middle East economies to suffer as well.

- Remittances on private transfers fell to USD 63.1 billion in 2015-2016.

84. Global data consultancy firm Gartner indicated Indian government will observe 3.1 percent uptick in the IT spend at USD 7 billion for 2016

- Government will spend USD 7 billion on IT products and services in 2016

- This includes spending on internal services, software, IT services, devices data centre and telecom services at all levels of the government

- IT services include consulting, software support, BPO, IT outsourcing, implementation and hardware support are set to grow at 8.8 percent in 2016 to USD 1.16 billion

- BPO segment will also grow at the rate of 22 percent.

85. CAD will widen to 1.4 percent of GDP in FY 2017 according to Nomura India which said the figure would widen from 0.9 percent in 2015-2016.

- The Japanese financial services firm has indicated that global demand is likely to remain sluggish but imports will rise towards year end

- Following this, country's trade deficit is expected to widen

- Imports continued to rise towards end 2016.

- CAD narrowed to 1.4 percent in April-December 2016 from 1.7 percent in 2014-2015.

- Exports fell by 0.79 percent to USD 22.17 billion indicating an 18th straight month fall in May 2016

- Imports too fell by 13.16 percent to USS $28.44 billion in the month under review.

86. Overall trade balance improved in May. Trade deficit for the month came in at USD 6.27 billion against USD 4.84 billion on a month-on-month basis.

- Taking merchandise and services together, trade deficit for April-May in FY17 came in at USD 5392.77 million which is 65.67 percent lower in dollar terms than the level of USD 15710.54 million during April-May 2015-16.

- Exports during May,2016 were valued at USD 22170.62 million or Rs 148336.31 crore) which was 0.79 per cent lower in dollar terms (4.04 per cent higher in rupee terms) than the level of USD 22346.75 million during May,2015.

- Imports during April, 2016 were valued at USD 7183 million (or Rs 47745.04 crore) registering a negative growth of 9.13 percent in dollar terms as compared to positive growth of 9.96 percent during March 2016.

87. RBI's new debt recast norms are credit positive for banks and will help in reducing gross NPO levels by 30-100 basis points after a year.

- Implementation of the guidelines will bridge the gap between actual expected losses and provisioning cover.

- New norms will also help in reducing reported gross NPA levels by 30-100 basis points from current level of 7.7 percent in March 2016.

- RBI issued guidelines on Scheme for Sustainable Structuring of Stressed Assets.

- Scheme allows the bifurcation of stressed borrow debt into sustainable and unsustainable portions.

88. Following rise of CPI and WWPI based inflation, RBI has launched the June 2016 round of Inflation Expectations Survey of Householders across 18 cities.

- This includes Ahmedabad, Patna, Chandigarh and Thiruvananthapuram

- Survey seek qualitative responses from households on price changes within the next three months as well as the next one year

- Quantitative responses were also sought on current three month ahead and one year ahead inflation rates

- RBI which factors in inflation while arriving at the monetary decision, said the results of the survey provide useful policy information.

- "Inflation expectations are subjective assessments of households covered in the survey and are based on households' individual consumption baskets," it said.

- RBI has been regularly conducting the survey.

- May retail inflation touched 21 months high in May due to rising price of food items.

- RBI also launched the June 2016 round of Consumer Confidence Index.

89. RBI has released a paper on stressed assets called Scheme for Sustainable Structuring of Stressed Assets. The aim of this paper is strengthening the ability of lenders to deal with stressed assets and place real assets back back on track by providing avenues for reworking financial structure of entities facing genuine difficulties.

- RBI will facilitate the resolution of large accounts which meet specific criteria. Accounts facing severe financial difficulties may be put for restructuring or write down or larger provision can be allowed as well.

- Paper describes resolution plans to be implemented for debt servicing.

- Overseeing Committee will also be formed by the Indian Banks Association in participation with the RBI for choosing stressed assets cases.

- Paper also mentions certain guidelines for choosing accounts falling under it.

- Accounts that have commenced commercial operations and projects in which institutional investors will have exposure of more than INR 500 crore are concerned.

- Amount will include any accrued sustainable debt and paper goes on to define sustainable debt when Joint Leaders Forum or consortium of financial institutions believe existing loan can be serviced or retained at the existing level.

90. India has beaten Japan to become the world's third largest oil consumer with oil demand galloping 8.1 percent in 2015, according to BP Statistical Review of World Energy released on June 8, 2016

- With demand of 4.1 million barrels in a day, India is the third largest consumer after the US and China at 19.39 million bpd and 11.96 million bpd.

- India accounted for 4.5 percent of world oil consumption in 2015

- India's demand growth surpassed China's 6.3 percent expansion.

- Japan slipped to 4th spot after oil usage contracted 3.9 percent to 4.15 million bpd in 2015

- In 2014, it used 4.3 million bpd ahead of India's 3.48 million bpd

- Review shows global demand for primary energy grew by 1 percent in 2015 which is slower than the 10 year average

- This shows continued weakness in the global economy and lower growth in Chinese energy consumption as the country shifts from industrial to service driven economy

- Oil is the world's leading fuel with 32.9 percent of international energy consumption and market share for the first time since 1999

- Coal is the second largest fuel in market share at 29.2 percent. Market share of private energy consumption stood at 23.8 percent.

91. Cotton exports from India, the world's biggest producer has nearly halted as local prices have rallied due to tight supplies because of drought forcing key importers like Bangladesh, Pakistan and Vietnam to turn to other suppliers. Freeze in Indian export will promote Australia, Brazil and the US to raise shipments and push global prices to their highest since August.

- Price rise could substantially push up fabric and clothing prices and put pressure on the margins of garment making.

- Landed cost is Indian cotton is around 75-76 cents per lb for Pakistan and Bangladeshi buyers and this is around 73 cents for Brazilian cotton.

- Pakistan and Bangladesh prefer Indian cotton due to low freight charges and local cotton spot market prices have risen by 10 percent from a month ago to 38,4000 rupees per 356 kg due to limited supplies after consecutive droughts cut production.

- India may produce 334.1 million bales of cotton in 2015-2016 starting on October 1 from last year's output of 38.3 million, according to estimates by Cotton Association of India.

92. RBI is setting up a multi-disciplinary panel to understand these companies and create the perfect ecosystem for them. The committee will have representatives from financial regulators and stakeholders from the industry:

- Fintech covers a large section of areas including transactions, lending and insurance.
- RBI is also looking at other technology based systems, trends for receivables sale and unified payment interface systems.

93. To reduce import dependance, the government has decided to establish 6 bulk drugs and medical devices parks which will entail combined investment of INR 60,000 crore. Government has also decided to establish six bulk drugs and medical devices parks, which will entail a combined investment of INR 60,000 crore.

- Government has decided to establish 3 bulk drugs and 3 medical devices parks across the country.
- Parks will require investment of INR 60,000 crore.
- As per various estimates, once parks become operational, they can bring down production of device and bulk drugs by at least 30 percent and in the long run, this will help the general public also.

94. Mobile data traffic is also expected to grow the fastest globally at 15 times by 2021. The country also grew most in terms of net additions in mobile subscriptions as per the March hurter over at 21 million, followed by Indonesia and Myanmar with 5 million net additions each and US as well as Pakistan with over 3 million net additions each. This is as per the Ericsson Mobility Report and the latest edition of the report reveals that globally IoT is set to overtake mobile phones as the largest category of connected devices by 2018.

- Between 2015 and 2021, the number of IoT connected devices is expected to rise by 23 percent annually of which cellular IoT is forecast to have the highest growth rate.
- IoT is now accelerating as device costs fall and innovative applications emerge.
- From 2020, the commercial deployment of 5G networks will also provide additional capabilities which are critical for IoT.

95. ICRA India's international traffic has logged a compounded annual growth rate of 10.5 percent in the past 10 years, according to rating agency ICRA. Besides a 16 percent growth in passenger traffic in the previous fiscal coupled with lower jet fuel prices has helped the domestic airline to improve performance during the period despite increased competition. ICRA senior vice president commended that in view of tight liquidity conditions in the past, airline strategies have moved from chasing market share to one focused on enhancement of profitability resulting in route rationalisation and cutting down on capacity expansion as well as fleet rationalisation and renegotiation of maintenance contracts.

96. Fiscal deficit in April came in at Rs 1.37 lakh crore, which is 25.7 percent of the Budget estimate for 2016-17.

- Fiscal deficit is the gap between expenditure and revenue, which for the whole fiscal has been pegged at Rs 5.33 lakh crore.
- The deficit in April last fiscal was 23 percent of the Budget estimate. For 2016-17, the government has set a fiscal deficit target of 3.5 percent.

- According to data released by the Controller and Accounts General, total expenditure of the government in April read Rs 1.61 lakh crore, or 8.2 percent of the full-year estimate.
- Of the total expenditure, Plan spending was Rs 45,543 crore while for non-plan spending was Rs 1,16,442 crore. Revenue collection was Rs 22,075 crore, or 1.6 percent of the estimate. Total receipts of the government - from revenue and non-debt capital - in April stood at Rs 24,659 crore.

97. Telecom industry's revenue grew by 6.5 percent last year, the lowest since 2010 despite the sector witnessing close to 79 million subscribers during the period, according to COAI.

- If one goes back to 2010, the industry has been delivering double digit growth of around 10 percent following constant revenue growth of double digit.
- Industry has also seen a fall in revenue from voice calls though overall subscriber base rose by 79 million in 2015.

98. New capacity addition by the wind power sector may decline to 2500 MW in current fiscal as against 3415 MW in the previous fiscal on account of challenges faced by segments in MP and Maharashtra, rating agency ICRA indicated on May 30.

- Long term outlook for the wind sector remained strong given favourable government support and large and untapped wind power potential.
- Wind energy sector is facing challenges of slowdown following signing of fresh PPAs and reported delays in payments by state owned utility.
- Headwinds could lead to a decline in fresh capacity addition to 2500 MW in the wind energy sector in FY2017.
- In FY2016, the wind power sector witnessed a record capacity addition of 3415 MW, an increase of 48 percent over the capacity addition of 2,308 MW achieved during FY2015.

99. Indian economy will grow 7.7% in this fiscal amidst likely improvement in the industrial and agricultural sectors performance on account of good monsoon. The investment cycle is to take 6 months to witness a pickup says the survey. The growth in 2016-2017 is expected to be supported by an improvement in the agricultural and industrial sector performance. Prediction of a good monsoon after consecutive years of sup optimal rainfall will back the improved outlook in the current fiscal.

- The FICCI economic outlook survey also puts across a median GDP growth forecast of 7.7% for FY2016-2017.
- RBI in the previous month forecast a 7.6 percent growth in the current fiscal with the onset of a favourable monsoon.
- Agriculture sector is expected to record a median growth rate of 2.8 percent in 2016-2017 with a maximum and minimum range of 3.5 and 1.6. Industrial growth is expected to grow by 7.1 percent in 2016-2017.

- Services sector is estimated to grow at 9.6 percent. The survey was conducted during April/May 2016 among economists belonging to the industry, banking and financial services sector.

100. Government of India has approved the establishment of a National Investment and Manufacturing Zone in Odisha. This is India's third NIMZ involving a massive area of 163 square kilometres.

- The project will come up at Kalinganagar industrial area in Jaipur district of Odisha.

- For execution of the project, the Union Ministry of Commerce and Industry has approved INR 4241 crore

- Of this, 3816 crore will be invested in the first phase of the project which will be completed by 2020.

- NIMZ will create job opportunities for 1.5 alike people and help Odisha grow as a manufacturing hub and help Paradip's growth.

- To boost the manufacturing sector, the Union Government in 2014 announced the establishment of 16 national investment and manufacturing zones under the National Manufacturing Policy.

- It aims to enhance the share of manufacturing in GDP to 25 percent and creating 100 million jobs over a decade.

Q.1 Loans and Project Agreement for WB has been signed between Government of which state and WB?

A. Kerala   **B.** Karnataka

C. TN   **D.** AP

Q.2 Paying monthly fees has been abolished for domestic shipping firms which now have to pay one time license fee of what amount?

A. INR 25,000   **B.** INR 20,000

C. INR 30,000   **D.** INR 35,000

Q.3 What does DEEP stand for with respect to power procurement?

A. Discovery of Efficient Electricity Price

B. Discovery of Effective Electricity Price

C. Discovery of Electric Efficient Prices

D. None of the above

Q.4 Minister of Railways has inaugurated a high speed Wi-Fi service at which railway stations:

A. Patna (Bihar)

B. Ranchi (Jharkhand)

C. Vishakhpatnam (AP)

D. All of the above

Q.5 SEBI has received 4 applications for InvITs of which 2 have been cleared. What are InvITs?

A. Infrastructure Investment Trusts

B. IT Investment Trusts

C. India Investment Trust

D. None of the above

Q.6 RBI has laid down rules allowing FDI up to 100 percent in CICs. What does CIC stand for in this context?

A. Central Information Commission

B. Credit Information Council

C. Credit Information Companies

D. None of the above

Q.7 Entities under probe for serious violation in which market can seek settlement of the case if they make good on losses suffered by investors to SEBI's satisfaction?

A. Share Market   **B.** Stock market

C. Capital market   **D.** Money market

Q.8 Which digital wallet service provider has been allowed to be part of BBPS of NPCI?

A. Coupon Duniya   **B.** Groupon

C. Paytm   **D.** Oxigen

Q.9 World Bank has approved USD 625 million for India's grid connected rooftop solar program and a front from CIF. What does CIF stand for?

A. Clean Technology Investment Fund

B. Climate Investment Fund

C. Climate International Fund

D. None of the above

Q.10 NDA has replaced 5 year plans with vision documents for how many years?

A. 8   **B.** 9   **C.** 10   **D.** 15

Q.11 BSE has eased norms for trading on which platform?

A. Stocks   **B.** Shares

C. Mutual Fund   **D.** None of the above

Q.12 What does FIU-IND stand for in the context of finance?

A. Financial Intelligence Unit- India

B. Financial Intelligence Union- India

C. Fiscal Intelligence Unit- India

D. FIscal Intelligence Union- India

Q.13 Deutsche Bank executive has taken over as CMD of MCX. What is his name?

A. Mrugank Paranjape   **B.** Mrugank Sen

C. Mrugank Singh   **D.** Mrugank Sinha

Q.14 Electricity consumption will touch 4 trillion units by which year according to the Ministry of Coal and Power?

A. 2020   **B.** 2030   **C.** 2040   **D.** 2050

Q.15 RBI will issue INR 1000 banknotes with the inset letter ______.

A. A   **B.** G   **C.** T   **D.** R

Q.16 What is the value of the trade deficit of the US with India?

A. USD 1.7 billion   **B.** USD 1.6 billion

C. USD 1.5 billion   **D.** USD 1.4 billion

Q.17 What is internationalisation of rupee include?

A. Savings on Foreign Exchange Transactions for Indian Residents

B. Reduced Foreign Exchange Exposure for Indian Corporate

C. Reduction in Dependence on Foreign Exchange Reserves for BOP Stability

D. All of the above

Q.18 Union Cabinet has given approval between RBI and Central Bank of which nation on currency swap agreement?

A. UAE   **B.** UK

C. US   **D.** None of the above

Q.19 People with annual income above INR 50 lakh will have to disclose acquisition cost of assets such as __________.

A. Land   **B.** Building

C. Jewellery   **D.** All of the above

Q.20 Which public sector bank has ranked number 1 when it comes to the highest willful defaulters?

A. PNB

B. SBI

C. Indian Overseas Bank
D. None of the above

Q.21 There has been a jump of 13 percent in budgetary allocation for _____ research in the present financial year.
A. Social science
B. Health
C. Scientific
D. None of the above

Q.22 RBI has issued a master direction on the merger of which banks?
A. PSU banks
B. Private sector banks
C. Development banks
D. Syndicate Banks

Q.23 RBI has allowed IDF to raise resources through bonds as well as commercial papers of less than 5 year maturity, what is IDF?
A. International Debt Fund
B. India Debt Fund
C. Infrastructure Debt Fund
D. Internal Debt Fund

Q.24 CBDT has opposed simplified _________ rules to permit companies to claim credit for tax paid overseas.
A. Foreign Tax Credit
B. International Tax Credit
C. Global Tax Credit
D. World Tax Credit

Q.25 Ministry for Power, Coal and New and Renewable Energy launched which services operation in India?
A. Power
B. Coal
C. Ancillary
D. Manufacturing

Q.26 Wholesale inflation for India for the month of March came to _____ percent Y-O-Y continuing the tryst with negative territory as against -0.91 percent in February.
A. -0.85
B. -0.75
C. -0.65
D. -0.55

Q.27 An ASSOCHAM SREI study has said which state has topped PPP projects across India?
A. Gujarat
B. Kerala
C. Maharashtra
D. UP

Q.28 DGFT has defined which form of commerce?
A. m-commerce
B. e-commerce
C. web-commerce
D. Both b and c

Q.29 India is going to experience which rate of economic growth according to CII in 2016-2017?
A. 7.4%
B. 7.5%
C. 7.9%
D. 8%

Q.30 RBI cut the key interest rate by what percent?
A. 0.25
B. 0.75
C. 0.55
D. 0.35

Q.31 India's coffee exports rose by what percent in 2015-2016?
A. 13.36%
B. 13.38%
C. 13.37%
D. 13.39%

Q.32 According to the Sixth Economic Census, which was released by the Ministry of Statistics and Programme Implementation, which state has seen the highest growth in enterprises and employment generation over the past 10 years?

A. Uttar Pradesh
B. Punjab
C. Maharashtra
D. Gujarat

Q.33 RBI purchased how much currency in USD to prevent rupee from strengthening too much?
A. 100 million
B. 5 billion
C. 50 billion
D. None of these

Q.34 India's external debt stood at _____ billion towards the end of December 2015, according to FinMin
A. USD 480 billion
B. USD 289.5 billion
C. USD 122.6 billion
D. None of the above

Q.35 ADB has cut India's growth forecast to what figure for 2016-2017?
A. 7.3
B. 7.4
C. 7.5
D. 7.6

Q.36 European Union will lend India USD 450 million through EIB. What does EIB stand for?
A. Europe International Bank
B. European Investment Bank
C. Europe Investing Bank
D. None of the above

Q.37 RBI has tweaked the rules for lending rates and stipulated that fixed rate loans of up to how many years will be offered by lenders based on marginal cost of funding?
A. 2
B. 3
C. 4
D. 5

Q.38 India will grow by what percent in 2016-2017, said ICRA?
A. 7.6
B. 7.7
C. 7.8
D. 7.9

Q.39 RBI has prevented banks for submitting data for NEFT transactions by walk in customers without an account with them. What does NEFT stand for?
A. National Electrical Fund Transfer
B. National Electronic Fund Technology
C. National Electronic Fund Transfer
D. None of the above

Q.40 Government has exempted whom from 1 percent excise duty in the jewellery industry on March 20, 2016?
A. Artisans
B. Job Workers
C. Both a and b
D. Jewellery Retailers

Q.41 Which category of people are classified as poor according to the Tendulkar poverty line?
A. Those earning less than INR 33 per day
B. Those earning less than INR 25 per day
C. Those earning less than INR 15 per day
D. None of the above

Q.42 Ministry of Tourism has launched a program to train college students as _________.
A. Tourist guides
B. Tourist facilitators
C. Paryatak Mitras
D. Both b and c

Q.43 Yes Bank has just signed a pact with IBCC for cooperation in knowledge sharing. What does IBCC stand for?
A. India Brazil Chamber of Commerce
B. India Botswana Chamber of Commerce

C. India Bangkok Chamber of Commerce
D. India Bangladesh Chamber of Commerce

Q.44 Government has made the decision to relax norms for which category of MSMEs?

A. startups
B. 10 year old
C. 5 year old
D. 3 year old

Q.45 IRDAI has said the insurer should assess the credit risk of any buyer contributing more than what percent of the total turnover of the policy holder?

A. 2%
B. 3%
C. 4%
D. 5%

Q.46 IMF has said India is the best among emerging economies. What are some of the concerns the country needs to address, according to the IMF?

A. Stress from leveraged corporate balance sheets
B. Quality woes of state run banks to sustain recovery process
C. PSB balance sheet issues and deteriorating corporate profitability at 10 year low
D. All of the above

Q.47 Fitch Ratings has lowered India's economic growth forecast for the next fiscal to what percent?

A. 7.4
B. 7.5
C. 7.7
D. 7.8

Q.48 Food processing sector has received how much FDI till December in the current fiscal, according to Minister of State for Food Processing?

A. USD 385.35 million
B. USD 385.45 million
C. USD 385.55 million
D. USD 385.66 million

Q.49 Which United States agency has issued a loan guarantee making it the first one from America for the Indian health sector?

A. UNAID
B. USAID
C. USTAID
D. None of the above

Q.50 Which business school has tied up with NHAI for ensuring development of managerial competence?

A. ISB
B. IIM-A
C. IIM-K
D. NMIMS

Q.51 NASSCOM and which state government signed an agreement to set up the first startup warehouse in the state?

A. Tamil Nadu
B. Karnataka
C. Kerala
D. Andhra Pradesh

Q.52 According to WEF's Global Energy Architecture Performance Index Report, India is at what rank in terms of energy security and access?

A. 90
B. 91
C. 92
D. 93

Q.53 GoI has approved Department of Investment and Public Asset management proposal for strategic disinvestment of CPSEs. What are CPSEs?

A. Central Public Sector Entities
B. Central Public Sector Enterprises
C. Central Public Sector Enclave
D. None of the above

Q.54 RBI has made amendments to the treatment of certain balance sheet items of banks for what purpose?

A. Boosting their regulatory capital
B. Aligning with the Internationally adopted Basel III capital standards
C. Neither a nor b
D. Both a and b

Q.55 Indian economy is projected to grow at what percent in the current fiscal according to FICCI and CSO respectively?

A. 7.4%, 7.5%
B. 7.5%, 7.7%
C. 7.4%, 7.6%
D. 7.5%, 7.6%

Q.56 RBI has extended currency Swap arrangement till November 2017 with SAARC Nations. This includes:

A. Maldives
B. Nepal
C. China
D. Both a and b

Q.57 What does VLE stand for in the context of Indian banking?

A. Voluntary Local Entrepreneur
B. Village Level Entrepreneur
C. Village Level Enterprise
D. None of the above

Q.58 Public Investment Board has approved INR 800 crore proposal from which government body/department for setting up payments bank?

A. DoT
B. India Post
C. Indian Railways
D. None of the above

Q.59 Government will map 1.5 lakh bridges through an integrated IBMS system. What does IBMS stand for?

A. Integrated Bridge Management System
B. Indian Bridge Management System
C. India Bridge Management System
D. Integrated Boat Management System

Q.60 What is Industry 4.0?

A. Fourth industrial revolution
B. Manufacturing industries in 4 sectors
C. Four fold sector specific industries
D. None of the above

Q.61 OECD, a Paris based think tank, has pegged India's economy growth rate at what percent in the next fiscal?

A. 7.2%
B. 7.3%
C. 7.4%
D. 7.5%

Q.62 RBI has revised norms for NBFC factor firms. What steps have been taken as part of this?

A. Guidelines for NBFC companies stipulates there should be board approval for underwriting commitments with an aim to mitigate credit risk
B. RBI also raised threefold of reporting frauds from INR 25 lakh to INR 1 crore for NBFC
C. Factoring services should be extended in respect of invoice which showcases genuine trade transactions
D. All of the above

Q.63 Which project has been launched by Geographical Survey of India in collaboration with Ministry of Mines and Steel?

A. Operation Khanij Khoj/ Discover

B. Operation Khanij Kosh/ Explore
C. Operation Khanij Khazana/Excavate
D. Operation Khanij Khoj/Uncover

Q.64 Quick Estimates of IIP with base 2004-2005 have been calculated for the month of December 2015 using data compiled from how many source agencies?

A. 12   **B.** 13   **C.** 14   **D.** 15

Q.65 AP government has inked a pact with USTDA for developing which city as a Smart City?

A. Vizag   **B.** Medak
C. Hyderabad   **D.** None of the above

Q.66 Inflation has reached a 17 month high recently. To which year has CSO revised the Base Year of the CPI?

A. 2011=100   **B.** 2010=100
C. 2012=100   **D.** 2013=100

Q.67 US Chamber of Commerce has just released its 4th Annual Global IP Index. What does IP stand for?

A. Immediate Possibilities
B. Infinite Possibilities
C. Intellectual Possibilities
D. International Possibilities

Q.68 CSI released the AE of National Income for FY 2015-2016 indicating that growth in GDP will be around _____.

A. 7.3%   **B.** 7.4%   **C.** 7.5%   **D.** 7.6%

Q.69 India's economy is likely to grow by what percentage in Fiscal 2017, according to CRISIL?

A. 7.7   **B.** 7.8   **C.** 7.9   **D.** 8.1

Q.70 TRAI has ruled in favour of?

A. Net Neutrality   **B.** Free Basics
C. Airtel Zero   **D.** None of the above

Q.71 Maharashtra will be setting up the first international arbitration centre in which city at the start of the Make in India Week from February 13th to 18th?

A. Mumbai   **B.** Nagpur   **C.** Solapur   **D.** Pune

Q.72 RBI will purchase back indexed bonds maturing in which year?

A. 2022   **B.** 2023   **C.** 2024   **D.** 2025

Q.73 Indian economy will grow at 7.4% in which fiscal according to NCAER?

A. 2016   **B.** 2015-2016
C. Current fiscal   **D.** All of the above

Q.74 IT exports are pegged to grow at a slower pace of 10-12 percent in which fiscal, according to NASSCOM?

A. 2017   **B.** 2016   **C.** 2015   **D.** 2018

Q.75 Cabinet has approved the formation of JV with states for which projects?

A. Rail   **B.** Road   **C.** Air   **D.** Port

Q.76 RBI has relaxed several rules including ______ norms for boosting startup activity within the country.

A. FII   **B.** FDI   **C.** SDR   **D.** GDP

Q.77 India has overtaken Thailand to become the world's largest exporter of which grain?

A. Rice   **B.** Jowar   **C.** Bajra   **D.** Maize

Q.78 Exports at the half of the sector of the 30 closely monitored by the Commerce Ministry were in the negative zone in December. Exports declined by 15 percent in December to what number?

A. 22.2   **B.** 22.3   **C.** 22.4   **D.** 22.6

Q.79 RBI has allowed banks to take which action?

A. Sell Indian Gold coins
B. Buy Indian Gold coins
C. Both a and b
D. Neither a nor b

Q.80 India's CAD narrows to 0.5% of GDP from which percentage in 2015 leading to lower commodity prices?

A. 0.7%   **B.** 0.8%   **C.** 0.9%   **D.** 0.10%

Q.81 India has signed a USD 250 million with the World Bank for which project?

A. Bihar Kosi Basin Development Project
B. Damodar Basin Development Project
C. Odisha Mahanadi Basin Development Project
D. None of the above

Q.82 EXIM Bank of India has entered into MoU with which state for promoting exports from the state?

A. Andhra Pradesh   **B.** Karnataka
C. Kerala   **D.** TN

Q.83 India's trade deficit with China has risen to how much in 2015 as it has touched a record high?

A. 44.87 billion   **B.** 44.86 billion
C. 44.85 billion   **D.** 44.84 billion

Q.84 India's IIP for November contracted how much while CPI for December rose to 5.6%?

A. 3.1%   **B.** 3.2%   **C.** 3.3%   **D.** 3.4%

Q.85 Urijit Patel, Deputy Governor of RBI has been reappointed for 3 years. How many deputy governors of RBI are there?

A. 3   **B.** 4   **C.** 5   **D.** 6

Q.86 Union Cabinet has provided the approval for the creation of CGFMU. What does it stand for?

A. Credit Guarantee fund for MIDRA
B. Credit Guarantee fund for MADRA
C. Credit Guarantee Fund for MUDRA
D. None of the above

Q.87 India produced how many tonnes of sugar during the 3 months up to December 2015-2016, according to ISMA?

A. 7.95 MT   **B.** 7.97 MT   **C.** 7.98 MT   **D.** 8.01 MT

Q.88 Government has abolished export duty on iron ore pellets to 0 from what percent?

A. 3   **B.** 4   **C.** 5   **D.** 6

Q.89 Retail information for farm labourers rose in November to what percent, on account of increase in food items prices?

A. 5.02%   **B.** 4.92%   **C.** 4.43%   **D.** 4.65%

Q.90 Growth in FY16 has been pegged at which percentage, according to HSBC?

A. 7.2   **B.** 7.3   **C.** 7.4   **D.** 7.5

Q.91 e-Commerce industry is estimated to be worth USD 38 billion by 2016 according to which industry body?

A. FICCI

B. ASSOCHAM

C. PHDCCI

D. None of the above

Q.92 GoI recently released the MTDS to better manage public borrowings. What does MTDS stand for?

A.   Medium Term Debt Management Schedule

B.   Medium Term Debt Management Scheme

C.   Medium Term Debt Management Strategy

D.   None of the above

Q.93 Growth in 8 core sectors of the economy declined to what percent in November?

A. 3.2   **B.** 1.4   **C.** 1.3   **D.** 1.2

Q.94 Securities and Exchange Board of India proposed fresh norms for public issues of REITs. What are REITs?

A.   Real Estate Indian Trust

B.   Real Estate Investment Trust

C.   Real Estate Investing Trust

D.   Realty Exchange Investment Trust

Q.95 Global economic growth will be below par next year according to IMF MD. Who is she?

A. Christine Lagarde

B. Janet Yellan

C. Angela Merkel

D. None of the above

Q.96 Government will be setting up a INR 40K crore NIIF. What does NIIF stand for?

A.   National Innovation and Infrastructure Fund

B.   National Investment and Infrastructure Fund

C.   National Innovation and Investment Fund

D.   None of the above

Q.97 RBI released which report on the medium term path for financial inclusion on 28th December 2015?

A.   Kelkar Panel Report

B.   Mohanty Panel Report

C.   Shah Panel Report

D.   None of the above

Q.98 Indian bank loans rose by what percent Y-O-Y in 2 weeks to December 11th, as per RBI?

A. 10   **B.** 11   **C.** 12   **D.** 13

Q.99 NPAs have jumped by 50 basis points to what value between March and September quarters?

A. 5.2%   **B.** 5.1%   **C.** 5%   **D.** 4.9%

Q.100 RBI has set up a helping for guiding start ups on which matter?

A. Debentures

B. Shares

C. Forex

D. None of the above

// Smart Answer Sheet //

Correct — Indicates percentage of students who answered questions correctly.

Skipped — Indicates percentage of students who skipped questions.

Q.	Ans.	Correct / Skipped
1	B	21.88 % / 18.74 %
2	B	31.25 % / 37.5 %
3	A	25.0 % / 34.38 %
4	D	34.38 % / 37.5 %
5	A	37.5 % / 40.62 %
6	C	18.75 % / 40.63 %
7	C	31.25 % / 37.5 %
8	D	18.75 % / 40.63 %
9	B	31.25 % / 37.5 %
10	D	28.12 % / 40.63 %
11	C	28.12 % / 37.5 %
12	A	37.5 % / 37.5 %
13	A	34.38 % / 37.5 %
14	B	37.5 % / 37.5 %
15	D	21.88 % / 37.5 %
16	A	15.62 % / 37.5 %
17	D	40.62 % / 37.5 %
18	A	25.0 % / 40.62 %
19	D	65.62 % / 25.0 %
20	B	37.5 % / 25.0 %
21	B	31.25 % / 31.25 %
22	B	15.62 % / 34.38 %
23	C	21.88 % / 25.0 %
24	A	21.88 % / 34.37 %
25	C	21.88 % / 40.62 %
26	B	28.12 % / 43.76 %
27	D	15.62 % / 28.13 %
28	B	21.88 % / 34.37 %
29	D	15.62 % / 37.5 %
30	A	28.12 % / 34.38 %
31	D	15.62 % / 40.63 %
32	A	25.0 % / 37.5 %
33	A	18.75 % / 28.13 %
34	A	21.88 % / 37.5 %
35	B	21.88 % / 40.62 %
36	B	56.25 % / 37.5 %
37	B	15.62 % / 40.63 %
38	B	18.75 % / 43.75 %
39	C	46.88 % / 37.5 %
40	C	28.12 % / 40.63 %
41	A	40.62 % / 34.38 %
42	D	34.38 % / 40.62 %
43	A	18.75 % / 37.5 %
44	A	40.62 % / 37.5 %
45	B	31.25 % / 37.5 %
46	D	40.62 % / 40.63 %
47	C	15.62 % / 40.63 %
48	B	25.0 % / 40.62 %
49	B	21.88 % / 43.74 %
50	A	21.88 % / 43.74 %
51	A	25.0 % / 34.38 %
52	A	18.75 % / 37.5 %
53	B	46.88 % / 37.5 %
54	D	34.38 % / 40.62 %
55	C	15.62 % / 40.63 %
56	D	46.88 % / 37.5 %
57	B	28.12 % / 40.63 %
58	B	40.62 % / 40.63 %
59	A	31.25 % / 37.5 %
60	A	25.0 % / 34.38 %
61	C	28.12 % / 40.63 %
62	D	37.5 % / 40.62 %
63	D	15.62 % / 37.5 %
64	D	12.5 % / 40.62 %
65	A	25.0 % / 40.62 %
66	C	34.38 % / 37.5 %
67	B	18.75 % / 37.5 %
68	D	15.62 % / 40.63 %
69	C	21.88 % / 43.74 %
70	A	31.25 % / 40.63 %
71	A	21.88 % / 31.24 %
72	B	25.0 % / 34.38 %
73	D	25.0 % / 40.62 %
74	A	25.0 % / 40.62 %
75	A	18.75 % / 37.5 %
76	B	43.75 % / 40.63 %
77	A	31.25 % / 37.5 %
78	A	15.62 % / 43.76 %
79	C	43.75 % / 28.13 %
80	A	15.62 % / 37.5 %

Q.	Ans.	Correct	Skipped
81	A	25.0 %	31.25 %
82	A	31.25 %	37.5 %
83	A	15.62 %	37.5 %
84	B	28.12 %	43.76 %

Q.	Ans.	Correct	Skipped
85	D	15.62 %	37.5 %
86	C	46.88 %	40.62 %
87	C	34.38 %	40.62 %
88	C	37.5 %	40.62 %

Q.	Ans.	Correct	Skipped
89	B	21.88 %	43.74 %
90	C	21.88 %	43.74 %
91	B	37.5 %	40.62 %
92	C	25.0 %	40.62 %

Q.	Ans.	Correct	Skipped
93	C	25.0 %	40.62 %
94	B	46.88 %	37.5 %
95	A	40.62 %	40.63 %
96	B	25.0 %	37.5 %

Q.	Ans.	Correct	Skipped
97	B	31.25 %	40.63 %
98	B	15.62 %	43.76 %
99	B	34.38 %	40.62 %
100	C	53.12 %	37.5 %

Performance Analysis

Avg. Score (%)	16.0%
Toppers Score (%)	87.0%
Your Score	

//Hints and Solutions//

1. The Loan and Project Agreements for World Bank (IBRD) assistance of US$ 100 million for the Karnataka Urban Water Supply Modernisation project were signed between Government of India/Government of Karnataka and the World Bank on 24th May.

- The objective of the project is to provide city-wide access to a continuous piped water supply in the eligible cities in the State of Karnataka and to strengthen the service delivery arrangements at the city level. KUIDFC is the implementing agency for the project.
- The project would have four broad components: (i) Capital Investment Program; (ii) Institution Building; (iii) Technical Assistance for Sector Development; and (iv) Project Management.

2. Paying monthly fees is a tedious process as one has to repeatedly encounter red tape. The government said domestic shipping firms will have to pay only a one-time licence fee of Rs.20,000 to own foreign flag vessels, in a bid to give a boost to the maritime sector.

- The government said the move would boost the Indian Controlled Tonnage Scheme and be a step towards promoting 'ease of doing business' in the maritime sector.

3. First e-bidding process through the recently launched DEEP (Discovery of Efficient Electricity Price) e-bidding portal for short term power procurement has been found by Uttarakhand and Kerala and for the State of Bihar. The early adoption of the e-bidding portal has resulted in substantial savings as price discovered through e-bidding are significantly lower than the prices at which power was procured during a similar period in the last year.

4. Minister of Railways Shri Suresh Prabhakar Prabhu inaugurated the high speed Wi-Fi services at Patna, Ranchi and Vizag through video conferencing from Rail Bhawan, New Delhi.

The Wi-Fi facility for the visitors & rail users at these stations has been commissioned by RailTel in association with Google for providing high speed state of the art world class internet experience to the commuters.

- India is heading towards digitalization, Internet has become the basic need of every individual for which they are entitled to.
- To bring the railway stations to world standard and to keep pace with the latest technology, provision of high speed WiFi is the first step in this direction.

5. SEBI has received four applications for InvITs or Infrastructure Investment Trusts with two of the applications received for setting up such entities approved.

- No application has been received for REIT or Real Estate Investment Trust though regulator has been getting enquiries.

- These instruments will help to garner funds for further investment into infrastructure and real estate projects.

6. Aiming to attract more foreign investment, RBI on May 19th laid down rules permitting FDI up to 100 percent in credit information companies if ownership of the investor company is well diversified.

- RBI also said it considered allowing higher FDI limits to entities with track record of running a CIC in a well regulated environment.
- FIIs/FPIs investing in CIC should not seek representation on the board of directors based on their shareholding according to RBI.

7. Entities under probe for "serious violations" in capital markets can seek settlement of case only if they make good on their losses suffered by investors as per the consent of SEBI.

- Regulations provide settlement of cases where proceedings have not been initiated.
- Regulations provide for settlement of cases where proceedings are yet to be initiated.

8. Digital wallet company Oxigen announced that the RBI has given approval for the firm to be part of Bharat Bill Payments Systems as commissioned by the National Payment Corporation of India.

- Oxigen has in the past processed bills through connection directly to numerous vendors.
- Getting the license will help Oxigen widen all its vendors falling under BBPS.

9. World Bank has approved USD 625 million aid for India's solar programme. The WB's Board has approved USD 625 million loan to support India's grid connected rooftop solar programme to generate clean energy.

- Board also approved a co-financing loan of USD 120 million in concessional terms and a USD 5 million grant from the Climate Investment Funds Clean Technology Fund.
- Project will finance installation of 400 MW of grid connected rooftop solar photovoltaic GRPV across the nation.
- Solar OV installations will provide clean, renewable energy and reduce GHG emissions by displacing thermal generation.
- Project will also strengthen the capacity of key institutions and support development of the overall solar PV market.

10. The National Democratic Alliance government at the Centre, led by Prime Minister Narendra Modi, has decided to get rid of the Nehruvian five-year plans, and replace them with 15-year vision documents.

- These will be framed keeping in mind the country's social goals and the sustainable development agenda.
- The NITI Aayog has been directed to prepare a vision document at the earliest. The current 12th Five-Year

Plan will be terminated in the current financial year, 2016-17.

- The first 15-year vision document will start from 2017-18, along with a seven-year National Development Agenda which will lay down the schemes, programmes and strategies to achieve the long-term vision.

11. To get more participants on the MF trading platform, top bourse BSE has eased registration norms by leaving out minimum paid up capital and net worth requirements for applicants

- Changes would be applicable for BSE STAR Mutual Platform- electronic segment allowing individuals and HUF to trade

- The following conditions were discontinued: minimum paid-up capital requirement for corporate applicants, self-certified networth, individuals having a minimum tangible assets of Rs 1 lakh for the registration of mutual fund distributors.

12. Financial Intelligence Unit - India (FIU-IND) has signed Memorandum of Understanding (MoU) with 30 counterpart FIUs of other countries for sharing the information pertaining to money laundering and terror funding.

- FIU-IND is also a member of Egmont Group of FIUs, an international organization with a membership of 151 FIUs.

- Besides, India is also a member of the Financial Action Task Force (FATF), an intergovernmental body which makes recommendations relating to combating money laundering, terrorist financing and serious tax offences.

- India participates in various regional/global meetings to put India's position with regard to steps taken to combat money laundering and terrorist financing.

13. Deutsche Bank executive Mrugank Paranjape took over as CMD of MCX or Multiple Commodity Exchange which had previously been without a head for 2 years.

- MCX is an independent commodity exchange based in India established in 2003 and is based in Mumbai.

- It is India's largest commodity futures exchange and the turnover of the exchange for the year 2015 was 55.52 trillion rupees (865.55 billion US dollars).

14. Indian electricity consumption will increase four times from 1.1 trillion to 4 trillion units by 2030. Despite energy efficient schemes, a possible 10 percent jump is there in electricity growth annually for the next 15 to 16 years. Emphasis given to domestic manufacturing activities will increase power consumption despite improvements in energy efficiency.

- India has set a target of 175 GW of renewable energy generation capacity by 2022 of which 100 GW is to be obtained from solar.

- Solar power capacity at 6.7 GW will touch 20 GW.

- As the solar power sector is on track, the government will focus on encouraging new hydropower and wind power capacity.

15. RBI will be issuing INR 1000 banknotes with inset letter R in both number panels. Banknotes will also have other security features such as ascending size of numerals, bleed lines and enlarged identification mark

- Bank notes bearing the signature of Governor Rajaan will also have year of printing 2016 printed on the reverse.

- Design of banknotes will be similar to INR 1000 banknotes in Mahatma Gandhi Series 2005.

- All banknotes in the INR 1000 series will have identifying marks and remaining notes will remain legal tender.

16. US has a USD 1.7 billion trade deficit with India in March. It also has a USD 26 billion trade deficit with China during the month of March. Goods and services deficit was USD 40.4 billion in March down USD 6.5 billion from USD 47.0 billion in February

- March exports were USD 176.6 billion, USD 1.5 billion less than February exports while imports in the month were USSD 217.1 billion, USD 8.1 billion less than February

- The Commerce Department also indicated that exports from China increased USD 0.1 billion to USD 8.5 billion and imports decreased USD 6.1 billion to USD 34.4 billion

- March figures also show a surplus with South and Central America, OPEC, UK and Saudi Arabia.

- Deficits were recorded with China, EU, Germany , Japan, Mexico, South Korea, India France, Brazil, Italy and Canada.

17. Integration of rupee will facilitate greater degree of integration of the Indian economy with the rest of the world in terms of foreign trade and global capital flows.

- Key benefits of internationalisation of rupee include savings on forex transactions for Indian residents, reduced foreign exchange exposure for Indian corporate, reduction in dependence on forex reserves for balance of payment stability.

- An important driver for internationalisation of currency is country's share in global merchandise and commercial services trade.

- Indian government has put in place a framework for issuance of rupee denominated bonds in international sphere by Indian corporate.

18. The Union Cabinet chaired by the Prime Minister Shri Narendra Modi has given its ex-post facto approval for the Memorandum of Understanding (MoU) signed in February, 2016 between Reserve Bank of India (RBI) and Central Bank of United Arab Emirates (UAE) on co-operation concerning currency swap agreement.

- The MoU commits that RBI and Central Bank of UAE will consider signing a bilateral Currency Swap Agreement on mutually agreed terms and conditions, after undertaking technical deliberations, subject to the concurrence of respective Governments.

- The MoU will further strengthen the close economic relationship and cooperation between India and United

Arab Emirates. The swap agreement is also expected to facilitate invoicing of bilateral trade in local currencies.

19. Persons with annual income of over INR 50 lakhs will have to disclose acquisition cost of assets like land, building and jewellery in the IT return forms for assessment year 2016-2017

- Luxury items disclosed will also include silver, gold, platinum or other precious alloys or metals, according to a CBDT announcement.

- As per the directives, for items received as gifts, the assessed will have to declare the cost of acquisition by the previous owner along with value additions.

- Where the cost at which assets are acquired by the previous owner is not ascertainable and no wealth tax return may be filed, value estimated should be at circle or bullion rate.

20. State Bank of India has ranked Number 1 in the list of public sector banks with the highest number of wilful defaulters stood at 1164. Total amount outstanding in the bank was INR 11,705 crore according to the Finance Ministry. PNB came in second with 904 defaulters owing INR 10869. Indian Overseas Bank bucked the trend with number of wilful defaulters shrinking to 70 in 2015 from 517 in 2012.Total amount in outstanding public sector banks has shot up to INR 66190 crore in 2015 and INR 27749 crore in 2012.

21. Close to 13 percent jump has been reported in budgetary allocation for health research in 2016, according to the government. Total budget allocated for the department of health and family welfare for financial year 2016-2017 is INR 40657.57 crore while INR 1144.80 crore had been allocated to the department of health research. The 12.44 percent increase in allocation over the financial year 2015-2016 was discussed, as the budgetary allocation for health research stood at INR 1018.17 crore in 2015-2016.

22. RBI came out with a master direction for merger of private sector banks and between NBFCs and banks. Another master direction indicated that a compilation which consolidates instructions on rules and regulations framed by the RBI under numerous acts including banking issues and foreign exchange transactions.

- Scope of the master direction on the merger will cover the amalgamation of 2 banking companies and amalgamation of NBFC with banking company.

- In these cases, the voluntary amalgamation will become effective following approval from RBI.

- According to the direction, the decision of the amalgamation shall be approved by respective boards by a 2/3rd majority and not just members present and voting.

23. RBI has allowed infrastructure Debt Fund to raise resources through bonds and commercial papers of less than 5 year maturity. Currently, IDF-NBFC was created for raising funds for primarily fund infrastructure projects. RBI has capped the average exposure limit for IDF-NBFC at 50 percent and maximum at 75% of the total capital fund apart from limits on issuance to only PPPs successfully operational at least for a year.

24. Central Board of Direct Taxes has proposed foreign tax credit rules to assist corporates. For providing relief to corporates with income abroad, simplified Foreign Tax Credit rules were introduced. These have been formulated to help companies claim credit for taxes paid overseas.

- CBDT said tax credit can be availed by entities paying taxes in the nation including those with Double Taxation Avoidance Agreement.

- Foreign tax credit will be determined by conversion of currency of payment of foreign tax at telegraphic transfer buying are on dates when the tax has been paid or deducted.

25. Shri Piyush Goyal, Union Minister of State (IC) for Power, Coal and New and Renewable Energy released Report of the Technical Committee on Large Scale Integration of Renewable Energy, Need for Balancing, Deviation Settlement Mechanism (DSM) and associated issues on April 18.

- Shri Goyal also launched Ancillary Services Operations in India.

- The Ministry is set to take 'one nation, one grid, one price 24X7' on mission mode

- India has set an ambitious target of achieving 175 GW of renewable generation capacity. In order to integrate such high penetration of renewable energy and address the concerns of the stakeholders in renewable energy

- A high level Technical Committee was constituted with members from Ministry of Power, Central Electricity Regulatory Commission (CERC), Central Electricity Authority (CEA), renewable rich states like Gujarat, Rajasthan, Tamil Nadu, West Bengal, Power Utilities like PGCIL, Power System operation Corporation Ltd. (POSOCO), NTPC, State Generating companies and Private generating companies and Institutions like India Meteorological department (IMD), National Institute of Wind Energy (NIWE), National Institute of Solar Energy (NISE), GIZ, Ernst & Young (E&Y), etc. The committee had extensive deliberations and has recommended 15 point action plan.

26. Wholesale inflation for India for the month of March came in at -0.85 percent Y-O-Y continuing the tryst with negative territory as against -0.91 percent in February. This number measured by WPI index was fired by Y-O-Y increase in primary articles, steep fall in fuel and power group and less change in manufactured products.

- WPI basket weightage for primary articles, fuel and power and manufactured products stood at 20 percent, 15 percent and 65 percent respectively.

27. Uttar Pradesh has topped PPP project investments with the highest share of 15 percent followed by Maharashtra and Gujarat. UP has the highest share of 22 percent in terms of value of total PPP investment projects under constriction across India followed by Maharashtra (11 percent), Haryana (8.5 percent), Gujarat (6 percent) and Madhya Pradesh (4.5 percent)

- Most PPP investment projects have been terminated in Maharashtra (13 percent) followed by Chhattisgarh (10

percent), Gujarat (9 percent), Kerala (7 percent) and MP (7 percent).

28. Commerce Ministry Today announced that online transactions of goods adhering to e-commerce norms will get duty benefits under MEIS or Merchandise Exports from India Scheme. For MEIS, e-commerce has been defined as the buying and selling of goods and services (including digital goods) over electronic or digital network.

- Under MEIS, government provides duty benefits at 2,3 and 5 percent depending upon products and country.

29. Terming GDP calculation as an imprecise science, CII has pegged the economic growth of the country at 8 percent for the current fiscal, higher than 7.6% pegged by the RBI. GDP growth of 8 percent is expected in 2016-2017says CII President Naushad Forbes. The basis for this economic prediction includes strong macroeconomic fundamentals and good business sentiments as well as downward trend in interest rates. CII's new president also highlighted the need for focusing on regulatory mechanisms.

30. A host of measures have been introduced to smoothen liquidity supply so banks can follow productive sectors for lending and have an accommodative stance going ahead

- Weak private investment in face of low capacity utilisation has spurred the need for a reduction in policy rate by 0.25 percent and introduced a host of measures to smoothen liquidity supply.

- RBI's repo rate or the rate at which it lends to the financial system has come down to 6.5 percent- this cut is in line with expectations as the stock market has reacted, however the BSE Sensex was down 300 points.

- A host of measures were also taken on the liquidity front with the narrowing of the policy rate corridor to 0.50 percent from earlier 1 percentage point.

31. India's coffee exports rose by 13.39% in 2015-2016 with coffee exports jumping by 13.39% to as high as 3,19,7333 tonnes in the 2015-2016 fiscal over the previous year. There has been slight increase in shipment of instant coffee and other varieties.

- India has shipped 281987 tonnes of coffee in the previous fiscal according to the Coffee Board

- Instant coffee exports rose to 97,000 tonnes from 94,000 tonnes in the same period

- In value terms, total exports rose to INR 5204 crore in the previous fiscal from INR 4877 crore in 2014-2015.

- The board also indicated high value exports in markets like Japan, US, Canada and Australia.

32. Among the larger States, Uttar Pradesh has seen the most massive growth in enterprises and employment generation over the past 10 years, outperforming Gujarat, Punjab and Maharashtra.

UP has seen a 67.4% in the number of economic establishments in the state between 2005 and 2013 compared to national average of 41.8 percent. It fared better than Gujarat, TN, Karnataka, Maharashtra and West Bengal.

UP has been placed third in terms of employment growth over a decade ahead of other states like Gujarat, TN, Karnataka, Maharashtra and West Bengal.

- Urban India performed better seeing a growth of 47% in the number of establishments and 42% growth in employment over the last decade. Rural India saw the growth of 38.4 and 34.8 percent. UP bucked the trend.

- A third of the 36 states and UTs saw numerous establishments in rural areas grow faster than urban centres, with UP leading in this respect.

33. RBI bought as much as USD 1 billion (100 million) to prevent rupee from strengthening too much after the currency hit three-month highs as investors poured funds into emerging markets, and despite the buying, the rupee struck a three month high of 66.1700 per dollar on 31st March and was on course to post a gain of 3.2 percent in March - its biggest monthly gain in 2 1/2 years.

- The rupee's appreciation reflects a broad move into high yield emerging markets by investors, as central banks for major economies - notably the Bank of Japan and European Central Bank - have adopted a more dovish stance.

- Traders said they expect the rupee could appreciate further, after foreign investments into Indian debt and equity surged to a one-year high of USD 3.3 billion in March, reversing outflows from earlier this year.

34. Finance Ministry has calculated that India's total external debt has risen to USD 480 billion towards the close of December as compared to March in 2015. Total external debt stock at December end recorded a rise of USD 4.9 billion over level at end March. Government external debt stood at USD 90.7 billion in December 2015 while non government debt equaled USD 389.5 billion.

- Effective external debt policy has helped in controlling rising external debt and maintaining comfortable external debt position.

- Long as well as short term debt will be focused on by the policy.

- It will also study raising sovereign loans on concessional terms with longer maturities, regulating ECBs, and rationalising interest rates on Non-Resident Indian deposits.

35. ADB has cut India's growth forecast to 7.4% for 2016-2017 and global headwinds will pull down the growth rate in the next fiscal. ADB has pegged growth at 7.8% in the earlier instance.

- ADB's Asian Development Outlook also projected a rise in consumer inflation.

- This is chiefly on account of the impact of salary hike on government employees and likely mid pick up in global oil prices.

- Indian Finance Ministry has estimated growth to by between 7 to 7.5 percent in the next fiscal year and India is currently one of the fastest growing economies in the world.

36. The European Union, through the European Investment Bank (EIB), will lend India €450 million (approximately INR 3,300 crore) towards constructing a 23-km long Lucknow Metro rail line and a purchasing a fleet of new trains.

- The EIB is the EU's official bank and the world's biggest international public bank, and its loan will cover half of the total project costs for the Lucknow Metro.

- The first tranche of €200 million was signed on March 30th, during Prime Minister Narendra Modi's visit to Brussels, as part of the 13th India EU Summit.

- The remaining tranches will be disbursed over the course of the project.

- Lucknow's Metro is expected to increase the public transport mode share from 10% to 27% in the city of 3 million.

- This marks the largest transport loan outside Europe for 10 years and EIB's first sovereign loan to India.

37. RBI has tweaked upcoming new rules for lending rates. The central bank said on 29th March 2016 the fixed rate loans of close to three years offered by lenders will be linked to the marginal cost of funding. Loans above that tenor should be exempt. Earlier, all fixed rate loans have been exempted from being set based on marginal cost of funding. The change will apply to new rules implemented from April 1, 2016.

- The new rules force lenders to base lending rates on marginal cost of funds.

- It is not based on average cost of funding.

- New rules will force lenders to adjust lending rates in relation to market rates removing the sector's discretion in making a decision as to how much to charge for loans.

38. Indian economy will grow 7.7% in 2016-2017, according to rating agency ICRA. It projected Indian economic growth to improve to 7.7% in the coming fiscal led by domestic consumption demand against the backdrop of OROP recommendations and 7th Pay Commission. The agency also said that though fresh project pipelines appear robust, commencement of work will lag announcement provided moderate capacity utilisation is there in some sectors.

39. Reserve Bank of India is discontinuing a two year provision where banks have to submit data in association with NEFT transactions by customers who have walked in and do not have an account with them. Bank should continue to maintain relevant records, however adding the necessary details when required.

40. To prevent further agitation by jewellers against imposition of 1 percent excise duty, finance ministry has asked artisans and job workers to not pay this levy. Artisans and job workers not covered by this duty are not required to take registration, pay duty, file returns or maintain a book of accounts. For jewellery manufactured on job work, the liability is on the manufacturer and not the job worker, the government decided.

41. Niti Aayog's Task Force on Eliminating Poverty has argued the poverty line is not the basis of identification of the poor. Instead, it is the BPL census on the basis of which state governments identify the poor. Main criticism of the Tendulkar line is that it is low...but other estimates of poverty say little about what is happening to households in utter poverty. Committee chaired by former Chairperson of the PM's Advisory Council and the National Statistical Commission, late Suresh Tendulkar calculated poverty line for 2004-2005 at levels that were equivalent in PPP terms to one US dollar per person per day. This was the internationally accepted poverty line at that time. Tendulkar computed poverty lines for 2004-2005 at a level that was equivalent in PPP terms to INR 33 per day.

42. The Ministry of Tourism has launched a programme open to college going students to inculcate in them appropriate tourism traits and knowledge, to enable them to act as Tourist Facilitators (Paryatak Mitra).The development and promotion of tourism is chiefly the duty of the State Governments/Union Territory Administrations.

43. Yes Bank has inked a pact with India Brazil Chamber of Commerce for cooperation in knowledge sharing and B2B covering the core sectors of sports, media and entertainment with special focus on IT infrastructure, broadcast driven business opportunities and special innovative business integrations.

44. As per the decision, MSMEs can deliver goods and services as per prescribed technical and quality specifications and norms on prior experience and turnover will be relaxed for them. This will assist startup MSMEs to take part in 20% public procurement from MSMEs and relaxation has been made for creating a conducive start up environment in India.

45. IRDAI has said on 10th March 2016 that the insurer should assess the credit risk of the buyer which adds more than 3% of the total turnover of policy holders while revising guidelines with respect to the credit insurance business. The regulatory body has revisited 2010 guidelines which regulate the credit insurance market to give a much needed boost to growth of the credit insurance market. Listing conditions for trade credit insurance, it has said that trade credit insurance policy should not be issued to lenders, financiers or banks.

46. India has performed best among the emerging economies though health of PSBs and corporates is a major worry. Vulnerabilities in corporate financial positions and public bank asset quality pose a risk to economic recovery and financial stability if not addressed in time. Corporate profitability is at a 10 year low, large companies are too leveraged and stressed assets in the system are over 14% with state run banks contributing the plan's bulk.

47. Fitch Ratings lowered the economic growth forecast of India for the next fiscal to 7.7 percent and maintained GDP projection for present fiscal at 7.5 percent. Fitch has forecast an 8% growth in December for the year 2016-2017 on account of capex spreading and gradual implementation of broad based structural reform agenda. 2016-2017 and 2017-2018 would be supported by greater amounts of real disposable income, leading to a normal monsoon after deficient rainfall for the past 2 years and the implementation of the recommendations of the 7th Pay Commission.

48. Food processing sector has received USD 385.45 million in FDI till December FY 2016 according to Minister of State for Food Processing Sadhvi Nirajan Jyoti. Total FDI in the previous fiscal stood at USD 515.86 million from April 2012 to December 2015. Government has also announced 100% FDI in marketing of food and products related to food produced and manufactured in India. 100% FDI will be allowed through the FIPB route leading to marketing of food products manufactured in India, benefiting farmers and generating employment.

49. The loan guarantee has been issued to RBL Bank Limited providing loans totalling USD 9 million to Wellspring Healthcare Private Limited (Healthspring). This is the first loan guarantee that USAID will provide in the country's health sector. High quality primary healthcare would be provided through this.

50. NHAI has tied up with Indian School of Business, Hyderabad for the development of competence of its technical and managerial manpower. The programme called Leadership Programme in Infrastructure Management relates to multiple disciplines namely economics, finance, law and social as well as environmental issues.

51. NASSCOM and TN state government have signed an agreement to establish the first startup warehouse in the state spread over an area of 8000 square feet. It will accommodate close to 50 startups and provide resources to the new companies. Information Technology Department and Electronics Corporation of TN have exchanged documents with NASSCOM for the warehouse which will be set up under the NASSCOM 10,000 startups initiative aimed at scaling up the startup ecosystem in the nation and funding the growth of 10,000 startups in the field of technology over the span of the next 10 years.

52. India has been ranked as 90th in a list of 126 nations compiled by World Economic Forum based on ability to deliver secure, affordable and sustainable energy. The Global Energy Architecture Performance Index Report of the WEF was topped by Switzerland followed by Norway. Sweden, France, Denmark, Austria, Spain, Colombia, New Zealand and Uruguay. Brazil was the top performer among BRIC nations followed by Russia, India and China.

53. GoI has approved Department of Investment and Public Asset Management for laying down the procedure and mechanism for strategic disinvestment of CPSEs or Central Public Sector Enterprises. Previously, strategic disinvestment would be associated with recommendations of the Disinvestment Commission. Government has also approved setting up of CGD or Core Group of Secretaries on Disinvestment under the Cabinet Secretary to implement the CCEA decision. NITI Aayog will perform the role of the Disinvestment Commission.

54. RBI has made amendments to the treatment of specific balance sheet items of banks boosting regulatory capital and aligning the same with globally adopted Basel III capital standards. According to the new riles, banks will be permitted to recognise part of real estate assets, foreign currency assets and deferred tax assets as capital with suitable hair cuts. This is in light of regulatory forcing banks to associate more stressed assets as NPAs leading to enhanced capital requirements. Existing capital adequacy guidelines were reviewed for aligning the definition of regulatory capital with internationally adopted Basel III capital standards issued by the Basel Committee on Banking Supervision. The amendments to be carried out with immediate effect include revaluation reserves due to change in carrying

amount of bank property will be considered as Tier 1 instead of Tier 2 capital and continue to be reckoned at 55% discount. Foreign currency translation reserves due to translation of financial statements of the bank's foreign operations to reporting currency may be considered as Tier 1 capital and reckoned at 25% discount. Foreign exchange translation reserves will suit banks with operations which have foreign operations such as SBI and BoI.

55. Indian economy is expected to grow at 7.4% in FY 2016, slightly lower than 7.6% projected by AE of CSO. FICCI's Economic Outlook survey puts across a media GDP growth forecast of 7.4% in the current fiscal. CSO had earlier estimated that Indian economy will record a 5 year high growth of 7.6% in 2015-2016 based on enhanced performance in farm and manufacturing sectors. FICCI poll was conducted in Jan/Feb 2016 and it estimated that agriculture sector will experience record growth of 1.7% in 2015-2016, 0.3 percentage points lower than what was the estimated growth in the round before this. The median forecast for Wholesale Price Index based inflation rate for 2015-16 has been put at (-)1.8 percent, with a minimum and maximum range of (-)2.8 percent and (-) 0.4 percent, respectively. The Consumer Price Index based inflation has a median forecast of 5 percent for 2015-16, with a minimum and maximum range of 4.6 percent and 6.3 percent, respectively.

56. To enhance economic cooperation and strengthening financial stability, RBI has extended USD 2 billion currency swap arrangement to SAARC nations till mid November 2017. As per the arrangement, RBI is to provide swap arrangement for up to USD 2 billion in foreign currency and Indian rupee. SAARC swap arrangement was offered by RBI to SAARC nations in November 2012 and facilities will be made available to Afghanistan, Bangladesh, Bhutan, Maldives, Nepal, Pakistan and Sri Lanka. The swap amount available to various member central banks has been arrived at broadly based on two months import cover subject to a floor of USD100 million and a maximum of 400 million per nation.

57. Common Service Centres are being channelised and withdrawal facility introduced here in order to provide banking services to each village of the nation by leveraging technology. Facility has been introduced so that banking access point is there in every village. Village level entrepreneurs have earned INR 438 crore as commission so far, financing the startup revolution in India and making the gram panchayat digitally literate.

58. Public investment Board has given the approval for an INR 800 crore proposal from India Post for establishing a payments bank. This bank will target unbanked and under-banked customers in rural, semi-rural and remote areas, with a focus on providing simple deposit products and money remittance services. The pilot for the payments bank is set to start from January 2017, and the full-fledged operations may start by March. Close to 40 global financial conglomerates including the World Bank and Barclays have shown interest to partner the postal department for setting up the bank.

59. GoI will be mapping 1.5 lakh bridges through an integrated system called IBMS. This stands for Integrated Bridge Management System. When completely operational, it will be the largest such system across the globe. Around 46,645 bridges have been digitally mapped by Germany. IBMS has mapped close to 50,000 bridges and culverts numbering 1.5 lakh in the nation. System that is an initiative under the Make in India drive will have smallest details of culverts and bridges and address safety as well as security concerns. IDEC Engineers have been appointed as project consultant for this and the system will contain data such as national identity number, latitude and longitude classifications and SES.

60. India's average economic growth rate was 7.5 percent in 2015 and India grew at a faster rate than China for this year, just as IMF had estimated. India is currently well on its way to a 4th Industrial Revolution/Industry 4.0 where the new face of global industries has come to the fore. This is the age of advanced manufacturing, robotics, 3D printing and quantum engineering.

61. Indian economy is set to grow at 7.4% within the next fiscal. OECD says Indian economy will grow at this robust rate though modest recovery is expected in advanced economies. Organisation for Economic Cooperation and Development has raised the Indian growth forecast as against 7.3% projected in November 2015. India is set to grow by 7.4% in 2016 and 7.3% in 2017 according to the Interim Economic Outlook released by the OECD. It also said that China would continue to rebalance its economy from manufacturing to services and growth is forecast at 6.5% in 2016 and 62% in 2017.

62. RBI has revised norms for NBFC firms stipulating that there should be on board approved limit for underwriting commitments with the aim to mitigate credit risk. RBI has also raised threshold for reporting frauds from INR 25 lakh to INR 1 crore for NBFC. Another point is that factoring services should be extended in respect of invoices which represent genuine trade transactions. Factoring business is a financial service whereby firm sells accounts receivable for the factoring company which then pays discounted value to seller under receivable receipts. As far as NPA classification is concerned, factoring with resource basis is where exposure would be reckoned on the assignor.

63. Minister of Mines and Steel, Mr. Narendra Singh Tomar launched the Khanij Khoj/Uncover project of the Geographical Survey of India. This is one of the flagship programmes of the draft NMEP. The project will be carried out in two selected parts of the country to look for buried/concealed mineral deposits. The main components of this initiative are as follows:

- Characterising the geological cover of India.
- Studying lithospheric architecture.
- Resolution of 4D geofynamic and metallogenic evolution.
- Isolating the distal footprints of ore despots.

64. CSO has released Quick Estimates of IIP or Index of Industrial Production with the base year of 2004-2005 for December 2015 compiled using the following 15 source agencies:

- Department of Industrial Policy & Promotion (DIPP);
- Indian Bureau of Mines;
- Central Electricity Authority;
- Joint Plant Committee, Ministry of Steel;
- Ministry of Petroleum & Natural Gas;
- Office of Textile Commissioner;
- Department of Chemicals & Petrochemicals;
- Directorate of Sugar & Vegetable Oils;
- Department of Fertilisers;
- Tea Board; Office of Jute Commissioner;
- Office of Coal Controller;
- Railway Board;
- Office of Salt Commissioner and Coffee Board.

General Index for the month of December 2015 was pegged at 183.4 which is 1.3 percent lower as against December 2014. The Indices of Industrial Production for the Mining, Manufacturing and Electricity sectors for the month of December 2015 stand at 137.5, 192.0 and 183.2 respectively, with the corresponding growth rates of 2.9 percent. 10 of 22 industry groups in the manufacturing sector showed negative growth during the month of December 2015.

65. USTDA and the Andhra Pradesh government have inked pact to develop Vizag as a Smart City. The US Trade and Development Agency has inked an agreement with the AP government for developing infrastructure, data systems and communication in Vishakhpatnam for it to become a smart city.

66. CSO has revised the Base Year of the CPI from 2010=100 to 2012= 100 w.e.f January 2016. In addition to this, Consumer Food Price Index (CFPI) for all India Rural, Urban and Combined are also being released for January 2016. Inflation rates (on point to point basis i.e. January 2016 over January 2015), based on General Indices and CFPIs are given as follows: General Indices (Provisional) for the month of January 2016 for Rural, Urban and Combined are 128.1, 124.2 and 126.3 respectively. CFPI for Rural, Urban and Combined for the same month are 131.1, 131.0 and 131.1 respectively.

67. US Chamber of Commerce has ranked India as 37 of 38 nations in the 4th annual International IP Index -Infinite Possibilities- which measured the IP environment in India alongside 37 other economies. Only Venezuela has scored low. Index was produced by GIPC or Global Intellectual Property Centre and India's overall score fell from 7.05 to 7.23. Report also noted a decrease through introduction of Global Measure of Physical Counterfeiting in the current edition, in which India was ranked 7th.

68. Central Statistics Office under Ministry of Statistics and Programme Implementation has released Advance Estimates of National Income for the current fiscal along with QE of GDP for Q3. Growth in GDP during 2015-2016 was projected at 7.6% as against growth rate of 7.2% in 2014-2015. Real FDP is likely to reach the value of INR 113.51 lakh crore rupees, according to AE and QE figures.

69. According to CRISIL, the Indian economy is expected to grow at 7.9 percent in the fiscal commencing April which is much less than earlier forecast of 8.1% on account of intensification of international economic downturn. Economy's modest recovery has been shaped by excellent fortune on crude oil and commodities. Economy has weathered two successive monsoon failures apart from slower economic growth cycle. Next fiscal will also see implementation of OROP and 7th Pay Commission.

70. Telecom Regulatory Authority of India on 8th February 2016 barred TSPs from charging differential rates for data services prohibiting Free Basics and Airtel Zero Platform. TRAI has ruled in favour of Net Neutrality. While no service provider can provide discriminatory tariffs for data services in association with content. no service provider can also enter into discriminatory tariffs for data services and reduced tariff has only been permitted for accessing or providing emergency services. Financial punishments will also be imposed for regulation contravention and the regulation may be reviewed after a period of 2 year. Fine of INR 50,000 will be levied each day, subject to maximal value of INR 50 lakh for violation of regulation by service providers.

71. Maharashtra has made the plan to set up the first international arbitration centre in Mumbai ahead of the maiden Make in India Week to be held from February 13 to 18. Overseas disputes arbitration is set to yield revenue worth INR 2 billion. Singapore International Arbitration Centre showed in 2013 that of the total 259 new cases, Indian companies made the contribution to the highest number of filing at 85. MCIA will open up avenues for business as well as legal talent across the state and evolve framework in accordance with global standards followed by SIAC, ICC and LCIA.

72. Reserve Bank of India said the government will buy back inflation indexed bonds/IIBs maturing in 2023 via reverse auction in February 11th. Not so effective bonds have received a below par response due to lack of marketing and associated tax issues. GoI has also notified repurchase of 1.44 percent inflation indexed government stock 2023 via a reverse auction for total amount of INR 6500 crore. Bonds were launched as alternative to gold as an investment in high current account deficit. Repurchase will be prematurely held to redeem government stock through utilization of surplus cash balance and it was an ad-hoc move.

73. According to the National Council of Applied Economic Research, Indian economy will grow at 7.4% in the current fiscal (2015-2016). GDP growth rate forecast is 7.4% for 2015-2016 and 2016-2017. Prospects for agriculture sector in 2015-2016 were poor due to a deficient rainfall. Agricultural growth during the first half of the current year fell to 2.0% from 2.4% for the first half of 2014-2015.

74. IT exports are all set to grow at a slower pace of 10-12% in the fiscal 2017 according th NASSCOM. The export will be hit by currency fluctuations and the weakening of the rupee against the US dollar. IT export industry is looking at 12.3% growth in 2015-2016 closing on March 31.IT services and software industry body had forecasted a growth of 12-14 percent in exports. Rupee industry had fallen to a 29 month low against the dollar, in recent times. Currency movement influences the industry which earns close to 80% of the revenue from US and Europe. Currency movement also influences the industry which earns close to 80% of the revenue from EU and US.

75. Cabinet has approved the formation of JV with states for rail projects to ensure wider participation of states. Railways has formed JV companies with state government for mobilisation of resources for quick implementation of rail projects. JV companies will now be responsible for project identification, land acquisition and financing in addition to government funding and monitoring. Cabinet presided by PM Narendra Modi has taken the decision that JV companies would be formed with equity participation of Railways Ministry and concerned state governments. Each JV will have paid up initial capital of INR 100 crore associated with the project quantum of projects to be undertaken. The initial paid up capital is limited to INR 50 crore for each state.

76. RBI has relaxed numerous rules including FDI norms for boosting start up activity within the nation. Start ups will now be allowed to receive foreign venture capital investment regardless of which sector they operate in. New norms will permit share transfer from foreign venture capital investors to other residents/non residents. Proposal for permitting startups to get foreign venture capital investments is a positive step as presently.

77. India has overtaken Thailand as the largest rice exporter in the world. It is the world's largest rice exporter in 2015, shipping 10.23 MT according to a top Thai rice exporters body Thai Rice Exporters Association. Thailand has exported 9.8 MT of rice in 2015 down 10.8% Y-O-Y. They attributed downturn to global economy contraction with high rice demand and Thailand ended up second position in terms of overall exports. Vietnam won the third position globally while China was the leading importer of rice.

78. Exports of half of the sectors out of the 30 closely monitored by the Commerce Ministry were in the negative zone in December on account of fall in global prices and demand. Outbound shipments of close to 15 key sectors such as leather, engineering and petrol have dipped last month due to ministry data. Exporters body FIEO indicated that the pace of fall has moderated in December. India's exports fell about 15 percent in December to USD 22.2 billion, placing trade deficit to USD 11.66 billion, which is the most massive in the past 4 months. In November, it fell by 24.43 percent and continuous export declines will impact jobs and place pressure on CAD. Government should address inverted duty structure in sectors in the Budget besides exemption of exports from service tac and export development fund. FIEO has indicated that the top 2 sectors engineering and petrol products fell by 15.68 percent and 47.69 percent respectively in December 2015. Gems and jewellery exports shrank by around 7.75% to USD 2.46 billion in the previous month. These 3 sectors make 55% of the country's total exports in 2014-2015 which was pegged at USD 310.5 billion. Agri products that constitute over 10 percent of the country's total shipments has recorded negative growth during the month in review.

79. RBI permits banks to sell Indian Gold Coins with Ashok Chakra minted by MMTC via their branches. This terms and conditions shall be as per a contract between MMTC and designated banks. MMC has made the decision that gold used for IGC will be mobilised domestically under the Gold Deposit Scheme and Gold Monetisation Scheme. Coins are available in denominations of 5 and 10 grams while a 20 gram bullion is being manufactured by MMTC. India imports 1000 tonnes of gold each year, draining out the foreign exchange and plain pressure on fiscal deficit.

80. India's current account deficit may narrow to 0.5% of GDP in 2016 from 0.7% in 2015 on account of lower commodity prices especially oil. Given lower oil prices, one expects CAD to narrow to 0.5% of GDP in 2016 from 0.7% in 2015. As per official figures, exports contracted for the 13th month in the row in December 2015. Outward shipments shrank 14.75% to USD 22.2 billion and

global demand slowdown. Imports can plunged 3.88 percent for USD 33.9 billion in December ober the same month in the previous year.

81. India has signed a USD 250 million loan agreement with the World Bank for Bihar Kosi Basin Development Project for enhancing resilience to for floods and enhancing agricultural productivity. Objective of the project is for enhancing resilience to floods and enhancing agricultural production and productivity in targeted districts in Kosi River Basin and enhance the capacity of Bihar to respond effectively to an eligible crisis or emergency. FM has indicated this in a statement. Primary beneficiaries will be rural producer and households in the Kosi River Basin who are exposed to floods, it is indicated.

82. EXIM Bank has entered into MoU with AP to promote exports from the state. MoU was signed by EXIM Bank CMD Yaduvendra Mathur and Shamsher Singh Rawat, Secretary and Commissioner for Industrial Promotion, AP. EXIM Bank aims to support exporters possessing operations in the AP in attaining higher exports by facilitation of market linkages through market advisory services that will assist in identification of suitable partners.

83. India's trade deficit with China has risen to 44.87 billion in 2015. India's trade deficit with China has reached USD 44.87 billion in the past year and exports shrank to USD 13.38 billion as bilateral trade registered a considerable increase adding up to USD 71.64 billion missing out on the USD 100 billion target established by leaders of the nations. India-China trade has reached USD 71.64 billion according to reports released by Chinese customs. Bilateral trade registered a marginal increase as against USD 70.59 in 2014. This year China's exports have increased to USD 58.25 billion as against USD 70.59 billion in 2014.

84. India's Index of Industrial Production for the month of November has fallen by 3.2% as against 9.8% in October while CPI has risen for the month of December to 5.6% compared to 5.41 percent for November. As per the CNBC TV 18 poll, CPI has come to around 5.5% while consensus was expecting IIP to come down to levels of 1.8 to 2 percent.

85. Urijit Patel, Deputy Governor of RBI in charge of the monetary policy department, has been appointed for a term of three years for the second time. Patel, 52, will finish his 3 year term on January 10, and has become the longest serving deputy governor in 2015-2016 if he serves the full three year term. Many of the recent deputy governors served a maximum period of only 5 years. A deputy governor can serve for the period of three years w.e.f taking on the charge on or after January 11,2016 or till further orders, whichever is earlier. A PhD from Yale University in Economics and graduate of the University of London and Oxford, he has served as the head of the U. Patel Committee proposing inflation targeting as the prime objective of the central bank. As per the agreement, RBI will target 4 percent inflation at the close of the financial year 2016-2017 and for subsequent years, with a band of +/- 2 percent. Other deputy governors of the RBI are H. R. Khan, R. Gandhi and S. S. Mundra.

86. Union Cabinet gives approval for Credit Guarantee Fund for MUDRA (Micro Units Development Refinance Agency) loans and conversion of MUDRA Ltd into MUDRA SIDBI. Fund will generate more than 100,000 crore worth of loans to micro and small units within the first instance.

87. India has produced 7.98 MT sugar and exported 0.3 MT till December 2015-2016. Country's sugar output rose to 7.98 MT in a percentage increase of 6.5 during the first three months of 2015-2016 while exports were 3,00,000 tonnes during the same period, according to industry body ISMA. As per the latest production data released by Indian Sugar Mills Association, overall output of the country rose to 7.98 MT in October-December 2015-2015 up from 7.49 MT in the same period a year ago. Sugar output in top sugar producing state Maharashtra rose to 3.37 MT from 3.26 MT in the review period.

88. Government of Indian abolished export duty on iron ore pellets, from 5 to 0 percent in a move that will make the commodity more competitive amidst weakening prices and falling demand. In the year 2014, government has levied a 5% export duty on iron ore pellets which are value added products of leftover low grade iron used in still making. Notification in this regard was issued by Central Board of Excise and Customs. Pellet Manufacturers Association of India Secretary General, Deepak Bhatnagar has said that industry had been lobbying the withdrawal of export duty since 2014 when it was first levied and that pellet industry's capacity utilisation has fallen to 35%.

89. Retail inflation for farm labourers and rural workers in November increased to 4.92% and 5.02% respectively on account of increase in food item prices. Corresponding inflation in October was 4.43% and 4.65%. Food inflation under CPI-AL and CPI-RL came at 4.79% and 5.15 percent in November 2015. All India CPI numbers for agricultural and rural labourers for November rose to 853 and 857 points respectively. CPI-AL and RL of TN registered the maximum increase while Meghalaya saw the maximum fall.

90. Foreign brokerage firm HSBC said the country is current amidst a credit less recovery and policy reforms were the main step to attaining higher growth. Economists have also expressed dissent with the new method of GDP computation and said the economy will clock 7.4% in FY16 and remain stable in FY17 as well. During this phase of credit less recovery, sectors like investment which rely on external funding take the longest to revive. The macro side is facing fiscal trilemmas according to economists where the main challenge was funding higher wages at the same time, lowering fiscal deficit and continuing government capex.

91. This is a 67% jump over USD 23 billion revenue for 2015 as per industry body ASSOCHAM. Indian e-commerce market was worth USD 3.8 billion in 2009 and went up to USD 17 billion in 2014 nd USD 23 billion in 2015. It is expected to touch USD38 billion mark by 2016. Enhanced internet and mobile penetration as well as increased acceptability of online payments and desired demographics will provide the e-commerce sector a chance to connect with customers. ASSOCHAM predicts a 5 to 7 fold increase in revenue generated via e-commerce.

92. To better managing public borrowing, government has taken the decision to switch to INR 50,000 crore high cost debt in 2016-2017 and 2017-2018 into fresh instruments of longer term maturity. In terms of releasing Medium Term Debt Management Strategy, Finance Ministry has announced the objective of debt

management strategy is obtaining government funding at all times at a cost which is low in the medium/long term. MTDS is put together for the period 2015-2016 to 2017-2018 associated with outstanding government market borrowing as noted on March end 2015. Switches of INR 30,000 crore are conducted in 2015-2016 and INR 50,000 crore in 2016-2017 and 2017-2018 as part of the scenario analysis of the MTDS. Reversal in the interest rate cycle is set to lower borrowing cost in the domestic market in 2015-2016. MTDS is in accordance with the Medium Term Fiscal Policy Statement.

93. Growth in 8 sectors of the economy fell 1.3 percent in November, as against 3.2 percent growth in October. This showcases the uneven nature of economic recovery. While cement, crude oil, steel and natural gas production declined M-O-M, electricity production was unchanged. Pace of growth was slower as carrying refined products, fertilizer, refined petrol products and coal output rose. Fiscal deficit for April to November rose to INR 4.83 lakh crore and is currently pegged at 87% of the FY16 Budget estimate.

94. For providing new avenues for raising funds, capital market regulatory body SEBI on 31st December 2015 proposed fresh norms for public issue of Real Estate Investment Trusts. This includes a cap of 75% allocation to institutional buyers. Proposed norms for the public issuance of REITs pertain to appointment of merchant bankers, disclosures within the offer documents and filing of draft papers, keeping them in public domain for a minimum of 21 days. For issue made via book building process or otherwise, allocation in public issue should equal maximum 75% to Qualified Institutional Buyers and 25% to other investors, according to SEBI. Investment managers can allocate close to 60% of the portion available for allocation for QIBs to anchor investors subject to specific conditions. Anchor investors need to create applications for INR 10 crore minimum in public issue and allocation to investors should be on discretionary basis subject to minimum of two investors for maximum allocation up to INR 250 crore and 5 other such investors for over INR 250 crore.

95. Global economic growth will be disappointing within the year, according to head of IMF MD Christine Lagarde who said the prospect of rising interest rates in the US and economic slowdown in China would lead to economic vulnerability worldwide. Additionally, growth in global trade has lowered considerable and decline in raw materials is an issue for economies linked to these. Moreover, financial risks are rising in the emerging markets. Start of normalisation of the US monetary policy and shift towards consumption led growth were needed to be carried out smoothly.

96. Government will be setting up a INR 40 k crore National Investment and Infrastructure Fund. Its chief executive will be finalised towards the end of January. IIFC has been appointed as the investment advisor and IDBI Capital Market Services Ltd has been appointed as advisor. NIIF has constituted a search cum selection committee under CCEA Secretary Shanktikanta Das for selection of the CEO of NIIF.

97. RBI on 28th December 2015 released the Mohanty Panel Report on medium term path for financial inclusion. Financial inclusion is aimed at delivering financial serves at affordable cost to disadvantaged and low income segments of society. The key aim is to improve the credit system for the underprivileged and focus on poorer agricultural households to ensure shift of credit demand from informal to formal sector. As per the report, banks have to make special efforts for opening up accounts for women and girls and a unique biometric identifier such as Aadhaar will be linked to every individual credit account. The report also stressed on improving last mile service delivery.

98. According to RBI, outstanding loans rose INR 981.80 billion to INR 69.66 trillion rupees in two weeks leading up to December 11. Non food credit rose INR 977.20 billion to INR 68.57 trillion rupees and food credit rose INR 4.60 billion rupees to INR 1.09 trillion rupees. Bank loans rose 11# while deposits rose 11.5% according to the RBI weekly statistical supplement.

99. Between the March and September quarters, NPAs jumped 50 basis points to 5.1% between March and September quarters. Gross naps rose to 5.1% as of September quarter from 4.6% in March 2015. As per the Financial stability report released by RBI, net NPAs as percentage of total net advances increased to 2.8% from 2.5% in March. The end of the Corporate Debt Restructuring (CDR) cell, led to restructured standard advances as percentage of gross advances declining to 6.2 from 6.4, but stressed loans ratio increased to 11.3 from 11.1 percent in the same period. Public sector lenders recorded the highest level of stressed assets at 14.1 percent followed by private sector banks at 4.6 percent and foreign banks at 3.4 percent, as per the report.

100. RBI has created a dedicated helpline to assist start ups undertaking cross border transactions. Enterprises should provide complete information to RBI and mention other issues on which they need guidance. Helpline will assist in timely and effective dissemination of information.

// Notes //

// Notes //